CHILD

of

LIGHT

———

A BIOGRAPHY
OF ROBERT STONE

———

Madison Smartt Bell

DOUBLEDAY

New York

Grateful acknowledgment is made to Houghton Mifflin Harcourt Publishing
Company for permission to reprint "Children of Light" from *Lord Weary's
Castle* by Robert Lowell. Copyright © 1945, copyright renewed 1974 © by Robert
Lowell. Reprinted by permission of Houghton Mifflin Harcourt Publishing
Company. All rights reserved.

Unless otherwise indicated, photographs are courtesy of the Robert Stone Estate.

Book design by Maria Carella
Jacket photograph by Nancy Crampton
Jacket design by Emily Mahon

Library of Congress Cataloging-in-Publication Data
Names: Bell, Madison Smartt, author.
Title: Child of light : a biography of Robert Stone / Madison Smartt Bell.
Description: First edition. | New York : Doubleday, [2020] | Includes index.
Identifiers: LCCN 2019022780 (print) | LCCN 2019022781 (ebook) |
ISBN 9780385541602 (hardcover) | ISBN 9780385541619 (ebook)
Subjects: LCSH: Stone, Robert, 1937–2015 | Novelists, American—
20th century—Biography.
Classification: LCC PS3569.T6418 Z54 2020 (print) | LCC PS3569.T6418 (ebook) |
    DDC 813/.54 [B]—dc23
LC record available at https://lccn.loc.gov/2019022780
LC ebook record available at https://lccn.loc.gov/2019022781

MANUFACTURED IN THE UNITED STATES OF AMERICA

10 9 8 7 6 5 4 3 2 1

First Edition

CHILD OF LIGHT

FOR JANICE STONE

AND IN MEMORY OF BOB

Nations exist not only as geographic entities and political divisions but also as living stories. The national mythology is always there; its relationship to reality may be dubious but no one can understand a country who does not understand its self-image, its story about itself.

—ROBERT STONE, "1984"

I do not claim to know much more about novels than the writing of them, but I cannot imagine one set in the breathing world which lacks any moral valence. In the course of wringing a few novels from our fin-de-siècle, late-imperial scene, I have never been able to escape my sense of humanity trying, with difficulty, to raise itself in order not to fall.

—ROBERT STONE, "THE REASON
FOR STORIES: TOWARD A MORAL FICTION"

CONTENTS

PREFACE

R obert Stone is one of the most powerful and enduring writers of the late twentieth century, also called
sometimes the American Century, and in the latter aspect now thought by
many to have come to an ignominious end. Stone's work chronicled both
the peak and the decline of a great many aspects of U.S. world dominance,
as practiced abroad and reflected at home. In recounting the struggles of
the particular individuals that peopled his imagination, he also told us the
story of our time. Stone was an artist, not a reformer, but he had a very
unusual ability to engage his fiction with the most urgent social issues of
his time and ours, while living in the midst of them, and to do so without
artistic compromise.

When Stone mustered out of the navy in the late 1950s, the United
States had perhaps reached its zenith in terms of economic success and
dominance, political hegemony worldwide, and a vibrant and vigorous
culture, ripe for exportation in multiple embodiments: from serious literature and high art to B movies, pop music, and Coca-Cola. It seemed
a national moment free of self-doubt—although a considerable dysphoria
would soon begin to express itself, as the social upheavals of the 1960s
began. Stone, who did not begin the world from a position of privilege,
was quicker than most to see the shadows cast by the rising American star.
In his work, he would repeatedly portray those bright aspirations set off
by a surrounding darkness which was likely in the end to devour them.

Stone's novels each capture the zeitgeist of a particular period. *A Hall
of Mirrors* slashes into the underbelly of American racial anxieties as the
civil rights movement, and resistance to it, get underway. *Dog Soldiers*

somehow captures the whole spirit of the Vietnam era while barely setting a scene in Vietnam. *A Flag for Sunrise* delves into the dark side of the Monroe Doctrine, following the most corrupt machinations of American influence into the bloodiest crannies of Central America. *Children of Light* stages the cocaine-fueled, illusion-rich culture of 1980s Hollywood. *Outerbridge Reach* swings the 1990s boom-and-bust stock market cycle by the tail, shaking out its scariest social consequences. *Damascus Gate* discovers the sinister side of the U.S. engagement with Mideast politics in general and Israel in particular—among other things, as one must always say of any Robert Stone novel . . . a great many other things. Stone's fictions are all human stories, first and foremost, driven by characters invested with remarkably rich and dense inner lives—characters we are compelled to recognize as our close cousins. There but for the grace of God (or just good luck if you prefer) go we.

Bob Stone sometimes described himself as a "slothful perfectionist," though his body of work conveys perfectionism more than sloth. All of his fiction—multifaceted and with unsuspected depths—repays multiple readings, and handsomely. There is little in even the best of contemporary fiction that can claim this quality; however brilliant on the first read, it is not likely to offer fresh insights on a second. The reward Stone offers to the reader is much larger than usual, though he was genuinely hard to please and often found it hard to please himself. He was a conflicted, sometimes tormented personality in both life and art. His disposition was choleric at times; he suffered fools with very small patience, and he confronted the world with the bright, acidic irony of an extraordinarily perceptive, bitterly disappointed idealist. Although Stone was never an autobiographical novelist in the relatively narrow sense that writers like Richard Ford, Saul Bellow, and Ernest Hemingway are, some variation on his own qualities usually gets projected onto at least one major character in all of his novels (Rheinhardt in *A Hall of Mirrors*, Holliwell in *A Flag for Sunrise*, Walker in *Children of Light*) or sometimes the Stone personality is split between two protagonists (Converse and Hicks in *Dog Soldiers*, Browne and Strickland in *Outerbridge Reach*, Brookman and Stack in *Death of the Black-Haired Girl*). His unusual personality, his restlessness, and his ambition for his work caused him to lead what his widow has called "a hell of an interesting life."

Stone borrowed the title of his fourth novel from a poem by Robert Lowell, and used the entire poem as the epigraph of his first:

CHILDREN OF LIGHT

Our fathers wrung their bread from stocks and stones
And fenced their gardens with the Redmen's bones;
Embarking from the Nether Land of Holland,
Pilgrims unhouseled by Geneva's night,
They planted here the Serpent's seeds of light;
And here the pivoting searchlights probe to shock
The riotous glass houses built on rock,
And candles gutter in a hall of mirrors,
And light is where the landless blood of Cain
Is burning, burning the unburied grain.

Enigmatic, quasi-impenetrable, rich with half-realized, tormented thought, it is not Lowell's best-known poem, nor his best, but it did serve Stone as a sort of chthonic treasure map for his extraordinary exploration of the grandly ambitious, vexed, and troubled American society we all have shared with him.

Born to a single mother, decades before such situations became socially acceptable, Stone was raised an outsider. Throughout his hardscrabble childhood, he and his mother were each other's sole allies in a struggle against forces out to separate them for their own good. Young Stone spent time in orphanages when his mother could not keep him; he also logged a good deal of time on New York and Chicago streets. His conflicted relation with the American dream has to do with the fact that it was never his by entitlement.

Stone's life and work reflect the evolution of America's sense of itself—from the naïve ebullience of the 1950s to the tenebrous uncertainties of the post-9/11 twenty-first century—and in this process, Stone's novels were always just a little ahead of the curve. His childhood left him with the street kid's hardwired alertness to threat, a preternatural sense of trouble on the way, before it has quite crested the horizon. His first fully realized fiction (an oral performance) was composed to outwit Child Protective Services. He spent four years as a very small boy in a Catholic orphanage in Manhattan, plus a few months in a Booth shelter in Chicago; these experiences gave him a sense of how such institutions can warp personality. A three-year hitch in the navy he began at age seventeen was a different sort of institutional experience, and in some ways corrective of the ones he had before.

At the end of his military service, Stone returned to New York for a brief run as a newspaperman and college student. Within a year he married, dropped out of school, went with his wife to New Orleans and then to California, where he took up a Stegner Fellowship at Stanford University and began writing his first novel, *A Hall of Mirrors*. During those early West Coast years he fell into the orbit of Ken Kesey, who was then beginning his experiments with LSD. Stone partook with enthusiasm, while resisting the cultish qualities of the Kesey circle. By 1964 he was back in New York with his wife and two children working at various short-term jobs while he finished the novel.

After *A Hall of Mirrors* was published in 1967, the Stones moved to London where they lived for four years, during which Stone went to Vietnam to gather material for his second book, *Dog Soldiers*. In 1971 he returned to the United States and a teaching career, first at Princeton and then at Amherst College. *Dog Soldiers* won the National Book Award in 1975, and the publication of *A Flag for Sunrise* in 1981 consolidated his reputation as a significant voice of his time.

By midlife, Stone had assimilated into the mainstream of American society as much as serious artists ever do; he was a respected novelist, a college professor, the head of a prosperous middle-class household—quartered in Westport, Connecticut; Block Island; Key West; Sheffield, Massachusetts; and Manhattan's Upper East Side. The Stones always divided their time among two or more residences, while Stone himself incessantly traveled all over the world, for outdoor activities, research for his books, journalistic assignments, and representation of American letters in other countries, sponsored by various avatars of the U.S. Information Agency. His book contracts grew ever more lucrative as his reputation expanded with the big novels of his peak career, especially *Outerbridge Reach* and *Damascus Gate*. Still he could never entirely shake the financial anxiety his insecure childhood had instilled in him and was always eager to pick up a little extra income through teaching and journalism— distractions from fiction writing which he often seemed to welcome. Dependent on alcohol from his teens, Stone embraced most recreational drugs that came his way, and by the end of the twentieth century his alcohol and prescription narcotic use had begun to wear down his remarkably strong constitution. In the early 2000s he rallied; there were several more books he wanted to write and for that he needed to take better care of his health than had been his custom. For a time, he returned to full strength as a writer. Then damage from the smoking habit he'd broken in the 1980s caught up with him, and he died of chronic obstructive pulmonary disease in 2015.

Stone's formal education was incomplete; he was to all intents and purposes an autodidact, and despite the many years he spent in academia, he trafficked very little in received ideas. His outsider's instincts gave him a longer view of the world of which he had become a part. Each of Stone's novels confronts a peculiarly disturbing problem of the period in which it is set. His technique of splintering his own personality into several different characters allows him to surround each issue with a circle of penetrating views. A Robert Stone novel is an artistically closed system in which the social issues of a given period play out in an experimental form.

———•———

I became a devout admirer of Stone's fiction in the early 1980s. We were very slightly acquainted then, and during the 1990s got to know each other better. During the last fifteen years of his life we were close friends. We shared, among a few other things, an addictive personality and a vocation for letters. In both cases, his were much stronger than mine.

PART ONE

———

A HALL OF MIRRORS

1

A New York Childhood

I was born in Brooklyn on President Street, the border of Park Slope and South Brooklyn," Robert Stone recalled in midlife, for a book of essays on Catholicism. The day of his birth was August 21, 1937. "My mother was a schoolteacher in the New York public school system. My father worked for the old New Haven Railroad. My mother's family had been on the Brooklyn waterfront, working on the tugboats, for several generations. When I was still small, my parents separated. I moved with my mother to Manhattan and grew up then in Yorkville and on the Upper West Side. My mother was schizophrenic, and when I was about five she was hospitalized for a while. I went to St. Ann's at Lexington and Seventy-Seventh Street, which later became Archbishop Molloy High School. St. Ann's was somewhere between a boarding school and an orphanage, run by the Marist Brothers. I was at St. Ann's until I was nine and then I was out again."

This account exaggerates the stability of Stone's early years somewhat. Supposed to have been a railroad detective, the C. Homer Stone who appears on Robert Stone's birth certificate is a cipher. Sometimes Bob Stone spoke of him as if he had occasionally appeared on the scene of his early childhood . . . and sometimes not. His mother, Gladys Grant, apparently never married anyone and raised her only child as a single parent.

In the late 1970s, Stone agreed to be interviewed, at length and in deep detail, by Ann Greif, who was researching a dissertation in psychology. Greif, who took a psychoanalytic tack in her questions and commentary, was particularly interested in Stone's early childhood and his relationship with his mother. Some visceral recollections were prompted.

"My mother didn't have an honest bone in her body, God bless her. She really was, if she had been a little more together she would have been in the game, she was a real outsider. . . . She really didn't give a shit about anybody except me and her. But she did care about me. . . . She didn't relate to other people, she really didn't care about other people. . . . I mean she did not care about the government and she didn't care about the war, whether Hitler won the war or Roosevelt won the war was all the same to her, whether the government carried on and saved the world or whether the world didn't get saved, whether the Russians took over, she really couldn't care less. I mean she was looking out for herself and to give her credit she was looking out for me."

Jim Maraniss, a close friend of Bob's since the 1970s, recalled that Bob sometimes seemed to believe that his father had been a foreigner, perhaps a Jew, not quite a peddler but someone who ran a stand or storefront in one of the East Side neighborhoods where Bob lived with his mother. "I am very unclear about this, because my mother was not very confiding in me . . . she was sometimes delusionary and she was sometimes making up stories so it is very difficult to be very clear."

In *A Flag for Sunrise*, Stone created a cameo role for "Sy; he had once run a newspaper stand on the corner of Dyckman Street and Broadway. Sy lived almost across the hall from Holliwell and his mother in a cheap hotel in Washington Heights for ten years and Holliwell still half suspected that Sy had been his mother's lover." The boy Holliwell sometimes helps Sy in the newsstand; Sy teaches him to sing "The Internationale" and mocks his Catholic education.

In the early 1960s, when her son was grown, Gladys told him various stories of his origin. Sometimes Bob encouraged her with drink. Once she told him that his father had been a Greek, a Jew, or a Lebanese, and on another occasion she claimed that his father had been quite another person who was killed in the 1937 bombing of Shanghai. Again using alcohol as an interrogative tool, Bob got her to admit this story was untrue, and yet she had saved bar receipts which proved that she really had been in Shanghai in the 1930s. "For years," Bob wrote later, "I had been coming across identity documents, apparently referring to her, but representing the bearer under a variety of names. Passports, visas, bar bills in Tokyo, even the deeds to two cemetery plots in two different cemeteries. The documents were signed in her handwriting but affirming two different names."

Another time Bob was told "that my father was a guy she met somewhere around the New York Public Library and I presume made it with,

I have to presume made it with, but I don't think she ever saw him again. No, she told me he did come around once in a while, but she didn't want anything to do with him. I really don't know who he was. The odd thing also is that I don't think my mother was very sexually active. In my life-time she was not at all ever. She had no boyfriends, no men friends of any kind, all the time I was growing up, never. It would not surprise me too much if I found out that was her first sexual experience and that it took place at the age of forty or what not."

Stone's own accounts of his paternity were inconsistent. Eventually he settled on the idea that he had never met his father at all, except for one occasion when a man came to the door—but his mother didn't let who-ever it was in. The uncertainty was such that Gladys might just as well have been fertilized by a shower of light—as Zeus impregnated Danaë. Bob once found something his mother had written about his birth in the heart of a bright moonlit night. The account had a numinous quality, but that was as much as he ever knew about it. Despite all the difficulties of his childhood he always had the sense that his mother was completely devoted to him, and only to him.

———

Gladys's father was a tugboat captain; a Scots American Protestant, while her mother was a Shanley—a lace-curtain Irish family hailing from the Finger Lakes region of upstate New York. There was some cross-religious tension in this Catholic-Protestant marriage (the surviving chil-dren leaned to the Catholic side). Captain Grant plied his trade in New York Harbor. For a while the Grant family had settled in Manhattan's East Sixties, probably moving there around the time that the rail line that ran up Park Avenue through Harlem was put underground in the 1870s. Not all of their many children survived. In this period, diseases like scar-let fever and diphtheria took many young lives, including those of Glad-ys's twin brothers and a third and favorite brother, John.

Gladys Grant was born on October 16, 1894. She told Bob "about going out in her father's tug boat early in the morning in the harbor dur-ing the time they were building the Brooklyn Bridge" (a detail which must have been one of her fantasies, since the Brooklyn Bridge was completed in 1883). Gladys remembered "going to bring him cans of beer from the saloons" around the harbor, and "going with pails to a ketchup factory."

She described for Bob the reconstruction of Park Avenue into "a desirable neighborhood" after the rail line went underground, although she could not have been an eyewitness to that since it happened almost twenty years before she was born. As an adult Stone speculated that Captain Grant's position in the harbor must have given the family some prestige, but in Gladys's recollection they were not always prosperous: ". . . she would go on sometimes about how poor they were, some of the time, tales of poverty and so on. It really obsessed her a lot. She was always struggling with money, and she had a great fear of poverty. It seemed to be something she had grown up with."

A schoolteacher in her prime, she probably attended Hunter College. Somewhere along her way she picked up a rather patrician New York accent, which her son absorbed from her in the course of his difficult childhood. She had traveled widely for a woman of her class and generation. She was acquainted with people in Canada and took Bob there when he was small, as well as taking him sometimes to Block Island. Her connection there remains a mystery, but those visits were regular, and when Bob got older he was able to get summer jobs on Block Island, working in and around the vast, barnlike tourist hotels.

Gladys's claim to have studied at the Sorbonne may or not have been true, but she had certainly been in France. Her story of having been in Shanghai and Japan in the 1930s seemed even less credible, yet Bob confirmed it by finding those bar receipts from Shanghai and Tokyo hotels. She had a story about having had to climb out a porthole of a ship for some reason—while pregnant with Bob. Where that vessel originated or was bound has been lost.

Gladys once informed Bob's wife that "a gypsy fortune-teller told her that she would have a wonderful son. 'So,' she added, 'I decided to have this one.'" Whether that "this" alluded to previous undelivered pregnancies will never be known. She was forty-three when Bob was born in 1937—an extremely late age for first-time childbirth, with or without climbing out of portholes.

When he started school at St. Ann's, Bob began to get a sense of the difference between his mother and other people: "it became pretty clear to me that there was a separation between her and all the other people in the world, and that if I was going to have to choose up ultimate sides, although my sympathies were all with her . . . I would prefer to be like all the other people in the world, rather than like her. . . . I couldn't hang in there with her and be crazy too. . . . Her way of seeing things and her way of dealing with the world was as far as I could tell the wrong way to do it. . . . I was not getting any real advice. I was getting plenty of support in the sealed world of me and her, but I was not getting anything that was very useful to me outside that world."

Gladys's mental problems inhibited any social life she might have had with anyone beyond her son, although "she was really kind of lively, she was very charming even when she was crazy. . . . A lot of people liked her, she was likeable but she, she just didn't have any friends. . . . She was not without wit . . . she was a little mischievous, she had a habit of being able to say very wacked-out things in a kind of serious fashion which was engaging." As an older child, Bob began to find these qualities embarrassing. "I used to tell my friends that she was deaf when I got to the age to bring people home because it covered up her eccentricities. I mean she just could not deal with other people at all. She had no way of composing herself into a relatively respectable anonymous presence. . . . I got that impression that relations with other people were always kind of strange, and I pretty early learned to be embarrassed by it. But I liked her. I didn't not like her."

Despite this fundamental affection, "I cut myself off from her fairly early because there was a center I could not contact." And even as a small child, Bob was astute enough to register the risks of some of Gladys's survival strategies: "I mean I was much more scrupulous than she was, she didn't have any scruples, she collected welfare and unemployment under three different names. She would report checks lost." But "she never got caught. I used to tell her that you are going to get caught and you are going to go to jail, and she would go into a flap, she would say that is a wish-thought, you are wishing me into jail. Well, she used to tell me stories about mothers who chopped up their children while they were asleep and there was a time I used to go to bed thinking she was going to chop me up when I go to sleep. . . . She was a great actress."

There was no contact at all with whoever Bob's father's family might have been, and very little with the Grants. Gladys's parents were both dead by the year of Bob's birth. Gladys was sporadically in touch with her sister Grace, though the two sisters seemed to get along poorly. Grace was a devout Catholic, while Gladys, in breaking relations with most of her family, had also fallen away from religion. "My mother, who disliked religion, found her sister hard to take for that reason. She was not particularly kindly . . . she was a rather abrasive woman. My mother used to hit Grace up for money. They had some kind of ritual going involving her going to Grace for money which there never was, which she never got much but she disliked doing it and I guess Grace disliked giving it to her but that was the basis of their relationship."

Gladys saw nothing of her surviving brother, though he lived just across the Hudson, in Edgewater, New Jersey. "She didn't have anything to do with any of her other siblings," Bob recalled after her death. "She was really a very secretive and not at all gregarious woman. She had no friends to speak of at all and she had no contact with her family." Essentially, Bob and his mother had no one but each other. They were *two against the world*—a paradigm Bob would later invoke as a model for his marriage to Janice Burr.

———

Gladys's schizophrenia was a matter of speculation. No one knows what treatment she received, in the 1940s, for whatever mental illness she had. Her paranoia was florid later in life, and both Bob and Janice assumed that was a schizophrenic symptom. But a doctor who treated Bob in his sixties diagnosed him as bipolar and guessed that his mother had probably been bipolar as well. Gladys's loss of her job as a schoolteacher involved "various hearings." Bob's childhood memories of her hospitalizations were not rock-solid either, to the point that Janice wonders "if she wasn't just unable to cope with a very active and intelligent child who was probably not very well behaved."

Bob recalled afterward, "I was very talkative. I went into rages. I had very bad tantrums, I think. I really used to throw things around and get very angry. I have clear recollections of being really just as angry as I could be for the size I was." As an adult he remembered beating up his teddy bear: "I used to punch him a lot because I was frustrated and angry a lot of the time. So without getting mad at him I would punch him around and he would be somebody else for a while so I could punch him out. . . . I would make him be somebody else because he had a real personality to me so I would make him be somebody else before I would punch him around."

For a single mother in the 1940s, a son acting out in uncontrollable ways would have been a difficult problem, but St. Ann's Academy was there to help solve it. It was not so unusual for parents in hard times to farm out children who were too big to be handled as infants but still too young to be managed by reason.

To be immured at St. Ann's was no picnic for Bob, who may have been as young as four when this experience began, though he was not alone in his age group there. The regime was penitential to the point of resembling an actual penitentiary: "you get up in the morning and you say your prayers directed by a brother, and then you go and have your cereal, and then go to class, and then you go and have your lunch, and you come out and have ten minutes in the yard and then you go to afternoon class and then you get out and take your books back to the dormitory . . . and everywhere you go you line up and you walk in lines. Everything is organized, and you are never by yourself, everybody is trucking along more or less in a line 'in silence and in order' which I can still hear. You did everything in silence and in order and zipped around this complex. . . . It was all very grim, physically very grim, and I guess in all ways pretty grim. I mean everybody was very unhappy there . . . there was a lot of sniffling and snuffling and unhappy little kids there. I mean that was the scene.

"The Marists were savage, but in those days I don't know where they stood in terms of savagery—you were always hearing about some order of Irish troglodytes down the road who were actually permitted to use flails. They certainly slapped people around right and left; it was very dreary, very tiresome. . . . One of my earliest anxieties was whether I was going to be lined up outside the prefect's room at night to get my hands slapped with a razor strop. There *was* a strop and he actually did sharpen his straight razor on it, and he had these little kids of five and six lined up outside his room to hit them on the hands."

The classes themselves provided little relief from the regime of general misery. "Especially the teachers who taught the little kids were just completely ignorant. They didn't know anything about kids and they didn't know anything about anything much. All they knew was 'in silence and in order.' They just couldn't teach anything. . . . At least they couldn't teach it to me because I just bloody never learned it." Despite this poverty of instruction, Bob, combining his natural intelligence with a desire to please and escape the nightly punishment ritual, got good grades for the most part, though success as an elementary student at St. Ann's was a tricky business: "It was not approved of to have the answers all the time, it was not approved of to be too smart, and it was not approved of to go around using words that you weren't supposed to use that were beyond your age capacity." The Marists chased him out of the school library, considering him to be too young to read without supervision. Instead, Bob managed to find comic books he remembered as being "scary, and uncontrolled . . . extremely violent and extremely chauvinistic."

Before his mother's collapse (whatever its nature), "she had her job as a teacher and we lived in apartments that were quite comfortable and middle class, including finally one in Yorkville on Lexington and Eighty-Fifth. With the hospitalization, she lost her job and since she was no longer a teacher, she couldn't get any leases. From then on we lived in furnished rooms, but before that life was very comfortable and middle class, which figured for me as a kind of lost paradise." Even in this Eden there may have been a couple of serpents. Gladys needed sitters for Bob while she was teaching, and one of these, in Bob's recollection, "had boyfriends who went in for things like hiding me in the closet while they went at it sort of thing. There was some kind of bad scene but I don't remember." Gladys believed that one of Bob's ears was bigger than the other because of a sitter pulling on it. "There were various unpleasantnesses of different kinds," but Bob didn't blame his mother for them: "I know because I was covering up for some of the things she was doing, for my mother's benefit."

Time spent with his mother in Bob's early childhood was precious and often pleasant as well. The attachment between them was strong. Gladys liked books and would read to him. "Bless her scattered mad Irish bones, she lived by the books. I remember from infancy strange words she spoke. ASOKA. TURGENEV." She taught Bob to read before he entered first grade, an accomplishment that put him in the wrong place in the book once he did enter school and was likely as not to earn the disapproval of his teachers at St. Ann's. From the beginning, though, he saw his early reading skill as an instrument of liberation. In return (or in fact from a mixture of motives) Bob told her stories of his own invention. "If I would tell her things that had happened to me, small kid adventures, her reading of them would be cock-eyed. . . . I could never make the point that I wanted to make and I could never get the reaction that I wanted to get. I could make things up for her which would get the reaction I wanted because I knew finally how she worked. So if I wanted a certain reaction I had to make up an adventure that would produce the reaction . . . because the real stuff she always got a wrong reading of. I could never get it through."

Bob had imaginary friends as well, "one called Jerry, why Jerry, I don't know. I think he was better at everything than I was, smarter than I was, tougher than I was, bigger than I was." His teddy bear, despite the regular battering, "I think was more important than my imaginary friends . . . it was my best friend, I mean I really had a thing going with that bear."

Weekdays for preschool Bob must have been very solitary, spent with none-too-attentive caregivers, while his mother was out teaching school herself. "I think I spent a lot of time inside as a kid. . . . I think because I was supposed to be taken out and I wasn't taken out." Frustration with confinement sometimes produced the childish rages and beatings for the teddy bear. But living at St. Ann's felt even worse to Bob. Decades later, he portrayed the St. Ann's experience in "Absence of Mercy," one of his few strictly autobiographical short stories, as having "the social dynamic of a coral reef." Although the Stone character in the story is "able to laugh off much of the brothers' absent-minded battery . . . the statutory evening punishments he would never forgive or forget. . . .

"Ten minutes to a quarter of an hour after the lights had gone out, the prefect would emerge from behind his curtain and eye the quivering scholars like a high priest inspecting the offerings. He would then make a withering remark at their expense; one of his favorites was to address them as 'mother's little darlings,' a characterization hardly appropriate, since they were in fact orphans about to be beaten."

In 1998, after the publication of the story in Bob's first collection, he received a letter from Brother Vincent Jerome, writing on behalf of Archbishop Molloy High School in Queens (the institution St. Ann's had morphed into): "Please allow me to apologize for the unfortunate experiences you had while with the Marist brothers. In no way will I defend certain actions." Bob replied in a conciliatory tone: "I don't think I carry any real bitterness. Like a great many veterans of Catholic education in the forties and fifties, I suppose I dine out on atrocity stories. Of course I don't think being smacked around was good for our characters, but in retrospect I realize how lost and confused so many of my young teachers were—as the Church herself was in those days of uneasy triumphalism. And of course as a teenager I had no compassion, no mercy for people I thought were all-powerful but who I now realize were suffering more than I."

Bob would identify later in life the real-life model for the fictionalized prefect in "Absence of Mercy" as "just a nut," a malfunctioning cog in "this kind of Second Empire French system of prefects and procurators." Also in real life, Bob's mother came regularly to take him out of St. Ann's for excursions, sometimes keeping him overnight or for a whole weekend. "He said if she took his shoes off in the evening he knew he was staying," Janice Stone recalls—and how he must have longed for that signal.

Back at St. Ann's, Bob distracted himself by fantasizing. "I was getting into imaginary games very heavily at this point. In fact the more time I could fill with imaginary life the better off I was as far as I could tell. So I could work the whole day and the whole number around imaginary trips and games and what not and just keep one ongoing story going." Sometimes the fantasies were written down: "like all kids I was writing little stories about trips to Mars and I just kept it up."

Sometimes the games were shared: World War II was happening overseas and in the news, and the boys at St. Ann's invented ways to reenact it; Bob joined the group that played the Nazis. "I didn't really know how much I was supposed to support the war effort because I had the war worked in with the school. I really was inclined to believe things like if they were for it I was against it. I began to vaguely suspect that the Germans and the Japanese must be doing something right if they had enemies like the people I was going to school to."

There were few opportunities for play during the day at St. Ann's, but at night the boys were sometimes allowed to listen to the radio, and Bob made a friend, Douglas Nash, on the basis of their mutual ability to expand on the radio stories. "Nash was going to be a kind of minor crime figure in New York when he got older. I had a lot in common with him . . . he got shoved around a lot because he was fat and because he was kind of scroungy. . . . But he was a bullshitter, he was a very gifted bullshitter and I liked that. And he was also enormous fun to work out imaginary games with. . . . Nobody else could do it on as sophisticated a level as he could, I mean for my purposes. . . . We were just better at it so that we got to realize after we had played with various other people in imaginary games that we could get much further into it if we played with each other because we could feed each other and work out these complex running story games to play out."

Just short of ten years old, Bob left St. Ann's as a boarding student permanently, though the "lost paradise" was not to be regained. Her teaching job gone forever, Gladys now eked out a living by addressing envelopes at home, a lifeline too slender to qualify her for a lease on the sort of apartment she and Bob had lived in before. "I lived with my mother in SROs [single-room occupancy hotels] and rooming houses mostly on the West Side. They weren't as bad in those days as they later became, so I can't say I was really in there with junkies. There was more variety in the poverty of New York at that time—layers and layers. It was very interesting to live on the West Side when it was only seedy, before it became totally lethal," Stone recalled in the late 1980s. "Now it's much more dangerous and less interesting, which seems kind of unfair." But life would certainly have been tough enough for the Stones. The envelope addressing was poorly paid, crippling to Gladys's hands, and socially isolating. Bob learned to pick up a little money by volunteering himself as a guide for visitors to museums like the Metropolitan Museum of Art, and he also learned a lot about the collections in these places, information which would later impress Janice. "I knew various spiels about different paintings. I used to approach people and offer to guide them around if they could put up with me. I mean I must have been pretty obnoxious I would think. I don't know why anybody would go to a museum and take on this kid, but some people did. . . . I knew a little bit about painters, about Renaissance painters."

He continued as a day student at St. Ann's, a situation more bearable than living in. Mistreatment of day students was less severe: "they only slapped you around in the classroom." Not all instruction at the school was completely terrible, and Stone would later give St. Ann's credit for training in a writing style that was "practical, down-to-earth, and basic—in its way good." At some point he came down with scarlet fever, which must have been terrifying for Gladys, who'd lost at least three siblings to such diseases. Bob himself was frightened. "For a couple of months, I really thought I was going to die," he told Bruce Weber in an interview many years later. "It got me in kind of an elegiac mood. It may be I was too young to realize there was such a thing as death. I realize it now." If the illness did give Bob a sense of his own mortality, that might have helped inspire the period of intense Catholic devotion he went through during his early teens. When he was fourteen, he was shaken again by the death, from spinal meningitis, of a friend who had been in St. Ann's as a boarder with him. "I was in that very difficult position you get in when you really believe in God, and at the same time you are very angry: God is this huge creature who we must love, know, and serve, though actually you feel like you want to kick the son of a bitch."

Gladys, though not a practicing Catholic herself, supported Bob's episode of religious fervor. Stone recalled many years later that, as for herself, "it was just not in her temperament to be religious," but although "she was sort of anticlerical . . . she liked the idea of Catholicism. She thought it gave kids something to adhere to—she was quite right—so she sort of elected me to be the house Catholic. . . . She went to church only when she went with me. I think she went only to please me, whereas I thought I was going to please her. So finally we were both going to accommodate each other, and we both quit when I did. But I took it seriously enough to imprint quite deeply a lot of aspects and attitudes that I think are religious and Catholic. . . . It's very hard to escape that take on the world. And when you come right down to it, the world *is* like that, after all. . . . So the preparation probably had some usefulness after all, some grim utility. . . . In some ways Catholicism is very good training for making the best of a hard world, which is what you have to do."

————

However difficult it was to keep him, Gladys seemed unable to bear the thought of another separation from Bob, who himself was terrified at the idea of confinement in another institution. When he was ten or eleven, Bob's situation caught the attention of the child welfare services of New York City. "We lived in . . . this tiny, I mean *tiny* room, the two of us, and she was going around being weird, etc., trying to get work addressing envelopes and so forth and working at maids' jobs when she couldn't get anything else. So . . . to some of the more affluent people who lived on the lower floors in bigger furnished rooms, it looked like a pretty rough deal for a little kid. This crazy lady. And they reported us to the Society for the Prevention of Cruelty to Children. Now I was in good shape. . . . God knows she was not cruel to me or if she was cruel to me she was cruel in a subtle fashion and I was quite capable of being cruel back, so I mean there was no need for this."

At the society's headquarters in East Harlem, Bob had a private interview, "a little separate session with this jerk who was a do-gooder . . . a social worker, a do-good asshole fool who knew from nothing and my business was to convince him that 'No sir, I am fine, I am doing just fine, I don't need you to put me into this goddamn place,' which I could see just walking into it was a goddamn snake pit and if they ever glommed me and stuck me in there I was going to be in big trouble. So my business was to just get back safe to the pad and get the hell out of this institution which these idiots in the name of taking care of the poor and oppressed were running. . . . I was scared . . . because I thought she was so crazy that I thought, 'Okay, they are going to see right away that she is demented and I am going to get scooped up by these fools and institutionalized again,' and I didn't want it."

Desperation can be a mother of invention: "They felt I was super together because I put a rap on them that turned them around. My rap was that I was going to be the most articulate fucking eleven-year-old they ever conversed with and that is what I did." This performance may have been Stone's first direct concrete experience (outside his encapsulated relationship with Gladys) of the power of words, of rhetoric and persuasion—the power of a story to reshape reality. And it was a triumph (despite the unfortunate fact that Gladys attended the interview wearing mismatched shoes); the society dropped the case.

Still, Gladys and Bob were unnerved enough to flee to Chicago, to get out of range of New York's institutional child-catchers, and in the hope that Gladys might resume teaching school there, where no one knew her problematic record. Mostly likely Gladys didn't know anyone in Chicago either; the best she could manage was doing menial work around a Salvation Army shelter to earn her keep and Bob's. The contrast to St. Ann's was considerable: Bob "had the Salvation Army to contend with, whom I didn't like a bit better and who were different, who were these weird kind of Midwestern people who I couldn't make sense of, and who also tended in odd moments to slap me around, like when I was trying to teach other kids to play cards, which they disapproved of violently. So you were always finding something that somebody or other disapproved of that made them hit you."

The Chicago shelter was ahead of its time in accepting an interracial population, so Bob found himself in companionship with black children for the first time in his life. "Chicago in 1948 was a relatively segregated city and it got us into a lot of trouble with other kids. To be associated with that shelter was to be of low status and the fact that there were black kids in there made it all the more troublesome."

For orphan boarders, the Chicago shelter was much less confining than St. Ann's had been: "the kids there were gypsy-kids in a way that I was sometimes but not always: I went in and out of that life. In a way there was a lot of stability in mine. This was a taste of what happened and what you came up with when there weren't any systems." As an adult, Bob told an interviewer the gist of what he learned from the St. Ann's boarding situation and the Chicago shelter: "As I grew up, I began to see the institutional personality, people right around me who were going that way, affectless sociopaths. There is a certain reverence for the sociopath as a major cultural type in American society, along with the frontiersman, the puritan and the outlaw. I was trying to recognize that very fact: the importance of the rootless, emotionally crippled individual in American life."

In Chicago, Bob could spend time out on the street, where he developed a flimflam selling *Life* magazine subscriptions on the pretense that the proceeds would go to Catholic charities. "I don't know what in my small devious mind possessed me to think it up, but it worked. I got fascinated with the idea of the con. It also became apparent to me that I could really lay a rap on people even at that early age, and that if I perfected this I could think up all sorts of numbers that would get me lots of money." However, "I was really fairly scrupulous or at least sentimental so that if I ended up taking money from people I felt bad about it. . . . I didn't hate people enough. . . . I didn't have that whole bit of alienation that I recognized in others."

One of those "others" might have been Gladys, and despite his scruples about her scams, Bob sometimes played a role in them. In Chicago they went together to beg from a Catholic priest, and another time the two managed to get on a radio program in quest of charitable donations. Stone reprised the radio episode in *Outerbridge Reach*, when the filmmaker Ron Strickland plays a tape of the show for a character named Pamela: "They listened to the dulcet tones of Strickland's late mother as she described her dedication to the education of youth. The host had an old-time carny accent, a vanished mode of speech full of secret inflections. Strickland heard his own adolescent voice. He sounded a little like the carny and that was all wrong because he and his mother were supposed to be straight citizens. . . .

"My mother and I were begging," Strickland explains to Pamela. "We were being the deserving poor."

The population of the Salvation Army shelter overlapped the criminal classes in a way completely different from that of St. Ann's. "There were a couple of kids around from the shelter whose families or whose absent fathers were actual con men, in the great middle-western tradition of con-ning." Small-time hustlers of this ilk would later turn up in Stone's fiction.

An astrologer doing Bob's horoscope in 1963 discerned that "1948 was a year of great upheaval for you. Some kind of awakening then, with good and bad aspects, but quite eventful." A perspicacious description of Bob's brief Chicago period.

Despite Bob's attraction to the confidence game (and his sense of his own talent for it), he also felt a longing to belong to "the straight world," probably reflected from his mother. A social iconoclast at heart, Gladys preferred to sustain a facade of middle-class respectability—the culture from which she had come. Though she would sometimes work as a maid when she could get nothing better, she hated doing menial work in the place where she lived. After a few months in Chicago they returned to New York, and to Bob's first experience of raw homelessness: for two nights they slept on the roof of an apartment building on Lexington Avenue. Once Gladys found some sort of work, "we got into a crummy hotel, but crummy hotels in those days didn't mean what a crummy hotel means now. There were junkies around but the junkies were discreet. There was theft but if you were careful and kept your door locked it wasn't danger-ous. It didn't feel dangerous, my mother didn't feel that it was dangerous, it was just unconnected and lonely, solitary people." Bob returned to St. Ann's as a day student, though by now, in his early teens, he had the con-fidence and experience to go truant, spending many days in pool halls or on the New York subway with other boys in similar situations. Gladys would make a couple more attempts to escape to a life outside New York, taking Bob once to New Mexico and once to Montreal, but none of these excursions lasted long.

In the winter of 1948, Bob and his mother took a room at the Endi-cott Hotel, between Eighty-First and Eighty-Second Streets on Colum-bus Avenue, probably moving there from the "crummy hotel" into which they'd descended from their rooftop perch. It was "the Christmas of the Great Snowfall." Bob and his mother bought a scrap of Christmas tree on December 24 and smuggled it into the room, while clerks and bell-men "looked the other way." They put lights on the tree and watched the snow, listening to the radio. It was a watershed moment in Bob's struggle through childhood. "I grew up in the Endicott," he later wrote. He and his mother managed to stay there for several years, throughout all or most of Bob's high-school career; from the Endicott he commuted across town to St. Ann's. He and Gladys shared a single room at the back of the build-ing, with "four windows, so even in winter there was a plenitude of light." There was no kitchen and the rule against hot plates was one they didn't break: "my mother didn't cook, which to her, I think, was the point of liv-ing in New York and not getting married."

The establishment had opened in the late nineteenth century as an elegant hotel. "The Endicott, when I lived there, was in the process of an accelerating descent that would last most of the century. From being a fashionable hotel it must have slipped, gradually, into becoming the sort of place in which Mr. Hurstwood in Dreiser's *Sister Carrie* set up with his mistress at about the same time she was finding it necessary to patch his hand-tailored suits, the day he first found an extra drink at the mir-rored bar more comforting than a fresh flower in his lapel." The hotel's downward drift had conveniences for adolescent Bob: "Like a city cat I crammed myself into every space not completely secured, and everything the old place offered was mine, to the extent that I could experience and comprehend it." There were only a couple of other children in the build-ing, though at thirteen Bob got a heavy crush on "a girl my age who lived there, alone like me, with her mother. Presumably they too were drifting down from something more conventional." Their connection was limited to gazing, probably one-sided gazing. Then, "in some kind of adolescent fit I left a Valentine under her door on February 14. Then I was so appalled at my own sickly, humiliating gesture that I lived in fear she'd find out I'd sent it. For a year afterward I watched from, as it were, afar." The feeling is so closely similar to the longing the narrator of James Joyce's "Araby" feels for Mangan's sister next door that it may partly explain Stone's life-long admiration for that story.

"Every school day morning I took the cross-town bus from the corner of Columbus and 81st. After school I often went to some schoolmate's apartment for a few hours of hanging out in bad weather, or stickball or street hockey in good. I'd meet their parents and be polite. Then I'd pick up my mother at the Endicott and we'd go down to 77th under the maples along the Columbus Avenue side of the Museum of Natural History." It seems a picture of normalcy, though given the cramped quarters Bob shared with his mother, he probably didn't receive his friends at home.

In the typical SRO hotels of the day, the bathroom would be down the hall, which presented what Bob reported as "the ghastly dilemma of the in-room sink. The idea was not to piss in it—or if you did, keep on believing that you hadn't. Once you had pissed in the sink of your bath-less double you belonged to the fallen world around you. It was no lon-ger a question of passing through on the way to better things. Many a dapper bachelor, lady or gent, fastidiously turned out, secretly gave way, demoralized by disappointed hopes, by solitude and drink. To know this struggle in the dark was to know more than you needed about Original Sin, natural depravity and the thin pretenses on which the maintenance of human dignity depends.

"Being roomies with your own mother, striving to preserve her naïve but sacred trust (by for example not pissing in the sink), believing with all your might that *she* would never do such a thing, all this takes its emo-tional toll. All the intimacies and evasions attendant on sleeping a few feet away from a most proper-minded, actually quite prudish former school teacher, were, as I now realize, the source of some stress and confusion to me."

Gladys had a lot invested in Bob, to the point of encouraging his ado-lescent fling with Catholic devotion, as much as she disliked religion. As he moved through his teens, however, Bob was on his way to becoming an apostate, and more than a bit of a rogue in the St. Ann's classrooms. He enjoyed swimming and running for their own sakes but in the form of organized sports, not so much. His performance in school track meets seems modeled on Alan Sillitoe's "The Loneliness of the Long-Distance Runner." "I would get to the flats where at the end everybody would stand around and yell and I would let about eighteen guys pass me at that point. It really used to shake me up. I didn't like running against people and I didn't like people cheering at me. It just made me feel self-conscious in an unpleasant way." Offered a swimming scholarship to another high school, he turned it down, continuing instead at St. Ann's. Throughout his life Bob loved almost everything to do with water: swimming, snorkeling, diving, fishing, traveling in any kind of aquatic vessel, but he wasn't inter-ested in racing people in it. His decision to stay on with the Marists was moved by a sudden "fondness for Catholicism," as well as his distaste for competitive sports.

When he became friends with memoirist and fiction writer Frank Conroy later in life, Bob discovered that he and Frank had lived in the same East Side neighborhood as adolescents. They didn't know each other then, because Frank attended a private school, automatically rendering him Bob's class enemy. As Bob had told Janice, "Some of the parochial-school kids preyed on the private-school students, fighting with them and perhaps stealing their lunch money. Bob did not behave this way, but he remembered that if he and his schoolmates were noticed too far west (for example, on Fifth Avenue) the police would tell them to get back where they belonged."

Teaching in most subjects continued to be poor at the upper levels of the St. Ann's program. Many of the teaching brothers were "French Canadians and they had rather strong Quebec accents and idiosyncrasies which were reinforced by their own personal idiosyncrasies," a situation which fostered a good deal of mutual incomprehension. Bob had no luck in math, but in subjects where his interest and talent enabled him to teach himself to some degree, he did better. The study of Latin, where the Marists were naturally stronger than elsewhere, did interest him. He read Ovid and Cicero, probably also Caesar and Virgil. As an adult Stone recalled that he "really enjoyed learning Latin and I still read poetry in Latin." One of his juvenile fragments of writing is set in the Roman world. In his 1998 letter to Brother Vincent Jerome, Bob mentioned "some wonderful teachers among the Marist brothers, who encouraged my writing though exasperated by my indiscipline," and mentioned that Latin was "to this day the only foreign language in which I've ever had a true literary experience."

The Marists also assigned students to read classics of the nineteenth century, including *The French Revolution: A History*, by Thomas Carlyle, "the first person who gave me what I would call a literary experience, who taught me something about how language works and what writing is about. . . . My first reaction to it was 'I can't understand a word of this, it doesn't make sense to me, what a strange way of writing this is.' But as I read it, I began to really enjoy it, and I began to understand it more. It really struck me as most unfamiliar, provocative, and strange." Stone's coursework included contemporary Catholic intellectuals like Cardinal Newman, which gave him some grounding in twentieth-century prose style. At home, his mother continued to share her reading matter, introducing Bob to Thomas Wolfe among others (his classmates thought him a "weirdo" for reading Wolfe).

With his quick wit, sharp tongue, and the contempt and even hatred he felt for the schoolmasters, Stone was a dangerous pupil—less a class clown than an agile gadfly. "There were a number of people who thought that I was amusing and who kind of liked me in school. And the school didn't like that because they saw me as subversive, which I was. I really was subversive to everything they stood for. . . . I think I was basically pretty aggravated with them for hitting me all the time." For the amusement of his classmates Bob wrote satirical caricatures of some teachers, bashing them out on a manual typewriter. One, called "The Vulture," has survived:

"Inside her first grade classroom her pupils were strewn about, consuming the sun in carefree abandon. Rising, she smoothed down her pink skirt and addressed the class.

" 'I may be new around here but I'm not stupid.'

"Shocked by such insolent behavior, the more radical faction of the class arose and began proceedings to have Miss Vulture impeached. Cooler heads won the day, however, and instead she was placed on thirty days probation ending her trial. She placed her head on the desk and said, 'Jesus Christ, what have I done to deserve this!' Then she began picking threads off her black suit."

Close physical and psychological observation made these lampoons extremely volatile stuff. Finally Bob had to abandon the series when a piece featuring "one particularly dimwitted French Canadian" was traced to him. "And I mean there was really nowhere to go after that . . . I mean I think his feelings were very hurt but of course at that time I didn't care. It didn't matter to me that his feelings were hurt because I had no mercy. They were just so powerful, these people, that I didn't have any mercy for them at all."

In 1998, an Englishman named John Gavin read a profile of Robert Stone and recognized his classmate from St. Ann's, where he'd attended high school from 1951 to 1953. "I seem to remember we were pretty close at one point," he wrote. "Certainly I was very much under your influence. You introduced me to politics, and we had some great discussions on life and philosophy, though I don't remember winning any arguments." Eventually, Bob's influence over his fellow students would get him into the worst trouble St. Ann's was capable of delivering.

During Bob's high school years, the Endicott "nose-dived. One day we were outraged to find that the welfare department had begun to place its clients in the hotel. Who did they think we were? Who did we think we were? Who were we?

"The old people lived on Social Security. Many of the rest of us were working alcoholics, inhalator freaks, schizophrenics who moved from job to job, in vanished niches of diminished industries where temporary jobs were always available. Many of the lone women like my mother were hand-addressers of envelopes or hand-inserters, work that cut their hands to shreds and twisted their fingers into arthritic stumps, or petty office workers in the garment district without the skills to sew." Bob and Gladys's way of life involved eluding the welfare system, or gaming it (sometimes both at the same time). "So the idea of sharing the Endicott with congenital, regular welfare clients infuriated us."

Coming down the stairs from the roof one winter night, Bob surprised a couple of men who "fled, leaving spread across the stairway a pale beautiful girl. She looked like the sensuous murder victim in *Spicy Detective*, a contemporary publication. She was dressed as if for work in a sheath suit. One of the arms of her jacket was rolled up, and in the crook of her elbow was a hypodermic needle full of blood." Both excited and alarmed by "the fatefulness and cheap drama of the scene and the girl's good looks," Bob slipped outside and notified police of the overdose by pay phone.

Bob began to skip school more and more regularly, or sometimes showed up stoned or drunk. "One of my party tricks to amaze my friends I did a number of times when I was about sixteen was to drink four or five cans of beer and show up for class drunk, completely plastered, to show that nobody was more crazy or out to lunch than I was. That was my way of demonstrating my self-destructiveness and willingness to do any crazy shit." In the same spirit, he joined the Saxons, an Upper West Side, mostly Irish street gang, around the same time he stopped going to Mass. In his middle teens he was fully initiated and became the gang's "war counselor." For the competitive sports he disliked he could now substitute more or less ritualized street fights with Puerto Rican gangs on adjoining turf. In the mid-1950s, these battles were unlikely to involve firearms and seemed to have the light operatic flavor of similar episodes in *West Side Story*; this fighting was, in Stone's recollection, "incredibly decorous, chivalrous, and safe by today's standards." At the same time, racist ugliness was on the rise, as the white gangs contested black and Hispanic youth for primacy in Central Park.

As a Saxon, and with the certain status he had in the group, Bob was able to meet girls more freely, though such romances were still constricted by 1950s Catholic morality. "I was really fond of one girl I used to date who was really a friend and who I liked in all sorts of ways. . . . She had kind of a square jaw, she was cute, and intelligent, she was smart and in some ways liberated from that scene but in other ways she was a bit of a trial because every time we necked which is what we both wanted to do she would have gone to confession and . . . the priest would have told her not to do this, and this of course was a drag. And I began to feel like an occasion of sin."

Apparently the girl's family (a regular Irish Catholic household with mother, father, and children all on the scene) accepted Bob without much reservation (though one imagines that his modest outlaw status had some attraction for the girl herself). That access gave him a taste of the "straight life" he often aspired to, though at the end of his high school years, his impulse to blow up his chances at that kind of life proved stronger.

A couple of years later Stone projected "an idealized version" of this relationship into a story called "The Two Smartest Kids on the Block," in which a neighborhood bystander, dully aging in a dead-end job, considers the fate of Tone Dolan and Margie Donnelly. It's easy enough to recognize a self-portrait in Tone Dolan, who "played a great deal by himself down on the East River Drive, and though he never spoke much to other people, he was always talking to himself." Though the neighbors consider him "a feeble-minded kid" whose parents are "such nutty people," Tone Dolan does surprisingly well in grammar school, ending each week with "a fist full of the Holy Pictures that they gave out for the highest marks. His mother carried them around in her pocketbook."

In high school Tone begins to drink and get in trouble: "when he talked, it was always to be on the wrong side of arguments." He leaves "a good Catholic academy" for public school, then more or less drops out. "People would spot him in crazy parts of town walking up and down streets, any hour of the night, sometimes drunk, sometimes sober, talking to himself. So, before very long the word went out that Tone Dolan had become an eight ball. An eight ball is a guy who acts in a way other than people think he should."

The character of Margie may be somewhat further from the reality of Bob's Irish girlfriend: "you know that in every neighborhood there is one particular golden girl." Like Tone a precociously promising student, Margie wins a scholarship to "a very posh Catholic girls' school near Park Avenue," a success that causes the neighbors, however paradoxically, to frown on her for getting above herself. Perhaps it makes sense for her to fall in with the roguish Tone ("what the Irish call a dark sort of man, meaning that there was a barrier between himself and the world"), with whom she shares a fondness for eight-ball subjects like music and art and "books which were considered dangerous to faith and morals."

The couple quietly plans for a future that involves, as a preliminary step, Tone joining the navy. "They had discussed it and agreed that he should go in and sort of organize and brace himself for a possible assault on conventional living, and she would take dramatics at Columbia and when he got out, they would get married and try things together." Instead, Margie is killed in a car wreck and Tone sinks into despair and complete dissolution. The story fizzles out in the mind of the narrator, who reflects on the blighting of a somewhat hopeful future from the point of view of never having imagined much future at all for himself. Aside from an astute rendering of the oppressive mind-set of the 1950s working-class neighborhood of its setting, this retrospective framing of the story is the only glimmer of what the mature Robert Stone would achieve.

———•———

Despite his rebelliousness, frequent truancy, and showing up drunk to class on occasion, real-life Bob was doing well academically, at least in subjects that interested him. His involvement with the Saxons was of course frowned upon by school authorities, but he began, on his own, to back away from the group. The street-gang culture was changing, with increased involvement with organized crime and hard drugs; many Saxons had begun to use heroin. Though Stone would develop a taste for narcotics later in life, in his teens he only used alcohol and marijuana. In his role as war counselor for the Saxons he did diplomacy with the Puerto Rican gangs, and discovered he liked the Hispanic boys more than not; there seemed less point in fighting them.

Gang conflict was becoming more dangerously violent; lethal weapons were more likely to appear. In an unexpected clash with another gang near the Central Park obelisk, knives came out and "a lot of people got cut." One of the Saxons had a dangerous stab wound, so Bob and his party took him to the nearest hospital, a Fifth Avenue establishment that turned them away. Finally they dropped him off, still breathing and still bleeding, at the doors of a down-market hospital more likely to receive the poor. Bob came away from the episode thinking "this is foolish. If I'm going to get killed, I'm going to get killed over something worthwhile." He did spend part of the next year hanging out with an Italian gang in

East Harlem: "They would do things like exchange fascist salutes and paint 'Viva Il Duce' on the walls, more to bust balls than anything else."

In school he was preparing for the Regents Exam, at the time a tool for identifying high-school graduates with potential for college education. Bob took a dim view of the Marists' guidance for the Regents. "Where I went to school, the whole of artistic endeavor in human history was something that you tried to cram into the college preparation course when you prepared for the Regents scholarship test. They just fed you all this information that you were supposed to memorize, without actually exposing you to the contaminating influences of the art itself. Basically they were saying, Here's a whole lot of stuff that the Gentiles believe and various shibboleths and names that you ought to know because they'll be on the test the Jews will give us." Since Bob had already acquired a good deal of knowledge about Western art history on his own, while lurking about New York museums as a smaller child, this bleakly cynical approach to the subject must have put him off even more. "It was all totally external from life, from the course of our being prepared for our careers with Hartford Accident and Indemnity and for Calvary Cemetery."

A senior now, Bob took the test, and went on performing as "house crazy" at St. Ann's; he had now (having cast off the chains of organized religion, the Roman Catholic version in particular) also begun to preach his new enthusiasm for atheistic secular humanism to his fellow students, some of whom were swayed by it. One of them, Freddy Vassi, refused to go to Mass with his parents and invoked Bob's arguments as the reason why. Now there was some real trouble; Bob became the target of a "grand inquisition."

In a way he enjoyed it. "I felt like Luther or something. I really thought I was a superhero." In the midst of the interrogation ("a full-scale inquisition at night that I had to go in for") it was somehow revealed that, though he was failing math at the time, Bob had earned the highest score of anyone in his school on the Regents Exam (and even qualified for a college scholarship)—information the Marists had kept from him until then. They solved the exquisite paradox of this situation by expelling Bob from the school.

Though he "thought it was all very exciting," Bob was "a little bit disturbed at the effect on my mother of my being thrown out of school." Despite the Regents Scholarship, the doorway to college appeared to be closed. He knew he wanted to be a writer, and had even won a couple of literary prizes during the year before his expulsion from St. Ann's. His short story "The City Is of Night" won a First Class Gold Medal publication prize in the Washington Square College annual prose writers' contest; if Bob had entered again as a high-school senior he would have had a shot at a four-year scholarship to New York University. Around the same time he also won first prize in a TV script-writing contest sponsored by the American Cancer Society, for a short play featuring Napoleon Bonaparte, largely based on Bob's eighth-grade reading of Carlyle's *French Revolution*. Still, a writing career didn't really seem feasible to him at that time. "I didn't think that being a writer was economically possible; I'd come to share from somewhere, not from my mother, the sense you had to make a living in a more solid way."

"I don't like to talk about my early life very much," Bob told Ann Greif many years later. "It is a very mixed bag and it wasn't unmitigated unpleasantness . . . I mean in all the obvious ways it could be bad, it was." It was obvious enough that his mother's mental illness and her precarious social situation had mixed effects on Bob as a small child—bringing out a whole host of precocious capabilities but also burdening him with the enormous stress of being reliant almost entirely on his own resources. "I wasn't scared of very much when I was that age . . . I was probably more competent with dealing with stuff than I am now." At fourteen he began to suffer cyclical depression. "I would get *really* bummed out for long periods of time. And the fits of depression would be accompanied by irrational fears of one thing or another. I would get scared of people, and then it would pass. . . . I would go back to more or less normal. I mean I really did surround myself with all kinds of fantasies and dreams. I was all the time off somewhere in my head."

Some of these feelings are reflected in Stone's first prizewinning story, "The City Is of Night," which his mother clipped and surreptitiously submitted to *The New Yorker*, though without success. Gladys didn't in fact think it was impossible for her son to become a writer. She had shared her taste for reading (sophisticated for the time) with Bob, and she wrote a bit herself from time to time. In his teens Bob read some of his mother's prose, though his opinion, at least in retrospect, was not very high: "Her writing wasn't very good as I remember, because it was very sentimental, but it wasn't illiterate. It was quite literate . . . but very mannered and artificial." Much later, Stone ruefully recalled that his mother had raised him to think he was so brilliant he didn't have time for her. Gladys's support for Bob's artistic vocation couldn't help but be erratic, but it was also authentic, and in a way that counted.

"The City Is of Night" is a nearly plotless story that represents Stone's first of many assaults on the ineffable. "Nothing spectacular has to happen, no big celebration or anything like that, but on the most quiet nights you get a feeling which is hard to describe and you wake up the next morning feeling older." In its style of conversational ingenuousness the story owes something to Sherwood Anderson and maybe a little to Thomas Wolfe (though without any of Wolfe's bombast). Later on, Stone guessed it was "probably written a couple of weeks after I finished reading *The Catcher in the Rye*, and I have a feeling if I read it now I would find it intensely Salingeresque." Wrong: Even in this fledgling effort the writer Stone is immune to Salinger's sentimental *preciosité*.

As in much of his mature work, in this story Stone scatters his own qualities over more than one character. His narrator is acutely interested in language and has a habit of going to the library to read the encyclopedia. But it's another character, Ed McLanahan, who's famous for his good "school marks," and a third, Charlie Egan, who "would give out with the damned oddest things, even poetry and stuff like that and sometimes he was silent and moody like early that night." A fourth character, Jamey DiScioli, has recently left a Saxon-like street gang and ends up voicing a lot of what was probably in Stone's mind at the time about his own situation.

Dramatic action is scanty, but the image of late-1950s New York City grows extraordinarily vivid as Stone's narrator roams the Upper East Side, picking up one acquaintance after another until the group is quite sizable. Killing time is the order of the evening. They spend a couple of hours in a pool hall, then trundle a quantity of beer to Pilgrim Hill in Central Park. Though the New York skyline is panoramic as always, there's a pervasive sense of the future's foreclosure.

DiScioli talks about quitting the gang: "those guys—all day long they just push a dolly around down in the garment district or make deliveries for some cheap grocery. Then, on Sunday, they put on their thirty-dollar suits and walk around the park acting tough. There must be more to living than that. . . . Those guys are scared, see? All of them—because they know if you take them out of the gang they won't be anything but a punk pushing something down Thirty-eighth Street. So they get together—a lot of frightened little guys who make a lot of noise because they have to use their damned club jacket for a soul. . . . That's it. That's why I'm out."

Poet-philosopher Charlie Egan remarks, "I think they get us all behind something sooner or later. . . . We'll be pushing things through the streets, yet."

Because of the high cost of joining the union, the young men figure that the merchant marine is no longer a viable escape route. But Charlie's brother is going into the military, still an option open to anybody. "Maybe it'll settle him down, huh?" Charlie says, to which Stone's narrator replies, "He's just a little wild because he doesn't know what to do with his time."

Although *The New Yorker* rejected this story when Gladys sent it to them, they did invite Stone to send more of his work. "That really set me up," Stone said later on. "But I think with very few exceptions the teachers and friends I had really didn't look at the life of the arts except as an excuse for not working. . . . A writing career was unstable, and what I was really after on some level was stability. I really wanted to be something absolutely solid, something uneccentric, perfectly acceptable and secure."

2
VIEWS OF THE WORLD

Expelled from St. Ann's in May of his senior year, Bob found himself at loose ends. He worked briefly as a clerk in a department store, and fretted that members of a rival gang might be out to get him. He spent his spare time hanging around Greenwich Village and observing the beatniks, then made an about-face in the direction of stability. At seventeen he got his mother's permission to enlist for a three-year hitch in the U.S. Navy, "known as a minority enlistment or colloquially as a kiddie cruise." Without much in the way of competent adult advice, he didn't see any better option; the enlistment also represented a conscious putting away of childish things. Besides, "I wanted to go to sea. I was romantic about the sea, and I wanted to see the world. Corny old Navy stuff."

Boot camp was a rough ride for Stone, who turned eighteen early in his navy hitch. After a few days, he quipped much later in life, "I was wondering where the Society for the Prevention of Cruelty to Children was, now that I really needed them. . . . Bainbridge, Maryland, and it was absolute hell. It was summer and so uniform was whites. The only way you could wash your clothes was with a scrub brush and Ivory Soap. My mother was an old lady; I wasn't very handy at keeping my gear together and I was also kind of dreamy and unfocused, not ideal Navy material at all. It was really traumatic for me. The up side was that though they terrorized me, they didn't hit me. And I was in boot camp from August until November; I got sent back and had to do part of it over again."

The survival skills Bob had picked up at St. Ann's did not transfer well to military training. The regime of senseless, arbitrary punishment he'd suffered as a small boy had created in him what in behavioral psychology is called "learned helplessness." In the 1960s, within the context of operant conditioning, a series of remarkably cruel animal experiments established that a creature afflicted with random punishment no matter what it does will sink into a sort of trembling apathy. When Stone endowed his fictional alter-ego Mackey, the protagonist of the short story "Absence of Mercy," with this quality, he called it "an instinctive cringe." Navy training, with its own particular brand of behavior modification, eventually made this problem go away: "when I was being subjected to their stuff, I really shocked them"—the boot camp noncoms, that is. If it took longer than usual, the boot camp experience finally did free Stone of that damaging reflex, encysted in him since early childhood.

Next, "I went to a technical air patrol squadron at Norfolk Naval Air Station and from there I went to radio school in Norfolk. From there I went aboard the USS *Muliphen*, during September of 1956. The ship was an AKA (attack cargo ship) that looked like one of those ships off Normandy: big A frames and landing boats stacked up on the hull." The AKAs were World War II vintage vessels, armed with five-inch cannon and antiaircraft guns in some cases; "their form grimly followed function and they were as plain as dumpsters." AKAs were the workhorses of what was then called the "Gator Navy," after the amphibious functions of its fleet.

Bob Stone boarded the *Muliphen* with the rank of seaman first class. The personnel clerk who had given him his orders turned out to be a New Yorker himself, and confided in Bob that he was "going to a problem ship."

" 'They're always falling off ladders,' he said," which must have been a coded message. "Certain ships were dominated, prison-style, by cliques of sailors—sometimes men from the same tough town—who enforced a code

of their own below decks. . . . Such a ship's officers might be only vaguely
aware of the system that prevailed in the enlisted quarters. Masters-at-
arms and senior petty officers either looked the other way or, like crooked
cops, made some political accommodation with the de facto leadership."

An older man, a third-class boatswain's mate, soon marked Stone as
"tender gear," a term applied at the time "to sailors of youthful appearance,
when imagined as passive partners in prison-style 'facultative' homosexuality or as the victims of rape," as Bob wrote several decades later. A dol-
lop of homophobia was standard equipment for the average young male
psyche of the 1950s, and Bob had had an unpleasant experience shortly
before leaving New York when a male friend had tried to trap him into
a sexual encounter—unpleasant enough that he was still disturbed by it
when talking to Ann Greif some twenty-five years later, though more by
the element of entrapment than by the sexual overture per se: "He was . . .
a manipulative person given to all sorts of intrigues, a game-player who
set up all kinds of numbers. I think he was probably pretty sick. . . . I am
still angry about that." The intriguer had also managed to convince Bob's
then girlfriend that the two boys had "some kind of scene going on, which
made me feel very bad indeed."

In any case it would plainly not do to be raped aboard the *Muliphen*.
Stone took an extra bunk chain to sleep with him that night; when the
attack came he used this weapon to fight it off. "A few men were awake
and silent or laughing; I was new, nobody much cared." When Bob told
me this story in the 1990s, he made it sound like a weary ritual—his assailant didn't really offer much resistance, but Bob just had to beat him
up, to assert a survivable level of integrity, while feeling miserable about
every blow of the chain. An account written later for *The New York Review of Books* makes the struggle sound more challenging: "In those days
I was always blundering into fights only to be reminded that it wasn't
like the movies, to be amazed by the strength and determination of my
opponent." Misery, though, is common to both versions. Stone said that
when he crossed paths with his attacker a few days later the man claimed
"You cried just like a cooze," during the encounter, and though Bob didn't
remember that "it occurred to me that I might well have. I didn't care for
the picture the reflection summoned forth, me whacking Flem repeatedly
with a bunk chain, weeping away 'like a cooze.'" But at least there were
no more attempts to molest him.

The *Muliphen* sailed to Rapallo, where the sailors got shore leave and young Stone set foot on European soil for the first time. He was on liberty in Rome when a recall order came; the Sixth Fleet was being dispatched to protect and extract civilians from the Suez Canal zone.

On July 26, 1956, President Gamal Abdel Nasser of Egypt had nationalized the company operating the Suez Canal, a critical conduit for shipment of oil and passage of military shipping from the Mediterranean Sea to the Indian Ocean via the Red Sea. This route was a key point of interest for France, Britain, Israel, the Soviet Union, and the United States. After months of unsuccessful diplomacy (fraught with the complexities and confusions of the early Cold War period), Egypt was invaded: by Israel through the Sinai Desert and by combined British and French forces at Port Said, where the Suez Canal opened into the Mediterranean.

Stone was transferred as a radioman to the USS *Chilton*, another elderly attack cargo vessel, and shipped to Port Said. He was in the emergency communications room when the French air attack on the harbor began. "I had just learned Morse Code. . . . I was developing a fist, and I was seeing how fast I could send it. In order to do this, I would shave my own personal keyboard until it had a kind of hair trigger, so I could make it go faster and faster and faster and faster. And I could blow the other guy away, because he wouldn't be able to copy me, because I'd be so fast in this little game we played." Stone was diverted from "filing away at my tap board" and ordered on deck to set the sight on the *Chilton*'s five-inch gun, which "sits up on a little platform all by itself amidships. You climb up it on a little ladder. I didn't know how to set it. Nobody had ever taught me. I had no idea. Fortunately, it didn't matter one way or the other. It was the French against the Egyptians. But when I first got on deck, the first thing I saw was that the sea was red."

The French were slaughtering the Egyptians like shooting fish in a barrel. "A French jet would go in. You'd hear it, I don't know how many minutes later. It was going along the corniche of Port Said, and it was killing every living thing. A man was sitting in a boat saying 'Allah Akbar Rachman, Allah Akbar Rachman, Allah Akbar Rachman,' all by himself in a reed boat, rocking back and forth, completely out of his mind. . . . And so I climbed up on my little five-inch, and all around me was this red water and exploding reed boats and Port Said being absolutely blown apart. And I thought, 'This is what I always thought it was like. This is the real thing. This is the way it is.' "

Since the Americans were not combatants in this action, Stone and his shipmates were not directly in danger, and he like the rest of them was more thrilled than appalled at first. "I thought to myself, 'God, I'm glad I'm here. I'm so glad that I'm here.' And it still didn't occur to me that anybody was doing anything wrong. . . . And the illumination rounds being fired against the sunset, I thought was the most beautiful thing I'd ever seen."

After nightfall the mood aboard the *Chilton* changed when a French Mirage jet shot out the vessel's anchorage. "So we were anchored basically to nothing. So we began to go to general quarters and we'd track them with our little five-inch and our fifty-millimeters every time, until more and more, every time they came over, they came over, it seemed, lower and lower; and we really wanted to kill them, because it began to penetrate our consciousness that the harbor was filled with dead people."

At eighteen years old, Stone's "overwhelming response . . . was 'I always knew this was the way things were.' I always thought that the world was filled with evil spirits, that people's minds teemed with depravity and craziness and weirdness and murderousness, that that basically was an implicit condition, an incurable condition of mankind. I suddenly knew what was meant when Luther said, 'The world is in depravity.' "

Later the same night, the awfulness of it all started sinking in, and Stone began to process that "something terrible was happening. But when I figured it out, I thought, 'This is the way it is. There is no cure for this. There is only one thing you can do with this. You can transcend it. You can take it and you make it art."

That didn't happen right away; the small amount of fiction Stone wrote shipboard related to his previous life in New York. Some of his navy experiences would later be translated into short stories written for a class at New York University, but not the one at Port Said. After seeing the Suez action, he was transferred back to the *Muliphen*, which continued to cruise the Mediterranean.

Shore leave happened in pleasant places: "In the fifties, especially, the eastern Mediterranean was a pretty exotic location. People in the mid-fifties didn't often get to Greece, for example." In Athens, Stone pissed in the Temple of Zeus, an act which he later joked might have worsened his future luck, due to the god's displeasure. On one of its Atlantic crossings, the *Muliphen* laid over in Cuba, and on riotous shore leave in Havana, Bob was "one of a group who had gotten into trouble for having pissed on the statue of Jose Marti—an act of drunken hilarity, not political," as he later told Jim Maraniss. Bob found another use for his equipment while in Cuba: "The place was called the Blue Moon. It had a curving wall of translucent glass bricks and a bar with a travel-poster photo of the Havana skyline. Young women came out to be bought drinks and taken upstairs. One of them approached me. I have many recollections of that day, but I can recall neither the woman's face nor her name nor the details of our encounter. I do recall there was a certain amount of laughing it up and pretending affection and also that there was paying. The bill came to quite a lot of money. I presume I was cheated in some way, but everyone was nice."

There was more to that first Cuban experience than frivolity and dissipation. "All this Spanish tragedy," he wrote much later, "leavened with Creole sensuality, made Havana irresistible. Whether or not I got it right, I have used the film of its memory ever since in turning real cities into imaginary ones."

After his enlistment ended, Stone assayed the liminal experience of the sailor on shore leave in forty-odd pages of a never-published story called "The Good Neighbor," set in Mariposa, a fictitious, Spanish-speaking Caribbean locale. The narrator leaves his vessel in quest of a legendary bordello, the House of Love, but perhaps not really knowing exactly what he's after: "I felt as though I had come somehow to the naked edge of the world. It seemed all like the dawn of that morning, all things carried to their ultimate extremes, a hell of lost human jetsam, a paradise of palm and whitecaps—the chiaroscuro of the waterfront square, with its unbearable sun and creeping black relentless shade." The sailor falls in with another American who's settled in this place, "a faintly Babbitty character from Denver," and a person of wealth and influence in Mariposa, therefore called "the Captain." In the course of a twenty-four-hour barhopping odyssey the narrator keeps crossing paths with the Captain, who eventually conveys him to the House of Love, where instead of springing for the notorious "Deep Six," the narrator only drinks more rum. The venue and the scene taking place there is somewhat reminiscent of the Consul's visit to the Farolito in Malcolm Lowry's *Under the Volcano* (of which Stone wrote admiringly late in life).

The House of Love bartender predicts that the Captain "will take you to his house for a drink. He is always taking people there. He used to take me. My friend, he lives in the jungle. Out in the jungle. You will see. Sometimes I am frightened when I think of it." The narrator is duly conveyed to the Captain's domicile in the hour before dawn: "The place had a luring, dangerous beauty, like a mountain pool, or the bottom of the sea." Indoors, he greets the Captain's wife (whom he's crossed paths with earlier in his bar crawl) and is offered nothing more sinister than a ham sandwich. And yet:

"There was no mystery now. It was terror. A black relentless terror as palpable as the scented night outside. It had hung over the Captain as he weaved through the streets of the old city, and over the Captain's lady as she sat alone with her gin. It mixed with the smell of the elephant grass and the orchids, seeping from the jungle outside into their tasteful living room. I felt it fill me as I stood before them—a blend of this jungle, this night of orchids and moonlight, the red and yellow bacchanal of the old city, the stench of El Triano. I felt almost reverent in its presence. And as we drove through forest and back toward the city and my ship, I remember that the sun came up again—fierce and unbidden, out of the lovely, deadly night." It might be going a little too far to say that "The Good Neighbor" represents Stone's first completely mature work, but it is certainly a harbinger, forecasting Rheinhardt's drunken wanderings of New Orleans in *A Hall of Mirrors*, and Holliwell's brushes with nameless terrors in the tropics of *A Flag for Sunrise*; it also succeeds in suffusing its exotic locale with the sort of dark ambivalence that would characterize his later work.

———

Shipboard, Bob read copiously. "Everybody on a ship reads, whether it's comic books, or Westerns, or the Bible, or whatever." Stone read *Moby-Dick*, which "might strand me in passages as tedious as Sunday routine in mid-Indian Ocean, but I kept at it, through the overwrought, white hot language, the leaden dirty jokes and general absurdity. I had started young enough to enjoy the mysteries and to ponder the prophecy at its core." He also read Joyce's *Ulysses*, a lot of Joseph Conrad, and whatever poetry he could lay hands on. "I had an anthology of poetry with some Wallace Stevens poems in it and I will never forget the morning (maybe it was Sunday) when after innumerable false starts 'Sunday Morning' stood open to me. I understood it!" Not all his shipmates restricted their reading to comic books or the Bible. "Those huge ships, you always found people who had read the same books that you did. There was always somebody on the ship who had read *The Great Gatsby* or had read Hemingway. You always found people to hang with."

Stone composed "The Two Smartest Kids on the Block" and submitted it to *Esquire*, where it was rejected. He did the necessary courses to earn a high school GED, and also passed a test to become a navy journalist, which came with a promotion to petty officer third class. "Because I passed the test, I was officially certified Third Class Journalist. I had the insignia on my arm to prove it. Essentially I was a correspondent for the Armed Forces Press Service; that was my last year and a half in the navy."

Aboard the *Muliphen*, Stone was editor of the ship's newspaper and editor in chief of the USS *Muliphen* Cruise Book, the equivalent of a yearbook for high school or college, featuring photos of the officers and crew and Stone's text describing the voyage. While still on the Mediterranean tour, he also wrote a story on the marine residence station in Beirut. Then he volunteered for an expedition to Antarctica: Operation Deep Freeze III, aboard the USS *Arneb* (another AKA). "We started in Davisville, Rhode Island, in November and we went around the world by way of the canal to Port Littleton [*sic*], New Zealand, and then down to Antarctica, then to Sydney, to Durban, South Africa, then Montevideo, and we got back in the Spring of '58. We were in Antarctica for two periods: the first at Cape Hallett on the Pacific side for almost two months, then to Sydney for a liberty, then back down for a couple of more months. The ship's mission was taking off old Seabees, putting new Seabees on, giving them new equipment. Also we had scientists aboard; we were tracing cosmic rays. We had these receptor instruments. The University of Chicago had apparently supplied a course for us to follow and we were tracking cosmic rays. I think that there was also some kind of secret military function but I can't remember what it was."

Before sailing to Davisville to take on supplies, the officers and crew of the *Arneb* were treated to a fancy lunch, catered by Longchamps, on their mooring in New York's North River. The ship went into port at Norfolk for the Thanksgiving holiday, then sailed through the Panama Canal and down South America's west coast. Sailors crossing the equator for the first time went through some initiatory hazing. Thanks to crossing an international date line, the *Arneb* actually missed New Year's Eve of 1957.

In Lyttelton, New Zealand, Stone went ashore in the company of Bob Bell, an operations office yeoman working as a secretary in the same shipboard office as he. (Bob had decorated his desk with a photo of the New York skyline and another of Brigitte Bardot, representing at the time "the poles of my desire.") Though Bell had finished college, Stone was the more experienced writer and able to lend him a hand with his secretarial chores; they had become friends on that basis at first. Stone confided to some extent in Bell, who reports the detail that "he and his mother were living in cardboard boxes in New York at one point. . . . He could be somewhat elusive, but we enjoyed going out to dinner and chasing girls in New Zealand and Australia." Their first move in Lyttelton was to buy civilian clothes, but they were still recognizable as Americans and got a friendly reception for it. "I said, 'Bob, you don't have to chase these girls—just walk down the street and they'll tap you on the shoulder.'" Bell had acquired this intelligence from older salts aboard the *Arneb*, and it turned out to be true. Amiable New Zealanders bought the sailors meals and drinks; "we weren't allowed to pay. Early evening we met two young nurses and took them to a movie."

According to Bell, Stone changed his life by giving him a copy of *The Magic of Believing*, a 1948 proto-self-help book by Claude Bristol—and an unlikely fit for Stone's library. "He told me about a sailor who ran down the passageway and quickly handed him this book, insisting that he read it. Then, the man just disappeared." This tale too seems a little unlikely. Conceivably Gladys might have sent Stone the book. She did send other titles to Stone while he was in the navy, including *Arrowsmith*, *The Prophet*, the writings of Ashoka (a Buddhist emperor of the Maurya dynasty), and Jack Kerouac's new novel—Stone said later, "I am probably the only person who had *On the Road* recommended to him by his mother."

The Magic of Believing purports to be a manual for winning success through marshaling one's willpower; beloved of Liberace and Phyllis Diller, among others, it is still in print today. Though Bob Stone was not likely to be seduced by a tract of this kind, he may have read at least some of the book before passing it on to Bob Bell. The book does express a formulation of the American dream which was fairly widespread in the 1950s and which would become a factor in much of Stone's mature fiction. "America has long been the greatest of El Dorados, the stage upon which the most numerous of self-found men worked their bonanzas and their miracles of thought to the enrichment of themselves and mankind at large," Bristol quotes (extensively) from the 1932 issue of the *Commercial and Financial Chronicle.* "Man individually and collectively is entitled to life in all abundance. It is a most evident fact. Religion and philosophy assert it; history and science prove it. 'That they might have life, and that they might have it more abundantly,' is the law. What do you seek? Pay the price and take it away. There is no limit to the supply. . . ." This peculiarly American sense of entitlement is a submerged plot engine in several of Stone's novels, and the idea of "life more abundant," though usually framed in cynicism, remains captivating for some of his protagonists.

The crew got cold-weather gear and winter survival training as the *Arneb* sailed out of Lyttelton on January 8, though the ship was entering the Antarctic summer, and in Stone's recollection "The weather often didn't get much colder than a winter day in New York." He finished *On the Road* "while we were anchored off the shelf ice at Cape Hallett. Around us was a painfully gleaming landscape, black and white and a supernal blue. We had icebergs the size of cathedrals to seaward. Ashore, an army of Adélie penguins clucked and waddled their birdie lives away in a state of endless contention. The smoke of Mount Erebus twisted up into a Krazy Kat sky. Now and then the southern aurora would transform the visible world into a landscape beyond imagining.

"After four hours of copying encoded Cyrillic letter blocks, mainly weather reports from the Soviet polar station at Mirny down the coast, I'd pop up to check the horizon and find a free chair in the radio shack then I'd put JJ Johnson and Kai Winding on my headphones and join Sal Paradise and Dean Moriarty and Carlo Marx tooling toward the outskirts of Cheyenne." The *Arneb*'s crew was split between two twelve-hour shifts, "because it never got dark. Sometimes we'd have these shore parties where we'd go in and hang out, drink a couple of cans of beer and look at the penguins."

Not all the shore parties were so lighthearted; at New York University a year or so later, Stone fictionalized one that involved the recovery of a shipmate's corpse. The protagonist, Coleman, is a journalist tasked with writing a letter to the dead man's next of kin, but Stone assigns the rawest reaction to the death to a different, minor character:

"There was a thin coating of ice over Clifford Eubanks. His face and hands were totally blue, not in the way that one thinks of a human body being blue, but actually, objectively blue. A length of frozen wire was coiled around his neck.

" 'What a place to die,' Rudy Insley said. He was seventeen. 'What a goddamn lonely place to die.' "

On the upside, Stone got to visit the Russian base at Mirny, where vodka was served to the guests at eight in the morning, along with fresh apples and oranges. Mostly decorated with images of Lenin, the Mirny base was otherwise homey, "somewhat like a second-rate rooming house," as Stone reported to his friend Bob Bell. Along with the fresh fruit, the Russians had the benefit of a modest herd of pigs.

The *Arneb* embarked "last year's wintering-over personnel" from Wilkes station, along with twelve Adélie penguins bound for San Diego. On January 30, the ship got underway north toward Australia. "I had the wheel," Bob wrote years later; "we used to trade off watches and it was always fun to take the duty helmsman's trick in the open ocean, up on the lighted bridge where a man could feel like a real sailor instead of a military puppet. On the sharp cobalt horizon was a wave of some kind, a quiver, etching itself low against the ice blue sky, sort of like an undulating wave on a sonar screen.

"The captain was called to the bridge. He was an incurious man by nature, but the sight, like many things about that voyage, annoyed him. He ordered a change of course in the direction of the pulsating line. When we came near enough we saw that the wave was composed of penguins, surfing, porpoising along. They were Adélie penguins migrating north for the winter from the continent itself to the sub-Antarctic islands. There were miles of them and their passing took hours and their center seemed to be outrunning our pathetic twelve knots. At the end of the line, the rear of the flotilla, the numbers decreased, the mass split into separate lines. Straggling groups followed the rest, smaller and smaller groups, then individuals, some of them missing flippers or eyes, some with injured beaks. Casting their shadows over the stragglers, following the fleet, were the big, wide-ranging predatory seabirds, pterodactyl squadrons out of time, the skuas. It was a beautiful, terrible sight."

On February 8, the sailors picked up American music on the radio as the *Arneb* sailed into port in Australia. The ship moored in the Garden Island Navy Yard for repairs to a boiler, allowing the crew a couple of weeks to see the capital. En route to Fremantle, the *Arneb* had more and worse boiler trouble, and put in to Melbourne for more extensive repairs — four weeks' worth, in the end. At liberty, Bob Bell used powers acquired from *The Magic of Believing* to get games with "a great Melbourne tennis player," while Bob Stone made time with his fencing-team girlfriend, Denise O'Brien. He'd scraped acquaintance with the tall redhead by offering to carry her foils across Hyde Park in Sydney. It happened she was bound for Melbourne herself, to train for the upcoming Empire Games in Montreal.

Thanks to the *Arneb*'s long layover, Bob and Denise had a month together. He went to watch her fence in "the dingy gym" and, when he could, would sneak her out early enough to hit the bars—which in the 1950s closed at six o'clock sharp. They spent time at the beach—one without shark nets, which the Australians preferred because it was less crowded. "Although he was always afraid a shark might get him, he didn't want to look chicken in front of the Australian girls," Bob admitted to Janice later. He took Denise to see a film of the ballet *Giselle*. Friendly as Australian girls were, they were also practical enough to know that American sailors would not remain in their ports forever, but Bob was in Melbourne long enough for the relationship to turn semi-serious and even to develop an edge of conflict. Denise awakened him to the idea that there was something different about Americans when seen from the point of view of other nationalities. In fact she thought Americans were mercenary, worshippers of the dollar, though she gave Bob a pass as an "artistic type," as indicated by his "long sensitive fingers. Not like most blokes."

They wrote to each other after Bob sailed away and made tentative plans for the future. Bob would be discharged from the navy by the time Denise got to the Empire Games, so they might have met in Montreal, though in the end, they didn't.

Work on the boiler was still going on when the *Arneb* left Melbourne for Durban, South Africa, a situation which unnerved some of the crew— powering across the Indian Ocean with a single boiler was not considered safe. After two days the other boiler came back into service; the ship picked up speed and completed the two-and-a-half-week voyage without incident (except that one of the engineering officers was quietly taken off the ship in a straitjacket once the *Arneb* was safely moored).

Apartheid was in full force in Durban—a factor that made the town a much more obviously alien place than any landfall in New Zealand or Australia. It bothered Stone but he didn't let it dampen his spirits too much. On the strength of a lucky phone call he and his friends managed to score a blind date with three girls studying at the University of Natal. Half drunk, he and his friend Galen, "a literary type with more than one grand theft auto behind him," persuaded a Zulu rickshaw driver to board his own vehicle and let the sailors race him up and down the Marine Parade, finally stopping just short of flinging the whole apparatus over a cliff into the ocean. They paid people off and walked away; Galen, who had also read Joseph Conrad, quipped, "The horror. The horror."

For some reason about half of the *Arneb*'s crew was able to get drunk on shore the day the ship set a course for Uruguay; getting the ship out of port turned into a vaudeville comedy, though with its dangerous aspect, including one sailor falling off a ladder to land on his face on the steel deck. The men had sobered up by the time the ship rounded the Cape of Good Hope. They reached Montevideo with no trouble, though the boiler room was still a worry. After three weeks there the *Arneb* steamed north again, reaching Norfolk, where much of the crew dispersed, on May 23. Elvis Presley's "Hound Dog" played on the radio as the ship came into port; after their seven-month voyage, far from the United States, many of the men were hearing Elvis for the first time.

Stone drew duty at Norfolk's Marine Corps base. "I was technically a prisoner chaser for about a week. I'd go to the brig at Camp Allen where the Marines had the court-martialed prisoners. I had to march them along the military highway to breakfast. We'd have ours and see that they had theirs. They'd relax and get out of hand, and I was always afraid they'd pull some dangerous thing on us when we were bringing them back to the Marines. Admirals would be going to work and we wanted to make it look good. We had these .45s we were passing around. It was stressful to eat with these .45s with these guys who were fighting with us; it was no way to have breakfast."

His kiddie cruise was almost up. Stone had enjoyed it, learned a great deal, and matured considerably. He could have reenlisted and did consider doing so. "Back in the States, I had one more trip out, training reserves to Halifax and back. Training them meant getting them to do all our unfinished work. Then, unbelievably, I walked away."

Stone left the navy on July 14, 1958—Bastille Day. Carrying his discharge papers off the Norfolk base, he hauled into view of the *Lafayette*, one of the French carriers in action at Port Said two years earlier, and in fact one of the vessels Stone had tracked with the *Chilton*'s five-inch gun. Small world. "That day I had no beef with the French," he wrote later, and he thrilled to the sound of "La Marseillaise," which a band was playing on the flight deck.

———

"I had found a home in the Navy and out of its canvas and timbers I had put together an education," Stone wrote retrospectively. It helped that a good many of his shipmates were "people whose history was like mine. They had been busted for stealing hubcaps, their father was in prison, and their mother was living alone; something like that. So I actually had a pretty good time in the Navy. I can't say that I had a bad time."

During his voyages he learned about differences among people from others than Denise O'Brien: "Being thrown together with a whole lot of people from all over the country, especially since this was at a time in the mid-fifties when the country was less homogeneous, when for example the South was still the South and all that it entailed, and people from Appalachia were much more distinct, regional types, when there was much more contrast between New York and kids from West Virginia. It was very interesting and tremendously helpful" to Stone's mature writing later on. He had made a few like-minded friends and learned that he could manage on his own. "It gave me time to think and it gave me some experience of the world, certainly in terms of the world outside the United States. It gave me time at sea, a lot of time to reflect. . . . I don't believe I was an adolescent any longer when I came out." And furthermore, as he commented wryly: "The Navy did not engage my tendency to fuck up. They didn't bring that out in me."

3

A NEW YORK COURTSHIP

Back in New York, Stone reunited with his mother, though not to the extent of moving back in with her. "I didn't think I was in a position to sign a lease. . . . Apartment living wouldn't have occurred to me. Wherever I lived I lived in furnished rooms or cheap hotels because they were no hassle." The room he took at the Hotel St. George in Brooklyn cost him only $15 a week, and within a few days of his discharge he'd found a job writing for a magazine in Brooklyn that circulated among the navy's enlisted men, relying on a fine blend of cheesecake and antique seafaring stories. "Life on the beach was manageable although I still missed the Navy sometimes, wondered if I'd done the right thing in leaving. But when I dreamed, as I did often, that I'd shipped over, I was always glad to be awake and free again."

With some of his navy friends he had joked about starting, once their enlistments were up, a motorcycle gang to be called the Weirdbeards. But in fact he didn't keep in touch with any of those people. He didn't try to find them in civilian life and was just as happy that they didn't appear to be trying to find him either.

———

In the fall of 1958, Stone got his job at the *New York Daily News* (a tabloid that then enjoyed the largest circulation in the entire United States), took up his Regents Scholarship, and started classes at New York University. Now he definitely wanted to write—something beyond journalism. In the navy he'd collected a small sheaf of rejection slips, from *Esquire* and others, notably the standard form from *The New Yorker* with its handwritten addendum, "Try us again," for Stone "an anthem for some years to come." He was equally interested in the theater in those days— taking acting classes at the Herbert Berghof Studio and able to attend shows with his serviceman's discounts, sometimes in the company of one of the girls he'd dated in high school. An actor's life appealed to him in part because it seemed less solitary than a writer's.

In the late 1950s, "The *Daily News* was the last of the old-time newspapers. They still had these superannuated reporters of Damon Runyon's generation. Gene McCabe had covered the Legs Diamond trial; two other reporters disguised themselves as a doctor and nurse and got a picture of Ruth Snyder in the electric chair." Stone's official job title was "copy boy," which might summon an image of Jimmy Olsen from the Superman comics, "but there was more. I did get to judge a poetry contest." One of the contestants (though not a winner) was Hugh Romney, later to be known as Wavy Gravy. The *News* had other uses for him, as Bob recalled: "The idea with the copyboys was that they were also a kind of talent reserve; some people did features for the big thick Sunday section. Sometimes they would send you out as a kind of substitute reporter.

They would send you to places they didn't want to go, the morgue for instance."

The general attitudes governing the paper were grimly alienating for Stone. "I mean there was a kind of New York, working class authoritarianism that I don't seem to get on with. That was the prevailing ethos. The *Daily News* in those days was like an extension of a police department. One of the things about the *News* which in those days made it special was its paranoid and vicious political position. It has no politics any more but in those days it was a rabid rightwing affair with some of the most wicked and devious editorials ever written. Some critic commenting on the contents of TV provoked an angry editorial: 'We're all for culture, my dear.' 'My dear' implying the limp-wristed aesthete. If they had a choice of coming out for life or coming out for death, they'd come out for death." As a closet aesthete, though not so limp-wristed, Stone could feel uncomfortable at times, though he could quietly cultivate an admiration for Little Orphan Annie ("an institutional child like me") in the comic strip that ran in the paper at the time. And the *News* reporters' hard-drinking habits were more congenial to him. A bottle of Gold Leaf cognac was standard equipment in City Room desk drawers. After their shifts (and probably also sometimes before) reporters would make the rounds of the nearby bars, and trade tips on horses at the Yonkers track.

———————

The American 1960s—starring Joni Mitchell, Charles Manson, the Chicago Seven, and so many, many more—was still waiting in the wings when Robert Stone met Janice G. Burr in New York City. Like Bob, Janice was a birthright New Yorker and was taking classes at New York University, while working a kaleidoscope of part-time jobs to make ends meet.

Janice had been born in the Bronx and raised there until the age of ten, when her parents moved the family to Bogota, New Jersey (pronounced *buh-GO-ta*, unlike the capital of Colombia). She stayed there through her junior year of high school, then came to live with her maternal grandparents, Alex and Hilja Mattson, on Amsterdam Avenue in Manhattan, where Janice graduated from the High School of Commerce. She hoped to enroll in Hunter College, tuition-free at that time for New York City residents, but her parents' New Jersey address scotched that possibility. With some difficulty Janice persuaded her father, who didn't see much use in college for girls, to pay her first year's tuition at New York University.

Janice was "a very shy girl" by her own description. "When I wasn't working or in school, I read, mostly novels and poetry. The complaint at home was that I always had my nose in a book." In fact, Janice was the first in her family to attend college at all, though her brothers and sisters later followed her into higher education.

Like Bob Stone, whom she hadn't yet met, she enrolled in New York University in the fall of 1958.

Alongside her classes Janice waitressed and worked as an usherette in a Manhattan movie theater, and later as a "guidette" at the RCA building, a pillar of Rockefeller Center at the end of the 1950s. In print, Bob Stone made fun of the "quasi-military *Star Trek* uniform" Janice wore for the RCA gig, but in private he thought she looked cute in it. Of Finnish extraction, Janice was a beautiful young woman, though you might have needed to look twice to get the full effect: tall, willowy, with the long straight hair parted in the middle which would become emblematic of the next decade. Her large clear eyes often seemed to be looking at something a long way off—something no one else could see, but if she turned her mind to you, her gaze was penetrating.

"I aspired to the bohemian life," Janice recalls, with a touch of irony. "My school friend Barbara Schreiber and I wore black stockings and hung out at coffee shops—Rienzi's on MacDougal Street, Cafe Figaro at Bleecker and MacDougal. We made the acquaintance of assorted raffish characters." She was then an usherette at the Little Carnegie movie theater on West Fifty-Seventh Street, and also at the Baronet Theatre, where "occasionally illustrious people attended." Marlon Brando, "my idol of the mid-'50s," didn't approach Janice, maybe because he was escorting an Asian woman to the show, but Henry Cabot Lodge was struck to see her reading Nabokov's *Lolita* at the Little Carnegie candy stand.

Anatole Broyard invited her out to the Cedar Bar, where he announced "that he was glad I was not one of the girls who came to the Village to go out with black guys. I was nonplussed. I was exactly the kind of girl who came to the Village to go out with black guys. I had a serious crush on one of them, in fact. But I said nothing." Of course Broyard might have satisfied this interest himself, if he had chosen, as the world was later to learn. "I admired him very much," Janice said later, "but there was no spark there for me, physically. And he plainly was tired of waiting for me to become more affectionate. And then I met Bob."

Bob Stone had been floating around in her vicinity, though without any apparent purpose yet. "We were both freshmen," Janice said, sitting on a sunlit couch in the Stones' Key West home, a few weeks after Bob's death of obstructive pulmonary disorder, "but since he had spent three years in the navy, he was three years older." Bob was dating Elaine Root, a friend Janice knew from her Classical Civilizations class, and in the late 1950s college women, still called co-eds, didn't poach their girlfriends' boyfriends. "So *I* wasn't paying any attention to him," Janice recalled. "But he was paying attention to me, apparently."

———

Bob and Janice both got As in the first semester in separate sections of a required freshman writing course, which meant they could skip the second semester of composition and enroll in a higher-level course— Narrative Writing with M. L. "Mack" Rosenthal. Rosenthal was a poet, the author of numerous books on modern British and American poetry, and for some years the poetry editor for *The Nation*. His Narrative Writing class was a sort of proto-fiction workshop—the universal adoption of the model in academia was still a couple of decades off. "He was a lovely, compassionate teacher," Janice remembered. "He would take everyone's submissions and read them aloud and critique them, and he assigned a few things for good examples."

Rosenthal's tactic of reading student manuscripts aloud in their entirety would become standard practice for the first generation of writers teaching their craft in the academy. His class met in the morning, just before the PE class that Janice was required to take. "I had opted for bowling rather than fencing, the other choice, because it required less aggression and technique." Bob fell into the habit of walking Janice from Rosenthal's class to the bowling alley, on University Place near the Cedar Bar. "I hated bowling, and was terrible at it, but I liked to walk with Bob."

Meanwhile, Bob seemed to be struggling in Rosenthal's class. "He spent the entire semester not producing anything," Janice recalled, "until the very last minute just about, the last class or two." That pattern would repeat throughout Stone's working life; he always wrote with difficulty, and if he had deadlines he was apt to crowd them, if not simply blow them out of the water. For Rosenthal's group, finally, "he produced a short story that he'd been working on, based on his navy experience, at which point it became apparent that the only person in the whole damn class who could write was Bob."

———

By this time, Bob had given up the St. George's salt-water swimming pool and found an SRO hotel in Manhattan to ease his commutes. Still "my shuttle between NYU and the *Daily News* had the rhythm of a treadmill." The bright spot was Rosenthal's class, where Bob, whose conscious ambition still involved acting, began a serious apprenticeship to what would be his real life's work.

To his students, Rosenthal was an immensely charismatic figure. The poet Grace Schulman remembers "when I enrolled in Mack's enormous course, heard that first lecture, and knew I would be lost to poetry for the rest of my life." The class was smaller and permitted meticulously close readings of students' work. Stone wrote later, "In every respect that I can think of, as a writer and even as an individual, Mack changed my life. And I remember the day that I first, as it were, recognized him, and strangely I remembered it without words. Strangely because Mack was, among other things, a man of words, and words are what we compress our exchanges into. One day in class, though, I'd written a story which had some particular hideously embarrassing clanger, something—a kind of dangling modifier, somebody hanging on the horizon where no land belongs—something along those lines. Mack said something. I can't remember quite what he said because I was so filled with fury at my having written this, and so humiliated. He looked across the table and he saw me fuming, and he simply broke up and laughed, and said something further. I can't remember what the words were. I remember the wit of it. I remember how funny it was, and how kind it was, and how reassuring it was. And I thought, this is the poet for me. This is the teacher for me."

Judging by his comments on a couple of Stone's surviving manuscripts from the class, Rosenthal was a nurturing reader but also a tough one. On "A Walk in the Street," a rambling account of a sailor's solitary night out in Norfolk, fueled by much alcohol and culminating in a pointless fight, a beating, and a ride to the brig in care of the Shore Patrol, Rosenthal wrote: "You get a good number of these 'effects' nicely, but aren't they pretty standard effects by now? & how interesting can a figure who stands for nothing but getting beaten up be?" He approved certain "poetic passages" in the story, while also marking many of them as wordy. In fact, the main value of this story is in its texture, which is somewhat uneven, containing various half-digested influences: Kerouac-style extended riffing and some familiar hard-boiled flavors, expressing a world-weary cynicism that was itself, in Rosenthal's term, "pretty standard." Still he was sufficiently struck by the raw talent to give the piece an A, and Stone sufficiently encouraged to publish it, under the title "Shore Party," in the college's literary magazine, *The Apprentice*.

"The Trojan Letter," a story drawing on Stone's Antarctic voyage, drew less-qualified praise from Rosenthal: "This is excellent, though more a story about Coleman's self-consciousness than about his actual response to the death." True enough; the elaboration of such characters' self-consciousness would become a hallmark of Stone's mature work. An early Stone alter-ego, Journalist Coleman is tasked to write a condolence letter to the family of a seaman who has drowned when his Sno-cat slips through a hole in the ice. He chokes on the assignment, and after several false starts, decides to go ashore and view the body. En route he and his companions warm themselves with quasi-medicinal brandy. On arrival Coleman feels illuminated enough to perform extreme unction on the corpse, using diesel oil and the brandy dregs. The act is parodic, maybe even blasphemous, but at the same time holds enough sincerity to steel the reporter to his duty. "Okay," Coleman said. "Let's go back and write the letter."

What's striking in "The Trojan Letter" is the emergence of Stone's original voice. There are still literary allusions: Coleman quotes a few lines of Yeats and tries to distract himself from looming thoughts of mortality by listening to a recording of *Peer Gynt* while reading Ibsen's text at the same time. "The absolute effeteness of this, he thought, smiling to himself. . . . Artsy decadence in the wilderness. Oscar Wilde-ism."

Self-conscious indeed! But the moment dissolves into the transparent purity of the following description. "He looked through the port at dead still, half frozen Mowbray Bay. A few yards from the ship, a seal dove from an ice bridge, leaving a small round hole in the fragile rim-ice on the water's surface and the sound came clear through the air. Then slowly the hole began to freeze again, and the ripple of sound was frozen in silence." Rosenthal marked some such passages as "fine writing," but did not complain that they were "wordy."

Notwithstanding its slightly sententious title, "The Dark Winter of Corporal Rafferty" gets Stone's whole working toolbox open on the table. Like Stone at the end of his enlistment, Rafferty is posted to an onshore military prison, shepherding Corps of Military Police prisoners with a billy club and a .45 pistol. Behind his back, other guards accuse him of being "an eightball. . . . He sweats the CMPs. He feels sorry for them. He loves the bastards." Rafferty's intellectual bent is also suspicious in this context. He happens to be reading James Branch Cabell's *Jurgen: A Comedy of Justice*. The prison is one of the navy's pockets of complete corruption, as Stone described one of the early ships he sailed on.

On night duty, Rafferty gets wind of a nasty bit of business: an informer among the CMPs, betrayed by another of the guards, will be beaten by the others during his shift. He's told, "Just don't hear anything around twenty-two hundred. Read your book." Nevertheless, the corporal tries to intervene, but the cell-block enforcer, Brachok, explains to him exactly how helpless he is—in a situation where corruption is seamlessly complete: "Don't try to mess with a system you ain't part of." As advised, Rafferty returns to his book, which offers cold comfort: "the part where the Man with Queer Feet shows Jurgen Things As They Are but Jurgen refuses to believe it because it is too horrible."

Here Stone hits upon one of his great subjects: the man of compassion and goodwill stymied by a corrupt and monolithic system, and sinking into unwilling resignation.

" 'You know,' Brachok said, 'you're an intelligent guy. For a while there, I thought you were gonna make some trouble or something.'

"Rafferty walked instinctively to the dormitory window. The prison yard was deserted. The snow had stopped. What a long winter it was, he thought, what a long dark night of a winter. As he turned his hand brushed the steel stock of his pistol and he quickly pulled it away. It has to pass, he thought, this winter—all these winters, have to pass. Maybe if you sit very quiet and still they pass over you. Maybe you can look the other way. . . .

" 'No, not me,' he said. 'I'm an intelligent guy.' "

Such finely tuned ironies would become the stuff of the masterpiece fiction Stone was destined to write. He didn't stay at New York University very long, but long enough to find his voice. And more: "I had been fatherless as a child. As a writer I was no longer so. . . . I would never have become a writer if I hadn't been in Mack's class. I can also say I would not have worked so hard to show off not only for Mack, but for one of the girls in the class who I subsequently married. . . ."

———

Near the end of the spring 1959 semester, Janice and Barbara Schreiber were waiting at the Washington Square fountain to meet a former boyfriend of Barbara's. When he arrived, he paid no attention to his ex, but invited Janice to meet him at a coffee shop later. Janice was furious for her friend's sake, though Barbara said she ought to keep the dubious date, or anyway not refuse on Barbara's account. Janice thought she would go after all, but only to give the fellow a piece of her mind. "Bob, who somehow appeared, offered to go with me. I thought that was a fine idea, because Barbara's ex-boyfriend was a bit of a shady character."

Whatever he was, he never showed up, or possibly he just decided to walk on by when he saw that Janice was not alone. Waiting—for a couple of hours—Bob and Janice had a more involved conversation than their short walks to the bowling alley had given them time for. "By then it was late afternoon and Bob took me out for a drink—several drinks—and proceeded to talk a lot as we got drunker. I got drunker, anyway." At eighteen, Janice was barely of age to drink legally in the state of New York, and her experience of alcohol was a good deal less than her companion's. "In those days, I thought drinking was romantic, at least for artists, writers, and bohemians." She'd been with Barbara to see Jack Kerouac at Hunter, when Kerouac "was so intoxicated he could barely speak . . . the evening degenerated into incoherence. Kerouac's beat friends pranced onstage as the evening ended. I found it all very exciting. . . ."

Janice was not without some inhibitions, however. "I was raised in a very proper family, with old-fashioned values, and I was having trouble developing the bohemian attitude toward sex. I'd done enough fooling around with my high-school boyfriend that I wasn't exactly a virgin, but the guys out in the real world, and even at college, were too pushy, and I rejected them all."

Bob Stone seemed different, in spite or perhaps because of the fact that he was still technically the property of Janice's friend Elaine. They'd drifted up to midtown from Washington Square; the bar was probably near the *Daily News*, where Bob was now working. "We'd spent hours together that day. We were at a table, both of us sloshed, and Bob was trying to impress me. Putting his best effort into impressing me. I was being distant." That was a tactic for Janice in her romantic situations then, or maybe more of a reflex. "If a likely suitor appeared, I took my position on the glass mountain and waited to be rescued." Meanwhile Bob "was very earnest and had a lot to say. He seemed somehow vulnerable, and I didn't feel I had to be wary of him the way I usually had to be with the guys I met. At some point I stopped listening and just watched him."

At twenty-one, Bob Stone had no bohemian pretensions in his dress, grooming, or demeanor. He was neat and nice-enough looking, though not a matinee idol. His sandy hair was still cropped almost as short as the navy would have required. However, one could get a taste of iconoclasm in his manner, as well as in his conversation. Overall he had a sort of elfish appeal, and his eyes, when he was excited about something he was saying, took on a captivating gleam. "He seemed so sincere, and he was trying to connect with me, through the noise of the bar and the alcoholic haze. And I suddenly thought there was something familiar about him. I barely knew him, but I recognized him somehow. It was a recognition, as if I had known him, from somewhere. It seemed possible to me that we were going to know each other now, and maybe for a long time."

It was late by the time Bob took Janice home to her grandparents' apartment on the Upper West Side. At their parting he said, with a mysterious conviction, *It's been so long.*

Rosenthal was impressed enough with Stone's semester-closing story to give him "a little talking-to after the class ended," suggesting he apply for a Stegner Fellowship at Stanford University. The Western novelist Wallace Stegner had founded the program in 1946. "I arrived at Stanford just as the GI students were flooding back," Stegner said. "Many of them were gifted writers. They had so much to say and they had been bottled up for two or three or four years. They were clearly going to have to be handled somewhat differently from the ordinary 18-year-old undergraduate." Bob Stone had served in the peacetime navy, more than a decade later; still, the Stegner formula seemed well-suited to his maverick disposition.

But Stone didn't act on Rosenthal's suggestion right away. There were distractions, some of them large. Janice had been present for the conversation about the Stegner opportunity, "but somehow, he didn't apply right then, because I got pregnant and we got married and we dropped out of school, and we went to New Orleans, and we didn't think of it, or at least I didn't remind him."

Janice had intended to switch from NYU to the University of California at Berkeley, most likely working her way through, as she doubted her parents would support the project. She had applied and been accepted. When she started seeing Bob she wondered "if he might conceivably care enough about me to go west. And if he didn't, if I would go, leaving him behind."

None of that happened. Bob began his second year at NYU, while Janice, who had not reenrolled because of her Berkeley plan, kept working as a waitress and RCA guidette. Bob had moved from Brooklyn to the Madison Square Hotel on Twenty-Sixth Street—the sort of SRO where he'd lived with his mother as a child. He was still working as a copyboy at the *Daily News*. An NYU adviser had recommended that he reduce his course load because of the job, but since his scholarship required him to be a full-time student, he lost it; his third semester at NYU would be his last. He and Janice frequented the midtown bars near the *Daily News* building, where "you could buy 50-cent drinks at such places as Culkins, on Third Avenue. At Culkins I was usually the only female in the place. Neither of us earned much money, and for Bob, drinking was already a necessity."

———

It's been so long, Bob had said, at the end of that first night. "I wasn't sure what he meant, exactly, but I felt the same way." In the morning Janice called a friend, the photographer Martus Granirer, and told him she thought she had fallen in love. She didn't quite think it was a good idea to notify Bob Stone—not yet. "Bob told me sometime later that when he used to phone me, I would sound so cool and uninterested that he thought I really didn't care about him and he was wasting his time. But I was feeling truly in love, and I was scared."

With Janice living at her grandparents', and Bob in an SRO where "he figured he was not supposed to entertain female guests," opportunities for accidental pregnancy were not obvious. They managed their first tryst by coming to the hotel separately and pretending they didn't know each other on the elevator. "Probably no one gave a hoot, but there we were; it was the 1950s, and we weren't sure what we could get away with." Out of the corner of her eye, Janice registered that Bob's room "seemed to be about knee-deep with discarded newspapers and socks. And I thought, this guy could really use some organizing. And then I thought—me, I can do that." As it turned out, she would be organizing Bob Stone for the next five decades.

In the summer of 1959, Janice moved out from her grandparents' and took an apartment with Barbara in Hoboken, near John Rapinic, who was the manager of the Seven Arts Coffee Gallery, at Ninth Avenue and Forty-Third Street, where Janice was working as a waitress. Hoboken was cheaper than Manhattan, and Bob came to visit often. "We were all short of money, and a date might consist of going out for rice pudding at a local diner."

Both Bob and Janice had learned their way around New York City as children, though Bob, whose childhood was less stable than hers, had been the more adventurous of the two. One of his boyhood enterprises had involved presenting himself as an ad-hoc guide at the Metropolitan Museum of Art, so he knew the collections there extremely well. They went to the Central Park Zoo and attended the weekend poetry readings at the Seven Arts Coffee Gallery. At one of these occasions, Janice gathered and saved some shards of a coffee cup flung by Gregory Corso in a fit of pique. "A real poet!" she thought at the time. "Real poetic temperament!"

The Seven Arts was a somewhat self-consciously bohemian place (even espresso was at least slightly avant-garde at that time), exhibiting expressionistic paintings and playing, between poetry readings and such, a soundtrack ranging from the Weavers to Lotte Lenya. Rapinic (who may have had an interest in Janice himself) did not think Bob Stone contributed positively to the intended ambiance. "If he had the money for a cup of coffee though, John couldn't keep him out. He was considered a bit bourgeois, I think," mainly on account of his appearance. At the end of the 1950s the *Daily News* ran well to the right of the *New York Post* (the latter then considered to be the *liberal* tabloid) and had an anti-bohemian dress code, which required Bob to wear a suit and tie on many workdays. The beard he briefly tried to grow proved beyond the pale for his employers, who ordered him to shave.

Janice usually got off work earlier anyway, and would walk east across Times Square to the *Daily News* and wait for Bob to come downstairs. From there, they could hit the pressmen's neighborhood bars. Bob's conversation had entertainment value too; if Janice had been too conscious of his effort to impress her during their first long encounter in the spring of 1959, she was now beginning to be genuinely impressed. Though his relationship to formal education would never be too warm, Bob read a great deal on his own, especially history during the time of their courtship. His autodidactic erudition was already forming, and Janice was genuinely struck by how much he knew, and by his "beautiful speaking voice. . . . He courted me with the poets I'd loved in high school, Keats and Coleridge," and especially Matthew Arnold's " 'Dover Beach,' the one with the tidal rhythm concluding with the verse that begins, 'Ah love, let us be true / To one another!' "

Alongside his wide reading, the three-year age difference and the navy experience made Bob more worldly-wise than Janice. He had gifts and accomplishment as a raconteur, and could talk amusingly about his travels—penguins in Antarctica, a mosque in Izmir. It didn't really bother Janice that Bob seemed to have had, as sailors aspire to, a girl in almost every port, from the navy officer's teenage daughter to the member of the Australian fencing team.

They were close to broke most of the time, to the point of having to walk out early on a Miles Davis/John Coltrane show at Birdland for want of funds to pay the cover charge. Still, Bob contrived excursions for them, some of which involved hitchhiking if there was no money for a bus. He took Janice to Block Island, where he had been with his mother sometimes. They rented a room over a drugstore, but after that their money ran out, as it usually did. On the ferry back a friend of Bob's who noticed the couple sharing a cheese sandwich gave them $10 (which they scrupulously repaid later on). Still, the Block Island trip was a harbinger: "It was one of the places from his childhood that he really loved, and he wanted to show it to me." Later on, the adult Stones would have a Block Island residence for several decades.

Bob also found a way to take Janice to see Puccini's *La Bohème*, performed by the City Opera at New York City Center on Fifty-Fifth Street, a domed, Moorish-style building originally constructed to house Shriners. "I identified with Mimi," Janice said later, "and thought Bob was just like Rodolfo." Bob had seen the opera once before, in Italy when his ship called at Bari. They both found a point of identification in "the life of the starving artist."

However much Janice's heart went out to Mimi, she was not really the fainting kind; in fact she was rather more practical than Bob, who was then earning just $55 a week at the *Daily News*. He usually spent at least part of this money before he got it, sometimes by borrowing from his mother, who was living on a fixed income of her schoolteacher's pension and needed to be promptly repaid, or by playing the ponies. The *Daily News* had a resident bookie to whom Bob was likely to owe a portion of his tiny paycheck. Janice enjoyed helping him pick horses ("I favored the ones with exotic names"), but she could see it wasn't a sound financial strategy. Though she herself was working two jobs and no longer had NYU tuition to think about, since she had left her grandparents' apartment she did have to think about money for rent. At Seven Arts she worked mainly for tips; also, Seven Arts was failing and about to shut down. The guidette post at Rockefeller Center paid $50 a week. Selling tickets to the roof of the RCA building from a desk across from the entrance to the Rainbow Room, Janice could watch New York's high society going in and out of the club, beginning to sport furs as the weather grew chilly.

Bob and Janice agreed to pool their resources, "so I could keep an eye on where the money was going." They had decided to live together once Janice and Barbara's summer rental in Hoboken ran out. Bob found an apartment for $95 a month on East Fourth Street between First and Second Avenues, in a building called the Garden of Eden, with "an appropriate mural on the wall in the lobby." The apartment itself was less edenic; a single room unfurnished except for a stove, sink, and refrigerator gracing the left wall, and painted battleship gray. Bob and Janice bought a bed and a can of paint, "pumpkin orange. I don't know what we were thinking. It was an aesthetic error. Bob used to spend a lot of time in the bathroom and I figured he was probably trying to escape from the orange glare. I hoped it wasn't to escape me." For most of his young life Bob had lacked the luxury of a private bathroom—such facilities were down the hall in the SROs where he and his mother had lived. "He joked that maybe that was why he got married."

Like Gregory Corso, Bob had occasional bursts of "real poetic temperament," which the orange apartment was sometimes a little small to contain. He once "threw a bottle of whiskey. It hit top first, broke a hole in the wall, and stuck there, unbroken. He pulled it out and poured himself another drink."

"The tantrum wasn't directed at me." Janice was definite about that part. "He always treated me kindly." In October 1959, they took a brief vacation to Vermont, at the height of the leaf season. Money saved by hitchhiking allowed them to spend a night at the Middlebury Inn, where they signed in as "Mr. and Mrs. Stone." Janice bolstered the imposture with a gold-colored band bought for fifty-nine cents at Woolworth's. Bob's whiskey made her feel ill that night. True, Janice normally preferred gin, but the real problem was that "Mr. and Mrs. Stone" were expecting.

Here (never mind the odd bottle chucked at the wall) was the young couple's most serious trouble so far. Neither felt ready for a child, though Janice, with five siblings, did want children some day. She imagined getting married at twenty-six, "after education and career and travel." Bob's father had not figured in his childhood, "and being a father wasn't on Bob's radar at all, as far as I could tell."

The situation was doubly frustrating because Janice thought she had it under control; having obtained a diaphragm from Planned Parenthood and diligently following the instructions. "I didn't trust Bob to be organized enough to consistently protect us against pregnancy. But I somehow slipped up."

Diaphragms don't have a hundred percent success rate anyway, but Janice, in blaming herself for the failure, also felt humiliated by it. "My ideal bohemian couple did not get pregnant—stupid girls with no ambition and no sense, who wanted to get married right after high school. Sometimes to entrap their boyfriends." But entrapment didn't come into Janice's relationship with Bob. "We were inseparable by that time, and he showed no more sign of leaving me than I did of leaving him.

"So, what to do? I offered to end the pregnancy if Bob could get information on exactly how." Fifty years later, their ignorance, or innocence, seems oddly touching: "There was rumored to be some potion a woman could take. He promised to ask around at work. But I guess he didn't." Giving the baby up for adoption didn't appeal to them either.

Twenty years later, Stone described his reaction to the predicament as "ambiguous. Like, 'Oh Christ,' and on the other hand I wanted to be with her, and I wanted to help her out and I wasn't even too brought down by the idea of a child, by the marriage and everything it entailed, and yet I felt trapped. . . . I think we just got through on our mutual good feelings for each other."

At first the pregnancy didn't slow them down. "One night we rode around on a motorcycle with Bob's friend John Gregg, and the guys proceeded to act like a couple of bikers and try to drive the motorcycle into a coffee shop on East Sixth Street, called the Dollar Sign." It was a somewhat shady place, and in 1960, the proprietor, Barron Bruchlos, was found dead in the basement of another coffee shop he managed, the cause of his death never fully explained.

Peyote, "the psychedelic drug of the time," was sold under the counter at the Dollar Sign. Bruchlos's supply (from Laredo, Texas) was legal to the point of bearing U.S. Department of Agriculture seals; still, a certain discretion seemed warranted. Bob might have tried the drug before; there was an incident when "I remember being on peyote and seeing a wrestling match for the *Daily News* in Madison Square Garden; seeing this on peyote may have changed my life." Under the mistaken impression (conventional wisdom then) that "no substances passed through the placenta to the unborn child," Janice tried a dose, along with Bob. "We did the drug indoors. It did not improve the orange color, but I found a fascinating rhythm in the imperfections of the walls." Tripping, Janice sent a message to her child in utero. "Basically it was—get out of there. I don't want to be pregnant. This had no effect, and I was relieved. Plainly this was out of my hands. Nature would take care of the pregnancy and the birth too, no matter how young and foolish the parents were."

Still, "an illegitimate child was unthinkable." Janice's conservative Protestant family, of German and Finnish stock, would never accept her going so far. And Bob's mother also set store by respectability, perhaps because as an unwed mother herself, Gladys had trouble meeting its conditions. The best and only solution was marriage, though Janice "deeply felt I had betrayed Bob with this—how would he get to write, if we had to support not only ourselves but a child?" The idea that they would both devote themselves to Bob's writing had been part of their commitment from the start.

Janice broke the news to her grandmother first. She was "OK with the idea, though she did ask me, after meeting Bob, if I didn't think he was crazy. Of course not!" There was some insanity running on the distaff side of Janice's family, though, which had recently touched her mother, who was never quite the same after being treated with electroshock for a nervous breakdown in 1955.

Meanwhile, Janice had never met Bob's mother, but only talked to her on the phone. "I decided to do Thanksgiving dinner, even if we had to eat on the bed." The turkey (the first one she cooked on her own) proved edible. The success propped up Janice's determination "to act like a good wife, if that was what I was going to be. And Gladys seemed agreeable to our being together. She was in her sixties then, gray-haired, retired, living on a pension, maybe two pensions. Bob thought she might have two social security numbers. She was always nicely dressed, purse, makeup. She had a dramatic air, and strong voice, a pleasant voice when she wasn't registering suspicion or anger. Her accent, Bob pointed out to me some years later, was actually upper-class New York. More like the Roosevelts than the neighborhoods. . . . Though she was not upper-class. Her father was a tugboat captain of Scottish descent, and her mother came from an Irish family upstate—lace-curtain Irish." Still, Gladys's personal history was so very colorful that she couldn't have found a rational objection to Bob and Janice's predicament, and though her behavior was not always rational, she didn't make trouble now.

The toughest nut was Janice's father, who at first seemed as if he wouldn't crack at all. His initial dislike and distrust of Bob was entirely mutual. Stone characterized the elder Burr as "a man who is really solitary and has never had any friends in his life, and whose manner of dealing with people is entirely bull. So his *bonhomie* which he projects and so forth is purely phony. . . . He is unquestionably the most boring man I have ever met in my life. I once tried to imagine if I could lose consciousness by holding my breath while I was in a conversation with him." (Burr did in fact have friends and was close to several he knew from work, but these men were not of Bob's stripe.) Curiously, Bob had been notorious for his ability to hold his breath for an extremely long time, during his childhood visits to Block Island.

A good many of Janice's young-adult choices had been acts of rebellion against her father. "Our worst fights were when I quit going to church (Lutheran). But I rejected most of his opinions. He was right-wing politically, so I was a socialist, and flirting with being a communist. He was racially prejudiced, so of course I was hanging out with black guys in the Village. He was anti-Semitic and all my best friends from childhood on were Jewish. And Daddy didn't care for Catholics either—the Irish, the Italians, ethnics of all sorts. The Burrs, Protestants, had been in this country for many generations, and the immigrant side of his family, on his mother's side, was German, Protestant, and had been in the U.S. for almost a hundred years."

Our social conflicts in the early twenty-first century are so very different from what they were that it can be hard to remember just how narrow the American mainstream was at the end of the 1950s. How long one's family had been in the United States counted enormously; membership in the Daughters of the American Revolution was a social chip as valuable as a Krugerrand. Barriers between closely related European ancestries (shanty Irish versus lace-curtain Irish) were remarkably impenetrable. Differences between Protestant churches which would be indiscernible to most people today then made for matters of life, death, and desperate letters to Dear Abby. And the exclusion of anyone outside the Euro-American gene pool went for the most part without saying.

Burr's social ideas seemed backward to Janice, and seem even more so now, but at the time they represented aspiration to a style of American-ness almost as powerful as post-revolutionary French citizenship in its capacity to level differences and erase the past, while at the same time allowing the American individual much more latitude for nonconforming self-expression. The contradiction inherent in this social model would provide subject matter for Bob's first novels; certainly it drives the motor of *A Hall of Mirrors*.

At the moment, Bob and Janice's problem was not artistic but practical: how to go forward in a life together without completely alienating their families. "So now I was going to marry a Catholic," she sighed, in the face of her father's disapproval. "And even worse, I was a fallen woman. He asked me sarcastically if I was going to wear white." Janice is a generally forbearing person who, if provoked to retaliate, does so with style. Following her father's jibe, "I went out and bought a red dress, wine-red, flared skirt, Elsa Peretti I think it was."

Bob and Janice went to city hall for a marriage license. "There was a couple younger than we on line. She was fourteen, and there with her mother. The groom was sixteen. We felt older and more sophisticated, not at all like them." Still, Bob couldn't persuade any judge to marry them. "One judge's clerk told him to get married in church like he was supposed to." At the time of their wedding Bob was all of twenty-two and Janice just nineteen.

Janice now had to go to her father for help. Burr must have softened slightly, for he arranged for the wedding to take place at a Lutheran church on Ninety-Third Street and Broadway, and also organized a reception at a hotel nearby. "He asked me if a chicken dinner at the reception would be a problem for Bob, since the wedding was set for a Friday evening. Bob told me to tell him that if such a thing was a problem for him, he wouldn't be getting married in a Protestant church." One suspects that, at some level or other, Stone and Burr might have enjoyed the tart flavor of these exchanges, despite the hostility of Bob's description of his father-in-law. Moreover, if Burr had been as socially toxic as Bob reports, he probably wouldn't have succeeded in making all the necessary arrangements.

The wedding took place on Friday, December 11, because that was the only day that Bob and Janice could both get off work. A Lutheran pastor, John G. Gensel, officiated; "he was known as the Jazz Pastor because he catered to jazz musicians." However jazzy, Pastor Gensel was as fretful as anyone about the risks of a "mixed" Protestant-Catholic marriage, and required a private interview with Bob beforehand, "though neither Bob nor I were believers at that point. Bob must have persuaded him, I guess, since he did agree to marry us." The interview was bound to have been a tense one, as Bob's view of Pastor Gensel was considerably more acerbic than Janice's: "this hip Lutheran cleric, this asshole . . . he was just a kind of I-am-with-it cleric, I understand you kids, you might think because I am a cleric I am not hip but actually I am really hip and Dizzy Gillespie is one of my best friends, like man I am with you, I understand you, I dig your point of view, like man wow. . . . He told us how lots of people wouldn't marry us but he would 'cause he was so. . . ."

In spite of all that, the deed was done. Janice wore the red dress, and Bob (eventually) ate the chicken. Gladys was in attendance, along with Janice's parents, several of her brothers and sisters, John Rapinic, and Martus Granirer, who unfortunately for posterity did not bring his camera. "Bob was late. I thought this was annoying but no big deal, since Bob was always late. Pastor Gensel had an appointment to counsel a couple who were considering divorce, so he wasn't happy. My poor father was pacing up and down outside the church, no doubt thinking that his fallen daughter was about to be left at the altar. Somehow it never occurred to me that Bob might get cold feet at the last minute. I had absolute faith in him. If he didn't want to get married, he would have told me, and we wouldn't have been there that night. When he finally arrived, he was accompanied by some friends from the *News*, and he was drunk. We knelt at the altar, to repeat our vows to each other in front of Pastor Gensel. When we got to the part about 'plight my troth,' we both started to laugh and had to suppress it. I'm sure the pastor didn't think our marriage would last a year. And in truth, I think we both felt like lambs being led to the slaughter."

For Janice, the reception was an ordeal, and she was relieved to escape and head downtown to the orange apartment with Bob, though she didn't actually know the cluster of people from the *Daily News* who tagged along with the newlyweds. "One of them made some wisecrack that I didn't hear that offended Bob, and he got angry and threatened the guy with one of our kitchen knives. The guests left in a hurry. Bob went drunkenly to bed and fell asleep. This was not my idea of my wedding night."

When asked years later how he felt during his wedding, Bob replied succinctly, "Drunk." His recollection of the fracas afterward is less casual than Janice's: "Later on that night I got into a fight and I almost killed someone . . . I am not kidding, it is the closest I have ever come to killing somebody in my life. That reflected the negative side of my reaction to getting married. . . . I felt awful about what had happened. I felt very badly about it the next day."

Janice's response, typical of her, was both more tempered and more positive. "It did cross my mind that I might have made a mistake, marrying him. But we were both OK in the morning."

4

HARD TIMES IN THE BIG EASY

During their courtship, Janice had been enchanted by Bob's seafaring stories. "I wanted so much to travel. He promised to take me to Europe. Stick with me, kid, he'd say, putting on a B-movie tough-guy accent—I'll take you places." So she was willing enough, soon after their marriage, to up sticks and head for New Orleans—not quite a European city, certainly, but one with cosmopolitan flavors very different from those of New York. And New Orleans was, as Bob later wrote, "the most exotic but affordable destination the Greyhound Corporation afforded romantic newlyweds." Also, the prospect of parenthood may have put a rabbit in Bob's foot.

They embarked on the three-day bus trip in January 1960. Janice had trouble sleeping on the bus and discovered that "she absolutely hated grits." To pass the time she read William James's *Varieties of Religious Experience*, passed on to her by Bob, surely a work durable enough for the journey. Arrived at last, they found a hotel on Canal Street.

"Bob went out the next day to check out the scene. When he came back he seemed bothered by something. 'Janice,' he said, 'I don't know if I can do this—a baby, all that.' " Fatherhood would be especially unnerving to a man who'd never known his father, but Janice put to herself that "Bob was an only child and had never known any babies. I thought that was the problem. I put my arms around him. 'Don't worry,' I said. 'It will be OK. We will be fine.' "

Later he let her know that during his first ramble in the New Orleans streets he'd seen an advertisement for roles in a traveling Passion Play and been sorely tempted to try for one. It would have put his acting training to practical use, and also permitted him to hit the road, leaving his pregnant bride behind. This moment was such a powerful watershed that in later life Stone reported to Ann Greif that he actually *had* joined this production and temporarily skipped town. The fantasy was worked out in full novelistic detail: "I was playing the head of the temple guards, which also made me responsible for a lot of the setting up of the scenery cause they used to hire local kids from Bible groups and put them to work for practically nothing doing necessary pull and tote type labor. So as commander of the temple guards I was also informed to head these operations. . . . I was being had. Well, I was being paid nothing particularly. . . . I mean if I wanted to do a number on my wife and kid and run off like some people did, like practically this whole company had done . . . as a writer there was a certain attraction but I was not going to do that, that would have been really dirty" to Janice and their unborn daughter, for whom Bob had chosen the name Deidre well before he or Janice had considered that she might actually get pregnant.

"I wanted the crazy life I was looking at more than anything," Stone wrote of the episode in his memoir *Prime Green*. "The last trace of gypsy life on the continent. I did not want to be stuck in New Orleans with my pregnant wife. . . . I wanted feverishly to climb aboard this absurdity and I wanted the ruthlessness and sangfroid to try." The matter was discussed a little, with Janice trying to imagine how she might get by on her own in New Orleans for a few months while Bob toured with the play—now visibly pregnant and, as she was beginning to discover, almost unemployable for that reason.

In the end Bob proved neither ruthless nor cold-blooded enough to bolt. The couple took a furnished apartment on St. Philip Street—at $55 a month the two furnished rooms were a step up from their last domicile in New York, "and oh what luxury, it had a table and chairs. . . . It had a balcony, with that French Quarter ironwork that gives the neighborhood its character. We felt like Stanley and Stella, in *Streetcar Named Desire*." From their ironwork balcony they could watch the Mardi Gras parades. Bob had for some reason "sort of dreaded" the Mardi Gras bacchanalia, but found it "disarmingly cheerful and sweet, observed by both whites and blacks."

When the party was over the Stones remembered they were broke. Their $55-a-month apartment was blessed with air conditioning, which wasn't much use in the dank and chilly New Orleans winter. And "work was hard to find. There seemed to be some sort of prejudice against Northerners." Janice, who had been holding down some sort of job since her middle teens, was turned down by the New Orleans telephone company, which insulted her; with her expanding pregnancy no one would take her as a waitress either. Bob found employment repairing drums, then in a coffee factory and later a soap factory, but wasn't able to stick to factory work any longer than his character Rheinhardt in *A Hall of Mirrors*. The soap factory fired Bob for "Attitude," which puzzled him. On the way out he noted to the cashier, "I never said a word to anybody." As a Yankee, he probably wouldn't have had to.

However brief, the factory jobs "gave me a look at the American assembly line, and no tour of American life in the twentieth century would be complete without a little time on the assembly line. You had to see one of those to know what the system was about." In the short term, no living could be wrung from this insight. Bob worked briefly at a bookstore on Canal Street, but he'd fictionalized his résumé a little to get the job and was let go when that deception was discovered. Janice answered an ad for 1960 federal census takers and passed the exam. Here there was no apparent prejudice against her origin; Janice's supervisor, John Marshall, was also a New Yorker. During the interview, her try at disguising her pregnancy under a long shirt failed, but Marshall thought it over and said, "OK, I'll find you a neighborhood without too many steps." Marshall and his wife, Gail, lived in the Quarter nearby the Stones, whom they soon invited to dinner. Presently Bob was working for the census as well, assigned to "elusive citizens living in places like the railroad yards," with the group that called itself "Marshall's Raiders." The job was structured as piecework, not to say bounty-hunting: "We got hired at a buck eighty a household to go all over town and just talk to the population of New Orleans—which is some population!" as Bob later told an interviewer.

Janice went door-knocking in the French Quarter, where she enumerated the famous burlesque queen Blaze Starr, then practicing her vocation on Bourbon Street, "a few years older than I, really beautiful. . . . She was very friendly, and answered the census questions readily." Janice also collected census data "back of town," a euphemism for the black neighborhoods where "people treated me quite well, if not in an overly friendly way." Bob's previous experience of the South was thin, limited to brief shore leaves south of the Mason-Dixon Line and the Southern sailors he'd known in the service—while Janice had none at all. "Black people still sat at the back of the bus. What was surprising to me was how smoothly the system seemed to work, how everyone seemed to accept it and know where they fit in. I couldn't figure out where you would hit it, to change it. When I invited a black child to sit next to me on the bus, her mother wouldn't let her."

Bob had had a glimpse of apartheid when the *Arneb* was docked in a South African port. In 1960, the situation in New Orleans wasn't quite like that. "At the time I thought New Orleans was as residentially integrated as any city I had seen." Public housing projects "were segregated in that their tenants alternated white-black-white-black. I had never seen people of different races, poor people at that, living in such proximity." The injustices of Louisiana race relations were buried under the same smooth surface that was puzzling Janice as well. Bob was finally shocked into a higher consciousness by his own behavior when he happened onto a death watch in a black home—a jackpot for a census taker because it brought a large extended family together at one time and to one place. "In my brisk impatience to record the statistical details of everyone's life, it took me a moment to realize that these people were strangely unforthcoming. . . . Their eyes were calmly questioning, almost humorous. I stood and stared and returned to my jotting until suddenly it hit me. . . . That had this been a white middle-class household I would never have dreamed of entering a sickroom, of approaching a deathbed, asking cold irrelevant questions of people who had come to mourn and pray."

The census kept the Stones employed through the spring of 1960, though payment lagged behind services rendered, as checks were mailed from some sluggish, distant borehole of the federal bureaucracy. Their landlord, Joe Ruffino, though thought to be a connected guy in the local Mob, was patient with late payment of the rent. "We weren't getting much to eat either," Janice recalled, and during that spring Bob's mother materialized in the Quarter; advised that the couple couldn't put her up, she found a single room in the neighborhood. Janice wrote to her mother that year: "Bob is one of those people who can't live happily with *anyone* (except for me)—not even his *own* mother. (His mother can't tolerate him for too long either, luckily)."

But even while living down the street, Gladys made an effort to help the expecting couple. "We pooled our resources, to the extent that she would contribute to buying a steak, say, and I would cook it. The largest piece I gave to Bob, and somewhat less to Gladys, and the smallest for me. Gladys complained about her portion. Steak cost about a dollar a pound, and hamburger fifty cents. Bob used to joke that this was a time and place where you crossed the street to avoid someone to whom you owed a quarter."

They both hung on to the census job to the end of May, scouting for the last "folks who were hiding or who didn't answer the door." Someone had ordered Marshall "to get rid of that pregnant census taker," but he kept Janice on, stipulating that she "stay away from the Federal Building." She suspected Bob had begun "to invent people, something I wouldn't dream of doing."

At last the census was definitively over. Though late paychecks continued to drizzle in for a few weeks, Bob soon had to find a new job, this time selling Collier's encyclopedias. The work took him out of town and sometime out of state "with whatever money he had in his pocket," so when Janice went into labor, a friend had to collect money in the neighborhood bars for her to take a taxi to Charity Hospital. Bob later characterized this institution as "Huey Long's gift to his private tinhorn republic. It was segregated, which meant that everything had to be done twice, replicated. Only the poor went there." Janice's view was somewhat more . . . charitable. "If you need a hospital, that's where you go, no?" If you couldn't pay for it, that is.

Janice exaggerated the length of time she had lived in New Orleans to make herself eligible for admission to the hospital. Little Deidre was born whole and healthy a couple of hours later. Later still, Janice fainted in the bathroom and broke a tooth in her fall. The broken piece of tooth went missing; when the doctors decided to X-ray to be sure she hadn't aspirated the fragment, they found instead a spot on her lung and decided to keep her in the hospital for a week to test her for TB. In fact Janice already knew about the spot on her lung and, years earlier, had already been through TB testing because of it, but there were no records handy to prove all that to the New Orleans doctors. So she couldn't be discharged; moreover Charity Hospital kept mothers and newborns separate, so the only contact Janice could have with Deidre was gazing through the window of the nursery.

When Bob finally returned to the Quarter from his encyclopedia-selling run, a friend let him know where Janice had disappeared to, but Charity Hospital didn't allow visitors either. Gladys dropped in on him but had no helpful ideas. After three days of this impasse Janice borrowed a nickel from a nurse, called the pay phone in their apartment building, and told Bob to bring a suitcase with clothes for herself and baby, on the theory that an orderly might bring it to her room. "The orderly said, 'What's in it?' 'Clothes for my wife,' said Bob. 'No,' the orderly said—'I mean, what's in it for me?' "

Deidre was finally brought to Janice, who dressed herself and the infant and began her escape against medical advice. "I had to gather enough strength to carry baby and suitcase down a long hallway and into the elevator. I was feeling very weak, and wondered if I might not fall and break another tooth." But she made it as far as Bob in the waiting room, and together they took the baby home.

Tropical summer: "Luckily it was so hot by then in New Orleans that not many baby clothes were needed." Janice's mother came for a week or so, and "was marginally more helpful than Gladys. . . . She did mention that she was pregnant too. I didn't believe her—she was prone to delusions and besides she was forty-four years old. But my brother Tim was born four months later." The visit helped the Burrs accept the Stones' marriage, and its first fruit, a little more easily than before. Previously, Janice had received at least one reproving letter from her family, to which she replied with vigor, "to say I'm sorry to be causing anyone any embarrassment— and I mean you and Daddy, *not* aunts, uncles, cousins, neighbors and so on. . . . I really couldn't care less who is raising their eyebrows at me, but I never wanted to hurt anyone, and I'm afraid you and Daddy have been hurt, and there is no way I can ever change that. Nor can I ever tell you that I regret anything and that I wouldn't choose to relive my life exactly as I have chosen to live it, if such a thing were possible, because I would. Bob and I have to live in our own way—we're that sort of people—even if our way isn't everyone else's."

For only $10 more in rent the Stones found a slightly larger apartment nearby on Chartres Street, but "we neglected to notice it did not have air conditioning." The last checks from the census work were petering out. Still Janice "felt we were a real family now." They had acquired a radio, on which they heard Floyd Patterson defeat Ingemar Johansson in the June 1960 heavyweight rematch. They adopted a stray kitten who proved to be an expert cockroach hunter. "When there were no more in the apartment, Mickey would go out and catch one on the patio, and bring it inside to play with."

For the last few days of paid-up rent, the Stones loaned their St. Philip Street apartment to old New York friends John Rapinic and Barbara Schreiber, who had come down for a visit. The guests were careless enough to leave the sink full of shrimp shells when they departed, stewing for days in the dense New Orleans heat, and by the time that situation was discovered the apartment required fumigation.

Bob found himself yanked off the Barracks Street sidewalk into an air-conditioned black Cadillac; the cool was agreeable; the company—the Mob-connected landlord from St. Philip Street—not so much. "'What you do that to me for?' Mr. Ruffino inquired. He was referring to the shrimp in the sink. 'I ever do anything like that to you?'" For a moment, Janice recalls, "Bob thought he might end up in the Mississippi, but Ruffino was not really such a bad guy."

There were plenty of hazards for a young man with a New York accent drumming Louisiana back roads—selling encyclopedias or anything else. Or maybe encyclopedias were especially risky. The buyer of the one set Bob managed to sell "made him swear that the books contained nothing about 'evolution or the mixing of the races.'" Voter registration drives, often staffed by Northerners, were going on in the area at the time, Bob wrote decades later in *Prime Green*, "assisting local initiatives that were sometimes creating African American constituencies where none had existed since Reconstruction." To white locals, Yankees purveying any kind of information must have all seemed equally seditious. On the outskirts of a Mississippi turpentine town, the whole sales team was arrested and jailed overnight "until a local lawyer was retained by Collier's to spring us."

It was not the first time Bob had found himself at gunpoint while pursuing his career with Collier's. There were other arrests, in the Louisiana towns Bogalusa and Covington. Bob gave up the job. The forgiving Mr.

Ruffino introduced him to one Dominick, who owned a bar on Dumaine Street and engaged Bob and others to do jazz poetry readings. Bob was writing a good deal of poetry at the time, but the bar audiences were not always receptive. "Sometimes, after Tulane football games, the players would come in and throw bananas at us. This cost them nothing, since the bananas, in bunches off the dock, were hung from the ceiling and the bar pillars." Afterward, the poets could eat the bananas, along with any other fruit that might have been hurled; this haul was often better than what they took from the tip jar.

There was not much future in this kind of thing, and by September Janice was still not completely recovered from childbirth. Using her grandparents' Manhattan address, she applied to City College of New York, and negotiated, through her sister Marge, for her father to finance their return. Her grandparents had agreed to let the young Stone family stay in their Amsterdam Avenue apartment. Mr. Burr sent money enough for one train ticket. Janice and Deidre embarked, but because of a strike, they were diverted to a bus in Washington, DC, where they had to leave much of their luggage behind. When Janice finally recovered Deidre's canvas baby carriage, "all the books I had stashed in the bottom, under the mattress, had been stolen, except for my Bible. The thief must have been superstitious."

Ruffino, who must have developed a real soft spot for Bob, helped him get into the merchant seaman's union. Bob stayed on in New Orleans, hoping to get on a ship, but because of his low seniority he mostly did pierhead work. Despite being short of cash, he managed to go on the kind of alcoholic benders Rheinhardt would undertake in *A Hall of Mirrors*. New Orleans was the first situation where he could drink more or less without limit (whiskey before breakfast is not considered pathological there). Without Janice, Bob's uncontrollable boozing became frightening even to himself.

By October he was hitchhiking back to New York to rejoin his wife and child. Rides being scarce in Mississippi, Bob hopped a freight train, having picked up a little rod-riding instruction from a surprisingly friendly yardmaster in Picayune ("always put a two-by-four in the freight car door to keep it from slamming shut forever"). In Birmingham, Alabama, he left the rails to return to the highways and was briefly jailed for vagrancy in the Carolinas; Janice wired money to get him out.

He reached the nation's capital on the day of the first Nixon-Kennedy debate, but passed through quickly, hastening for "the Apple and Janice, wanting nothing so much as to see her again." And there was the infant Deidre. Bob had intellectualized his ambivalence about fatherhood, using Francis Bacon's idea that in having children "we give hostages to fortune." Ann Greif, Bob's interlocutor at the time of this observation, misunderstood the Bacon quote and asked for clarification, which Stone provided: "it means you have given fortune, a capricious entity, hostages. Like you have handed your loved ones over to the mercy of this unpredictable, all-powerful force who may do with them as he chooses." This idea would emerge fairly often in Stone's later fiction; in the fall of 1960 he concluded that it was better to be near his hostages to fortune than not.

———

Despite the opéra bouffe quality of the performances at the Dumaine Street bar, Stone was serious about the poetry he was writing at this time, not on a par with his mature work but "a cut above a lot of the stuff that was going down in New Orleans." He was also seriously interested in playwriting. Of this ambition little survives but a few pages of a sort of morality play set within an abstract socialist government, and a scrap of one sheet with the opening scene of a religious drama set in Germany's Black Forest.

During the weeks he spent alone in New Orleans, Stone wanted to concentrate on his writing, but the effort was not entirely successful, maybe because he sensed his real vocation was neither to be a poet nor a playwright, and that in that sense he was on the wrong track. There were technical difficulties too. "I had a c-key missing on my typewriter and I had to put an 'x' every time I wanted to make a 'c.' I found this finally very frustrating, finally to the point where I threw the typewriter out the window and burned the poetry," most of it, anyway.

"And it was quite a while, I think," Stone later told an interviewer, "before I was able to get enough of the sense of life lived in time to begin a novel." His New Orleans sojourn—brief, intense, and extraordinarily different from any experience he'd ever had before—was catalytic in that regard. "I wasn't really ready to write a novel when I went down there. But I got a certain vision of American reality from that particular city and my life in it that made me ready to deal with this country and people's lives lived out in time and in a special kind of place. It gave me the arena that

I wanted, and I was able to draw from my experience of a lot of different people and put them together in the three main characters in my first novel. I put a great number of people together—not precisely, for they're finally imagined characters. But they're based on my experience of people. So it was very valuable for me to go there."

5
BLACK-AND-WHITE WORLD

It was much easier for Bob and Janice to find work in New York. Janice, who'd returned to college at City College of New York, waitressed briefly at Figaro's and then trained to keypunch IBM cards, a skill that would be durably in demand for the next couple of decades. Bob wrote ad copy for furniture "of the sort that was sold on time to poor people," a desperately dull job with a trailing consequence he disliked even more: "As a registered loser on every sucker list in New York, I could be sure of receiving my own overwritten, chiseling copy in every weekend mail, pitching myself with my own scam." Janice wrote to her aunt Helen, "Bob thinks work is phooey too. But he is sticking to it like a good boy. I wish he would write a book or something so we would be rich and he wouldn't have to work."

Still, with both of them earning they were able to save, and after Janice's grandfather died in November, they rented a third-floor walk-up at 13 St. Marks Place, in an East Village area whose demographic had recently shifted from Jewish to Polish and Ukrainian. Heroin was established in the neighborhood, more or less discreetly. "The superintendent of our building was obviously a junkie, with his dark glasses and uncommunicative manner. He didn't seem to work very hard, but he didn't bother us. The regular Bowery bums on our street didn't hassle us either."

The Bowery proper was a few blocks south, a skid row inhabited by alcoholics (then called winos), many of whom (in sharp contrast to the hordes of hapless homeless folk who would turn up in the early Reagan years) appeared to be there by choice. Many were educated, and some received trickles of money from the middle-class nests they'd toppled out of—enough to pay their way in the Bowery's numerous flophouses and dirt-cheap bars. At the end of 1960 Stone began to notice a change. "Black down-and-outers, whose absence few neighborhood whites had noticed before, began appearing at corners, and in the doorways of the chicken-wired hotels." There had previously been a de facto segregation of Bowery bums, heretofore all white. The newcomers were younger ("black men faced impoverishment more frequently and at a younger age than most whites," as Bob later wrote) and more likely to have been in prison, often doing very hard time.

Drugs, and "more serious fighting" cropped up. "Older men of all races fled the Bowery and looked for relative safety. But there was no protection for anyone. The Darwinian quality one glimpsed was as shocking as anything I ever saw." Bob's eye for racial discrimination and its consequences had been sharpened by his time in Louisiana, and the census-taking months had broadened his view. He was trying to write about New Orleans now, but finding it difficult to stick to it in his limited free time. "I was afflicted, it seemed, with some kind of pathological laziness. Maybe it was depression. Maybe just bad character. Somehow your worst characteristics stay with you when your good stuff goes." While living on St. Marks Place he did manage to hammer out a draft of "The Good Neighbor," but never got it quite in shape to submit to magazines.

The Stones were leading a lean life, but a manageable one. "We could afford food and rent and beer for Bob. I had pretty much given up drinking, as an unaffordable luxury, except for special occasions. Bob took charge of the laundry—the laundromat was near McSorley's bar. Women were not admitted to McSorley's. He could have a couple of beers while the laundry was in the machines." Janice's routine had its quaint features also. One of the tamer Bowery bums "used to watch Deidre, left in her carriage downstairs while I carried the groceries up two flights. I would give him a dime, for which he appeared grateful. My reasoning then was that someone might steal your groceries but it was inconceivable that anyone would steal your child."

If sloth or depression had had their way, Bob might have sunk into a career as an adman—a path that even offered some upward mobility for a man who never finished college. Around this time he got some slightly more interesting work, writing promotional copy for books published by George Braziller, a small but tony independent publisher. A life of quiet desperation was open before him.

Then, on a winter walk in Washington Square, the Stones ran into Mack Rosenthal, who was glad to see them. Bob's story "Shore Party" had appeared while the couple was in New Orleans and was relatively fresh in Rosenthal's mind. He reminded Bob about the Stegner Fellowships at Stanford, and that they didn't require an undergraduate degree.

Janice encouraged Bob to apply. It didn't happen overnight. Bob felt the need to write something new and more substantial for the purpose, and he was still having difficulty writing well in scraps of time whittled off the edges of his work-for-pay routine. The following fall he took a trip alone "to think about it," possibly somewhere in upstate New York; Janice never knew for sure. "He wasn't gone but maybe a few days, a week at most, and when he got back he wrote three chapters of a proposed novel, each about a different character—Reinhardt, Geraldine, and Morgan Rainey."

Probably Stone took a copy of Fitzgerald's *The Great Gatsby*, which he had read as a boy, on his bus trip to wherever in the fall of 1961. "It was a rereading of *The Great Gatsby* that made me think about writing a novel," he claimed later. "I was living on St. Mark's Place in New York; it was a different world in those days. I was in my twenties. I decided I knew a few meanings; I understood patterns in life. I figured, I can't sell this understanding, or smoke it, so I will write a novel." By that time, his experience of "life lived in time" had matured enough for him to begin.

"When a letter from Stanford arrived in the mail a few months later, Bob took it into the bathroom and shut the door. Then he let out such a yell that I teased him later that I thought Stanford had turned him down and he'd cut his throat with a razor. But Stanford's answer was yes, not no, and Bob would be in the 1962–63 class. There was money involved too—not a lot, but a few thousand dollars, so Bob wouldn't have to work. We were incredibly elated. Bob was going to be a writer at last. And we were going to California!"

6

FULL-COLOR SATURATION

The Stones arrived in California in the summer of 1962, both Bob and Janice feeling that, after they'd spent the past decade in black and white, their world had burst into Technicolor—as it had for Dorothy in *The Wizard of Oz*, spooling out the Yellow Brick Road and a limitless rainbow horizon. Years afterward, Bob analyzed this time of transformation in an interview: "When I first knew the guys who were the Grateful Dead they were students at the San Francisco Conservatory of Music, and they used to wear their suits to the train. So it's a mystery to me what happened. I mean, I know what the operative forces that created the '60s at the beginning were. Part of it was the civil rights movement and its various spiritual components. Some of it was the coming of age of the red-diaper babies, of which there were many in California." This confluence was the making of a kind of cultural revolution.

Janice and Bob wanted to see San Francisco, and as the Stegner Fellowship would not begin until September, they first rented a small apartment on the corner of Filbert Street and Van Ness Avenue, installing Deidre's crib in the closet with the Murphy bed (the first of these they'd encountered outside of Laurel and Hardy movies) that folded out from the wall. They were in walking distance of the bay and its panoramic views of Alcatraz and the Golden Gate Bridge.

And as usual for those days, they were broke or the next thing to it. Janice soon found work doing keypunch for Bank of America on the night shift. Bob became a "management trainee" for a clothier, using his acting ability to convince the employer that he meant to make a career of it—and feeling a little guilty about the charade. Working opposing shifts, they saw little of each other during the week, or not when they were both awake. The bank sprang for a taxi to take Janice home every night when her shift ended at two in the morning. The staggered schedule had its advantages for childcare. It fell to Bob to get Deidre fed and dressed in the morning. Images of sunny California had moved the Stones to come without their winter clothes, so they were often a little chilly in San Franciso's fog-bound climate.

On the weekends they walked all over San Francisco (being New Yorkers, neither could drive and in any case they had no car), sometimes ranging as far as Sausalito. There was a pizzeria a little way up the Filbert Street hill where they could afford to order Chianti with their meal. Fred and Olga Kiers, friends from New York University, came to visit on their way to resettle in Los Angeles, and filled the tiny apartment merrily to the brim. Gladys appeared in San Francisco, soon after the Stones' arrival, and moved into a downtown hotel room. How she financed this relocation is a permanent mystery. Gladys preferred to visit Bob and Deidre in the evenings when Janice was at work, but she would also babysit Deidre from time to time, to give the Stones an occasional evening out.

On August 21, Bob gave himself (and Janice) a birthday surprise by staying home from work. The surprise turned out to be bigger, and more durable, than intended. As Janice recalls, "I did a quick mental calculation, and figured we were in a safe period for lovemaking. The rhythm method was notoriously unreliable, we should have remembered. It was a most inconvenient time for me to get pregnant, but we'd done it again. And again I felt I'd let him down. I was determined that this pregnancy would not interfere with Bob's writing."

With that priority in mind, they invited Gladys to move in with them in September, when they found a two-bedroom house to rent, reasonably near the Stanford campus, on Willow Road in Menlo Park. Though Gladys maintained a steady baseline of antagonism to Janice, she could manage Deidre while Janice worked, and Janice needed to work as long she could; in May there'd be another baby. She found another keypunch job, at a Palo Alto temp agency, a mile's walk from 231 Willow Road. Bob took up his fellowship and began a writing class with Dick Scowcroft.

Born in 1919 and raised in a Mormon family in Utah, Scowcroft had come of age during the Great Depression. Apparently his family was touched by the economic collapse more lightly than some, because his parents' solution to the lack of jobs for young men in the 1930s was to give him $500 for an extended trip abroad. The youngest of thirteen children, and also the first of his family to graduate college, Scowcroft spent two years in Europe, returning before World War II broke out. A tremor exempted him from military service, and he did graduate work at Harvard, where he later became a Briggs-Copeland lecturer. The first of his many novels, *Children of the Covenant*, appeared in 1945. In 1947, Wallace Stegner recruited Scowcroft for the writing program he was beginning to build at Stanford. Older and further along in all aspects of his career, Stegner wanted to teach only one semester annually; Scowcroft was deputized to hold up the other end of the academic year.

At the time, the Iowa Writers' Workshop, housed in the Iowa City branch of the state university, was the only other writing apprenticeship program in the United States that granted a degree. Stegner's original writing students were Stanford master's candidates. Stegner got funding for the first fellowships from Dr. E. H. Jones, a Texas oilman who happened to be a brother of the then-chair of the English Department. The plan was to award five fellowships a year, though in practice the numbers varied, and the writing workshop mingled fellows with master's students, and once in a while a talented undergraduate.

Robert Stone arrived in the fifteenth year of the program, in a class including three other fiction writers (Merrill Joan Gerber, Ed McClanahan, William O. Walker) and two poets (Michael Miller and Henry T. Kirby-Smith). His novel in progress made a deep impression on Scowcroft right away. In those fledgling days of writing instruction in academia, students and faculty spent a great deal of time reading each other's work aloud in the classroom. Scowcroft is remembered to have wept while reading part of the text Stone had drafted for his Stanford application back in New York: an episode where one of the principals, Geraldine, reflects on the probability that her deranged lover, from whom she's hiding in the restroom of a Galveston dive bar, will in the next few minutes kill her with the .38 pistol she knows he carries.

"It might be like getting hit. That didn't usually hurt too much. Something to be got over with. It seemed very natural and right that Woody would shoot her when she went back out. She hadn't much idea why or what over—but Woody was the sort that killed you, she thought. 'I don't know,' she said to the mirror. . . .

"If he does it without talking, she thought, if I don't have to listen to him or look at him then I'll just be dead and that'll be it."

As the scene plays through, things turn out better than *that* for Geraldine (after all, there's a whole novel ahead of her) . . . but not really all that much better. The passage isn't written as a tearjerker—it has rather a hard-boiled cast—so what moved Scowcroft to tears must have been its powerful sense of truth rendered and probably the skill of the rendering.

Stone's classmates would also have been impressed, though none of them were lightweights. Several would go on to distinctive careers—notably Merrill Gerber (the only woman in Stone's crop of fellows), who was already publishing short stories when she got to Stanford and would go on to publish more than thirty books. And, since many recent Stegner Fellows stayed on in the area, the community was larger than just one year's group. Gurney Norman, like Ed McClanahan a native of the hardscrabble parts of Kentucky, had been a fellow two years before; he took to the Stones in part because of their shared working-class background (which he was able to detect in spite of the fairly patrician New York accent Bob had absorbed from his mother). Larry McMurtry, a fellow from Norman's year, was still living nearby. Janice hit it off particularly with an Australian fellow, Michael English, and his wife, Gail. And McClanahan, via mutual friends, introduced the Stones to Ken Kesey and his wife, Faye. McClanahan had previously spent two quarters in the Stanford graduate creative writing program in 1955, rooming with Jim Wolpman and Vic Lovell, who by 1962 were, "respectively, a labor lawyer and a grad student in psychology, living next door to each other in a dusty, idyllic little bohemian compound called Perry Lane, just off the Stanford campus," and had incorporated the Keseys into their circle a couple of years before.

Bob remembered meeting McClanahan this way: "In the autumn of 1962, I found myself seated in a California classroom across from a man in a two-tone cotton jacket and wraparound sunglasses. I noted that his shoes actually seemed to be made of blue suede. These were the days when native costume was still to be seen worn by the inhabitants of out-of-the-way regions and the man was an alarming phenomenon in his. He seemed to combine in person and outfit some ghastly time-past and an unimaginably weird time-future." Who better to bring Bob Stone to Ken Kesey, who was about to inject that unimaginable future weirdness into an astonished present.

Kesey had been working on his first novel while a Stegner Fellow in 1959. *One Flew Over the Cuckoo's Nest* was published in 1962, to sufficient acclaim to make Kesey the brightest star rising out of the Stanford program at the moment the Stones moved into the neighborhood. His natural charisma increased this effect a hundredfold.

"I was then a neurasthenic youth," Stone said of himself at the time he met Kesey, "morbidly sensitive and haughty. I had read *One Flew Over the Cuckoo's Nest* with great pleasure and admiration. But at the time I had spent most of my adult life in the Navy, and I had no idea how to talk to people. I can't remember the first thing I said to him because I've repressed it. I do remember he thought I was a Communist. Anyway the world was black and white for me, the color of subtitled movies at the Thalia.

"Some time later I found myself stoned, wearing a pot on my head, waving a neoprene boffer and trying to hit him on the head with it as part of a two-man re-enactment of the battle of Lake Ladoga scene from *Alexander Nevsky*. I think I was the Teutonic knights. Eventually there were thirty people rolling around the imaginary ice on that balmy California evening. You had to be there."

Eventually, a lot of people were. The golf course between Stanford and Perry Lane became the theater for Kesey's proto-Prankster experiments in making weird and wonderful things happen among large groups of people, well before the Acid Tests and the cross-country bus trip immortalized by Tom Wolfe. A lifelong friendship between the Keseys and the Stones was in the making.

The Perry Lane scene of the early 1960s was bigger than Kesey, though Kesey became one of its principal animators. At the end of the 1950s the area still had some rural qualities; denizens ate crawfish out of the local creek. In this way and many others it was just outside the boundaries of "normal." Perry Laners were early adopters of recreational marijuana use, and a free love ethic took hold there well before it spread all over California and the nation. If most of the householders arrived as conventional couples (one man married to one woman, etc.), a lot of other people passed through, sometimes lingering. Perry Lane harbored a good number of young women who were not so much runaways as temporarily AWOL from some more conservative situation. The attitude toward these was pre-feminist, so to speak, though the community tried to take reasonably good care of them, exercising its own variation on the concept of in loco parentis.

In "The Perry Lane Papers (II)," Lovell classed these guests as "wayward girls." As an alumna of the early scene put it, they weren't as wayward as all that: "We would cut school, change our convent oxfords for white bucks, and go to the city where it was easy to meet men. . . . Because we were, as Vic said, hung up on sex. We would neck for hours but anything else was what 'bad girls' did. . . . School was where we went to recover from hangovers; home was where we went to sleep; the pad was where we went to live. We all read *The Prophet* and Allen Ginsberg and none of us dared to say we did not understand all the words." Bystanders, slightly misinterpreting the depth of such behavior, began referring to Perry Lane as "Sin Hollow." This appellation did attract a few predatory men with false expectations. "What was more likely to be found was a slightly tacky cottage in the trees with people wandering about having babies and writing papers."

In the background there was a good deal of what the disapproving might have called promiscuity, but the effects of it seemed generally benign. If as a matter of fact "everybody was sleeping with everybody," as Chloe Scott put it, the net effect (according to Jane Burton, an undergraduate philosophy student at Stanford, later to become a lawyer) was "an incredibly supportive group love affair." Born to the British aristocracy, Chloe was already a veteran of a couple of previous countercultures by the time she became "one of the reigning free spirits on Perry Lane," including the outer circle of orgone-box therapist Wilhelm Reich and Jackson Pollock's inner circle in New York. As McClanahan wrote: "Chloe is at all odds the most glamorous woman I've ever known. A professional dancer and dance teacher, redheaded and fiery, a real knockout and a woman of the world. . . . At Chloe's anything could happen. And, as they say, it usually did."

———

Kesey had begun to refashion his own mind with the help of Lovell, who'd introduced him to the LSD experiments quietly underway at Menlo Park's V.A. hospital (where both Lovell and Kesey worked as orderlies) in the late 1950s. The semi-cryptic dedication of *Cuckoo's Nest* probably refers to that watershed moment: "For Vic, who told me there were no dragons, then led me to their lairs." Kesey must have thought of those dragons as friendly, for the early experiences with LSD among his circle were recorded as extremely benign. The government-certified lysergic acid diethylamide he was able to quietly subtract from V.A. supplies (ostensibly straight from Sandoz Labs in Switzerland) was much purer and safer than the street versions of the drug that would become ubiquitous later on.

"We'd recently been initiated into a new head space when we smoked pot for the first time," says Jane Burton, who'd first visited the neighborhood shortly before the Keseys appeared there. When Kesey brought LSD into the mix, there was already a foundation of communal solidarity laid in that new head space. "I don't remember anyone having a bad trip," Burton recalled. "I remember one night a bunch of us (about five of us—Ken Babbs was there, and Chloe) were lying out on the ground under a tree and we began to hallucinate these beautiful brightly lit red cherries growing up in the tree. We all hallucinated the same thing! It was grand!" According to McClanahan, "The commonplace would become marvelous; you could take the pulse of a rock, listen to the heartbeat of a tree, feel the hot breath of a butterfly against your cheek."

———

Bob didn't relax into the freewheeling Perry Lane lifestyle without some initial difficulty. Burton recalls a first impression of him as "a rather dour fellow with a grim outlook on life," when Kesey introduced him to some of the Perry Lane group for the first time. "It's a brief visit and after he leaves we look at each other and think, this is a grim, pessimistic sort of guy. Not love at first sight." Burton heard Stone read from his work in this early phase of their acquaintance: "Again it seems he impressed us with how dark he was, how bleak his vision. However it was only a short time after that we were all completely taken with him. His pessimism, his dark vision, had become lovable quirks. He knew it too and didn't mind."

Bob's luck with hallucinogens was not always good; he was in no way immune to bad trips. In the fall of 1962 the Stones and friends planned to go hear John Coltrane in San Francisco. With luck they might have also caught a bit of Lenny Bruce, performing at another club near the Coltrane concert. One of the Stones' companions had cooked some peyote and put it in capsules, but no one was sure of the right dose. "Bob always tended to overdo things," Janice said dryly; he dropped twelve capsules while the others took six. "On peyote there are no metaphors," Stone wrote later. The drug made Coltrane's music visible to him, though not in a pleasant way. "From each instrument in its kind issued some manner of bright spectacle, not one of which I could handle remotely. Bracing in the terrible wind, stepping carefully over the bright music that was piling up on the floor, I made for the street. I tried to be cool, and showed everyone who glanced at my walkout a grinning rictus of terror." Janice and another friend (more than sufficiently stoned on a mere six peyote capsules) followed him out of the club and into Chinatown, where Bob discovered he'd been walking on a nail in the tip of his shoe. "When I took my shoe off it seemed that my sock was drenched in blood—bright blood, the color of John Coltrane's soprano sax riffs." He investigated the shoe with a finger and cut that too. They didn't make it to Lenny Bruce.

Stone had a taste for marijuana and alcohol (and for quaaludes and opiates later on). Hallucinogens appealed to him less, though he did "receive LSD sacramentally," from Lovell's friend Richard Alpert, aka Ram Dass, who dosed a group of communicants with an atomizing throat spray. But Bob's propensity for bad trips discouraged him somewhat. He ran a morbid joke about an imaginary organization that parodied the AA buddy system; "the idea was, if you're feeling paranoid, contact Paranoids Anonymous and they'll send you another paranoid." Janice, meanwhile, was more circumspect, since she had the care of a small child and was pregnant to boot.

Bob's attitude to recreational drugs was generally hedonistic, but his "sacramental" reception of LSD did have some other effects. It "impelled me to re-examine my attitudes toward religion because my experiences with acid were very much charged with religion. I guess it would have been strange if they weren't. I was taking acid, and I was taking it seriously. I felt very much that I was consciously developing a view of the world, and when I had these religious experiences as a result of taking acid, I really felt that they demanded to be reconciled with my intellectual attitudes generally. So it made me less able to develop a totally secular intellectual system of my own. I again had to make allowance for the numinous—if not the supernatural, at least the nonrational, the extrarational. I think this probably served as a process through which my adolescent religious attitudes were transformed but somehow reinforced. My adult secular life was subverted again by something very intrusive and very strong. I began to have to afford to the extrarational a certain importance in terms of how I saw things, and as a result these religious areas of experience came to be reflected in my writing. The drug experience forced me not to dismiss those things as simply part of my childhood gear but to realize that I had to continue to think about and deal with them." And further, "Even though drug mysticism is a vulgarization of the real thing, I think it made me come to terms with my own religious impulses. There is some sort of religious impulse in every novel I've written"—although in Stone's first two novels, that impulse is fairly well camouflaged.

———

Janice could walk to her job in Palo Alto, but the Willow Road house was farther, about three miles, from Perry Lane and the Stanford campus. So the Stones bought their first car, a secondhand Hudson, from a writer acquaintance. How they learned to drive the vehicle has not been recorded, but Bob passed the test for his license easily: "he said he used the Zen approach, taking the test as if he had already failed it." Janice had more difficulty, which annoyed her since she believed (as later history tends to prove) that she was the better and safer driver.

The Hudson gave the Stones some range, though it was not roadworthy for longer trips. They took a train to Los Angeles to visit Fred and

Olga Kiers, who had settled in Compton, "not a good neighborhood even then." Fred drove the party to Las Vegas, where Olga had a cousin. En route, Fred pulled off the road briefly to play one of his horns across the desert sands. In Vegas, "Bob went straight to the roulette table—it was his favorite game. Unfortunately the maximum he could play with was $5. Bob got it up to $10 before he lost it all. We went back to Olga's cousin's house, where we slept on the floor until she went to work, and then we got to sleep awhile in a bed."

In October, the Cuban missile crisis unnerved many in the Stones' new social circle. Merrill Gerber feared that her husband, Joe Spiro, would be called to return to service. Gurney Norman was still in a military reserve corps and Ken Babbs was already flying a helicopter in Vietnam, though officially described as an "adviser." Bob was fretful that he too might be called up again. Janice, already beginning to be noticed for her cool head in this group of volatile personalities, "decided not to worry about it on the theory that the people running things (President Kennedy) had to be trusted to get it right. They did."

As Janice's pregnancy approached its term, tension with Gladys came to a head. Janice's mother, who was, so to speak, a different kind of crazy from Bob's, was coming West to help with the baby, on Janice's father's insistence more than her own. Told that she needed to move out, "Gladys took the news badly. She threw a fit, in fact, and said she wouldn't have anything to do with the new baby." After a brief stay in San Francisco, she returned to New York on her own.

With her work, child-rearing, and everything else, Janice had little time for prenatal care. Though doctors had given her a due date of May 8, she was sure that conception had happened on Bob's birthday, August 21, and that the child would come later. She worked through the first week of May "and then we waited. As the days passed, it seemed less likely rather than more likely that the event would ever happen. We began to wonder if this child was going to be born at all." On the evening of May 23, the Stones went with Kit McClanahan to see the film *Long Day's Journey into Night* at a Palo Alto theater, leaving Deidre in the hands of Janice's mother. Back home, Bob sat up talking to Kit into the wee hours. She had just left around 3:30 a.m. when Janice woke up to discover that her labor had started. Bob was not in good shape to drive and neither was Janice, "because I had started shaking uncontrollably. My dear crazy mother didn't know the area very well, and didn't offer to drive, but she delivered one of her cryptic comments: 'Women soon forget what men never know.' We took a taxi." Ian Stone was born in good health, within an hour of their arrival at the hospital. "The doctor in the delivery room introduced himself, rather sarcastically, as the one I hadn't met on my three prenatal visits."

Janice didn't return to work for a few weeks after the birth, and the Stones took time for an excursion to some hot springs in Big Sur, accompanied by Marge Burr, the McClanahans, and Peter and Karen Demma, who also had a new baby. "Deidre, just turned three years old, was surefooted enough to climb from rock to rock on the shore of the Pacific. . . . California had never looked more beautiful. And our life looked very promising."

Despite all these obligations and distractions, Bob was making progress on the novel that would become *A Hall of Mirrors*. Stegner had taken over the fiction workshop for the spring semester of 1963. A master teacher, he tended to lie low in discussions, as Merrill Gerber put it: "Though Stegner could perceive in an instant the flaws in a piece of fiction (the weak link, the parts we'd hurried over, the emotions we didn't understand and tried to sail past, the sloppy construction of a sentence or the misfit of even one word), he preferred to keep silent at first, to remain in the background and allow the class to thrash out their differences. Only when he observed we were not even close, had missed the fatal flaw, did he step forward and offer his advice." Also in Gerber's recollection: "In the workshop, Bob's papers were always in a mess, pages out of order, as he gathered them together to read from *A Hall of Mirrors*. He was so scattered, his fingertips yellow from tobacco, yet when he began to read, the class was transfixed."

Stegner had a mixed reaction to Stone. Bob had been in Kesey's orbit for months before he began working directly with Stegner, and Stegner had come to disapprove of his former student, despite or perhaps because of Kesey's success as a writer. Stegner looked askance at the whole Perry Lane scene, with its drug-drenched communal solidarity and incipient cultish quality. Kesey was not yet officially known as the Pied Piper of the psychedelic generation, but Stegner may well have foreseen what was to come and been alarmed by it. "In any case, Bob did not feel the warmth from Stegner that he did from Dick Scowcroft." Nevertheless Stegner was too astute a reader to overlook the magnitude of Stone's talent and potential and used his influence to get the beginning of "his still largely unwritten and untitled novel" read by editors at Houghton Mifflin in Boston, with the hope that Stone might be awarded a Houghton Mifflin Literary Fellowship, a prize intended to fund completion of "significant manuscripts" and thus conferring some prestige, as well as a fair sum of money.

Malcolm Cowley, who had previously taught in the program and paid a visit to Stegner and the new crop of fellows in the spring of 1963, also took an interest, and wrote to Bob in March: "I didn't get a chance to read the 28 pages of your manuscript while I was at Stanford, so I carried them East with me and read them on the plane. I was much and favorably impressed by them, and decided to have them read by three of the Viking editors." Cowley suggested that if the Houghton fellowship didn't come through, Stone might well get an offer from Viking, though he'd need to complete another hundred pages first. But in April, Stone got news from Paul Brooks, Houghton's editor in chief: "It is a long time since I have read sample sections of a first novel that showed so much sheer ability to create situation and character. All this has a freshness and life and strength that promise very well for the future. It seems not to depend at all on the fashion of the moment, but I don't think it is any less effective for that." Brooks did have a caveat: "We should like to see some more of the manuscript before deciding one way or another on a literary fellowship," a very reasonable condition if Brooks was working with the same twenty-eight pages that Cowley had seen. Nevertheless, Houghton was prepared to offer an ordinary contract on the spot: an advance of $1,500 with $1,000 up front and the balance "on receipt of a satisfactorily completed manuscript."

As well as a big boost in morale, the Houghton contract was a financial shot in the arm for the Stones, who had never had such a large lump sum in their hands before. Bob found a new house for them on Stowe Lane. It was much closer to the Stanford campus and just around a curve of the golf course from their friends on Perry Lane. "It was also, we found out later, sitting right on the San Andreas Fault, but there was no earthquake activity while we lived there." Proximity to the Perry Lane crew could produce other kinds of seismic phenomena. "One night Bob went out on the golf course with, I believe, Jane Burton and Roy Sebern, among others. I stayed home with the children, and listened to whoops and hollers from outside—they were, Bob told me later, having a lion hunt. I wondered if we'd all lost our minds. Bob ran in after a while—someone had called the cops, and the hunting party had fled." High jinks and impromptu community theater frequently spilled out of Perry Lane onto the golf course, where Diana Shugart Barich, another member of the group, remembers "our great friend Sandy [Lehmann-Haupt] being chased by a horse, and climbing up in a tree & playing my flute." In Bob's recollection, these events were accompanied by a brush fire: "We had not started the fire but we tried to make the best of it. A beautiful girl sat on a limb playing Bach on her flute until the aromatic smoke of burning leaves drove her down. Horses appeared and chased us until one of the women, an equestrienne, chased *them*."

Ed McClanahan: "The parties were just good, clean, demented fun. At any moment the front door might burst open and into the celebrants' midst would fly Anita Wolpman, Jim's wife, with the collar of her turtleneck pulled up over her head, hotly pursued by Jim, brandishing an ax gory with ketchup. Or Bob Stone, a splendid writer who has also done some Shakespeare on the stage, might suddenly be striding about the room, delivering, with Orson Wellesian bombast and fustian, an impromptu soliloquy, a volatile irreproducibly brilliant admixture of equal parts Bard, King James Bible, *Finnegan's Wake* and (so I always suspected) Bob Stone. . . . At one party, Gurney maneuvered ten delirious revelers into the backyard, looped Chloe's fifty-foot clothesline around them, and endeavored to create the World's Largest Cat's Cradle. 'Awright now, men,' he kept bawling at his troops, 'I want all the thumbs to raise their hands!' "

In the midst of the carnival, some serious writing was getting done somehow, and on the East Coast, Bob's work was being read with attention. The Stones had no phone at Stowe Lane, and had given out Gerber's number for important calls. In the summer of 1963, Gerber took a message from Dorothy de Santillana at Houghton: "She entrusted me with the news and asked me to get it to Bob. My husband and I hurried over to his little rented house and I fairly banged the door down with excitement. When I told him about his award, we danced around together on the rickety wooden porch in jubilation."

The Houghton fellowship more than doubled Stone's contract, increased to the value of $5,000, of which $2,000 was an outright grant and the balance an advance against royalties, payable in twelve monthly installments beginning in December 1963. Altogether, these payouts would support him for sixteen months to finish the book.

The news made Bob the most successful of his class of fellows (though

Gerber was also flush with the sale of a couple of stories to *The New Yorker*). Within the Perry Lane circle, he was now in some sense anointed. Diana Shugart Barich writes: "Imagine: It is 1964. I am 22. I am in a small gathering of kindred souls. We have smoked some dope and munched some munchies, and tripped out, made really silly jokes & laughed a lot. We are high, but more than that, happy. And then, Bob reads pages 182–183 of *Hall of Mirrors*, and I am there—in the glorious 'California of the mind.' I didn't know life could be this good." On group LSD excursions, Bob was apt to be "a kind of leader . . . a bit into his actorly mode, given to large gestures and silly monologues. . . . There was always an edge to his humor, but we all appreciated it, and it was a great antidote to all the 'flower child peace & love' stuff that was starting up."

Diana also remembers "thinking he'd never live to be 35 because he loved drugs so much. Didn't know at that time that he had the constitution of a . . . something." But the "special bond" she felt with Stone went well beyond shared drug experiences. "Up close he was always sweet, soft-spoken, gentle, and astoundingly open emotionally. And I think he did have a gift of making people feel special—I never felt I was the only one."

———

Jane Burton remembers "the first time I got a hit from Bob's magnetism. Bob could communicate more with a look, even a glance, than any other person I've known. One afternoon I was working in my house on Perry Lane. My front door was only a few yards from the Keseys' front door although there were bushes and trees growing between them. A path through the greenery connected them. Bob had stopped by at Kesey's and as I was working I saw Jim and Mike Hagen and Bob pop out of the Kesey screen door and troupe over to my house. I had been reading books by James Baldwin and Bob and I started discussing *Go Tell It on the Mountain*. I was critical of what I thought was an overuse of the word *love* in the book, saying that talk about love had to be used sparingly to be effective. Bob's answering look was one of agreement, but much more. It conveyed the excitement (thrill, really) he felt (and which I then immediately felt) that we could think so alike about something so important. It was very flattering too, and made me feel he admired me for what I had said. He certainly could telegraph admiration that way much more eloquently than anyone can with words. This must have been part of his tremendous charm for women."

Janice maintained an island of calm in the Day-Glo swirl of creative confusion.

According to Diana, "she didn't party with us so much because she had an infant," and Jane recollects, "One evening when I was at Kesey's, Bob and Janice came in with Deidre. The Keseys had offered to babysit and they were dropping her off for the evening. The drop-off was happening very quickly and Deidre was showing signs of getting upset about being left and Janice said in a reassuring tone that D would be fine as soon as they were gone, and she was. I saw that ability Janice had—of getting people to chill out—repeatedly over the years." Gurney Norman considered that quality more systematically. "For me, our mutual working-class background was a primary ingredient of connection, especially with Janice. It was nothing we talked about much, more of a felt thing for me in my affection for Janice and admiration of her strength. Toughness might be a better term. We men were goofy as boys much of the time. Janice was always fun to be around, great d.s. buddy (code for dope smoking), and general hilarity comrade. She had the sharpest political perspective of the whole tribe, along with Jane Burton."

Toward the end of 1963, Janice was beginning to wonder if all the good times were really good for the prospect of Bob finishing his novel. Aside from possibly excessive partying, Bob was exercising his penchant for distracting himself with other work, including a story called "The Lord's Hunter," aka "Hunter's Moon," which he contributed to a collaboration with the Stones' New York friend Martus Granirer, who used the story as a treatment in his application for funds to make a film. Granirer had written a payday for Bob into the application, but the project didn't score. The story itself, a near plotless rendering of a God-bothered youth rambling through a Southern pine barren and the landscape of his own derangement, has a peculiar Flannery O'Connor flavor unlike anything else Stone ever wrote, and stands as an anomaly in the development of his mature style. Gordon Lish, rejecting the piece for a little magazine called *Genesis West*, told Bob, "I KNOW you're a heavyweight—of this I'm convinced. I'm simply not persuaded that this story scores a knockout."

Much of the Perry Lane neighborhood was plowed under in August of that year, clearing ground for the development of more expensive housing. The demolition didn't entirely stop the party, though the nucleus was disrupted. A sense of lost idyll developed around the dissipating scene; as Jane Burton would recall years later, "We were all in love with each other on Perry Lane during the time I was there—or so it seemed to me."

The Kesey house was bulldozed with other Perry Lane dwellings; Faye and Ken moved fifteen miles away to a house in La Honda, which backed up into woodland and where Kesey soon began construction of the more ambitious psychedelic funhouse that would be immortalized, in different styles, by Tom Wolfe, Robert Stone, and others. The Stones, who had replaced their old Hudson with a '51 Chevy they got from Vic Lovell, visited often, though the high switchbacks of the road were hazardous even for better-practiced drivers than they (a sister of their friend Peter Demma had a fatal crash on that route). "One evening Bob drove us down the mountain and into the intersection at Alpine Road. We ought to have realized that the brakes were going, but we were both too inexperienced with cars. No brakes, and we plowed into the van in front of us, full of cans of paint and driven by a black guy. That stopped the car. The driver ran out, took a look at us and said, 'Thank God the children is okay!' And they were indeed okay. Deidre had bumped her nose."

The La Honda place, where Kesey had laced his wooded mountainside with the materiel for psychedelic light and sound effects, became the new setting for mind-bending sessions among Ken, Bob, Jane, and others. "There were many memorable days and evenings, but we were probably too stoned to remember them," says Janice. "Bob always attributed a verse to Ken that I thought was really Jane's invention—

> *Of offering more than I can deliver,*
> *I have a bad habit, it is true*
> *But I have to offer more than I can deliver*
> *To be able to deliver what I do.*

Whoever came up with that ditty, whether Jane or Ken or even Bob, it referred to Kesey, the Master of Revels."

Dirk van Nouhuys believes that Bob, as enthusiastically as he joined in the fun, always felt himself a little apart from the charmed circle evolving out of the Perry Lane set. "I think there were roughly two sorts of people. I'll call the first dilettantes, and that includes me, who basically were looking for a good time, escape, and moderate adventure. Then there are people I'll roughly call the revolutionaries. Vic was one although that's complicated, and Kesey was another. . . . Bob was none of these. . . . He was, I think, at heart ambivalent and felt he was to a certain degree caught up in something he didn't want to be. That may be because he, as I'm sure you understand, had more real demons in himself than any of the other people."

In charge of budget and planning for the now quite sizable Stone family, Janice thought it might be wise to distance themselves a bit from all the psychedelic revelry. Bob needed to complete his novel before the Houghton advance ran out, while Janice wanted to return to college, in part to prepare for some better career than being a keypuncher. According to this idea, Janice would go back to New York with the children and stay with her grandmother on the Upper West Side, while resuming classes at City College. Bob would use a free residency at Villa Montalvo, an artists colony in Saratoga, California, to finish the book, which he thought he could accomplish by the spring of 1964 if he had no distractions from family or friends.

There was a different kind of distraction: "He thought he had an eyelash in his eye and went to Stanford Hospital to have it removed. I was waiting for him, doing the laundry, at home on Stowe Lane, and a thought crossed my mind. That guy, my Robert—it's always drama—he'll probably come home and tell me he has a brain tumor." Then Bob returned, seriously shaken; he was indeed suspected of having a brain tumor. The problem was complicated by the fact that since the Stanford fellowship had run out, the Stones had no health insurance. Bob went to the V.A. hospital (the same one where Kesey had discovered LSD) to see if he could be treated as a navy veteran. When results there were not encouraging, he took the problem to Stegner, although the two were not particularly close. Stegner arranged to extend the fellowship, so that Stone could get top-flight care from Stanford Hospital.

"Bob was being incredibly stoical," says Janice. "I was expected to be stoical also, and I tried to be, not always successfully." The two of them decided that their plan for the next few months was too far advanced to be abandoned; Janice had already registered at City College of New York and given notice on their rental at Stowe Lane. "I went East, by train, with the children. Our friends all said goodbye, and gave me a stash of marijuana cigarettes to take with me."

CT scans and MRIs were a thing of the future, so Bob was scheduled for exploratory surgery. If a tumor were found it would be removed. Janice left the children in New York and flew back to California—her first time ever on a plane. With Jane Burton, she sat in the hospital waiting room. "Poor Bob looked so awful, when they wheeled him out, and I was in such a state of anxiety, that I didn't recognize him. But Jane did. And she was together enough to speak with the surgeon, while I sat there practically catatonic. There was no tumor. What the doctors had seen on Bob's X-ray was merely a calcium spur."

Stone's symptoms were caused by a "pseudo-tumor," aka "benign acute intracranial hypertension," more simply describable as unaccountable pressure in the skull. The solution was to drill two holes in his head. "The reason for two holes instead of one," Stone wrote, "was presumably based on the physical principle that required us back then to make two perforations in a beer can instead of one. This is a principle I vaguely grasp and probably another indication of intelligent design at work on the big picture. Air, inserted and released through these taps, seemed to produce the notes of a steam calliope to replace the rattle of the drill. Maybe I imagined it. . . . Anyway, the transformation of the patient's skull into a ceramic flute resolves the pressure. A cure."

Bob's California friends were as rattled by the episode as the Stones themselves. Burton: "Vic and I went in to see him in the hospital after the surgery. We (and everyone else) had been afraid he might not survive, but he had. We were emotional to a fault.

"Then we went up to where they had Bob in the hospital. He was lying in a darkened room with his head shaved and his eyes closed but when we approached the bed he raised his eyelids slightly and reached out with both arms and grasped our hands. Again, he conveyed with a look things too complex to put in words. I can see it yet. Relief, love for us that we were there at that moment, and exultation that we were all still here and could continue our lives together, our incredible, transcendent friendship."

Janice stayed with Bob in Palo Alto until he recovered his equilibrium, then returned to New York, the children, and her classes. Bob took up his residency at Villa Montalvo, where he was not quite so immune to distraction as he and Janice had intended. He was recovering from the aftereffects of his surgery, but still had headaches and some trouble with vision in one eye, symptoms that delayed his settling down to steady work. "Every time I take a walk around here and see something I dig, I commence missing you wildly," he wrote to Janice on Valentine's Day.

He intended to buckle down on the book on a "heavy schedule Monday morning at 9 promptly," but also thought he might spend the weekend "up at Kesey's," about thirty mountainous miles from Villa Montalvo.

Despite totaling a couple of the junkers he drove—"I hate those pig iron cocksuckers to the depth and breadth my soul can reach"—Bob had a couple of big excursions; first a roving acid trip with the Keseys and Burton, who'd "got some LSD for five bucks a cube," then a trip to Mexico in the same company, with the addition of Ken Babbs and his wife. Stone flew with Burton to Los Angeles, then drove with the rest of the party first to San Juan Capistrano and then across the border. Bob had picked up some Spanish in the navy and in Tijuana he managed to get his party off the tourist track and among "ordinary Mexicans who weren't hustling anything." He was proud of finding a really good restaurant, patronized by upper-class Tijuanans and free of American thrill-seekers, and only wished Janice had been there to "show off to." After the party's return to L.A., Bob dropped Burton at the airport and got lost for hours on and off the freeways, then caught a ride back to Villa Montalvo with the Keseys; "we arrived the following morning hallucinating wildly from fatigue."

"I'm going to have to stop taking off weekends," he said in reporting these adventures to Janice. In fact his restlessness had a lot to do with missing her. "Goddam this separation is a rougher scene than I quite thought, it really takes the stomach out of me. Whenever I think about you which is often I get a terrible pang which I can hardly deal with. We are almost one third of the way through, though—that's not a bad way to look at it."

In New York, Janice was working for the common cause. In the winter of 1964 she took the hundred pages she had of Bob's manuscript to Candida Donadio, on the strength of an *Esquire* article Ed McClanahan had showed the Stones back in California, where "Ed was listed as a new and talented writer, and Candida as a hot young agent." Rust Hills, the famed *Esquire* fiction editor, had located Donadio in "the Red Hot Center" for what the magazine headline termed "The Structure of the American Literary Establishment."

Born to Italian immigrants in Brooklyn in 1929, Donadio had plenty of Bob's New York grit. As a fledgling agent working for Herb Jaffe, she had sold Joseph Heller's *Catch-22* in 1957 (the number, legend has it, derives from her October 22 birthday). She was an agent at Russell and Volkening when Janice brought her that chunk of Bob's first novel.

Donadio read (and also numbered) the pages, and then took Stone on as a client (their friendship would last until her death in 2001). She whipped up some immediate excitement by sending Stone's manuscript to *The Saturday Evening Post*, where Rust Hills had just begun to acquire fiction. "She says they have literary aspiration and pay solid gold," Bob enthused in a letter to Janice, but he turned satirical when the sale fell through: "they wanted to see more and the More, by the natural structure of the book turned out to be wild sick scenes involving pot and crippled nymphomaniac lady numbers runners, I doubt that even the Hip Swinging Jazz Baby New Saturday Evening Post is up to plastering the godly drugstores and supermarkets of America with that action."

Houghton had given Stone some kind of deadline structure, but as he wrote Janice, Dorothy de Santillana, his editor, "is being solicitous, she tells me to forget about deadlines and finish at leisure. This, of course, I disregard, because it is necessary to proceed at great speed simply in order to get done—" and yet it was becoming apparent that he was unlikely to finish by June. Janice had bought them tickets on a student charter flight to London, imposing a deadline that meant more to Bob than his publisher's. "He had been promising me this trip since we first met, and had told me endless stories of his travels when he was in the Navy. . . . Yes, he said, he would finish the book by summer."

As that date drew nearer, Bob wobbled a bit, flirting with the notion of joining Janice in "a pad in the Mexican mountains" where he could keep writing. But in the end it seemed better to stick to the European plan. A good number of their friends were also planning to be abroad: the Wolpmans in Florence, Chloe Scott in London, and Michael Horowitz (a friend from Mack Rosenthal's writing class) in Paris. And Janice was set on it: "I saw this as our chance to live *la vie bohème*, as I had always imagined it." On the mundane side of things, she was also trying to find them their own apartment, to which Bob reacted, "Oh, man those New York pads seem dreary—the same old shit." The idea of a European summer was an antidote to that.

During his last weeks in California, Bob wrote, sometimes furiously, but his restlessness continued. When he was wheel-less at Villa Montalvo, Diana Shugart sometimes rode her Honda 50 motorcycle down to visit him. Neal Cassady, a Perry Lane habitué celebrated for his fictionalized role as Dean Moriarty in Jack Kerouac's *On the Road*, lived in nearby Los Gatos, so Bob could catch rides with him to call on the Keseys at La Honda. Their route traversed the Santa Cruz Mountains, on a road that "wound like a fairytale lane through redwood, fields of tule grass, and live oak. Here and there it would pass through valleys filled with ferns that would haunt your dreams."

As the psychedelic era developed its dark side (a process to which Stone was peculiarly sensitive), dream could sometimes dissolve into nightmare. A slaughter of the innocent appeared to be in the offing. "Police parlance developed a sporting metaphor to describe the method of psychos in search of prey. They called it 'trolling.' The kids talked about 'bad vibes.' The Santa Cruz became a sinister lonely place. . . . Administrators and residents at my colony at the foot of the mountains became extremely concerned that the gates be locked at night. Leaving them unsecured was a major dereliction."

Stone began to find it easier to work back in his old Stanford neighborhood, in Burton's new place on El Camino Real, where she'd moved after demolition dispersed the Perry Lane community. "I was commuting down to San Jose State every day where I was an assistant professor in philosophy and while I was gone Bob worked on his novel in my house. When I got home in the afternoons he was sweating and I could tell how concentrated his efforts had been all day." Later that spring, Jane found herself pregnant. "When I knew that I was, I told him. He didn't ask whose it was. We both knew it was his. He said, 'I don't want to stand in the way of the life force.'"

By this time Bob and Janice had decided, in the interest of staying together in the long term and in the light of the fact that they had married so young and then been plunged into the social and sexual upheavals of the 1960s, "not to be possessive of each other." (That strategy was successful, or something was; theirs is one of the most durable literary marriages of the American twentieth century.) Jane didn't mean to be possessive of Bob either. The prospect of single motherhood didn't alarm her, or not much, and there was solid support available from her community of friends. "Faye Kesey dropped by soon after, maybe the next day. I told her and she called Ken. I overheard her say, 'No, she's pretty happy about it.' And I was. Faye was beaming as no one else can. Abortions weren't legal then and if they had been, I'm not sure I would have done that. I wasn't worried. Life was incredibly easy in those days if you weren't very materialistic. . . . But when Bob left to join Janice in NY I cried copiously—though it was not because I wanted him. He and Janice belonged together and I wasn't interested in changing that."

7

TOO LONG AT THE FAIR

In the middle of May 1964, Stone caught a Greyhound to go back East. "I'd been riding the Dawg since my mother's first month as a single mom and it was home on wheels to me." As soon as the bus rolled away from the coast, however, he began to sense that something was dodgy about his appearance, at least in the eyes of others he encountered, in Sacramento and in Salt Lake City. The post-navy motorcycle gang he'd imagined had never left the realm of fantasy, but Bob was sporting a strikingly Weird Beard, rakishly combed into not one but two little points, and his style of dress, unremarkable on the West Coast, made him look like a beatnik in the heartland.

On a leg of the bus journey east of Chicago, he attracted the hostile attention of a gaggle of navy recruits—which struck him as only ironic at first, since as "an ex-petty officer with a little brace of service ribbons," he ought really to have been a senior member of their fraternity. Of course he wasn't wearing his decorations, though he did have his "old Navy seabag in which I'd stowed everything I owned, including the manuscript of my ongoing and ongoing first novel." It didn't help.

When the bus stopped in Highspire, Pennsylvania, Bob was accused by the sailors of having stolen his own bag from their group, and had to show his Naval Reserve card (with the serial number also printed on the bag) to justify his possession of his own gear to the sailors and some equally hostile bystanders who'd begun to gather. It didn't help. The sailors continued to stalk him, and in the small hours of the morning trapped him outside the bus terminal. "My one scoring point, perfectly legitimate in parking lots, was an elbow to the mouth of the guy who was trying to steal my bag from between my feet. But that was it, from then on it was them over me and I was covering up, on one side with my knees up, clinging to the seabag that contained the manuscript of the great work in progress." He hung on to both the bag and his bus ticket through the beating, but battered and bloody as he was, it took him several tries to convince a driver to let him board the vehicle that finally got him back to New York.

Janice had settled on a new apartment, at the corner of Ninety-Seventh Street and Riverside, with the advantages of an elevator and proximity to "one of the better public elementary schools in Manhattan," and only ten blocks from Grandma Mattson's place. "I could bring the children to her when I had classes and Bob was working." Facing the wall of the next building over, the three rooms had no view and little daylight; also, "One of our neighbors was a screamer. I never saw the man, but nearly every day he would let out a heart-stopping yell. Bob and I were so glad to be back together, even in what he later referred to as New York's ugliest apartment, that the screamer was a minor annoyance." With what was left of the Houghton fellowship money and six monthly payments still to come on the advance, Stone didn't have to find other work right away. "Bob wrote on his typewriter at the kitchen table, while I studied for my classes in the living room, and the children were banished to the bedroom and ordered to be quiet." Gladys, who had remained aloof until Bob returned from California, began to visit the Stones on Riverside Drive. At first she chose moments when Janice was at school to drop in on Bob, but now that the children were a little older it turned out that Gladys could be a real help with them.

If the Stones were back in a black-and-white world, an infusion of West Coast color was coming their way. Back in California, Kesey and friends were strapping themselves in for a madcap cross-country odyssey. Ed McClanahan "wistfully waved goodbye as Ken's psychedelically retrofitted 1939 International Harvester school bus lumbered off eastbound up Highway 94, the Good Ship Further—'Furthur,' if you're a purist—adorned stem to stern with luridly amorphous abstract expressionist psychedoodles and psychedribbles, Ray Charles's 'Hit the Road, Jack' blaring from the loudspeakers mounted on the poop deck, and all my most audacious pals—the Merry Pranksters, they'd lately taken to calling themselves, Ken and Faye and Jane and Babbs and Hassler and Zonk and George and Hagen and them, and the Real Neal (Cassady that is) at the Wheel—gaily waving back from every porthole, setting sail across the trackless wastes of America for the World's Fair in exotic, unspoiled New York City."

Jane Burton caught the Good Bus Furthur with the practical goal of getting herself to New York, where she had some prospect of a job at City College, plus friends like Janice Stone, plus a-little-more-than-just-a-friend Bob Stone. Jane was by then substantially pregnant, though the loose dresses of the flower-child mode became her, and also camouflaged her condition to casual inspection. If she had thought it would be more comfortable to travel with friends, that soon turned out not to be quite true.

Furthur's route to New York City was epically indirect, passing through Los Angeles, New Orleans, Pensacola, etc., in a style mostly innocent of advance planning. Chauffeur Cassady, needless to say, was doped to the eyeballs all the time, and so were most of the others. Near Wikieup, Arizona, they went off-road, mired the bus in sand, and whiled away their wait for rescue by dropping acid and stirring Day-Glo paint into the swampy waters of a nearby pond. By that time Jane's close friend Chloe Scott had already bailed; dismayed by the chaos, she left the bus in San José—before there was time to bestow on her a Prankster moniker such as others soon acquired: Hassler, Intrepid Traveler, Speed Limit, Gretchen Fetchin', Stark Naked (who lived up to her *nom vaillant* by dancing in the state described on the bus's outdoor observation platform).

The nicknames reinforced the cultish quality growing around the Prankster group, as Kesey (Captain Flag, Swashbuckler, etc.) evolved into the role of psychedelic shaman. *On the bus* or *off the bus* became loaded terms denoting faith or apostasy vis-à-vis Prankster-hood. Jane, dubbed Generally Famished thanks to the fact that she was eating for two, soon wanted to get off the bus but couldn't. Somewhere along the way she'd lost her purse with all her ready money and identification, and there were other good reasons not to be left behind in the heartland. The Pranksters, driving an extravagantly unsafe vehicle loaded to the gills with illegal and not-yet-illegal mind-altering drugs, escaped arrest by being too numerous (and too puzzling) to jail; local law enforcement always found it better to speed them on their way.

———

Until Bob's return from the West Coast, Janice had been living a quiet life in New York, taking care of her children, going to school, and socializing very little. Once in a while she saw Martus and Jean Granirer, old friends from her grandmother's neighborhood on the Upper West Side.

She tried calling John Rapinic, the Seven Arts manager who might have been a bit jealous of Bob back in the day (though he'd also attended the Stones' wedding), "to invite him over to Grandma Mattson's apartment, planning to share my stash of marijuana cigarettes from California. When he arrived, I asked John if he still smoked pot. He responded with disapproval, lecturing me that I was now a mother and should not be using drugs. So I didn't offer him any."

Despite all the social changes the 1960s were beginning to wreak, that sort of double standard was still in effect, and in more ways than one. In his last months alone on the West Coast, Bob really had had a hard time managing without Janice. "I've needed all my resources and working concentration I now think," he wrote to her from Villa Montalvo, "to keep myself from the kind of degeneration I fell into after you left New Orleans. I am apparently as organically connected with you as you are with me, no way around it. I miss you most painfully. I also miss the kids." Bob pined, asked for pictures, and complained that the pictures weren't as good as the real thing. Everything he wrote along those lines was true, if not the whole truth.

Paradoxical as it may seem, his missing and really needing Janice might have been a factor in bringing him closer to Jane. His letter announcing Jane's pregnancy wrapped the subject in camouflage: "Faye is pregnant again. Jane thinks she is too (Confidential) nominees being Danny North, Roy or Carl's brother Sandy. She's pretty pleased about it, I think. Kesey encourages her. That good old Perry Lane pastime continues to hold its own. Me, I live in Papal splendor." The last phrase, oft-repeated in Bob's letters from Villa Montalvo, appeared to be an oblique reference to the celibacy of the Catholic priesthood—code to Janice that Bob wasn't sleeping around during their separation.

—◦—

Eventually, Furthur rolled up to the building at Ninety-Seventh and Riverside. The Stone family climbed onto the roof of the bus for a Prankster tour of upper Manhattan. Janice recalls: "We had to duck for low-hanging tree branches as we crossed Central Park. California craziness had followed us to New York City. And it was exciting. Kesey could be counted on to make things happen."

By then Kesey and his crew were exhaustively filming and recording their every move (though without paying much attention to the issue of syncing sound to picture). They shot the New York streets from Furthur's conning tower, capturing amazed, amused, or just purely astonished onlookers (some of whom were taking pictures back as fast as they could click their shutters). Bob Stone appears in a short segment, his beard trained into two Mephistophelian points, looking as weird and riotous as any other member of the Prankster set. "You felt like you were in an aquarium," he said later, "on the other side of the glass." More seriously, "Ken really felt that things could be changed, that consciousness could be changed. He saw himself as a kind of liberator for the generation." In Stone's interpretation of Kesey's thinking at the time, Ken saw Furthur's arrival in New York as something like Napoleon's triumphal entry into Paris.

It didn't quite work out that way. The New York World's Fair was too big of a circus for a Prankster hootenanny to make much of an impression there. Stone: "The irony is that curved, finned, corporate America as presented by the 1964 World's Fair was over before it began. Sixty-four! Things were changing. We didn't know that World's Fairs were a thing of the past."

By the time the bus reached the fair in Queens, the Stones had already left the caravan. Bob and Janice did go to a party (hosted by Chloe Scott in her New York apartment) with Kesey and company, also attended by Jack Kerouac, Allen Ginsberg (two inspirational figures whom the Pranksters had hoped to meet and impress), and an imposter pretending to be Terry Southern. But these icons weren't tremendously impressed by all the tootling and capering (which in the fragments of surviving footage appear to be giving Kerouac a major headache). The Stones detached themselves and "went home to our bleak apartment."

There was the matter of Jane and her pregnancy, on which Janice had been left slightly behind the curve. "I'm not sure at what point it was unfolded to Bob. When he wrote to me, he said everyone was trying to guess who the father was. It might have occurred to him," she says with a ghost of irony, "that it was he. She probably told him, I would think. He was busy not dealing with it. I think it just gradually dawned on both of us that he was indeed the father. But we just went to Europe, you know, and Jane went back to California."

That might sound like sort of a vague non-solution, but if no conventional showdown took place, that's probably because none of the parties really wanted one. Decades later, Janice supposed that Jane's first wish was to have a child; keeping the father on the scene was not so important. "I guess she would have been happy if Bob had stayed, maybe. I don't know—Jane's such an independent person. She had a lot of great boyfriends, but she told me she never liked having someone else's clothes hanging in her closet. I wondered sometimes if *Kesey* would have liked it if Bob had stayed with Jane. I was certainly not exactly on board when it came to—I was as onboard as I could manage with that gang, but at some level I always distrusted Kesey. I thought that his interests and Bob's diverged, actually, and that if Bob spent much more time hanging out with Kesey the novel would never get finished. I mean, Bob once said, Kesey goes for life, but I'm going for art. And I thought he made exactly the right decision, because all those great nights of back and forth, you know, they disappeared into the ether."

8

GRAND TOUR

The novel was absolutely supposed to be finished before Bob and Janice took off for Europe. It wasn't, but the discounted tickets wouldn't wait. They took Deidre and Ian to Janice's parents in Bogota and caught their flight to London—nearly missing it, in fact, "when Bob wanted to have just one more drink at the airport bar—we had to run across the tarmac with our suitcase, just as the stairway was being pulled up."

The Stones spent a month in London, studying Arthur Frommer's *Europe on 5 Dollars a Day* and walking all over the city. Whenever she saw other people's children, Janice missed her own and felt guilty about abandoning them. Bob slipped into silent gloom, maybe fretting over his unfinished novel (he didn't try to work on it during the European tour), or maybe just yielding to a bout of the cyclical depression that would worsen for him later in life. Unable to snap him out of the mood, Janice brooded over lines of Randall Jarrell's "Cinderella," which had recently come her way.

> *A sullen wife and a reluctant mother,*
> *She sat all day in silence by the fire.*
> *Better, later, to stare past her sons' sons,*
> *Her daughters' daughter, and tell stories to the fire.*
> *But best, dead, damned, to rock forever*
> *Beside Hell's fireside—*

Dismal stuff indeed! Especially if one fills in the sort of "fire" provided in bedsits like the one the Stones had rented in South Kensington: a weak electrical apparatus fed by coins. Five years into a marriage contracted very young, the Stones were not immune to doubt. Bob, never at his best when not writing, used to dream he had reenlisted in the navy, "the symbolism of which," Janice said, "did not escape me."

There were distractions. Chloe Scott passed through, en route to Addis Ababa, with her daughter Jennifer, who'd taken care of the Stones' children sometimes in California; Jennifer was now mad for a new group called the Beatles. The Stones went to the Aldwych to see Samuel Beckett's *Endgame*, which while not exactly cheerful was cheering in the way great works of art can be. In Paris, Michael Horowitz arranged for them to stay on cots between the shelves upstairs in Le Mistral, George Whitman's Left Bank bookstore, later famous as Shakespeare and Company— with an excellent view of Île de la Cité and the facade of Notre Dame.

In Le Mistral's orbit they met Joan Michelson, an aspiring young writer who later made a career as a poet and who would be a close friend and copious correspondent with both Janice and Bob for many years to come. Joan described herself then as "a bit of a hobo-trail hitchhiker en route home after my junior year in Jerusalem. Bob was the guest writer in residence." Her father was a long-term friend of Whitman: "They were lovers of Dostoevsky and met as inmates in the stacks of Harvard Library." The Stones had to wait for the store to close to go to bed, but that, in the City of Light, was not a terrible hardship. "At night we would smoke hashish and listen to Radio Luxembourg play the Zombies—'She's Not There.' I asked Michael, what does that mean, She's Not There? He said—you know—she's not *there*."

Relative poverty is more easily romanticized in Paris than in London; Janice could plug in to her old Mimi and Rodolfo fantasy: "It was *La Bohème* in a garret full of books." Quick with languages, Bob could pick up enough French to get by and was adept at showing Janice around, as he had long promised her he would do. He took her to the landmark churches, applying the fund of knowledge from his Catholic childhood, plus his autodidact's erudition.

In the eighth week of their tour, the Stones went to Germany, stopping for a couple of days in Munich, where Bob's flair for language failed him to the point that they ordered both goulash and goulash soup for dinner. With their budget running low, they couldn't afford expensive mistakes. Encouraged by the manager of their youth hostel to move on, they went to Vienna, which was cheaper; they could afford a hotel if they lived on cold cuts. The discovery of Gustav Klimt's paintings cheered them. Bob called Candida Donadio, who wired them some money—welcome and unexpected relief.

With this shot of fresh capital they spent a weekend in Budapest, "where the earth did not seem to be rising on new foundations, nor did a better world seem to be in birth," Janice recorded. She had thought of herself as a socialist since her "rebellious youth," and had gone so far as to learn the words of "The Internationale" while at New York University. The disillusionment was compounded when the Stones, dressed in "our regular inexpensive New York clothes" had to produce their passports in the lobby of the tourist hotel, which the locals were not allowed to enter. Out of money and out of time, they went back to London to catch their flight home.

9

BACK TO THE SALT MINES

There was still the novel to be finished. Bob adopted a strategy that continued to be in use by the New York artistic community through the end of the twentieth century: work six months, get laid off (a step which could sometimes be tricky, for one couldn't simply quit), draw unemployment, write full-time for the next six months, repeat. Janice's father, whose career was in advertising, fumed, "If he wants to be a writer, why doesn't he get a job for a publishing company and work his way up?" Loyal to a fault, Janice had begun to fret a little herself. "I had never seen anybody write a book before, and I thought it was taking an awfully long time."

The months of a day job had to come first. Bob found his at *Inside News*, a tabloid that was part of the *Confidential* magazine group. Soon after, he made a lateral transfer to another tabloid, *The National Mirror*, which traded in reflections of morbid fantasies: for example, "Sky-Diver Devoured by Starving Birds" (a headline Bob briefly considered using as the title of his second novel). It was an absurd but in some ways entertaining post for a developing fiction writer—a situation where acid flashbacks, for example, could be reported as hard news—and doubtless it helped develop the surreal side of Bob's imagination.

Inventing such headlines was Bob's special gift. He pondered a photo of "a distressed-looking starlet whose mouth was a mass of slop. In black and white, the ink looked like blood.

"I started playing with ghastly headlines, sizing them in. All at once, driven by hysteria, by Satan, by my Friday afternoon craving for a paycheck, suddenly I had it:

MAD DENTIST YANKS OUT GIRL'S TONGUE

"By God, it fit like a nail!"

Dirk van Nouhuys remembers Gurney Norman quizzing Bob about this gig at "a party at Ed McClanahan's house when he had a big house in Palo Alto. As I recall, we were not stoned. Gurney had heard beforehand that Bob had worked for the *National Enquirer* or some similar sensationalist rag of the time. First thing, Gurney, in his polite and slightly formal fashion, asked Bob if he could ask him a question. Bob agreed readily. Gurney asked if the stories in the *National Enquirer* (or whatever it was) were true. Bob said some were and some weren't. Gurney said, in that case he wanted to ask about a particular story. The story portrayed a married couple where one of the members (I've forgotten how the genders lined up) could only have an orgasm if the other ran around their bed in circles quacking like a duck. Bob said he knew that that story was untrue because he had invented it."

—·—

Long afterward (and more soberly), Bob reflected, "Hemingway would always say that he learned his trade at the *Kansas City Star*. With this in mind I should reflect on what I learned . . . , beyond the depths of vulgarity of which I was capable. Certain laws obtain in all fictive enterprises, low journalism included. They are almost moral laws, the way grammar in its way is moral.

"I have come to believe that language, a line of print, say, is capable of inhabiting the imagination far more intensely than any picture. . . . Descriptive language supplies deeper penetration, attaches itself to the rods and cones of interior perception, to a greater degree than a recovered or remembered image. Language is the process that lashes experience to the intellect." So Stone really was improving his sense of craft while writing to tabloid deadline, though that process was completely disconnected from any idea of truth in reporting. The whole experience fed the portrait of Rheinhardt as an adept, conscience-free radio journalist in *A Hall of Mirrors*.

Bob's work on the novel continued, sometimes unsteadily. Finishing a degree in psychology at City College, Janice took an English course to justify time spent reading novels, including Norman Mailer's *The Naked and the Dead*. "I was impressed by it, and told Bob so. He responded by throwing the book out the window. I didn't even try to retrieve it. It was raining, and the Mailer book was now in the inaccessible courtyard below. And I realized Bob was having such a struggle with his own novel that he didn't want any competition. He was no doubt ready to throw the book out a second time."

By the fall of 1965, the novel to be published as *A Hall of Mirrors* was really, truly nearing completion, although Bob was confused about the ending. He knew in general what had to happen, that "there would be a riot, and that Rheinhardt was going to be inside the stadium. He also knew that Geraldine was doomed, and had to work out the details of that. And Morgan Rainey needed to be inside or nearby, and his story finished." Talking it out with Janice eventually solved the problem. "I was good at the logistics," Janice says, "who's inside, who's outside, where's everybody going?—but only Bob could have come up with a character like S. B. Prothwaite," the unaffiliated maniac who drives a truck bomb into a crowded stadium to produce the book's pyrotechnic finale.

Bob turned in the manuscript and shaved off his beard, prompting two-year-old Ian to inquire, "Where's my other daddy?" Dorothy de Santillana, the original editor, had by this time retired. The book was years late, and held up further by Houghton Mifflin's concern that one character (Farley the Sailor) might be a libelous representation of a real person.

Austin Olney and Paul Brooks were assigned to the project after de San-tillana's departure, but since both were based in Boston, Bob didn't have much contact with them, and moreover he really didn't want to look at the book at all after its submission. "It was as if he didn't have faith in it, or perhaps wouldn't be able to resist more rewrite." As he refused, ada-mantly, to read the proofs, Janice did the best she could with that job.

Any ideas for a second novel were still in early gestation. At loose ends in New York, Bob got an assignment from *Esquire* for a piece on Ken Kesey, who in the summer of 1966 had fled to Mexico to escape charges from a couple of drug busts in California, leaving a phony sui-cide note behind in his abandoned bus. No one was convinced by that gesture, and others were on Kesey's trail—not only law enforcement but also New Journalist Tom Wolfe, who would eventually publish his cov-erage of the story as *The Electric Kool-Aid Acid Test*. It was a race of sorts, and Bob, as a member in good standing of Kesey's circle, had the edge in the beginning. He got Jim Wolpman (one of the few who knew Kesey's exact location) to forward a letter to Kesey, and then "disap-peared into Mexico. Since we had no phone, it was as if he had gone into a black hole."

From his few weeks in Mexico, Bob produced a fifty-odd-page draft of a story as ambitious in conception as Wolfe's later work, intending to describe and explain what Kesey had become, and how. Kesey's evolution from literary fiction writer into a special sort of twentieth-century sha-man interested him in particular, because it was a road he himself would not take. "Many artists, needless to say, have arrived at rather original aesthetic conclusions and have quietly set out to employ their discoveries. For Kesey, artistic method is far too indirect. Like a Chautauqua preacher or country visionary from the Great Awakening he keeps happening, keeps coming on, an archetypical pitchman with real medicine in his elixir bottles—clown, minstrel, hypnotist, an intellectual Zorro." Report-ing and representation no longer interested Kesey; he wanted to be the event itself. For Bob, the gestalt of Kesey's new being had been captured by a young woman who'd earned the Prankster sobriquet Mountain Girl, "because she lived in a house on a hilltop in the wood near La Honda. On the first afternoon she walked into Kesey's house, she looked at the scene, listened for a while, and told him, 'You've turned on the Here.'"

Caught up in both of Kesey's drug busts (she had been the only other person caught in his second arrest, for marijuana possession on a San

Francisco rooftop), Mountain Girl followed him to Mexico—along with Kesey's wife, Faye, and their children; Ken Babbs, Gretchen Fetchin' (government name: Paula Sundsten), and their two children; one or two stray Hells Angels who'd hung around Kesey since the infamous La Honda celebration billed as "The Merry Pranksters Welcome the Hells Angels"; Neal Cassady and his later-to-be-notorious parrot; and more—an entourage that gladly embraced Bob Stone on his arrival. "Indeed, they are all powerful people, all physically attractive; they do not look a bit like Decadents or Parnassians or Aubrey Beardsleyesque laudanum heads." However, two of the group had been picked off by local police by the time Stone got to Manzanillo (an area believed by Mexican law enforcement to have become a gathering place for American drug users, with or without Kesey's magnetic presence). Kesey and his followers were being watched, and Stone's draft article created some darkly comic scenes from Pranksters' encounters with the Mexican police stalking them.

Kesey was given to vatic pronouncements during this period. "If your fantasy is big enough, you can change it. Everything." Or, "There's a Great Ear that is always open. All you've got to do is speak to it in terms that it will hear." To unbelievers, some of these statements might have smacked of paranoid delusion. On a flight from police through the jungle from Puerto Vallarta to Manzanillo, Kesey "found out that if I took my eyes off the chinches they attacked me. Everything in that forest was ready to strike me down if I got unwary. . . . I disciplined my awareness until I found that by concentrating the force of my attention I was in absolute control." Bob reported that Kesey's house in Manzanillo was papered with "many panels from Marvel comics, a strip in which a band of superheroes endowed with transcendent powers carry on a ceaseless struggle with a variety of fantastic opponents. It is Kesey's belief that the line employed in the artwork of this strip is keyed to that quality of perception which makes visible the world of the future."

Stone himself was not a true believer at this point, if he ever had been. He didn't "drink the Kool-Aid," in the latter-day sense of that phrase (though he didn't usually say no to LSD, and in Mexico couldn't have if he'd tried, due to Cassady's compulsive practice of dosing everyone's food and drink, which extended to the point of injecting a barbecue-destined pig while it was still on the hoof). Instead he observed, sympathetically but acutely, what was happening to the community of his California friends: "beautiful, fearless, strength-intoxicated" people who "strive for nothing less than a similar Superheroism. They have for quite a while employed Superpowers born in fantasy against the complications of the physical world in the name of the future." Baroque extrapolation of paranoid delusion was becoming part of Stone's stock in trade as a novelist, but he was a long way from buying into full participation in what Kesey and his inner circle were trying to become.

———

Thus far, Bob had had more obvious difficulties handling their long separations than Janice, but Janice wasn't doing so well this time on her own in New York. Visits from friends and family couldn't shake her mood. Along with sole care of their small children while Bob was in Mexico, she had obligations to school and also was still working substantial hours as a keypunch operator. Going to see a Bergman film on her own while under such stress turned out not to be a good idea. "*Persona* was about a young woman who has lost her mind and is either unable or unwilling to speak a word. I hated the film, though ordinarily I was a Bergman fan. And I found it disturbing. I was still someone who was very self-conscious, very shy. I often had difficulty speaking to others. I wondered if I too was losing my grip."

She found a Mexican telephone number that got through to the Kesey encampment, and asked Bob to come home. A Hells Angel hanger-on called him "pussy-whipped" for leaving at his wife's request, but Bob was happy enough for a hook to lift him out of the situation. LSD didn't always agree with him and in any case he liked to choose when he took it, rather than be a target of Cassady's clandestine dosing program. Bob's strain of paranoia was darker than Kesey's, and the Pranksters' Mexican scene did much to evoke it, as seen in "Porque No Tiene, Porque Le Falta," a short story written a few years later.

In any case, he had enough material for the *Esquire* article and then some. He returned quietly to New York, a few days following Janice's call. Not long afterward, Kesey himself, incognito, crossed back into the United States. Bob's draft article opened with a wonderfully comic rendition of the hambone performance Kesey turned in at the border. "He was Singin' Jimmy England, he explained, and he had been down to play an overnight country music gig and damn if the Mex's hadn't laid him out and cleaned him. Hell no, he didn't have no papers. He didn't have no money neither. Why, he didn't have nothin'. 'Cept (pat pat) his gitar. Yep, the women and the margaritas and the streets of Matamoros had laid Ole Singin' Jimmy low and all he wanted out of fortune was into God's country and then home to good old Boise."

"The Man Who Turned on the Here" had an epigraph from Marshall McLuhan: "I will stand on your eyes, your ears, your nerves and your brain and the world will move in any tempo I choose." This line adapted very well as a label for Kesey's ambitions of the moment. But Bob's editor at *Esquire*, Harold Hayes, thought Bob had gone too far into his insider's point of view. "Tell it to a neutral reader," he ordered, but Bob was unwilling or unable to do that (or believed he had in fact already done it). Eventually he shared the material with Wolfe, who based his chapter on Kesey's Mexican sojourn on it; Bob's article eventually appeared in *The Free You* (a Palo Alto publication edited by Gurney Norman and Ed McClanahan, among others) and later in *One Lord, One Faith, One Cornbread*, an anthology of writing by the pre-Prankster Perry Lane crew.

Without his beard, Bob looked considerably younger, and appears so in a couple of photos taken then, one by John Gregg, a friend from Bob's days on the *Daily News*. The shot ultimately used for the *Hall of Mirrors* jacket was taken by Christopher George, a friend of Jane Burton's. This image impressed Janice's friends at work, who crooned, "Where do you find one like that?" At the same time Bob came down with the first of many attacks of gout that would plague him throughout his life—puzzling for the Stones, who thought of gout as an old man's disease, and Bob was still, if barely, in his twenties.

In the summer of 1965, Martus and Jean Granirer had loaned the Stones their apartment on West Eighty-Sixth Street while they were on a trip to England—more commodious and agreeable than the ugly apartment on Riverside Drive. After Bob's return from Mexico they were able to make a more permanent move. New York's byzantine rent control laws made discounted "semiprofessional" apartments available to visual artists but not to writers. The Stones got themselves into one of these, on West End Avenue at Ninety-Eighth Street, with the help of the painter George Rhoads, a mutual friend of the Stones and the Granirers, who though he had his own domicile in the West Village agreed to co-sign the lease for the West End Avenue place. In the bargain the Stones got to hang three of Rhoads's larger paintings which they admired, and which wouldn't fit in Rhoads's West Village digs.

Jane Burton had come East again with her (and Bob's) daughter, living on a Vermont dairy-farm commune for a while, before taking a teaching job at Collaberg School in Stony Point, New York, where the Stones paid her a winter visit. Jane and the Stones still counted each other as close friends, and saw enough of each other for Emily to get to know her half-siblings a little (although none of the children knew about the relationship until several years later). Gurney Norman also stopped in; since the Perry Lane days he'd done a hitch as a forest ranger and had funny stories about spotting fires from the tower while stoned.

When Bob's unemployment ran out, he got a job as "assistant curator" at the American Congress of Artists Gallery on Fifty-Seventh Street; something in his personality having convinced the owner to take him on, despite his lack of any remotely relevant experience. He likened the job to being an assistant curator of shoes at Thom McAn; much of his time was spent reminding people (some as illustrious as Eartha Kitt) to pay for artwork they had taken away. His writing talent made up for "the startling lacunae in my art-appreciation background; I was kept on because I could write pay-up-or-else letters that were very polite but quaintly menacing."

ACA at the time "was what remained of a leftist art collective founded in the thirties," and the artists it showed during Bob's tenure—Anton Refregier, William Gropper, Raphael and Moses Soyer—still swung hard to the left. For many of them that style of political orthodoxy remained a point of pride. Bob managed to get a show for the Stones' friend George Rhoads, though the politicized ACA artists didn't think much of his work. Fundamentally immune to Stalinist fellow-traveling syndrome and related phenomena, Bob was more amused than anything by such pretensions. He quipped that Refregier "looked like he bought his suits in the Soviet Union, and had his hair cut there too. Bob wasn't intimidated by anyone."

Bob wrote to Jim Wolpman from his ACA job, describing the gallery as "full of peeling ladies from Great Neck." He congratulated Jim and his wife on the recent birth of a daughter, then: "For my own part I have more or less settled back into the urban ooze from which I emerged. But I did finish the book after all, in spite of heroic efforts on my own part to prevent it. . . . I work at the moment at the gallery referred to above, having spent last year editing A Sensational Tabloid With A Heavy Emphasis

On Sex. Janice is a Social Worker on the Harlem Futility Beat. She sends her love."

Since graduating from City College in 1966, Janice had been a caseworker for the New York City Department of Social Services, operating out of the Saint Nicholas Welfare Center on 125th Street and calling on clients in their west Harlem homes. "The job reminded me of taking the 1960 census" in New Orleans, "as, again, most of the people I visited were black. Another chance to be a white person coming around asking nosy questions. But I had known very few African Americans in my life. I wanted to get to know some better."

Janice was sympathetic to most of her clients, in more ways than one. She didn't earn much more than they did; real prosperity for the Stone family was still somewhere around the corner. Like many of the women she called on, she'd had her first child while still in her teens. "We commiserated with each other about the price of rent and groceries and children's clothes." Caseworkers like Janice had some latitude to recommend special grants for necessities like beds, kitchen equipment, and essential clothing. In spite of her shyness, she made some friends, "and I could come home and tell Bob stories about the lives of the people I met," some of which cropped up in his later fiction.

The finished novel was on the homestretch to publication. Houghton Mifflin nixed Bob's first title, *Children of Light*, on the grounds that it had recently been used for someone else's book. Looking for another advantageous phrase, Bob discovered that his source poem, which he had believed to be the work of Richard Eberhart, was actually by Robert Lowell. He may or may not have discovered at this time that Lowell had replaced the line "and candles gutter in a hall of mirrors" with "and candles gutter by an empty altar" between the poem's first appearance in a limited edition chapbook, *Land of Unlikeness*, and its later publication in *Lord Weary's Castle*, Lowell's first full-length collection.

"Hall of mirrors" might or might not be the better phrase for the intrinsic purposes of the poem, but for Stone and his novel it was clearly superior. He adopted the earlier version of "Children of Light," in its entirety, as an epigraph for this first book (in the long run it would seem equally appropriate for the whole body of his work). The comedy of titling errors continued, darkly. By coincidence the book's publication date was Bob's thirtieth birthday, August 21, 1967. He went to a bookshop near ACA to buy a copy and was offered *Hall of Mirrors* by John Rowan

Wilson. "Bob should have bought the book as a souvenir," Janice reflected decades later, "but it didn't seem funny at the time. For all he knew, the other writer's book would be a best seller, and his forgotten."

———

Norman Mailer was probably the last American novelist to completely fulfill the role of public intellectual. Not quite a whole generation later, Robert Stone would from time to time assume some aspects of that position (along with a highly ambivalent attitude toward it). Compared to Mailer, Stone is an artist of extreme indirection. Where Mailer liked to butt into the big issues of his time head-on, Stone was more inclined to ambush them. Stone's work included a take on most of the seismic social changes of his time, but as an artist he was less interested in political and cultural events per se than in the movements of chthonic forces underlying them. *A Hall of Mirrors* was his first effort to track those processes in a work of art—in fact, to use them as the rawest material of a work of art.

Some twenty years after its publication, Stone composed a brief retrospection on his first novel: "I wrote my first book after spending a year in the Deep South, a time that happened to coincide with the first sit-ins and the beginning of the struggle against segregation and also with the reaction to it. The novel centered on the exploitation of electronic media by the extreme Right, a phenomenon which we have not altogether put behind us. *A Hall of Mirrors* was not a strictly 'realistic' book, but as young writers will, I put every single thing I thought I knew into it. I gave my characters names with the maximum number of letters because I thought that would make them more substantial. I had taken America as my subject, and all my quarrels with America went into it."

———

10
A HALL OF MIRRORS

Technically, Stone used a technique of convergence here for the first time; the principal characters move into their encounters with hard winds driving them from behind. First to appear is Rheinhardt, a once-promising classical musician who no longer plays—still a relatively young man though no longer youthful in spirit, in flight from his abandonment of a young wife and child and from other, never-quite-specified disasters. When not on a bender, he has the skills to eke out a living at the low-power radio stations he blunders into during his plummet across the Southern states toward the Gulf. Rheinhardt's alcoholism is not just full-blown but wholly catastrophic; the young author's command of the nuances of that syndrome is frightening at times. Quick-witted and glib even during his blackouts, Rheinhardt has some of the unruly charisma of Shakespeare's Prince Hal, though he doesn't look likely to become king of anything.

Geraldine is running from Texas, the place most desperadoes run *to*. As a teenage bride she's seen her husband murdered and her baby die. We meet her as she's having her face slashed by a jealous, psychotic lover. With her scars still raw, she blows into New Orleans, where her damaged looks disqualify her from the kind of waitressing work she'd normally try for. When she tries to hustle in the bars, she gets stern warnings from the managers of the local pros. Once she and Rheinhardt run into each other, their broken edges fit together reasonably well; with her scars plain for all to see and his hidden in his psyche, a sort of sacred wound.

Rheinhardt is to some degree an alter ego of his author, intelligent, capable, talented, and worldly-wise. It's as if Bob Stone had asked himself, *What would it be like to waste all that, and in the most perversely self-destructive way possible?* Rheinhardt shares Stone's dangerous love of the bottle, and takes it further than Bob did at the time. Janice calls the character "a meaner, more cynical guy than Bob. Rheinhardt is farther along the path of alcoholism too. Maybe in retrospect I think not all that much farther along."

Bob's reference, in one of his letters to Janice from Villa Montalvo, to "the kind of degeneration I fell into after you left New Orleans," implies that he may have already shared his character's lowest lows. But Rheinhardt, even in the gutter, retains a sort of aristocratic gleam. As with Prince Hal, one senses he has elected low company for a reason, though in an early episode of free fall he quotes *Hamlet* instead—"Defend me, friends, I am but hurt"—at a time when he's abandoned his old friends and has yet to make new ones. But he finds an old friend when he bottoms out at the Living Grace Mission: Farley the Sailor, a con man of eel-like agility now posing as "Brother Jensen," a missionary to the "rum-dums" of skid row. From this hard landing he begins to put a few pieces of himself back together.

Rheinhardt drinks as anesthesia, to dull the pain of self-inflicted injuries: a squandered vocation and lost love. A Janice-like figure makes a brief but potent appearance in Rheinhardt's tormented memory: "but quite suddenly he saw very clearly a girl with gray eyes which were very sad and friendly, who smiled ruefully around a front tooth which had been broken in a fall in the wash room of the Knickerbocker Hospital the day after a baby named Rheinhardt was born to her—who used to break into a run suddenly when they were walking in the street, who liked to laugh and cried because she couldn't play the piano and Rheinhardt taught her to play a little of Chopin and who once wrestled with this Rheinhardt when he was berserk and paranoid with pot and he had slapped her three times until she cried from the pain and then put her hands on his shoulders and said, 'All right, all right,' and turned her face away—"

We see little more of her, but there she is. Rheinhardt has "a picture of them with her address on it; he was supposed to carry it in case he dropped dead." For Stone, this facet of Rheinhardt's history would have been a thought experiment on what might have happened in his own life if he had abandoned Janice and infant Deidre to travel with the Passion Play, rejoin the navy, or whatever.

Rheinhardt's other guilt-ridden agony is his lost artistic vocation. (Years later Stone told a journalist that he saw Rheinhardt wasting his talent out of a kind of spite.) Between bouts of boozing when he first hits New Orleans, he wanders into a library reading room and finds a youth reading sheet music for Mozart's Quintet for Clarinet and Strings, a strikingly difficult piece known to pros as "the Stadler." The chance encounter operates as a sort of PTSD trigger, catapulting Rheinhardt into a flashback of his audition as a clarinetist on the piece at Juilliard some years earlier. It's a tour de force rendition, and unexpectedly triumphant: "So it turned out that morning that just above the barrier of form was a world of sunlight in which he could soar and caper with an eagle's freedom, rule and dispense passion, where his breath was the instrument of infinite invention, yet not a pause was lost—not a note. He was not going to make any mistakes this morning; he found himself in control as he had never been. Because there was perfection in this music, something of God in this music, a divine thing in it—and the hungry coiled apparatus in Rheinhardt was hounding it down with deadly instinct, finding it again and again. . . ."

"At the end, in the final passage *allegro alla breve* he could feel himself—the brain, mouth, diaphragm, lungs and fingers of the musician Rheinhardt fused together in a terrible invincible unity. And as he and the strings came down together in the last lovely *tremolo*, he had thought—how beautiful, how beautiful I am!"

Stone never wrote an ars poetica more compelling than this one. But Rheinhardt, as the surrounding context makes painfully clear, had all that once but threw it away somewhere along his backtrail. For Stone protagonists, the two pathways to total destruction are losing the Janice-avatar and betraying one's talent. Sometimes the two paths can be taken together.

Rheinhardt and Geraldine get together in the opposite of a Hollywood "meet-cute," waiting for a bus to take them back to town from night-shift jobs at a soap factory. (Stone's short-term stints at similar jobs in New Orleans served him well in capturing the atmosphere of the fictional factory.) It's not much of a romance at first; Rheinhardt, exhausted from labor and alcoholic withdrawal, passes out on the cot in Geraldine's rented room, leaving her muttering, "Well I'll be goddamned." But within a few days he sallies out and lands a job at "WUSA—The Voice of an American's America—The Truth Shall Make You Free."

Another audition is required, and it's another tour de force—Rheinhardt has a sort of Delphic insight into exactly what kind of five-minute news spot his potential employers would desire and in twenty minutes cutting and pasting strips from the old-school news tickers he has "made some sharp one-liners out of the international stuff with a premium on Castro, stuffed the middle with the first or last paragraphs of the assembled racial routines and a sprinkling of the jazzier neutral items. The piece closed with a reverent thirty seconds on the lady from Tulsa"—a minister's wife raped by "the traditional six foot spade" in a New York subway station—"and a harmless Pete Smith style comedy accident that happened to a man in Venice fixing his roof. . . .

"Reading it through again, Rheinhardt felt a curious chill about the edges of his spinal column. How could it be so easy? The rhythm of instinct—that must be it; you didn't even have to think about it particularly and there it was ready to press, five minutes of sheer eagles and lightning." Stone had hit these kinds of grooves when making up stories for *The National Mirror*, but Rheinhardt's is a more sinister perversion of his gift: creating fake "Truth" for the dark purposes of the station and the people behind it—purposes Rheinhardt doesn't bother to examine until a long time later.

But it's a good job, especially compared to the soap factory, and on the strength of it Rheinhardt rents what appears to be the same apartment where the Stones had lived on St. Philip Street; he moves Geraldine in and the two embark on a sort of bohemian romance. It's not quite Mimi and Rodolfo, as both Geraldine and Rheinhardt (especially Rheinhardt) are too damaged to go very far in the direction of commitment. Still, it's touching to see these two walking wounded comfort and prop each other up.

Meanwhile the third character in the novel's structural pattern of convergence is moving along his own track toward the kinda-sorta happy couple. "Morgan Rainey shambled through the rain like an evil tiding; his face was suspiciously gray and drawn, his plastic raincoat far too small. The skirt of his topcoat reached below his shoetops. Schoolgirls flapping across the Civic Center in pastel boots giggled at him, motorists suppressed with difficulty a temptation to run him down; parking lot attendants ground their teeth at him."

Where Rheinhardt is wantonly self-destructive, Rainey is just haplessly unlucky, a quality that overlaps a bit with something similar in Geraldine. With Stone (whom he does not otherwise much resemble) he shares a strain of frustrated idealism and the experience of door-knocking through New Orleans black neighborhoods "back of town"—not for the census but for some obscurely motivated welfare survey, for which Stone borrowed something from Janice's New York social-worker job, though stripped of its helpful functions. "Your pay is regulated by the number of households you subjectivize so we expect you to motivate," his supervisor explains to Rainey. "You counsel no one. You evaluate nothing. We do that."

Rainey has a Harvard degree, plus "some background in field service overseas" (something like the Peace Corps is implied but not specified), which he hopes to bring to bear on actually doing some good for the people he visits. As his employer tries to explain ("How can I make that clear enough to you, Mr. Rainey?"), it just doesn't work that way. Among his coworkers, bald racism abounds. "To match this," says one, "you'd have to go to the black hole of Calcutta or a country very similar. You learn to steel yourself. When I go into one of those houses I say to myself—questions and answers and that's all. I don't look at them. I don't listen to their arrogance. I become absolutely impervious." Faced with this attitude, the welfare clients naturally become uninformative, as one might say. Rainey acquires a sort of Mephistophelian guide to the neighborhood to which he's assigned, "Lester Clotho, colored" as the survey bosses identify him. Intelligent, voluble, corrupt to the bone, Clotho escorts Rainey from one house of horrors to the next, mocking his good intentions the while: "But you're concerned aren't you Mr. Rainey? I use the word concerned in a sense of moral engagement. For example when you ask me a question like Do They Always Do Things That Way I think, I espy an uplifting reform-minded attitude."

Rainey turns out to live upstairs from Rheinhardt and Geraldine in the Quarter, but he doesn't actually run into them much; he and they are mostly found in separate chambers of the nautilus spiral that their ramblings through New Orleans create. Both parties move without much volition, conveyed by subterranean currents of which they are scarcely aware. Nothing in the novel pins down a precise date but the story appears to be set in the early 1960s, when the zeitgeist is charged with white racist reactions to the nascent civil rights movement (though the latter is never directly referred to). Stone's approach to the sociopolitical situation is utterly oblique; with the characters paying little attention to it, it simply builds itself out of inchoate dark matter, like the late-afternoon New Orleans rainstorms.

Of the three principals, Rheinhardt is most capable of insight into what's really going on (and also the most significant player in what's going on) but is not interested. The improvement in his circumstances has only camouflaged the depths of his despair. Getting through the day and night is good enough for him, blunting the pain with drink and pot and Geraldine's companionship (which turns out to mean more to him than he knows). "Nights betrayed him. He could get into bed with the girl, lose himself in the turns of her body, in the sweet gaming that was the only rest of his time in bed, in soothing and bringing her along."

The story is set too early for psychedelics to play a direct part in it, but Stone draws on his experience with the drugs to flavor Rheinhardt's alcoholic deliriums. "Which of us is the animation, dad?" Rheinhardt asks a passing motorist, then thinks, "I'm out here like Donald Duck walking around technicolored when it's supposed to be black and white. The driver was not the animation, because if he were, he would have dog's ears and white gloves, and there would be a balloon over his head with asterisks

and question marks and things." Rheinhardt's suicidal impulses are held
just off the screen of his consciousness. His Dostoyevskian reverie over a
display of straight razors in a shop window has that psychedelic gleam:
"The blade itself was music—something forged of a rare, transmuted ice-
like metal, secretly, at night. It was passion and science resolved; it burned
with a blue light that was not wholly in reflection . . .

"What a razor that is, he thought. That is the great American Razor.
He fairly could not turn from the blade." Rheinhardt can riff like that out
loud when he feels like it (a more restrained version seems to be a feature
of his radio show, though it's never directly quoted).

As for the book's apocalyptic finale, it is a very bad trip indeed.

Rainey's one extended encounter with Rheinhardt and Geraldine occurs on an afternoon when he offers to share with them a quart of ice cream
he's toting upstairs to his own apartment. Already pleasantly smashed on
gin fizz, Rheinhardt amuses himself by slicing and dicing Rainey with his
quick, sharp tongue (while Geraldine tries, ineptly, to restrain him). It's
a classic Stone conversational scene, resonant with dark and spiky under-
tones. Rainey recognizes Rheinhardt's voice from the radio and tries to
quiz him about WUSA's political stance (which is somewhere to the right
of Caligula). Apparently Rheinhardt has been folding attacks on welfare
recipients into his on-air routine. Advised by Geraldine that "He don't believe a word of what's on that station"—that is, the words that he himself
utters—Rainey responds, "Why I think that's fantastic. I mean between
the music that station is just all radical-right message. You must be up to
your nose in their politics—and yet you don't believe in it?"

"Belief is a very subtle and delicate thing," Rheinhardt teases, and a
few minutes later makes himself more plain: "I thought when I saw you
with your bag of ice cream that we were in the presence of virtue." Under
this malicious pressure, Rainey manages to reveal the true nature of his
quest, and with a certain conviction: "I want to find out about humanness. . . . Where mine is at and how I can keep it there when I find out."

Throughout his career Stone had the habit of splitting facets of his
own personality between two protagonists, usually setting them in opposition to each other. Rheinhardt really represents Stone's own worst
capabilities—in more than one way. The catastrophic alcoholism is a side-
show to the abuse of talent—a virtuosic verbal agility that can be put to
the service of anything, or (as in Rheinhardt's case) nothing at all. The

infection of Rheinhardt's self-inflicted psychic wound is corrosive enough to dissolve his last vestige of moral responsibility. On the opposite side of the equation, Rainey's drive to "find out about humanness" is really Stone's own, as he would declare (in somewhat different terms) from time to time throughout his life. Though Stone had nothing in common with Rainey's naïve sincerity, he did share the character's hunger for something credible, stable, durable, to believe.

The brush with Rheinhardt gives Rainey an inkling that evil is at work all around him and that he may have become its unwitting pawn. A customer at the bar/hotel/bordello that is Lester Clotho's headquarters enlightens him about the extent to which he is being manipulated. "Lester operates the Big Store for the White Devil. . . . He makes things happen back here the way someone wants them to happen. He shows the man whatever the man wants to see. . . . And your survey baby is a Big Store trip. Man there ain't no survey. Ain't nothing being surveyed. There's a white politician named Minnow who wants to please the white folks by getting a lot of niggers thrown off welfare. The survey is for him to do it. The results were in before the damn thing started."

The Big Store has something in common with "the Combine," a metaphor used by Ken Kesey in One Flew Over the Cuckoo's Nest for the establishment system for grinding individuals into conformity, then into dust. But Stone's Big Store shadow show is more richly, luxuriantly paranoid, tricked out with rococo exfoliations.

Throbbing with angry disillusionment, Rainey declares, "I'm going to strike this down," but of course he has no competence to do anything effective. An outraged visit to the scheming State's Attorney Calvin Minnow only gets him thrown out of the building. Adrift on Canal Street, "he walked along the crowded sidewalk with Rheinhardt's patter echoing in his ears; he had been hearing it for weeks while he made his rounds, from shoe-shine stands and stores, from passing cars."

Subterranean forces are about to break the surface. At the bottom of it all is Matthew Bingamon (a figure who at the time of this writing seems oddly predictive of Donald Trump), a tycoon who owns everything from the WUSA radio station to the soap factory where Rheinhardt and Geraldine were briefly employed. With his political coconspirators Bingamon has planned a RESTORATION RALLY and PATRIOTIC REVIVAL to take place in the Sport Palace, which happens to be situated in "a predominant nigger neighborhood," featuring celebrities like King Walyoe (a movie star who seems loosely based on John Wayne), the conscience-less con man Farley the Sailor providing evangelical ornamentation in his Brother Jensen guise, a Sicilian Mafia security team, and Rheinhardt him-self as the MC.

On top of the expected far-right rabble-rousing, some Big Store ma-nipulations have been planned. VIPs attending will be locked into a pen on the stadium floor, "in case you get some kind of disturbance. . . . It's just not reassuring to a crowd that's alarmed to see all the high-paying guests down below sort of bolt for the exits." The disturbance (also pre-planned, at least in part) is to be delivered by "groups of extremist niggers" furnished by Lester Clotho.

As excitement builds for this extravaganza, Rheinhardt and Geral-dine, coming toward the end of Rheinhardt's limited possibilities for her, get separated in the wake of an ugly quarrel. Rheinhardt looks for her haphazardly, in bars he's more likely to frequent than she, without suc-cess. On the big night Geraldine is drawn into the vortex of the RESTO-RATION RALLY; even though she can see Rheinhardt at his podium and shout to him from the gallery, she can't make him hear her. Drunk, stoned, and panicked by apparitions she sees in the crowd, she bolts and finally gets herself arrested for an end of a joint she has in her purse. In jail, feeling herself utterly abandoned, she hangs herself with the same kind of bunk chain that Bob Stone had once used to fight off his predatory ship-mate Flem.

At the rally, the Big Store provocations spin out of control, the con-spirators having stirred up more dangerous elements than they could foresee. Behind the theatrical race demonstration scripted by Clotho, a real riot is unfolding, and behind that the ultimate unpredictable wild card: the free-lance lunatic S. B. Prothwaite, moved by a thorny cluster of grievances against the powers that be, who appears at the wheel of a truck bomb. His bad luck holding invincibly, Rainey blunders into Prothwaite's passenger seat as the driver waits for a chance to make his move.

As the VIPs struggle to escape from their cage, Rheinhardt, called to calm the crowd with his magical voice while deep in his cups, hallucinates that he's conducting a concert: Mozart's Symphony in G. Independent of his volition, an extraordinary oration emerges from his mouth:

"Americans . . . our shoulders are broad and sweaty but our breath is sweet. When your American soldier fighting today drops a napalm bomb on a cluster of gibbering chinks, it's a bomb with a heart. In the heart of that bomb, mysteriously but truly present, is a fat old lady on her way to see the world's fair. This lady is as innocent as she is fat and motherly. This lady is our nation's strength. This lady's innocence if fully unleashed could defoliate every forest in the torrid zone. This lady is a whip to niggers! This lady is chinkbane! Conjure with this lady and mestizos, zambos, Croats and all such persons simply disappear. Confronted with her, Australian abos turn to the wall and die. Latins choke on their arrogant smirks, Nips disembowel themselves, the teeming brains of gypsies turn to gum. This lady is Columbia my friends. Every time she tells her daughter that Jesus drank carbonated grape juice—then, somewhere in the world a Jew raises quivering gray fingers to his weasely throat and falls dead."

The riff continues to inflate, conjuring psychopornodelic imagery that prefigures Ralph Bakshi's animated feature *Fritz the Cat*. From the depths of white America's fear of miscegenation, Rheinhardt conjures a black rapist hot on the fat lady's trail:

"The spade who's steaming up against that bus window wants her, men. He wants to run her out of her comfy relaxo-seat and fuck her to death in the hot tar of the highway.

"If he does, baby, it's gonna rain bearded men. The Great Lakes will turn into little brown people. Our boys in uniform all over the world will turn queer and toss up their hair in sequins and there'll be no more napalm bombs, Americans. The threat is internal. It's a hideous threat.

"Help! They're going to get her. No world's fair for her. O horrible! Iowa's never so pretty as in May."

This satirical address has the flavor of the wild, stinging riffs Bob Stone used to improvise in the midst of Perry Lane festivities a few years before. It's also a funhouse-mirror image of the Lowell poem used as the novel's epigraph. And in fact it expresses the intended message of Bingamon's RESTORATION RALLY fairly accurately (perhaps with a few minor exaggerations), encapsulating the brew of racism, xenophobia, fear of homosexuality, miscegenation, and the communist menace that the right-wing conspirators intended to manipulate for the manufacture of their own political theater.

Maybe there is no politics at all, only political theater. Anxieties of this kind run through the whole of Stone's work. Maybe deception and illusion are an infinite recession from which there is no exit. "Rheinhardt raised his hand to his head but was unable to feel anything there." He might be trapped in the hall of mirrors forever.

In the event, the crystal is shattered by Prothwaite, who drives his truck bomb into the center of the stadium and sets it off. The situation devolves into what Stone called, elsewhere, "primary process." Rheinhardt falls into the wake of Farley the Sailor, whose cynical ruthlessness is even greater (and much better organized for action) than his own. "You've got to recognize special situations and act accordingly," Farley remarks, having looted one of the downed VIPs for a $600 roll. "His survival is not my survival and so forth." Armed with red, white, and blue ax handles (furnished by the organizers for a preplanned episode of Negro-bashing), Rheinhardt and Farley thread their way through the chaos. "Free enterprise, baby," Farley pronounces as he smashes Bingamon's skull. "Individual initiative." In this manner, they eventually make their escape.

The novel's denouement phase requires Rheinhardt to identify Geraldine's body in the morgue, a procedure he completes in novocaine-like numbness. In the same way that he has trouble finding his own head at the rally, he has trouble finding any authentic emotion; it's Philomene, a crippled and mildly deranged acquaintance of his and Geraldine's, who asks him pointedly, "Doesn't it make you feel sad?" Rheinhardt embraces this idea, and repeats it to himself and others. There is a genuine pathos in it. Rheinhardt ends where he began, author (like Lear, evoked in a brief quotation from the play, "What, dead?") of the destruction of all he might hold dear, ready to resume his aimless wandering, and cursed, like a cockroach, with survival.

Rainey, denied martyrdom in Prothwaite's explosion, disappears from the story by passing out and getting hauled away in an ambulance. The only man of genuine goodwill in the whole story, he has proved himself completely ineffectual. Rheinhardt, possessed of all the capacities to operate in the world that are missing from Rainey, never has any will to act.

One senses the author's loyalties divided between these two protagonists. Staring into a frighteningly deep fissure in American society, Stone identifies both with the man who fervently (and perhaps futilely) hopes for humanity in spite of the odds and with the man who opts out and turns his back.

A long time later Stone reflected on his first completed novel: "That book was like a process. It existed in, and parallel with, my life for a number of really important years. I was learning to be a novelist, and I was developing a style, and I was also pursuing a vision of things. I thought a lot about my attitude toward the world, toward fear and violence, and that I had something to say about these things. If you had asked me then what I was writing about, I would have said, in a kind of Kerouac-like romantic vein, 'America.' If you'd asked me about a writer I was thinking of emulating, I would have said Gogol."

During *A Hall of Mirrors* prepublication season, Bob quit his job at ACA and went for a few weeks' residency at Yaddo, the well-known artists' colony in upstate New York. Elderly descendants of the robber baron Spencer Trask, whose legacy had founded the colony at the turn of the twentieth century, still visited from time to time. "Mrs. Trask was considerably deaf. Bob tried to make conversation, and asked her whether there were any bears in the area. 'Only blackberries,' replied the old lady."

At Yaddo Bob got to know the writer Ivan Gold (who happened to have an assignment to cover *A Hall of Mirrors* for *The New York Times*) and John Marquand Jr., both of whom would be close friends of Bob's for the rest of their lives. A scion of the local aristocracy, Marquand took Bob to a nearby cemetery to show him what was vulgarly known as "the Sedgwick Pie"; the family "had arranged to be buried in a circle, so that when they arose on Judgment day they would have to see no one else in the cemetery except other Sedgwicks." Bob, always devoted to playing the ponies, also spent plenty of time at the Saratoga racetrack. Janice didn't think he got much writing done.

In the fall, Bob's first novel took off with a very respectable roar. Stegner had furnished a generous quote: "Stone writes like a bird, like an angel, like a circus barker, like a con man, like someone so high on pot that he is scraping his shoes on stars." (Any residual disapproval of pot-smoking was barely detectable in the glow of the other high-flying comparisons.) The novel won praise in both a review and a personal letter from Joyce Carol Oates. "The nightmare is the author's vision of America," wrote Christopher Lehmann-Haupt in *The New York Times*; the *Times* also hailed *A Hall of Mirrors* as "one of the best books of the year." The *Newsweek* review, crediting Stone with "the gift of tongues," had a solid insight into the author's special fusion of the political and personal: "In a time of superficial thinking about violence and dislocation, Stone provides a hard, clear, lucid, bitter, comic vision of the pressures which, after years of underground incubation, have begun to erupt with lethal force from the psyche to the body politic."

Gold's coverage in *The New York Times Book Review* captured the novel's complicated flavors with a witty, and telling, cascade of comparisons: "*A Hall of Mirrors* is, one could say, *The Day of the Locust* as told to Malcolm Lowry and edited by Frantz Fanon, the shade of the young Dos Passos benignly gazing on the while. And with such namedropping I mean less to imply influences—which in any case are of interest chiefly to academics and biographers—than to indicate what league Stone is playing in. His voice and his world are his own." Gold, too, understood very well the novel's ambition to capture the gestalt of the American national psyche in the midst of a very turbulent time: "The characters through whom we must finally recognize ourselves, seem for a while to make less ambitious claims, but long before the horrid and accurate ending, we know that we have been witnesses to and participants in our own finish, deeply implicated spectators to the steep way down this nation has traveled since its bright inceptions, an historical moment ago."

High praise indeed, and well-deserved. After the long haul to completion, Stone could be forgiven for wanting to repose on such laurels for a little while. There were parties. Bob and Janice had befriended Jack Gelber, whose play *The Connection* they had seen a couple of years earlier, and his wife, Carol, who lived upstairs from them at 250 Riverside Drive. At the Gelbers' one evening Bob fell in with an English painter, Eleanor Brooks; she and her husband, the playwright Jeremy Brooks, would become close friends of Bob and Janice in the months to come. The Stones threw a sort of book/bon voyage party in their own apartment, inviting among others Ivan Gold and Joan Michelson, who revealed herself as an enthusiastic dancer. "I always thought of Joan when I saw one of Jules Feiffer's cartoons of the dancer flinging into 'A Dance to Spring.'"

In fact the Stone family was on its way to London, where *A Hall of Mirrors* was soon to be published by the Bodley Head. "Bob decided we should go to London for the publication. After all the years of work writing it, he wanted to enjoy the publication. Twice." The excursion seemed affordable—just. On the strength of the first novel's success, Candida Donadio had got Bob a contract with Houghton Mifflin for a second book, to be titled "The Dog Soldier," for a total advance of $10,000, with

$3,000 paid on signature in October 1967 and the rest payable in sixteen monthly installments of $400 to begin in January 1968. (Having learned that their author could sometimes be dilatory, the publishers made the monthly payments contingent on proof of progress with the work.) Despite the cash injection and the guaranteed monthly income, the Stones didn't feel they could keep the "semiprofessional" apartment. In any case they might not be returning to New York at all. Bob planned to take up a teaching position at the University of Iowa (where he'd recently been featured at a writers' conference) when they came back from England, where they planned to stay for six months.

PART TWO

———

DOG SOLDIERS

1

THE LONDON YEARS

I used to say I felt I went to a party in '63," Bob once told an interviewer, "and the party followed me out the door and filled the world. By '67 it was all over. The Summer of Love killed it. I went to Europe for four years. It certainly happened in London, and Kesey came over there for a little while, but it was entirely different."

———

October 21, 1967. Close to a hundred thousand people marched on the Pentagon and kept it surrounded for nearly two days, in a protest against the Vietnam War. Celebrity pediatrician Benjamin Spock inveighed against President Lyndon Johnson. Allen Ginsberg, Abbie Hoffman, and friends attempted to levitate the building. Norman Mailer and nearly seven hundred other people were arrested and jailed. "A man took my photograph without saying a word," Janice Stone recalled, "and I wondered if I looked memorable in anyway. Later I realized it must have been an FBI photographer taking pictures of all the subversives." Maybe her beauty and poise had been enough to attract a random paparazzo, but in her modesty she never considered that possibility. Janice had driven down to Washington, DC, with Jane Burton and some of Jane's friends from Collaberg School. It wasn't her first antiwar demonstration. With Bob, she had marched on the United Nations, to a rally where Martin Luther King Jr. was one of the speakers. But Bob by this time was in London, where on the day of the Pentagon march, three thousand people in a parallel demonstration tried to storm the U.S. embassy.

Leaving Janice to wrap up their New York apartment, Bob had gone ahead to England to find them a place to live, armed with most of the family's ready cash. A delay in closing their bank account made him nearly miss the *Queen Elizabeth*. He'd packed in his by now extremely well-traveled navy seabag, which, when he did manage to board the ship, caused him to be mistaken (and chewed out because of late arrival) for a member of the crew.

While Bob dawdled in changing the Stones' savings into English currency, the exchange rate happened to turn in his favor by about forty cents on the pound. "It was one time when Bob's procrastination and tendency to be late paid off," Janice said; she and the children were then crossing the Atlantic on the *Franconia*. The windfall encouraged Bob to check into the Cumberland Hotel, a posh, pricey billet facing the Marble Arch at the northeast corner of Hyde Park. He took Janice and the children there when they arrived in London by train from the Liverpool docks. The flat he'd arranged for them in Hampstead wouldn't be available for another month, so a few luxurious days in the Cumberland seemed a good way to acclimate.

Soon enough the Stones moved to a temporary flat on Greville Place in Maida Vale, near the Abbey Road Studios of Beatles fame and not too far from the Regent's Park and the London Zoo. The dank English autumn was dissolving into a wet winter, the sun describing an ever-smaller arc, far away on the southern horizon, on days when it appeared at all. Ian and Deidre took to calling their street either "Dribble Place," for the chronic London wet, or "Gravel Place" by preference of Ian, four at the time, who mainly remembers that the flat was cold and the lights didn't work. Getting the electricity on was a project; hot water was dispensed by a coin-fed meter, and the meager heat came from a "paraffin stove," the British euphemism for a device actually fueled by kerosene, which Janice believed, correctly, to be quite dangerous.

Ian and Deidre couldn't start school before the family was settled in Hampstead, but the outgoing tenant in the Hampstead flat kept delaying his departure on grounds of ill health. With little to do, the children grew stir-crazy. But that move was still a long way off. "Christmas came and went, and we were desperate to get out of dreary Greville Place." Their landlord-to-be in Hampstead, the Reverend Andrew McCulloch, offered them another temporary rental: a small stone row house in Port Isaac, on the Cornwall coast. The Cornwall seaside is not a holiday destination in winter, but it was sunny there, if cold; the village was picturesque, and views of the sea spectacular. A coal fire made the little house much warmer than the flat in Greville Place. In earlier centuries, Port Isaac had been stalked by the British navy's press-gangs, as recalled in a folk song Janice grew fond of:

> *The king must have sailors*
> *To the sea he must go*
> *So they left me lamenting*
> *In sorrow and woe . . .*

Bob for his part adopted a new view of the U.S. Navy, as a civilian reporter this time, traveling to Sweden to report (for *The Saturday Evening Post*, he hoped) on a group of navy deserters who'd jumped their ship in Japan. He had to buy a new overcoat to face the Swedish winter, as Janice had either thrown his old one out before they left the States, or given it to the Free Store run by an anarchist group called the Diggers. Interviewing the fugitive sailors brought Bob as close to the background of his novel-in-not-very-much-progress-so-far as he had as yet been able to come. "The Dog Soldier," as Stone's contract entitled it, would be set in the United States and was meant to be flavored with fumes from the dark underside of late 1960s peace'n'love utopianism, for which Bob had a bloodhound's nose, but he was having big trouble fleshing out a story. Absorbing the motives of the young deserters might have helped.

The deserter story was also one of Bob's first forays into real reporting (as opposed to the lurid fantasies he'd written for *The National Mirror*).

Shortly before leaving New York he'd been hired by *Cosmopolitan* to write a piece on Faye Dunaway, then cresting a wave of celebrity following the release of the film *Bonnie and Clyde*. It's safe to say that Bob, a man who loved women with discernment and fervor, enjoyed the knockout actress's company, but much of his copy was . . . dutiful: "Faye Dunaway alights from a taxi and walks into a chill wind. Feeling the cold, she knits her brow in an expression which is at once petulant and humorous and clings to her fiancé's arm. . . ." Bob trolled around New York in the wake of her limousine for several days, though he sometimes seemed more interested in watching people watching her: "A gaggle of teeny boppers has gathered at the Salvation's door; with big, cooled out eyes, they watch Faye pass inside. The teeny boppers make no demonstration because, of course, they are the new kind of kid."

Thanks to the movie, Dunaway was blowing out a new style; the

"Bonnie Look" would be *it* for a season in both New York and London. Bob got her to say the background stuff to his notebook, and sketched her in the available settings. Once in a while he caught a sharp insight, noting that *Bonnie and Clyde* had positioned her "as the gorgeous feminine center of a strangely beautiful, brutal pastoral. Under Arthur Penn's direction she brought the role a perverse animal vitality that matched the violence of the outlaw legend. Her combination of innocence and malice made her seem, in the dreamlike setting, a beautiful woman desirable and dangerous." Dunaway's own perception of a star's situation in Hollywood interested Bob too: "They used to be able to take you and make you into their creation. They could bend you and make you into whatever they thought you should be. It's really frightening to think that they could do that." A good few of these observations coalesced (some twenty years later) into Stone's creation of the actress Lee Verger as the heroine of his novel *Children of Light*, but celebrity profiles were not really his meat, and *Cosmo* didn't run the piece.

The navy deserters were a more congenial subject, and Bob had an eye for the Stockholm scene: "Life in Stockholm is not unpleasant for twenty-year-olds. The loveliness and liberality of Swedish girls are well known. . . . In the streets of the Old City there are discotheques and poster shops displaying the latest groove from San Francisco. Stockholm has hookahs and mandalas and hash. (The Animals were in town while I was there; Jimi Hendrix was due.)" Bob's subjects, "the Intrepid Four" (Craig Anderson, Michael Lindner, Richard Bailey, and John Barilla) were navy airmen who got their moniker for jumping ship (the aircraft carrier USS *Intrepid*) in Yokohoma, after a combat tour of the Gulf of Tonkin.

Like Stone, they'd joined the navy at the end of their teens; unlike Stone, they had enlisted in wartime and under pressure of the draft. Anderson, the most radical among them, was antiwar from the start and had chosen the navy as the easiest service from which to get a quick discharge, a plan that didn't quite work out. The other three were alienated from the war effort in the course of active service, and in conversation with one another when they "met regularly after working hours to listen to rock music, occasionally to smoke pot (a pastime which has become hardly less common among young servicemen in the war than it is among university students) and above all to engage in long nightly bull sessions." Lindner: "There were bombs everywhere. . . . You couldn't get away from the sight of them. Sometimes you could go out on deck and see explosions on the coast, mountains burning, tremendous fires going up. You think, we're killing a lot of people over there. And how do they know the difference between a Communist and a farmer?" Bailey: "But what the hell are we supposed to be saving those people from that's any worse than what we're giving them?" Lindner carved a peace sign on his belt buckle and was told to grind it off. Anderson refused to serve on the flight deck and was reassigned to janitorial work below.

After leaving the *Intrepid* on October 23, 1967, the four burned their uniforms and military IDs—a symbolic demonstration, like civilians burning their draft cards back in the States—but this action also cemented what they had done as desertion rather than the lesser offense of going AWOL. They expected to be arrested and sentenced to federal prison. Instead, sympathetic Japanese put them in touch with a local peace group that sheltered them and eventually helped smuggle them onto a Russian vessel. In Moscow the four were briefly paraded as propaganda assets, then allowed to ship out to neutral Sweden.

Stone's article presented the young deserters transparently, letting them speak copiously for themselves. (He was also writing very fast in hope of scooping the other reporters who'd flocked to Sweden at the same time.) If Bob felt any cynical response to his subjects' intensely serious naivete, he kept it almost entirely in check. In his implication, their youth and relative innocence was part of whatever point was there to be drawn. "To the propaganda mills of the Communist world, their lonely gesture was a gift to be exploited; to American apologists, a shameful, embarrassing piece of willfulness to be explained away into inconsequence." Between these polarities, the folks back home were still confronted by a "disturbing fact. Four of their young countrymen, from quite average backgrounds, who differed little from millions of their contemporaries at home, chose to invite prison, exile, and disgrace for themselves and their families in order to disassociate themselves from a war which their society declared to be a crusade. Like so many other incidents in the Vietnam War, it is unfamiliar, confusing, disheartening to most Americans."

In this atmosphere—in this fissure in the American social fabric—Stone's novel *Dog Soldiers* was about to take root.

Bob hadn't got very far with it yet. The monthly payments on Houghton's advance still had a little over a year to run—though they were contingent on proof of progress, which Bob at the moment could not very well demonstrate. Apart from the Intrepid Four interview, he'd been spending most of his writing time on the short story "Porque No Tiene, Porque le Falta," a south-of-the-border, drug-driven extravaganza very loosely based on his sojourn with Kesey and company in Mexico, featuring an intensity of paranoid delusion to rival Malcolm Lowry's *Under the Volcano*. Though eventually published in the *New American Review* in 1969, the story was not going to pay any bills in 1968. The London publication of *A Hall of Mirrors* proved something of an anticlimax—nothing like the splash the book made when released in the States—and a typo on the Bodley Head cover brought Stegner's pyrotechnic quote down to earth, reducing the pot-high author to scraping his shoes on the *stairs*, instead of the *stars* as intended.

Janice had kept the coal fire burning in Cornwall during Bob's excursion to Sweden. In February they were finally able to occupy their digs in Hampstead, "an elegant red-brick building" at 89 Redington Road, where the Stones took the former servants' quarters on the top floor, complete with a disconnected buzzer board. "Tired of packing and unpacking," Janice was happy to be settled in one place for a good while.

The Hampstead place had better heat and three bedrooms, one of which Bob could adapt for a study. With the children enrolled in Christchurch School, he could settle into a steady work rhythm (although he was already beginning to think he would need to visit Vietnam to see the heart of his subject firsthand). In the meantime he was "drinking quite a bit, not working on a novel, but thinking about it. When he was back in London, he would drink in the later afternoon in his study, take a nap after dinner, and then wake up if the Brookses were coming over or we were going out." Privately Bob was beginning to feel like "a frustrated one-novel novelist."

With four flats below their quarters, 89 Redington Road was a lively place, and an internationally mixed bag, with South Africans and Hungarians as well as the English. On the next floor down were Martin and Bunny Blaine, whose teenage children were at boarding school; Martin taught four-year-old Ian to play rudimentary chess. Across the hall from the Blaines, Mickey and Caroline Morgan fussed about the noise the Stone children made, running about on the top floor. When Deidre got back at them by eavesdropping, she was disappointed to find that "All they talk about is money." At ground level were Michael and Mari Winton, and in the other flat Vic and Jan Meyer, one of whose two boys, Conrad, was Ian's age and became his friend (and chess partner under the tutelage of the Hungarian Martin Blaine). Bob thought Jan was "dishy," and Janice thought Vic was interesting—Vic was a Polish refugee who'd been an RAF pilot during the Battle of Britain, and now practiced as a psychologist, in Janice's view proving a point made by a friend back in New Orleans days: "Don't think all psychiatrists aren't crazy."

But the Stones' closest friends in the beginning were Jeremy and Eleanor Brooks. Bob had been taken with Eleanor since meeting her at the Gelbers' party shortly before the Stones left New York, while Janice met the couple for the first time when the Brookses called at the Cumberland Hotel. Ten years Bob's senior, Jeremy had published a handful of novels, notably *Jampot Smith* and *Smith as Hero*, and in 1968 was working as the literary manager of the Royal Shakespeare Company (which had produced the version of Beckett's *Endgame* which the Stones had seen in London in 1964). He'd been in the British navy during the war, then studied under C. S. Lewis at Oxford. By the time the Stones moved to London, Brooks was spending most of his artistic energy on stage projects and, with four children to support, increasingly writing for film.

Polly, youngest of the Brookses, was Ian's age, while William, Margaret, and Josephine (Joey) were in their middle teens. Eleanor told Janice "she had learned to simultaneously paint and talk to little Polly, keeping the child amused with just half her attention," while the older three were out at school. "This was a skill I admired." She admired a little less the discovery that Jeremy kept a mistress: "a glamorous and blonde woman with theater connections," and two children of her own. Eleanor seemed to accept the fact that her husband divided his time between their home on Bartholomew Road and Trix's place somewhere in Saint John's Wood; Trix was even a welcome visitor at the Brooks establishment (though Eleanor balked at the proposition that the two families combine in a single dwelling). To Janice, the whole situation was puzzling, despite her sojourn in the free-love environment of Perry Lane: "Eleanor and Jeremy didn't seem to be beatniks, and London was not much like California. These people were respectable citizens, they were grown-ups!" Still, "I don't think I admired the Brooks family any less for their unorthodox family setup. I was just surprised by it."

The Stones had dropped into the Swinging London of the 1960s, but also into a sort of new New Grub Street situation, where artist and writers scrabbled fairly hard to get by. There was an exhilaration to it. The Brookses' house was full of art and literature, and with their artist and writer friends—even fourteen-year-old Margy was a professional actress in 1968, on her way to Tanzania to star (with Louis Gossett Jr.) in *The Bushbaby*.

Through the Brookses, Bob and Janice met Fran and Jay Landesman, American expatriates and a theatrical team—he a sometime playwright (also novelist, editor, memoirist, and all-around hustler) and she a lyricist best known for "Spring Can Really Hang You Up the Most." Jay was twenty years older than Bob, "who came home from his first encounter with Jay rather bemused. Jay had greeted him with the question, 'Don't you care how you look?' Jay was what was once called a snazzy dresser. Unlike Bob." Landesman had a quick, often bitter wit, and one of his preferred social tactics was "working the room, from embarrassment to humiliation." In that aspect he was not unlike Bob, whose verbal agility and often very dark view of the world enabled him to slice and dice with the best of them.

A strong friendship grew between the Stones, the Brookses, and the Landesmans, with Angus Wallace and his wife, Mary, soon added to the mix. An artist and inventor, Angus was an alumnus of the experimental Summerhill School, known to detractors as the "Do As You Please" school, but in Janice's view probably the only school that could have coped with him. Angus was "always off on some kind of tangent," prone to manic enthusiasms, excesses, and escapades. In fact the Stones met Mary before they met her husband, at the Brookses' house where she was sheltering temporarily "because Angus had run off somewhere and left her and the children homeless and penniless. . . . This was *La Bohème*, I thought, English-style, featuring poverty and drama."

A little over three miles separated the Stone and Brooks households. Jeremy would usually drive the Stones back to Redington Road after an evening *chez* Brooks, in a Bentley that counted a bar among its luxury features. "Drunk driving was common in England then." Jeremy had chronic pain from an accident with a drunken American driver years before; his doctor had actually prescribed alcohol as a painkiller. The Brooks children sometimes referred to Bob as "the man with the rice in his beard," but because the three eldest could look after little Polly on their own, the Brookses were more likely to come to the Stones, who had no built-in babysitting for Deidre and Ian. These were convivial evenings. "Bob and the Brookses drank whiskey, and finished off a bottle every night. I drank gin or vodka. I had always wondered how much alcohol we would consume if expense weren't a consideration."

Still inhibited by considerable shyness, Janice was more likely to listen than to take full part in these heady conversations. "The guys were all interesting and articulate, and so were Eleanor and Fran. I didn't have to say a word, but just pour the drinks." If well-lubricated, the conversations weren't necessarily ephemeral. Jeremy, especially, could talk brilliantly about the art and craft of fiction.

The Stones went to parties at the Landesmans' in Islington, where Jay and Fran "had what amounted to a literary/show-business salon," featuring the Australian screenwriters Ian Stocks and Jane Oehr; the comedian Irwin Corey; John Steinbeck IV, journalist, Vietnam veteran, second son of the novelist John Steinbeck; someone Fran presented as "John Simon the good [a composer and producer], not John Simon the bad [the New York theater and literary critic]"; and proto-pop psychologist R. D. "Ronnie" Laing, who "was usually so drunk we didn't get to know him." They met Arthur Kopit, an American playwright with a connection to Jack Gelber, and his wife, Leslie, when the newlywed couple came to London in 1968. This friendship was cemented years later when the Stones moved to Amherst, where Leslie came from and fairly often returned.

Frank Conroy, whose iconic memoir *Stop-Time* had appeared in 1967, turned up in London with an introduction to the Stones from Candida Donadio, whose client he was. A serious jazz pianist himself, Conroy took Bob and Janice to a concert by Rahsaan Roland Kirk. Ken Kesey also materialized, with a couple of Hells Angels in tow. Bob and Janice introduced Kesey to the Landesmans' set—but not the bikers. Bob was mistrustful of their social behavior, having been present "when visiting Angels hung someone upside down from the living-room ceiling" of the Keseys' house in La Honda. "Faye had made them turn him loose." Landesman and Kesey, both outsize personalities in different ways, hit it off well enough that the Landesmans eventually visited the Keseys in Oregon.

In the midst of these frolics, Janice's grandmother Mattson, back in New York, suffered a stroke and died soon after, leaving small legacies in a trust for Ian, Deidre, and a couple of Janice's younger siblings. (Janice herself had received some money her grandmother had saved for her at the time of her marriage to Bob.) There was no time for any of the Stones to cross the ocean before her demise. Janice had been close to her grand-mother, moving in with her more than once when she needed somewhere to lay her head in Manhattan, and was distressed that "she never got to see my children again." In this frame of mind, Janice and Bob decided to bring *his* mother, now in her seventies, to England for a three-week visit. Gladys accepted, then (true to her usual MO) cashed in her return ticket and rented a room.

It was easier for the Stones for Gladys to live on her own, and by this time she had a functional sense of how to live in London. "She still can't figure out the money, but people are more honest here than in New York and I don't suppose she'll be cheated very much," Janice wrote to her parents. "More likely she'll be accusing people of cheating her all the time. But she'll muddle through, I'm certain, even though she's operating on an idea of England twenty or thirty years ago, and can't read a map to save her life." One way or another, Gladys did manage; she never went back to the United States.

At that moment it looked like the Stones might not either. They were fitting happily into the international artistic milieu to which the Brookses had introduced them. The wintry plains of Iowa looked dour by compari-son, and Bob did not pursue the prospect of a teaching job there. Janice "thought it ridiculous to even think of exchanging our life in England for one in Iowa City. I was in love with London, North Wales, and the Brooks family."

Love was a many-faceted thing, with cutting edges here and there. The Landesmans had an "open marriage," a term of art that would be-come official with the publication of a book so titled in 1972, and encour-aged their friends to do likewise. (For example, they prompted Jeremy Brooks, already occupied with a wife and an official mistress, toward a fling with the novelist Iris Owens, the author of the black comic classic *After Claude*, when she was passing through London; in that particular case, Jeremy declined the honor.) Bob Stone didn't necessarily need a lot of encouragement along those lines, although the Stones were not the sort of couple who'd make an ideological declaration in favor of open marriage. Their attitude was more practical; because they had married extremely young, on the brink of a maelstrom of changing manners and mores, they had tacitly agreed to cut each other some slack in this area, or in slightly more elevated language, "not to be possessive of each other," in Janice's phrase. Thus minor flings could be shrugged off, and the understanding meant that Bob's extremely serious relationship with Jane Burton hadn't shattered the Stones' marriage.

It also meant that Janice had some amorous freedom of her own if she chose to exercise it—though her choices were often rather passive. She had never been as taken with Ken Kesey as Bob, and actively disapproved of his career as a "serial seducer of his friends' wives." In the Perry Lane days, she'd kept clear of him. But in London, Kesey managed to corner her (Bob having retired early): "Hospitality and friendship seemed to require that I be a good sport about it. I thought of the Native Americans who used to offer their wives to guests. Or maybe it was the Eskimos. . . . I can't say I didn't like Ken, or that his making love to me was unpleasant. He said, 'You're a thoroughbred.' Well no, I thought, I'm a workhorse."

A brief encounter with Angus Wallace was flavored with similarly faint enthusiasm. Janice, in New York for a brief visit from London circa 1970, was persuaded to accompany him to a meeting at the UN where Angus pitched his recent invention, an inflatable tent for refugees. Afterward he pressed her to spend the night with him. Janice demurred, but he followed her to Port Authority and when she missed the last bus to Bogota, she took the path of least resistance.

Both Kesey and Wallace boasted of their conquests afterward, not very much to their credit. In Kesey's case it was hardly noticeable, but Mary Wallace was seriously upset by the news of her husband's outing. "For months after that, when Angus was late coming home, Mary would phone and demand to speak to him. She wouldn't believe he wasn't with me. How awful it must be to be jealous, I thought." Bob, who stepped out more often and more willingly than Janice, didn't object to any adventures she might have; on the contrary, "he encouraged such escapades of mine."

Janice's lukewarm attitude toward her one-shots with Wallace and Kesey wouldn't have given Bob much cause for jealousy. There was something a little more serious on another excursion from London to New York. "At a party with Jay and Fran I met one friend of theirs, an unemployed jazz drummer, and ended up taking him back to Ivan and Vera Gold's apartment in the Village. I had the use of it while they were away. The drummer later introduced me to cocaine. At first I thought it was a terrific drug, and bought some to take home to Bob. But before long I decided I didn't like it. It tended to lead me to say things I wouldn't have said, and do things I wouldn't have done. I gave up on coke but got quite obsessed with the drummer for a while."

The drummer was rooming with Iris Owens at the time, which might have been a giveaway considering the Landesmans' matchmaking interests for their friends, but Janice didn't consider at first that Fran and Jay had quite likely set the whole thing up. She did write letters to the drummer in New York, off and on for a couple of years, "like a silly girl" as she put it much later. "At least one of those letters got sent to the Landesmans in London. Maybe by the drummer. Or, for all I know, they were intercepted by Iris Owens before they reached him, as I never got any sort of reply." Eventually it appeared that the Landesmans had shared some of Janice's billets-doux to the drummer with Bob, although that was another aspect she didn't learn about until a long time afterward.

"I sometimes felt I was falling short of living my part of the bohemian life that I imagined I wanted. But the only one of the guys I felt comfortable with, besides Bob, was Jeremy Brooks, and I didn't want anything to interfere with our four-way friendship." Of Bob, Eleanor told Janice, " 'He is magical.' I totally agreed with that." After Bob and Eleanor went for an overnight stay to the city of Bath, Janice accepted Jeremy's invitation to spend the weekend with him at the Brookses' cottage in Wales (where the two couples had already spent some happy times together). At the end of the day, "Jeremy protested that he would feel like a complete fool if we slept in separate beds. So we slept together."

If it wasn't exactly her own idea, Janice felt considerably more positive about this encounter than the ones with Kesey and Wallace. Jeremy was her real friend and to a degree a confidant. He certainly wasn't playing for points; by his own account, "he had reached the age where if any of his friends, male or female, wished to have sex with him, that was fine. For friendship's sake." Jeremy also told her, "tentatively, that some men found it exciting when their wives slept with other men. He didn't follow through on this idea, nor did I. But it registered with me. I had received nothing from Bob but gentle encouragement and strategic absences of himself when I had opportunities to spend time with other guys. He encouraged me to go to New York on my own, and to Wales with Jeremy. But. This wasn't unusual? Other men might feel the same way? I wasn't sure that this was true. I filed the idea away for further thought." There were times when Bob "was interested—too interested—in what I was doing, and though he was always cool with it, and tried to not be intrusive, I sometimes found it difficult to keep an area of personal privacy."

While Janice "was not a success as a swinger," at least in her own opinion, "Bob cut quite a swath through swinging California, swinging London, and everywhere else he went. . . . We had a sort of 'don't ask, don't tell' arrangement as far as his relations with other women were concerned. Except for Eleanor, who was my friend, who was no more going to steal my husband than I was going to run off with Jeremy, I would have been quite happy to have Bob all to myself. But he plainly was inclined to wander.

"Bob's great gift for friendship gave him an advantage. He connected with people. And he didn't let his other relationships interfere much with our life. He never made me feel that I was being replaced as the love of his life. As he was the love of my life, always, whatever else may have been going on at the time."

———

In the spring of 1968 the Stones went with the Brookses and their children for the first of many visits to Gelli, the Brookses' cottage in north Wales—an idyllic experience though in many ways also a rugged one. "There was no indoor plumbing to speak of. Water to the four-century-old stone cottage came from the Croesor River, which was nearby, directly to the kitchen, through a rubber hose." Bathing and laundry were done either in the sink or the river, which by American standards was more like a creek, "quite shallow and easily crossed on foot over the rocks." A diminutive outdoor latrine was jocularly referred to as "the pixie shithouse." Still, Janice thought it "the most beautiful place I'd ever seen. The main room in the house had a huge stone fireplace, with a kettle on a chain hanging within. There were flowers blooming, and sheep wandered through the garden, munching grass. It was paradise."

That Edenic quality of Gelli was sometimes given a substantive boost. "I do not know if I can fairly describe my father as a nudist," says Ian Stone (who was a small child at the time). "What I can say is that a few of the summers in Wales involved hippie nudism, marijuana, and mushrooms for the older groups. Other freedoms must have been occurring, but I did not see them."

The Stones formed a regular habit of spending school holidays with the Brooks family in Wales. Sometimes the Landesmans and other friends from the London set would join the house party. There were outings. Ian Stone: "I remember visiting a castle in Wales with my father and Jeremy Brooks and it seemed to me at least that they began performing a Shakespeare play right there on the ruin with great dramatic silliness. As I recall, they really had the lines and it totally knocked me out."

By Janice's recollection, "It must have been in the summer of 1968 that we took the last of our LSD there with Jeremy and Eleanor. I had smuggled our few tabs in from the U.S. wrapped in aluminum foil, at the bottom of a jar of baby cream. It was not a street drug. It was 1960s acid, and this lot was reputed to be the real Owsley product." (Owsley Stanley, a soundman for the Grateful Dead, was also known for making quality LSD for similarly elite consumers.) "We would not all take it at the same time, because we had the children with us. Somebody had to, as we put it, mind the store."

Despite the preplanning, Jeremy (never an enthusiast of drugs other than alcohol) managed to take a classic bad trip. "Late at night, Bob and Eleanor had to make Jeremy understand that he wasn't God, and had no special responsibilities as such." Bob and Eleanor had taken their doses together, on a different day, and had a happier experience, sitting on the bank of the Croesor. As a painter Eleanor was especially enchanted by the visual phenomena, while Bob, in an uncharacteristic fit of euphoria, "had an insight that he was, actually, good. As opposed to bad. His usual feeling about himself seemed often to be negative, that he was guilty of something, lazy, etc. He shared the news with Eleanor, that he was good. She laughed. No, she said—you're rotten. She was teasing him from the happy heights she was experiencing, I'm sure. But it somewhat derailed the benediction from the heavens. Of course you're good, I assured him. But I don't know that he ever believed it."

Janice took her tab alone, with Bob and Jeremy as non-tripping escorts, to the tunes of Phil Ochs and Joan Baez on a portable cassette player. "I sat on the grass on the far side of the river, the sunny side, and detached myself from the human reference point, the human experience, more than I ever would again. . . . I just looked up at the mountain far above me and watched the sheep grazing. They looked so small, and the mountain seemed so high. My insight was that whatever it was that kept the sheep fixed to the mountain, kept them from falling—I supposed it must be God." It was an authentic religious experience, and a durable one. "After that, I could no longer call myself an atheist."

2

FIRST TASTE OF HOLLYWOOD

Toward the end of 1968, Bob, ever restless and making little progress on his novel, decided to accompany Jeremy Brooks on a trip to Canada. Jeremy had a fledgling project under discussion with the Canadian director John Trent, who'd recently wrapped *The Bushbaby* in Tanzania, featuring the Brookses' daughter Margy. Bob was mid-Atlantic on the *Bristol City* when Candida Donadio called London with the news that Paul Newman's production company wanted to purchase the film rights to *A Hall of Mirrors*. Janice had to locate Bob with a shore-to-ship call, alarming him terribly at first since he assumed that some catastrophe must have befallen his family back in the U.K. In fact, the film deal offered "more money than we had ever seen in our lives." Bob received $50,000 for adaptation rights to the novel, and his contract to write the screenplay was a step deal adding up to more than $70,000—fantastic sums for a couple who'd been living in real poverty less than ten years earlier.

Once he landed in Canada, Bob went to Indianapolis to meet Newman, who was on location for *Winning*, an auto-racing movie costarring Newman's wife, Joanne Woodward, with Robert Wagner to fill out the love triangle. Newman was hooked on race-car driving for its own sake, but *A Hall of Mirrors*, with its depth, darkness, and subtle nuance, fascinated him in other ways. He had played his share of bad boys, but Rheinhardt was a much more complicated and introspective bad boy than he'd had a chance to play before.

Back in London, the script went on Bob's front burner. His previous screenwriting experience was zero, "but there was the book already, with all that dialogue," Janice thought. "How hard could it be?" Harder than one might think, in fact—good screenwriting is a more demanding endeavor than it looks to people who haven't tried it.

In January 1969 Bob went back to the States, to consult his partners and bosses in Hollywood, and to do some location scouting in New Orleans. Notoriously, writers get no respect in the Hollywood hierarchy, a factor that has inspired reams of jokes.

Janice thought that Bob came in for extra disrespect because of his youth, although he was then slightly over thirty. He looked younger than his age, and by his own account "gave the appearance of a not very with-it graduate student." Certainly there were demeaning moments, as when a Paramount secretary summoned him to the phone with the line "Front and center for Mr. Foreman." There were comedies of conflicting manners too. When Bob brought a hippieish young woman, with whom he'd shared the occasional *petite amourette* in the Perry Lane days, to stay with him in his hotel, he was startled to find this maneuver frowned upon by his employers. Their solution—rather a strange one—was to offer "him the services of a prostitute, or semi-prostitute (probably some poor young starlet). That was not what he wanted. Hollywood mores met beatnik mores. He was just not on the same wavelength as those people."

Nevertheless, Bob had enough pull to get Janice's way paid for a visit from London. Having engaged a friend of the Brookses' older children to look after Ian and Deidre for a couple of weeks, she flew over the North Pole into L.A., high on hashish and reading a novel by Edna O'Brien. Bob conveyed her to the Chateau Marmont Hotel where he was in residence.

At Newman's forty-fourth birthday party, held at his Benedict Canyon house, the Stones met Henry Fonda and Cloris Leachman. And Jay Sebring, a celebrity hairstylist who wore a snake ring on every finger, sold Bob a quantity of weed; he would be murdered by the Manson Family in the doomed house on Cielo Drive, in August 1969. Janice bought bell-bottoms in three different colors and had them altered to a skintight fit, with the declared intention "to pass myself off as part of the scenery," though probably that was not the effect, or at least not on Bob. The producer John Foreman introduced Janice as a character from Bob's novel and script—"the real Geraldine." Maybe he was stoned at the time. The Stones were surprised that dope-smoking was as prevalent in Hollywood as in other places they'd recently been, though Newman and Woodward didn't indulge.

Bob thought Joanne Woodward disapproved of him, possibly because of the girl in the hotel episode; his commitment to drinking and recreational drugs might also have been a factor (if the disapproval was real), but Bob and Paul were becoming friends. Both played pool, and Newman had a pool table in his home, where he also liked to cook for people. He taught Janice how to eat an artichoke leaf by leaf, and took Bob out in a VW Beetle he'd refitted with a Porsche engine to astonish and one-up L.A. drivers.

Janice returned to London alone. She sat for three portraits by Eleanor Brooks. Eleanor was always keen for new subjects, and would later paint a striking image of Bob palming open a weighty volume, wreathed in biblically overgrown hair and beard and the smoke from his cigarette, looking out into the room with the mad eyes of Rasputin or an Old Testament prophet. Earlier, Lou Gossett had enriched their marijuana supply with an importation from the *Bushbaby* set—"the sort of grass that, when you smoked it in Africa, you would then just crawl under a truck and sleep." Bob got back to England in time to taste it before the supply was exhausted.

The Keseys returned to London in the spring of 1969, this time for a long-enough stay to enroll their three children in the same school that Deidre and Ian attended. Ken's Lord of Misrule antics continued, but Janice didn't have much time for lotus-eating or Pied Piper shenanigans. Her mission was to get organized to rejoin Bob in L.A. for the duration of the screenwriting, taking the children with her this time.

She left Deidre and Ian with her parents in Bogota, where they could finish the school year, and continued to the West Coast on her own. Where she had devised her riposte to Hollywood's demand for glamour, Bob resorted to "an invisibility suit which enabled me to disappear like a squid in threatening situations." This was a costume he'd devised after his beating by the sailors on his bus ride back from California to New York at the end of the Stegner years: "a Fisher Body cap, a blue work shirt over a white undershirt, jeans, and Sears work boots. . . . If it didn't transform me into an outright yokel, it did give me a distinctly out-of-town quality that would have been spotted and mocked by Nathanael West."

Thus disguised, Bob studied the evolution of Hollywood culture and tried to match it to what was going on nationwide. "Anyone paying attention in those days remembers institutions that had seemed immune to public pressure appearing to give way at an angry cry from the street. Responsibility was demanded from quarters that had hitherto answered to no one, 'empowerments,' statutory or otherwise, of all kinds were defined and appeared about to be enforced. Nearly fatal crises of corporate culture suddenly struck outfits such as IBM and the Detroit carmakers, threatening their dominance, and even their survival. The quaintness of Japanese industrial traditions all at once seemed less otherworldly. On the other hand, the annoying eccentricity of the high-tech start-ups in northern California offered competition that had a faintly extraterrestrial quality. And always, Vietnam, engendering between elements of the population hatred not seen in America for a hundred years. Could all these phenomena be somehow connected?"

Bob was working and didn't always have the luxury of the long view. He had to fold himself somehow into the culture of his new employers, often uncomfortably (a metaphor for that awkwardness was the closet-size room he was assigned on first arrival at the Beverly Hills Hotel). He watched the "many long-haired kids from all over" who'd first turned up in San Francisco, beginning to swarm the L.A. streets, "heading, as they thought, for Movieland. The infantile association of the place with fun was of course a commercial delusion. Money, sex, and privilege were brandished. . . . Bohemian style, or an imitation of it, was not much admired. People worked hard, hustled hard, and stole just as they did anywhere else, but the stakes seemed higher. And the place had a culture of predation all its own."

As for the lifting of conventional constraints on the movie business, Bob's feelings were mixed, more on the negative side. "Everything from experimental lighting to scatological language and 'adult' themes annoyed the technicians and secretaries at the reorganizing studios. At the same time, liberation from the failing grip of the censors did not seem to be making pictures any better. In fact, it seemed increasingly permissible to trivialize on a more complex level, and to employ obviousness in treating stories whose point was their ambiguity."

That was a bad augury for Bob's adaptation of *A Hall of Mirrors*. Although he and his star actor were on a similar wavelength, Bob's first few conversations with the director Stuart Rosenberg were enough to let him know "that we had very little in common in terms of the stories we wanted to tell." (Janice mistrusted Rosenberg to the point of thinking that his last picture with Newman, the iconic *Cool Hand Luke*, was a failure, a view at odds with the audience that shelled out $16.2 million to see it.) To Bob's "astonishment, a full-scale reproduction of the house Janice and I had lived in on St. Philip in New Orleans was being constructed on a Paramount sound stage. It was a very peculiar frisson," and not a happy one—a harbinger of obviousness, in fact, and the sort of literalism that would drain the ambiguity from Bob's novel as it made its way into film.

On the upside, Bob had acquired a California license, so he and Janice could "drive around in the hills sometimes." Writing to the children in Bogota, Janice took a less jaundiced view of the Paramount set than Bob: "They have built a whole New Orleans house inside one of their enormous buildings—it has a patio with plants in it, and a balcony and everything—and when they want it to rain outside in the patio, they have the most clever way of squirting water on it, so it looks and sounds just like real rain!"

Submerged in Hollywood's warped reality, both Bob and Janice were sometimes homesick for England, whence Eleanor Brooks sent news, and commiseration on "headaches with the script. Suppose you have pretty good luck so far but I hope they don't muck it up. I thought the original script you produced was such a strong clean neat job I hope it hasn't gone too far off that by now." All the Brookses missed all the Stones (the children were particularly at loose ends without Deidre and Ian), and in parting Eleanor noted, "Blowing grass is not the same without you here."

In May 1969 Bob took a break from Hollywood and went with Janice to collect the children from Bogota. They stayed a week at the Plaza Hotel in New York, which vastly impressed Janice's father (and at least temporarily relieved his doubts about Bob as a provider). Then the four of them returned to California by train on the Super Chief and moved back into the Chateau Marmont. Their suite boasted a small kitchen, where Janice cooked a meal for Anthony Perkins (who played Morgan Rainey in the movie). While Bob labored on rewrites for the script, Deidre and Ian got acquainted with American TV for the first time. Deidre learned to swim in the hotel pool, and both children got a trip to Disneyland, "a horrible drive, down the smoggy freeways, with no scenery worth looking at, but the kids had a really good time when we got there, so I guess it was worth it," Janice wrote to the Burrs. Ian remembers that Bob had rented a light-blue Thunderbird with some of the movie cash: "after the little trolley English cars, I loved riding in that sleek-looking sedan."

The film went on location "into the New Orleans kind of heat where it was too hot to think," although the idea did penetrate that the adaptation (now regrettably titled *WUSA*) would not turn out an aesthetic success. The family was staying at the Roosevelt, but whenever they left the artificial cool of the hotel they felt unable to "imagine how we ever lived here without air-conditioning." Janice had particularly looked forward to showing Deidre around the city of her birth, but "the children just wilted" in the crushing summer heat. The growing sense that the movie would be a failure was equally dispiriting. A long time afterward Bob remarked, succinctly, "I was progressively appalled and when I saw the rough cut I really knew it was all over." On another occasion: "They did what Hollywood always does, which is to assemble this kind of synthetic nearest equivalent cliché."

In mid-June, Bob took a break and went with the family up the California coast, where they found a house to rent on Stowe Lane, in their old Menlo Park neighborhood. The rental house had "a huge overgrown forest-like yard, and the creek runs behind it," with its "banks full of poison oak," which the children somehow avoided catching, though Janice got a dose. Many friends from the Stones' earlier sojourn were still around, including Chloe Scott, Vic Lovell, and Ed and Kit McClanahan, whose two children were the right ages to hit it off with Deidre and Ian. Jane Burton was off in Mexico, expecting the birth of her second child, but the Stones had visits from Joan Michelson (now using the name of her current husband, Barry Katz) and Jeremy and Eleanor Brooks.

Hippie revolutionism had swarmed over Palo Alto, and some of the Stones' old friends had temporarily turned Maoist. Ken Kesey was living on the ancestral dairy farm in Oregon. The Stones called on him there, in time to witness delivery of a quantity of heroin from a motorcycle messenger attired like "a time-traveling dispatch rider from the Marne."

Meanwhile, America was about to put boots on the moon. With Jim Wolpman and Peter Demma, Bob planned an earth-walk, on a route from the coast at Monterey across the Santa Cruz Mountains to a Zen monastery at Tassajara Hot Springs. They'd been warned by rangers about panthers and wild boars, and had glimpses of some of the latter. Stone and his companions were kept abreast of the moon landing by the transistor radios of their fellow hikers. "A network rapporteur tried to coax the astronauts a little toward poetry to honor the historicity we were about to witness," as Bob recalled afterward.

On the second day they outdistanced the crowds and on the third reached the hot springs, where they could soothe their battered feet. Janice drove up with a party that included Joan Michelson and the children to meet them. They all "spent a few days at the peaceful Buddhist community of Tassajara, eating a vegetarian diet and soaking ourselves in the hot baths," enlivened by a moment when one of the women tried an unsuccessful pass at one of the monks.

Jim Wolpman was involved with the Midpeninsula Free University, a sort of educational collective that had evolved out of the Berkeley Free Speech Movement and the teach-ins of the early 1960s. (Its house organ,

The Free You, published Bob's report on Kesey in Mexico after *Esquire* killed the piece.) Loosely connected to the loosely structured Midpeninsula Free University was "a small, crippled, Southeast-Asian, named Husain Chung," who "arrived in the area, set up shop as the Human Institute, and began conducting intense psychodrama marathons." Dirk van Nouhuys, a friend of the Stones from the Perry Lane circle, describes Chung "as a sort of John the Baptist to Werner Erhard." Indeed, Chung's tactics do seem to prefigure those of Erhard's EST training. Peter Smart, in a worshipful *Free You* article on Chung, describes his psychodrama as "a stripping away of psychic layers, a going deeper and deeper into the self. You come in wearing a face, but it is not your real face. All the psychodrama, the merciless zapping (why do you lie, why are you so weak, so impotent? why are you such a bitch?) all this is designed to strip away the mask and reveal the real face, the face contorted with hatred and rage, the face with all its marks of weakness and shame. The marathon is a true mirror and for once, you must look at your real face," etc., etc., until "on the other side, there isn't disaster, disintegration, madness, loss of self, but rather self-realization, strength, wholeness, peace. That underneath that ugly face there is yet another face, your true face, and it is a strong, loving face. After the hell, comes this incredible joy, love and peace." Apparently, the hellish phase of a marathon psychodrama could go on for several days.

Several of Bob's friends, possibly including Vic Lovell, Ed McClanahan, and Gurney Norman (it's one of those stories that everyone tells from the point of view of a friend who was actually there), decided to get high and attend a Chung psychodrama. The visit was either intended from the start as a shuck in which Bob would combine his skills as actor and fiction writer to present false faces to the "merciless zapping" of Chung and his team—or else something very similar happened by accident. Bob had to be persuaded to go, and his real personality was not a safe target for this kind of manipulation. Jim Wolpman: "Chung (who was indeed an extraordinary individual) immediately focused on Bob. In response Bob created an entirely fictional character for himself. They went round and round as Chung dug in and Bob invented. It ended with Bob storming out and the psychodrama in disarray." By some accounts, the Stone party actually had to fight its way out of the situation.

Following these adventures, Bob went back to Hollywood, which was now full of "horror stories about the kids who had appeared on Sunset. They were not like the beatniks down in Venice who knew their place. These kids were dirty, they said, the girls and boys were hustlers, sold drugs." Bob's secretary, "who sounded like Irene Dunne," was pestered by crank calls: "a wall of stoned giggles and a hang-up." Bob knew the calls came from friends of his amused by the idea of "their old pal apparently ensconced in moguldom," as he wrote years later. Still, an atmosphere of menace was building, and eventually discharged itself into the Manson murders. "Fear appeared in a handful of dust," as Bob paraphrased T. S. Eliot's *The Waste Land*. With a couple of actor friends Bob and Janice went to a height that looked down on the fatal house on Cielo Drive, and later returned to the Chateau Marmont to smoke a joint—still the dope Bob had bought from Jay Sebring, recently deceased by way of multiple stab wounds. Abigail Folger, another very slight acquaintance of Bob's, had also been slain in the Cielo Drive massacre.

Charles Manson was crazy, but he was also an intentional terrorist, and the terror he produced was very effective, at least in the short term. It seemed a good time to get out of California, and maybe out of the States altogether, if one had somewhere else to go. The movie, for better or worse, had wrapped.

———

Bob's first tour of Hollywood was done—not without a few regrets about the artifact he'd helped produce. The experience had taught him something about the hazards of film adaptation, from the literary novelist's point of view: "the thing in progress slid between incoherency and the nearest equivalent cliché. The novel aspired to a certain poetry and was made of words. The movie *WUSA* came out looking like such a novel rendered as a very indifferent episode of *Matlock*." Deemed an "epic flop" for both Newman and Rosenberg (hard on the heels of their great success with *Cool Hand Luke*), the film fared poorly in the press, such as the trashing in *The New York Times*: "*WUSA* feels more like poor theater than poor moviemaking—so that it continually suggests a failed version of *The Balcony*, even though it strives to fall short of *The Manchurian Candidate*." Nevertheless, Perkins was nominated for best supporting actor and Newman called it "the most significant film I've ever made and the best."

The loss of control that many, if not most screenwriters experience had soured Bob on this line of work. "It's very tempting to try and translate something from book into film, if you like film, and I like film. And I think the experience is very satisfying in a lot of ways, but it's also deadly, or it can be." Though the Stones remained friends with the Newmans for a long time after, Bob was extremely forceful in repudiating their joint venture: "Now if you saw *WUSA*, it has my name on it. People might think this is what Stone thinks is a good movie. And that bothers me. . . . And I feel that because it has my name on it I probably owe everybody who has ever seen it an apology, so I do apologize. It is a god-awful movie."

Despite all that, *WUSA* had given Bob the best payday of his life so far. (It also won him some valuable credibility from his father-in-law, who clipped the prerelease publicity pictures, underlining "that Bob's name is mentioned twice in the ad.") The Stones sailed back to London, a little sadder, possibly wiser, and certainly a good deal richer, at least for the time being.

3
A TOUR OF VIETNAM

The movie money had enabled them to purchase their flat on Redington Road, which Candida Donadio had advised them to do as an investment. Though Janice was startled by the concept at first—"An investment! I was a socialist!"—the sale went through while they were still in California. "Bob and I had never invested in anything, having never had any more money than we needed to live on, if barely that."

Kesey and company had been staying in the London digs for part of the time the Stones were in Hollywood; on their departure, Kesey or his cohorts put out the word that the place was generally available as a crash pad. A series of unexpected arrivals disconcerted the couple the Stones had actually invited to stay there, Ivan and Vera Gold, to the point that they decamped. Bob's mother contributed to the atmosphere of chaos by coming around at odd moments to look for Bob, "once sleeping on the doormat outside the flat." From across the Atlantic, there was not much the Stones could do about these escapades, since they didn't even know where Gladys officially lived.

Gladys's grip on reality had been loosening during the Stones' absences, and it didn't improve once they returned. She "couldn't seem to settle into a living situation, a room by herself, anymore. She kept turning up at our place, where the guest room was Bob's study, where he was trying to write. She would neither go back to the U.S. nor let us find her a room in our part of London." During the months of shuttling between London and Hollywood, Janice had persuaded Gladys to return to the States with her, but at the last minute, Gladys canceled the plan.

Bob, a cigarette smoker of John Wayne dimensions, had managed to quit. But the stress of Gladys's deterioration wore down his resolve to kick the habit. "He had always been able to talk to his mother, to reason with her. Now she seemed to be out of reach. She locked us out of the flat one night. Bob said, Ma, it's me! It's not you, she replied. I've lost her, he said, very sadly."

A psychiatrist's opinion made Gladys's dementia official. (For comfort, he told them in inimitably British style, "We shall all dement, if we live long enough.") Her symptoms now included "sleeping with a large knife in her bed, fearful of being attacked." Although Bob had a deep resolve never to abandon his mother, there now seemed no choice but to commit her. A place was found at St. Andrew's Hospital in Northampton (where James Joyce's daughter Lucia was also immured). Northampton was near enough to London that Bob and Deidre could visit Gladys by train, but Bob was deeply discouraged by the episode, his own sense of failure, and fear for the future. "I'm afraid I'll be just like my mother when I get old," he told Janice. "They were in many ways alike, mother and son, and he knew it and worried about it."

Around the time of Gladys's commitment, Bob went back to a multipack-a-day cigarette habit. It would be another twelve years before he managed to quit permanently, and at the close of his life he would sometimes particularly blame the strong Embassy cigarettes he had smoked in England for the emphysema that finally put an end to him. But in 1971 he was also on his way to a war zone, where reasons not to smoke can seem less compelling.

————

The Stones had not been enormously active in the U.K. antiwar movement, although they had marched in one demonstration in Grosvenor Square. Janice's father, identifying himself squarely with "the silent majority," wrote them irascibly on the subject: "I don't mean to hurt your feelings but I know both of you favor the student rebellions and the dissension that is so prevalent in our country today. I believe they are communist-inspired." Janice briefly sent small sums to sponsor a Vietnamese orphan and gave blood once for a related cause: "Bob teased me that I had donated blood to the Vietcong." Later on, however, Bob dedicated *Dog Soldiers* to the Committee of Responsibility, an organization that brought war-wounded Vietnamese children to the United States for treatment (and then repatriated them) and also operated a shelter for children in Saigon.

As the family accountant, Janice was in charge of withholding a percentage of the Stones' income tax as a protest against the war. Tax resistance (of which Joan Baez was an early popularizer) had been growing since the early 1960s. In 1967, Gerald Walker of *The New York Times* had organized the Writers and Editors War Tax Protest. By 1970, so many people were involved in tax resistance to the war (usually involving very small sums per individual) that it was not practical to prosecute more than a few. However, Janice's gesture did inspire an IRS raid on Houghton Mifflin's Boston office, too late to garnish any payments due to Bob, however, as his contract had run out the previous year. "I was very pleased to hear it," Janice said, "though it didn't seem to bode well for our finances."

Bob's second novel was going nowhere fast. "I kept running into the Vietnam situation late in the war. I had been away from the United States for a couple of years. I couldn't get this book written. It seemed to me that these people—my characters—must have been in Vietnam, even though I didn't know quite who they were. I thought, 'What is their relationship to this Vietnam situation that is filling everybody's life now, that is so much on everybody's mind?' It's all anybody could talk about when I was with other Americans. It was so present, looming large in everybody's consciousness. And I began to wonder suddenly if I couldn't get some work over there, go and have a look firsthand at what was going on, because it was such an attraction—the idea of Vietnam as a place and as more than a place." Although the book wasn't going well at all, Bob's ambitions for it were quite large, so that "I realized if I wanted to be a 'definer' of the American condition, I would have to go to Vietnam. In many ways it changed my life."

The Hollywood money was running low, and when Bob decided he absolutely had to go to Vietnam before he could make progress on the book, it didn't seem affordable to buy a second $500 roundtrip ticket to Saigon, not to mention the point that (as Janice put it), "if I were to go, we would risk orphaning our own children, should anything go wrong." Bob couldn't get journalistic accreditation from any established organ of the press, and finally got a card from a start-up (and very short-lived) London publication called *INK*. At the behest of a friend the Stones had invested $200 in the enterprise, but they were not thrilled with the first issue. "God what a crumby paper it is!" Janice railed to her journal. "*The National Mirror* was never so bad," and that was saying a lot. "Every word in it looks untrue—and it's a left-wing inside-dopester scandal sheet, poorly laid-out," to boot.

The first issue of *INK* touched off Bob's paranoia, always easy enough to provoke. He feared that accreditation would stamp him as a junkie leftist to CIA snoops and Saigon police. So he wrote himself a letter of accreditation on *Village Voice* stationery, and Mike Zwerin, a European editor of the *Voice*, obliged him by signing it, though this gesture did not make the credential any less spurious.

The prospect of the trip unnerved Bob to the point that he began spending more time with his children, in the belief he might never see them again. Going to get a visa at the South Vietnamese embassy didn't soothe his anxiety. A hostile official there was suspicious of him in general and particularly incredulous of the contention that Bob would go to Vietnam to research a novel. Bob came away from this encounter fearful that he might be set up for some bogus bust if he did make the trip.

Bob had been refraining from drink for a bit, perhaps as a sort of training for the trip, but under this stress he fell "off the wagon, with a crash." Infinitely patient Janice grew exasperated by his dithering. On May 13, his visa came through. The next day he decided he would not go. But in the following few days he and Janice continued to make arrangements for a flight to Saigon and finally bought his ticket for £220. Janice's diary tracks his vacillation. May 20: "He still says he can't do it. Wishes he was dead. He's in very bad shape. . . . He knows it will be nearly as bad if he stays as if he goes. I suspect it may be worse—he may actually have a breakdown." Saturday, May 22: "He says he won't know if he's going until Monday, when he gets drunk and gets on the plane or doesn't. He says actually he's going to Vietnam to get killed because he's impotent. And yesterday I caught myself daydreaming that he was going out there to get recharged mentally and physically, and would come home cured (and thanking me for pushing him out there). But I'm not pushing too hard—I'm afraid to. He might get himself killed for spite, or have a crackup. . . . But I don't believe for a minute he's going to die. It's either Vietnam or a psychiatrist as far as I'm concerned." Monday, May 24: "Robert has departed."

Not without trepidation, of course. In parting he told Janice simply: "I hope I see you again." Janice informed him that she had invoked the spirits of her ancestors to protect him. "Again, as when he went to Mexico, it was as if he had disappeared into a black hole."

In fact, Bob had checked into Saigon's Royale, "the hotel of choice of the 'third-country press,' meaning many of the European reporters and photographers who were not, as they say, on board." That style of alienation was congenial enough for him to adopt (and shared by a good number of the American press corps as well). The Continental, where Graham Greene had stayed, was now occupied by a television crew. Bob went there to confer about a possible trip to Cambodia, but if he caught any whiff of Greene's own special brand of ennui, he didn't write about it.

Though his flimsy credentials were accepted only by the South Vietnamese Ministry of Information (and not by the American military), Bob soon fell in with a coterie of journalists, whom he described as "all serious war reporters who have paid their dues," including Gloria Emerson, Dede Donovan, and Judith Coburn. He had a particular admiration for Michael Herr, for the unusual amount of time he spent close to the heavy action of 1968 and 1969. Herr had left Vietnam well before Bob got there, surviving to tell the tale in the enduring form of *Dispatches*, while others (Sean Flynn, Dana Stone, Larry Burrows, Kent Potter to name a few) were not so lucky. Other journalists kept away from the front lines (not that there were any fixed lines in this guerrilla conflict), did color reporting around Saigon, and imbibed their military information from MACV briefings. The acronym stood for Military Advisory Command, Vietnam, which Bob jocularly personified as a "many-faced, many-armed deity," which "declared elephants to be enemy agents since they were employed in logistical transport by the NVA and the Front. There ensued what might have been an episode from the Ramayana, in which MACV unleashed enormous deadly flying insects called choppers to destroy his enemies the elephants. Whooping gunners descended on the herd to mow them down with 50 millimeter machine guns, and even my scandalized informant remembers the operation with something like insane exhilaration."

By Stone and others, the war effort was apt to be portrayed as this kind of darkly comical, epic folly. "They laugh a great deal," Bob wrote of his colleagues. "There is speculation about the number of reporters who have gotten into smack and talk of acquaintances rightly or wrongly alleged to have habits or who have kicked their habits." Heroin and marijuana were handily available all over Saigon. Bob had previously tasted smack with Kesey in Oregon (and perhaps also while running the streets of New York in his teens, at a time and place when there was plenty around to be tasted), but the Vietnam trip was probably his first extended fling with the drug, though thanks to his aversion to needles he only snorted, smoked, or possibly drank it on one occasion in "a bar on Tu Do Street, a bar which had the reputation of serving heroin in beer on request." American soldiers on R&R were equally enthusiastic consumers. "Bands of GIs, many of them hopelessly out of uniform in headbands and Japanese beads, wander around checking it all out. 'Wow,' they're saying. 'There it is.' They're smoking Park Lane cigarettes, which are filtered packaged joints, 600 piastres for 20." In Bob's observation, "dope is so pervasive that the language of war has become head shorthand."

One of his introductions took him to the heart of the expat drug world. "When I arrived in Saigon I had one name to look up. A friend of mine told me you've got to look up this guy, so I spent a couple of weeks looking for him, and when I found him I found that he was a junkie, that he lived in a pad on Tu Do Street with a lot of famed journalists, some with Vietnamese girlfriends, and they were dealing in heroin. And also when I located other people that I knew there, nobody wanted to know him, or wanted him anywhere around. And I also discovered that in the hotel where I was staying people were doing a lot of opium smoking. I just generally found myself, as far as I could see, up to my ears in smack." Some of his discoveries were too outlandish to use. "It is a fact that heroin was smuggled into the United States in corpses, in the coffins of dead soldiers. It seemed to me that this was just too much. . . . The American dead were being sent to Aberdeen, Maryland, with heroin concealed in their coffins. So it's something that fiction can't possibly do justice to."

"Saigon—it was Babylon. I was seeing incredible things. This guy took me around to these incredible joints, like existentialist caves, full of

Vietnamese students, scenes of draft dodgers, cowboys, rooms beyond rooms, wheels within wheels. And everybody was stoned morning, noon and night. It was extraordinary. Stories of the most unimaginably baroque nature came out of the war, and my feeling is you can't discount any of them."

Bob wrote color with the best of them, better than most in fact, savoring the ironies of cultural confusion: "rock music is as thoroughly un-Vietnamese as bobsledding or gang rape (which seems to have been another innovation stimulated by the American presence) and watching CBC [a Vietnamese rock band taking its name from the CBC bar in Saigon] one is aware that the process through which a 25-year-old Vietnamese transforms himself into a San Francisco bass player must be extremely dislocating." Scenes like these (first published in the *Guardian*, since *INK* had evaporated, leaving scarcely a stain, by the time Bob got back to London) would make their way into the opening movement of *Dog Soldiers*. Even in his color reportage, moral nausea sometimes leaked through his lightly satirical tone.

"The previous occupant of my Saigon hotel room apparently had a thing about smashing lizards ... Since house lizards are useful insectivores, a cheerful friendly presence in every hot country on earth, it is difficult to understand why anyone should want to massacre them in this fashion. So the vision of my faceless predecessor stalking about his Sydney Greenstreet Colonial hotel wasting lizards with a framed tintype of Our Lady of Lourdes (on evidence, the hunter's instrument) is a disturbing one with which to begin the day." Later: "in the course of my short walk from the hotel I have seen several lepers, a couple of crippled ARVN soldiers and a begging cretin led by an ancient woman, but it still seems to be the lizards that worry me.

"Lights flash in my eyes—the carefully nurtured outraged humanism I brought with me seems to have stalled at 'Reptiles.' ... My fever is coming back, the low-grade fever I've been nursing for several days, along with that outraged humanism."

Bob collected bitterly telling anecdotes: The Great Elephant Stomp, the active-duty, uniformed ARVN soldier pretending to be blind to facilitate his begging. Tipped by Judith Coburn, he visited the scene of a bombed tax office (which Coburn had witnessed from a restaurant across the street). "Nearby buildings have their windows broken and there are still a few shards of dishware and the odd spoon lying around among the chips of concrete. The street seems to smell of Clorox. Here and there are sprinklings of dried white powder that someone says is chloride of lime and on one wall a brown smear that appears to be a washed-over bloodstain."

On one occasion Bob did get closer to the action, "by motorcycle with another journalist," by Janice's recollection, "and he scared himself quite a bit." The other man was a buddy Bob wrote about "under the name of Harry Lime . . . for so long I can't remember his actual name." They rode along the outskirts of Operation Dewey Canyon II, in which U.S. troops supported an incursion of South Vietnamese troops into Laos—the ultimate goal was to interdict the Ho Chi Minh Trail. This outing was sufficiently dangerous, and Bob got a glimpse of what in his later writings on war he'd call "the elephant," "going to see the elephant" having been an American Civil War expression for a green soldier's first experience of combat. It was not something he talked or wrote about directly (though John Converse's experience under fire in *Dog Soldiers* probably runs very close to Bob's own).

Even twenty years later, writing for *Esquire*, Bob remained elliptical about it: "When I had finished my business in Saigon, I seemed to feel, for reasons that now strike me as idiotic, that honor required my reparation to a point in-country where ordnance of some sort might be discharged in my general direction.

"Off I went, to a place whose name I've forgotten; I think it was about thirty kilometers northwest of Saigon. A grunt who briefly traveled with me expressed the hope that since I professed a moral responsibility to be shot at (or at least near), I might find it in me to get my ass killed outright. This was the fate he found suitable for the sort of people who were in Vietnam when they didn't have to be."

If the trip to a live-combat zone was unnerving, civilian life in Vietnam could be even more so. "I did get to know far more than I wanted to know about the Saigon underworld. I found that scene thoroughly scary—so scary that sometimes I felt safer when I went out toward the line than I did in Saigon."

"It was the spring of 1971," Bob wrote, decades later; "the war was lost. I had just taught my kids, in London, to ride their two-wheel bicycles. I didn't want to be there, in Vietnam; I didn't want to stay. I didn't want to leave, either, because it seemed betrayal." His experience in the navy gave him a sense of solidarity with the American combat grunts in

Vietnam, while he also sympathized with the antiwar sentiment common in the press corps to which he now belonged (and indeed there was plenty of antiwar sentiment among the combat grunts too). On his way back to London from Saigon, he stopped in Thailand and spent a night in the Buddhist monastery at Ayutthaya, where he "obtained and drank a bottle of Mekong whiskey.

"'Weakness of the strong man,' the chief monk said merrily as he prodded me awake . . .

"'There it is,' I said. Who knew what I meant by that? It was what everybody said in Vietnam when they thought they had glimpsed the dark antic spirit of the war."

Inscrutable, ineffable, irreducible, the expression stayed with Bob for a very long time. Back in London, he used it as the closer for his piece in *The Guardian* on the tax-office bombing. "There it is. A marginal incident represented by a day-old bloodstain. I stand in the street, getting in the way of pedestrians—the thoughtful tourist trying to draw a moral. But there isn't any moral, it makes no sense at all. It reminds me of the lizards smashed on the hotel wall."

4

AMERICAN AFTER ALL

June 10, 1971. Janice's diary reports: "Brushing my hair in the mirror yesterday, I saw the door open and a man appear. Robert, complete surprise—a week early. Looking red in the face, high on fatigue. He talked and talked. Did it all, he did, got the inside dope."

To show for his sojourn in Vietnam, Bob had the makings of an article to sell to *The Guardian*, enough direct experience of the climate of the war to push on with the writing of *Dog Soldiers*, a saffron wrist thread (which he wore until it fell off naturally, according to instruction) given to him by the monk who'd teased him about his drinking, and his South Vietnamese press card, which he cherished as a souvenir for many years after, until, finally, it was stolen, along with a modest stash of cocaine, from his desk drawer in Amherst. It was a good thing to earn a few pounds from *The Guardian*, because the Houghton contract for the novel had run out, the movie money was almost exhausted, and no further income looked likely from *WUSA*. As Bob had put it to himself shortly before his trip to Vietnam, "I was in London with no second book written and a pretty poor excuse for a movie headed for late night TV with my name on it." It was time to make some kind of move.

The Stones could not legally work in the United Kingdom. Their expatriate life looked to be coming to an end, and not only for financial reasons. Deidre and Ian had acquired British accents and "were beginning to think of themselves as English," like the Landesmans' sons, Miles and Cosmo. Bob and Janice began to consider that "we were Americans and wanted our children to know that they too were American."

Janice went briefly to Finland, to glimpse her ancestral homeland, and to Sweden to buy a Volvo that they'd ship to the States. The Stones would need a car in Princeton, where Edmund "Mike" Keeley, an American novelist of cosmopolitan background whom they'd met through Bob's U.K. agent, had arranged for Bob to teach for a year at the university. But something had to be done about Gladys. With the expenses of the move facing them, the Stones could no longer keep up with the fees at St. Andrew's Hospital. She was in no condition to return to the States with them or to live in London on her own. Janice found a reasonable nursing home in North London, "a family-run place with only a few residents, who did not appear unhappy or drugged. It offered home cooking and the staff seemed friendly. Gladys hated it. When we went to visit, she would yell the whole time." Bob planned to return to London to visit her during Princeton's winter break, so their separation would be only a few months—no longer than several they'd had in the past. In the summer of 1971, the Stones loaded their lares and penates and sailed for their troubled homeland.

———

The return had elements of shock for Bob: "I was getting my perceptions of the war through the medium of the English press and television. That is why I think, when I came to America, I saw the impact of the war on the whole country more clearly, because I had been away, and I hadn't experienced it as a gradually increasing thing. It was still going on when I came back in '71, the same year that I had been over there, and came back to what was the beginning of post-Vietnam America. To me it seems that, with the war and the drug explosion and everything that happened in the sixties, the world seems so different than it was before the Vietnam

War, before the drugs, the music, before all that wild thing went through. It's almost like living in the aftermath of a revolution—as one might talk about 'before the revolution' and 'after the revolution.' This is a different country." For *Dog Soldiers*, this shock was probably salutary. Meanwhile, the Stones' reentry also involved a return to the mundane.

Princeton University was proud of its four-year undergraduate creative writing program—the only one of its kind at the time. The program was set up as a track in the English major, and managed by two tenured English professors: poet Theodore Weiss and Mike Keeley. Other creative writing faculty members were in a revolving-door situation—working on one-year contracts renewable up to five years, with no option to continue past that point. Perhaps for that reason, many of them commuted from New York. In the 1970s, creative writing instruction in the academy had left its infancy to enter a sort of adolescent period, and New York City offered a sizable pool of well-published writers for Keeley and Weiss to draw on, people who were more than happy to earn some extra money by running out to Princeton to teach a couple of classes a week.

The Stones had no base in New York anymore and had sunk the remains of their capital into the London flat (now rented to friends of the Golds: Bill Broder, a novelist and playwright with Stanford connections, and Gloria Kurian Broder, also a writer, best known for her short stories). With rents rising sharply in Manhattan, Bob and Janice could not afford to return there. They found lodging for themselves and their children in the Magie Apartments, one of a pair of eight-story buildings recently constructed a short distance downhill from Princeton's main campus, on the shore of Carnegie Lake. This location was one of the better options for transient faculty and for some graduate students fortunate enough to move on from the Butler Quonset hut compound, which had been improvised to house such students with their families at the end of World War II. The Stones paid $256 a month for their place, just $6 more than they were charging their tenants in London.

The creative writing program was set up, appropriately, in a sort of no-man's-land between Princeton's central humanities campus and the Engineering Quadrangle a good deal farther east. The building at 185 Nassau Street was an old elementary school absorbed into university real estate and repurposed for visual arts, film, and creative writing. Students and faculty working there enjoyed a mild sense of subverting the sort of dull discipline that would have formerly ruled the building—as if the lunatics had finally got control of the asylum. The hourly bus to New York stopped almost on the doorstep. Bob had a large, airy office on the second floor—a good thing, since the apartment was too small for him to have a separate work room there. He kept a portable typewriter at his office, and pushed ahead on his second novel as hard as he could.

In what was standard operating procedure at the time, Keeley had hired Stone because he was impressed with Bob's work, and without worrying much about conventional credentials. Bob's formal education stopped with a GED from the navy, but he had mastered more knowledge and craft than the average PhD, and though he liked to call his teaching career "dropout's revenge," he was serious about his work with writing students.

Social life in tiny Princeton was a little thin for the Stones, who'd always lived in major cities: New York, New Orleans, San Francisco, London, and Los Angeles. They didn't make close friends among the writing faculty, which was quite small. Bob had his ticket to visit his mother in London, but before winter break freed him to go, Gladys died suddenly of a stroke at the age of seventy-seven. Bob was alone at the burial of her ashes in a North London cemetery, except for a couple of staff members from the nursing home and a priest who turned up, having belatedly discovered that the deceased had been a Catholic. There was something appropriate in that solitude, since for most of Bob's childhood he and his mother had been just "two against the world."

The priest rebuked him for not letting the clergy know his mother was there, but Bob claimed "she wouldn't have been happy if I had—she hated priests"—despite her own peculiar brand of intermittent devotion and her encouraging Bob in the faith in at least one phase of his youth. The rest of her story remained as mysterious, and there was not much with which to reconstruct it. Had she been schizophrenic or bipolar? Impossible to say, as Gladys diligently avoided doctors. A few papers that came to light showed she had traveled widely, and under different names. "I think she lost many things over the years," Janice mused, "left in storage spaces she couldn't pay for. There was not much trace of her life." And Bob in fact had lost *her*, as he admitted on the night she locked him out of the flat on Redington Road. "He said that she had lived her life before he was born, and he didn't know what that life was."

"Bless her scattered mad Irish bones," Bob wrote, late in his own life, "she lived by the books. I remember from infancy strange words she spoke. ASOKA. TURGENEV. When we last met, we two, she was a crazy retired New York schoolteacher, on and off the sauce. God forgive me, I pretty much put her aside as well. Selfish things some of us do. I think she brought me up to think I was so terrific I didn't have time for her."

———

Like many writers in the academy, Bob had some difficulty writing while teaching, although he was finally making progress on his second novel—now three years overdue. His current income was scanty; Princeton paid him $466 a month before taxes, more than half of which went for rent, and his writing income for 1971 was just $127 paid by *The Guardian* for his piece on Vietnam. The Stones were also struggling for relief from double taxation in Britain. Bob's mother had died intestate and also lost her savings account passbook. Recovering whatever money she might have left in the U.K. would not be simple, though Janice pointed out that "nobody else is going to do it." Closing her letter to the Stones' U.S. accountant, she noted, "It looks like 1972 is going to be another financially uneventful year," which was a mild euphemism for a lean one.

William Heath, a professor of English at Amherst College, was pulling for Bob to teach there the next year, and Bob snapped up the offer when it came. During the summer they took a detour to Maine, renting from a Princeton professor a house on MacMahan Island, off the Down East coast. Despite a stream of visitors, Bob worked steadily on the manuscript that was on its way to becoming *Dog Soldiers*. The house was capacious enough for him to have a private work room. His tour of Vietnam had given him a much clearer idea of where he wanted the novel to go, and although the family's various relocations in the early 1970s had disrupted his work rhythm, he was now making real progress.

"I didn't really research it," Stone said of his second novel afterward. "I didn't know what I was doing when I began it. I knew I had experienced certain people's lives around me, some of whom were fairly close to me, some people not. But what the moral of the damn thing was I didn't know. At a certain point I got the opportunity to go to Vietnam, and I had been sort of messing around with these people, with their story, and what their lives were like, and it occurred to me when I got there that I was seeing the other side of American reality in the Sixties, but this suddenly forced me into a sort of recognition of what things were actually about."

Stone had always intended to set this story in the United States, but it took him years of struggle to understand that its lodestone was in Vietnam—not so much in the combat zones, or even among the increasingly obscure issues and ideologies supposed to be at stake, but in the corrupt penumbra surrounding the American involvement. As in *A Hall of Mirrors*, he would find himself tracing the edges of a fissure in American society, in this case treating the Vietnam War as a wound.

———

At Amherst College in the fall of 1972, Bob was assigned a full load, with courses in writing, literature, and film, the latter course team-taught with the English professor Richard J. Cody. "They were both film buffs, and assigned their favorite noir movies to their puzzled students. I'm thinking these may have included *Kiss Me Deadly*, *The Asphalt Jungle*, and the documentary *Night Mail*." Some of Bob's most talented students from this period would later work in film, including Merrill Greene and perhaps most notably Ken Burns, "a long-haired Hampshire College student," who could take courses at Amherst under the five-college consortium arrangement, which also included Mount Holyoke, Smith, and the University of Massachusetts at Amherst. Then there was Michael Hardy, older than the rest, a veteran who'd returned from Vietnam with a crippled hand, a probable case of post-traumatic stress disorder, avant la lettre, and a fondness for grog, which he very much shared with Professor Stone.

The Vietnam War looked like it might never end; resistance to the draft was at its peak; and controversy over the war had moved to the storm center of American politics. In 1972, the prospect of being drafted hung over most young men in college at Amherst or anywhere else. Janice's brother John was exempt for bad eyesight, but she worried about her younger brother Peter, approaching draft age. The war issue was central to the 1972 presidential election. Janice went door-knocking with a group for George McGovern and his antiwar platform, riding a bus from Amherst to townships in eastern Massachusetts. "Bob said, If you have to canvass for McGovern in New Bedford, he's lost the election," and Nixon's landslide victory in all states but one proved the point, though Janice and others could take some cold comfort from a bumper sticker that appeared soon after: "Don't Blame Me—I'm from Massachusetts"—the only state that went for McGovern.

Their international tax troubles were complicated when the IRS attempted to garnish Bob's wages at Amherst, to recover taxes the Stones had withheld previously as a protest against the war. The matter was resolved, in favor of the tax authority, shortly before the Stones met Amherst's president, John William Ward, at a cocktail party. Though Janice (if not Bob) worried that he might frown on their attracting angry tax collectors to the college, Ward was against the Vietnam War and "in fact seemed amused."

The Stone family had moved into a good-size house at 43 Hitchcock Road in Amherst, on an exchange arrangement with the physics professor Joel Gordon for the Redington Road flat. The Hitchcock Road house was close to campus, and Bob could elude family chaos by working in his office there; he also had a carrel in the library, where colleagues and students were unlikely to pursue. That year he was distracted by attacks of gout so severe that he "had to bump his way downstairs sitting down so as not to walk on his excruciatingly painful foot." Advised to give up alcohol and butter to bring down his triglycerides, "Bob was good about eating the margarine," but about refraining from alcohol, not so much. "Dr. Brandfass retired a year or two later, thanks to a heart attack," and as Janice laconically remarked, "Bob went on drinking," often with his Vietnam vet student Michael Hardy. This friendship seemed to be helping him move forward on the book. Hardy's combat experience was bountiful, and though not much combat is directly depicted in *Dog Soldiers*, it's a factor in the sensibility of the co-protagonist Ray Hicks.

James Maraniss, another professor at Amherst, also became a close friend, though his acquaintance with Bob (who was considerably older) got off to a wobbly start. "I was a 28-year-old beginning Assistant Professor in Spanish who was favored for some reason by the English Department. I think he saw me as *the other*, a smug, privileged Ivy Leaguer. He later told me that he had hated me at first (which surprised me to learn, because if I was reticent I was never standoffish).

"He would try to talk to me about Borges, and I would agree with the things he said without getting deep into his preoccupations. He could read diffidence as hostility, I guess. Some people called him 'paranoid,' but that has never been my experience. He didn't stick with his first impression, of me, at least." Despite whatever initial antipathy there may have been, Bob and Jim became boon companions, cementing their friendship on trips to Central America, which furnished raw material for Stone's third novel, *A Flag for Sunrise*.

In the summer of 1973 the Stones went back to London briefly. They were able to reclaim their Redington Road flat for a short period, but spent most of the time with the Brookses at Gelli. With Jeremy and Eleanor they made an eight-day excursion to Ireland, leaving Ian and Deidre in Wales with the Brooks children, who were old enough to manage on their own. They traveled on the car ferry, and Jeremy drove them around the Irish Republic in his Bentley. Tourists were sparse at the time; "sometimes it seemed we had the entire country to ourselves. The troubles in the north, where there was IRA activity, seemed to have scared people away from the Republic also." But the Stones and the Brookses encountered few hazards, though a bed did collapse under Bob and Janice at one of the B&Bs where they stayed.

Bob's Shanley ancestors hailed from Ireland, but he didn't seem much interested in exploring those roots. He did have real interest, and a good deal of knowledge, "about Ireland's difficult history with the English, especially the details of the 1916 uprising." Though "he always identified with the Irish rebels," he wouldn't push the point in the company of his English friends. They visited the tower at Glendalough, and the Rock of Cashel, and a holy well in County Clare, "or maybe County Kerry," but didn't quite make it to the grave of William Butler Yeats.

Back in Gelli, Bob carried his typewriter outdoors and worked in the shade of the trees by the river. *Dog Soldiers* was going into the homestretch, and he was able to keep his momentum through the fall of 1973, though the Stones changed lodgings again in Amherst, moving into the house of the English professor William Pritchard and his wife, Marietta (who were also going abroad for the year), at 62 Orchard Street. "Their house was not as grand as the Gordons', but much cozier." Here Bob pushed to the end of his novel, and cut and pasted a final draft (which was the state of the editing art in those last decades before computerized word-processing became universal).

Janice proofread the manuscript but was too busy to type a clean version of the finished book, since along with housekeeping and childcare she was taking night classes for a master's degree in counseling at the University of Massachusetts Amherst. She found a student to do the typing, but forgot to specify that it be double-spaced. "There was no time for a do-over. Houghton Mifflin was not pleased." The publisher charged Bob a fee for retyping the manuscript in Boston.

5

Dog Soldiers *Goes Live*

The single-spacing fiasco was a penultimate bump on what had been a fairly rough and crooked road to the appearance of Stone's second novel. It had been seven years since *A Hall of Mirrors*, and the dubious quality of the film adaptation might have dimmed the luster of the novel in the public eye. Slow delivery may have worn Houghton's patience a little thin, and it looked as if the publishing engine was sputtering at the start. *Dog Soldiers* was announced by a packet of unusually strangled publicity-speak that somehow managed to make a rivetingly suspenseful story seem almost dull: "In an alienated world, where drugs are a leit motif [*sic*], where federal agents deal in dope, and old people bide their time by the flickering TV, Stone's characters make small gestures of love and loyalty toward each other." Bob had not been working especially closely with the editor, Austin Olney, though he did call on him a couple of times in the prepublication period. Houghton's Boston location seemed rather far away from publishing's gravitational center in New York. Absent from their hometown since 1967, the Stones in Amherst felt a little out of the loop themselves. There were no plans for a book tour. When Bob asked about publicity, Olney replied, "We'll put a notice in the *Globe*."

Then, in November 1974, the reviews began to roll in. Richard Locke, in the all-important *New York Times Book Review*, sneered at the plot as "melodramatic" and was inclined to disparage what he called "a narrative meditation on the counter-culture. Its subject and complex, ironic tone prompt the thought that the 1960's could be described in a chain of aphorisms, oldies but goodies: History is a nightmare from which I am trying to awake. Those who cannot remember the past are condemned to repeat it. Turn on, tune in, drop out. Blow your mind. The tigers of wrath are wiser than the horses of instruction. Sooner murder an infant in its cradle than nurse unacted desires. Let it all hang out. Let it be. Let it bleed. Sorry about that. Stonewall it.

"Or one could play the from-to-to waltz: from Martin Luther King and SDS to Angela Davis and the SLA; from Dylan and the Beatles to Alice Cooper and Charles Manson; from Laos and Vietnam to Greece and Chile; from Nixon to Exxon; from Watts to Boston. The beat goes on."

But then Locke began to take the book more seriously, noting that it is "the first novel by a man young enough to have been involved in the counter-culture and to have seen Vietnam as a journalist that makes intelligent, imaginative and horrifying connections between the war, the counter-culture and heroin." He compared Stone's novel favorably to earlier attempts to capture the 1960s in fiction by a pride of literary lions: Mailer, Bellow, Updike, Malamud. Quoting the whole of Stone's epigraph from *Heart of Darkness*, Locke noted the novel's descent from Conrad and (less accurately) Hemingway. With a few deft comparisons and contrasts Locke picked Stone out of the swirl of contemporary fiction writers (not forgetting a slash at one: "Joyce Carol Oates sounds like an effusive hysteric beside him"), gave him credit for being funny at times, complimenting "his ability to deliver real experience—physical, mental, moral, social, political; he's a real American novelist, like Bellow, not an esthete or a show-off or a simple confessor." Best of all, Locke seemed to understand the depth of thought behind the action, and finished by dubbing Stone "one of our best novelists under forty."

Dog Soldiers was covered by the *Daily News*, where Bob had once been a copyboy. A brief notice in *Newsweek* was most valuable for the prominence of its venue, but the novel got more substantial coverage in *Time*—two columns, including a startling comparison to Chaucer's "The Pardoner's Tale," with a headline, "Flowers of Evil," drawn from Baudelaire. In *Esquire*, Rust Hills, not yet the close friend of the Stones he was to become, compared the book to *The Maltese Falcon* and *The Thirty-Nine Steps*. Hills was the first to declare that *Dog Soldiers* had captured the essence of the Vietnam War: "All wars, I guess, are senseless; but the Vietnam war was archetypically senseless. And it's the very senselessness of it, the immorality of it to begin with, the—here, I've got it now, what I want to say—the perverse futility of all the death and violence of that war—that's what Robert Stone somehow manages to capture in *Dog Soldiers*." The *St. Louis Post-Dispatch* compared Stone to both Raymond Chandler and William Faulkner. "We don't get reviews like this!" Austin Olney exclaimed, perhaps with as much embarrassment as satisfaction (at least as Bob and Janice understood him). The cherry on top of what was shaping up to be quite a nice cake was delivered via *The Washington Post Book World* by William McPherson, who called *Dog Soldiers* "the most important novel of the year."

———

For the structure of *Dog Soldiers*, Stone uses a convergence pattern similar to the one deployed in *A Hall of Mirrors*, though in the case of *Dog Soldiers* all of the principals know each other before the story begins. John Converse is married to Marge (née Bender), an antiheroine of dark allure, and well enough acquainted with Ray Hicks to trust him to deliver an extremely valuable package of heroin to Marge for resale in the United States. It's a simple plan, as one might say. Hicks, a combat veteran now serving aboard an aircraft carrier, will smuggle the package to Converse's wife; Converse will join her after the offload of the drugs; everybody cashes in and lives happily ever after.

There's some evidence here of Stone's habit of scattering various traits of his own around a cast of characters. Marge Converse, though she shares the gray eyes of Rheinhardt's lost love and also the name of one of the Burr sisters, really is not in any way a Janice avatar. So far from being able to pull some Bob-like character back from the brink of utter ruin, she has very little power to do that for herself. When the story opens she's working a dead-end job in a triple-X movie theater, desultorily caring for their small daughter, Janey, and dabbling in narcotics (Percocet and the far more dangerous Dilaudid) even before a virtually unlimited supply of pure heroin falls into her hands. Still, Marge is not, or not yet, the sort of desperate street addict held up by the mid-1970s media as an example to avoid. She has a reasonably stable middle-class background: her father a successful proprietor of a clutch of tabloid newspapers; her husband the author (albeit quite a while ago) of one successful play. What Marge has in common with Robert Stone is the addictive personality, a hapless attraction to narcotics, and a capacity for total irresponsibility when caught in the coils of such drugs.

In fact Marge is an instigator in the drug-smuggling scheme, writing her husband in Vietnam: "—why the hell not? I'm prepared to take chances at this point and I don't respond to the moral objections. The way things are set up the people concerned have nothing good coming to them and we'll just be occupying a place that someone else will fill fast enough if they get the chance." That last line is a rather clean iteration of ethical relativism. Once she has high-grade heroin in her veins, Marge will go a step further: "I'm just a little slip of a thing, but I'm all primary process. I live the examined life. Not one funny little thing gets by me."

Most obviously an authorial alter-ego, John Converse shares Stone's early-1970s sense of himself as a directionless one-hit wonder. Converse inherits his author's experiences in Saigon, inhabiting the same sort of demimonde populated by dubious international journalists, hustlers, adventurers, and adventuresses, not to mention a wide spectrum of local talent. Many details of the *Guardian* piece, including the lizard-smashing anomaly, the Great Elephant Zap, and the service of heroin in girlie bars, are reprised in the novel's meander through the "existentialist caves" of Saigon. Converse, during a period of employment in his father-in-law's tabloid consortium, has been responsible for producing headlines like "Skydiver Devoured by Starving Birds" (for a time used as a working title for *Dog Soldiers*). His demented mother very much resembles Gladys in her dotage—her decaying pretensions to gentility wrapped around an odor of death. A scene in which Converse takes her to lunch is probably as close as Stone ever came to portraying the late stage of that mother-son relationship.

Unlike Stone, Converse considers himself to be a complete physical coward, especially after his one experience under fire has flattened him to the ground in abject terror, "a little stingless quiver in the earth. That was all there was of him, all there had ever been." This episode is very likely based on whatever had happened to Stone during his observation of Operation Dewey Canyon II. Converse comes away with "several insights," notably this one: "the ordinary physical world through which one shuffled heedless and half-assed toward nonentity was capable of composing itself, at any time and without notice, into a massive instrument of agonizing death." It's very different from Stone's own reaction to the battle in the harbor in Port Said in the 1950s: "God, I'm glad I'm here. I'm so glad that I'm here." Plainly, Converse would prefer not to have been there. He emerges as "the celebrated living dog, preferred over dead lions." Thenceforward, "fear was extremely important to Converse. It was the medium through which he perceived his own soul, the formula through which he could confirm his own existence. I am afraid, Converse reasoned, therefore I am."

As for any moral objections to the procurement of heroin, he can simply tell himself, "if the world is going to contain elephants pursued by flying men, people are just naturally going to want to get high."

Ray Hicks, the third principal, is sometimes said to be entirely based on Neal Cassady. Like Cassady, Hicks is a man of action, and the setting of his climactic death scene probably relates to Cassady's 1968 death while walking a railroad track out of San Miguel de Allende, very possibly overdosed on Seconal at the time. After that the resemblance fizzles out; Hicks is relatively closemouthed (a long way from the sort of speed-fueled chatterbox Cassady was); though he shares Stone's weakness for alcohol, he's not much of a recreational drug user, and he operates (usually) with a steely self-discipline based on a martial reworking of Zen similar to that of medieval Japanese samurai. "Dog Soldier" designates a member of a Cheyenne warrior society renowned for fighting stubbornly to the death. The fact that the original title in the Houghton contract was singular— "The Dog Soldier"—suggests that Hicks may have been the first character Stone conceived.

As in Stone's case, Hicks's discipline can be eroded by alcohol rather quickly. On the eve of his delivery of the package to Marge, he goes on a long barhopping expedition during which his guard drops very low and he comes close to blowing the whole operation. At the end of the novel, Stone infuses Hicks's memory with his own formative childhood experience. Meeting Hicks for the first time, Marge is repulsed, thinking of him as "this scented death's head harlequin." It has gotten back to Hicks through a mutual friend that Converse once called him a "psychopath," something which bothers him from time to time.

But Hicks's martial discipline and his capacity for swift, unreflecting violence come in very handy when the Converses' apartment in San Francisco is attacked by a couple of bandits who are after the heroin, soon after Hicks shows up to deliver it. (Converse has not yet returned from Vietnam.) The action scene is done with Stone's charcoal palette, through the eyes of a stunned Marge watching maneuvers she can hardly understand, as if they were skits from the Keystone Kops. Hicks subdues the attackers with their own weapons and shackles them to the plumbing with their own cuffs. It's a good samurai victory, if temporary. Hicks and Marge grab the drugs and some money from the bank, ditch Janey with a woman friend of Hicks's (who will later deliver her to Marge's father), and flee south in the direction of Los Angeles. According to Janice, the escape of Hicks with Marge in tow was originally inspired by an episode in the

Ramayana, where Ravana, King of the Demons, kidnaps Princess Sita, the wife of Rama.

Converse is endowed with Stone's gift for mordantly evocative repartee. Leaving Hicks with the heroin in Vietnam, he announces, "As of now it can rain blood and shit. I got nowhere to go." Both halves of this statement are proved out in the States, where as Hicks warns Converse, "it's gone funny." Funny peculiar, not funny ha-ha. Hicks further warns Converse, "I don't know who you're running with but I bet they got no sense of irony."

But maybe they do. When Converse gets home to find his apartment trashed and his family missing, the bandits have left "a devil on the wall above Janey's crib. It had horns and bat wings and a huge erect phallus." There's got to be a touch of irony in that. For a couple of days Converse manages to stay a step ahead of his pursuers, Keystone Kops–style again. He shakes them off by running through Macy's, and shelters for a night in the office of the tabloid he once worked for, where Marge's father and other erstwhile colleagues milk a few more bizarre headlines out of him. The surreal lunch with his demented mother is part of his evasion strategy.

But finally the pursuers, Danskin and Smitty, do catch Converse, drug him, and drag him to a motel room where they torture him to discover the whereabouts of the heroin. Danskin wisecracks, does accents, performs obscure parables. The television, playing *Only Angels Have Wings*, is turned up loud to cover Converse's screams while his captors are burning his face on an electric stove. "You're not gonna make it, kid," says the television, then, "Our land is your land." There's all the irony you can eat.

A backpack full of pure heroin makes the perfect MacGuffin (doubtless the reason Rust Hills's review invoked *The Maltese Falcon*) because it doesn't have to be artificially infused with attraction; in real life as in this fiction, everybody really does want a panacea for any kind of pain, physical or psychological, plus a cure for desire—once you have enough pure heroin, you really don't want anything else. At the same time, in the manner of Mark Twain's "The Million Pound Bank Note," it's perplexingly difficult for Hicks and Marge to get rid of it.

Their escape route tours the dark side of hippiedom—first stop Hicks's remote mountain cabin, which they find infested by a couple of young outlaws in charge of a pair of probably kidnapped teenage girls. After flushing them out, Hicks counsels Marge, "we're not in a position to make a big thing over something like those kids. You walk around these canyons enough you'll come across a sleeping bag full of bones. . . . Fuck up a little bit once and the next bag of bones is you."

The cabin and environs make a good set for psychopathy; Hicks has stashed there a Land Rover and an M16 assault rifle complete with grenade launcher and plenty of ammo. He considers betraying Marge to facilitate his own getaway, but instead falls in love with her, after his fashion. "Because of his nature and circumstance, the most satisfying part of Hicks' sexual life had come to be masturbation—he preferred it to prostitutes because it was more sanitary and took less time. He did not take it lightly when, rarely, one woman pleased him, and his deepest pleasures were intellectual and emotional. He became a hoarder, careful and slow to the point of obsessiveness, a thinker."

Next stop L.A. and the moviemaking milieu that Stone had learned about while scripting the ill-fated *WUSA*. Of interest here are the fixers and fakers who flit through the shadows, incarnated in the person of Eddie Peace, an old connection of Hicks's who promises to find a buyer for the smack but instead delivers a couple of dilettantes: Jody and her husband, Gerald—who's writing a novel! . . . of all things, and "wants to do something honest and real about the heroin scene." Annoyed by the uselessness of the encounter, Hicks furnishes a lethal dose of honest reality, hitting Gerald in the vein with the high-grade pure, then walking out with Marge, leaving Eddie to dispose of the body and also (more interestingly) the hysterical screaming wife. (Bob had not intended for Gerald to die in this scene, though most readers think that he did.)

On to a different mountaintop near the Mexican border, this one crowned by an old mission church, surrounded by a psychedelic compound devised by Hicks's "old roshi" Dieter, and built by his followers, who seem to have all departed by the time Marge and Hicks arrive, leaving Dieter alone with his son Kjell. The setting, tricked out with lights and loudspeakers spun through the woods descending from the mission, resembles the Prankster kingdom at La Honda, but Dieter doesn't take after Kesey all *that* much, though the feeling of post-guru-hood may have some root in Stone's visits to the Keseys in Oregon, after the Pranksters had dispersed.

Dieter hasn't moved on anywhere, but remains forlornly perched on the ruins of an unfulfilled dream, if one doesn't go so far as to call it a hallucination. Below the mission structure are caves once sacred to precolonial Indians and much later to pupils (among whom Hicks was once a star) of the cultish version of Zen that Dieter espouses. The caves also serve as secret passageways, and Hicks, on his way to ambush the pursuers who have traced him and Marge to the foot of the mountain, discovers inside "a Day-Glo detritus of old highs. There Are No Metaphors, it said—in violet—on one wall. Everywhere he turned the light there were fossilized acid hits, a riot of shattered cerebration, entombed."

By this time all the principals have converged on the point of climax. Now in charge of their master, a crooked federal agent named Antheil, Danskin and Smitty have recaptured Converse and brought him to the foot of Dieter's mountain as a hostage. A standoff ensues, and when Converse is pushed forward to plead for the other party to give up the dope, Marge decides to comply, but Hicks secretly gives her a decoy package and hides the real one. Before Antheil's group can discover the deception, Hicks has crept down through the caves and opened fire on them with his assault rifle and M70 grenade launcher.

"It was Dienbienphu, Stalingrad," Converse thinks, rolling for cover after an inconclusive struggle over Smitty's handgun. "The din of battle swelled over them—bazookas, mortars, rockets, tank guns—" Then Converse realizes that Dieter, at Hicks's request, is broadcasting these sound effects through speakers in the trees. The firefight has turned magnificently psychedelic—although some of the bullets are real. In a reprise of the television's coincidentally apt commentary on the previous torture scene, Dieter turns to reciting koans of his own device over the sound system: "Form Is Not Different From Nothingness. Nothingness Is Not Different From Form."

Converse, less fearful than previously but acutely interested in adhering to his corporeal form, alerts Hicks to his friendly presence with the Vietnamese phrase "*Chieu hoi*" (which means something like "welcome return" and was the title of a PSYOPS program during the war). Hicks is wounded and at least some of the assailants have gotten away, thus remaining a threat. Hicks tells Marge and Converse to go get his Land Rover and head for a railroad crossing a few miles away, while he recovers the real package and walks the track to meet them there.

Heroin in hand, Hicks shoots up for the pain, then has Dieter help bandage his dangerous thoracic wound. Dieter tries to talk him into getting rid of the drug, going so far as to run for the edge of the cliff with the package. Hicks, believing Dieter is trying to steal it for his own profit, shoots him dead. "Lousy stupid thing," he thinks when he recognizes his mistake. "Like everything else."

Hicks's long solo march to the horizon, known to aficionados as "the Zen death scene," is an extraordinary tour de force. "He closed his eyes to the moonlight and began to erect a blue triangle against the base of his skull. The background was deep black and there was some effort involved in delineating the borders of blue. At the heart of the triangle, he introduced a bright red circle and within the circle he concentrated his pain." This meditation permits him to keep going, down the mountain, through the woods, and out across the salt flats, following the railroad tracks. Pushing on into daybreak, he rehearses the key points of his life: his failed marriage to a Japanese woman, and a bleak little comedy he calls the Battle of Bob Hope, in which most of the men in his squad were pointlessly killed. Also, "there was a child around somewhere. . . . He knew immediately that the child would be the most dangerous thing he had to face, the hardest thing to get by."

In fact it's the boy Bob Stone from the Chicago shelter, masquerading as Hicks's child self: "A turned-around kid who made up stories—wise guy, card player. They all made up stories in the Booth Shelter, they all told lies about themselves." Hicks rebukes the kid, who's accompanying him as a full-blown hallucination at this point. "I know you. I wish I didn't but I do. You better do something about the way you cringe and whine. I don't want to see you do it." These are in fact qualities of both Stone's and Converse's worst versions of themselves—which Hicks has used Zen and the Marine Corps to purge out of his own being.

Both reality and the meditation fade. The triangle is "distorted in heat. It can't hold its shape. Another hallucinatory companion asks Hicks what he's carrying and he replies: 'Pain, man. Everybody's. Yours too if you only knew it.'" The Christ-like overtones of the pain-bearing passage are obscured by the fact that Hicks is still humping heroin. With the world's pain, he's also carrying the ultimate painkiller, but is too impaired by his wound to unstrap the pack. Not long afterward, Hicks is dead.

Marge and Converse, meanwhile, are enjoying a subdued reunion and a sort of rebirth, in the sense of finding slightly better versions of themselves. Though still in as much danger as he ever was, Converse is no longer running on fear alone. He's not so craven in the hands of Antheil and company, and bold enough to save Marge from a bullet by snatching down Smitty's gun at the beginning of the previous night's firefight. Marge is impressed by his unfamiliar competence in tasks like hot-wiring Hicks's Land Rover. Previously indifferent to moral arguments, she now makes one herself, persuading Converse to meet Hicks not to keep trying to complete the drug deal but to help a friend in need. "Sometimes," she argues, "people do simple-minded things like that. They take a chance to help their friends."

If the novel affirmed that assertion outright it would be sentimental, and *Dog Soldiers* is definitely not. Although Converse and Marge do find Hicks's corpse and the heroin on the tracks (and decide to leave the latter for Antheil to enjoy), Converse's response to Marge's argument is oblique in the extreme. "I don't know what I'm doing or why I do it or what it's like." Then, with more confidence, "Nobody knows. That's the principle we were defending over there. That's why we fought the war."

These characters have come a very long way from "an ethics of humane metaphysics and natural virtue." In fact, the absence of motive is striking in all the main actors of the story. Asked by Charmian, his sometime lover in Saigon, what he'll do with his payment for moving the heroin, Converse admits he doesn't know.

"Shit, you *don't* know, do you? You know you want it though, don't you?"

Converse's reply is unclear even on the second point.

"I desire to serve God," Converse said, laughing himself. "And to grow rich, like all men." More snappy, empty repartee. Later in the States he tries telling a colleague at the tabloid, "All this shit. It was because of Charmian." The colleague suggests that he must be in love with her but Converse tells him, "No. Not at all. I was over there and there was this girl and I wanted to please her." This intention too seems remarkably weak. Later still, though, when Converse is held hostage by Antheil and company on the slopes of Dieter's mountain, "He felt intensely aware and alive, the way he had felt in the moment when he decided to buy the dope for Charmian." It's as if his secret purpose in the whole extravaganza was to blast himself out of some kind of moral torpor.

Minutes after meeting her for the first time, Hicks makes a pass at Marge, and "it came to her clearly that it was what she wanted. Suddenly the whole terrifying enterprise had composed itself to incarnation—this man, this scented death's head harlequin, with his fingers in her flesh, was embodiment to it all.

"There was no power in her. She sought the stale mouth, warmed to the beak across her belly, curled herself into the fear, the danger, the death. The thing itself."

It's all rather similar to Converse's credo: *I fear, therefore I am.* But on the slopes of Dieter's mountain, he begins to feel a faint possibility of acting on some other principle. It emerges from a story he once wrote about an idealistic young medic killed in the war. Though he published the story in a mood of pure cynicism, the medic's life and death "had provided for him a solitary link with an attitude he publicly pretended to share—but which he had not experienced for years and never thoroughly understood. It was the attitude in which people acted on coherent ethical apprehensions that seemed real to them. He had observed that people in the grip of this attitude did things which were quite as confused and ineffectual as the things other people did; nevertheless he held them in a certain—perhaps a merely superstitious—esteem."

Though Converse doesn't recognize it, Hicks actually is such a person—as Dieter tries to explain to Marge, calling Hicks "your natural man of Zen. . . . He acted everything out. There was absolutely no difference between thought and action for him." In some contexts this quality can get you called a psychopath, but in Dieter's context it is admirable, and he credits Hicks with "enormous self-respect. Whatever he believed in he had to embody absolutely." In this sense, the Zen death scene is not simply a suicidal act but also a successful self-actualization.

The heroin itself, the ultimate painkiller, is much more than a mere MacGuffin. But the characters commonly call it "shit," because that's also what it is. Marge, declaring, "I want to get straight," has just enough willpower to leave it behind. One senses that she and Converse may have painfully, indeed comically, stumbled into some possibility of redeeming their lives. But there is no close-up of their departure from the stage; they are last seen in the distance, through the harsh eyes of Antheil, as he collects the heroin from Hicks's corpse.

There's a special horror in actions like those that compose the plot of *Dog Soldiers* being undertaken for no reason at all. The entire story stems from its actors being morally at sea, a situation that in turn derives from the way the Vietnam War and resistance to it had scrambled the American moral compass, confusing everyone's previously automatic sense of the right way to navigate the world. But it's a chicken-and-egg question; maybe the nausea of moral uncertainty was endemic to American society all along and the war only brought the symptoms to the surface. With all civilized adornment stripped away, the reader is left to confront *primary process. The thing itself. There it is*, irreducibly. No point has become the point.

———

On January 22, 1975, Austin Olney wrote cheerfully to Bob that *Dog Soldiers* sales had "passed the 19,000 mark." He also pointed out that Houghton had spent or was committed to spending $17,000 in advertising—an issue that both Bob and his agent had complained about. Candida Donadio could be blistering on such subjects, and Olney's February letter to her had a more pronounced defensive flavor. Late delivery, and that single-spaced manuscript glitch, meant that "we were publishing late in the season, and had the problem of bridging the book over Christmas. In addition to all of this the sales force was having a hard time getting the book into the stores against the complaints of Vietnam and drugs."

This sense of unsavory subject matter may have contributed to Houghton's apparent under-confidence in the book at the beginning, though Olney argued to Donadio that the gradual build of promotion had been deliberate from the start. "Our whole strategy, as you will recall, was to start off modestly and wait for the quotes to come in because we had no particular selling handle and no one was going to believe Houghton's enthusiasm for the book as much as they would objective critics'. The quotes came in but they were slow in coming. . . . On Bob's next, for example, the strategy might be different because now he has a large and passionate following, but would it have worked on *Dog Soldiers*?" In any case, Olney insisted, "we have really broken our backs in advertising the book." The ad budget, by then increased to $19,000, "amounts to darn near a dollar a copy sold and I don't see who can complain about that." This caviling over relatively small sums could cease once Ballantine paid $100,000 for paperback rights to the novel in August 1974.

Dog Soldiers had proved a winner, whatever wobbles there may have been along the way. The seal of success was affixed that fall, when the novel became a finalist, and then the co-winner of the 1975 National Book Award. The company was distinguished in the extreme; other finalists were Philip Roth, Donald Barthelme, Mark Smith, Grace Paley, Toni Morrison, Gail Godwin, Joseph Heller, and Vladimir Nabokov. In the event, *Dog Soldiers* split the prize with Thomas Williams's *The Hair of Harold Roux*. Split decisions are rare in the National Book Award. One of the judges, the novelist Stanley Elkin, had held out to include the Williams book, and was proud enough of having done so to leak the information.

For the first time, Bob's acceptance speech showed a consciousness of his role as spokesman for an era (or maybe it was just the first public expression of such an awareness). The nine paragraphs seemed meant to lay claim to the mantle of novelist as public intellectual (a garment that Hemingway was probably the last to completely fill out, and to which Norman Mailer was still, erratically, clinging). This very short essay reveals the depth of Stone's historical thinking and the particularly potent way he applied it to the contemporary scene.

"In its confident moments, the American liberal middle class is capable of bringing to bear immense reserves of practical moral energy. During the early nineteenth century, for example, when the transcendentalist spirit which had been incubating in the chill womb of Calvinism, shaped by Calvinism's alternating certainty and doubt, came forth proclaiming an ethic of humane metaphysics and natural virtue. The Genevan darkness broke up under all that pure American light and slavery was driven from the land. If the spirit thereafter lay buried under the carcass of Mammon, it remained alive." Not half bad for an autodidact, or maybe only an autodidact could have produced this synthesis.

"The era of the sixties began with its renaissance," Stone continues. "Many tears of liberation were shed. There was a lot of embracing. You would have had to have been without a heart not to be moved by some of the things that were said and done. You would have had to inhabit a hell of your own despair not to believe in the hope that the consciousness of a generation was being gentled and enlarged, that, however minutely, the perception of the nation would become more responsive to what was best in itself." If these seemingly idealistic statements are tempered with a touch of satirical skepticism, the darker embitterment that would come later has not yet arrived; at the time of this writing, Stone was still young.

The snake in this reborn Eden was, of course, the Vietnam War. "One might say that it was an era dominated by the good intentions of the American middle class; abroad it was a time of chaos and war because those good intentions, while they are a generally progressive force domestically, do not travel well." Inevitably, Americans thrown into turmoil by the war, the resistances to it, and the larger destabilizations of society that followed, "were forced to rediscover one of the harshest and irremediable facts of life—that the universe belongs to the strong. That weakness always fails; strength prevails. Confronting this, many looked within for the core of strength and certitude that would sustain the vision and found that it wasn't there." Surely there's a shadow of lapsed Catholicism in these sentences, for Stone is describing a world without God, though invoking no holy name, unless in absence.

In Stone's view, the loss of inner certitude requires starting the quest for it all over again. "It was an old simple story, a breakthrough and a fall from grace, a few steps forward and a few steps back, man's fate. We'll go on enacting it of course because it has to be acted out and we're all there is. We'll go on because we have no choice and we'll go on creating myths for ourselves, taking our sustenance where we find it. We'll choose, some of us, to believe that there's some level of our common consciousness where it's all known, everything necessary—nothing forgotten, nothing lost sight of. And that this old process—the description of which is the justification of our literature—is our infinitely comic, infinitely painful stumbling toward it."

We're all there is rings out as a definitive declaration—any and all of the rest is no more than mythologizing, on that point the speaker is clear. "What a misfortune," a character in Stone's next novel will declare, "that we have only each other." Neither Stone nor most of the people of his invention seem to be expecting guidance or salvation from any deus ex machina or coming from anywhere else. And yet, however paradoxically, between the lines of the conclusion of this 1974 speech is some support for the claim Stone would make much later, that he was the only theological novelist working in America.

———

Dog Soldiers was an outlier when published in 1974, or it might be better to call it a harbinger. The bulk of combat-centric Vietnam War novels (most of them written by veterans of the military, rather than the press corps) did not begin to be published until several years later, and that wave crested in the early 1980s. In the mid-1970s window, Stone's book was regarded as the definitive work of fiction on the war by readers who found it both curious and curiously appropriate that only a small percentage of its action took place in Vietnam, and practically none of it in combat.

In the 1980s, Stone recalled for an essay in *Harper's Magazine* that "working in Vietnam, I found myself witnessing a mistake ten thousand miles long, a mistake on the American scale. I began to write a novel set in Saigon. As it progressed, I realized that the logic of the thing required that everybody make his or her own way back home, into the America of the early 1970s. The early to mid-'70s still seem to me, in retrospect, like a creepy, evil time. A lot of bills from the '60s were coming up for presentation. *Dog Soldiers* was my reaction to the period."

In a letter written in 1999, more than twenty years after *Dog Soldiers* first appeared, a writer friend of Stone's named Bettina Drew reported that she had recently watched a videocassette of the film adaptation, *Who'll Stop the Rain*. "Dan Benvenuto, a Medusa handyman who stores stuff in my garage, watched it with me. His verdict: 'That was deep. They brought the war home with them. I know a lot of guys like that.'"

PART THREE

A FLAG FOR SUNRISE

1
HOLLYWOOD, TAKE TWO

In March 1974, the Stones bought their own property in Amherst, an old farmhouse at 360 South Pleasant Street, complete with its own large barn. In June they moved in, and with the help of Michael Hardy (a scion of rural Pennsylvania) used residual manure from the barn to fertilize a substantial vegetable garden. Hardy himself was living in one of two apartments the house contained—one in the basement and one in the attic. The attic apartment was soon occupied by Erika Hollister, a University of Massachusetts student and the sister of Hardy's girlfriend Alexis Hollister, who shared the basement with him. Income from the apartment rentals covered most of the Stones' monthly mortgage payment (although Erika sometimes defrayed part of her rent by cooking for the family)—which was a relief, since Bob's income and employment were both unpredictable. The Stones had borrowed a little over $40,000 to make the purchase, a few months before the publication of *Dog Soldiers*, without knowing how the novel would perform.

So the venture was both exciting and alarming. Writing her parents soon after the deal was closed, Janice noted that "we are really going to be starting from scratch again in terms of furniture and household gear," and planned to come to Bogota to retrieve some of her own things stored there, plus anything useful the Burr household didn't happen to be using. She predicted the sellers would leave some of their furniture when they moved out. "I hope we end up with something that looks like a home, rather than a gypsy campsite. If it doesn't work out, we can always fill our barn with hay and live out there for the summer." Another household acquisition was a two-month-old German shepherd named Dougal, "not quite housebroken yet but trying to cooperate."

Bob took an involuntary hiatus from teaching at the end of the spring semester of 1975. He had been on a three-year contract at Amherst, and there were no courses available for him in the academic year 1975–76. That $100,000 advance from Ballantine for a paperback edition of *Dog Soldiers* was coming in very handy. Candida Donadio was working on a film sale for the novel and a couple of scriptwriting deals for Bob, one for *Dog Soldiers* and another to be based on a 1974 short story, "Aquarius Obscured."

The story appears to have begun as an unwritten episode or outtake from *Dog Soldiers* in which Marge (high on Dilaudid) and her daughter, Janey, visit an aquarium shortly before the arrival of Ray Hicks at the Converse apartment (an event referred to in the novel but not rendered in full). In the short story the situation changes substantially; the mother, now called Alison and taking synthetic hallucinogens instead of Dilaudid, receives a long world-historical lecture from the porpoise in a tank. Though Donadio first hoped to sell "Aquarius Obscured" to *Playboy*, it eventually landed in *American Review*; not long after she brought in a $25,000 deal for Bob to adapt the story for Universal (although in the end the script was never written).

There were a handful of foreign sales for *Dog Soldiers*, and, most substantially, Donadio (apparently unconvinced by Austin Olney's protestations) had arranged for Bob to leave Houghton for a much more lucrative deal at Knopf for his next novel: a $135,000 advance to be paid out in monthly stipends of $3,720—income that would keep the Stone family afloat for three years. This deal was sealed in January 1976, with a stipulation that Bob must deliver the book by December 1978 or be liable to refund the money (and also a clause requiring demonstration of "suitable progress" in December 1977). The package partnered Stone with Robert Gottlieb, then a star in the editing world. Negotiating the contract was apparently rough: according to Janice, Donadio "told Bob that after the stiff telephone discussions, with her demanding better terms, she would hang up the phone and go throw up."

Gottlieb for his part retained a very long memory of "Candida's ultra-tricky ways," but his enthusiasm for Bob's fiction was unqualified. "I know the book will be very good," he wrote to his new author, "and I know we'll try our best for us. The rest will be in the lap of the gods—as good a place as any I guess." "Untitled Novel" was the only definition of the expected book in the contract, but Stone had apparently described a sixteenth-century historical novel to Gottlieb.

With these streams of income the Stones were flush enough for Bob to take a break from teaching (and also Janice planned to get another job in social work when she had finished her master's degree). The house on South Pleasant Street was the first home they had owned since their flat in London, and they wanted to stay in one place for a while, to give Deidre (fourteen) and Ian (twelve) a stronger sense of stability.

——•——

The new house was in easy walking distance of the Amherst campus, but also backed into a large expanse of pasture and woodland, stretching south to a sizable stream called the Fort River. Despite his fondness for grog and a very heavy smoking habit, Bob was not a sedentary person, and he took considerable advantage of this new proximity to the great outdoors. In winter all four Stones took up cross-country skiing, though "Bob found cross-country a bit boring. He was always looking for a hill that he could ski down, as fast as possible. He thought he might take downhill skiing lessons at Mount Tom [a few miles south in Holyoke], but never got around to it."

Hardy was a hunter and also a fisherman, who sometimes took Ian, Bob, and Janice's younger brother Peter (now enrolled in UMass) fishing in a rowboat on the Quabbin Reservoir, a good-size body of water about twenty miles east of Amherst. He also kept two vizslas, Hungarian hunting dogs that resemble Weimaraners, but with a stockier build and reddish-brown coats, and would hunt pheasant with Bob in the fields and woodlands south of the house.

Presently a swimming pool was installed, over Janice's objection that pools were "unattractive and pretentious"—as a compromise it was located a good distance from the house. Bob's argument was "that as a Hollywood writer, he should have one, was entitled to one." Having failed to reach him by phone with some compliments about the story "Aquarius Obscured," Candida Donadio quipped in a letter, "all you guys are probably at poolside," in the classic Hollywood manner. "Yeah." The pool's location was remote enough that Peter, who lived with the Stones while completing his engineering degree, felt comfortable starting a marijuana patch behind it, though "the crop wasn't very potent," in the view of local consumers.

Then, in 1976, Bob did go back to Hollywood—with enthusiasm. Donadio had signed him up to write a screenplay for a *Dog Soldiers* movie, to be directed by Karel Reisz, starring Nick Nolte as Ray Hicks, Tuesday Weld as Marge Converse, and Michael Moriarty as John Converse. Reisz was a prestigious director, a Czechoslovakian Jew who'd escaped Nazi Germany as a child in 1938. He had served in the British Royal Air Force during the war; his parents died in Auschwitz. His first feature film was an adaptation of Alan Sillitoe's novel *Saturday Night and Sunday Morning*; his most recent, *The Gambler*, loosely based on the Dostoyevsky novel of the same title, had been a successful vehicle for James Caan.

Since *WUSA* Bob had written an original screenplay, *Phosphorescence*; inscrutable and nearly plotless, the film was never made, but the project left him feeling more experienced and confident as a screenwriter. Optimistic (and very happy about the fresh income stream), he took Deidre with him to California for the first set of meetings with the filmmakers. But the first draft of the script ran into trouble with the producers (Herb Jaffe, a literary agent turned producer who'd once been Donadio's employer, was prominent among this group) over the character of Marge—in the novel an instigator of the Converse couple's drug scheme, and a reasonably willing, if passive, partner in Hicks's later effort to sell the heroin for profit. She also, before the main action of the novel begins, already has a considerable narcotics habit of her own. The producers felt, adamantly, that Marge had to be rewritten as an innocent dupe of Converse and Hicks, in order to win the sympathy of the movie audience. (Preserving Weld's star quality might have played some part in this urgency as well.) It was also true that Bob's draft of the script weighed in at 175 pages, substantially too long, but he quit the picture over the Marge controversy. Judith Rascoe, a friend from the Stanford and Perry Lane days, was brought in to carry out the makeover and finish the script.

Bob shared credit for the screenplay, however much the end result displeased him, and stayed friends with Rascoe. He still got a good payday (not quite as good as it might have been), but as the aesthetic coup de grace, the producers did some sort of research which demonstrated that no one would buy tickets for a movie with the words "dog" or "soldier" in the title. The picture, which featured a number of Creedence Clearwater songs, was rechristened (anemically and irrelevantly) as *Who'll Stop the Rain*. From this fiasco, Bob claimed to have learned never to title a movie with a Swedish diphthong.

However alienated he felt by these developments, Bob still followed the picture on location in Durango, Mexico, where a Hollywood version of the novel's fictional version of Kesey's Prankster compound at La Honda had been erected. Janice later came to join him, noting from the corner of her eye that Bob's flirtation with Weld did not appear to be very serious. Bob would later draw on his position as ex-screenwriter on location to create a similar situation for Gordon Walker in his fourth novel, *Children of Light*.

During this second Hollywood project, Bob did form a more durable attachment to Lucy Saroyan, an actress and photographer, the painfully estranged daughter of the writer William Saroyan. Reisz had introduced them. This relationship was one of several that Janice felt she could tolerate. In fact she found Lucy to be likable the couple of times they talked on the phone. Also, Bob had told Janice "the relationship was about drugs, not about sex," which was likely to have been at least partly true, given that Lucy died at fifty-seven from a convergence of cirrhosis of the liver and hepatitis C.

2

DIONYSUS REDUX

Bob developed appendicitis during one of his trips to L.A. to work on the script. He had an appendectomy, and somehow came away from the ordeal with a prescription for quaaludes, a drug that had been developed to treat insomnia but was becoming popular for recreational use. He returned to the East Coast eager to share the discovery with Janice, who was not enthused. "What's the big deal? I asked. You take a sleeping pill and you don't go to sleep? Quaaludes made me want to take a nap. I decided to leave them to Bob, since he liked them so much."

For the next several years, quaaludes were on Bob's menu of intoxicants. Cooperative doctors on both coasts kept him supplied. Also, Lucy had introduced Bob to a West Coast dealer who would mail drugs to Amherst from time to time. Bob, who worried about the extent of his drinking while continuing to drink, may have thought of quaaludes as a substitute for alcohol in the beginning, but in practice he was likely to use both at the same time. On one such occasion, a policeman followed Bob home, presented Janice with Bob's driver's license, "and ordered me not to let him out again that night"—this in a period when the law enforcement attitude toward driving under the influence was far more lenient than now.

Bob's habits impaired the Stones' social life to some extent. It was not unknown for him to pass out at parties. Having over-celebrated the good news of his being hired for the *Dog Soldiers* screenplay, he went to sleep on the couch of the hosts of an Amherst faculty dinner, to Janice's embarrassment. But when alert (which he could remain through the early and middle stages of intoxication) his incisive intelligence and cutting wit made him scintillating company. By the mid-1970s, Bob had acquired a great deal of erudition about subjects that interested him, and a great many subjects interested him. Because most of his knowledge was self-taught, through voracious reading and endlessly curious exploration of the world and the people in it, he trafficked very little in received ideas, unlike many other writers and most other academics. Talking with Bob was very likely to refresh the ideas of the people he knew.

A redoubtable conversationalist, he could also be a dangerous verbal sparring partner. Generally speaking, Bob detested Graham Greene, perhaps because of some superficial similarities between them as writers, which sometimes led to inept comparisons. Yet his description of Greene, from an introduction to *The Quiet American*—"Along with his insight into a fallen world, Greene maintained a lifelong capacity for rage. It is expressed in his virtuoso torrents of sarcasm and loathing"—could as well have been applied to himself, at least on certain occasions.

In 1976, amidst frequent runs to the West Coast for the *Dog Soldiers* script, Bob went with Janice to a writers' conference in Sun Valley, Idaho, where their New York friend Jack Gelber was teaching too. They stayed in Ketchum, where Ernest Hemingway had his last residence—and finally, fatally, shot himself. Many of the Hemingway family still lived in the area, including his fourth and last wife, Mary; son Jack; and granddaughters Joan, Margaux, and Mariel. The Stones met all the Hemingways briefly but did not get to know them well. They spent much of their free time with Carol and Jack Gelber, hiking the mountains and exploring the area—a ski resort in winter and a hunters' and fishermen's paradise. Both couples had brought their children along. In general, summer writers' conferences were in a growth stage, incidentally providing far-flung writers, many of them ensconced in academic programs all over the country, with paying work in pleasant settings, free (or nearly free) vacations for their families, and opportunities to reunite with each other. Bob and Janice left Sun Valley owing some money on their Ketchum condo (thanks to a misunderstanding over the point that the conference did not in fact cover all their lodging expenses), but they returned the following summer.

In the early 1970s, Bob befriended a poet from the Amherst faculty, Anne Lathrop Fessenden, whose eccentricities reminded him of his recently deceased mother. Anne was living with her own ancient mother, who died while riding in Anne's car. She told the story laconically: "And then I realized my mother had died." When one of Anne's other friends on the faculty committed suicide, the phone rang incessantly in her empty office, "with Bob listening next door, wondering who it could be." Much later, he would use this detail for a scene in *Death of the Black-Haired Girl*. At the time, "Bob made a joke of 'the annual faculty suicide.' We didn't know any of them personally but it did seem to be an annual event."

Social demands from students could sometimes be taxing. "One night in 1978 I went with him to dinner at the home of an Amherst student, John Monroe. I wanted to be there so Bob wouldn't drive home drunk. After some hours of drinking and talking, I suggested to Bob that it was time to go, that I was tired. J.M. was displeased, and insisted Bob should stay. I realized that everyone wanted a piece of Bob, and that his students especially felt entitled to his company, day or night. And it was not only the students. He seemed to give himself to everyone. He was like Dionysus, I thought. The world was going to tear him apart, eat him alive."

Bob had the occasional Dionysian episode before a wider public too. Philip Tsiaris, another Amherst student, remembers "one evening while the *Godfather* movie was first playing in the theater in town, Robert came in the theater while the film was on completely drunk and yelling to everyone, 'Why are you watching this shit. This is bullshit. Fucking criminals. These guys are nothing but thugs, don't glorify these animals,' and probably much more said to that effect, replete with expletives." Stone was a writer who, after all, took aesthetic judgments seriously.

———

The Stones' marriage had its tensions during this period. In Amherst, as she improved her professional qualifications for social work, Janice was making efforts to emerge from her perennial shyness, "to become more outgoing and assertive." She joined a Gestalt therapy group led by

Jack Canfield, later to be celebrated as the author of *Chicken Soup for the Soul* and many of its innumerable sequels. She attended a lecture by Ram Dass (government name: Richard Alpert), an early LSD acolyte whom the Stones had briefly encountered in California, now setting himself up as a guru, promoting a fusion of fragments from Eastern religions with assorted hippie platitudes. At the New England Center, which hosted her Gestalt group, she was the subject in a demonstration of Rolfing (chosen for her slender build, as the Rolfer on duty was a woman on the small side) and later went through the whole course of treatments, though seeing little effect after the first.

Bob was not wholly supportive of these activities. When he had known Richard Alpert years before—none too happily—on the periphery of Kesey's Perry Lane circle, he was not impressed by the new Ram Dass avatar. Enticed to a New England Center event, he "made a couple of skeptical, bordering on hostile, remarks." Bob's cynicism, when aggravated, had a real cutting edge; hostile remarks from him could definitely draw blood and be too well and surprisingly constructed for the average person to respond to effectively. The volatility of his temperament, exacerbated by increasing dependence on drink and downers, sometimes caused trouble between him and Janice.

A connoisseur of women of all varieties, Bob was far from above the occasional fling, and Janice, despite their standing agreement to allow each other some latitude in this area, was not above being irked by some of them. Bob's extramarital adventures during this period didn't seem serious enough to threaten the marriage, and the two could even laugh together at certain absurdities, as when Bob was interrupted by a security guard while embracing a student on the floor of his Amherst office. Less amusing to Janice was when she caught Bob kissing one of the Stones' lady tenants in the kitchen. "I was offended. In my own kitchen I didn't want to be running into girls smooching with my husband"—reasonably enough, though the lady in this case assured her the encounter was meaningless.

If such brief passages could be dismissed as trivial, it would have felt more like a betrayal when Bob left Janice alone on South Pleasant Street with Angus Wallace, a challenging houseguest for anyone and with whom she had her own uncomfortable history, to call on Judith Rascoe in New York. But before he had driven very far he thought better of it, made a U-turn, and came home to take care of his wife.

Moments like these proved to both of them the strength of their commitment to each other. "I knew that Bob and I tried to provide a place to stand, for ourselves, for each other. Bob said to me at least once, 'Two against the world is better,' " an idea derived from his embattled childhood alone with his mother. "We stood together, but the ground sometimes seemed less than solid." Janice bought a couple of teddy bears as an anniversary gift: Mimi and Rodolfo from La Bearhème. "We're Our Bears" was the motto for their cozy times; Bob even translated the phrase into Latin. Yet Janice saw that "we were now out of our Mimi and Rodolfo stage of life, and well into what I thought of as our Stanley and Stella (*Streetcar*) phase."

Janice was no teetotaler, but she could control her drinking when Bob could not, which was a subject of many an argument. "I did pitch a sugar bowl at him once. I never wanted to hurt him, and I threw it over his head." This gesture might or might not have been a benefit of the various forms of assertiveness training Janice had undertaken around the same time. "I identified with Grace, the wife in 'Helping,' when she said, 'You got everything I had, Chas. What's left I absolutely require.' But I was never so eloquent. Anyway, most of the story is fiction."

3
THE WORK IN HAND

When teaching at Amherst, Bob had the option of working in his office on campus or in a carrel he was assigned in the library basement. He preferred the latter, "where no students would interrupt. He would wander among the stacks of books," as he described it to Janice, "thinking, talking to himself, startling people. He could also drink there." He also did a lot of real writing there. David Blistein, a student at this time, remembers "being up around six a.m. one morning (which means, undoubtedly, I'd been tripping all the night before), and seeing him walk across the campus to the library. Clearly he was going to work. That's when I knew that writing was work. Wonderful work, but work. He could have been carrying a lunch pail and a hardhat and walking to the coal mines (although I'm sure he looked forward to it more, and was probably hard at it even while walking across campus)."

Without access to those campus work spaces, Bob did his writing at home, first in a room of the barn that "though heated, seemed too dark and depressing to spend much time in." He installed a pool table in the barn instead, and began working in a room by the kitchen, overlooking the backyard. There he typed on an enormous IBM Selectric (the instrument of choice for many writers of the period), "leased for the purpose at great but tax deductible expense," while listening to Robert J. Lurtsema's classical programming on NPR.

The novel in progress was historical—a story based on the career of Jan of Leiden, the illegitimate son of a tailor (a detail that probably appealed to Bob), who was an Anabaptist leader of the Protestant Reformation in Germany during the early sixteenth century. (Anabaptists believed that Christians ought to be baptized as adults capable of reasoned choice, rather than during unconscious infancy; the born-again Christian movement of the twentieth century has a thread of its origin here.)

Jan of Leiden was a flamboyant, potentially tragic figure who arrived in Münster in 1533, soon after the city (previously a Catholic cathedral town) was recognized by treaty as Lutheran. Attracted by inspired ministers already there (including Bernhard Rothmann and Melchior Hofmann), Jan also sent for Jan Matthys, who had baptized him and was considered a prophet. Matthys took power in Münster, expelled the Catholics, and began setting up a communal system of government on principles derived from the Gospels (abolishing money and outlawing private property, for example). The army of a Catholic prince soon laid siege to Münster, and after Matthys was killed during an Easter Sunday sortie, Jan of Leiden proclaimed himself King of Münster and continued developing Matthys's government in the direction of pure theocracy. Some say Jan of Leiden's social system was also openly and expansively polygamous (Jan himself was supposed to have taken sixteen wives in just a couple of years), while others suggest that the polygamy story was mere propaganda circulated by Catholics to justify the sack of Münster in 1535 and the execution of Jan of Leiden and other leaders by extraordinarily savage torture.

Jan of Leiden afterward enjoyed substantial literary immortality, featured as a character in various works from the late sixteenth century to the twenty-first, by writers including Marguerite Yourcenar, Anita Mason, and Richard Powers. The story offered Bob Stone the opportunity to work out aspects of his own religious ambivalence in a context where religious disagreements were literally matters of life and death, where religious leaders wielded real and sometimes absolute temporal power, and where martyrdom was far from being a metaphor. The charisma of cult leaders fascinated him, in part because of his experiences with Kesey. A couple of other twentieth-century pied pipers had recently made the news, including L. Ron Hubbard, the science-fiction writer whose masterpiece turned out to be the Church of Scientology, and Mel Lyman, a banjo and harmonica player from Jim Kweskin's jug band who, after writing a book entitled *Autobiography of a World Savior*, founded a commune called the Lyman Family in Boston's Roxbury neighborhood, thus earning the sobriquet "The East Coast Charles Manson."

The historical situation in sixteenth-century Münster literalized a lot of similar ideas and practices that Bob thought still held sway (in disguised forms) over twentieth-century life, and the dramatic properties of Jan of Leiden's story were attractive. But he could not quite make a full imaginative entry to a period four centuries in the past, and capturing the voices of those characters convincingly gave him enormous trouble.

The novel flagged, and finally fizzled. Surprisingly (or not), quite a lot of its fundamental ideas would make their way into the next book Bob actually finished—a twentieth-century novel called *A Flag for Sunrise*. That radical shift of setting and situation had been brewing somewhere in the back of his mind since a brief trip to Mexico in 1974, if he was not yet consciously aware of it.

4

SOUTH OF THE BORDER

He admires hippies, Celine, Conrad, Dos Passos, William Burroughs," quoth the *New York Post* in a profile of Stone promoting the U.S. publication of *A Hall of Mirrors*, "likes to talk, drink, walk, skin dive and does not disapprove of drugs." If Bob ever admired hippies, it didn't last long—he was more likely to blame them for destructive cheapening of the revelatory experiences he'd enjoyed in the company of Kesey and the original Perry Lane group. His other tastes were accurately reported. Stone was fond of water, in and out of large or small boats; he had never been the sort of sailor who doesn't swim. On the contrary, he was "never happier than in the water," by Janice's recollection.

The skin diving he did in the 1960s involved snorkels, not air tanks.

Not until 1976 did he begin learning to scuba dive. There was more to this interest than mere sport; the deeper dives possible with scuba equipment would attach to his next big subject, although he didn't yet know how.

"I went to Central America in 1978," Bob wrote in a 1988 piece for *Harper's Magazine*, "to go scuba diving while at work on a new novel, and returned to the region several times thereafter. I became acquainted with a few Americans working there. At that time relatively few people in this country knew where Huehuetenango was, and Managua, Nicaragua, was the title of an old Andrews Sisters song. The Somozas had been running Nicaragua for many years and they seemed quite secure in their power—at least to my touristic eyes. Everything was quiet there. One day I even semi-crashed a party at the Presidential Palace.

"The palace stood in the middle of what was literally a fallen city. From a distance, downtown Managua looked like a park—it was so green. When you got a closer look you could see that the green was that of vegetation growing over the rubble where the center of the city had collapsed two days before Christmas in 1972. The palace stood unscathed in the middle of the destruction. Around it was a kind of free-fire zone of scrub jungle where no one was permitted. The palace stood just beyond the effective mortar distance from the nearest habitation." Such striking images would coalesce into the setting of a completely different story.

Writing a decade after the fact, Bob had collapsed the chronology a bit. His Central American exploration actually began in March 1976, when he flew to Tuscaloosa to give a reading at the University of Alabama. Instead of returning to Amherst after his performance, he cashed his check and flew to New Orleans, where he stayed two nights in the Royal Orleans Hotel in the French Quarter, a couple of blocks from Jackson Square and not too far from the Stones' old digs on St. Philip Street. From there he phoned Janice (what sort of explanation he gave has not been recorded) and the next day caught a plane to San Pedro Sula, capital of the Cortés department of Honduras. Then he flew to La Ceiba, a hundred miles or so east on Honduras's north coast and about sixty miles south of Roatán, a Caribbean island that is a diver's paradise. He stayed three nights in the Pirate's Den Hotel, explored, and did some snorkeling in the reefs.

In Roatán or La Ceiba he made the acquaintance of a military attaché to the American embassy in Managua, who was vacationing with his wife and her sister. This group offered Bob a ride with them across the Nicaraguan border to the capital (an episode he would later fictionalize in *A Flag for Sunrise*, reworking the diplomatic couple as Tom and Marie Zecca). With them he attended a party thrown by Arturo Somoza, the brother of Anastasio Somoza, the dictator of Nicaragua. Arturo had the audacity to pull some peeling skin off Bob's sunburned nose—a sort of casual, semi-sadistic assertion of power which Bob had probably not encountered since his sojourn with the Marist Brothers at St. Ann's.

He returned from this adventure exhilarated, mostly by the idea for a completely different novel than the historical narrative that had him bogged down. The germ of *A Flag for Sunrise* was beginning to sprout. And Bob, since his visit to Roatán, was determined to learn to scuba dive.

His success with the latter project shows how strong his physical constitution must have been at that time, when he was still a very heavy smoker, not to mention other indulgences. He began taking lessons at the Springfield YMCA pool, driving forty miles round trip for the privilege. Certified in December 1977, he made his qualifying dive in the summer of that year, at New Hampshire's Spofford Lake. Reef diving came later and mattered much more. In 1978 and 1979 he made two trips to Bonaire, a divers' paradise in the former Netherlands Antilles, with Ian accompanying him both times. "He broke his eardrums diving," Janice says, "but he came back happy. The undersea world was wonderful to him. It plainly gave him great joy to have seen it, and he described it to me—the light, the tropical fish—as he would describe another country, a foreign country I had never seen."

Bob's own account was still more vivid: "One of the happiest days of my life was one on which I broke an eardrum scuba diving off the island of Bonaire and descending, a little too precipitously, on my first coral reef. It was as close to paradise as I ever expect to find myself. On the sheer joy of it, I made for deeper water, slipped over the reef and kept descending until my depth gauge registered over 90 feet. At that depth, the glorious colors of the sun-dappled reef began to disappear. Parrot- and angel fish were dun as mackerel. Purple fans lost their luster. I was approaching the levels of nitrogen narcosis and also a depth at which decompression time would be necessary to prevent an attack of the bends if I spent more than a few minutes. But I also felt at the border of a great mystery."

Meanwhile Bob needed to visit more above-water foreign countries to feed the ideas in formation for *A Flag for Sunrise*. In the winter of 1977 he planned a trip to Guatemala and Honduras with Jim Maraniss, who was fluent in Spanish. In Jim's recollection, "He said he wanted to go back to

Central America to get more ideas for a book, and I said that I would, too; I could be his interpreter and fellow traveler. He liked having someone else in his imagined world. And that is what it would be like in Central America for us."

Janice, who was going along this time, did the logistics. On the eve of departure, Bob got cold feet and wanted to cancel. Not unusual for him; he was an anxious traveler—surprisingly so, considering the number of hazardous places he visited in the course of his life. "He had a bad habit of scaring himself. Rehearsing all the things that could go wrong, in great detail," an occupational hazard of the writer's imagination. Stephen Crane had put it well, in one of Bob's favorite passages from *The Red Badge of Courage*: "A little panic-fear grew in his mind. As his imagination went forward to a fight, he saw hideous possibilities. He contemplated the lurking menaces of the future, and failed in an effort to see himself standing stoutly in the midst of them." (This characterization also fits Frank Holliwell, a principal in *A Flag for Sunrise*, almost perfectly.)

Janice threatened to go alone with Jim if Bob backed out. "I was bluffing," but that or something did the trick. The trio embarked on schedule, flying from Hartford to San Pedro Sula by way of Miami; their real destination was Guatemala but the Honduran airport was reputed much safer than anything in the neighboring country. Jim drove them across the border in a rented four-wheel-drive pickup.

"It was real third world," Jim recalled later: "beggars and shoeshine boys, soldiers everywhere, monkeys howling in the arboreal canopy (the '*monos malos*')," who would eventually put in their appearance in *A Flag for Sunrise*. In Honduras, "we were stopped at a crossroads and a peasant (Bob called him a *machetero*) asked for a ride. I said (in Spanish, a language Bob thought he could understand, although he did not, or no more than Hemingway did: no grammar and little vocabulary) climb in the back. Our luggage, such as it was, was back there. He got in, along with about ten more *macheteros*, who rode with us down toward the coast. While they were back there, they went through our stuff and stole some little things, like toothpaste. Bob was beside himself the whole time, rolling up the windows, locking the doors, convinced that the *macheteros* were going to climb around and murder us. He was in a panic. He may have been right, though his attitude toward everyone had been distrustful, which goaded me into acting the opposite: comradely as it were, trusting. . . . Characters like me were of course the naïve fools of his books.

This never offended me. Bob and I loved each other, like brothers. He insisted that we stop in front of the police station at our destination to let the peasants off and roll down the windows."

Janice's version of the episode differs in detail: "Jim said it would be all right. We let the Hondurans off, one by one, until there were just two. When we stopped to let those last guys get out, they took a couple of our suitcases and ran off. What they got, I'm sure they were sorry to discover, was only old clothes, toothbrushes, etc."

"Every time we entered a cantina or restaurant," says Jim, "Bob would ask the mariachi band to play 'El Rancho Grande.' This was one of our amusements. When we drove into a shit town, such as Progreso, Honduras, we would say to each other: 'No es Paris' (with an accent on the i)." Such japery was not necessarily endearing to the locals. Of Bob's displays of satirical wit, Jim remembers, "People didn't take a liking to him, to say the least, but nothing bad ever happened." (In a key scene of *A Flag for Sunrise*, Holliwell alienates a Central American audience with an improvised satirical monologue very much in Bob's style.) According to Janice, meanwhile, someone "told Bob to warn Jim not to speak about politics so audibly in public. That was considered dangerous in Guatemala." Certainly none of them needed to be mistaken for political actors of any kind; Bob was there to observe, in Jim's view "to be able to give a convincing landscape to his fantasy," that is, to nurture the imaginative medium for *A Flag for Sunrise*.

"Guatemala City was ugly," says Janice, "and I'd never seen the kind of poverty we saw in Guatemala and Honduras. Those countries were beautiful nevertheless. . . . The Mayans in the villages of Guatemala carried their poverty like the burdens they carried on their heads, with dignity and grace." The latter quality is a transitive property of peasant cultures the world over; in *Damascus Gate*, Bob would describe it as "the mystical patience of the very poor."

Ranging out from Guatemala City, they stayed in a hotel on Lake Atitlan (which *was* a beautiful site). In Antigua, they saw a religious procession that struck Janice "like something from the Middle Ages of Europe." In the Indian village of Chichicastenango, the church "was dark and seemed to be lit by smudge pots or candles rather than electric light. There was a strong religious charge inside." The Stones didn't officially subscribe to any religion at this time, but Janice, in the Chichicastenango church, "knew that people prayed there with great faith, because I could see it, and feel it." Bob was less susceptible, more warily ambivalent, but (especially given the intense experience of his Catholic childhood) such demonstrations of the palpability of faith meant something to him too.

Jim Maraniss: "I think that he was more attuned to the difference between rhetoric and actual manifestations of the divine spark than anyone else I knew." Faith "was drilled into him relentlessly in his youth, and his childhood was so beset with worries (for his mother and himself) that he needed belief to stay whole. Later he lost it and was essentially (like most of us) an atheist who hoped to believe in God (truth, love, warmth, sweetness) and suffered in His absence."

For another angle on the grandeur of ancient Mayan civilization and the religion that had once informed it, the Stone party went by bus to the ruins at Tikal, climbing up and down the pyramids there by "holding on to a chain." They'd come by bus, but during the visit a heavy rain washed out the roads. A solution materialized in the form of a smallish plane. "The pilot reminded me of the Hells Angels in his leather jacket," Janice recalls—perhaps not a reassuring resemblance. Also, there were more people stranded than the plane could carry back to Guatemala City, but "that problem was resolved when one couple with children, Germans, I think, decided not to board, concerned about safety. The plane took off, circled around and landed again at the airstrip. The pilot had forgotten something. The manifest, Bob said. We finally got on our way late in the afternoon. We had to reach the city before dark, we were told, because the airport in the capital had no lights. And we did, but barely."

What they were seeing in Central America put both Jim and Bob in mind of the Spanish Civil War, which they discussed frequently during the journey. (In Guatemala it might have been another unsafe topic.) "Bob, and I also, but to a lesser extent, was anti-Communist in that context, and distrustful of Marxism in practice. In this regard, Bob's politics were much influenced by Arthur Koestler, *The God That Failed*, etc. (There was never any question of embracing the right wing; he was an anti-Communist leftist.) In any event, he held the Spanish Republic as an example of what might have been in the twentieth century, but had been betrayed by the Communist Party, and abandoned by the West." In *A Flag for Sunrise*, some similar ideas are discussed by leaders of the revolution in fictional Tecan; the elders among them are saturated in the memory of the Spanish Civil War, as the American characters tend to be drenched in traumatic disorders stemming from Vietnam.

During the May trip to Honduras and Guatemala, Jim had also wanted to go to El Salvador, to visit one of his college classmates who was living there, but they were warned off; the country was too dangerously unstable in 1977 (and would remain so for a good many years to come). "In Guatemala," says Jim, "we were accosted by a few men who said they were Salvadorans. They told us that they couldn't go back, that they would be killed. It was as if we should do something, at least be witnesses. They were almost weeping.

"There was of course nothing we could do, but listening to so much pain and supplication was something we always referred to later, and I think it was their voices that made the novel real and concrete." The Salvadorans made an extremely durable impression on Bob, as Jim recalls. " 'I haven't forgotten those guys,' he would say. He was referring to the actual sensation of hearing them, the quality of their voices. In a language he didn't really know."

The Central American excursion was a cusp experience, and after it, Bob knew what he wanted to write and was ready to write it. Still, as with most of his other books, *A Flag for Sunrise* did not come quickly or easily. And by the time his ideas for the new novel were beginning to coalesce, he was dangerously behind on his contract with Knopf, which called for him to deliver a finished manuscript by the end of 1978. On the upside, if Bob Gottlieb was worried about the delay, he kept it to himself. Candida Donadio had shown him fifty pages of manuscript in the spring of 1977. Gottlieb wrote Bob, "I was surprised (not to be somewhere in the 13th century), but certainly not disappointed. . . . It left me acutely frustrated, wanting more." All that was enthusiasm; Gottlieb concluded by assuring Bob, "I'm as unworried about this novel as I have ever been about a book at this stage of development. In fact I'm thrilled."

Such confidence was surely encouraging; still, Bob's fresh energy to write had arrived none too soon. There was more research to be done as well, though somewhat less arduous than the Central American trips had been.

In 1975, Bob had reviewed Peter Matthiessen's Zen-Caribbean novel *Far Tortuga* for *The New York Times Book Review*, describing it as "a series of moments captured whole and rendered with a clarity that quickens the blood." Now he wanted to find his own way into the world of twentieth-century Caribbean seafaring in which *Far Tortuga* was set. He wrote Matthiessen and got some introductions to people in Key West—one to Dink Bruce, the son of Toby Bruce, who'd provided similar guidance to Ernest Hemingway when he lived in Key West. Dink arranged for Bob to spend a few days on a shrimp boat, one of the Singleton fleet based in Tampa. This brief voyage became the basis of the shrimp-boat sequence in *A Flag for Sunrise*.

It was Bob's first trip to Key West, and the end-of-the-world atmosphere of the place appealed to him. There was already a substantial community of writers and artists in formation there. Bob met Thomas Sanchez (a chronicler of the Key West scene in his novel *Mile Zero*) and his wife, Stephanie (a painter), and also the novelist Tom McGuane. When Bob returned to Amherst, he asked Janice, "I wonder what it would cost to buy a house in Key West, what it would be like to live there."

To get a sense of his heroine, Sister Justin Feeney, Bob went to Northampton to talk to nuns there. "He was very impressed with them. He had positive feelings about nuns, if not about his childhood teachers" at St. Ann's, who had all been men. Among religious women, Bob could find an easier release for the Catholic doctrine hammered into him as a boy—in the person of Sister Justin, this material could be shaped artistically. At the same time, Janice had an inkling that the fictional Justin's surname might be a nod to a woman with whom Bob had had a brief affair.

Meanwhile Bob's schedule was hectic enough to make it hard to find time to write (especially for someone with a penchant for procrastination). Apart from the research trips south of the border in the spring and summer of 1977, he spent a chunk of May in Hollywood, went on location for *Who'll Stop the Rain* in Durango in June, then in July to Sun Valley with Janice, for another round of the writers' conference quartered there.

From Sun Valley, Bob drove with Janice, their children, and Janice's youngest brother, Tim, to the West Coast. Tim and Ian went to San Francisco with Janice's sister Ginny and her husband, while Bob, Janice, and Deidre stayed on the Keseys' Oregon farm. They visited the house Faye and Ken had recently bought, on a bluff above the Pacific, where Ken had installed editing equipment with an eye toward finally completing a film from the disorganized footage that survived from the Prankster cross-country bus trip thirteen years earlier. Aside from that project, work on the farm could be strenuous; Kesey's irrigation system required a ritualistic "moving the water," that is, shifting a network of hoses several times a day; all able-bodied men on hand were expected to assist in the maneuver. Apart from these activities, Ken was slightly in the doldrums. The Pranksters had disbanded, and he wasn't writing much. His enthusiasm for drug experimentation was unabated, and he used a little heroin sometimes—judiciously; Kesey never became a prisoner of addiction. Bob, by nature a more addictive personality, was protected again by his dislike of needles, though Janice thought he might have snorted a little scag with Ken.

Southbound, the Stones stopped at Port Orford to visit Mountain Girl, a Prankster muse prominently featured in Bob's long piece about Kesey's drug arrests and flight to Mexico (government name: Carolyn Walker). Her daughter with Kesey was named Sunshine, and Mountain Girl was in the process of taking up with Grateful Dead guitarist Jerry Garcia when the Stones called on her. Three hundred miles south they stopped at a commune on the outskirts of Fort Bragg, where Janice's sister Marge was living with a new husband, his son, and her daughter from a previous marriage. They were also able to see Michael Horowitz, their old friend from New York and Paris, now married to Cindy Palmer and raising their daughter, who would eventually be known as Winona Ryder.

Next stop was to collect Tim and Ian from Ginny in San Francisco, and visit a younger Burr sister, Alison, who with her husband had recently become a disciple of the guru Ciranjiva Roy—a colorful figure even in the company of Indian swamis operating in the States at that time. For fundraising, Roy exhorted his followers to be fruitful, multiply, then draw welfare on their children and turn over a portion of that income to him. At the time of the Stones' visit, Alison and her husband had contributed two little boys to this system and were soon to have a third. There might have been some material here for a novelist of Robert Stone's predilections, but at the moment his attention was elsewhere, and he and Janice never met Ciranjiva Roy. Many years later he began plotting a novel that traced the course of pilgrims through such milieux of the 1960s and '70s, but the project was never completed.

At summer's end, the Stones flew back to Amherst. In August, Bob turned forty. His strong constitution was still serving him well, although his doctor declared, on an application to the Minnesota Mutual Life Insurance Company: "I am aware that Mr. Stone has a history of excess alcohol consumption and some slightly impaired liver function, type II hyperlipidemia, and gout in the past." But Bob scored a clean bill of health on a 1976 physical and a 1977 follow-up; incidentally he "reported that he was limiting his alcohol intake to very light amounts and on weekends only." This rate of consumption was possibly somewhat understated—although Bob could cut his drinking down quite drastically for short periods and might have done so in anticipation of the insurance physical. His affection for quaaludes was not mentioned at all.

Bob was back in the Amherst classrooms in 1977–1978, and with his teaching a distraction from writing, the reconceived Central American novel was moving slowly. Although by then he had done all or most of the necessary legwork, it always took a very long time for an idea to mature to the point that he could execute it to his own very high standards. Jokingly, he would refer to himself as "a slothful perfectionist," but in fact it was no joke, and this odd combination of qualities could sometimes put him in very painful positions.

There were other distractions—one of them sizable. In the spring of 1978, Bob, whose interest in acting went back at least as far as his abortive relationship with the Passion Play in New Orleans, took a leading role in Harold Pinter's *The Homecoming*. The play was performed on the Amherst campus and the actors other than Bob were students, but Helene Keyssar, a member of the Department of Dramatic Arts who had become friendly with the Stones, gave it a professional-grade production. In a recommendation written for Keyssar a couple of years later, Bob mentioned that he'd been inspired by "a fit of insanity" to try out for the part of Max, the sour, sadistic paterfamilias and the lead role in the show. During rehearsals, he was dealing with hearing loss and pain from his dive-damaged eardrums, which meant that prescription painkillers had entered his mix, alongside alcohol and quaaludes, to the point that Helene's husband, Tracy Strong, called Janice "from their house one night to say he thought I should pick Bob up, that he wasn't making sense. Bob was offended. He didn't seem conscious of how drunk and incoherent he seemed when under the influence of quaaludes."

Despite such wobbles, Bob rose handsomely to the occasion when the curtain went up. The Gelbers came from New York to see him in the part, and Arthur and Leslie Kopit also traveled to see the play, which was favorably reviewed by a couple of local newspapers. *The Amherst Record* opened its coverage by calling Bob's performance "the most fascinating" surprise of the production: "He plays the mean and mercurially sentimental old father with a British working-class accent that doesn't always ring true—but nonetheless he's magnificent, and interest, always high, perks up when he's on." Another article praised Bob as "extremely effective" in conveying the "temperament of an embattled crustacean" attributed to the character of Max; this writer was familiar with other performances of what was then a popular and often-produced play.

Mercuriality came naturally to Bob (as did, sometimes, a sort of throttled anger), and he had his own reasons to be interested in what *The Amherst Record* called a "study of the effect of women in the lives of men—men's attitudes toward them, their need for them, what happens when they aren't around—and how a woman responds to them." A conversational mean streak was also not difficult for Bob to portray.

Already skilled in the art of verbal laceration, Bob surely relished the quick vicious turns in Max's speeches, as well as the savory language Pinter had furnished the character. The *New Yorker* critic John Lahr wrote (at the time of the play's fortieth anniversary performance, long after Bob had played the part in Amherst), " 'The Homecoming' changed my life. Before the play, I thought words were just vessels of meaning; after it, I saw them as weapons of defense. Before, I thought theatre was about the spoken; after, I understood the eloquence of the unspoken." These qualities of the play had real relevance to Bob's project of constructing scenes for *A Flag for Sunrise*, the novel that for the moment had him stuck.

Major artists like Robert Stone and Harold Pinter influence each other by expanding their ideas of what's possible. Stone is fundamentally a realist, while Pinter is fundamentally not, but internalizing a large chunk of Pinter by performing it enlarged Bob's sense of what could be done with speech, not to mention "the eloquence of the unspoken." Certain episodes of his work in progress would push the borders of the real extremely hard.

5

DEALING WITH DEPRESSION

Jane Burton had brought her two children, Emily and Jacob, to visit the Stones during the Christmas season of 1977. Once as heavy a smoker as Bob, "in the three- or four-pack-a-day range," Jane had recently broken the habit, which put her on edge; she also had the capacity to match Bob drink for drink. Her son's father, Herbert Wickenheiser, came down from Vermont to join the party. "Jane could be contentious when drinking, and gave him a hard time. Herb was wearing an incongruously formal dark suit. You look like an undertaker, Jane told him." Jane, whose independent spirit was slightly ahead of her time, never married anyone, sticking to what she'd once told Janice: She just didn't want to see a man's clothes hanging in her closet.

Bob had not had much contact with their daughter since her birth, although he kept her photo in his study and would sometimes acknowledge to visitors that Emily was his out-of-wedlock daughter. Ian and Deidre had met Emily briefly a decade earlier, when Jane was teaching at Collaberg School, but without having any idea that she was their half-sister. After the 1977 Christmas visit, Janice decided to disclose the relationship to Deidre, and in the summer of 1978, the Stones invited Emily to accompany the family on a visit to London and to see the Brookses.

The London flat had by this time become something of an albatross, because the Stones' ownership kept involving them in wrangles over U.K. income tax—although its investment value had increased a great deal. Bob and Janice still entertained the idea of moving back to London full time, but for the moment it was rented to "a Canadian millionaire, whom we found after running an advertisement in *New York* magazine." This tenant was elsewhere during the summer of 1978, so the Stones and their children could use the flat. The visit to the Brookses' cottage was a more uncomplicated pleasure, bringing back the flavor of certain good old days. Janice: "Emily said then that she thought the valley in North Wales was the most beautiful place she had ever seen, which was the way I felt when I first went there." Emily was getting to know her half-siblings for the first time.

There were good times, but the summer in England was "one of our rougher periods. Bob was quite depressed," likely because of slow progress on *A Flag for Sunrise.* "Of course, the more depressed he was, the less writing he did." He'd had a similar bout of depression during the Stones' first visit to Europe, when he was stuck on *A Hall of Mirrors,* but the 1978 episode was considerably worse. It had also been brewing for a while. "Bob had seen a psychiatrist earlier that year, at my urging," someone who'd impressed Janice favorably when she saw him in action in the course of her own study and practice. "He seemed to be a sensible, not stuffy therapist. Bob saw him a few times, but was put off when Jack Roseman asked him when he had last been to church."

A few years later, in a sunnier mood following the success of *A Flag for*

Sunrise, Bob joked with a *New York Times* interviewer about this brush with psychiatry: "I'm not much crazier than anybody else, but I'm not much saner. So one day I felt really crazy and thought, I'll go see a shrink. I called my GP, and he recommended this guy I knew from around town. He was everything that a psychiatrist should be, very humane and very together. I went to him, and I talked to him, and he said, 'What you need is religion. What you should do is go to Uttar Pradesh in India, because in Uttar Pradesh the ground is so holy that as you walk on it, the vibes coming up from the ground will clear your head.'"

Bob's lengthy conversations with Ann Greif, which had taken place just a little earlier, didn't amount to therapy as such (though Greif did include some therapeutic commentary in the text she delivered to him in the fall of 1978), but the detailed rehearsal of his childhood in his meetings with her might actually have contributed to destabilizing his mood. In any case, he met Roseman only a time or two, and had stopped seeing him before the summer trip to England.

In London, "one night he miscalculated the pills he was taking, along with alcohol, and overdosed himself. He had swallowed, it seemed, quite a few tranquilizers, and in the morning he still seemed to be drugged. The rest of the bottle was spilled on the bedroom carpet." The scene was alarming enough for Janice to take Bob to Middlesex Hospital on the recommendation of one of their old Hampstead neighbors who was a nurse.

The hospital visit was inconclusive. "Bob had himself checked out. By that time the drugs had worn off. I wondered if it might be a suicide attempt. He couldn't remember his state of mind. I asked him to please let me know if he felt suicidal, and let us deal with it together. I reminded him that our children were not grown up yet, and needed him to be in their lives. He promised me that he would not kill himself without telling me and giving me a chance to talk him out of it." Perhaps, after all, he had never intended suicide. Decades later, Ian vigorously rejected the idea: "Did you not sense my father's essential character and courage? He would never have hurt us." That much is completely true. And at some point: "My father told me that the way to deal with suicidal feelings, should they arise, was to postpone any decision. This pits despair against its equal, procrastination. Time sorts things out just well enough."

—•—

In conversation with Greif, Bob had said that he thought of children in general, and his own in particular, as "hostages to fortune," following Francis Bacon's opinion that "He that hath wife and children hath given hostages to fortune, for they are impediments to great enterprises, either of virtue or mischief." In fact, he didn't follow Bacon all the way, as he always had the sense to remember that Janice was the opposite of an impediment to his great enterprises. At the same time the anchor of family life sometimes seemed to restrain him too much, though his use of the "hostages" phrase might refer more narrowly to a difficult truth all parents learn: no diligence can completely protect one's children from the grinding of fortune's wheel.

"Deidre and Ian were well into a sometimes rocky adolescence, Deidre eighteen and Ian fifteen" in the summer of 1978. Still Janice, at thirty-six, "envied my pregnant friends," a group that included Leslie Kopit, Alexis Hollister, and Jim Maraniss's wife, Gigi Kaeser. "I asked Bob whether we might try for another baby." Bob invoked the hostages-to-fortune principle, then "thought about it for a few days. All right, he said. Then he added, We'll get this one baptized. His saying this surprised me."

The Stones' life was in considerable flux at the end of 1978. Their season in Amherst was winding down. They'd enrolled Deidre and Ian in private schools in the area, hoping to improve their grades, but Ian was close to finishing high school by this time, and Deidre was already reaching for some kind of independence; at summer's end she found herself a job as an au pair and stayed on in England after the Stones returned to the States. Old friend Joan Michelson caught a glimpse of her at the Brookses' London digs a few months later: "Deidre was at that time adrift between an au pair job and the unknown."

Who'll Stop the Rain was released in August 1978. In May the film had been featured at Cannes, but Bob was too disenchanted with the project by then to have any interest in attending (although it did appear under the title *Dog Soldiers* for this debut). In the States, the movie got some good reviews; Roger Ebert gave it a thumbs-up, defining it as "a well-assembled chase movie—a thriller, with a few existential notes left over from Robert Stone's *Dog Soldiers*." In fact Ebert, who seemed to have read the novel, found a substantial amount of Stone's intention preserved: "it is a war movie, in a way; a story of people at war with themselves after the one in Vietnam screwed them up." The critic praised Nick Nolte in the role of

Hicks, and found that as Marge, Tuesday Weld turned in her best performance "in years." A friend in Maine, the poet Ken Rosen, wrote Bob that the movie was "highly okay . . . admiring how Converse in such a sneaky way looked like you, trying to figure out what pissed off Penelope Gilliatt," who'd panned the picture in *The New Yorker.*

In London, where the movie ran under the original title, reviews were much more favorable, as Tom Rosenthal, Bob's editor at Secker and Warburg, wrote in January—enough so to stimulate a 15,000-copy paperback reprint of the U.K. edition of the novel. Despite some positive attention, the movie failed at the box office, meaning there was no new income from that source. Bob, still struggling with the third novel, needed to keep teaching to make ends meet. He put together a package to teach at Stanford in the spring of 1979, then move on to the University of Hawaii at Manoa for the academic year 1979–1980.

In December 1978, Bob and Janice took a room at the St. Moritz in New York and invited her parents to dinner at Luchow's, a restaurant her father remembered fondly from business dinners before his retirement. Bob needed to brace himself for encounters with his father-in-law, and while Janice was picking up the elder Burrs in Bogota, he did so, to excess. "To make matters worse, Luchow's had become a tourist trap, and we had a long wait for our reserved table. Bob had nothing much to say during the meal, which Dad nevertheless seemed to enjoy. As I drove them back to New Jersey, I half apologized. Dad defended Bob, saying he was 'a good provider.' Male solidarity, I thought. I told Bob the next day that Dad seemed to have accepted him into the family at last. Bob replied, rather bitterly, Good, it only took him eighteen years."

6

HAWAII

At the end of March 1979, soon after Bob had returned from a fishing and diving trip with Ian to Bonaire, he and Janice loaded up their blue Buick Skylark and started the long drive to California, leaving Deidre and their two sets of tenants on South Pleasant Street. As Bob and Janice crossed Pennsylvania, news of the Three Mile Island nuclear incident lit up the radio. The news didn't trigger Bob's travel anxiety; "nuclear meltdown was not the sort of scene to preoccupy him." Their plan was to ship the Skylark to Hawaii later on.

Soon after their arrival in California, Janice flew back to Amherst to begin preparing for their move off the continent. While teaching at Stanford, Bob stayed again at Villa Montalvo (now rechristened the Montalvo Arts Center), where he'd spent some time struggling to finish *A Hall of Mirrors* in the 1960s. From the point of view of peace and quiet, the residency was unluckily timed. "The fucking Montalvo people are determiting, drilling through the foundation to spray. It sounds like a steel mill in full operation." To complicate the situation, Bob was having some difficult encounters with Jane Burton, whom he perceived to be "getting set to ask for money," as he wrote to Janice soon after. "She wants to go to law school and reckons she can't hold her present 14,000 a year job. While drunk, which she always is when I see her, she told me how poor she was. Then she blew it by having to tell me how poor Kesey was too, which always gets my back up. I went into a rage, carried on about how I was not made of fucking money, was not Louis G. Mayer, did not own a beach house or a Moviola, that some people had absurdly exaggerated ideas of my great wealth. She apologized, cried—I totally out-awfulled her. Then she called me up in the middle of the night to apologize some more. I hit the roof. She's afraid I've joined the many people who aren't speaking to her."

Bob's anger may have had some source in an uneasy conscience. His parentage of Emily, though no secret among close friends, had never been legally established, and he paid no regular child support. "He made an occasional voluntary contribution, but we were usually pretty tight for money ourselves." Jane never asked for child support per se—her commitment to her own independence worked against that—but considering all the circumstances, it was reasonable for her to feel, sometimes, that she was owed more than she was getting.

Bob's letter to Janice made no report on progress with the novel. "Nice weather's finally here," Bob signed off. "Another goddam day in Paradise."

———

Hawaiian paradise was the Stones' next stop. At the end of August they flew to Honolulu and moved into an upper-story apartment of the

Mauna Luan complex, overlooking Hanauma Bay. They'd stretched a bit to get there, paying $1,000 a month for a larger place in a better location than had otherwise been available. The apartment complex boasted a racquetball court, swimming pool, and covered garage. Though Janice at first felt mildly uncomfortable living in a gated community, "security-conscious Bob didn't mind the guard at the entrance." Once, he slept off most of a drunk locked in the blue Skylark in the covered garage. Ruth Pratt, the Stones' host the previous evening, "had given Bob and Janice the leftovers from dinner. When Bob woke up in the morning, he still had the leftovers on his lap, so he sat in the parking garage and ate them."

Overall, Bob liked the Mauna Luan enough to fantasize about buying into it, but the Stones were in one of their lean years and there was no way to finance that idea. "Bob had to settle for Hawaiian shirts. He wore them for years, a unique fashion statement in Amherst, and later in Westport."

It took Bob half an hour to drive to campus, but his teaching schedule was light so he didn't have to do it every day. Writing time was plentiful, and dive opportunities verged on the miraculous—nearby Hanauma was a popular location, among others. Bob found a dive partner in Kim Woodard, who was attached to the East-West Center in Honolulu. Janice's sister Ginny and her husband, Paul, were both divers and joined Bob and Kim on the reefs when they visited from San Francisco. So too did Elliott Anderson, the editor of the literary review *TriQuarterly*. One time Janice and Jack Gelber waited on the beach for Bob, Kim, and Elliott to resurface. "They were delayed for so long that I began to get worried, but finally the three of them appeared, hiking down the beach with their gear. Bob told me later that Elliott had been diving with a bad hangover and ran into trouble during the dive. He and Kim helped Elliott get ashore, climbing out over the volcanic rock at the end of the bay. Bob thought that Elliott had had a close call."

George Walker, a member of the Kesey coterie, "was living on a sailboat with his girlfriend at Ala Wai Harbor. The boat was beautiful, a real antique, polished mahogany with gold-plated trim. It had needed repairs, and George was working on restoring it. He took us out on that boat a few times before he sailed it across the Pacific to California. He was trying to escape from the owner. George figured he could put a lien on the boat for the unpaid work, and perhaps get ownership of the vessel." Before this great escape took place, "Bob picked up some sailing skills," useful knowledge for the writing of *Outerbridge Reach* years later, as was the general idea of disappearing into the ocean on a sailboat.

Janice couldn't find work in the counseling field, possibly because she was frank in telling employers that she only intended to stay in Hawaii for one year. With the high rent on their apartment, and direct income from Bob's novels mostly dried up for the time being, they needed to find extra money somewhere. It seemed finally time to sell the London flat and take what would have been a considerable profit, but their Canadian tenant announced his refusal to leave—a position that his wealth and U.K. tenancy laws made easy to defend, especially against rightful owners an ocean away. Bob was infuriated by this play, but there was nothing he could immediately do about it, although the strain of maintaining residences in Amherst, Hawaii, and London was beginning to feel like too much.

Janice got work at Kuapa Preschool taking care of a group of two-year-olds—replacing a woman who'd quit after a week's hospitalization for a venomous centipede bite. She befriended Sylvia Golomb, a Chinese American from Oakland, who was in charge of the three-year-olds at Kuapa. "She was pregnant, and I rather hoped her condition was contagious." It didn't seem to be, but managing ten two-year-olds gave Janice "all the kid action I could handle." The job paid only minimum wage, which was still something, and was in walking distance of the Mauna Luan.

"There were more surfers and sports fans in Bob's class than there were scholars," but he generally found his students likable, and there was an advantage to having less pressure from them than from more ambitious students at Stanford and Amherst. The Hawaiian students, who probably didn't have much idea of Bob's growing stature in the literary world, didn't want to intrude into his personal life. Nor were they involved with the kind of politics Bob's first two novels had engaged.

The Stones, however, were for the most part happy. Work was congenial, and Bob and Janice "hung out with a partying crowd," whose libation was "mostly Olympia beer," plus the local marijuana, which "was very good, really mellow. It seemed impossible to have a bad time smoking it." Janice was usually ready for a beer and a toke "when I had spent a long day herding two-year-olds, and then walking home in the sun. But Bob always overdid it."

There was some kind of party for the Stones to attend almost every weekend, and often more than one. Along with the incident when Bob passed out in the parked Skylark, "one night at Ruth Pratt's after drinking quite a bit, he walked through a door to nowhere, in the dark, and fell out of the house entirely. It was a drop, probably four or five feet. I held my breath." Ruth remembers: "Before Bob fell out of my door to nowhere, he had announced to the party that, if anyone had a question they had better ask it because his next toke was going to render him useless. That was his amygdala making him polite in the face of possible bad behavior. Bob fell out of the house through the legs of a tripod holding a broken telescope so that, when he rose, he was wearing it."

There's a photo depicting the Stone circle stoned on the North Shore beach: Bob and Janet Onopa, Ian and Susan MacMillan, and Janice and Bob—Bob looking more like Poseidon than Dionysus this time, if Poseidon could get cross-faded. "Earlier," in Ruth's version, "we had huddled around the kitchen table in a cloud of cigarette and pakalolo smoke with a gallon of screw-top wine. When a woman opened the door to scold us for sitting in the kitchen when the sun was shining and the ocean was outside, she seemed to be from another world. Bob, before going to the beach, turned into the room and said, 'All I ever wanted was to be held in the palm of God's hand.' "

Though very far from being a tract, *A Flag for Sunrise* is steeped in Catholicism, or rather in some of many ways that the Catholic experience can continue to affect those who have departed from the church and its dogma, sometimes to the point of outright apostasy. Hawaii (oddly) gave Bob a chance to explore a variety of religious experience previously unknown to him: "one of the Catholic churches there used to have joint services with a Pentecostalist church—I mean, this was sort of Holy Rolling. Nuns and seminarians really got off on this. It was a chance to carry on and speak in tongues and the whole number, which certainly seems to me on the face of it to be the very opposite of everything that Catholicism is all about. I guess it was forbidden fruit for Catholics. They got to sing 'There's an Old Rugged Cross' and they got to talk in tongues and things like that."

All things considered, Hawaii turned out to be a good writing environment for Bob. He had sufficient time and less pressure from his academic job than previously. His drinking and dosing pattern was still a

manageable liability, while regular diving kept him healthy and happy—
the dive experiences fed directly into the novel as well. By the time the
Stones returned, somewhat reluctantly, to the mainland, Bob was close to
finishing *A Flag for Sunrise*.

7

HELPING PROFESSIONS

After the Stones returned to Amherst, Janice "found a job
doing child protective service work for a private agency in Springfield. It
didn't pay much but it was interesting work," and provided a circumstantial background to Bob's short story "Helping," written a few years later.
Bob, not teaching in the fall of 1980, pushed to finish *A Flag for Sunrise*.
Janice "read it through for him, and I think I did some retyping. But he
required no editing on this one from me, or from his editor, Bob Gottlieb.
The novel seemed near-perfect."

Bob got hired to teach two workshops at Harvard in the spring semester of 1981—at $15,000 for the pair it was a better-paying gig than some
he'd had recently. He could commute from Amherst, with the university
putting him up two nights a week in Adams House. "Teaching in Cambridge made for a regular work week, and he was not drinking when he
drove the ninety miles or so on Tuesday and Thursday mornings."

Provisional sobriety is one of the conditions of "Helping." The heart
of the story is a vicious marital quarrel provoked by the husband's alcoholic relapse, but the atmosphere is suffused with the worst late-twentieth-
century humanity has to offer in terms of bad faith, casual cruelty, and
downright degeneration. There was some suffering involved in the composition too. Bob lost his finished draft of the story in a computer crash
and could only retrieve it "a few words at a time, and all out of order," as
Janice recalls. "Rather than do a jigsaw puzzle of the results, he sat down
and rewrote the story."

Elliot is a counselor in Boston, his wife, Grace, a lawyer engaged with
the most hopeless human services. A session with a malingering phony

drives Elliot to leave work and visit his erstwhile local, where he termi-
nates a period of sobriety with a couple of shots, then purchases a bottle
of scotch for the road. By the time he gets home he is loaded . . . for bear.
Grace returns from a bad day in court, her disappointment in her husband's lapse soon turning into despairing rage. Their dialogue is lacerat-
ing. In an action plainly drawn from life, Grace is provoked to wing a
sugar bowl at Elliot.

Elliot's acid account of his reason for drinking is very likely also true
of Bob.

> "What do I mean? I mean that most of the time I'm putting
> one foot in front of the other like a good soldier and I'm out of
> it from the neck up. But there are times when I don't think I will
> ever be dead enough—or dead long enough—to get the taste of
> this life off my teeth. That's what I mean!"
> She looked at him dry-eyed. "Poor fella," she said.
> "What you have to understand, Grace, is that this drink I'm
> having"—he raised the glass toward her in a gesture of salute—
> "is the only worthwhile thing I've done in the last year and a
> half. It's the only thing in my life that means jack shit, the closest
> thing to satisfaction I've had. Now how can you begrudge me
> that? It's the best I'm capable of."

And also:

> The liquor seemed to be giving him a perverse lucidity when all
> he now required was oblivion. His rage, especially, was intact
> in its salting of alcohol. Its contours were palpable and bleeding
> at the borders. Booze was good for rage. Booze could keep it
> burning through the darkest night.

After Grace retires from the fray, Elliot stays up, fondling his rage and
a loaded shotgun. At dawn he carries the weapon out into the snow, con-
templates wasting a couple of neighbors he meets on a ski trail or killing
himself. Catching sight of his wife in a window of their house, he begins
to hope for the grace of her forgiveness.

The couple's quarrel is drenched in sour irony. Both Grace and Elliot
live in a circumstantially bad world—disappointed in their childlessness

while acutely aware that children brought into such a world are doomed to suffering, *hostages to fortune*, as it were. Grace, though, is supported not so much by religion itself (Elliot baits her about that, most cruelly) but by an ethical template derived from the habit of faith, which furnishes her a reliable moral compass. Elliot has nothing of the kind himself (so the cruel baiting is rooted in envious despair). Instead, "nothing but whirl inside him. . . . He could not control the headlong promiscuity of his thoughts." For such a condition, alcohol (not just for this autobiographical protagonist but for a great many alcoholics) is a palliative—until it stops working that way.

In the first agony of his morning after, Elliot "realized that now there would be whole days to get through, running before the antic energy of whiskey. The whiskey would drive him until he dropped. . . . Getting drunk was an insurrection, a revolution—a bad one. There would be outsize bogus emotions. There would be petty moral blackmail and cheap remorse. He had said dreadful things to his wife. . . . There would be damn little justice and no mercy."

A miniature masterpiece in its own right, "Helping" gives a frighteningly clear picture of Bob's "drinking life," and also a pretty good idea of what a no-holds-barred fight between the Stones would have looked like. Having learned to know his partner very well indeed (through loving her, ironically enough), the husband knows exactly where to place the low blows when love, catalyzed by alcohol, has turned to anger. It's especially noteworthy that he focuses the attack on the very qualities in her that she regularly uses to save him from the worst in himself. Mornings after such explosions must have been very terrible indeed.

There's a Janice avatar somewhere in almost every Robert Stone novel, but the character usually operates in the wings. After "Helping," she doesn't appear in a connubial fight scene until *Bay of Souls* in 2003, and in that episode her husband doesn't have a lot to say.

The real-life Janice never withdrew her support from the real-life Robert Stone (and Bob, till the end of the twentieth century, never quit drinking for long enough for a relapse to provoke disappointment as bitter as Grace's). Bob could certainly hold a lot of liquor without betraying any impairment, and when he did overrun his capacity, Janice unfailingly saw the two of them as two against the world. There were incidents, some she witnessed and some she did not: "He told me that he had, one night, driven into Harvard Square in the wrong direction, on a one-way street.

He did a terrific imitation of the Boston accent of the cop who stopped him. 'Look at all those people lookin' at you, mockin' an' jeerin'.' I don't think they did breathalyzers in those days, and Bob probably had a Harvard ID. The cop let him go."

In the early 1980s, cocaine was making one of its periodic eruptions into (relatively) polite society. In New England it was suddenly "around in a big way, as it had been in Key West when Bob went there in 1977. He told me that in one place in Boston there was a thin film of cocaine all over the bar." For deeply devoted alcoholics, though, the chief virtue of cocaine is to enable them to stay up and drink longer. At the end of the 1970s, Bob "much preferred quaaludes, and of course alcohol." Sometimes he used his social-engineering skills to coax prescriptions for narcotic painkillers from his dentist and from doctors treating his periodic gout attacks. But cocaine would be a big factor in the drinking life of Gordon Walker, the protagonist of novel number four.

In Hawaii, the Stones had been friends with Tom Riley, another member of the university faculty. In the fall of 1980, Riley turned up in Massachusetts with his wife, Karma, who was performing a one-woman show in Northampton. "We had dinner with Tom before the show, and Bob drank so much that he fell asleep during the performance and was snoring. It was infuriating, because Karma Riley was a good actress—she portrayed nine different women, one after another. Bob was annoying our fellow theatergoers. I would pinch his nose when he began to snore. This move would temporarily stop the noise."

On the way out after the performance had ended, "a couple of women decided to give me a half-friendly lecture about the unacceptability of his behavior. I'm pretty sure they were lesbians from Northampton's large gay community. I was so pissed off. I wasn't sure if I was angrier with Bob or the self-righteous women." Closing ranks with Bob came naturally. "I told them that over the years, my husband and I had become used to a certain amount of social disapproval. It was true enough."

Two against the world. Afterward, Bob incorporated the incident into his raconteur's repertoire as a self-deprecating comic set piece. "He would say, pantomiming expressions of disapproval, that the two lesbians had said they were very sorry that 'this,' indicating himself as the drunken lout, 'had come between us,' our solidarity as fellow females. He knew I was trying to defend him. But he seemed to have no actual memory of the evening at all."

Tom Riley, writing to thank the Stones for the preperformance dinner where Bob had had his few too many, was forgiving, and in a way even sympathetic: "Karm's play went over well enough for her to pick up a couple of other east coast bookings for it. It is funny, but the feminist group that booked her had real problems with her 'aloofness.' Almost as much problem with that as they had with your snores, Bob."

At the end of the day, an artist capable of creating *A Flag for Sunrise* could be forgiven . . . a very great deal.

8

A FLAG FOR SUNRISE

To organize his third novel Stone uses a structural device similar to that of his first two, setting two of his three principals, Frank Holliwell and Pablo Tabor, on courses bound to converge on a tiny mission run by the Devotionist order in the fictitious Central American country of Tecan. Among these three, Holliwell most obviously resembles the author in his background, qualities, and present situation. Stone makes him an anthropologist, a useful substitute for fiction writer. Holliwell is fatherless in all but name, and far more embittered with that condition than his author ever expressed. Holliwell's unhappiness with his bastardy approaches that of Edmund in *King Lear*. He teaches anthropology at the university level, and is married to a Janice avatar somewhat similar to Grace in "Helping"—a spouse who tactfully remains offstage.

En route to an academic junket to Compostela, a fictitious country somewhat resembling Honduras, Holliwell ends a period of abstinence by slamming a couple of Bloody Marys before getting behind the wheel of his car. In New York he has a sodden lunch with Marty Nolan, a spymaster he served under, albeit informally, during the Vietnam War. "I wasn't an intelligence specialist, or even a contract employee. I mean, you know how it is. . . . They come to you." He's completely cynical about the value of any information he ever produced: "it all goes into the hopper. Nobody gives a shit about it—maybe nobody ever looks at it. But it ends up— pardon the expression—intelligence." Nolan wants him to slip over the border from Compostela to Tecan to check out that Devotionist mission, but Holliwell turns him down.

A shadow of the Vietnam War looms over Holliwell wherever he goes. For an interview in *The New York Times*, Stone told Charles Ruas that during his own trips to Central America, "I was sensing the American presence in all its variety and aspects. The situation began to remind me of Vietnam. I was again seeing this irrational sense of mission which Americans are consumed with when they are about their business in the underdeveloped world." And also, "I think everybody must be aware that this society is a whole lot shakier now than it was before the war." Parting from Nolan, Holliwell reflects, "A great deal of profoundly fractured cerebration had gone on in Vietnam. People had been by turns Fascist mystics, Communist revolutionaries and junkies; at certain times, certain people had managed to be all three at once. It was the nature of the time—the most specious lunacy had been enacted on both sides of the Pacific."

Holliwell feels his sense of self slipping the farther he travels from the stabilizing conditions of his Stateside life; it's as if the whole Vietnam experience could begin again for him. In a state of drunken paranoia, he makes such a hash of his lecture in Compostela that he fears he may be attacked in its aftermath, but instead he's rescued by Tom and Marie Zecca, Foreign Service types posted to the U.S. embassy in Tecan (and loosely based on the American couple who had given Stone a lift into Nicaragua in 1976). Like Holliwell, both Zeccas served in the Vietnam War, a point disclosed soon after they meet. He reads the Zeccas' helpful offer of a ride across the Tecanecan border as a shove from the spymasters in the direction of that Devotionist mission on the coast.

———

"During my trips to Central America," Stone wrote for *Harper's Magazine* several years later, "I began to make a point of listening to as many stories as I could. After a while the stories began to form a pattern that conformed to my sense of Mesoamerica's history. This band of republics between the Andes and the Grijalva [a 300-mile-long river in southeastern Mexico] seemed placed by its gods in a very fateful situation. The region seemed to have attracted the most violent conquistadors and the most fanatical inquisitors. When they arrived, the Spaniards found holy wells of human sacrifice. Here, racial and social oppression had always been most severe. The fertile soil of the place seemed to bring forth things to provoke the appetite rather than things to nourish—baubles and rich toys, plantation crops for your sweet tooth or for your head.

"These lands were eventually yoked to labor-intensive, high-profit products, bananas, of course, and coffee, chocolate, tobacco, chicle, emeralds, marijuana, cocaine. I decided to put down the book I was writing and begin a new one. My subject was again America; the United States had been involved here for so long."

"It's easy to create a country," Stone told Ruas. "All you have to do is to think of a name for it." He might well have been thinking of real countries (Yugoslavia, Iraq) created in almost exactly that manner, though his Tecan is a fiction, a geographical scramble of Honduras, Nicaragua, and Guatemala. "It's representative of all those places in the world, particularly in Latin America, that are beset by the American presence and that are ill-governed. In another way, it is the world."

Stone goes on with a quote from Porfirio Díaz: " 'Poor Mexico, so far from God, so close to the United States.' Every time this colossus of the north turns in its bed, poor little Tecan is practically overthrown. The American presence is serving its own interests as it sees them, but without actually meaning to it is inflicting great hardship on Tecan," which the novelist had created as a stage for presenting "a due bill coming up for payment. Nothing is free, and we've been getting our bananas, so to speak. We've been getting our potassium to stave off our sense of existential dread. We've been sending in the marines and pushing people around in Central America, and we're going to eventually have to pay the price for it."

Tecan, like a good many U.S. client dictatorships in Central America at the end of the 1970s, has been simmering with leftist revolutionary movements for a considerable time—among the intelligentsia and the urban poor. As Holliwell rolls into the country, tension has been vastly increased by the government's thoughtlessly greedy seizure of copper rights in the mountains, which has "given every anti-government faction a common cause," according to Tom Zecca's analysis.

On a collision course with this situation is Pablo Tabor, AWOL from the U.S. Coast Guard after shooting his fine hunting dogs, terrorizing his wife with another firearm, and abandoning his son with her to take flight—all the while cranked to the eyeballs on the popular amphetamines of the period. Pablo's surname, and some aspects of his personality, are recycled from one of the corrupt, sadistic guards in Stone's unpublished story "The Dark Winter of Corporal Rafferty." He has a tremendous capacity for violence, and some talent for it.

It's possible to read Pablo as a version of Ray Hicks in *Dog Soldiers*, but without Hicks's discipline, which makes a very big difference. With Hicks he shares military training and a mystical disposition, but in Pablo's case the training didn't properly take and the mysticism is too disorganized to do him much good. One would see little of his creator in Pablo, except that he is a sort of fun-house reflection of Holliwell, who is very clearly cast in Stone's image. It is more than possible that Stone invented Pablo as a sort of there-but-for-the-grace-of-whatever-go-I figure. Pablo is an "institutional personality," the sort of "affectless sociopath" he told Ruas he'd begun to recognize in childhood, an expression of "the rootless, emotionally crippled individual in American life."

The key institutions in Stone's youth had been orphanages, the navy, and the Catholic Church. Pablo has experienced versions of the first two, while his religious sensibility is all the more dangerous for being ungoverned by any rational doctrine. His personality is well-described in this scrap of dialogue from Bob's unfinished play about Bernhard Rothmann: "Such men do not know themselves. They call their own fits and notions as signs from God. Their whole spirit is in their spleen. Satan easily enters into such a man and when he does the world becomes sweet with love."

Adrift in Vizcaya (another fictive locale on the Central American coast), running low on amphetamines and confidence, Pablo is recruited by Jack and Deedee Callahan, a sleekly epicurean, piratical couple with a plan to use their discreetly souped-up shrimp boat to run guns into the Atlantic coast of Tecan. (Bob took the trouble to sketch modifications to the Callahans' vessel on a yellow legal pad: secret compartments and a false hull.) The crew consists of their old friend Fred Negus, a white Bahamian, and his black sidekick Tino, but for the delivery they need an extra piece of muscle. Callahan is looking for "a bad guy I can keep in line," that is, a sociopath almost (but, fatally, not quite) exactly like Pablo.

———

If Pablo is a man of almost pure action, Holliwell and Sister Justin Feeney, the young American nun tending the clinic of the Devotionist mission, may seem to represent opposite extremes of the *vida contemplativa*. With nothing positive to enlighten it, Holliwell's contemplation has turned bitterly cynical, his inner life gone badly to seed. An idealist, activist, and nursing nun, Justin would appear to have the advantage over him. However, all is not well with her either. She is stationary in her mission, with the two other principals driving blindly toward her, but she is far from still.

The mission is in the doldrums, with no congregation and not even any patients in its clinic. Devotionist superiors have ordered Sister Justin and Father Egan to shut the place down and come home. Aside from the mission's idleness, a revitalizing fruit company has recently bought the land out from under it.

Justin is reluctant to abandon the mission for reasons obscure even to herself. Father Egan, an elderly alcoholic visionary, wants to stay on till he can finish an interminable tome of theology he's working on. To Justin he says, "You've been morally spoiled. There's always been someone around to take your good intentions seriously." If the comment is cutting, Justin is hard enough on herself to have come up with it on her own. She's in a state to question everything about herself and her vocation.

For distraction she goes with a younger Tecanecan priest, Father Godoy, to take some children to a carnival in nearby Puerto Alvarado. A sense of renewed mission comes to her via Godoy (on whom she happens to have a nunnish little crush); some revolutionary action may happen soon along the coast and Justin's infirmary would then be needed. Holliwell, meanwhile, drifts into a resort on Tecan's Atlantic coast, not far from French Harbor. His itinerary has a feel similar to Stone's first spontaneous trip to Honduras, and Holliwell does a bit of diving himself.

Something tempts him to go over a deep drop beyond the pretty, sunlit, shallow region of the reef. And something goes wrong. "Turning full circle, he saw the same shudder pass over all the living things around him—a terror had struck the sea, an invisible shadow, a silence within a silence. On the edge of vision, he saw a school of redfish whirl left, then right, sound, then reverse, a red and white Catherine wheel against the deep blue. It was a sight as mesmerizing as the wheeling of starlings over a spring pasture. Around him the fish held their places, fluttering, coiled for flight.

"Then Holliwell thought: It's out there. Fear overcame him; a chemical taste, cold stone on the heart. . . .

"As he pedaled up the wall, he was acutely aware of being the only creature on the reef that moved with purpose. The thing out there must be feeling him, he thought, sensing the lateral vibrations of his climb, its dim primal brain registering disorder in his motion and making the calculation. Fear. Prey."

The menace is all the more terrifying for being invisible. Holliwell suspects a shark but the dive master scoffs away the idea, pointing out that Holliwell never saw it. This episode is a linchpin for images of primitive predation veined all through the novel. Heath, a cosmopolitan corporate assassin whom Holliwell meets at his resort, encourages him to eavesdrop on other guests, Buddy and Olga, as they regale each other with anecdotes about pedophile murders carried out by friends of theirs back home. Lieutenant Campos, chief of the Guardia Nacional in the Puerto Alvarado area, is in the habit of slaying hapless hippie-girl tourists who fall into his clutches—forcing Father Egan to bury one of those corpses at sea. (Campos also has a sinister eye on Sister Justin, stalking her as Holliwell imagines or knows the shark to be stalking him on the reef.) Some malevolent intruder has taken to murdering small children from the coastal villages nearby, inspiring the surviving kids to chant *mono malo, mono malo*, naming their predator *bad monkey*—a suitable title for *Homo sapiens* gone wrong.

Subjective insight into a sociopath (in less full bloom than those above) comes through the characterization of Pablo, who, though he does many stupid things, is not exactly stupid. Indeed, he is extremely cunning but without much power of insight, which means that as much as he wants to be an actor in the world he is always more acted upon by it. Pablo is acutely aware of the structures surrounding and controlling him—to a paranoid extent (paranoia being a trait he shares with his author) and sometimes inaccurately, though his perceptions are often close enough for rock and roll. For example, he figures out fairly quickly that the Callahans don't trust him much and are prepared to kill him at the end of the run.

When Pablo senses they are toying with him ("turning me around," in his own private lexicon), he's quite correct—and in a more sophisticatedly sinister way than he can imagine. At the top of their game, the Callahans could dance rings around a Pablo, but in fact they are drinking and smoking too much dope for the occasion, as is their cohort Freddy Negus, though he reproaches the other two for it. In these circumstances Pablo can try running a game of his own. When the guns are loaded, he eavesdrops and gets some information about the supplier, Naftali, and decides to go ashore to try robbing him. By dumb luck, Pablo happens to inter-

rupt Naftali in the process of committing suicide by Nembutal overdose
with a brandy chaser. Entering his last delirium, Naftali makes him the
surprising gift of a very large diamond. Then, as his drugged mind soft-
ens, Naftali slips a strange ichor into Pablo's astonished ears.

"There is a creature in another dimension whose jewelry is dead
worlds. When this creature requires more of them it plants the seed of light
on a tiny planet. After a while there are people and then nothing—a pa-
tina." And then: "Brain coral . . . It's only the outer coral of the brain. . . .
There are reefs outside, Pablo. And reefs inside—within the brain of the
diver." It's as if Holliwell's experience on the reef is being filtered through
psychedelic kabbalah. "In the brain coral you see the skull of the earth, the
heaping of the dead. You pass it going out . . . you see it in your mind . . .
it's your own brain. Sometimes among the brain coral . . . the casing of a
skull. It rolls under the reef."

Pablo is fascinated by this mystification because it implies the existence of a coherent worldview behind it, though all he can articulate to
himself is "he had scored in spite of everything. Had made an idiotic over-
play and scored all the same. He felt forgiven, favored by God."

Tino, having heard a rumor of Naftali's death and Pablo's involvement, jumps ship. The Callahans lose their one sober and competent
crewman without knowing the reason why. Nevertheless they carry on.
Deedee is deputized to keep Pablo occupied and calm as the *Cloud* sails
toward the Atlantic coast of Tecan. Masquerading as fishermen, they net
enough shrimp to cover the crates of guns in the hold, then repair to Pablo's berth to consummate the seduction Deedee has been nursing along
since Pablo boarded in Vizcaya.

The scene (a good deal more explicit and less delicately nuanced in
draft versions) expresses Stone's interest in female sexual predation, a
subject underrepresented in American literature, though for the novel's
larger purposes there's more to it than that—it ties in to a larger pattern
portraying the ways human beings devour each other. Jack has a clear
understanding of the way Deedee satisfies her taste, to the point of being
her collaborator. "She likes edges. She thinks he's a stud. He's got shit between his toes and he's going to be dead tomorrow. That's what she likes."
In the end it's just a more epicurean version of the Eros/Thanatos cocktail
quaffed by Buddy and Olga's murderous child-molesting friends, or as
Jack concludes, "you can't have sex without mortality."

However, the slightly misjudged and underestimated Pablo recovers from postcoital *tristitia* in time to remember that his shipmates are planning to kill him soon, and sets about killing them all instead—successfully, though not without taking a bullet through the muscle of his leg. Alone, wounded, high on speed and the fantastic amount of pot he smoked with Deedee before her demise, Pablo now has to bring the *Cloud* through the reefs toward the light which Sister Justin has been told by emissaries from the revolutionary Father Godoy to leave burning on the dock of the mission at French Harbor.

Holliwell, snorkeling in the shallows near the mission, manages to impale a knee on venomous sea urchin spines. The accident flushes Justin out with her nursing kit and allows Holliwell to scrape acquaintance with Father Egan as well. In this scene Holliwell reveals to Justin that he's something of a Catholic himself and has been schooled by Jesuits. Holliwell comes away with a strange attraction to the nun. He makes a couple of returns to the mission, sounding out Justin exactly as a spy would do. They dine together, she tells him her relatively thin life story, and he imagines falling in love with her. Though much of this feeling amounts to projection, some of his perceptions of Justin are legitimate. "*More* was what drove her. Whatever the world afforded in the name of virtue, sacrifice, good works, she wanted more, wanted it all, as though she deserved it."

Life more abundant, in spiritual terms. Holliwell's notion is not so far off of Father Egan's idea that Justin has been morally spoiled. What she's done most recently is replace the expectations of faith, to be fulfilled in the indefinite future if at all, with waiting for the revolution to launch, which could happen the next night or the one after and will give her a definite, constructive role to play. She can't shake her concern about what will be left of her personal being if she succeeds in the spiritual life, "if I win, if I crush myself." Elsewhere, Stone ruminates about "that sense of being in touch with the numinous, with something transcendent. In a way it's vain and foolish and sort of spoils everything for you because you're expecting too much—that kind of spiritual orgasm is what you're always going for." Justin turns toward the brewing revolutionary action to find a target for this kind of frustrated expectation. "To do penance and amend my life, amen. To struggle unceasingly in the name of history. Gimme a flag, gimme a drum roll, I'm gonna be there on that morning, yes I am."

Concerned, attracted, and guilty in more ways than one, Holliwell toys with the idea of confessing to Justin that he's been sent as a spy. "If he did not tell her, it might be more dangerous for her. . . . If he did tell her, it

would quite likely be dangerous for him." Heath and the other "contractors" that are beginning to fill up Holliwell's resort have begun to quiz
him, not quite casually, about the nun and the mission. Holliwell, though
extremely drunk during most of his waking hours, can still perceive
that this group of profiteers is totally in with Tecan's dictatorship and
the Guardia Nacional defending it—thus involved in the threat to Justin.
When he calls Tom Zecca, hoping to get the dogs tracking Justin called off
from a higher level of authority, Zecca pretends not to understand him,
and Holliwell knows that, as a spy, he's been turned out in the cold.

So Holliwell returns to the mission to declare his love for Justin and
then make love to her. Their love passage is infinitely more high-minded
than Deedee's with Pablo, but it does involve Holliwell's awareness that
Justin has a good chance to be dead tomorrow. Still it is expressed in different terms. When Justin quotes Emily Dickinson ("A Wife—at Daybreak,
I shall be—Sunrise—Hast thou a flag for me?"), he begins to understand
that he has maybe mostly been an instrument for something she wanted
to do for herself. Not long afterward he finally tells her that he and others
have been spying on her and tries to persuade her, unsuccessfully, to flee
the grave danger she is in.

Drunk in his resort that night, Holliwell is snatched from his bed by
Heath and Soyer (the latter a local representative of international corporate interests), who hustle him to the Puerto Alvarado police station. In
the course of a fairly standard third world interrogation, with the civilians and Lieutenant Campos taking turns, the veils (fairly flimsy to begin
with) fall away and the real structure of relationships is revealed. What's
really running Tecan's corrupt government and its enforcement mecha-
nisms is not the U.S. State Department or the CIA but entities like Inves-
tors Security International, represented by Heath, who's now plainly in
charge of the local situation. (The big villain of this play is no particular
person, state, or government, but transnational corporate capitalism.) In a
moment alone with Holliwell, Heath declares, "I'm the shark on the bottom of the lagoon. You have to sink a long way before you get to me. When
you do, I'm waiting."

———

During the same dark night, Pablo has by dumb luck (or in his own
belief the grace of God) fumbled the *Cloud* through the coral reef to the

rendezvous point just off the mission's dock. He hands over the weapons to the revolutionaries, sets the *Cloud* on a collision course with the reef, and watches her sink from a lifeboat. On shore, he limps into the group of pre-Columbian stelae near the mission, where Father Egan has assembled a congregation of international vagabond youth, including but not limited to Weitling, the young renegade from an inland Mennonite mission who's under a compulsion to murder children: the *mono malo* in flesh and blood.

Now high on a cocktail of speed and pain pills, and possibly feverish from his leg wound, Pablo fits right into this assembly. He seems to be responsive to Egan's strange ministry, though really their conversation would be funny if it wasn't so scary: a spectacle of two delusions, talking past each other. "Pity the Weitlings of this world, Pablo. They're victims of things as they are. That's what Satan is, Pablo. Satan is the way things are."

Pablo drinks it all in happily enough. "Something's going on Pablo," Egan tells him, and Pablo concludes, "I'm in this. Me. I am." Like all good sociopaths, he knows that everything is really all about him.

———

Egan takes Pablo back to the mission for treatment of his wound. There they find Justin running her little corner of revolution and Holliwell dosing himself on medicinal brandy. It's decided that Holliwell and Pablo—strange bedfellows that they are—should head out toward the shipping lanes in the mission's boat (the same vessel used by Egan, in the novel's opening sequence, to bury one of Campos's victims at sea), in hope of being rescued. Egan will remain at the mission while Justin, with the revolutionary group, goes forth to meet her destiny.

Father Godoy has told her, not quite warning her, that the rising on the Atlantic coast is planned as a diversion from more serious maneuvers in other regions. That turns out to mean that in the short term the revolutionaries around Puerto Alvarado are defeated and Justin is captured and turned over to Lieutenant Campos. As Campos beats her to death, she returns unequivocally to faith and discovers her vocation for martyrdom in its purest form, telling him with her last breath, "Behold the handmaid of the Lord."

———

Locating Justin's election of martyrdom in the whole context of what this novel has to propose about the order which may or may not govern the world we live in is something of a challenge. Father Egan, whose occasional gift for inspired simplicity is one of the novel's lodestones, takes it at face value when he gets the news from Campos (a frightened, helpless, probably doomed fugitive now that the revolution has succeeded everywhere else in Tecan). "She said that, did she? ... Good girl. She *was* special, young Justin."

In the guise of spiritual counsel, Egan advises Campos to "imagine a world in which you don't exist." For his own part, the priest finishes the story in a state of Zen-like acceptance of things as they are—or one might call it a version of Kierkegaard's infinite resignation: "His moments were never dull since he had come to occupy them one by one. . . . The truth was a fine thing, but it had to be its own reward."

That last line could stand as a late-twentieth-century novelist's credo.

———•———

Many years later, in conversation with the interviewer Peter Occhiogrosso, Stone announced, "When I once said, 'In a sense I'm a theologian, and so far as I know, the only one,' I meant that in terms of American writers . . . I felt at various times that I was taking seriously questions that for most educated people were no longer serious questions, and I ascribed that to my Catholic background. I mean specifically the question of whether or not there is a God or whether or not you can talk about life and its most important elements in religious terms, the question of the absence of God—Heidegger's postulating God as an absence—all these things are, for the most part, not taken too seriously by educated people."

Although Bob never had the same sort of religious reawakening that Janice experienced during her last acid trip in Wales, his use of psychedelics under Kesey's wing in Palo Alto "impelled me to re-examine my attitudes toward religion because my experiences with acid were very much charged with religion. I guess it would have been strange if they weren't. I was taking acid, and I was taking it seriously. I felt very much that I was consciously developing a view of the world, and when I had these religious experiences as a result of taking acid, I really felt that they demanded to be reconciled with my intellectual attitudes generally. So it made me less able to develop a totally secular intellectual system of my own. I again had to make allowance for the numinous—if not the supernatural, at least the nonrational, the extrarational. I think this probably served as a process through which my adolescent religious attitudes were transformed but somehow reinforced. My adult secular life was subverted again by something very intrusive and very strong. I began to have to afford to the extrarational a certain importance in terms of how I saw things, and as a result these religious areas of experience came to be reflected in my writing. The drug experience forced me not to dismiss those things as simply part of my childhood gear but to realize that I had to continue to think about and deal with them."

For a literary novelist who (in some ways like Dostoyevsky) uses some of the mechanics of thriller plots to build narratives of much more serious intent, Catholicism also has some useful features built into it. "There it is. Obviously, if you think about the iconography and the principal mysteries of the rosary, you have an awful lot of blood, an awful lot of violence. . . . So it's appropriate, in a way, that Catholicism and its iconography reflect all this, because the world, after all, *is* like that. It tells you that you have to accept this, it tells you that the world is this way."

A Flag for Sunrise isn't an illustration of Catholic doctrine, as many Flannery O'Connor short stories are, nor is it limited to an exploration of the influence of Catholic faith on human behavior, the way so many Graham Greene novels are. If Stone had finished his Jan of Leiden novel, it might very well have turned out more like the examples above, because all the characters would, necessarily, have been acting quite consciously in the light of religious dogma and the conflicts inherent within it. *A Flag for Sunrise* is by contrast an intensely realistic novel—its texture of the real is carved in deep relief—whose foremost concern is always the way we are with each other. The novel is a study of human being, but along the way Stone is able to capture a good many varieties of religious experience, simply because they are of acute concern to the characters.

The complete sentence in Luke 1:38 reads: "Behold the handmaid of the Lord; be it unto me according to thy word." What the sentence expresses is absolute and unconditional surrender to divine will. Few are capable of that even in propitious circumstances; that Justin can produce it from the experience of being beaten to death by a malevolent third world military troglodyte really is "special," in Father Egan's term. Justin's dying declaration is a transcendent moment and, as such, irreducible; one may disbelieve entirely in the idea of Christian martyrdom and still be forced to acknowledge that she has suffered . . . just exactly that.

Transcendence on this order is obviously not available to everyone. A more common relationship to Catholicism is exemplified, oddly and often almost comically, by Lieutenant Campos, a brute with a transactional relationship to faith and practice. Campos wants Egan to broker deals with the Divine for him—in his view that's simply what priests are for (a view widely shared by faithful peasantry from the Middle Ages on up).

———

Some believers require more. Pablo, whose brand of unorthodoxy is probably no crazier than Egan's (but is distinctly more naïve and far more violent at the personal level), has like Campos a transactional relationship with the superstitious vestiges of belief that remain to him; he's always trying to cut a deal with his destiny. To call his beliefs a system would be going too far, but whatever it is has something in common with primitive magic, Weitling's compulsive murderousness, and whatever was the point of the human sacrifices conducted long ago among the stelae near the mission. "Poor Pablo," said the writer actually in charge of his destiny, "he's such bad news—that's the secret of life that he never discovers, that he's just terrible bad news."

That leaves Holliwell, and Pablo's bad-news quality is no secret to him after the two have spent a couple of hours in the open boat. Pablo treats him to a stream of monomaniacal raving. "Nothing can stop me now, Holliwell. I got it all together. Like there are ten million people think they got it all together but I'm the one who has. That's how it was meant."

In reaction, Holliwell "felt the force he had encountered over the reef.

"The stuff was aqueous, waterborne like cholera or schistosomiasis. He had been around; he had seen it many times before. Among swarms of quivering fish, in rice paddies, shining in gutters. It was as strong as anything in the world. Stronger perhaps, when the illusions were stripped away. It glistened in a billion pairs of eyes. Comforting to think of it as some aberration, as perversion of nature. But it was the real thing, he thought. The thing itself."

That situation is easy to read as *kill or be killed*, so Holliwell acts on the principle by stabbing Pablo with his own diver's knife and dumping him out of the boat. "Just another one of us," he thinks, watching Pablo go down. "We're all the joke. We're the joke on each other. It's our nature. . . . What a misfortune, he thought, that we have only each other." This rejection of anything beyond the mortal world of human interaction is underlined by a couple of hallucinatory sharks that appear in Holliwell's dream that night as he continues to drift on the open ocean.

" 'What is there?' the shark asked his companion.

" 'Just us,' the other shark said."

The eye you see with is the one that sees you back is the sort of koan of which Stone was fond—derived and simplified from a longer, less mysterious sentence once pronounced by the medieval mystic Meister Eckhart. After killing Pablo, Holliwell incorporates it into his own delirious monologue. He attaches it to a news item he once used in his teaching: "An experimenter endeavoring to observe chimpanzee behavior had fashioned a spy hole in the door of the animals' chamber through which he might watch them unobserved. Putting his eye to it, he had seen nothing more than what he finally identified as the eye of a chimpanzee on the other side of the door." One might as well say that our notion of God's omniscient eye on the sparrow or anything else is merely our own regard reflected back. "Ape stuff," Holliwell thinks with a shudder. The only godhead is some *mono malo*, preying on the hapless ordinary monkeys. Just us.

Still, as much as Holliwell resembles Stone, and although he is the last man standing at the story's end, it would be a mistake to assume that his truth is the only one out there. Holliwell's perceptions are not always correct; for example, he mistakes Naftali's diamond for a rhinestone and tosses it out of the boat. At the very moment when he's thinking that "He, Holliwell, was things. There was nothing better. The absence of evil was the greatest horror," something rather peculiar occurs:

"Then out of the sky suddenly blue as the eye of things there came in dogged laboring flight, heavy-winged, a pelican with a spot of blood at its breast. His head snapped back to follow it, but he dared not turn full round and face the eye in the sun." This thoroughly naturalistic image is also a hard-edged chunk of medieval Christian iconography that would have been instantly recognizable to all the characters in Stone's Jan of Leiden novel: The maternal pelican was believed to pierce her breast to nourish her young, a pattern representing Christ's sacrifice of his body and life for the redemption of humankind.

What it may mean to Holliwell we just don't know. We see him see the iconic presentation, but we don't know what he sees in it. A few minutes later, material salvation presents itself when his boat drifts to the shore of an island. There's even another boat with occupants whom he can address: "I require rescue here." The novel ends in this ambiguity. Redemption (an idea that became important to Stone toward the end of his life) is contrasted with simple survival. Redemption and rescue are not the same thing. If Holliwell is in need of redemption, he doesn't get it here.

————

Robert Stone's third novel appeared in the fall of 1981. *A Flag for Sunrise* launched with front-page coverage in *The New York Times Book Review*, and was a finalist for the Pulitzer Prize and the PEN/Faulkner Award for Fiction, and twice for the National Book Award (most unusually): once for the hardcover and once for the paperback edition the following year. In a winner-take-all literary culture, the fact that *A Flag for Sunrise* didn't actually win any of these accolades meant that it didn't sell as well as the enthusiastic reception warranted. Nevertheless, the splash was sufficient to reestablish Robert Stone (who had not published a book for seven years) as an important and unusual spokesman for the Americans of his time, and the book sold a very respectable 40,821 copies in hardcover.

"[The] violence seems very right, made inevitable by the tone of dark historical despair underlying everything," said the prepublication review in *Kirkus Reviews*. "No American writer does crazy dangerous people better—perhaps because no American novelist finds the strain of pusillanimity in contemporary Americans quite as scary as Stone does. . . . And, more agonized than even a Naipaul over history's black holes, Stone lights every page with the superiority of his prose: the great descending speed of his paragraphs, hipness turning ecclesiastical, the extraordinary cynical ventriloquisms of much of the dialogue."

Richard Poirier delivered a long, somewhat patronizing essay for *The New York Review of Books*—overly dependent on the weak metaphor of its title ("Intruders")—and sometimes capable of mind-boggling historical errors like this one: "the Vietnamese, by introducing a generation of Americans to hallucinogenic drugs, intervened in America, creating thereby in Southern California a replica of the nightmare landscapes of their own ravaged country." What? But Poirier's piece is consistently astute about the remarkable craftsmanship of the novel, both in detail and on the grand plan. There's an incongruous invocation of Pynchon's *Gravity's Rainbow*, which *A Flag for Sunrise* resembles not at all, as well as one of those glancing comparisons to Graham Greene that so irritated Bob: "He populates both this novel and *Dog Soldiers* with predominantly Catholic characters, apparently drawn to the tradition of violence and debasement that includes such Catholic novelists as Mauriac, Graham Greene, and Flannery O'Connor. But while Stone, who said in a recent interview that he was brought up a Catholic, sporadically reminds us of the traditions of Catholic nonconformism, his novels are given neither structure nor meaning by them."

Poirier (adept in picking out the novel's most subtle literary allusions) includes a similar but somewhat more interesting discussion of Stone's relationship to the literary tradition behind him. "While most of the allusions are to the literature of despair, that literature in the past usually found ways to affirm redemptive possibilities not offered in this book. In fact, when Stone echoes earlier writers he seems to imply that what looked like down to them may look like up from here." And finally: "*Flag* is a disturbing book in many ways, some of them not intended. I'm not referring to Stone's politics as such but to the degree to which they may reveal more about his opportunism as a novelist than about his anxieties as a citizen. The opinions that can be inferred about America or its uses of power or the possibilities of resistance to either—none at all, I would suppose, in his view—are so implicated in his creative energies that they don't as yet offer themselves to argument. They are nonetheless available to suspicion. As a writer he is an inveterate showoff, and it ought to be said, in order to keep an important writer an honest one, that novelistic imperialism such as his—I mean that desire for the glamour of ruin that can be articulated only by first discrediting and then disposing of whatever might challenge it, including a clear head—may be worth worrying about, like any other kind of imperialism."

———

But the caviling scarcely mattered; to have such an extensive review in *The New York Review of Books*, complete with one's caricature (Bob was made to resemble a cross between the very late Tolstoy and one of the crazier Old Testament prophets—with a film clip rolling out of his typewriter, even so), was incontrovertible evidence of having "arrived." Un-qualified validation for *A Flag for Sunrise* was produced by John Leonard for *The New York Times Book Review*, though for much of the review it's difficult to predict where it might be going—Leonard's flamboyant prose suggests that the critic might have celebrated his enthusiasm for the book by taking all the hallucinogens Bob Stone had ever consumed at once: "Hold on to your tricornhat, or your cruciform, or your Uzi. In his third novel, after *A Hall of Mirrors* and *Dog Soldiers*, Robert Stone decides to be Dostoyevsky. Perhaps, on conceiving 'A Flag for Sunrise,' he was more modest. He would be Graham Greene, sending various quiet, stupid Yan-quis to Central America. He would be Joseph Conrad, hyperventilating near a convenient pyramid. He would be Herman Melville, reversing Billy Budd, as if Christ were a black hole or a woman's glove. But he thrashes his way—spaced out on ideas and angry love, possessed by comparative religion, punished by God and history—to Fyodor and a blue eye that turns into a blind sun. He swaggers in evil."

Hang on to your hat, indeed. But in his conclusion, Leonard's ap-proval is clear, and unreserved: "*A Flag for Sunrise* is the best novel of ideas I've read since Dostoyevsky escaped from Omsk." Also, when your nov-el's review lands on the front page of *The New York Times Book Review*, the reviewer's opinion matters far less than this glorious placement. With this kind of momentum, even pans (Bob got a nasty one from Jonathan Yardley of *The Washington Post*, who "found the novel too left-wing, even un-American") turn into assets.

There were reviews in *Time* and *Newsweek* and in most of the big-city dailies. Knopf sent Bob on a substantial book tour, with stops in Bos-ton, New York, Charleston, and Atlanta among others, plus a run to the West Coast. At the time, publishers reserved this sort of thing for writers with a shot at bestsellerdom, and *A Flag for Sunrise* did make *The New York Times* bestseller list for one week—though only because of an error that the *Times* corrected the following week. (Bob had bet against his own chances with somebody at his publisher, and the *Times* list quirk left the winner unclear.)

The book's strong performance closed a string of lean years for the Stones, when for example "paying Ian's private school tuition had been difficult"; now "the financial pressure was off us for a while." With their friends the Gelbers and the Kopits, the Stones had a celebratory dinner in the Rainbow Room, whose entrance Janice had admired two decades earlier from across the hall, while selling tickets to the roof of the RCA building. "I had never been inside the place before. The Rainbow lived up to my fantasies of it, a glittering cave of luxury."

With *A Flag for Sunrise*, Stone consolidated a body of work that amounted to a whole greater than the sum of its parts. *A Hall of Mirrors* and *Dog Soldiers* had also, each in its own way, plugged into the zeitgeist by tapping into what most troubled the American psyche during the periods in which each was set—and so releasing tremendously strong currents. In *A Flag for Sunrise* it was more apparent than ever how fusing topical issues to eternal questions had become Stone's way of shaping an enduring work of art. With the completion of this masterpiece, he came to a stronger awareness of his own powers—in spite of the immense struggle to get there, the long periods of tormented inaction, dark passages from which it had seemed he might never emerge.

———

Of *A Flag for Sunrise*, Tim O'Brien said simply, "I wish *I'd* written it." This sentiment would be shared by writers in Robert Stone's vein for generations to come.

In the summer of 1983, my mother handed me a paperback copy of *A Flag for Sunrise*. We were on our way to spend a few weeks with friends in the Roman Campagna and a couple of other places. It was my first trip to Europe; my first novel had been published a few months earlier. Before I got on the plane, I had never heard of Robert Stone. By the time the wheels touched down in Rome, he was the writer I wished I could become.

PART FOUR

---·•·---

CHILDREN OF LIGHT

1

EMBOURGEOISEMENT

He reminded himself that he had his business like everyone else," Holliwell reflects, trying to shake the creeping existential horror of his plunge into Central America. "His business was done in University Park, a perfectly real place though recently constructed. It was to husband and father, to teach, even to inspire, and to endure. These things were not trivial. A monstrous pride might despise them, but honor could not. Because who does one think one is?"

Who indeed? In the lead to his 1981 interview, Charles Ruas defined his subject this way: "For the past 10 years Robert Stone has lived with his wife and two children in northern Massachusetts. . . . Now that the children have grown up and are preparing to leave home, he and his wife are considering a move themselves. He leads a rigorously healthy life with disciplined work habits. He's out in the woods walking with his dog as soon as it gets light. After drinking a quantity of tea, he starts work and goes as long as he can. His wife is the first to read his work in manuscript, and he consults her if a decision of style is too close to call; except for his editor and his agent, she is his only reader of work in progress.

"Robert Stone, now in his early 40's, is of medium height, slender, with the ruddy complexion of the country." This picture was accurate as far as it went—not so far as to mention that Bob's ruddy complexion might be related to drinking a quantity of something other than tea.

Then there was *People* magazine, presenting Bob to its vast readership with the headline: ROBERT STONE LIVES IN PEACEFUL SECLUSION, BUT HIS NOVELS INHABIT A SHADOWY AND VIOLENT WORLD. Not quite *National Mirror* material, but sufficiently pumped up to unnerve its subject slightly. Bob was induced to pose for a picture: scuttling across the Hartford airport in a trench coat and carrying a briefcase, wearing also the fretfully suspicious expression of a minor spook or a small-time Mafia bagman. Past the headline, the *People* piece painted a picture of Stone leading a modest and industrious life—with nods to Bob's unstable childhood, Prankster days, and Vietnam adventures. (Asked if he smoked heroin like others in Vietnam: "'That stuff is illegal, isn't it?' he says with a smile.") But all of that was in the past, Stone implied: "It's hard not to think of yourself as young and indestructible, but my proper business now is writing. Besides, the people in my books are alternates for me—they go through all that horrendous stuff so I won't have to."

It was an image he wanted not only to present to the public but also to enact in private life. "These things were not trivial," as Holliwell had put it. Stone told the interviewer he was working on a novel "closer to home than" *A Flag for Sunrise*, "a book about the effects of the Industrial Revolution on a small New England mill town." He had possibly made this project up on the spot, along with a bit of fictitious detail about his father. Stone sometimes went fairly far in planning out historical novels but never actually finished one.

Some of his friends would call Bob paranoid (Ken Kesey thought the quality a virtue, at least in his friend, and had incorporated it into his quote for *Dog Soldiers*). Maybe someone else would not have reacted as strongly to the profile locating him (not very specifically, in fact) "in a small college town in Massachusetts. . . . The novelist wants his exact whereabouts kept a secret," the piece chattered on. "'I write about a lot of strange people,' he reasons, 'and I don't want them coming around to hassle me.'" The idea that mildly or severely disturbed people Stone had never heard of might decide they were models for his characters had bothered him since *Hall of Mirrors*. There was the woman who identified intimately with Geraldine because "I have a scar on my face, too," and there were others, less innocuous than she.

Bob's real problem with the *People* profile was that it put his person, rather than his work, in the spotlight (which was after all the magazine's declared mission as well as its well-known technique for manufacturing celebrity). Bob wanted success for his work, but celebrity for its own sake did not interest him. And even in the pre-Internet 1980s it would not have been too hard for some loose fool, or a pack of them, to figure out what "small college town in Massachusetts" that was.

Besides, Bob was temperamentally inclined to be a rolling stone, and he'd already stayed in Amherst for longer than anywhere else in his adult life. By now, the need to keep a stable home for the children had decreased. Ian was off to Beloit and Deidre, though still living on South Pleasant Street, was leading an independent adult life, supporting herself with Nefertiti's, a perfume shop in Amherst that the Stones had purchased. It looked like a feasible time for a change.

————

Bob had a habit of taking Ian on fishing trips to Block Island—the happiest province of the world of his own boyhood. Old-timers remembered Bob from when he was a lad, and some remembered his mother too. Return to Block Island was a kind of homecoming.

Alongside the appeal of fishing and nostalgia, there were signs that some sort of writers' and artists' community might be beginning to coalesce. As early as 1975, Daphne Ehrlich (a member of the *Dog Soldiers* editorial team at Houghton) wrote Bob, "I thought I'd let you know that we are recreating our 'scene' in Block Island this summer if you and your family were thinking of coming out again." A few years later the Stones were thinking in more permanent terms. They were already in the habit of scanning the real estate section of *The Block Island Times*, but "prices always seemed to go up faster than our income did."

Now Bob got in touch with a childhood friend on the island to try to find an affordable place, and in June 1981, they bought a house for $82,000. "The house on Pilot Hill Road was over a hundred years old, located uphill from the Block Island School. There was a large empty lot, as well as Payne Road, between our house and the school. A line of evergreen trees in the front yard had inspired the owners to call the house Misty Pines, a name we dropped immediately." The property featured a small outbuilding that could be converted for Bob to use as a studio. The Stones were to keep the Block Island compound for many years, longer than any of the several other properties they owned.

Proprietorship of a second home was part of what Bob somewhat satirically defined for the *Washington Post* Style reporter as his ongoing process of "embourgeoisement." In keeping with this motif, twenty-one-year-old Deidre teased her father during the interview: "I bet he didn't tell you he watches *Days of Our Lives*, did he?" Bob was quick to clarify that he'd watched the soap only a couple of times, for experimental and research purposes. In the same conversation Deidre, perceptively, undercut the embourgeoisement theme, cautioning the reporter: "He looks very quiet and well-mannered, but actually he's very angry." True enough, Janice confirmed decades later: "Bob had regular fits of anger. He is very funny writing about them, but watching him could sometimes be alarming. He would pace the room for a few seconds, growling softly, and he gnawed on his index finger until, over the years, it became calloused. I'd sometimes ask him if anything was wrong, even wondered if he was angry with me, but he would say no. I got used to it, and tuned it out. It was a brain glitch, I decided—maybe the flip side of his depression." This spontaneous flowering of rage became a motif in "Available Information," a trippy occasional piece Bob published in *Rolling Stone* at the end of 1981, discussing how radio crosstalk, among other media phenomena, could push his anger buttons. Deidre, whose observations of her parents sometimes took a satirical turn, had once told Bob and Janice that they needed to see Stanley Kubrick's *The Shining* because "it's about our family"—though Bob's brain glitches never went so far as Jack Nicholson's character.

In fact the Stones could not use their summer home the first summer they owned it, as Janice had no vacation time from her job at the Children's Study Home. They rented the Block Island house to their friend Carol Southern (the ex-wife of the novelist and screenwriter Terry Southern), a maneuver that serendipitously produced a telephone listed in her name, screening Bob's connection to the house without the expense of an unlisted number; the Stones kept that listing for the next couple of decades. As *A Flag for Sunrise* publicity ballooned, Bob grew ever more uneasy about staying on in Amherst, but he didn't want to live on Block Island full time. "In winter," he told Janice, "there was nothing to do on Block Island but attend church on Sundays," seldom one of Bob's preferred activities. "He wanted to be closer to New York City, or maybe in the city itself." They began to tour houses along the Connecticut coast of Long Island Sound, without finding anything workable. Then they visited old friends Arthur and Leslie Kopit in Westport, a fashionable enclave between Norwalk and Fairfield. Paul Newman and Joanne Woodward had owned a compound there since the early 1960s, featuring a colonial house and a barn they converted to a screening room. Janice and Bob "didn't think we could afford to buy there, but as Arthur drove us around town we passed a modest house on Hillspoint Road with a real estate company sign. 'How much could that place possibly cost?' Arthur asked. We decided to find out."

The final answer was $155,000. In fact, the house was a perfect find for the Stones at that moment. The owner was an architect who'd bought the place and remodeled it with the intention to flip it (a good many years before that term of art came into general use). The location on Mill Pond (an area the Stones would jocularly call "the Bronx of Westport") brought the price within their range. The Stones were having a couple of fat years, with money from *A Flag for Sunrise* still coming in, and Bob having recently signed a new $300,000 contract with Knopf for a novel that would eventually become *Children of Light*. A Westport bank approved them for a mortgage, their second after the one they'd undertaken to buy the Block Island house. Janice was at that moment making $11,000 a year as a social worker, the highest salary she had ever earned, though one she was soon to give up.

2

BEHIND THE IRON CURTAIN

In the summer of 1981 Bob went to London to consult with his U.K. publisher and agent and to struggle with the recalcitrant tenant now more or less squatting in the Stones' Redington Road flat. In August Bob flew to Bucharest, capital of what was then Ceaucescu's Romania, still an Eastern bloc totalitarian state. His trip was sponsored by the United States International Communications Agency.

Although the role of literary fiction writers as public intellectuals was in decline in the early 1980s, USICA cultural programs abroad continued to present writers like Robert Stone in that light. In Bob's case the social engagement of his first three novels helped. In the spring of 1982 he'd received, via David Rosenthal of *Rolling Stone*, an article clipped by an Amnesty International staffer about the recent political murder of a nun, Victoria de la Roca, in Guatemala.

"It's hard to really think of this as life imitating art," went the cover letter to Rosenthal; "It's more that once again one is reminded that what he has created in his book, through compelling imagination and imagery, the story of the net closing around just one woman, is also an everyday event in Guatemala." Based on some discussions of another novel, the staffer had adopted the idea that "one novel, one story well-told, could do more to awaken public consciousness about Guatemala" than any standard political reportage. "Stone's is frightening in a different sense, because as I said to you, the fantastic unreality of what is actually happening in Central America, seems to me to be heightened, made somehow more disorienting in his book because you can't really be sure which country (if any) he's talking about at any particular point. . . . I think Stone's book is not only a 'good story' but important and timely in a political sense, with Central America now the object of so much international attention."

Victoria de la Roca was neither the first nor the last nun to be slaughtered in the chaos of Central American politics. Two nuns had been similarly slain in El Salvador in 1980 and there would be more to come. But for a writer like Bob, and for his U.S. Information Agency handlers, the implication was that a novelist like Robert Stone could become a player of some significance on the world stage.

The trip to Romania had been some months in the planning. *A Hall of Mirrors* and a couple of Bob's short stories had been translated by Andrei Brezianu, a Romanian novelist and intellectual. They had first met when Brezianu toured the States in 1979, under the auspices of USICA. The two writers hit it off and made tentative plans to meet again. "Talking to a translator," Bob wrote later on, "is almost always a pleasure for writers. You're with a person who has special interest in exactly what you intended in a book line by line, one who is trying literally to get on your wavelength." As the Romanian visit began to take shape, Bob wrote to his hosts, "I'm rather taken with the notion that I have this translated existence in what, to my provincial mentality, is such a far-flung place."

The publisher of the Romanian translation of *A Hall of Mirrors* was expressing tentative interest in *A Flag for Sunrise*—so long as the novel involved no "unspeakable practices, unnatural acts," that is, in Brezianu's interpretation for Bob, "drugs, gays, etc." Apparently the drug-running, drug consumption, and peripheral gay-bashing in *Dog Soldiers* had rendered that novel unacceptable to Romanian arbiters of taste. Bob was also owed some royalties on the Romanian edition of his first novel and the publication of the two stories, although at the time it was uncommon for foreign authors to be able to collect.

"Bucharest under Ceaucescu was one of the most ghastly places on earth," Bob reported afterward. "Its atmosphere partook of true horror; he was Dracula, the real thing, the Prince of Transylvania, ruler of the undead. No tour of the twentieth century would have been complete without a stop in Ceaucescu's Bucharest." As for his own position there: The "literateurs" attached to the Romanian state, "reading my morally convoluted pessimistic fiction, had somehow decided that I was what they referred to as a progressive. Between one thing and another you had to wonder about their idea of progress." Still, there was an advantage to the misperception: "My work was seen as critical of American society and consequently I was perceived as a potential foreign friend."

This theoretical friendliness (discreetly supported by USICA, no doubt) did not produce a completely comfortable situation. Bob was assigned a guide and minder, Gabriela Gheorghiu, an occasional journalist believed by the writers he met on this trip to be an informant for the Romanian state. An "interview" she later published on "The English Page" of *Tribuna Românei* invested Bob's speech with an uncharacteristic stiffness: "The Romanian readers are marvelous. I like them and I shall always treasure the memory of that meeting." In fact, Bob was genuinely interested in free exchange with Romanian readers and writers, beyond his growing friendship with Brezianu, though Gheorghiu's alert presence inhibited that. However, she liked to clock out early, so Brezianu could visit Bob in the evenings, quietly slipping him notes for rendezvous with other writers.

There was plenty in Romania for paranoia to attach to. Control on native writers was extremely tight. "Romanians needed a license to buy a typewriter, and if they disposed of it they had to turn in the keys to the police." Aside from his official minder, practically anyone Bob ran into was possibly a spy. Food was scarce to the point that Gypsy children lingered around restaurants, hoping for leftovers as the plates were cleared. More ordinary citizens, warming themselves during the winter nights by their intermittently supplied gas ranges, sometimes died if the gas went off, then came back on, unlit, while they were sleeping. By night, according to Bob's notes, "the streets were without light" and "a pall of dirty smoke hung in the air like evil itself."

In addition to appearances in Bucharest, Bob went to various other places around the country—Cluj-Napoca, Mangalia, Constanta—usually attended by Brezianu and always by some minder/spy. Brezianu alerted Bob to the nature of one new companion by introducing the man as "Gabriel." Bob understood him to mean that the man he was meeting was the equivalent of Gabriela, thus suspected to be in the security service. The new man was confused. "My name isn't Gabriel," he protested. Escorted by such a Gabriel, Bob and Brezianu went to a Black Sea beach. At Brezianu's signal, Bob walked into the water, fully clothed, to converse with another Romanian writer waiting for him, by prearrangement, beyond the surf line. The Gabriel of the day could think of no pretext to follow.

Less comical was Bob's discovery that Brezianu had another translation in hand: Thomas à Kempis's *The Imitation of Christ*, which for whatever reason was an extremely dangerous enterprise in Ceaucescu's Romania.

Brezianu asked Bob if he would help move his Kempis translation out of Romania—to Brussels, where "an émigré typesetter" had been lined up to print it. Bob agreed, not without some trepidation. Gheorghiu's unexpected appearance at the hotel added some suspense to the hand-off, but finally Bob picked up the package without alerting her and took it as far as the airport by streetcar. "In the end our little improvised network picked someone else to carry the book the rest of the way through the rigorous airport security. . . . All my life I would be tempted to say I had actually taken it out to Brussels but to do that I would have had to lie and undo all the merit I had acquired in helping out in the first place."

Reflecting on the experience many years later, Bob wrote: "Some kind of irony was being visited on me—in my pursuit of good times I was evolving a theology of suffering. . . . It might be more correct to call it an aesthetic of suffering. Over the years I had glimpsed some essentials and one was the trolley ride in Bucharest, another was the night in October 1956 when I watched the French jets bomb Port Said from the USS *Chilton*, another was Dewey Canyon Two at Lang Vei in 1971"—the place where Bob had come closest to combat in the Vietnam War. Gathering these three experiences together, he drew a provisional conclusion: "We want human suffering to mean something. . . . We think it must. We insist on it."

One of the dissident writers Bob had semi-secretly met in Romania had given him a bottle of brandy on his way out. He was meant to drink it in memory of their community, but the bottle was broken in transit.

3

PROFESSOR STONE

Back in the States, life was calmer, in spite of Bob's travel commitments running through the fall of 1981, most of them to do with promoting *A Flag for Sunrise*. Janice left her job in social work to become, at Bob's request, his full-time assistant. The change was affordable; despite having taken on two new mortgages at the high interest rates of the early 1980s, the Stones were more financially comfortable than they had probably ever been. The sale of *A Flag for Sunrise* paperback rights to Ballantine brought $250,000 (enough to earn out the Knopf advance with plenty left over for Bob), and the Knopf contract for his fourth novel guaranteed (after a $50,000 payment on signing) monthly payments of $5,000 for fifty months—albeit with a clause that had become standard in Stone's contracts: After eighteen months, evidence of "satisfactory progress" must be shown to the publisher to keep the cash flowing.

Tom Jenks (later to become among many other things Bob's editor at *Esquire*) had been in his first year of the Columbia MFA program when Bob came to teach a sample class in 1980. "On the appointed day Bob arrived in the classroom, and without much prelude read aloud James Joyce's 'Araby' to students around a seminar table," Jenks wrote several decades later. "At several points Bob paused and humbly passed a consecrating hand over the pages and made short comments, expressing admiration for a word, phrase, or image. The class ended, and the students wandered out into the hall. 'What the fuck was that?' one said. 'I didn't learn anything.' There was a general murmur of agreement in the hallway, graduate writing school—art!—being the uncertain, anxiety-prone path that it is. In Bob's class that day, there were no notes given or taken, no pedagogy per se, no list of rules to follow, nothing more concrete than Joyce's words, Bob's voice, moving in that sacred and profane story from blindness to sight."

Though he never embraced the academy completely, by the time of this encounter Bob was well-seasoned as a teacher. He'd jotted his basic principles for leading fiction workshops in one of the spiral notebooks he also used for sketches and fragments of his novels. Jenks's "no list of rules to follow" had a variation in Bob's heading:

> No body of knowledge to impart
> Reading, writing, criticism

The latter phrase listed the three fundamental components of writing workshop activity—by 1980 there was a fairly general consensus to that effect.

> For reading—take it where you will—enjoy it, try to learn
>   why you enjoy it—which shouldn't interfere with your
>   enjoyment—
> Writing—the more you do of it, the more you learn about it—
> Criticism should be a part of what you learn—not a place for
>   upmanship or malice—but part of a cooperative effort—you
>   must accept your writing as a public premeditated act.

These were simple and flexible principles, universally applicable for students willing to cooperate. Bob, who never suffered fools gladly, had small patience for mediocre student work, but at Columbia he wouldn't have seen much of that. Located within the nerve center of national publishing, the School of the Arts MFA of that period was one of the top three most selective such programs in the country, and (thanks to very limited financial aid combined with New York City's perennially astronomical cost of living) the most expensive. Students had to be extremely talented to win admission, and they had to be extremely ambitious to assume the cost. Such students were well able to make the most of what Bob's teaching, unconventional as it might sometimes be, had to offer.

"Ten years later," Jenks continues, "I was teaching at the Iowa Writers' Workshop and Bob came to do a short gig. I suggested that he read 'Araby,' in part because I wanted to hear him voice it again, and in part because it was one of the best lessons students could hope to receive. Forty or fifty assembled, and their response was very much the same as that of my classmates at Columbia ten years earlier. It can be hard to know what you've received until later. In life, Bob knew something about that. And he raised it to art."

Westport, when Bob had time to linger there, was a calm environment, suitable for a writer settled in his life and habits as Bob claimed to interviewers he was and probably wanted to be. "The view clear across the Mill Pond to Sherwood Island was beautiful, and we felt that living on the water was uplifting to the spirit. The light changed from hour to hour, day to night. Bob had a work space in the attic, on the third floor of the house. We had his desk from the Amherst house moved upstairs. The space was entirely private." The attic office featured a second phone line, to isolate Bob's business calls for tax accounting, but its listing in the name of I. A. Crock (the name of the Stones' long-ago real estate partnership with Fred and Olga Kiers) made it unlikely for inbound calls to intrude.

Despite working conditions close to ideal, Bob did not yet have a good start on the fourth novel. His travel schedule for 1982 was as busy and hectic as in the year before. In February he gave a reading at the University of Kentucky, the linchpin and pretext for a tour of the eastern part of the state with Gurney Norman, an old friend from the Perry Lane crowd, who had grown up there. On his return to Westport he met some concern from another set of long-term friends, the Gelbers and the Kopits, about the extent of his drinking.

Interventions as such were not quite yet in vogue, but Bob was induced to talk the issue over with Stuart Shaw and Jill Schary Robinson (he an Englishman, playwright, and memoirist; she the daughter of a president of the Metro-Goldwyn-Mayer studio and the author of the Hollywood memoir *Bed/Time/Story*, a work much concerned with recovery from addiction). Stuart and Jill urged Bob to try AA, and Janice would have liked him to try it, but he was not willing, despite or because of a "hard sell" from Stuart. Bob snarled to Janice, "He threatened me with death." Jill persuaded Janice to attend an Al Anon meeting. "Bob was so horrified that I had gone to Al Anon that he cut down on alcohol for a short time." In spite of this friction, the Stones enjoyed the company of Jill and Stuart and continued to socialize with them until they moved to England.

Bob and Janice were on the move too, next to California where Bob would teach the spring semester at the University of California at Irvine. This university town, still under construction in the early 1980s, was "new and rather alienating" in Janice's eyes. They found a house to rent at 1298 Anacapa Way in Laguna Beach, "a gem of a town, reaching up into the hills of the Pacific." Their neighborhood backed into Laguna Coast Wilderness Park, part of which Bob could drive through on his fifteen-mile commute to the university.

At UC Irvine, there was a young writer, described by one of Bob's colleagues as "'a long drink of water,' who had left a fat manuscript in Bob's office." The colleague assured Bob that the author was not one of his students and that he was not obliged to read the work, or even open the package. In fact this "long drink of water" was a writer named Kem Nunn, and the package contained a draft of his first novel, later published as *Tapping the Source*. This work, sometimes characterized as "surf noir," owed something of its style to Robert Stone's fiction, and something of its plot structure to Roger Corman's biker movies. Nunn was a late bloomer, from the academic point of view. Nearing thirty, he hadn't finished his undergraduate degree, but Oakley Hall, the director of the writing program, let him sit in on MFA workshops at Irvine and gave him a copy of *Dog Soldiers* with the news that its author was coming to teach.

"I read the book," says Nunn, "and was blown away. It was noir, it was action, but it was also a book of ideas, a book about America. I also felt . . . I could do something like this (or at least try) and it became one of those books that, as an aspiring writer, you really start trying to dissect and to imitate. And I began writing *Tapping the Source* and pushing really hard to have a finished draft that maybe Bob would read when he got there."

There was every chance Bob wouldn't read Nunn's manuscript, given the irregularity of Nunn's situation in the program and the fact that "Bob didn't much enjoy reading student work most of the time. . . . But he had a moment of boredom one day and thought he'd have a look." He packed the manuscript for a trip to Mexico to visit Nick Nolte on the set of *Under Fire*, a film set in the midst of the 1979 Nicaraguan Revolution. Bob and Nolte had hit it off during the *Who'll Stop the Rain* shoot. They shared a taste for Rabelaisian excess; as Bob later told Steve Goodwin, Nolte's "idea of a good time was to drink a bottle of tequila and lie down in the middle of the main street and see what happened." Nevertheless, Nunn's manuscript did get read somehow, and Bob came back with the idea of trying to get a movie deal for Nunn's story; if it went through, Bob would write the adaptation.

That scheme didn't come to fruition, though for Nunn at the time it was "pretty heady stuff, way more than anything I'd imagined." Whether

Bob had consciously recognized the extent of the influence of *Dog Soldiers* on *Tapping the Source* is unknown, but the episode shows the spectrum of his response to apprentice work—from relative indifference to unstinting enthusiasm, often paired with this kind of concrete support. In this instance, Bob's intervention helped launch Nunn's long and successful career.

4

THE DUKE OF KENT

Bob and Janice had intended to return to Westport in late May 1982, but an odd happenstance changed that plan. Kristen Peckinpah—the daughter of the notorious director Sam and the wife of Gill Dennis, another screenwriter/director whom Bob knew from his various Hollywood stints—was auditioning for the role of Cordelia in a production of *King Lear* coming up in Santa Cruz's summer Shakespeare festival, and she invited Bob to read with her. "Bob immediately agreed. He loved reading Shakespeare. The way it turned out, Kristen did not get the part of Cordelia but Bob was offered a part—the Duke of Kent, Lear's faithful companion. He could not resist." His role in Harold Pinter's *Homecoming* had been a memorable experience in Amherst years before; to play Shakespeare was an even better opportunity.

The Santa Cruz Shakespeare festival was to open in July. In June, Bob went to the Midnight Sun Writers' conference in Fairbanks, Alaska, where he met John Hildebrand, a younger writer who knew the Alaskan territory well. Hildebrand already had a regard for Robert Stone, enhanced by Bob's reading of the opening chapter of *A Flag for Sunrise* at the conference, "where the Canadian girl is kept in a cooler of beer. To me, Bob was the great American novelist, a man of the world, someone who'd seen the things he'd written about—Hemingway with a conscience and a sense of humor."

It was a hard-partying conference and Bob didn't want to stop; he changed his return ticket to join a road trip with Hildebrand and Edward Hoagland (who was also featured at the conference). Hildebrand borrowed a pickup truck and took them on a long circular route for several days of camping and fishing. This wild hare through Alaska was the first of many excursions Bob and Hildebrand would share. Since the Stones' return from England in the 1970s, Bob had acquired a taste for hunting, fishing, and outdoor adventure, much of it in the company of Michael Hardy, who had died in a car wreck in the spring of 1982.

Late in June, Bob and Janice moved down to Santa Cruz where they shared accommodations with other players in the Shakespeare festival. Bob poured himself into learning the part of Kent—a substantial role that includes the first line and the next to last line spoken in the play— practicing tête-à-tête with Janice, before full-scale rehearsals began. The play opened in early July and ran into mid-August. It was an ambitious production, with two members of the Royal Shakespeare Company, Tony Church and Julian Curry, playing Lear and the Fool, respectively, for several shows (roles otherwise undertaken by lesser-known actors).

Press coverage noted, perhaps charitably, a "range of acting abilities," but with a favorable nod toward the portrayal of Kent by "the celebrated novelist Robert Stone." Predictably, the Royal Shakespeare Company pros Church and Curry got most of the ink, but there were other professional actors in the production, including "the lovely Kate Rickman" (so described by the *Santa Cruz Express*). Playing one of Lear's disagreeable daughters, Regan, Rickman had her picture in a couple of the papers.

"It was a good experience for Bob," says Janice. "Less so for me. The actors were close, socializing with each other nearly every night. Kate Rickman was smart, talented, beautiful, mischievous, and unhappy," certainly a very dangerous combination of qualities, which Bob found intriguing, at least up to a point. "Bob liked Kate, and responded to her attention, showing off a bit." How serious his response really was is somewhat unclear, but it was sufficient to start and sustain a lot of very widespread gossip.

Kate was married to Tom Rickman, "the screenwriter of the film version of *Coal Miner's Daughter*, whom Bob had met at Squaw Valley. Perhaps he had met them both. The song that summer was Willie Nelson's 'You Were Always on My Mind.' Kate called it 'the guilty husband song.' The Rickmans knew Willie Nelson. They were going to divorce before too long, but we didn't know it. Maybe they didn't know it either."

This cocktail was for once a little too much for Janice. "My usual strategy for dealing with this sort of thing was to be elsewhere, to wait for the flirtation to blow over. But here I had nowhere to escape, as Bob was depending on me for everything from practicing his lines to driving him around. For the first time I found myself jealous. It was like catching a disease, and I hoped I would recover quickly, because it was making me a bit crazy." Level-headed as always, and fair-minded perhaps to a fault in this case, Janice "didn't want to do anything to make Bob unhappy, or Kate either, in such a stressful time, when their focus had to be on their stage performances."

Eventually there was a bit of a showdown. Bob told Janice "that Kate had asked him if he had slept with Tuesday Weld, during the filming of *Who'll Stop the Rain*. He said he didn't know why he said it, but he told her he had. He sounded surprised at himself. He had never slept with Tuesday Weld, he said, and he wasn't sleeping with Kate either. He tended to be truthful, and I believed him." Bob and the lovely Kate went their separate ways with no more ado. Janice, driving back to Santa Cruz from a visit to the Barichses' in San Francisco, realized she was pregnant—something she had quietly hoped might happen since 1978.

———

In September Bob made that quick trip to Oaxaca to visit Nick Nolte and Roger Spottiswoode on location for *Under Fire*. Spottiswoode, who'd been assistant director for *Who'll Stop the Rain*, was directing *Under Fire*, and Bob might have had some idea that the team could be reassembled to shoot *A Flag for Sunrise*. (There was some movie interest in the novel, notably from Kathleen Turner's production company, but no picture was ever made.) However, Spottiswoode was scheduled for the next James Bond movie. Perhaps somewhat seriously, he asked Bob if he wanted a part, but Bob laughed that off, saying, "Don't you think I'm a bit old to play Bond?" The practical value of this trip was to give Bob the experience of another Mexican movie location he could incorporate into his not-quite-yet-conceived next novel. He took the trouble to sketch some movie gear into one of his spiral notebooks, in case he'd need to visualize it later on.

Back in California, the Stones packed their Skylark and aimed it east, driving through the Napa Valley wine country and stopping over for a spa experience in Calistoga Hot Springs, where Bob and another guest entertained each other and Janice by "quoting Ovid to each other in Latin, as we all floated one night in the warm water pool." Less happily, as they were leaving Calistoga, Janice realized she'd had a miscarriage, at not quite two months.

Further east, the Stones spent a night with Oakley and Barbara Hall. "Bob learned that gossip about him and Kate had reached Squaw Valley." Perhaps the story had not crossed the Rockies, though, and at any rate it was over. In Wisconsin, they stopped to see Ian, who was attending Beloit College. The visit to her living child might have put Janice in mind of the one she had just lost. "As we drove through western Pennsylvania the next day we found ourselves in tears. I was crying for the baby I would never have. Bob was crying for Michael Hardy," whose fatal car crash had happened in this terrain, only a few months earlier.

———

The good news was that Bob had a novel taking shape in his mind— something a long car trip can sometimes engender. The recent acting experience and the trip to the *Under Fire* location, added to the knowledge of the moviemaking world he'd acquired as a screenwriter, had coalesced into a plan for a Hollywood novel. "He told me one of his characters would be a crazy actress, and I said, oh no, not her! Not Kate, he assured me." In fact the eventual heroine of *Children of Light*, Lee Verger/Lu Anne Bourgeois, turned out to be almost entirely a creature of Bob's imagination (though it's possible some shadow of Lucy Saroyan lies over her). Before leaving California in May, Bob had picked up a copy of Kate Chopin's *The Awakening*, which he'd read previously when Deidre was assigned it for a class. A screenplay based on the Chopin novel would be at the center of the novel Bob had in mind—creating a whole new hall-of-mirrors effect.

5

DEATH AND OTHER TRIPS

Bob was having trouble with his voice in the fall of 1982, probably exacerbated by repeated declamation of Kent's lines in the Santa Cruz *Lear* production. The Stones still had their health insurance in Massachusetts; Janice drove him there to have polyps removed from his vocal cords and sent for biopsy. A three-pack-a-day smoker at this point, he had reason to fear cancer in this situation. "Driving back to Connecticut, Bob was planning for his death. Will you go with me?" he asked Janice. "Of course, I said. I couldn't imagine life without him. Sure I'd go with him. Why not?"

In some ancient cultures it was common enough for prominent men to be accompanied by their wives and retainers on the final voyage, but in late-twentieth-century America the notion was unusual, to say the least. Yet Janice took it seriously—indeed, seemed captivated. "When Bob wanted to do something, I always tried to figure out how to do it. Just in case worst came to worst, I began to plan, or at least to fantasize, but with the mental reservation that I had to think what to do about the children. They were now grown up but hardly launched into their lives. . . . I was still under the influence of the Duke of Kent, so beautifully portrayed by Bob. I thought I would not say no, if called."

The polyps weren't cancerous after all, so the imagined death trip didn't have to happen. Life was going to go on. The Stones were mostly done raising the two children they'd had so young, and it was now clear there would be no more. They were still in their early forties, with who knows what ahead of them, including books to be written and lives to be lived.

The health scare alarmed Bob enough that he finally quit smoking. Janice had quietly given up cigarettes more than ten years before, but for Bob breaking the habit was "the hardest thing he'd ever done," in part because smoking was entwined with his writing. "It had been so many years that he had sat at his typewriter with a pack of cigarettes at hand, smoking whenever he stopped to think." Fighting this addiction "interfered with his writing for months," and at a bad time, when he should have been getting the new novel off the ground. "He said later that he didn't understand how he did it, but whenever he felt tempted to smoke, bummed a cigarette from someone, he forced himself to break it in half rather than light it. He began to drink more, but I couldn't pressure him about drinking when the project in front of us was quitting tobacco. Doing both would surely be impossible."

Bob was not teaching that fall, and in November he set out on another European tour, again sponsored by USICA but this time also involving the launch of *A Flag for Sunrise* in foreign editions. Planning had begun the previous summer with a scheduled trip to Denmark; Bob's itinerary was later expanded to include Hungary and Germany. The tour would take up the last three weeks of November and distract Bob from any lingering cravings for tobacco (as well as from the novel he was trying to write).

A slightly quaint feature of USICA sponsorship was a requirement that Bob report on the trip—one thousand words for $100. The guidelines for the report suggest a sort of Cultural Espionage Lite: "If noteworthy, what were each group's most notable misperceptions or misunderstandings?" and "Toward which of your views and ideas did they show most skepticism or intellectual resistance? Could you determine the reasons for their reaction?" The report Bob filed was conscientiously compliant up to a point, while tending to stray in the direction of his own somewhat different interests.

Robert Stone, Jayne Anne Phillips, Elizabeth Hardwick, and Marilynne Robinson landed in Copenhagen in November—a quartet which in Bob's view delivered "as wide a range of views, literary, social and political, as you can get between four American writers." (Bob maintained a friendship with Marilynne Robinson, a worthy intellectual sparring partner, for the rest of his life.) For three days they attended a conference with Danish writers at the somewhat puzzlingly titled Louisiana Museum of Modern Art—this name had nothing to do with the state on the Gulf of Mexico but derived from the fact that the nineteenth-century owner of the country house around which the museum complex expanded had serially married three women named Louise. Bob gave a lecture at the University of Southern Denmark in Odense, two hours west of Copenhagen, on "contemporary trends in American writing, with particular regard to the distinctions, which I regard as eroding, between the mode of realism and that of fantasy and surrealism," and another at the University of Copenhagen, where he found students in the English Institute to be "very knowledgeable and conversant with contemporary English literature."

There were parties, doubtless well lubricated, following the programs at Louisiana, and "many opportunities, well taken advantage of, for extending the official sessions into a private discussion." The official topic of the three-day seminar was "International Provincialism—Is the Global

Village Becoming a Mere Village?," which as Bob reported, dryly again, "could not be adhered to with much strictness in a discussion between Americans and Danes whose definitions of 'Provincialism' differ so radically, nor is the McLuhanesque concept of the Global Village particularly viable these days."

Bob formed an attachment with Inge Eriksen, a Danish novelist and science-fiction writer, about his own age, and with something of Janice's rangy Scandinavian allure. Eriksen's first novel was "a cartoon of words dealing with an imaginary Latin American revolution," so it was natural for her to be fascinated with *A Flag for Sunrise*. What exactly had gone on in those six days is opaque, but from the letters, the Stone/Eriksen connection seemed more a passionate writers' friendship than a romance. "You reach me all right, Robert Stone," she wrote, "I have met a few male writers with whom I share what I have never shared with a woman: some queer desperation, which is very difficult to articulate." Like her correspondent she drank more than a little, while claiming "I'd never write seriously on booze, I drink to keep myself upright, which was pretty difficult with this book, *The Whore from Gomorrah*." Eriksen made Bob her confidant, through the mail if not in person, letting him know in December 1983 that she had left her husband. "Of course I have fallen in love too, I guess it is inevitable when you're so raw after a book, etc. I need not talk about that, I can't bear it, but it is serious and I feel like I'm playing Russian roulette with my life now. But maybe you have to do that once to become a real human being."

That last sentiment was one Bob Stone could share, and was indeed a factor in the book he was struggling with in 1983. Eriksen was bold enough to inquire into his state of mind. "Busy? Depressed? Happy? Bored? I don't know what to hope for you except that the book is good. I guess it is, you opened up for something with the last one and such things tend to unfold in the next." Bob replied, confidingly, "Since we got back from Europe during the summer, I've been trying to hold my life and work together, stay married, keep from falling in love, keep from drinking, from dope. I've also been trying to write seven days a week a novel about a drug-addicted film writer and a schizophrenic actress. I keep deciding to shake off this winter and its discontents, but I never do. . . . So I'm maintaining a low grade bourgeois crisis, analogous to a low grade fever, and I imagine once you've seen one bourgeois crisis, you've seen them all."

———

Sometime after his European trip was planned, and the tickets purchased, Bob had learned that *A Flag for Sunrise* was the winner of the *Los Angeles Times* Book Award for fiction. Determined to accept in person, he flew from Hungary (the second stop on his USICA tour) to L.A. on November 18, enjoyed himself royally at all the festivities, then on November 21 flew to Frankfurt for the third and final leg of the tour. This whiplash turnaround proved too much for even Bob's rugged constitution, especially given the recent surgery to his vocal cords. After two days in Germany (and one lecture on "Fiction and Journalism" at the Johannes Gutenberg University in Mainz), Bob lost his voice. He had been looking forward to the first readings from his own fiction in Germany, but it was clearly impossible for him to perform them. Exhausted, he canceled the last two days of the tour and went home to Block Island.

———

In Bob's absence, Janice had been spending time with Jeremy Brooks, who had stopped in on the Stones in Westport on his way to rehearsals of his dramatization of Dylan Thomas's *A Child's Christmas in Wales*, then being produced in Cleveland. While Bob was in Europe, Janice took Jeremy for his first visit to Block Island, where they explored the defunct apple orchard behind the house and planted some tulip bulbs. "We ducked out of sight when propane tank replacements were delivered, so that the gas man wouldn't notice that I was in the house with someone other than my husband. This event was reimagined by Bob when he wrote *Outerbridge Reach*, and Anne Browne takes Strickland to Browne's island getaway."

Bob turned up at his own island getaway, jet-lagged, fatigued, and out of sorts. "He and Jeremy got into some kind of argument the night he arrived, though they were very good friends. I can't recall what they argued about, but I remembered Joey Brooks, Jeremy's oldest daughter, referring to big guys sharing small spaces, usually teenage boys and the older men at the Brooks cottage in Wales, as engaging in 'male antler-rattling behavior.'

"I didn't want to hear my two favorite guys hassling each other, so I went out. I walked to the cliffs and climbed down to the beach. When I went home an hour or two later, they had both gone drunkenly to bed." In the morning, the quarrel was forgotten.

6
TECH DEVOLUTION

In 1983, Bob joined a wave of American writers who were switching from typewriters to word processors of one kind or another. Between constant travel and the ordeal of quitting smoking, he had not really been making "suitable progress" on the fourth novel and "was determined to do something to write faster. It was seven years between the publication of *A Hall of Mirrors* and *Dog Soldiers*, and another seven before the publication of *A Flag for Sunrise*, and he said he was going to stop writing his books 'in biblical cycles.' "

Encouraged by their friend, neighbor, and early adopter Arthur Kopit, Bob acquired a Vydec word processor, a behemoth produced by Exxon during that company's brief foray into manufacturing office equipment. The Vydec wouldn't pass through the tight stairways of the Westport house, so Bob had to give up his pleasant attic office for a small room on the ground floor, where, cramped under the bulk of the machine and bathed in the blue-white fluorescent glow of its screen, he claimed to feel "like he was working at the Dnipropetrovsk hydroelectric plant."

Bob's established writing habits included rewriting key scenes a great many times, often more than twenty drafts. When the typewriter was his most sophisticated tool, every word of every draft had to be retyped. Early and intermediate drafts were festooned with xxxxxxxxxxxxxxxxxxxed-out deletions and often scrawled over by hand as well (not to mention cigarette burns and coffee stains). He had used scissors and paste to assemble a final draft of *Dog Soldiers* for the hired student typist—an old-school method he'd doubtless picked up while editing *A Hall of Mirrors* with the Houghton team.

Parts of *Children of Light* were written before Bob acquired the Vydec. These pages had the palimpsest quality of the drafts of his earlier novels (and various structural plans for *Children of Light* were scratched out by hand in spiral notebooks or on yellow legal pads). When he switched to the word processor, draft pages got cleaner but there were no fewer of them. Bob printed frequently (ream after ream of dot-matrix print on fanfold paper). Sometimes he'd mark the printouts by hand, but not as often or as heavily; it was faster to revise and improve the previously printed version by working directly on the screen. Walking behind him, Janice frequently pushed Print herself; she worried that material might get lost, especially after a first draft of the story "Helping" did vanish into the ether.

The word processor soon became an essential tool, and presently the Stones got a "portable" one. "This machine was a Texas Instrument, and it weighed 38 pounds," according to Janice. "I know its weight because I often carried it." Around the same time Kopit retooled an early word-processing program, XyWrite, to make it more user-friendly for himself and his writer friends. Kopit taught his version of XyWrite to the Stones, who became so attached they continued to use it well into the twenty-first century (when they had to scavenge for junked computers still capable of running the program).

In Westport the Stones' social circle included the Kopits, plus a new friend, their neighbor Noel Parmentel, a writer originally from New Orleans who'd built a reputation in New York as a satirical political essayist (contributing to *The Nation*, *Esquire*, and *National Review*). He'd taken a young John Gregory Dunne under his wing for a time, and later Dunne's wife, Joan Didion. Dunne credited Parmentel with the style "of an axe-murderer, albeit a funny one." By the time he met the Stones, Parmentel was a recovering alcoholic—"alcohol tried to kill me," he was wont to say—but "unlike some of our friends, didn't seem to be bothered about Bob's drinking." And the two men had complementary acidic visions of the late-twentieth-century American scene.

Another Westport neighbor was the publisher Seymour Lawrence, who was "sharing a house with Joan Williams, the novelist. Joan's special claim to fame was that she had been the very young girlfriend of William Faulkner toward the end of Faulkner's life." In fact, the romantic interest had been entirely on Faulkner's side and remained unconsummated; the two kept company for a few years but the relationship ended when Joan married another man in 1954. Still, "Bob used to say that Sam had collected her, as he would a rare book, because of the Faulkner association." Such cynical aperçus aside, Bob genuinely respected Lawrence for having "no conversation and no interest except his writers."

The Stones saw the Newmans fairly often, if Paul and Joanne were around, and they continued to see a good deal of the Keseys, who came east in 1983, stopping at Westport on their way to some sort of celebrity ball in New York. (Newman had starred in the film of Kesey's second novel, *Sometimes a Great Notion*, so the two men knew each other fairly well.) Bob and Janice drove them into the city. Ken had adopted the cause of West coast hemp farmers and had brought "a giant ball of hemp" from Oregon, which he directed Janice to babysit while he and Faye checked into their hotel. "Sit on it, he said. So I sat at the door of the Waldorf Astoria, dutifully sitting on a huge ball of rope, feeling silly and trying to look nonchalant. Why did I always do what Kesey told me to do?" The answer, and not only for Janice though her perception of it was clearer than most, was that "he made his view of things inevitable, at least in the moment."

Kesey came twice to Westport in 1985—once in July with Gurney Norman and again in October with Faye—and on the second occasion *Esquire* recorded Bob and Ken in conversation, then garbled the transcription and published it with some of Bob's remarks assigned to Kesey (a goof which annoyed Bob considerably). Since the couples had last been together, Faye and Ken had lost their son Jed, killed in the crash of his wrestling team's bus at age twenty-one. Remembered by Janice as "a sweet child," Jed was exactly Ian Stone's age, and had been his childhood companion. "Ken and Faye buried him on their farm in Oregon, where they could visit the grave every day. Not everyone thought that was a good idea."

———

In London, the Stones' struggle with the man who had used U.K. laws protecting "sitting tenants" to squat in their Redington Road flat, had come to a head in 1983. Emotions ran sufficiently high that at one point (according to Bob) Deidre (as yet unencumbered with husband and child) "volunteered to go down to Sanibel Island, the tenant's American residence, and kill him." But instead they played through the problem by the book. "Bob asserted, through his lawyer, that he needed the flat back in order to reside there himself, and that 89 Redington Road was his primary residence in the U.K. The projects he would be working on, he stated, would include a play based on the story of Donald Crowhurst, an English sailor who was lost during a solo race around the world"; this idea was later spun into Bob's novel *Outerbridge Reach.*

Though wealthier than the Stones would ever be, "the tenant asked for a payoff to relocate to Switzerland, a place where, we were sure, he already had a home." Bob and Janice clenched their teeth and paid him anyway, reasoning that this capitulation would be quicker, and probably cheaper, than the protracted court battle that was their only alternative. Janice went to London in April 1983, where she found that the tenant had finally departed from Redington Road.

Margy Brooks and her French Israeli fiancé were staying short-term in the Stone flat (installing new carpet in lieu of rent), and Janice bunked in with them for a few days. Most of the old neighbors in the building had by this time moved on, encouraged to take profits from the rising real estate values of the 1980s. Bob and Janice planned to sell. After a few weeks in Italy, they returned to London together, to spend time with the Brookses and begin breaking up the flat. Janice, who found she "could part more happily with my things if they were going to friends," gave sundry household items to Valerie and Michael Herr, then living in London while Michael worked on a Stanley Kubrick project. Books, ever difficult to transport, went to a couple of friends who had opened a bookstore. Jeremy Brooks, an enthusiastic and able cook, got the kitchenware.

Eleanor Brooks gave the Stones the portrait she'd done of Bob in the kitchen of the Gelli cottage in 1978. The portrait went to Westport along with a couple of antiques that Janice didn't want to part with. "That painting captures Bob so uncannily, but he had mixed feelings about it and would never let me hang it. He said he didn't want to be confronted every day with his younger self." That he was smoking a cigarette in the portrait may also have been a factor. Eventually the painting found a wall in the Manhattan apartment the Stones bought in the 2000s and owned through the end of Bob's life.

7

DOORS OF PERCEPTION

Bob's enthusiasm for drugs other than drink had been noteworthy even in the Perry Lane circle, where it was shared to some extent by everyone around him. Prone to bouts of depression since childhood, Bob, because of his perfectionism and the difficulty of bringing his work to the high standard he required of it, didn't get the relief from practicing his craft that many writers do. That situation left him with an abiding interest in altered states by any means necessary.

He was also often looking for a drug to substitute for alcohol, something that might make it easier for him to drink less, or not at all. His excesses could be embarrassing and sometimes troublesome. Returning with the Keseys to Westport from New York, Bob passed out on the train and there was real difficulty getting him down a steep staircase from the station. "The Keseys were used to wrestling cows at their dairy farm and were strong people, but Faye nearly lost her footing going down the steps, holding Bob up by his left arm as Ken held his right." During a flight delay, en route to meet Janice for a Bellagio residency, Bob had a few too many and was helplessly drunk by the time he got to Milan.

Back in England, he showed up drunk at a party the Brookses were giving, moving Janice to a crisis of doubt. "I was upset, and began to wonder if I was contributing to this situation in some way. Was I an enabler? And what did that mean exactly? Did he have to be drunk to live with me? Should I leave him? I asked Jeremy and Eleanor for their opinions. They told me that if I left Bob he would only get worse. I thought they were probably right. And I didn't want to leave him."

While the Stones were resident in England in the 1970s, a British doctor had suggested that Bob wean himself off alcohol with narcotic painkillers. At the time Bob wasn't interested. Later on, drugs introduced as substitutes for drinking (including quaaludes, perhaps) were more apt to become additions, rather than alternatives, to his consumption of grog. (Gordon Walker, the protagonist of *Children of Light*, is seen seeking downers to help reduce his drinking—a dangerous and potentially fatal program.) For many years Bob had on occasion really needed opiate prescriptions for his painful attacks of gout. That was a situation that could be gamed, and in the early 1980s, with a growing interest in this family of drugs for their own sake, Bob was able to find cooperative doctors. In London "was an agreeable man who was willing to write Bob the odd scrip for pain pills. And in Wales, Bob could buy kaolomorphia in Port Madoc without a prescription. It was a diarrhea treatment, a mixture of clay (kaolin) and morphine, not awfully strong. Bob would let the bottle sit until the clay settled, and he could drink the morphine off the top."

Substance issues notwithstanding, Bob banged steadily away on the Texas Instruments word processor back in Westport (portable enough that he could move it back into his attic office), churning out pages of *Children of Light*—until he got distracted by a project for an HBO script based on the career of Dr. Tom Dooley, a navy doctor who'd served in Vietnam in the mid-1950s (before escalation filled the country with American soldiers), then left the military to set up a private clinic in Laos. A devout Catholic (as well as a closeted homosexual, according to a voluminous CIA file on him), Dooley was the sort of outlier who could not help but fascinate Bob Stone. Bob accumulated a couple of crates of Dooley-related material and traveled all over the country interviewing people connected to him, but the project finally came to nothing.

After this long detour, Bob returned to the novel he was supposed to be writing, and decided he had made a "wrong turn" somewhere. A good number of alternative structures for *Children of Light* had been sketched since the inception, one of them designated as "Plan Charlie." Bob refined a new plan, discarded a good number of pages, and made a fresh start.

Helene Keyssar, the director of the Amherst production of Harold Pinter's *The Homecoming* in which Bob had starred, had moved to California with her husband, where both were teaching at the University of California at San Diego. Bob was invited to teach there for the spring semester of 1985. Noel Parmentel, an avid and effective fixer who seemed to know helpful people everywhere, helped the Stones get "a terrific apartment on a cliff above the Pacific, in Encinitas." They hauled thirty-eight pounds of Texas Instrument word processor into the new place. Bob went into the homestretch on the novel, and to the astonishment of all had finished by the time his teaching stint was over—comfortably ahead of the contractual deadline. "This was a first for him. He was usually years late delivering a novel." Word-processing power had increased his rate of productivity much as he hoped—but not only that. "He was assisted by XyWrite, and also cocaine, which both he and Helene were using at that time." Janice, who was the Stones' household accountant among her many other roles, dryly observed that Bob had spent about $6,000 on the drug during their stay in San Diego; a serious cocaine habit could be ruinous in more ways than one.

8

CHILDREN OF LIGHT

Children of Light is a cocaine-fueled book, with the drug stirred into the metabolisms of not only the writer but also his protagonist, Gordon Walker. Stone was led in this direction both by his own shifting taste for intoxicants and by his unusual instinct for tracking the zeitgeist. Cocaine was, indeed, both the engine and the metaphor for the greed and gusto for gain and for instant gratification that characterized the American 1980s.

In the novel, Gordon Walker is a sometime actor (who like his author has recently played in a production of *Lear*) making his living mainly as a screenwriter . . . which is to say he is for the most part a well-paid hack. His wife, Connie, another offstage Janice avatar, has recently gotten fed up enough to leave him. His addictions are gaining on him as he lurches into middle age.

"For the past few weeks, he had been getting by on alcohol and a ten-gram stash of cocaine and he had begun to feel as though he might die quite soon." Glimpsing himself in a bathroom mirror, he quotes "Thou art the thing itself," from *Lear*. "Unaccommodated man is no more than such a poor bare forked animal as thou art." Taking further stock of his condition, Walker reflects "that in the brief course of his waking day he had consumed Valium, alcohol and cocaine." Cut from the published book is the next line: "It was a regime that killed and quickly; Walker had seen the bodies." Stone would try this regime from time to time, sometimes on medical recommendation, sometimes not.

Bill Barich remembers that his friend Bob Stone was in much the same shape as his protagonist at around the same time—toxic from his recreational substances and "paralyzed with the fear of death." Stone himself, reminiscing about the cocaine days with some old friends on Ballast Key in 2010, recalled his " 'research' for *Children of the Light*, which involved eight-hour coke-and-writing binges after which he would, sensibly, feel completely out of his mind, 'and then I wouldn't have any idea what to do now that I was so out of my mind and so usually that meant I'd have to make a drink, and, well, there you go.' " And *where* you go in such circumstances is downhill, fast.

Nevertheless, "Walker thought of himself as a survivor. He knew how to endure, and what it was that got you through." (In this conviction he has something in common with Holliwell in *A Flag for Sunrise*.) "There was work. There were the people you loved and the people who loved you." The rest of the novel shows Walker, deliberately and perversely, severing all those lifelines, although he has a notion of recovery in his mind.

"A dream, he thought. That's what we need. . . . A plan and a dream, somewhere to go. Dreams were business to Walker, they were life." He's pinned his dream not to his filmscript being shot in Mexico (though in fact it's one of his more artistically ambitious efforts) nor to Lee Verger who's performing the lead role, but to Lu Anne Bourgeois, the real person behind the Lee Verger stage name, and his companion in considerable craziness "in the days of mind drugs and transfigurations." Though his writing services are no longer required, he has a strong impulse to visit the set.

Having persuaded his agents to broker his reception on the Mexican location, Walker drives south, making a couple of calls along the way— hoping to pick up something that might help him retreat from alcohol. "I'm on this fucking thing," he explains to Quinn, a friend of his youth, an aging stuntman and dealer to the stars. "I'm doing a lot of blow and then I'm drinking. I need downers." When Quinn, regretfully, can't oblige, Walker drives south of the border to a Laetrile clinic run by Dr. Er Siriwai, "formerly the film community's most eminent writing doctor and on two or three occasions something like a medical hit man." Siriwai furnishes quaaludes, along with some well-considered warnings.

But Walker is notoriously impervious to warnings. He drives farther south, arriving at a cliff above the beach area of the Mexican location late in the day. Below, "he saw a woman remove a bandanna from around her head and toss it onto the sand. He saw her walk on, remove her bathing suit and stand naked and golden in the sun. He was seeing, he supposed, what he had come to see." Walker is a longtime laborer in the Hollywood dream factory, and as cynical as any of the rest, but for once the illusion being fabricated captures him. "He had never been so in love, he thought, as he was with the woman who stood on the beach in front of that camera and several dozen cold-eyed souls. It was as though she were there for something that was theirs. . . . Tears came to his eyes. But perhaps it was not poetry, he thought. Only movies . . .

"What had it been, almost joy, he thought, a long lost thing, something pleasurable for its own sake. It had slipped away.

"Fuck it, he thought. I got something almost as good."

But the cocaine he takes doesn't restore the moment. It brings him an unwelcome flash of clarity instead. "When he went out on the cliff again and fixed his binoculars on the naked figure he saw it was not Lu Anne but a younger woman who somewhat resembled her. There's your poetry, he thought. Your movies."

———————

Like Stone's previous novels, *Children of Light* has a convergence structure. Walker's wandering toward the Mexican location is crosscut with scenes of Lee/Lu Anne negotiating with the film crew on the set; she has stopped taking her antipsychotic medication in hope of turning in an uninhibited performance. She's being watched, with a certain unease, by the directors and others of the crew. The presence of Dongan Lowndes, a one-shot novelist now writing celebrity coverage for a slick reminiscent of *The New Yorker*, alarms her, and not for no reason. Even before Walker turns up, she's close to running off the rails. As the effects of her medication fade, her hallucinations begin to return. Termed by her "the Long Friends," these frighteningly, vividly rendered phantasms derive from her Louisiana childhood and the witchy, Vodou-flavored culture from which she sprang.

The value of the work at hand might be her salvation, as Walker believes it might be for himself. They're shooting Walker's script of *The Awakening*, a novel by the nineteenth-century Louisiana novelist Kate Chopin. It's a sort of proto-feminist work, featuring Edna Pontellier, the daughter of a Kentucky Confederate general, who has married into the upper-crust Creole society of New Orleans, whose culture she understands poorly. Edna is beautiful, intelligent, sensitive, pampered by her wealthy and ambitious Creole husband, Léonce. With two small children, at the age of twenty-nine she seems to have found her security as a well-to-do young matron. But she is not as stable as she seems.

The lucid, frank clarity of Chopin's writing would certainly have appealed to Robert Stone, so too Chopin's seemingly effortless portrayal of a young woman's evolving sensibility (something Stone could sometimes find a little difficult). "In short, Mrs. Pontellier was beginning to realize her position in the universe as a human being, and recognize her relations as an individual to the world within and about her. . . . But the beginning of things, of a world especially, is necessarily vague, tangled, chaotic, and exceedingly disturbing. How few of us ever emerge from such a beginning! How many souls perish in its tumult!"

In her confused effort to pry her way out of her chrysalis, Edna abandons conventional social pursuits, indulges a far too serious crush on a younger man, and is finally captured by a notorious seducer. The result, in her time, place, and culture, is ruin.

Returning to the Grand Isle beach resort where her young crush previously taught her, to her deep delight, to swim, Edna enters the ocean out of season. "The water was chill, but she walked on. The water was deep, but she lifted her white body and reached out with a long sweeping stroke. The touch of the sea is sensuous, enfolding the body in its soft, close embrace." The sea itself has become the longed-for lover. The final passage is written with such subtlety that it's difficult to define Edna's action as a suicide, but she does not return to shore.

This scene is the one Walker observes from the cliff, when he first arrives in sight of the location.

As Walker works his winding way toward her, Lu Anne struggles to find someone safe to attach to. Her husband, Lionel, is the best option—he functions for her as Connie does for Walker (or Janice for Bob). But he's leaving the location with their children, and the rest of the crew are jackals, more or less.

Lu Anne retreats to her chamber to prepare for the day's shoot and brushes her hair before the mirror, "hoping to see Rosalind and not some ugly thing." Rosalind of *As You Like It* was her first great success as an actress and the character has durable numinosity for her. But "It was Edna in the glass now, not Rosalind." As it should be; she's conjured up the role she's meant to play. Lu Anne sees "the inhabited mask of Edna Pontellier before her." Sinking deeper into character has its hazards for Lu Anne. Edna's carelessness of her children, in her nineteenth-century milieu, can actually be taken as one of her conventional qualities. "She was fond of her children in an uneven impulsive way. She would sometimes gather them passionately to her heart; she would sometimes forget them." Thus, "Edna was independent and courageous. Whereas, Lu Anne thought, I'm just chickenshit and crazy. Edna would die for her children but never let them possess her. Lu Anne was a lousy mother, certified and certifiable. Who the hell did she think she was, Edna? Too good for her own kids? But then she thought: it comes to the same thing, her way and mine. You want more, you want to be Queen, you want to be Rosalind."

Digging her way deeper into Edna's character brings her into contact with Walker and his works. "Edna walking into death was conscious only of the sun's warmth. So it was written. Walker had her dying for life more abundant. All suicides died for life more abundant, Walker's notes said." There's another fillip from Claude Bristol's *The Magic of Believing*, which Stone had briefly harbored in his consciousness while sailing on the *Arneb*—ironic in this context but still very dangerous, be it to Edna or to the woman playing her: *it comes to the same thing . . . you want more.*

As the afternoon shooting schedule goes on, Lu Anne's mental state deteriorates, although she may be turning in better performances to the camera. A camera-bearing crane, which Stone had sketched in his notebook on his last visit to a Mexican location, hovers over her. When Lu Anne's alone in her trailer, she's in trouble. "*Malheureuse*, a Friend whispered to her. The creature was inside her dresser mirror. Its face was concealed beneath black cloth."

Lu Anne looks for succor. "Her pills were on a shelf of the trailer lavatory. She went in and picked up the tube. Her body convulsed with loathing at the sight of the stuff." Abandoning the antipsychotic meds, she cruises her friends on the set for downers and reflects on Walker's directions for Edna in the script.

"She senses a freedom the scope of which she has never known. She has come beyond despair to a kind of exaltation."

Lu Anne works on the idea of exaltation. "You're walking into the water like our Edna and bam! Life more abundant.

"That's a trick, she thought suddenly. That's a mean trick, because Walker was right about the lure of life more abundant. To go for it was dying."

———

By the time shooting has wrapped for the day, Walker has driven down from the height above the beach location and been welcomed, half-heartedly, at the production's hotel. While Lu Anne is tormented by her hallucinations, Walker is besieged by simpler illusions. He spots Lu Anne in the gloaming of the hotel garden and approaches. "She was wearing her hair as she had worn it fifteen years before, he thought. He knew her silhouette, her moves, her aura." When he comes closer, he realizes he has mistaken her body double, the Australian Joy McIntyre, for Lu Anne—and for the second time that day. A man with Walker's feelings for Lu Anne ought to be able to identify "his dark angel" correctly at least fifty percent of the time, but then Joy's whole job is to foster the confusion—that class of illusion is the very stuff of Hollywood.

Walker attends dinner with the cast and crew. Dongan Lowndes, whose profiling of Lee Verger is faintly reminiscent of the then one-shot novelist Robert Stone doing the same with Faye Dunaway, needles him about screenwriting necessarily revolving around "the cheap shot." Walker defends the craft a bit more fervently than might have been expected. "You have to believe it's worthwhile, and you have to accept the rules. You can't be a solitary or an obsessive. You can't despise your audience. It requires humility and it requires strength of character." One senses Stone speaking through his character here.

Truth to tell, Stone was only a modest success as a screenwriter. The stories he needed to tell (this one very much included) depend almost entirely on the interior state of his characters, and while such qualities can be captured in film, the screenwriter is seldom in a good position to make that happen. But Walker's speech shows how Stone respected screenwriting as a good journeyman would, with skills to be conscientiously acquired and honorably practiced. In writing about filmmaking he took the same approach. He did his own research and used consultants to ensure a firm grasp of the technical side. As for moviemaking's social aspect, Stone knew every dark cranny of that firsthand, and made the most of what he knew in the novel's many scenes of public and backstage scheming.

The following day, Walker has to do a few contortions to evade a production assistant who's been tasked to prevent him from reaching Lu Anne. They spend the day sequestered in her cabana, drinking mescal and talking Shakespeare—fantasizing about her playing the Fool to Walker's Lear. "They made love over a daylight hour or so." Then Lu Anne catches him cutting lines of cocaine in the bathroom, and, most dangerously for herself, claims a share.

Unbeknownst to them, they are being photographed. "The photographs were sunlit shots of Lu Anne and Walker naked in bed. Walker was holding a small shiny rectangle while Lu Anne sniffed at its surface through a drinking straw." There ensues a small but elegant blackmail subplot in which the photos are recovered from the disaffected, aged-out publicist who took them, but not before one print has been slipped to Lowndes. One such image, of course, would be more than enough to sink the production, along with Walker's and Lee Verger's careers.

So to another dinner party, only this time Lu Anne's psychosis is amped with cocaine, while Walker, having most likely ruined himself absolutely, has no further reason to exert any self-control whatsoever. An uninhibited Walker in a social situation gives the idea of what Stone in similar circumstances was like, especially if cranked on whiskey and coke. (In fact, Walker's verbal slicing and dicing of the publicist the night before helped provoke the blackmail photo session.) Here he carves up an almost random victim: Ann Armitage, a once-famous aging actress present as a guest of the producer.

"Miss Armitage was the only person in America actually hanged during the McCarthy period. She was strung up at the height of her career from the witching elm at the Hamilton horse trials. . . . Miss Armitage is a student of sexual prowess in males, and a major Mexican art critic. She combines in her single self the principal attributes of Eleonora Duse, Eleanor Roosevelt and Eleanor of Castile. Also Rosa Luxemburg, Sacco and Vanzetti. If a passing divine hadn't noticed her dangling there during the dressage competition and recognized the visible manifestation of grace, her poor alcoholic impotent husband might be alive today. Pretty soon she's going to write her memoirs and we'll see a parade of virtue as long

as Macy's at Thanksgiving but with twice as much gas and imagination."
This sort of thing raises serial insult to the level of avant-garde jazz improv.

Fleeing this scene, Walker and Lu Anne charter a small plane and then
take a bus toward a shrine she believes to be on a mountain above a tiny
town in the interior, Villa Carmel. On the bus, "Walker underwent a peculiar experience. He was examining what he took to be his own face in
the rearview mirror, when he realized the roseate, self-indulgent features
he had been studying were not his own but those of the man in front of
him. His own, when he brought them into his line of sight, looked like
a damaged side of beef. The odd sense of having mistaken his own face
remained with him for some time thereafter."

When they reach the supposed shrine, Walker recognizes it as a piece
of Hollywood detritus from a previous Mexican shoot. "It isn't anything
or anywhere," he tells Lu Anne. "It's fake." A moment later he's discovered the shed has been converted to a different use: "For God's sake, Lu
Anne! It's a fucking corncrib on a pig farm."

Lu Anne won't be denied her mountaintop apocalypse. "This is a
holy place," she insists. "Sacred to me." She cuts herself—superficially but
enough to bathe them both in blood. Nature cooperates; a storm strikes
the mountaintop just as she has persuaded Walker to disrobe with her—
throwing his cocaine stash away into the rain at the same time. Their antics resonate with the classic scene of Lear on the heath, though their overt
Shakespearean allusions are to *As You Like It*.

Finally the storm forces them into the shelter of the corncrib. Once
it has passed, Lu Anne pulls Walker into a manure pile. "She reached out
and rubbed the stuff on his forehead in the form of a cross. 'In the name of
pigshit and pigshit and pigshit. Amen. Let us reflect in this holy season on
the transience of being and all the stuff we done wrong. Let's have Brother
Walker here give us only a tiny sampling of the countless words at his
command to tell us how we're doing.'

" 'Not well,' Walker said.

" 'Yeah we are,' Lu Anne told him. 'We're going with the flow. This is
where the flow goes.' "

It's a long complex, difficult passage, involving on the one hand an
authentic, Catholic-infused, religious experience for Lu Anne, and on the

other an absolute desecration of all that. Stone rewrote the scene more than a dozen times.

Following a rescue by Mexican police, Lu Anne has a whim to complete their return to the location by walking on the beach. Walker doesn't think to dissuade her, or can't. They watch the sunset over the sea. Then Lu Anne wants a swim. She slips out of her clothing again. Once she's put some distance between them, he has no chance of catching her, and once she's in the water, he has no chance of finding her, though he tries for a long time. When help arrives, too late, he can only say "I lost her."

The catastrophe is heartbreaking in its simplicity. Walker had only to stay near her to prevent it. But even that single provident action is beyond him.

Children of Light is in its way another hall of mirrors. "I'm your actress, that's right," Lu Anne tells Walker on the height of Monte Carmel. "I'm wires and mirrors. See me dangle and flash all shiny and hung up there?" But the novel is not an indictment of filmmaking in itself, though merciless in its depiction of social corruption in the ad hoc communities that make movies. The critique of the medium as inherently cheap is dismissed in the disagreeable personage of Dongan Lowndes (an unusual example of Stone building a sort of Frankenstein's monster from distortions of some of his own qualities). Something rather different is at stake.

There's a lot of Robert Stone in Gordon Walker, and maybe just as much in Lu Anne Bourgeois. Anyone who wants to see the "secret eyes" the actress finds in her makeup mirror can take a look at the author photo on the jacket of the hardcover's first edition. Stone's gaze is penetrating, and he might well be looking at something no one else can see. Janice remembers that "Bob said at least once that all his characters were himself, even the women."

Certainly Stone set out to produce a tragic romance between Walker and Lu Anne (as he had done with the Rheinhardt-Geraldine and Holliwell-Justin pairings in previous works). And he had a grand good time satirizing the Boschian creep show that exfoliates, like some psychedelic mold, all over his Mexican location. (Readers and reviewers concentrating too narrowly on that aspect found the book trivial because it didn't engage the national/international political predicament in the way that Stone's first three novels had done.) Beyond those two quite obvious interests, *Children of Light* is, rather less conspicuously, an ars poetica in which Stone asks and tries to answer the artist's existential questions: How does one practice the craft honorably in corrupt situations? How can one extract artistic authenticity from a medium like film, whose dependence on sensory illusion always carries with it the risk of phoniness? How, indeed, does one retrieve a worthy artifact from what Yeats, in a slightly different context, called "the place of excrement"?

There are those who give their all to create artistic illusions, and others who merely traffic in them. The platoons of people it takes to produce a movie can mostly be grouped in the second class. As Walker puts it in one of his conversational assaults on a colleague, "You're talking to the right crowd. There are people at this table who could vulgarize pure light."

——•——

Though the phrase is wrenched well out of the context of Lowell's poem, *Children of Light* is the perfect title for this novel, which is all about a kind of people who can't materialize without a projector bulb. No more than shadows on the cave wall, one might say, but to dismiss this book as an insubstantial story about show people would be a big mistake. Here, every bit as much as in his previous work, Stone is driving hard at the essence of the American character, suggesting that our assumed entitlement to become bigger and better versions of whatever selves we started with requires us, as a step in the process, to project an illusion of ourselves forward, as if onto a screen. Such is the magic of believing. Life more abundant becomes a lure as toxic as heroin or cocaine.

9
MOUNT SINAI

No doubt it felt like a great idea to go somewhere else after finishing a book like that. And Bob was a restless soul, a man in as constant motion as he could be. He had borne down hard for a long time on *Children of Light* and was looking for a new destination.

Meanwhile Tom Jenks, whom Bob had first known as a student at

Robert Stone pretends to be a baby.

GLADYS C. GRANT

OCT. 16, 1894   NEW YORK, U.S.A.

5   FEET   6   INCHES   WHITE   GRAY

X X X   OCT. 1, 1968

X X X

VALID UNTIL SEPT. 30, 1973   CANCELED

(ABOVE) Gladys Grant's passport, valid until September 30, 1973.

(LEFT) Gladys Grant and Bob Stone at the Statue of Liberty, early 1940s.

Robert Stone

Robert Stone

(TOP) Bob Stone, boy patriot, Wall Street, early 1940s.

(ABOVE) Autographed yearbook photo, St. Ann's eighth-grade graduation, 1951.

(ABOVE) Janice Burr at the Seven Arts Coffee Gallery, late 1950s. © *Burt Glinn/Magnum Photos*

(BELOW) Bob and Janice Stone at Michael Horowitz's wedding reception, Greenwich Village, 1965. *Courtesy of Cynthia Palmer*

Deidre, Ian, and monkey,
London, 1967.

Jane Burton, Stanford,
early sixties. *Courtesy of
Jane Burton*

M. L. "Mack" Rosenthal,
Stone's writing teacher at
NYU, in his later years.
Maria Politsky

(ABOVE) Jeremy and Eleanor Brooks at Gelli, circa 1970. *Courtesy of Margaret Leclere*

(RIGHT) *The Prophet Stone* (portrait by Eleanor Brooks), Gelli, 1974. *Courtesy of Eleanor Brooks*

(BELOW) Robert and Janice at the Gelli swimming hole, August 1994. *Courtesy of Margaret Leclere*

Inscrutable Stone, Westport, 1980s.
Courtesy of Gigi Kaeser

VYDEC word processor used by Bob in Westport, early 1980s.

Stone and Ken Kesey, flower children, 1979.

Bob and Janice and friends, Hawaii, 1979 to 1980.
Courtesy of Ruth Pratt

Stone spooks his way down a Hartford sidewalk, 1981.
Susan Aimee Weinik/The LIFE Images Collection, Getty Images

(RIGHT) Stone performing the role of the Duke of Kent in a Santa Cruz Shakespeare festival production of *King Lear*, 1982. *UC Santa Cruz, Special Collections*

(BELOW) Stone on the Denali Highway, Alaska, 1982. *Courtesy of John Hildebrand*

(ABOVE) Bob and Janice with tiny cars and distant pyramids, Egypt, 1985.

(ABOVE RIGHT) John Hildebrand with damned nice speckled trout, Quetico Provincial Park, Ontario, 1987. *Courtesy of John Hildebrand*

(NEAR RIGHT) Janice as Calliope, "Enter the Muse," *Esquire*, 1990. © *Michael Tighe*

(BELOW) Bob and Jim Maraniss in Cuba, 1991.

(From left to right): Raymond Carver, Stone, unidentified child, Tobias Wolff, and Morris Bond.

Stone in Haiti, Morne Rouge, June 2000.
Courtesy of the author

Bob and Janice embraced Ballast Key, 2010.
Nance Frank, courtesy of Gallery on Greene

Columbia, had become an editor at *Esquire*, where "one of the challenges was how to convince the top editor and publisher to make room for literary work on its own terms, or, conversely, how to match a literary author's talents and interests to the magazine's desire for a particular type of piece. Space was always limited and mainly allocated to articles pegged in one way or another to encourage advertising. Focus groups with readers routinely placed fiction and literary pieces as the least read items, yet *Esquire* prided itself on its long-standing literary reputation, so it was not impossible to keep the margins open for Bob, whose work accorded with both the magazine's masculine persona and its iconoclastic counterculture ethos, though by the 1980s, *Esquire* was a much tamer publication than it once was.

"Bob sometimes lamented in a resigned way about the length of time it took him to write a novel, and between *A Flag for Sunrise* (1981) and *Children of Light* (1986), I wanted to keep him appearing in the magazine. One afternoon, we met at a now vanished wine bar, Oenophilia, which he chose, on the Upper West Side. The dark little spot was on an otherwise nondescript block of Amsterdam Avenue, which was years away from being gentrified. Bob appreciated good wine but didn't need to be at the Four Seasons to enjoy it. He briefly studied the wine list and ordered a bottle of white Burgundy, a William Fèvre Chablis Premier Cru, and we proceeded to get pleasantly drunk. I asked him what he might like to write next for *Esquire*, and he drew a map of the Middle East on a cocktail napkin. We agreed on a travel piece to Jerusalem, the Red Sea, Egypt, a voyage on the Nile, and so on."

The Stones set out in April 1985—separately, as Janice was not on the *Esquire* expense account for travel. She "flew to London on Kuwait Airlines, a flight which was probably such a bargain because they served no alcohol. Then I bought a bucket-shop ticket to Cairo via Sofia." Plenty of alcohol was served on Bob's flight. His itinerary had been booked by the prestigious British travel firm Abercrombie and Kent, whose Cairo representative upbraided Bob "about arriving drunk, telling him that people did not behave that way in Egypt." Though alcohol was not illegal in Egypt it could be a challenge to procure, and Bob perforce cut down on his drinking during the several weeks he and Janice spent there. On a camping trip in the Sinai desert, Bob went five days without a drink, which proved that he could do it.

From their hotel in the Zamalek district the Stones made the inevitable Egyptian visits: the Temple of Luxor, the Valley of the Kings, the pyramids. Bob and Janice were persuaded by a guide to be photographed on a camel. Bob went scuba diving in the Red Sea. "All the dive shops could get you down, our Israeli guide said, but if Bob wanted to be sure to come up again" he needed to go with Rolf Schmidt, a German dive-shop operator. "Diving at Sharm el Sheikh, at a site known as the Tower, included a sheer drop-off into deep sea, and as he descended the wall he became aware of a shark below. So there was that thrill of danger," and of life imitating the crucial and quite similar shark-menaced dive scene in *A Flag for Sunrise*.

Mike Keeley and his wife, Mary, who had grown up in Alexandria, showed the Stones around that city. When they dined with friends of the Keeleys, they were served wine by a Muslim servant: "our hosts told us the man was very disapproving of their use of alcohol, and they feared he would quit." Bob much later used this episode, with some other Alexandrian elements, in an early-draft opening scene to *Damascus Gate*.

There's some dispute about which is the true Mount Sinai where Moses received the Ten Commandments, but the Stones climbed one of them, beginning the ascent at two in the morning, "guided along a sandy camel track by a blazing Venus and the crescent moon," as Bob recorded it. On the peak a little after sunrise, "we stood at our vantage point, not wanting to move, hardly able to tear our eyes away from the scarlet mountaintops. A few ravens rode the updrafts as the sunlight spread across the granite cliffs, but there was a curious scarcity of carrion birds. A few days before, on a late afternoon hike, we had seen a female gazelle at the end of a *wadi*, and there were fox droppings around, presumably the detritus of those foxes for whom the unrighteous shall one day become a portion. But for the most part, these mountains seemed unwelcoming to life.

"The top of Sinai is a place for the geologist or the metaphysician. Its exposed strata display the skeleton of time. It's also a temple, and not the Wee Kirk o' the Woodies either, but a place where those on legitimate business go at the summons of the Most High God and are told what to do and damn well do it.

"It was quite in the spirit of Sinai that the Lord gave instruction to Moses thus: 'And thou shalt set bounds unto the people round about, saying, Take heed to yourself that ye go not up into the mount or touch the border of it: whosoever toucheth the mount shall be surely put to death.' Since I had a packsized Bible conveniently to hand, I was able prayerfully to reflect on that very text when I climbed on up to the summit and the clouds of hash smoke hit me and I saw the piles of tin cans and all the people. There was lots of photography in progress and shutterbugs were backing and filling, colliding, quarreling and apologizing as they herded their subjects over the rocks. Family groups were backing arm in arm toward sure annihilation at the edge of every precipice.

"Boys moved among the throngs selling rocks with fake Nabatean inscriptions. In one quarter of the ancient ruined fortress on the summit, a tall man with a Grant Wood face was reading from Exodus, his Texas voice rising and falling in the din: '. . . scarlet, and fine linen, and goats' hair, and rams' skins dyed red, and badgers' skins and shittim wood. . . .' In another section, a priest in a blue ski jacket read mass in Swiss Italian. Two slim young women from the north of Europe were trying to squeeze between the bars of a closed Orthodox chapel through the windows of which was visible an icon of horned Moses casting down the tablets of the law in rage. In an abandoned mosque beside it, one O'Toole had inscribed his clan's surname over the mihrab (the prayer niche that indicates the direction of Mecca) in what against all odds appeared to be green spray paint. A couple of dozen Orthodox pilgrims, who had come by bus from Cairo, wandered about unhappily, trying to ignore this crush of heretics." By the time Bob sent *Esquire* the piece (a draft that involved a close comparison of the Stones' voyage with a Christmas trip Henry Adams took with his young wife, Clover, in 1873), Jenks had moved on and the magazine had lost interest. Bob's version of the Sinai ascent was much rewritten for *The New York Times*, and the ironic layering of old and new in the scene forecasts the palimpsest effects of *Damascus Gate*.

Bob and Janice spent only two days in Israel, with a brief visit to Jerusalem by way of the evening bus. From Israel, they flew to London on separate itineraries as before. Janice's route, by way of Cairo and Sofia, looked to the hair-trigger Israeli security agents of that decade like one a terrorist would take. "I was asked to explain myself—what I had been doing in Israel, where I had stayed, why I was traveling separately from my husband, why I was going by way of Egypt and Bulgaria. I nearly missed my plane." But the episode made for a good story and Bob dined out on it for months, "saying that the Israelis were looking for my poison umbrella."

His Middle East article eventually appeared in *The New York Times*

Sophisticated Traveler, much diluted to conform to the travel-writing requirements of that section. Meanwhile, the trip had fulfilled another research purpose. Bob had been ruminating on a novel set in the Middle East since well before he sketched that map on the cocktail napkin for Tom Jenks, though most of another decade would pass before he settled into writing it.

PART FIVE

OUTERBRIDGE REACH

1
CHILDREN OF LIGHT,
RECEPTION AND PROMOTION

Bob's delivery of the *Children of Light* manuscript came out more or less even with Knopf's advance on the book. He committed to teaching another semester at Princeton in the fall of 1985. The Stones took an apartment in the Hibben-Magie complex where they had briefly lived in 1971—the place seemed seedier to them now, perhaps because of poor maintenance, perhaps because they had grown used to living at least a little higher on the hog. Bob's teaching schedule was light enough that they could spend part of each week in Westport and sometimes even Block Island.

On Valentine's Day in 1986, Bob was off to Australia on another cultural junket, sponsored by the U.S. Information Agency. This trip lasted nearly six weeks, taking him to various cities in Australia and New Zealand. Traveling without Janice, Bob got in a scrape or two. While in Sydney, he scored prescriptions for oxycodone and Indocin—for gout, ostensibly, though he was not above putting a prescription narcotic to recreational use. He burned his hand on a tea towel he'd set on fire on his hotel-room stove, and while diving in Perth cut himself on coral. These wounds were infected by the time Bob passed through Sydney again, the infection serious enough to make him ill for a few days; he was still feeling a little sick from it when he did a phone interview from Adelaide with Barth Healey of *The New York Times*.

The general drugginess of *Children of Light* prompted certain questions. "I come out of the generation of drugs when we were all experimenting with LSD—a bunch of artists experimenting," Bob told Healey. "Drugs marked my generation very strongly. But I lost a number of friends, by which I mean they are dead." Asked if he took drugs now, Bob gave a lawyerly response. " 'I don't use illegal drugs,' he said. 'I am a social drinker, and even that I regard as a waste of my creative energy. I write good prose. I wouldn't be able to do that if I were dependent on drugs and alcohol, which I use progressively less and which I anticipate using not at all.' "

The lines from Healey's interview were appended to an insightful review of the novel by the biographer Jean Strouse, which ran on the cover of *The New York Times Book Review* on March 16. Strouse took Stone's career and the novel seriously: "Critics have compared Mr. Stone to Conrad, Faulkner, Hemingway, Graham Greene, Malcolm Lowry, Nathanael West; all apt enough, but there's a James T. Farrell, Raymond Chandler, Dashiell Hammett strain as well—a hard-edged, lonely intelligence that sets bright promise off against stark failure and deals its mordant hand lightly." (She also dubbed him "the apostle of strung out.")

Bob was still Down Under then, and also well away from the flap over his U.K. publisher André Deutsch having "jumped the gun and published a few days before Knopf, infuriating the Knopf people." Janice was deputized to smooth that situation out as best she could, until Bob's return on March 25.

———

The Stones carried out the *Children of Light* tour as a team, though Janice didn't make all the trips that Bob did in the spring of 1986. The day after his return from the junket to Australia, they rushed to New York for two days of promotion, bookstore readings, and interviews. Bob then did a three-day whistle-stop run on his own, to Washington, DC, Boston, and Chicago. At home, Janice phoned bookstores to check on their *Children of Light* stock ahead of his arrival, and also marshaled her friends to do the same all around the country.

On April 8 they flew to the West Coast. Alongside promotional events in L.A. and Berkeley, they had time to see friends from the Stegner Fellowship days: Merrill Joan Gerber and Joe Spiro, and Bill and Diane Barich. They drove to Gill Dennis's Malibu home to discuss film and television projects in which Bob might take an interest. They had dinner with Margot Kidder at Warszawa in Berkeley. Kidder was interested in playing Lu Anne Bourgeois in a possible adaptation of *Children of Light*. Janice remembers her "doing Lu Anne impressions" over the meal and doing her best to impress Bob that *I'm your actress*, as Lu Anne tells Walker in the finale; I'm your stone-crazy actress if that's what you want. Her interest in the character was durable, and the Stones continued to see her occasionally for the next couple of years, at the Boxing Day party she hosted at Ding Dong House, which overlooked the Hudson River from the Palisades.

Probably best known for her role as Lois Lane in the *Superman* movies of the 1970s and '80s, Kidder, like Lu Anne, was pushing forty in 1986; no longer getting the best film parts, she'd begun to work more in television. In 1996, Kidder went missing for several days in which she apparently lived in the shrubbery of Glendale, an L.A. suburb, where she was found " 'dirty, frightened and paranoid' in bushes behind a suburban home and was taken for psychiatric testing," an episode that suggests she may have shared something of Lu Anne's mental instability. These qualities might have made her perfect for the part, but no such movie was ever made. Hollywood doesn't much like being satirized, and Bob Stone never signed another screenwriting contract, although there continued to be attractive overtures.

———

Enthusiastic as he had been about *A Flag for Sunrise*, Bob Gottlieb at Knopf didn't think so much of *Children of Light*—which he termed, to Bob Stone, "your not-too-adorable book." Bob Stone in his turn was unhappy with what seemed to him a lackluster promotional effort. When he suggested to Gottlieb that it might be pitched as a "Hollywood novel," Gottlieb made the somewhat puzzling reply that he didn't want to "mislead readers." Since *Children of Light* is among other things a comprehensive, thorough, and biting analysis of Hollywood moviemaking and the people who do it, perhaps he meant that it could not be read as a roman à clef, mapping its characters onto real-life Hollywood figures.

Stone was never one to base his fictional characters narrowly on any real person, as much as he poured himself into all of them. Thus he was startled by a rumor that the Drogues' father-and-son directorial team was based on Walter and John Huston, whom he had never met. Some of the piquant anecdotes in the novel were lifted from real life, and Janice remembers "a real-life counterpart to Shelley Pearce, and the San Epifanio Beach Hotel, when we lived in Laguna Beach." Although he disclaimed that Kate Rickman had any influence on the characterization of Lu Anne, Bob knew more than one troubled actress, and very likely did draw on his long friendship with Lucy Saroyan for the creation of Gordon Walker's "dark angel." But it was himself he relied on most.

"The character of Gordon Walker is so much like Bob in the 1980s," says Janice, "subject to attacks of anger and fear, drinking too much, using cocaine and pills, risking his health if not his life." There were other strong resemblances too: the taste for the racetrack; the broad and deep knowledge of Shakespeare, whom both Bob Stone and Gordon Walker constantly quote (with a particular obsession on *King Lear*); "the verbal brilliance, oiled by alcohol"; the seeking restlessness and need for "a plan, a dream, somewhere to go; and the increasing number of things he sought to banish from his consciousness." For Janice, one of Lu Anne's lines evokes her own first meeting with Bob: "One day many years ago I think you said something wonderful and you looked wonderful saying it." "If all his characters, in all his books, were himself, finally, Gordon Walker seems to me to be the one most closely channeling Stone."

Robert Stone was not the sort of celebrity that a mass audience would want to scry into by way of a fictional character, and if Lu Anne could be called a composite character, she couldn't be pinned to a single model. That *Children of Light* couldn't be sold as a Hollywood roman à clef (in the way that *A Flag for Sunrise* could be sold as a south-of-the-border thriller/romance) may have contributed to Gottlieb's disaffection, or the new novel may simply not have been to his taste. Also a factor, *Children of Light* sold roughly eighteen thousand copies, less than half the performance of *A Flag for Sunrise*, and nowhere near earning out that $300,000 advance. The press tended to be tepid, with critics making disappointed comparisons to Stone's previous work. In a lengthy *New York Review of Books* piece, Al Alvarez dismissed *Children of Light* as "self-indulgent." *People* denounced it as "a novel that is as tedious and annoying as its characters . . . 258 pages of hopeless bitterness." Even reviews that were more positive failed to draw ringing conclusions, devolving into mere description and quotes from Stone interviews.

Over the course of the next year, Bob quietly began to disengage from Knopf. In addition to his discontent with Gottlieb's response to *Children of Light*, there was a rumor that Gottlieb might leave Knopf to assume the editorship of *The New Yorker* (a move that later did take place). Candida Donadio arranged some meetings with other editors: Gerry Howard of

Viking Penguin and John Herman of Weidenfeld and Nicolson. Since it always took Bob a good while to concentrate his focus on his next big book, the editors were bidding on a pig in a poke; the poke might have contained the WWII Italian novel that Bob had been contemplating off and on, or any number of other potential projects. In August 1986, Bob signed a contract with Weidenfeld and Nicolson "for an untitled work of literary fiction, the subject of which is a teenage daughter of a murderer who is befriended by a middle-aged man." The advance was $400,000, most of it to be paid in monthly installments of $7,500, as was habitual in Stone's previous contracts. Weidenfeld and Nicolson, a well-established publisher in the U.K., had just started up in New York via a partnership between George Weidenfeld and Ann Getty—Stone's remarkably large advance was underwritten by Getty money. Bob was not alone in getting an unprecedentedly generous contract; Weidenfeld and Nicolson was spending enormously to acquire name authors and the next books they'd write, to the point that their editors were taking gambler's chances.

2
EGGHEADS IN SICILY

By April 19, the Stones were back in Westport. Janice's diary records, in a fine blend of exhaustion and delight, "Day off!" Bob spent a few days working on his untitled short story, and took a stab at converting the opening into a play or screenplay. By April 22, though, he was in New York, discussing future travel plans with Harvey Shapiro of *The New York Times*; Shapiro wanted to send him back to Eastern Europe, while Bob hoped for Zimbabwe. The trip that did materialize was a conference in Sicily, sponsored by PEN American Center. "This one I really didn't want to miss," says Janice, "and I managed to deal myself in."

After a quick trip to Wisconsin to see Ian graduate from Beloit, the Stones flew to Palermo on May 18. The conference ran from May 19 through May 23, housed at different palazzi all over Sicily, to which participants traveled by bus. Along with Stone, the American writers included Mary Gordon (whose stance toward Catholicism interested Bob), Jay McInerney, David Leavitt, Richard Gilman, Elizabeth Hardwick, and the *New York* magazine book critic John Simon. The American writers met, or to some extent collided with, Italian and Soviet delegations; it was a spicier mix than Bob had found in New Zealand and Australia. The Italians all seemed to be captivated by the then-fashionable theory of deconstruction (a joke played on the Western literary world by a couple of French philosophers). Janice thought that the young fiction writer Leavitt "made an articulate case for deconstruction." The Italians were another matter, and it wasn't just an issue of translation. "Listening intently through earphones, I tried and failed to hold on to one coherent statement. Bob also had trouble with the speeches; he felt the Italians were speaking only to each other. He did comic imitations of them with a broad Italian accent."

Nonetheless the American delegation took its mission seriously, staying up late at night to strategize and refine responses. Bob, who was formally representing American PEN, spoke relatively late in the conference, from a fair copy made by Janice from his notes scrawled on the "Letteratura, Tradizione, Valori" stationery printed for the occasion. To stand under such a banner, Bob declared, "is to become part of a paradox— consciousness-conditioning reality, the reality of one afternoon at least.

"Life in collision with language produces the necessity of interpretation. We cannot take things whole all at once; we would be swept away. We would find ourselves simply out in things, confronting an infinity of primary process. The self could not survive." Bob went on to quote Conrad: "Fiction must justify itself in every line," with the gloss, "His statement concerns the esthetics of prose, and consequently it is a moral statement. In the practice of fiction, esthetics and morality are closely connected.

"The subject of every genuine work of literature is the same as that of the simplest joke—nothing less than how it is. If we laugh together at a joke, we're sharing a glimpse of the universe." Implicitly he was making an argument against the literary gamesmanship proposed by deconstruction. "There is an American saloon proverb that states, 'there is no such thing as a free lunch.' It's quite right; nothing comes gratis in this world. Conventionalization, vulgarization, meretriciousness, all have to be paid for somewhere down the line. If writers are in fact performing a moral function they will not succeed in doing so through complacency." These ideas, stimulated by friction in the Sicilian conference, were to be expanded into "The Reason for Stories," an essay Bob published in *Harper's Magazine* in 1988.

By way of denouement, Mary Gordon (who had a drop of Sicilian blood) told a dirty Sicilian joke and danced the tarantella with the mayor of Taormina. The conferees scattered. Bob and Janice toured Sicily for a few days, visiting the island of Stromboli where they climbed halfway up the volcano there. "Then we went to Milan, and on to Trento, on the Adige River. Bob was still thinking about the Italian historical novel he might write."

———

He was also working, though with difficulty and growing frustration, on the novel his Weidenfeld contract described, while still tinkering with the idea of a play or some kind of narrative inspired by the solo sailor Donald Crowhurst's disappearance at sea. Bob had most recently used the latter project in a feint at reestablishing his U.K. residence, so as to dislodge the tenant from the Redington Road flat, but he was serious enough about it to take a course at the Longshore Sailing School in Westport in the summer of 1987.

By the mid-1980s the crack cocaine epidemic had taken hold all over New York. Where heroin users were tranquil when they had their fix, and only hunted when they needed money for the next one, crack users became more aggressive when they were on their drug, a factor that worsened the quality of New York street life considerably. Bob had taken note of this issue and begun sketching a piece on "cocaine's coloring of the American psyche" for *Harper's*. Though well aware of the increased risk to civilians in Manhattan, the Stones sublet a two-room apartment from Marin Hopper, the daughter of Dennis, who was moving to California. The building was in Greenwich Village, on West Eleventh Street between Waverly and West Fourth. The neighborhood was safer than most in Manhattan in those days. Thanks in part to the large community of gay men in the area, whose members were apt to be abroad at all hours, there was relatively little assault on the street, though the Stones' car was broken into a couple of times while parked nearby (they lost the radio, a typewriter, and Ian's clothes), and also rammed by a tow truck while Bob was driving it.

The Stones were away from their Village pied-à-terre a good deal. Bob spent a week teaching at a conference in Santa Fe (he was thinking about setting a portion of his novel in progress in New Mexico). He spent most of the rest of August with Janice in Block Island working alternately on that manuscript, now variously called "Opus 5" or "Charlie Manson's Gold" (both placeholder titles) or the cocaine article for *Harper's*, to be published in December as "A Higher Horror of the Whiteness." Janice prepared a book of characters for a possible *Children of Light* screenplay.

There was interest from the writer-director Neil Jordan and the producer Paul Gurian, and Bob went so far as to draft a few pages of a script, although no deal was ever made. A good number of other film projects were being toyed with: an adaptation of *A Flag for Sunrise* meant to star Sam Waterston, and a screenplay revolving around the John Marquand character Mr. Moto. Fran Landesman, on a visit to New York with Jay, tempted Bob with the notion of turning *Children of Light* into a musical. Bob also got as far as contract negotiations with CBS Films to adapt a nonfiction book called *'Ludes*, by Benjamin Stein, for a picture Paul Newman would direct. That project foundered because it looked for a moment as if the production company might fail, also because Bob, fond as he was of the drug itself, wasn't so interested in the book. For lack of time, he turned down an offer to adapt an Edna Buchanan story for Martin Scorsese. He was so busy during this period that he began asking Janice to read the many books sent to him for comment.

Alongside all the maybe schemes, Bob had a clutch of piecework deadlines: the *Harper's* cocaine piece, which he delivered in early October; the Egypt travelogue commissioned by Tom Jenks, rejected by *Esquire* and finally published in *The New York Times*; an essay on photo-portraiture commissioned for a coffee-table book being produced by Polaroid. These obligations, plus increasingly hectic travel, left him little time to work on his novel under contract. And he had become the chairman of the PEN/Faulkner Foundation, a post that he would hold for the next thirty years, and which gave him cause for frequent trips to Washington, DC.

It mattered for him to attend the Wheatland Foundation conference in DC—funded by Ann Getty and thus connected to Bob's new publisher. Getty money assembled a star-studded group of fifty writers from all over the world, most deploring the current state of letters, but from different points of view. Such events, along with his frequent USIA-sponsored excursions around the world, helped Bob sustain an international presence, not to mention a consciousness of what was going on outside his own country.

The Americans talked about aesthetics; William Gass complained that "an idea was treated like a cockroach in a basket by up and coming American writers," and there were complaints about the "whoredom of the lecture circuit." The Americans were all getting uneasy about the growth (exponential in the late 1980s) of the academic workshop system for training new writers (although this system provided most of them with steady employment—thus relief from pimping themselves out on the lecture circuit).

The Peruvian novelist Mario Vargas Llosa expressed more social concern, which was common to many of the South and Central American writers present: "We still have great illiteracy, great poverty, but never has literature meant so much to Latin Americans. This may be our golden age." Some Russian writers had been allowed to travel from the Soviet Union for the conference, where they were able to meet refugee Russian writers who could not return home; logically enough their concerns were more political. "Andrei Siniavsky hushed the room when he noted that 'literature is a dangerous game, sometimes a bloody one, in Russia.' "

In such company American writers, who didn't have their lives on the line for what they wrote, risked appearing inconsequential or even frivolous (especially pure aestheticians like Gass). Stone, whose work had a more world-historical bent than most U.S. fiction of the 1980s, stood a little apart from his compatriots on this point. His contemporaries in American fiction mostly sprang from the well-educated classes, while Bob was mostly self-taught and also self-invented, given his working-class origins and desperate childhood. He inclined to identify with Joseph Conrad, whose background was checkered in a different way, but who had penetrated the world of English letters as an outsider.

3
OPUS 5

In the spring of 1988, Bob met John Hildebrand again for a tour of Quetico Provencial Park in Ontario, an expanse of over a million acres, with more than 2,000 lakes. In a letter listing what Bob should bring along, Hildebrand explained, "I try to strike a balance between the austerity of backpacking and the excesses of a safari with native bearers since on the portages you become the porter." This trip was logged as research for the Opus 5 novel, still in early stages on Bob's various desks, although the relevance did not become obvious until the week of paddling and fishing was over.

John had to get back to Wisconsin to testify as a character witness for a friend who'd been accused of child abuse in the course of an ugly custody battle. The case promised raw material for the "helping" aspects of Opus 5; Bob changed his ticket so he could attend the trial, which ended in a conviction thanks to the child's mute reenactment of the abuse episode with a doll. The accused lost custody and served some time, yet, somewhat to Hildebrand's surprise, managed to get his life successfully back together in the aftermath of it all. "I think people either forget or invent a new narrative about themselves that allows them to go on," Hildebrand said several decades later. "We have a deep-seated need for our stories to hold, to edit out the inconsistent parts—if for nobody other than ourselves." (This comment runs very close to an idea Bob was developing around the same time, that people require an "informing story" in order to live their lives coherently.) "I think Bob was interested in the trial because he often wrote about people who lie to themselves or find ways to override their own moral objections. His novels are full of good people who fuck up and attempt to rationalize it."

Bob kept roving, to events in Gainesville, Florida, and Carlisle, Pennsylvania. He made an appearance at the U.S. Naval Academy (picking up some background later used in *Outerbridge Reach*) and received the John Dos Passos Prize for Literature from Longwood University in Farmville, Virginia—this award had a particular appeal thanks to Bob's abiding interest in Dos Passos. At a conference in San Juan he tried his luck in the hotel casino. "He had enormous energy and restlessness in those days," says Janice. "As he had told me they said about him in the navy, 'Stone will go anywhere.' It was still true. I think the constant travel may have held off the depression which still hit him sometimes. And although it left him less time for his writing, I also think the travel somehow shook his creativity loose."

Janice had planned a research trip to New Mexico, where Opus 5 episodes were definitely going to take place, and the Stones did spend five days in the Santa Fe area in November 1987, although by then Opus 5 was running off its rails. In August Bob took a few days off from it to write the short story eventually published as "Absence of Mercy"—a rare event because he had written relatively few stories up to that time, and also for the relative speed of execution.

In September 1987 Bob enlisted Janice for a plot consultation; beginning with *Children of Light* she had contributed to continuity issues like keeping characters' names straight and making sure that Bob's classic converging plotlines were correctly scheduled. Nine chapters of Opus 5, about two hundred pages, had been completed by then; the several subplots were well underway, some important thematic tropes were emerging, and generally speaking this novel seemed to have enough momentum to get itself completed.

The first two chapters of Opus 5 sprang from the short story "Helping"; in the next few chapters Elliot continues to drink and yaw around East Ilford, getting involved with Clara, an underage damsel in distress whom Elliot believes is being turned out by a local pimp; he also believes she's AWOL from a local hospital with a wing for troubled teenage girls and tries to take her back there, sardonically insisting, "I'm here to help you. Help is my middle name."

This plotline appeared to be moving toward fulfillment of the description in Bob's Weidenfeld and Nicolson contract, but at this point the story lines began to metastasize, shifting into Clara's point of view and then entering the mind of her biological father, a convict who lost his child after his arrest for horrific murders during the breakdown of a Manson-like cult ("compounded of Ayn Rand novels, Fascism and astrology") of which he had been a leader.

Despite some redundancy, confusion of the timelines, and Bob's tendency to keep changing the names of some key characters (all relatively minor problems that Janice was getting used to solving as she went over Bob's works in progress), this large chunk of novel showed tremendous promise. The noirish criminal thriller plot was maybe even more potent than that of *Dog Soldiers*. Long-term thematic concerns were present, many of which Bob never addressed again in the same way.

Bob seems to have planned Elliot as a self-portrait even closer than Gordon Walker had been. The nuances of alcoholism and the bouts of inexplicable rage Bob shared with Elliot were going to get a fuller treatment than before, and the phases of Elliot's binge drinking are treated with much more depth and detail than in the case of Walker: "Bits and pieces of sobriety were crackling along the edges of his envelope, interfering with the process of his solitary revolution. He felt at the point of surfacing when his instinct was to sound, to dive as deep out of the light as he could go. He wanted to be where there were neither acts nor consequences but only the shadow of both."

Janice avatars in Bob Stone's fiction usually remain discreetly off-

stage, but in this novel Bob plainly intended to make Grace a central character. Driven apart by Elliot falling off the wagon (and to a lesser extent
by Grace's reaction to that), each is bewildered without the other. Loneliness (not something Bob had made much of in previous work) has a hold
on Elliot. Grace mirrors such emotions. Worried over absent Elliot (and
missing him despite her anger and frustration), "Alone was what she felt.
She began to imagine a life lived that way. Then it occurred to her that one
was always alone finally." Despite these pessimisms, the reader senses that
the plot will probably bring this couple back together.

Behind this poignant personal situation was an intention to contrast
an ineffectual secular system for redemption (the "helping professions")
with the old religious one. Elliot's attitude toward it all is bitterly cynical:
"This valley is absolutely lousy with Help," or "I'm Mister Help. You've
come to the right man." Grace, though not immune to her own style of
cynicism, can sometimes be pious about her vocation to do good. Grace
has religion, which Elliot mocks (a bit jealously maybe). Yet Grace can
also see the other side of the case quite clearly. "One simply had to see that
there were no metaphors and that things were only what they were. On
the field of folk it was all confusion, hope for the best and serve the ape. It
was freedom but it was so paltry."

The sterility of a world without God conflates with her own childlessness—a painful issue between Elliot and herself. "The godlessness of
things was plain enough, she thought. In the winter landscape outside she
saw a dead land spread out beneath the eye of vacancy. The churches were
empty, the songs still and the fields barren. She was barren. The world
was eminently uninformed, ruthlessly, blindly changing, promiscuously
spewing random systems, transmitting meaningless patterns of energy to
the stars, receiving back the same blank messages and reading them, loud
and clear. If the world died, she thought, every trace of the context in
which its survival had mattered would die with it."

This material was extremely potent, and it was clear that Stone meant
to use it to work through some of his own complex and ambivalent attitudes toward religion. But in the fall of 1987 he felt, for whatever reason,
stuck on the project. In September he had more "thinking" than writing
days. In October he began to reset his course in a completely different
direction.

4

CHANGING COURSE

Commissioned to write a piece on New York Harbor for the *Times*, Bob arranged a sail out of the Seventy-Ninth Street Boat Basin on the *Prelude*, a cutter-rigged ketch whose owner, Ed Bacon, made it available for charters around New York and New Jersey in summer and around the Caribbean in winter. If Bob still felt any nostalgia for a sailor's unattached life, Bacon seemed a man of his own kidney. The text of the *Prelude*'s brochure was deftly witty; under the heading "Captain" it read: "Ed Bacon has boated for over 40 years. He first skippered a rowboat on the Delaware River, skippered or crewed on over 25 boats, lived aboard (a womb with a view) at 79th Street Boat Basin for fifteen years, and sailed off into the sunset in 1985." Bob, who had been rethinking his next novel in a fundamental way, told Ed at least a little about his interest in the Crowhurst story during a sail around New York Harbor on October 26. It was a clear day in the middle fifties; if the Black Monday stock market crash the previous week had cast a pall on Manhattan's financial district, it was only metaphorical. Not long after this initial trip he wrote to Ed about scheduling a Caribbean cruise on the *Prelude* in January or February 1988, noting in his closing that "My researches on the voyage of Donald Crowhurst continue and I'm writing away," and in a postscript: "I still haven't written the article for the *Times*. My deadline is 15 December and my wife says inspiration had better strike me soon."

Bob and Janice began to draw up new schedules for research travel to Staten Island, the Caribbean, etc. Bob seemed a good deal more excited about writing the first chapters of what would become *Outerbridge Reach* than completing the *New York Times* assignment, but the article eventually got turned in, appearing as "Changing Tides" in April 1988. It underlined that "New York was intended from its foundation to be a moneymaking operation, and the harbor was its sole reason for existence. It would stand or fall on its facility for moving goods by water for profit. . . . By the middle of the 1840's, the shoreline of lower Manhattan displayed the forest of masts familiar to us today from old prints and the first photographs. This was the port known to Whitman and Melville; its enormously vital and brutal early industrial landscape is reflected in their work."

The piece goes on to imagine Bob's mother's childhood crossings of the harbor with her tugboat captain father to describe Bob's own passage under the Brooklyn Bridge in an Irish coracle, and his rather triumphant return to the city aboard the *Arneb* in 1958. Among such anecdotal entertainment, the piece never quite loses its focus on a mild sense of decline in the harbor, the Manhattan shoreline, and what they represent. The Black Monday market crash (which had stung the Stones a bit, as it would sting *Outerbridge Reach* protagonists Owen and Anne Browne) is felt, without being directly mentioned.

Bob's closing struck the root chord of the new novel he now had in hand. "New York Harbor grew in the name of profit, and some things, after all, don't change. In the old days, the raw business of the harbor was done right down the street; today, in our new-age fastidiousness, we prefer not to witness the primary processes of our economy. At the South Street complex, we preserve for our pleasure a fine romance of Whitman and Melville's grand, dark, Satanic mill of a seaport. I think it's too bad we could not do more to save the scale of lower Manhattan's striving towers now that the heroic age they represent is past. They expressed a great dream, commerce as a moral force, American power, an empire of peace-loving producers and traders whose ennobled common sense would astonish the world. They were cathedrals. For as long as anyone lives who understands the dreams they personify, they will stand, in good times and bad, reflecting and reflected by the great harbor whose prosperity raised them." Bob had been interested in the Crowhurst story for many years, but his study of New York Harbor showed him how he could recast it as an American, and specifically a New York, story. Once he figured that out, Janice remembers, "he became very excited and began writing it immediately." Only superficially would *Outerbridge Reach* be a novel about a sailboat race; its deeper thrust was to be aimed at the commercial underpinnings of the American dream.

5

FIVE YEARS OF FREEDOM

Amidst the swirl of potential projects—articles, screenplays, the oft-postponed musical-theater project with Fran Landesman—Bob had many conversations about teaching opportunities. The possibility of returning to the University of Hawaii, where the Stones still knew Bob and Janet Onopa among other friends, had a definite appeal. There was some discussion of going to the University of San Diego, where their friends Helene Keyssar and Tracy Strong were now teaching. And Bob had a firm offer from Frank Conroy, who'd just become the director of the Iowa Writers' Workshop, to teach there in 1988. But before that could happen Bob got word that he was to receive the Mildred and Harold Strauss Living from the American Academy of Arts and Letters.

Awarded to two writers at five-year intervals, this grant had been given for the first time in 1983, to Raymond Carver and Cynthia Ozick. The co-winner with Robert Stone in 1988 was the novelist Diane Johnson. Harold Strauss, who had been editor in chief at Knopf, believed fervently that writers ought to write and not teach, and the terms of the grant expressed, or rather enforced this opinion; recipients could not earn money from work other than writing (with an exception for a modest amount of lecture income) during the period of the grant, which paid each writer a total of $250,000 in monthly stipends over five years. For Stone, who'd just completely reconceived his plan for a long, important, and challenging fifth novel, the timing could hardly have been better.

Free of teaching for five years, Bob continued to push himself hard with travel as frequent as ever, to conferences and readings, research and pleasure trips, including more voyages on the *Prelude*; crewing for Ed Bacon helped him improve a knowledge of sailing that would feed into *Outerbridge Reach*. Also for the novel, he traveled to consult with boatbuilders in Newport and elsewhere. For other aspects of the work in progress, the fashionable novelist Jay McInerney (who had used the Stones' West Village sublet from time to time) helped Bob explore the New York club scene. McInerney had recently left his wife for the model Marla Hanson, whose celebrated facial slashes had an odd resonance with Geraldine's scar in *A Hall of Mirrors*. He hit it off with Bob and Janice, and took over the Village sublet altogether in 1989, when the Stones had had enough mishaps with their cars in the neighborhood and were also "a bit tired of hauling thirty-eight pounds of computer up and down the stairs."

In February 1988, Bob and Janice flew to San Juan to join Ed on his boat for a sail to Virgin Gorda, Saint Thomas, and Saint John. This trip allowed Bob to learn about satellite navigation systems and to get in a little snorkeling off of Cooper Island, though parts of the itinerary were canceled because of bad weather. Bob spent a good deal of time at the helm of the *Prelude* and picked Ed's brain about sailing a small boat in the Drake Passage, which connects the Atlantic and Pacific Oceans between Cape Horn and Antarctica, and might figure in the round-the-world race Bob was plotting for the novel. Bob sailed the Caribbean again with Ed (but without Janice) in late March and early April.

In May he flew to Portugal on Ann Getty's private jet, for a Wheatland-sponsored conference on literature. There he met his friend Ian McEwan and a new acquaintance, Salman Rushdie. The three spent a night "carousing around Lisbon" in search of fado; whenever they found any, Bob had to struggle "to get the voluble Rushdie to hush up so he could hear the music." Then a rising star in the U.K. literary world, Rushdie was on the cusp of the notoriety his novel *The Satanic Verses* would bring him. The book made a mockery of the prophet Muhammad in a way calculated to outrage Muslims the world over. Rushdie was prepared to profit from the scandal, to see his book burned and banned in various localities, and even to dodge a few brickbats flung at him when he walked the London streets—all in the name of artistic freedom—but he was not prepared for the Ayatollah Khomeini to issue a fatwa that called for faithful Muslims to kill him on sight.

The death sentence was cemented in place by Khomeini's death a few months later, and Rushdie spent the next several years in hiding (at a cost to British security services of £11 million). The scandal turned into the most polarizing crisis between Islam and the secular-humanist West until the 9/11 bombings a dozen years later. Writers worldwide, Bob Stone included, rallied to Rushdie's defense. In February 1989 PEN American Center sponsored a serial reading of the novel in Manhattan. Bob was advised by Edward Said that the excerpt he'd be reading was the most blasphemous in the whole book. This news perturbed him a little, though as luck would have it, in the TV broadcast of the event he was misidentified by a caption as Larry McMurtry. Standing up for Rushdie was not without consequences; some writers who publicly supported him saw their titles pulled from the shelves of bookstores that were receiving explicit threats—complete with lists of titles and authors to be withdrawn, or else.

The Stones spent much of the summer of 1988 on Block Island, where Bob could concentrate on *Outerbridge Reach* and also have plenty of exposure to sailboats. A small outbuilding was converted into a studio for him, as the house was often crowded with guests. John and Sharon Hildebrand came with their infant daughter, Rachel. Bob went out fishing with John, and in November he took to the woods with Hildebrand again, to hunt deer "in the Tiffany Bottoms where the Chippewa River bumps into the Mississippi." This time John sent Bob not only a list of what to bring along ("a compass, whistle, flashlight, knife and watch") but also a topographical map of the area: "As you can see, it's bottomland swamp with lots of sloughs and beaver canals. Every time I go in there I get lost a little bit." He further promised Bob "an interesting experience, a good dose of Midwestern Gothic anyway."

"There were four or five of us; except for Bob, everyone else worked at my university. The first night we crossed the Mississippi to Wabasha, Minnesota, and ate dinner at a restaurant in the old Anderson House, the oldest operating hotel in the state," a scene which Bob would later transform into the Hunter's Supper Club for his 2003 novel *Bay of Souls*. The party spent a night in a cabin owned by one of John's friends, and "very early in the morning paddled across a slough into the bottomland swamp. I remember we didn't have any luck until late in the day when I saw three deer crossing a beaver dam and shot the largest—a doe. Bob may have fired as well from behind me and missed—me as well as the deer." Hildebrand had furnished him "a twelve-gauge shotgun with a short slug barrel . . . it's very accurate though it looks like a riot gun and makes a terrible roar."

Next, "we ran into some Hmong hunters while we were gutting the doe." The Hmong are a mountain people indigenous to Vietnam's Central Highlands; the French called them Montagnards and many had fought with the Americans during the war. By the late 1980s Hmong refugees had, for whatever mysterious reasons, concentrated in Wisconsin in significant numbers. In *Bay of Souls*, Bob would turn this sighting of Hmong hunters into a haunting echo of Vietnam.

In the last couple of years of the 1980s, Bob kept flinging himself around the country and indeed around the world. August 1988 found him covering the Republican National Convention in New Orleans, which gave him a chance to return to his old stomping grounds and also produced a perceptive, biting article for *Harper's Magazine*. Two decades since *A Hall of Mirrors* first appeared, real-world political theater was now able to produce scenes that had looked over the top in the novel. Stone on President Reagan's convention speech: "It's the primal voice of the electronic age, the medium *and* the message, the voice that never sleeps, that cajoles, inspires, and commands wherever cathodes glow. We can no more resist it than oncoming night. For just about as long as Ronald Reagan has been alive, his voice has whispered in our dreams, a manifestation of American reality. Flick a switch and there it is, unresponding but constant, everywhere, every hour. It seems to emanate from some invisible consensus, the voice we have all agreed to hear. It is not the voice of a man; its name is legion. It is inside us. Our consciousness ebbs and flows to its undulation, obedient as tides to the moon. Hearing it, we mistake it for our own."

Bob found time for another USIA tour, which allowed him to consult a Finnish boatbuilder; and his relatively local hops, to New York or Washington, DC, on publishing or PEN/Faulkner business, were almost uncountably numerous. Despite the idea that she'd stop working in order to travel with Bob, among other things, Janice didn't end up accompanying him on a good many of these journeys—although she was able to keep plenty busy organizing his itineraries, along with his works in progress and everything else on his desk. "I liked to be free sometimes, and to have my grandchildren visit, which was easier to do when Bob was on the road." And if Bob saw other women in some of his many ports of call, she might have preferred not to know about it.

6

WOES OF THE FLESH
AND PUBLISHING FOLLIES

Bob's health at the end of the 1980s was beginning to be worrisome, at least sometimes. Entering his early fifties, he was not quite so indefatigable as he had been, although most of the time he tended to behave as if he were. In the spring of 1988 he returned from the Wheatland conference in Lisbon with pneumonia, and over the summer he had to cancel a good many engagements because of illness, including gout attacks. He had booked himself for a reading at the Manhattan Theatre Club on the evening of June 13—after which he had to rush to the airport for an overnight flight to a writers' conference in Ireland; as he quipped to his Dublin host, John Banville, "Surely the cause of international drinking deserves no less." In the event he had to cancel both the New York reading and the flight to Dublin. Janice's diary records him as too sick to work that day—unusual, since if Bob was housebound he'd almost always get some writing done. Later, he had to cancel a sail with Ed Bacon on the *Prelude*—too sick to make the trip. And in 1988 he'd even "had to cancel his appearance at the Academy of Arts and Letters where he was to be formally awarded the Strauss Living. His doctor in Westport, Dr. Cohn, was concerned."

Bob was having mysterious abdominal pains and gaining more weight than was healthy. Janice teased him that "he looked like Bacchus" in a photo taken in Australia, "chubby, happy, and probably drunk." There were times Bob embraced a Dionysian role, and times when Janice embraced him in it. But human beings can wear themselves out expressing the appetites of the gods.

The New York Public Library had started an annual fund-raiser, where the fat cats of the writing and publishing world put on their tuxedos and evening gowns, milled about the grand public halls of the building at Fifth Avenue and Forty-Second Street, and were wined, dined, and honored. Though most people called the event "Literary Lions," the honor involved dubbing certain people "*Library* Lions," in reference to the famous two marble lions which flank the Library's Fifth Avenue entrance.

Bob Stone was a Lion in 1987, and so was Raymond Carver. The two had met in San Francisco in the 1960s but didn't really become friendly till twenty years later, when they began to run into each other regularly at Toronto's Harbourfront Festival. "Bob walked up to him and clapped him on the back in greeting. Carver staggered. He was quite ill by then, and Bob had not realized it. Although he had given up alcohol ten years before, Carver had not given up smoking and was now dying of lung cancer."

Younger than Stone by just one year, Carver had come much more recently to wide recognition of his fiction (which he had only a few years to enjoy). Their writing was not very similar but they shared a Rabelaisian enthusiasm for grog and tobacco, with Carver struggling to give up the one while Bob struggled to give up the other. The coffin nails will kill you quicker; Carver was dead within the year. The loss was distressing to Bob in more than one way. In the months before he died, Carver tried to hit Bob up for pain pills (a false trail: if Bob sometimes scored pain pills, he didn't keep them long). Bob was shocked by how stingy Carver's doctors were with effective pain medication—fretting about the possibility of addiction in a terminal patient seemed completely absurd.

The two men had not been immensely close, but they had corresponded a little and Bob had gone fishing with Ray a time or two, from Carver's house in Port Angeles, north of Seattle on the Strait of Juan de Fuca, where Carver kept a boat. And Stone had a large respect for the way Carver stood behind his work, or even within it, telling an interviewer, "His writing was very much the way he was. You could admire and love the man in the same way you could admire and love the writing." Speaking at Carver's memorial service, Bob pulled out a couple more stops: "I went fishing with Raymond a few times and I never saw him walk on water but I know he walked through fire. I know this because many times reading one of his stories or poems I was able to follow him through it to the other side." These were lines of thoughtful praise, but Bob also admitted he was "alarmed and shocked" by Carver's swift decline, in part because it looked very much like a memento mori addressed to himself.

———

Another kind of stress came Bob's way in 1989, when it began to be disclosed that Weidenfeld and Nicolson had run into trouble and would be in for some restructuring. In October *The New York Times* ran a piece describing (somewhat satirically) "nearly four years of clashing egos, organizational mayhem and liberal spending (with the conspicuous absence of any noteworthy success in the bookstores)." Fun was poked at Ann Getty for being an amateur in the publishing world; the piece treated her, albeit obliquely, as a dangerous kind of dilettante.

Bob Stone's position with the publisher was complicated because he was no longer writing the novel his contract described. He had an understanding with John Herman, who'd received the first chapters of *Outerbridge Reach* in January 1988. He also had a clause in his contract allowing him to follow Herman if he went elsewhere, and indeed Herman was leaving Weidenfeld and Nicolson for Ticknor and Fields. The latter had been an independent Boston firm in the nineteenth century, and the publisher of Hawthorne, Emerson, Thoreau, and many other canonical writers—by the 1980s it was an imprint of Houghton Mifflin, with a reputation for literary fiction nurtured by Corlies "Cork" Smith.

Instability at Weidenfeld and Nicolson started a new flurry of competition for Bob's novel in progress. Sonny Mehta, recently arrived from London to take the helm at Knopf, would have liked very much to publish Robert Stone. Aaron Asher, another redoubtable figure in 1980s publishing, emerged at the head of a reorganized Grove Weidenfeld and very much wanted to keep Bob there, as did Ann Getty, with whom Bob had formed a pleasant acquaintance during the various Wheatland events. Seymour Lawrence, with whom the Stones were friendly, had his own imprint at Houghton and was also a contender.

The uncertainty dragged on for several months (though Bob was still able to keep working on the book, whenever he was in one place for long enough to settle into it). There was even some disagreement between Janice, who thought it better to stick with Grove Weidenfeld, and Bob, who was inclined to follow John Herman. Bob and Janice did a great deal of socializing with all the players during the fall of 1989. They also spent some time with Elena Castedo, a Spanish novelist (she wrote versions of her work in both Spanish and English, bypassing the need for a translator) who was based in Washington, DC, and whom the Stones had gotten to know in the PEN/Faulkner orbit. Castedo's family had come to the Western Hemisphere in flight from the Spanish Civil War, first settling in Chile; Elena came to the States in the late 1960s, where she earned degrees at the University of California, Los Angeles and at Harvard, and then published her first novel, *Paradise*. Possessed of luminous beauty and extraordinary charm, she also had an eminently practical side. When she talked to the Stones about how badly she thought Grove Weidenfeld was handling the novel she had in production with them, the Stones listened.

Bob decided to make the leap to Ticknor with John Herman, but the logistics of his departure from Grove Weidenfeld proved sticky. During the period of indecision, Candida Donadio had advised him to sign an amendment to his contract, extending his deadline for the novel to March 15, 1991. The ink on that item was scarcely dry when Ticknor and Fields began arranging to buy out the contract. Herman, who at this point at least knew what sort of novel he was likely to get (and had a portion of it in hand), managed to increase the value of the Ticknor contract over the previous one—substantially: Ticknor offered $600,000, a fifty percent increase. Asher had assured Bob that "they would not hold me against my will," but Asher didn't personally have the power to release him from the contract, and the business folk at Grove Weidenfeld stalled on this point through the summer and fall of 1990, despite a series of increasingly scathing letters from Donadio. Finally they produced a demand that Bob pay *compound* interest on advance payments he'd received since 1986, which they calculated at almost $75,000. Resolving this matter was a long headachy hassle—not good for Bob's health given that he was prone to fits of rage even without this kind of provocation, nor for his concentration on *Outerbridge Reach*, which he was now under increased pressure to complete.

7
KEY WEST AND BEYOND

In the fall of 1989, the Stones got word from their friend Liz Lear in Key West that the U.S. Navy had sold a portion of the Truman Annex, which was part of the Naval Air Station Key West, to a private developer who would soon begin constructing condominiums, and there was a good opportunity to buy in early. The tract was adjacent to the Harry S. Truman Little White House and to Fort Zachary Taylor, a nineteenth-century beachfront structure recently absorbed into a state park. The Stones had sold their house in Amherst so there was some cash they could consider earmarked for real estate. Two days after talking to Lear at a New York dinner party, they sent a deposit on the yet-to-be built condo, and signed a contract within a week. "I'd never even been to Key West," Janice said. "But Stone would go anywhere, and I would go anywhere with Stone."

Bob *had* been to Key West a time or two—first in the 1970s, for *A Flag for Sunrise* research, and again in 1989 as the guest of Seymour Lawrence, who had a house in Hidden Beach that was subdivided into four apartments for rental and the use of his friends. By then the writer/artist winter community had expanded a good deal and the island had been further developed as a destination for hard partiers from all over the country. For Bob Stone, the place combined elements of a writer's retreat with his long-past experience as a sailor on shore leave from the navy.

Janice "hoped that spending time in Key West, a tropical place on the water, would suit Bob, maybe cure his restlessness." She worried about his fitful health (probably more than Bob did), and she kept remembering Gordon Walker's bitterly brilliant remark about his own squandered vocation: "If I was that good, I would never waste a moment. I'd be at it night and day. I'd never drink or drug myself or be with a woman I didn't love."

For her own part, Janice entered the Key West project (details of which would of course be her responsibility) with a sense that "a new phase of our lives was about to begin. I was hoping for more peace, more serenity. I thought Bob should settle down and do nothing but write."

———•———

It didn't exactly happen that way. For one thing, the Stones' Key West retreat was yet to be constructed. Soon after they committed to the buy, Bob and Janice flew down to inspect the site, staying at the Hidden Beach house near the buoy marking the southernmost point in the United States. It was not the last trip Janice would make to try to keep track of the building.

Bob cut back on travel, at least a little; the trips he'd scheduled were a bit less frequent and he didn't leave North America for more than a year. When in Westport he worked steadily on *Outerbridge Reach*. A few days after Christmas in 1989, Bob's on-again, off-again abdominal pain got so severe he was briefly admitted to Norwalk Hospital; doctors suspected kidney stones but tests were inconclusive. The undiagnosed symptoms continued for most of the month; nevertheless the Stones went through with a plan to relocate to California for the winter—they'd rented the same Laguna Beach house where they'd stayed when Bob was teaching in the area.

Still on the Strauss grant, he wasn't teaching in 1990; Janice, travel agent and logistician, couldn't quite pinpoint "the rationale for this latest move.... There was no reason to go to California to look at boats. He could do that just as well in Connecticut," though admittedly it was warmer in Laguna Beach than in Westport (where insulation in the Stones' house was an incompletely successful afterthought on the part of the original builder). "Bob arranged a few readings in California, but I think the real reason for the trip was just his restlessness." In fact, Bob (in the midst of the Key West condo purchase) had been toying with the idea of moving to the West Coast more or less permanently, while Janice was quite clear that she wanted her base on the East Coast, near their children and increasing number of grandchildren (a fourth was born to Deidre in the summer of 1990). The Stones were in the habit of traveling by road, in vehicles loaded with books, files, and bulky 1980s computer equipment; at least once Janice made a trip to Block Island with mattresses lashed to the top of her car. For people changing lodgings in that style, a regular East Coast–West Coast commute would have been more than a notion.

Bob's symptoms persisted in Laguna Beach. Not feeling well enough to concentrate on the novel, he completed a short account of his court-ship of Janice for an *Esquire* ode to the "literary wife," published that summer as "Enter the Muse," also featuring Kristina Ford and, bizarrely, Joan Didion. Janice got a stunning full-page picture in the magazine, plus a heartfelt encomium from Bob: "I was drawn to her because her way of being had some quality of the forest, a sense of great strength and vital-ity under a covering of tranquility. It was in her walk and in everything about her. She seemed to have great wisdom and great intuition. As I got to know her better, I found that this was so."

About the same time, he finished another article about the war on drugs, which made a few rounds before being picked up by Alice Turner for *Playboy*, where it appeared as "Fighting the Wrong War." Wrong in Bob's view because it replicated a pattern of errors made in Vietnam, and was capable of doing comparable harm: "The egregious phoniness of this war on drugs does not mean that there is nothing to lose. On the one hand, the Administration carries on the same weary game of cops and robbers, running down tips, turning informers, bribing hit men for testimony. In other words, it tacitly accepts the status quo in the hope that the problem will generate sufficient political capital and then go away. Meanwhile, on the streets, where the real problem is being lived out, the user—the person most in trouble—has nowhere to turn."

None of that made him feel better physically. In California he was diagnosed with diverticulitis and given antibiotics to treat it. Advised to stop drinking while taking the drugs, he did so for a while but was still in pain. Admitted to Hoag Hospital, he was told he'd need surgery but decided to try a liquid diet first. This gambit brought little relief either. At the end of February the Stones decided to roll up the Laguna Beach opera-tion early, and return to the Connecticut doctors who knew them better.

Mid-March, Bob had a piece of colon removed at Norwalk Hospital. The surgery triggered a gout attack, and Janice "hassled the nurses about getting him pain relief until they lost patience and threw me out." Another victory in the war on drugs! By 1990 neither Bob nor Janice was doing much in the way of illegal consumption, though they'd smoke marijuana if it came their way. Quaaludes were more or less over by then, though Bob's interest in other prescription downers remained lively. For his recuperation he was prescribed Halcion, a drug known for its freakish side effects, though Janice remembers, "He liked it quite a bit." Still on antibiotics, Bob should not (and in fact did not) drink. Janice stopped with him, "out of solidarity," not for the last time.

At the end of summer everything took second place to the suicide of Janice's youngest brother, Tim, still under thirty when he died. Bob and Janice knew that Tim had a bad problem with cocaine, which in his somewhat unusual case seemed to activate symptoms of schizophrenia, but lately he had seemed to be doing better, and no longer to be using coke. After his death it came out that "his friends had encouraged him to use heroin, since cocaine made him crazy. This was a successful strategy, in that he was able to keep his sanity and his employment right up until his arrest" for possession of heroin. Unable to face the probability of a draconian jail sentence, Tim Burr died another "casualty of the war on drugs."

Bob accompanied Janice to the funeral in New Jersey, near the Burr home in Bogata, limping from sciatica, a new and sometimes excruciating problem that had cropped up not long after the section of his colon. Tim's open casket inspired Bob to tell Janice that "he never wanted to be exhibited that way when he died" and would much prefer a quick cremation. Janice got a grip on her grief (the sudden, awful loss of Tim was particularly hard on her parents, then in their seventies), and by September was wrangling with Key West contractors on the phone as she packed the Block Island house for a return to Westport.

Feeling better health-wise in the fall of 1990, Bob signed the contract with Ticknor and Fields—an act of some bravado since he would not formally be released from the Grove Weidenfeld contract until January of the following year. Endgame wrangling with Grove Weidenfeld went on through the holiday season. Bob was working very steadily on *Outerbridge Reach*—the high stakes of what that game had become seemed to encourage him to keep his nose to the grindstone.

On New Year's Eve, Janice and Ian picked up a rental van and the Stones began loading it for their first winter migration to Key West.

On January 13 they moved into the Truman Annex condo and a certain amount of settling down began to take place. Bob worked on *Outerbridge Reach*, picking up speed as he approached the conclusion. His health was better, apart from one brief episode of gout. They spent time with old friends who had begun to winter in Key West and began to make some new ones.

Bob seemed something like contented in Key West. The nearest bar was two blocks from the condo: the Green Parrot, frequented more by the sort of locals who call themselves Conchs than by tourists and snowbirds. Bob, with his beard and the slightly louche dishevelment he could summon without difficulty, fit right in. From January to April he made only two brief departures from what locals call "the rock" when they want to get off it. On April 1, at his Key West desk composed of a door dropped across two file cabinets, Bob finished his first complete draft of *Outerbridge Reach*.

That didn't mean the book was quite done, but he let down for a bit, traveling to Maryland and California for a couple of lectures, while Janice read and annotated the manuscript. He'd begun to work on revising the novel between these two trips, but paused in that project on April 24, when he and Janice loaded up their car and began a three-day drive back to Westport. There the reworking of *Outerbridge Reach* continued. Janice and Bob had become a smoothly operating editorial team for this phase of finishing a book. Bob rewrote with the help of Janice's notes, while Janice made a second pass, proofread Bob's refinished pages, and sent chapters to sailing consultants, Bruce Kirby and Dick Whetstone, for confirmation that verisimilitude was as it should be in those parts of the novel. Janice was generally in charge of policing the computer, where chapters were stored in separate files; as Bob completed his work on each, Janice would print and renumber them by hand to assemble a complete manuscript; she also did final proofreading.

In the first week of May, Bob attended the American Booksellers Association convention in New York—an appearance generally reserved to bestselling or hoped-to-be-soon-bestselling authors. "They rented us a room at the Waldorf Astoria," Janice noted. Evidently Ticknor had great expectations for *Outerbridge Reach*. On June 7, Bob and Janice drove into New York to deliver copies of the finished manuscript to John Herman and Candida Donadio—such physical deliveries had not yet been replaced by digital file transfer. Then for most of the summer they were free.

Summer rounds included several weeks in Block Island, plus brief runs to New Orleans and Saratoga, where, as had become traditional, Bob read at Skidmore and went with Janice and friends to the track. August the Stones spent in California, first at the Squaw Valley conference where Bob was working. At the end of the conference he dug into finishing work on the copyedited manuscript of *Outerbridge Reach*. Once Houghton's legendary copy editor, Larry Cooper, came aboard, Janice debarked, "because I didn't want to work on this manuscript myself with Bob. I knew next to nothing about sailing."

Cooper is unusual in his trade for being a holistic reader as well as a detail fanatic. He was working with Bob for the first time, but had been a fan of *A Flag for Sunrise*. His praise in the cover note to the copyedited *Outerbridge Reach* was more effusive than usual for him, calling the novel "superb. Strickland is an amazing creation with a wicked sense of humor. I'd definitely want him around after the nuclear mayhem. But there's so much else I loved about the book. The scenes with Pamela, and Thorne, who I really wasn't sure I could trust until the end. The contretemps with Dolvin: I used to be friends with a carpenter as self-righteous as that! Your ear is perfect."

That kind of review from one's copy editor can be taken as a good omen. A bit later, Cooper sent a quote from Horace in his cover note on the proof.

> Caelum non anima mutant qui trans
> Mare currunt . . . Quod petis hic est.

Bob applied his St. Ann's Latin to a penciled translation at the bottom of the sheet.

> *They change their sky, not their soul,*
> *who run across the sea . . . What you seek is here.*

The essential spirit of *Outerbridge Reach* could hardly have been captured more efficiently.

8
OUTERBRIDGE REACH

September the Stones spent in Westport—a relatively quiet period, with September 28 logged as "day off. Bob and Janice went for a walk." *Outerbridge Reach* proofs arrived two days later; Bob and Janice turned that package around in about two weeks. The book was now out of their hands till publication in the spring of 1992.

With the publisher having made such a large bet on this novel, dominoes were arranged to maximize its success. It helped that Robert Stone was now recognized as having a secure place in the American literary pantheon. In the winter of 1991, Mona Simpson's February 1991 *New York Times* review of the Denis Johnson novel *Resuscitation of a Hanged Man* opened this way: "There has always been a strain of American fiction that seems to grow directly from Melville and Conrad. The foremost voice of this sensibility in our time is Robert Stone."

If Simpson's line perfectly set up the seafaring plot of *Outerbridge Reach*, it did so by happy accident. More intentional was a long profile of Bob in *The New York Times Magazine* by Bruce Weber, who spent a good deal of time observing the Stones at home on Block Island and in Westport, and went sailing with Bob and one of his experts, Bruce Kirby, in Long Island Sound. Kirby and Bob told Weber sea stories, Kirby's mostly humorous, Bob's distinctly more grim: a sailboat capsized by a barge line, killing all but one aboard; a sailboat blown away from a group of swimmers careless enough to all go in the water at once, leaving their vessel unmanned.

He's "very dark, very dark," Jane Burton told Weber for the piece. Weber's own take found Bob "as much at the mercy as in command of a large intelligence," which fit with Michael Herr's description: "He's like this huge, walking, talking moral barometer." Ken Kesey, as usual, was expansive: "Bob despairs, and there's something noble about the way he does it. Bob used to get high, stand naked in broken glass and stare at the sky and shout. Somebody who does that has to be on the job or they'd strike him down." Here was a portrait of the artist as wild raving hero, with just a dash of Mister Natural thrown in (Kesey being very fond of extracting deep meanings from the funny papers).

Weber got Bob to talk about the convergence structures he favored—in Weber's phrase, "a construct of intersecting lives." Bob called it "the metaphysical view, the God's-eye view that you see these people about to collide." He talked to Weber about his childhood and his mother with a somewhat surprising frankness, and also about the "kind of backward, primitive Catholicism that the Marist Brothers literally beat into me," which he was happy to think he had escaped in his middle teens. But "of course I was to learn that I wasn't out from under it at all. It's not something you get out from under."

The profile makes a somewhat strained effort to identify the author with his single-handed sailor and would-be hero Owen Browne—though Bob had cautioned him, "I don't do life portraits, though I'll equip my people with characteristics of somebody I've known." Still, Weber reached for similarities between Browne's background and Stone's, and found the Stones' living situation in Westport similar to the Brownes'. His description of Janice Stone tends to map her onto the character Anne Browne, though without openly drawing the conclusion. About Janice, Michael Herr was quoted a second time: "She's the patron saint of writers' wives." Weber found in her "the manner of a country wife, with an aura of calmness and intelligence and secret rebelliousness.... Asked if she feels she's given up too much, she says, 'One always has regrets about the lives one doesn't live.'" That much is something Anne Browne might indeed have said, while Janice's next line comes from a different sensibility: "But how many lives can you live?"

A calculated confusion of art with life is a way to play to a larger common denominator, and in that sense the profile was surely good for business; Ticknor and Fields most definitely wanted to sell this novel to as many people as possible. *Outerbridge Reach* had a first printing of 75,000, much larger than any of Bob's previous books. In the spring of 1992 Bob went on tour for nearly two months, albeit with a couple of intermissions, during which he and Janice were able to see the New York Metropolitan Opera's production of *Parsifal* and to attend opening day at Belmont, where they won on a horse named Belle of Amherst.

From mid-April into June, Bob was on the road, appearing in Miami, Orlando, Northampton, Boston, Denver, Houston, Fort Worth, Iowa City, and Madison, with multiple appearances in New York and nearby communities like Stanford. Janice went along for the West Coast leg of the tour, where the Stones stayed a couple of days with the Keseys and saw old friends from Perry Lane and Prankster days. Somehow sandwiched into this period was a two-week tour of England: Janice accompanied Bob for that too. A year later Bob went out again to several more cities for the paperback edition. These efforts paid off rather well; *Outerbridge Reach* sold upward of 80,000 hardcovers (double Stone's best previous sales), and enough paperbacks to earn out most of that $600,000 advance. It would be fair to say this novel was a winner.

———

Winning versus losing is an overt subject of *Outerbridge Reach*, while financial wins and losses are woven into its background. Early in the novel Anne and Owen Browne overhear their teenage daughter, Maggie, and her friends mocking characters on a TV show: "losers, losers, losers." Anne is distressed: "it makes her seem crass." Browne argues: "I don't think kids should be taught that somehow winning is morally suspect. Or that losing is a nobler condition."

The conversation isn't trivial. The whole novel turns around all the ways in which the America of its period had become a winner-take-all society—the same attitude that trickles down to Maggie and her friends. To be a winner or a loser is likely to be construed as an innate trait. Browne claims that Anne, not himself, "is the compulsive winner around here. . . . You hate not winning so much that you can't stand the sound of the word 'loser.' But you were brought up not to let on." That line introduces a note of bitterness into what at this early stage of the story seems to be a strong and loving marriage. After lovemaking the same evening Anne laughs it off. " 'Is that winning?' she asked, laughing at him. 'Did you win that one?' "

Love is one game both players can win. In the structure of most other contests, though, any winner's victory requires a bevy of losers. In that sense, the promise of winning braided into the American dream starts to look like the pea in a shell game. In the 1980s cultural critics began to look askance at society's shift in the direction of simple materialism. The satirical term "yuppie" was coined; by the end of the decade, yuppiedom's upward mobility had reached or surpassed its peak.

The Brownes are cresting a wave of prosperity composed of Ronald Reagan's "morning in America" and the long bull stock market of the 1980s. They have a large house north of New York City and another on the fictional Steadman's Island. Maggie attends a posh boarding school. Owen owns a sailboat docked in one of his employer's marinas on Staten Island. He writes copy and sells similar sailboats for Altan Marine. Anne writes color pieces for a sailing magazine, *Underway*, and also plays the stock market, until, in an event reminiscent of Black Monday, she gets badly burned.

In early drafts, the Brownes' investment losses got more play; in the final version this issue hums more quietly in the background. Though Owen is instantly and absolutely forgiving, Anne is left with a sense of guilt and a taste of losing in her mouth (which she tries to wash away with wine). The reader is given to understand that the Brownes' financial situation has shifted from secure to precarious, or maybe was never all that secure to begin with. Owen starts to perceive his dwelling as "old and outsized, a mansion on the edge of a slum." The postcard views of a pleasant day sail morph into images of ruin.

In real life, a good many prosperous people slipped into precarity around this time (the Stones had a little skin in the stock market game, but were insulated by their real estate investments and by Bob's habit of taking payout on his advances in a long series of salary-like installments). In the world of the novel, Altan Marine's parent company, the Hylan Corporation, seems suddenly to be on shaky ground. Matty Hylan, the founding entrepreneur, has been wont to personify his enterprises in the same way Richard Branson did. On the eve of the market crash Matty was planning to sail a newly designed Altan boat in a single-handed round-the-world race sponsored by his own company. After the crash he simply disappears; nevertheless the race must go on.

Harry Thorne, the more down-to-earth partner in the Hylan Corporation, is left to sift damage and salvage assets. Appearances also need to be salvaged, so Thorne continues the Hylan Corporation's sponsorship of the race. Browne, an Annapolis graduate and Vietnam veteran who looks the part of the gentleman sailor to the point of appearing in Altan's promotional videos, is tapped to sail in Matty Hylan's place.

The decision whether or not to accept is tormenting not only for Owen and Anne but also for their oldest friends, a cadre of Annapolis veterans and their wives, who with the Brownes inhabit a small bubble of American idealism of a style that was mostly destroyed by the Vietnam War—during which, among other things, their courtships were conducted. Both Owen and his comrade Buzz Ward had their weddings at

Annapolis, "passing under swords into the June sunlight. It had been 1968 and the Navy at war."

Outerbridge Reach is as Vietnam-haunted as any of Stone's novels—maybe more so than most. Anne and Owen sometimes seem trapped in their nostalgia for their wartime experience, when romance was heightened by the imminence of real danger. Anne, prompted by her husband, recalls "the beach at Pattaya and mai tais at the Halekulani and all-night loving at the Navy's Waikiki Beach hotel. At dawn, his whispering, *Lente lente currite noctis equi.* They had been adolescents. She remembered the deliciousness of youth and the feeling of fuck the world, the proud acceptance of honor, duty and risk."

Less lovely is the memory of civilian contempt for the military: "midshipmen were cleaning spittle off their dress blues" in 1968. The Vietnam experience for Browne and his classmates is watching "America fail to win the war there." Buzz Ward, a navy pilot, had to eject from his plane over Dragon Jaw Bridge and spent five years as a prisoner of war. Browne's combat experience gets less detail, but the tone of his sensibility conveys the idea that when your team or your nation loses, it takes some mental agility not to feel like a loser yourself. The shock of the stock market crash, the destabilization of Browne's employer, and the invitation to race around the world bring some of these sentiments to the surface.

As comfortably as he seems to circulate in the leisure-sailing class, Browne does not belong to it by birth. His parents were servants, immigrants from England—his father a raging, maudlin drunk (thus Browne himself is almost a teetotaler). Though the role of the father is reduced from early drafts of the novel, one has the impression that Browne has inherited the spirit not of the hero but of the valet. In that context the ideas of honor, duty, and risk he acquired at Annapolis may look something like a veneer.

Anne for her part comes from real money, but somewhat dubiously gained. The aristocratic deportment that (with her beauty) turns heads when she enters a room is acquired (like Owen's idealism) by her in the first generation. Her father, "Smiling Jack" Campbell, is "presiding chief of a race of water ruffians—Irish and Newfie by origin—who had lorded it over certain sections of dockland since the last century." Thus neither husband nor wife is entirely to the manner born, though the same is true for most American aristocrats—a phrase that is itself contradictory in "the classless society" we often like to claim.

Browne, then, stands on the brink of the race in a state of midlife disillusion, longing for "a homeland that could function as both community and cause," but believing that "no such place existed." He "felt that his own country had failed him in that regard," and "was tired of living for himself and those who were him by extension. . . . He wanted more." Here is another variation on the Stone protagonist's drive toward life more abundant.

In this state of mind, the race strikes Owen, as he tells Anne, as "the way to recoup" and not just financially (though there are financial considerations—if Browne wins the race he'll not only secure his position at Altan but have opportunities for books, movies, licensing). Beyond that "he imagined freedom. It was a bright expanse, an effort, a victory. It was a good fight or the right war—something that eased the burden of self and made breath possible. Without it, he felt as though he had been preparing all his life for something he would never live to see."

Colored by feelings of this kind, the idea of Browne's voyage is hemmed in by doubts that persist right up until the moment of his departure. The truth is that he's radically underqualified, having done very little solo sailing—less than he, atypically, begins to claim. In ways of which he's scarcely conscious, the possibility that the venture may be suicidal is both deterrent and incentive. Browne is profoundly tempted to put himself to a kind of survival test. In a special note written for a Franklin Library collector's first edition of the novel, Stone defined the situation as "a diagram in which a man rashly acts out the impulses driving his inner life against the stark background of sea and sky, trying to impose on those terrible coordinates the intersection of his desires." In a great many of his stories, Joseph Conrad had done the same, constructing moral fables that played on a stage composed of those same few and simple elements. Talking to Bruce Weber, Stone went back to *The Bluejacket's Manual* he'd been issued when he first enlisted in the navy. "The sea isn't inherently dangerous," Stone quoted. "But it's unforgiving."

Anne (described in an early draft as "a penitent Jansenist princess") also vacillates on the matter of the voyage—at the same time that she throws herself entirely into the preparations as quartermaster and logistician (very much in Janice's real-world style). Her most devouring moment of doubt comes during the sleepless night they share before the sailing. "Of course he must not go," she thinks. "Of course his experience was insufficient and his preparations jury-rigged. She had always known it. It was time to say so." Sensing that Browne is "desperate . . . that she ask him not to go," she almost does it but is stopped by a second thought: "it will be with us the rest of our lives. He will regret it forever. She would always have stood between him and the sky-blue world of possibility. . . . Their lives would be like everyone else's and it would be her fault."

After Browne has sailed, Anne visits her father, trying with limited success to convince him of the worth of the enterprise (in an outtake, Smiling Jack snaps that "the sea is for children and fuckups"). Departing, she finds herself able to embrace "the solitude she would have to endure in the coming months. It would really be the two of them, each alone against the world, as it had been during the war." Even the isolation appeals to her now: "the thought of having to endure encouragement filled her with disgust. It was too much like consolation. Winning was all, she thought. It was the only revenge on life. Other people wanted reassurance in their own misery and mediocrity."

Confirming Owen's earlier estimate of her, Anne's reverie concludes, "She required victory." The nobility of the aspiration is fraught with a dangerous spiritual pride.

———

Into this rather simply drawn victory-or-death scenario strolls the documentary filmmaker Ron Strickland, a far more complex (and corrupt) character than either of the Brownes. Strickland is first seen wrapping a shoot in a Central American country reminiscent of El Salvador—amusing himself in his last hours there by flaying a couple of young female revolutionary tourists of their unexamined idealism.

Strickland has been engaged to cover Matty Hylan's round-the-world adventure, and after Hylan's disappearance, Harry Thorne, though a bit suspicious, agrees to keep him on board to film Hylan's replacement. Almost from the beginning, then, the Brownes are seen not only through their own eyes but also through Strickland's various lenses.

Strickland, the creator of a Vietnam War film called *LZ Bravo* and another on New York call girls, *Under the Life*, has a predatory attitude toward his subjects. He considers himself to be an artist of perception, but his perception has a cruel edge; his specialty is getting people to unconsciously betray the worst of themselves on camera. "Christ," says his sycophantic assistant as they watch Central American rushes, "you really open them up." Later, alone, Strickland congratulates himself on how well he can "make them spread, make them dance." (The invasive sexual language that both he and his assistant favor for this topic is not accidental.) But he also worries that "perhaps there was such a thing as knowing too much. He was fast to his perception like some flying creature to its paralyzed wings. Once tiring he could never rest."

"Horrible instrument," Strickland thinks of his camera at one point, "it never lied." His reflexive approach to Owen Browne is to probe him for weaknesses, trying to trap him on camera with questions like "What does winning mean to you? As a man?" Anne he quite simply wants to despoil. "I want Little Momma in a straight-backed chair, upright, *uptight*, got it?" he explains to his assistant—whose first question upon entering the Browne household is "How we gonna fuck 'em?"

Recognizable as a creep at a hundred yards, Strickland is also, well, a portrait of the artist. If Bruce Weber was correct in claiming that "the author is locatable in the novel," he's actually located in more than one place. Stone's Franklin Library note identifies Strickland as "a conscious artist." Stone admitted to having real difficulty in the creation of Owen Browne. "He's a householder, a solid citizen, the kind of person I don't write much about," Stone told Weber. "You really have to invent a kind of music for a character. You've got to get the sound of their cerebration. The writing should take on a sense of the personage. And I could not get the sound of Browne."

It was symptomatic of the problem that Stone changed the character's name several times before settling on Browne. Strickland, whose very name suggests toxicity, was Strickland from the start. Unpleasant a character as he is, Stone understood him much more easily.

Bent as he was on identifying Stone with Browne, Weber does note in his profile that Bob's very slight and occasional stutter is much more prominent in Strickland—who uses it as a tool to disarm people: "There were those who trusted him for the stammer, as though it should somehow keep him honest, and those, the stupider ones, who patronized him as a half-wit." Attentive to this small detail, Weber seemed not to notice as much that Bob had invested Strickland with much of his own childhood— passed in seedy hotels in the unreliable care of a half-mad single mother. In the fictional reprise, young Strickland and his mother are carnival types, and Strickland retains that sensibility as an adult, his work informed with ruthless carny cunning.

According to his established habit, Stone split aspects of his own personality between Strickland and Browne, but in a more extreme way than previously. Browne's pose is just too good to be true, and therefore it isn't. Strickland is for better or worse true to himself and well aware of what he is. He's repulsive in a way that facilitates analytic distance on the part of the author, though in the Franklin Library note Stone writes of him without prejudice: "Work occupies a place at the center of his life that for the others is filled by the need for a quest or a resolving love." Though he operates like a con man to get it done, Strickland's work itself is relentlessly honest, albeit in a disconcerting way: "his work was too much like things. People required their illusions. He had only the news they didn't want to hear."

Stone draws Strickland and Browne in a way that puts different aspects of his own personality in opposition. Browne's projection of himself as a sort of preux chevalier—white knight to Anne's incarnation of a princess—is something Strickland automatically wants to tear down, yet to do so requires a kind of sympathetic insight. Browne's "good looks caught one's attention," Strickland reflects, studying his subject at a restaurant to which Harry Thorne has taken the party, "but their blandness did not inspire the proper measure of respect." The personality inside Browne's bland handsomeness seems different live than in the footage Strickland has already shot: "he did not seem so easygoing. His moves were full of anger, something the camera could not convey in the absence of perspective. At rest, his face could look quite haunted and unsound. . . . All at once he understood why Browne, in spite of his clean-cut aspect and beautiful wife, had been given a bad table in an establishment like the one in which they sat. His physiognomy was unlike that of a winner, Manhattan-style. In one quick look he could be seen as naïve and anxious to please and remotely dangerous."

It's an impeccable set of insights, and in sum the very understanding of Browne that Stone himself had to struggle to reach. For all his perverse unwholesomeness, Strickland is strictly faithful to his artistic practice and the kind of truths that it can serve. He cares about absolutely nothing else—until, against all reasonable expectation, he falls in love with Anne.

The design of *Outerbridge Reach* is really opposite to the convergence structures Stone had used for his previous four novels. Here all the characters are tightly entangled at a quite early point, and once Browne sails their paths begin to diverge. The expectation that these ways will rejoin is to be frustrated; each of the three principals ends up alone.

Solitary after Browne has sailed and Maggie returns to boarding school, Anne indulges her creeping alcohol problem until she wakes up (albeit in her own bed in her own house) unable to account for the evening before or for a second bottle of wine that has somehow been emptied. Vague memories of a movie she must have watched in bed assail her: "lyrically pornographic scenes in which a greasy-haired, unshaven man in a leather jacket and lifter's gloves slapped an undressed, slack-mouthed blonde and called her a bitch." There's a touch of prescience in this dream, though Anne's first reaction is a decision to stop drinking altogether and for a good while she is able to do so. Sober, she finds some difficulty occupying herself. "At certain times Owen's absconded presence obsessed her."

Meanwhile she is regularly thrown together with Strickland, who continues to film Browne family gatherings and other situations relevant to the race. (Browne, meanwhile, is supposed to be taking video of himself and his experiences on the boat.) Strickland's ugliness is moral rather than physical; he is also a capable seducer, to the point that "most of the attractive women Strickland knew had been to bed with him." (In this line Janice, with a twinge, recognized one of the character's autobiographical features. On the other hand, a scene in which Strickland and Anne must, for the sake of propriety, hide from the gas man under the covers of the Brownes' bed on Steadman Island is closely based on the Block Island episode where Janice and Jeremy Brooks had to do the same—one of those cases when Bob and Janice could laugh over each other's amorous adventures and mishaps.)

The extraordinary verisimilitude that Stone infuses into every scene he writes prevents the Anne/Strickland affair from looking implausible. She is first drawn to the apparent weakness in him. Not without calculation, he shares with her the weirdness of his childhood, a nasty episode of bullying he endured in Vietnam, a peculiar, Mayan-influenced amulet he wears to represent the sacred artist's wound he's cradling. When he makes the critical unexpected appearance at her door, his stammer seems to be so bad he can't get out a syllable, "until she could stand no more of it. She put out her hand and covered his lips with her fingers." Moments later the situation, however inexplicable, becomes simple enough: "It turned out to be what she wanted."

Strickland can only relate to anyone, his lovers included, by picking them apart. His urge to debase Anne sexually goes back to his first sight of her, and now he is able to follow through. He alters her appearance and displays her in the demimondaine venues he frequents, from downtown Manhattan to Atlantic City, playing on her incipient alcoholism. In his company Anne begins to drink again, and "her intoxication had a rowdy, slightly dangerous quality that pleased him."

For Anne the affair amounts to an abdication of self, or maybe an exchange of the self she's carefully constructed for her life with Browne for another that might occur at random. Watching herself in a mirror, tricked out for Strickland, she has "a quick vision of her future as a blowsy middle-aged reveler, all booze and beige hotel rooms. A former wife and former mother easing into forlorn, privileged self-indulgence, bloated and shrill." For all his dominance of her, Strickland finds his attraction turning into a kind of attachment with which he's totally unfamiliar. He grows "afraid of losing her," suspecting that after all she may shake him off and return to Browne if and when Browne returns from his voyage.

Maybe for once, Strickland is the one being played. That anxiety leads him to argue with Anne that he is the stronger man of the two. It's true in a sense, for Strickland is ruthlessly capable in a way Browne is not, and knows himself and what he wants in a way that Browne does not.

———

Not only on the voyage itself but in the run-up to it, Browne is compelled to examine himself in unaccustomed ways. Pondering whether to sail or not to sail, he soon recognizes fear as a factor, but one he believes he has come to terms with. Though in the past "he had always regretted the lost chances, played safe and been sorry . . . now the action had come for him and he was afraid." Once recognized, that much can be overcome, but Browne has a deeper and more particular experience, one that he almost certainly shares with his author: "It was as though, he thought, some rat lived around your heart. But not a rat—a child, a brother. Your late brother, the infant reprobate, beaten senseless by the rod, by the drill sergeants and the good nuns of life. Smacked proper but always back for more, always appearing in the clutch, the stretch, the shadow of the goal, to ask who you think you are."

Though sufficiently courageous in real life (he has after all proved that much in combat), Browne like many men suffers dreams in which he is abjectly craven. Unlike most men, he has a real-world opportunity to discover which version of himself is real. "His fear was not of being overcome but of failing from the inside out. Discovering the child-weakling as his true nature and having to spend the rest of his life with it." The urgency of escaping that prospect is what finally drives Browne to sea, where, as Stone's note to the Franklin edition puts it, he will have the chance to "try himself against the world."

In the early days he nearly funks it. Feverish from an infected cut he got in a pratfall during embarkation and later neglected, he is tempted to pull the plug on the whole expedition and return to safety and shame. Instead, once he has ridden out the illness, he discovers that he's perfectly well up to the mechanical requirements of the solo sail, his lack of seasoning be damned. "Inexperienced adolescents had single-handed around the world and the winners always looked good after the fact." Browne's boat seems capable and fast and the course he's set more than good enough—in the first phase of the race he's actually in the lead.

"No one knows how he'll react to being alone," Browne reads in a letter from Buzz Ward (whose experience of the subject includes more than a year of solitary confinement as a POW). "My opinion is that we are much more alone in a human situation that is utterly alien to us than when alone at sea or lost in the woods or something of that nature. The point is to keep solitude from becoming a prison." It's a point of some anxiety for Browne, who's had hallucinations during briefer periods of isolation both in the woods and at sea. On this occasion he seems to be managing— getting a little punchy at times but not in an obviously dangerous way.

"The best entertainment, Browne discovered, was his own thoughts. And then, as a kind of puzzle, there was the radio." He develops a fascination with the missionary broadcasts he can pick up off and on in the middle of the ocean. A dramatization of the story of Jacob and Esau is programmed, with parts spoken by different players and the master narration delivered by a rather judgmental "English lady" who is the sole speaker in less special broadcasts. Browne plans to consume the performance as comedy but soon finds aspects of it "unsettling. . . . He was unaware of the tears that coursed down his cheeks." In her summary interpretation the

English lady insists on the absolute power of God's will, which "binds the world and everyone in it. There is no setting it aside. There is no pleading against it." At these admonitions "Browne stirred in his bunk, his teeth set in rage." Afterward, "it struck him suddenly that there might be some form of false thought, notions that had their origins outside the brain and even outside ordinary reality."

The Jacob and Esau story is also loaded with implications about the careless exchange of articles of great value for stuff of next to no worth at all, and about the manipulation of false appearances for the gain of some at the expense of others. These tropes are pertinent to the next thing that happens to Browne and his vessel. A storm strikes. Browne weathers it well enough but his boat does not. Matty Hylan was supposed to have sailed a custom-made prototype for a new Altan product—the prototype handcrafted by a virtuoso shipwright in Finland but never delivered because of Hylan's failure to pay. What Browne is sailing instead is the first stock boat off the line, built to the same design as the prototype but with infinitely inferior materials and shoddier craftsmanship, as the stresses of the storm reveal: "Bad workmanship and sharp practice. Phoniness and cunning. Fucking plastic, he thought, enraged. It sounded like a liar burning in hell."

Thus the novel's climax manifests not as a zenith but as a nadir. Browne himself is thoroughly implicated in the fraud of which he is a victim.

" 'Altan Forty! Master-crafted! A seasoned winner in the newest design! All the elements of the precision-designed racer—attainable! Affordable!'

"They were his own words. And of course he had approved the boat. More than that: in imagination he had invented a perfect boat for it to be. It had been salesmanship by ontology, purveying a perfect boat for a perfect ocean in an ideal world. The very thing for a cruise to a perfect island, the one that had to exist because it could be imagined. He had been his own first, best customer."

In this crisis Browne's sense of betrayal radically expands. Of course he has no way of knowing that at this moment his wife is betraying him with the scurvy, conniving filmmaker, but the rest of the package is unmistakable. He has been tricked and cheated by his employers, sponsors, manufacturers—by an all-encompassing system of illusory false values (ranging from throwaway products to ephemeral gains in the stock market), and he himself is absolutely complicit in erecting that system.

This moment of recognition takes him a long way from the sort of self-knowledge he had hoped to gain.

"*Res sacrum perdita.* He could not remember the origin of the phrase. Sold our pottage, overheated the poles, poisoned the rain, burned away the horizon with acid. Despised our birthright. Forgot everything, destroyed and laughed away our holy things."

Browne breaks up the fixtures of his cabin for material to shore up the disintegrating seat of his mast. The effort succeeds to the point that his boat can limp along but can no longer sail competitively. However, the storm has also destroyed a couple of key receivers and taken all the racers out of contact; for the moment nobody knows where any of them are.

With his boat incapable of continuing the race, Browne spends a few days circling an island he's happened upon, somewhere in the South Atlantic, not far from the Antarctic Circle. Imagining where he might be with a better vessel and better luck, he thinks about "the book he had imagined writing. The book of a stern, steady man, a man for long solitary passages.

"Browne was moved to consider the difference between the man he might pretend to be in a book and the one he actually was"—that is, the reconstruction of himself as a fictional character. Going a step further, he records a false position in a spare logbook. The game takes hold. He finds anchorage in a natural harbor of the island, removes the transponder that signals his location from his mast, and begins creating two different logs (as Donald Crowhurst had done before him): one recording his true positions and another the carefully invented positions that would take him around the planet comfortably ahead of the other racers. This program of elaborate deception could all be "looked at as philosophy, Browne decided—as a question of reality and perception. Everyone had to believe his informing story. Everyone had to endure his own secret. That was survival." It does not quite come into his consciousness that, having been so thoroughly betrayed by his world, he can, through the deception he's designing, reflect that betrayal back on the betrayers. But why not?

For R & R, he sometimes chatters in Morse code with a blind teenage ham operator. Ashore on the island, he finds a mile-long field of whale bones and a shed whose outer walls are scrawled with slogans he may well be hallucinating, to which he adds in invisible tracery "BE TRUE TO THE DREAMS OF YOUR YOUTH." There also seems to be a sort of settler's house and when Browne enters he hallucinates a woman there.

By now Browne's mind is quite thoroughly shipwrecked, though he still has competence enough to begin sailing north, taking an extreme shortcut to the race's finish-line port. The English lady on the radio batters him with God talk. But "his time was occupied in learning to live a life of singularities in which no one action or thought connected certainly with any other"—that is, a life with no possibility of meaning or integrity. Maybe he really has fallen prey to "false thought, notions that had their origins outside the brain and even outside ordinary reality." Whatever the process, it leads him to despair. He cannot follow through on his deception. Nor can he return to the truth.

"Too bad, but the lie had broken the covenants. He had made himself unworthy of his own predicament and the truth was no longer his to convey. It had to be served alone. Single-handed, he thought, I'll make myself an honest man."

He weights himself with a diving belt and prepares to go off the stern of the boat to drown. "And jumping, stepping into space, he had to wonder if something might not save him. Somehow he had always believed that something would. He had never realized how much he had believed it. Be out there for me. Stay my fall.

"Nothing did."

"I see this enormous empty space from which God has absented himself," Stone told Bruce Weber. "I see this enormous mystery that I can't penetrate, a mystery before which I'm silent and uncomprehending." He might just as easily have been talking about Ahab's white whale, or the wall that seals the view in "Bartleby, the Scrivener." But Owen Browne doesn't need a whale to personify his obsession; at the end of the twentieth century such a person can just as conveniently batter himself to pieces on the walls of his own psyche.

The denouement of the novel has a few surprises, although the surviving principals behave true to type. When Browne's empty boat is found in the wrong place at the wrong time, with the incriminating logs intact, Strickland of course wants to reorganize his film around the new revelations of cheating and corruption, while everyone else wants the film shut down—most especially Anne. Strickland, who had feared all along that she would drop him and go back to Browne, now realizes, in the bitterest frustration, that she intends to leave him, just as definitively, for the *idea* of Browne she'd prefer to preserve.

But then Strickland is used to having nothing but his work. He snatches up Browne's video footage, steals the logs, and makes for his New York studio. However, he has for once underestimated the forces arrayed against him. Smiling Jack Campbell, though never a fan of Owen Browne for his own qualities, is quite willing to defend the dead man's reputation for the sake of his daughter and his grandchild. In the cavernous warehouse where he has a storage locker, Strickland is intercepted by a couple of waterfront thugs who strip him of his materials and also break his hands with a baseball bat. Once he limps back to his studio he finds that the remainder of his film and sound has been stolen from there as well. Strickland has got by for a long time on his cockroach-like capacity for survival, but one senses that this time he may be absolutely and permanently defeated.

That leaves Anne, who has to suffer the loss of Owen (whoever he really may have been); she also suffers Maggie's bitter fury at the discovery of her father's dishonesty, and on top of that, what might seem a minor matter, the "lost regard" of Harry Thorne, who quite admired her until she sullied her purity with Strickland. Afterward, his view of her is absorbed into cynicism. "Hardly a surprise that Jack's daughter turned out to be a superannuated, angel-eyed colleen with a round behind and heels to go with it. As disillusionments went, it was survivable."

Thorne is a minor character in the novel, but what's interesting is that both he and Jack Campbell, of an older generation than the Brownes, are men of a certain rough integrity who live by their lights consistently without having to think much about it—in great contrast to Owen Browne's interminable, inconclusive, self-mutilating self-examination. Thorne and Campbell are both the sort of men of honor that used to be common enough in the Sicilian Mafia, the far West, the rural South, or rural New England, to name a few of the cultures that nurtured them. They were natural denizens of "that enormously vital and brutal early industrial landscape" that Stone described in his essay on New York Harbor, "the port known to Whitman and Melville"—and so by the time of this novel's publication pretty much a dying breed.

Owen Browne, for all his noble aspiration, is actually quite a decadent specimen—as much so as Strickland though in a very different style. That leaves Anne, the last person standing, now a penitential princess indeed, determined to recoup and redeem her husband's folly and failure by making a single-handed sail around the world herself. That project might seem absurd or even sentimental, except that Anne has been carefully established throughout as a better sailor than her husband, and, more important, we understand by the novel's end that she has a greater strength of character as well.

Browne and his author would agree that everyone has to believe an "informing story"—the story that shapes one's actions and one's very being. Such a story may seem to be imposed by inexorable circumstance or to be predestined by God's will. However, Anne's plan to launch herself into a different future from what the world seems inclined to allow her, at this story's end, demonstrates that thanks to human free will (and no matter if God is present or absent or if there is or ever was any God at all) a sufficiently strong and determined person can change, indeed rewrite her informing story, and use it to become, authentically, the person she wants to be. Stone meant something of the sort in these two lines from his note to the novel: "On some level we all deeply require our lives to mean something. We hope for moral coherence, for a meaning to our suffering."

This aspirational aspect, which does survive in some form to the very end of a very dark novel, stands in sharp contrast to Stone's bitter but unflinching critique of the decay of American society at the end of the twentieth century from its former . . . vitality, if not grandeur. As energetic as it was brutal, the nineteenth-century New York Harbor was a location of exchange for the concrete objects produced by the American economy: textiles, steel, and other soundly manufactured articles of real and durable usefulness. By 1990 that economy was well along with its transformation into a marketplace for the exchange of often dubious services and the manipulation of financial instruments whose relationship to real goods or sound currency had been attenuated to the breaking point. From the late-twentieth-century harbor, the view of lower Manhattan was choked with the Wall Street palaces where all that reckless alchemy took place—and in that sense, as in his previous novels, Stone had found a way for *Outerbridge Reach* to channel the spirit of the age.

The actual, physical Outerbridge Reach is a dismal place—a channel between Staten Island and New Jersey, fraught with a dark history and more recently become a sort of aquatic junkyard. On some obscure impulse, weeks before he enters the round-the-world race, Browne sails his pleasure boat into the channel. "In a still backwater off the Kill, ringed with light like a prison yard, wooden tugs and ferries were scattered like a child's toy boats. Some lay half submerged and gutted, their stacks and steam engines moldering beside them in shallows. Others were piled on each other four and five high, in dark masses that towered above the water. . . . The busy sheer and curve of their shapes and the perfect stillness of the water made them appear held fast in some phantom disaster. Across the Kill, bulbous storage tanks, generators and floodlit power lines stretched to the end of darkness."

Casually moored to one of the wrecks, Browne remembers "scraps of the place's history. Thousands of immigrants had died there, in shanties, of cholera, in winter far from home. It had been a place of loneliness, violence, and terrible labor. It seemed to Browne that there was something about the channel he recognized but could not call to mind."

Yet men still long for glory. Separated from its geographical reference, the title phrase throbs with a resonant grandeur. Stone wrote that it "is meant to suggest, literally, grasping, extension, an urge toward excellence and transcendence." A grand, ambitious reach which finally exceeds its grasp.

———

Outerbridge Reach appeared in the spring of 1992, with cover art by Rockwell Kent in the style of his illustrations for Melville's *Moby-Dick*, and on the back a full-page photo of Bob, bearded and looking most nautical at the helm of a sailboat which, to the private amusement of those in the know, was actually parked on a trailer somewhere on the Connecticut shore. The book was widely and for the most part well reviewed. In venues like *The New York Times Book Review* and *The New York Review of Books* Bob was treated respectfully as a major American author and one of the most significant voices of his time. Pulling out a lot of stops, William H. Pritchard summed up for the *Times*: "Robert Stone's blend of heroic aspiration and mordantly deflationary irony results in something like tragicomedy—maybe even something like Shakespeare, our best tragic comedian. But whatever you call it, 'Outerbridge Reach' seems to me a triumph—a beautifully and painstakingly composed piece of literary art."

In March, *Outerbridge Reach* claimed a place on the *New York Times* bestseller list.

While Bob was on the West Coast leg of his tour, he picked up a review of the book by Jonathan Raban in a Seattle paper, and to his great annoyance found Raban looking askance at his use of the Donald Crowhurst story. A mere murmur in the U.S. coverage, this very flimsy issue caught fire in the U.K. John Sutherland's piece in *The Times Literary Supplement* took a very different tone from the U.S. reviews, treating Stone as a novelist in decline since *Dog Soldiers* and formally accusing him of having failed to credit *The Strange Last Voyage of Donald Crowhurst* by *Sunday Times* journalists Ron Hall and Nicholas Tomalin, which had been published in 1970.

Bob's interest in the Crowhurst story predated the book. The Stones had been living in London when Crowhurst's racer was found adrift in 1969, carrying incriminatingly fake logbooks similar enough in character to those composed by the fictional Owen Browne. Bob had a very early interest in making some adaptation of the story, had discussed it with his U.K. agent Deborah Rogers, and even had some preliminary conversations with the filmmaker Nicolas Roeg. But the film project was stymied by Crowhurst's widow's refusal to cooperate. With that experience in mind, Bob had been circumspect in connecting his novel to the Crowhurst story. He also had another historical model for the Brownes: Leonidas and Mina Hubbard. Leonidas died in 1903 during an abortive exploration of Labrador; later on Mina completed the journey he had intended.

Stone's note to the Franklin Library edition does mention Crowhurst by name, but his brief head-note to the U.S. trade edition says only "An episode in the book was suggested by an incident that actually occurred during a circumnavigation race in the mid-1960s. This novel is not a reflection on that incident but a fiction referring to the present day." Sutherland's review quoted those lines and called them "vague to the point of shiftiness," then went on to make the claim (absurd from both the moral and legal point of view) that the 1970 book had somehow taken the Crowhurst story out of "the public domain."

Of course the character of Owen Browne has nothing to do with Donald Crowhurst, however much Bob might have used the Crowhurst logs and journals as source material. The obviousness of that point was not enough to stop the controversy, which was soon taken up by the British gutter press (then mostly the property of Rupert Murdoch). "By the time Bob got to London, in mid-May, to promote the U.K. edition of the book, *The Daily Telegraph* greeted him with a story captioned Best Selling Author Sails into a Copycat Storm. This was in the main section of the newspaper, not the book section." Nicholas Tomalin was dead by then—killed while reporting in Israel in 1973, which gave him something of a hero's aura. Ron Hall publicly stated that Stone had "changed it just enough to avoid copyright infringement"—which would do very well for a "shifty" claim if one were needed. Facts, a common resource for novelists and reporters alike, cannot be copyrighted.

Bob and his agents and publishers considered a libel action—difficult and expensive in the U.K. and likely to do more harm than good, in terms of prolonging the life of the controversy. Bob contented himself with publishing a rebuttal in *The Times Literary Supplement*, and as was often his case exceeded the occasion with a larger meditation on the relation of fiction, fact, and factual reportage: "Fiction's province is the moral imagination. Its function is not to detail the actual world but to create a parallel one. Image by image, phrase by phrase, through artifice and evocation it must then make that world at once credible and meaningful. In his preface to *The Nigger of the Narcissus* Joseph Conrad (who was inspired by a newspaper story to the writing of *Lord Jim*) wrote that 'A work that aspires, however humbly, to the condition of art should carry its justification in every line.' This, I think, is the heart of the matter. No great work is remembered for its plot, that clumsy replication of 'real life.' "

That said, Bob's fury at the vilification began to subside, though the embers could still be provoked into flame. Years later, when he and I were traveling in the north of Haiti, we stopped to cut the dust at a half-derelict hotel on the road a mile or two south of Vaudreuil. We sat in the untended garden, drinking Prestige beer from squat brown bottles wrapped in white napkins and watching the lizards run in and out of the vines that covered the crumbling concrete-block walls; now and then one would pause to inflate its ruby throat. I don't recall how the subject of that old scandal came up—I can't think why I would have raised it, but if I did, it was a big mistake. Bob instantly erupted into a state of choler that I never saw in him before or after, snarling in a rage-choked voice, *I wrote that book with my blood!*

PART SIX

———

DAMASCUS GATE

1
But First, Cuba

Bob and Janice had long planned "to take a trip for our-selves to celebrate Bob's finishing his novel. He always said that when he finished *Outerbridge Reach* he had promised himself 'perfect happiness.' Of course perfect happiness was another trip." The Stones thought about Istanbul, then settled on Italy, planning to visit places they hadn't been previously, plus a few they wanted to return to. Janice got as far as booking their flights for mid-October, but then Bob's eternal pipe dream of a trip to Cuba suddenly got real, and the Italian holiday had to be postponed.

In 1991 it was still against U.S. law for U.S. citizens to visit Cuba, but workaround routes had been well-established—many of them via Canada. Bob picked up Jim Maraniss in Amherst, and on October 14 the two flew from Toronto to Havana.

Janice, who had elected to stay home this time—"Cuba was never on my list of places I wanted to go"—logged the date as one of her infrequent days off. Bob arrived in Cuba armed with an assignment from *Harper's Magazine*, and he had a connection to Sandra Levinson, described by Jim as "a communist from Mason City, Iowa, who had come with a Venceremos Brigade in the sixties. Bob had known her when they were both in the Kesey crowd." The Venceremos Brigade began as a late-1960s collaboration between revolutionary Cuba and Students for a Democratic Society, bringing American students to experience the revolution firsthand, often by laboring alongside Cuban workers in the sugarcane fields. For most, the trip amounted to no more than revolutionary tourism, but Levinson kept up contact, becoming the head of the Center for Cuban Studies in New York, which continued to organize visits of Americans there. She had influence in Cuba, where she knew many people, and Bob's acquaintance with her proved very useful.

Papa Hemingway was still a presence in Havana when Bob had represented the U.S. Navy there in the late 1950s. In the literary color piece Bob turned in to *Harper's* (political observations were tactfully inserted between the lines), he discoursed both on Hemingway (with whom he sometimes felt certain affinities, up to a sharply limited point) and on Graham Greene (whom he consistently loathed, in part because Stone and Greene were often carelessly lumped together as Catholic novelists with an interest in the third world). Bob's report from Havana was scathingly cynical about both: "two macho coxcombs who had so much trouble staying at the right end of their own firearms. Both were elaborately proclaimed Hispanophiles, famous for their Latin friendships. Hemingway favored toreros and waiters. Greene, in his later years as nemesis of the American Century, became a junketeer and rosy ornament to the *cuadrilla* of Omar Torrijos, in whose translated conversation he professed to detect profundities.

" 'Both of them spoke exactly two hundred words of Spanish,' the Cuban émigré novelist Guillermo Cabrera Infante told me once, speaking of Hemingway and Greene. Cabrera Infante had been a Cuban diplomat during the early years of the Castro regime; today he is an opponent of Fidelismo. 'But Greene and Hemingway could never have conversed,' he went on to say. 'Each knew two hundred different words.'

"The Cuban novelist Antonio Benítez-Rojo, who during the Seventies and Eighties ran the publishing division of the state-run cultural center, Casa de las Americas, remembers Greene's hobnobbing visits with Castro in Havana; he recalls, too, how Greene and other distinguished foreign guests were referred to ungenerously as *come mierdas.*"

With Jim as translator when his own Spanish ran out, Bob had the chance to talk to a good many uncelebrated Cubans: "Many of those I spoke with were artists and professionals whose attachment to the government ranged from enthusiasm to sympathy to resigned acceptance. In a comfortable farmhouse outside the city I talked with members of a family whose large landholding had been taken over by the state and who had seen numerous relatives flee to the United States. It was clear they felt that the revolution had given them more than it had taken away. The same seemed true of another family I was introduced to in the old slum of the Barrio Chino. Many of the enthusiasts were people of principle who resembled not at all the cynical apparatchiks I used to encounter on visits to Eastern Europe." Some of these meetings would have been orchestrated by Levinson, who was still a partisan of the Cuban Revolution and lived in Cuba about half of each year. Despite this influence, Bob drew a few conclusions of his own.

"Still the mood of the city seemed forlorn and surly. In the downtown streets youths hassled tourists for dollars. Prostitutes were out in numbers near the Vedado hotels, and there were endless lines in front of the ubiquitous 'pizzerias' in which scorched cheese concoctions were dispensed, uninteresting but filling meals to augment the rationed goods available in state groceries. In one of those consumer crises that bedevil socialist economies there was an absence of soap in the city, eroding morale among the fastidious *Habaneros*, forcing people to wash their clothes, their dishes, and themselves in Chinese toothpaste. A surprising number of young people, encountered casually on the street, denounced the government in bitter and obscene terms. Many of these youths were poor and of color—the very people who, in theory, benefited most from the revolution. A story was making the rounds. A little boy stands on the Paseo del Prado watching the tourists comfortably sightseeing. Whatever he wants, he finds, is on sale only for dollars, to foreigners. Asked what he wants to be when he grows up, the boy replies: 'A foreigner.' "

As luck would have it, Stone and Maraniss had turned up in Cuba during the severest phase of "the special period," when the crisis precipitated by the dissolution of the Soviet Union, which had done a lot to prop up the Cuban economy, was wreaking great hardship on the populace. Jim took to quoting a Cuban folk proverb he'd learned from Benítez-Rojo, *"Lo que hay que hacer es no morirse."* A decade later, when Bob began to feel a more intimate proximity to death, the line became for him a sort of mantra: *The thing that you have to do is not die.*

One evening Bob, Jim, and Sandra dined at El Floridita, where Hemingway used to get his daiquiris. "The band was playing 'Guantanamera,' for the Europeans, who were the clientele," according to Jim. "The three of us were eating lobster (Caribbean *langosta*, different from the New England kind). Sandy said that there was no street crime in Havana. When we chuckled at that, she suggested that we take a walk down the street (Calle Obispo), which we then did (a little tipsy). We had got just to the Western Union sign which goes over the street, when a well-organized bunch of muggers attacked us. They grabbed Sandy's purse, which she didn't want to let go of, and dragged her for half a block. Bob and I were just knocked down, not at all hurt. Sandy was devastated because she lost her notebook with all the telephone numbers in it, and also her black Swiss Army knife.

"We went back to the Floridita, where a courtly old waiter, who must have known Hemingway, addressed us: *'Ustedes quieren tomar algo?'* " *Do you want to eat something more?*

Bob's reaction (in tranquillity, after some ineffectual measures, including a visit to the police station, had been taken): "As Che Guevara, Frantz Fanon, and Lenin himself would have agreed, there's nothing like a little violence to define the propositions." The mugging was not in itself very serious, though suggestive of a swirl of discontent beneath the surface. There were larger forces at work, also partially invisible; Cuban history had its sinister side. "Like much of America, its conception had a dark aspect, the shadow of genocide and slavery. What it offered to the world was not nourishment but the things of appetite." With some measured cynicism about the Castro regime, Bob also thought it possible "to hope for new beginnings. The final drama of Fidel Castro's Cuba may be that he has prepared a future for his country in which he and his ideologues serve no purpose, have no place."

———·—·———

Bob returned to Westport on October 20, and on November 11 he and Janice finally embarked on their Italian holiday, touring Venice and several small towns, capping it off with a couple of days in Rome. Back in the States, Janice acquired a second-generation Toshiba laptop—at about ten percent of the weight and bulk of the computers they had been used to traveling with, the new machine, once instructed in XyWrite, would make the Stones' journeying much easier. By the second week of January 1992, they were settled in Key West, where Bob began trying to figure out what novel he was going to write next.

Some pages of Opus 5, working title "Charlie Manson's Gold," got promoted to a folder labeled Opus 6, but Bob was now planning a different attack on the material. In July 1992, with *Outerbridge Reach* touring finally behind him, he sent to John Herman "my thoughts about a new novel, which I'd like to get going more or less at once."

The heroine would be Lucia Percy, "known as 'Luce'—as in 'loose,' " and about the age of Bob's children. Like the ingenue of Opus 5, Luce would grow up in foster care in mill-town New England. "One night in the early sixties," Bob wrote to Herman, Luce's biological mother "attended a party at Perry Lane. Neal Cassady was there (and me too). After the party, she left with Cassady's entourage. A few years later, Luce was born in a broken-down school bus outside of Tamanchale, Mexico. They called her 'Firefly.' "

Bob meant to retain the Manson-like drug-drenched cult from his Opus 5 draft, and a backstory revolving around atrocious murders. The ingenue's natural father is still an ex-con, but now in witness protection in Orlando, Florida, invested with some of his author's sensibility. As Bob wrote to his editor, "Butler lives as a solitary, alienated and bitter. The spectacle of Disney World's construction obsesses him, in the light of local history, the hellish turpentine camps and the ruthless war to the death against the Seminoles. Lonely, trying to salvage some moral direction, Butler survives by his perception"—two essential qualities of a Stone alter ego. "Music is lost to him but he's spent his life reading everything he could lay his hands on"—very much like his inventor—"he's a mixture of yardbird mysticism, true erudition and genuine insight," a sort of *perceptual athlete*, like Strickland in *Outerbridge Reach*.

Elliot and Grace, the Bob and Janice avatars of Opus 5, are gone from Opus 6 without a trace, Bob having displaced his own qualities onto the Butler character. The bitterly painful satire of the "helping professions" is gone or much minimized (some vestiges persist in the synopsis of Luce's foster-care situation). What's left is a haunting from the dark side of the 1960s, and now in sharper relief than before, the paradigm of a lost daughter and lost father half-blindly seeking each other—the latter motif of abiding interest to a fatherless novelist who'd had relatively little contact with the daughter born outside his marriage.

Bob wrote a first chapter, capturing the adult Luce as an established singer-songwriter with impressive verisimilitude, but ultimately went no further with this narrative. Instead, his attention began to return to the apocalyptic Jerusalem novel whose elements had been on one of his back burners since the trip to Egypt in 1985.

2

NOT A SILLY QUESTION

In the summer of 1986, Bob had given a long interview to Peter Occhiogrosso, for a volume published the next year as *Once a Catholic*, featuring Bob alongside twenty-some other artists, writers, and prominent people ranging from Mary Gordon to Jimmy Breslin to Frank Zappa. The project gave Bob occasion to reflect, in much more depth and detail than usual for him to record, on his own ambivalent (but intense) relationship to religion.

"When I once said, 'In a sense I'm a theologian, and so far as I know, the only one,' I meant that in terms of American writers," Bob told Occhiogrosso. "There is just more religion and more religious questioning in my work—it seems to me that I probably deal more with religion, that there is more overt Catholicism in the stuff that I write about—than in most writers that I am aware of, except Mary Gordon. I felt at various times that I was taking seriously questions that for most educated people were no longer serious questions, and I ascribed that to my Catholic background. I mean specifically the question of whether or not there is a God or whether or not you can talk about life and its most important elements in religious terms, the question of the absence of God—Heidegger's postulating God as an absence—all these things are, for the most part, not taken too seriously by educated people. I talk to my editor, for example, or most of the people that I know, and they aren't concerned with religious questions, not in quite the same way that I am. They might ask the same questions, but not in the same terms that I ask them. That's what led me to make that statement.

"I'm really concerned with the idea of there not being a God as a kind of dynamic absence that is a constant challenge. Now if it never meant anything to you, then obviously it isn't a challenge, it's just the way it is. As a result of having been a Catholic, I'm acutely aware of the difference between a world in which there's a God and a world in which there isn't. For people who either have not taken religion seriously or have not been exposed to religion, the question of whether or not there's a God is an obviated question, a trivial or silly question. It's not a silly question for me."

By no means trivial or silly, this question would be central to *Damascus Gate.*

———•———

Bob didn't start running with any novel right away. In the spring and summer of 1992 he was on the road more often than not. Hangovers from PEN/Faulkner celebrations in early May provoked a bout of melancholy. He wrote to Kate Lehrer, a journalist, author, and PEN/Faulkner board member, "The writing life is so lonely, so fraught, so demanding of energy and emotional investment that it hurts bitterly to be provoked or patronized. It's as though people are refusing what you know is the best part of yourself. In the end, of course, no matter how much recognition we get it's never enough, never seems to justify the labor. We always look down the wrong end of the telescope. Stone's law."

In the fall of 1992, Bob's selection of *Best American Short Stories* appeared, featuring work by Robert Olen Butler, Joyce Carol Oates, Mavis Gallant, Rick Bass, Reynolds Price, Alice Munro, and more. Editor Janet Silver passed along a *Publishers Weekly* review that harped on "depravity," "viciousness," and the "melancholy chords" struck by the book, remarking that "No doubt this reviewer would declare that my 4-year-old's illustrated dinosaur book is really a treatise on extinction." Bob's introduction to the volume, exceeding the occasion as he was wont, began with a concise analysis of the influence of Nathaniel Hawthorne, Edgar Allan Poe, Henry James, Ivan Turgenev, Ernest Hemingway, and Eudora Welty on the evolution of the modern short story, leading into a close reading of James Joyce's "Araby," whose mood of inchoate romantic longing related to parts of Bob's experience in his early teens at the Endicott Hotel. The essay doesn't make that connection explicit, but Bob's reading of the "Araby" narrator as the "intelligent and sensitive orphan" depicted, who perforce must have evolved into the "literate, eloquent adult" who is actually telling the story, is suggestive: "He seems to have gone from solitary motherless childhood to what one might guess to be the literary life."

On November 20 the Stones were in London, lunching at the Groucho club with the Landesmans and another couple. The next day they flew to Jerusalem and checked into the Mishkenot Sha'ananim, a cultural center in the Israeli section of the city, which hosted a good number of well-known American and international writers. They drank and dined at Fink's ("local color," Janice noted), went to museums where they saw among other things the Dead Sea Scrolls, visited the Church of the Holy Sepulchre, and wandered the Old City. Bob had come equipped with contacts and most of their meals were taken with one or more of those.

Though they'd originally planned to spend their whole stay at the Mishkenot, they later changed their dates so that they could spend a few days on the Palestinian side of the city, in the American Colony Hotel, where they relocated on November 30. From that base they were able to visit some mosques with a guide. They ranged outside of Jerusalem too: On December 1, they were given a tour of the Gaza Strip by UN personnel, an experience that would acquire some importance in *Damascus Gate*. They visited the Degania Alef kibbutz, whose earliest version had been established in 1909, on a beautiful site where the Jordan River flows into the Sea of Galilee, and also went to the Golan Heights. They went out toward the Syrian border, and with Irving Weinman and Judith Kazantzis, friends from Key West, took a swim in the Dead Sea. Or rather Bob and Irving and Judith did—Janice decided to sit it out while "the three of them got into the unpleasant, mineral-rich water, which they were advised not to even get into their mouths, to avoid swallowing any."

This foursome also visited Masada, a mountaintop fortress in the Judean Desert, where Jewish Zealots were besieged by the Romans during the war that resulted in the destruction of the Second Temple, and finally committed suicide en masse rather than surrender. "Irving walked up to the top, as a gesture, but the rest of us took the elevator." The weeks in Jerusalem gave Bob his first chance to develop the incredibly complex image of the city he would portray in *Damascus Gate*, and also the germ of a contrarian idea—*Jerusalem Has No Past*—which figures in the novel and which he also used as a title for a 1998 piece in *The New York Times*.

"Tip O'Neill liked to say that all politics is local. In Jerusalem, politics is local but also moral and cosmic. Of course, politicians everywhere employ an ethical diction, however ungrammatical. And the reality of power in every city has its source in a measure of combat. But nowhere is this as true as in Jerusalem. Millions of us, raised in three major faiths, grew up believing that even apparently trivial encounters in Jerusalem's narrow streets and within the shadows of its wall determine the human condition. Its sparrows were no mere sparrows. A broken promise in the Holy City, a night of lovemaking, an act of mercy, might be studied centuries to come as a guide to the will of the universe. The story of a nocturnal arrest and a felon's execution there might change eternally the notion of human responsibility."

After walking the reader through Jerusalem's most holy places, Bob concluded, "All of these spiritual sites followed the fortune of earthly empires, which is to say, the fortunes of war. The glories of faith, even the most sublime, were emblems of secular triumph. The eternal question has always been settled, directly or indirectly, by force. Whose Jerusalem?"

Alongside Bob's more mystical question concerning the existence of God, the pragmatic question of to whom the Holy City would ultimately belong is critical in *Damascus Gate*—it might be argued that friction between the religious issue and secular one is what generates the plot of the novel.

3

THE WRITING SEMINARS

Bob returned from Jerusalem knowing for certain what novel he wanted to write; in Key West that winter, he got down to work. He was at the end of the last year of the Strauss Living, and soon would again be eligible to teach. As luck would have it, a job was already waiting for him, this time at the Writing Seminars at Johns Hopkins University in Baltimore.

Founded in 1947, the Writing Seminars was one of the first fully fledged academic creative writing programs in the country. By the 1990s it featured a small, one-year M.A. program in fiction and poetry, and an unusually large undergraduate creative writing program, with around a hundred majors. Since metafictionist John Barth joined the faculty in 1973, the graduate fiction workshop had attracted students inclined to work in a similar vein to his. Although he was semiretired by the 1990s, his influence on the fiction side of the graduate program remained very strong, as he was the most constant presence there—teaching one semester of the graduate fiction workshop each year, while the other semester rotated among visiting writers and permanent faculty member Stephen Dixon.

Steve Dixon and Bob Stone were both New Yorkers and their acquaintance went back a ways; Dixon had first called on Janice and Bob in the 1960s, in the company of George Walker's ex-wife Lola, whom he was dating at the time. Though Stone and Dixon were not remotely the same sort of writer, they respected each other and each other's work. Johns Hopkins's courtship of Bob was mostly conducted by Steve.

A $50,000 salary to teach two weekly workshops in one semester with practically no other duties amounted to a dream job at the beginning of the 1990s. Bob was interested, but still bound by the terms of the Strauss Living until the end of 1992. Johns Hopkins proved willing to wait to make the star hire they wanted, with Barth bridging the gap in the graduate workshop. The deal was sealed by a letter from John Irwin, the director of the Writing Seminars, in the fall of 1991—which noted that Bob would begin teaching in the spring of 1993. In 1992, an anticipatory laurel was laid upon him by the Johns Hopkins Board of Trustees: Bob would be dubbed the "Alumni Centennial Professor in the Writing Seminars."

Prone as ever to tight scheduling, Bob taught his first class the day after he got back from a sail in the Caribbean that had been commissioned by *Condé Nast Traveler.* "He had to make a quick turnaround from travel writer to professor. It was his first teaching job in five years." Plenty of people at Johns Hopkins and in the general Baltimore writers' community were eager to lionize Bob and socialize with him (I not least among them). There were dinners and concerts and films with various configurations of Johns Hopkins faculty, plus a fairly busy schedule of events on campus.

The Stones saw a good deal of Jean McGarry, Mark Crispin Miller, Steve Dixon and Anne Frydman, and the poet Peter Sacks and his wife the painter Barbara Kassel. Janice notes, "I went to more social events with him than I usually did, because I thought we might actually know these people for a while. The JHU professorship was a permanent position, with tenure, and I wanted everything to go well." My wife, Elizabeth Spires, and I had gotten to know Bob and Janice a bit, just before they came to Baltimore. Beth had been invited to a Key West Literary Seminar on Elizabeth Bishop in January 1993, and I went along for the ride (and to take care of our two-year-old daughter). The Stones had us over to their condo, where Bob told a story about Neal Cassady's parrot, now in the care of some Prankster survivor, which was still emitting speed-freakish disquisitions in an imitation of the long-dead Cassady's harsh, grating voice—and likely to keep doing that for another half century.

Back in Baltimore, we invited Janice and Bob to dinner with some other Johns Hopkins folk. It was a pleasant evening, though because I am vain about my cooking it bugged me a little that Bob only pushed his food around the plate. On a later occasion, Bob accepted my invitation for an after-dinner drink, but when I went to pick him up from the house the Stones had rented from Steve Dixon in Mount Washington I found that he'd forgotten about it and gone to sleep. Perhaps a bit impishly, I asked Janice if she'd like to go instead—and I'd have been perfectly happy if she'd accepted. She declined, but with a smile.

I couldn't have blamed her if she'd lumped me in with those people who wanted a piece of Bob to the point that he risked being devoured altogether. Bob might well have felt the same about such importunities, mine and others'. I have never had nearly so many fanatical devotees as he, but talking to mine has always made me a little nervous.

Mount Washington was a shaggy neighborhood in those days, running to large overgrown lots with the odd sorts of houses one might find in Anne Tyler novels or John Waters films. Down by the bank of the Jones Falls stream was a four-block-square commercial district with a handful of bars, restaurants, and boutiques. Housing stock rambled away uphill on the west side of the waterway.

Redolent of that particular Baltimorean eccentricity, Mount Washington was quite a solid middle-class neighborhood—residents still felt all right about sending their children to the local public school—but the overgrown shagginess factor facilitated occasional break-ins and, less frequently, assault. While living there, the Stones had a burglary when both of them were away on separate trips. "I got back first, driving my two older grandchildren from Massachusetts," says Janice, "and found checkbooks, electronics, and jewelry missing. The police responded promptly and took fingerprints from the basement door glass. And to my surprise, they apprehended the thief within a few weeks."

Despite the startling success of Baltimore law enforcement, the Stones "found the incident unsettling." In any case their residence on Sulgrave Avenue was never intended to be permanent. Bob "considered renting an apartment in Washington instead of in Baltimore." His "PEN/Faulkner gang" was there, and Bob's interest in the move may have reflected an early disaffection with the Johns Hopkins social scene, which under the influence of Irwin and Barth and a handful of sycophants they encouraged was thought by some to resemble the Borgia court. Also, Bob "thought he might write a Washington novel."

But Janice persuaded him against that move. "I was sure he'd soon get fed up with the hour-long commute between the two cities. I worried about him drinking and driving, or else my having to drive him to school and back twice a week. And I found that I liked Baltimore, considered it a real city, a real place, unlike, say, Irvine, California, or Amherst, Massachusetts."

The Stones found an apartment at 100 University Parkway, across the street from the Johns Hopkins campus, so Bob could easily walk to work. "We agreed it was a perfect apartment, except for its not being in New York. We were still having New York fantasies and thought of that as our end destination, full circle, back where we started." The location was the sort of medium-rise multiunit building that's actually quite rare in Baltimore. The Stones' ninth-floor apartment had the high ceilings and general feel of an Upper West Side apartment in one of those prewar buildings (built before World War II) that were beginning to be coveted in Manhattan. Only their cat, accustomed to easy access to the outdoors, didn't like it.

In his first weeks at Johns Hopkins Bob was struggling to finish a Caribbean piece for Condé Nast, and to make progress on what would become *Damascus Gate*. A 1991 contract with Ticknor and Fields for an untitled collection of stories came with a June 1, 1993, delivery deadline, but Bob didn't so much mind being late with a volume like that, and the $25,000 involved was, at this point in his career, not the most significant sum in play. Along with tenure and the good Johns Hopkins salary, there was a $600,000 contract for Bob's next novel, signed in 1992, and payable in annual installments of $150,000. Still, the Stones' expenses (now including four residences) were also quite high—so Bob, not only to appease his chronic restlessness, took any paying gig he was offered, and also did a full-scale book tour for the paperback edition of *Outerbridge Reach*. There were pleasure trips as well, to Gettysburg and Manassas to see Civil War battlefields—Bob's interest in these had been aroused by a PBS documentary recently produced by his old Amherst student Ken Burns. And he went hiking in the Adirondacks with Mark Levene, the scholar who was writing about his work.

All pleasant enough, but there was some friction on the job. The students Bob was teaching had been picked to suit Barth's taste—as had long been the case in the Writing Seminars master's program. In November 1992, Barth wrote Bob a long letter introducing the group—more or less positively at first: "No real losers in the room, though of course some are more winning than others. . . . Esprit and morale are high." Barth was perturbed, though, that there were a couple more students in the group than usual and asked Bob's support in holding the number down in future. If Barth was on his way to retirement, what future was he talking about exactly? And then there was more worrisome news about the M.A. fiction writers: Bob would be taking over several students who were halfway through writing novels. "Deal with it as you please," Barth wrote; "I will provide you with copies of the novels-thus-far if you want them, but oy gevalt." Barth continued loquaciously on this and similar themes, in the archly flippant tone characteristic of his style, by which Bob Stone would scarcely have been charmed.

There was not much ground for compatibility between Barth and Stone, and to increase opportunity for abrasion, they were assigned to share an office—only until Barth's imminent retirement, of course. The office was "beautiful" in Janice's view, but "helping Bob move in, I could see that Barth was a very tidy man, keeping his desk clear and everything in its place. Bob was otherwise. I don't think Barth ever complained, but we worried about the office situation. There was only one desk, and Bob would invariably leave everything scattered about. I was neater than Bob, and I'd always avoided sharing office space with him myself. If I had occasion to visit his office at JHU, I would try to put Bob's things in better order."

Bob had a cluster of small to medium annoyances during his first semester at the Writing Seminars. Someone scrawled some slurs derived from the *Outerbridge Reach* plagiarism scandal on a poster for his spring reading taped to the door of the campus bookstore. It's possible that Bob never saw it (I might have been the one who tore it down before he could) but undoubtedly quite a few people did. During the question period following his reading in April, a heckler asked him if he still used drugs. Bob paused, significantly enough to suggest contempt for the question, but answered, carefully and slowly, with a blanket denial: He had not, did not, and would not use any illegal drugs whatsoever. This response, while not wholly credible with regard to the past, pleased other members of the Johns Hopkins faculty and also the Writing Seminars director.

Bob had a pair of mirrored teardrop sunglasses he wore a good deal during this period. He wore them on the way to his April reading, though he took them off at the lectern, and he was reported to be wearing them in his classroom when a journalist from *Baltimore Maga-*

zine visited his graduate fiction workshop in the fall of 1993. The article that appeared suggested that Bob seemed disconnected from the students and their work, that maybe he seemed altogether out of it; the sunglasses, which also appeared in a photograph, acquired a sinister, if silent, implication.

Hampton Sides, who wrote the article, later had considerable success writing up historical material for the popular market and also did a bit of screenwriting. Stone's work might have appealed to such a person (Sides had some praise for it), but much of the article was sneeringly hostile, describing Bob as "a rogue gypsy ghost . . . knitting his brow, stroking his fan-tail beard, and casting long inscrutable glances from behind dark sunglasses." Sides set up a scene in which Bob was quoted at some length, trashing a student short story by "Bill from San Francisco." The piece featured an invidious comparison of Stone to Barth (who edited student manuscripts more copiously, etc.) and expanded to a critique of creative writing programs in general, with slightly shopworn disapproval from Flannery O'Connor and Tom Wolfe, and a fresh pull quote from Jonathan Yardley: "In the closed culture of the writing schools, Robert Stone sufficed. If you ask me, the transition from Barth to Stone is the same as the transition from Tweedledee to Tweedledum."

The piece made some attempt (possibly more of pretense) at even-handedness, closing with "Bill from San Francisco" describing a private meeting with Stone, following that "brutal" critique, which had been more constructively helpful: also, Bob had "apologized for coming on too strong.

" 'Not that he owed me. I don't want Stone to pull punches,' he added. 'I'm not going to stop writing just because somebody didn't like one of my stories. If a single person can stop you, then you weren't a writer in the first place.' "

———•———

In 1993, it's just possible that Bob might have sometimes worn sunglasses to hide the fact that his eyes were "pinned"—pupils shrunk to pinpoints are a giveaway of narcotics use, which also might have explained his indifferent appetite in those days. During his first semester at Johns Hopkins, Bob was troubled much more than usual by gout, for which he was treated with allopurinol and colchicine. "The treatment didn't seem to work as well, and the pain kept returning," Janice records. "If he was fond of pain pills before this, he became even more so." On the upside, any opiates Bob might have been taking at this time came to him by way of prescription, and he had a medical reason to be taking them; such use wouldn't have risked revocation of his tenure.

But in other ways Johns Hopkins seemed to be a less than good fit. In fact, Bob didn't connect terrifically well with the whole group of graduate students handpicked by Barth. "It's not that they were any worse than the student-writer norm, but some of their work didn't appeal to Bob. Some of it that I read," says Janice, "I thought was dreadful. Bob did the best he could with it, but a few of the students felt unduly criticized and were unhappy." Some of that student unhappiness leaked into the hostile article in *Baltimore Magazine.*

If Bob had more of a hand in selecting the students, as over time he eventually would, he could expect to form a good rapport with more of them. However, there was a different and more durable problem—one that had not been made at all clear to Bob when he accepted the job offer, on the understanding that after that first spring semester he would hencefor-ward be teaching only in the fall. Barth wrote to Bob in the fall of 1992, indicating that he too preferred the fall semester: "The fair thing for us to do, I reluctantly acknowledge, is to alternate and so with a sigh I accede: You take the fall '93 semester; I'll take spring and fall '94; you take spring and fall '95, etc presumably ad inf."

There was no indication in that "ad inf." fillip that Barth planned *ever* to retire; on the contrary, Bob could probably look forward to sharing his office for as long as he remained at Johns Hopkins. But that was not all. M.A. fiction theses were normally read in the spring semester; Barth's let-ter dilated extensively on the point that he had done this chore for many years and intended to do it no more. Thesis-reading would now land in Bob's portfolio.

Although various accommodations were made later on, the Writing Seminars position was not turning out to be the simple one-semester com-mitment that Bob had thought he was making. (For one thing, Barth's schedule would have prevented the Stones, one year out of every two, from wintering in Key West.) Of course it was still a very good job— better than most of them out there, but the bait-and-switch factor might have been disconcerting to anyone. With Bob's chronic restlessness in the bargain, it was fatal.

———

Janice brought Deidre's three older children to Block Island for June and July 1993, and invited her niece Arwen to help look after them. It proved hard for Bob to work in a house brimful of busy little children; the Stones "converted the shed/garage to a fairly comfortable writing room." Here Bob finally finished the Caribbean piece owed to Condé Nast and got a foothold in the first movement of what would become *Damascus Gate* (the working title for the book, per XyWrite file names, was at first simply "Holy"). That much was accomplished despite the report of Deidre's eldest, Candace, "that she had peeked in the window and 'he's not working, he's sleeping!' No," Janice advised the girl, "he's thinking!"

In the fall Bob returned to teach at Johns Hopkins, with excursions: in October to the Harbourfront Festival in Toronto; to New York where he introduced Frank Conroy reading from his new novel, *Body and Soul*; and to the Caramoor Center upstate near Katonah, where (on Halloween as it happened) he read the first chapter of his "Holy" work in progress. His second semester at Johns Hopkins would prove to be his last. Late in 1993 he was offered a five-year contract at Yale and in the winter of 1994 he accepted that offer and turned in his resignation to the Writing Seminars.

———

I had managed to see a fair amount of Bob in the fall of 1993. On October 6, I roped him into a reading at Goucher College, where I and my colleagues were teaching some of his work, particularly *Children of Light* and the essay "On Moral Fiction." One Sunday afternoon later that fall, I contrived to take him out to hear a blues band at the Cat's Eye Pub in Fell's Point. I had by then figured out that Bob would be less likely to have nodded off at an earlier hour, and I also thought he'd like the neighborhood, which had been part of Baltimore's working port in the days of the clipper ship and later an entertainment district for sailors. In the 1990s the area retained a certain louche quality, although it was becoming expensive to live there.

I picked Bob up at the Polo Grill, the restaurant in a posh new condo building that had just opened on a corner about half a block from the

Stones' apartment building. We tarried in the bar for a drink, and Bob was recognized by an elegant older couple, who tried to engage him in conversation. In fact, they seemed in their patrician way to be needling him a bit, until Bob got off a line or two that hushed them, and we made a swift departure. There was a hall of mirrors effect. In the car I mentioned that it had been like a scene in a Robert Stone novel. Bob seemed puzzled at first, then said, "Oh—them being pissy and me being . . ." a lot like Gordon Walker at his cuttingest, though he didn't put it exactly that way.

It had rained hard earlier that day, and on the way downtown my little Honda sedan struck a surprisingly deep puddle; it threw up a bow wave that blinded us for long enough to release a big pulse of adrenaline. When the windshield cleared I looked out and saw the tenement walls behind the train station washed in that magical evening light that Edward Hopper liked to paint. "So there is a God," I blurted out; I hadn't planned to say it. Bob smiled, a little inwardly; I didn't know it then but with his work on *Damascus Gate* he probably spent a few hours every day contemplating that very point.

The Cat's Eye faced the waterfront across a street of eighteenth-century cobblestones. Some of the barmen were bikers. The band, which revolved around stride pianist Steve Kramer, was excellent, and there was nothing wrong with the grog. The harmonica player, Glenn Moomau, was a writer himself and was thrilled to meet Bob (I had been promising to bring him). We settled down in a corner and listened to the music and talked. Kramer's performance drew a fairly hectic crowd, particularly for the third and final set, when random wandering musicians might be allowed to get on stage and jam.

Something in the ambiance must have reminded Bob of his navy days; he told me the story of having to defend his virtue, aboard the *Muliphen*, with a bunk chain. "Oh," I said brightly, "that must be the bunk chain Geraldine hangs herself with." Bob looked puzzled again. After a moment I realized he'd forgotten the scene. (At the time I had no idea of the ten or so arduous years that had gone into the completion of that novel.) When he did remember, he seemed to be pleased to have forgotten, if only temporarily. His comment was, "So, after all, you can be free."

I came away from that encounter feeling like I had learned something of which I'd never before been conscious, although it was very much a part of my own writing life. That is, we write this stuff not so much to communicate it (that would be an intermediate phase) but ultimately to be free of it. That much was something that we shared, and it felt like a bond. However, I didn't see Bob again for several years after the Stones left Baltimore.

———

Janice was piqued by Bob's seemingly chimerical decision to up stakes from Johns Hopkins. "I did all I could to change his mind. It had been such a hassle to move to Baltimore, to furnish the apartment, to move the books from Westport. And I liked living in Baltimore. I couldn't believe I was going to have to do the whole moving project again, in reverse." It didn't happen right away. Bob would not take up his position at Yale until the fall, so he was free for the winter of 1994; Janice sublet the Baltimore apartment and they lived the next months between Key West and Westport.

Damascus Gate was a research-intensive project, requiring knowledge of the kabbalah, the Phrygian deity Sabazios, terrorist tactics for blowing up historic sites, and a whole lot of stuff in between. Bob had left Baltimore with a crate of related books from the JHU library—Janice would eventually see to their return, just a couple of years overdue.

She and Bob had planned a midsummer trip to visit Eleanor and Jeremy Brooks, who had permanently retired to Wales—Jeremy now afflicted by cirrhosis of the liver. "When we spoke by phone, he sounded not quite like his old self, but he assured us that he was going to be all right, that he would be in better shape by the time we arrived." In fact by the time they got there he was dead, aged sixty-seven. The Stones got the news in Block Island on June 27; by July 5 they were on their way to England. All the Brooks children gathered at Gelli; the Stones put up Margy and her husband in the house they had rented nearby.

They stayed in Wales through the month of July. "Bob set up his computer outdoors with an extension cord running from the house. He did a lot of hiking and had another gout attack. That sent us to the clinic in Penrhyndeudraeth, and then to Boots the Chemist to fill prescriptions and buy some Kaolomorphia. When Bob recovered, he climbed Mt. Snowdon with Will Brooks, which brought on a recurrence of sciatica. Nothing held Bob down for long."

But the next phase of the Stones' life was marked by many deaths.

Their old friend Angus Wallace passed away, as did Jerry Garcia, whom Bob had known slightly in the days when the Grateful Dead were minstrels to Kesey's Acid Tests. Bob wrote a piece on Garcia's passing for *Rolling Stone*, waxing elegiac on the 1960s Bay Area culture in which they'd both taken part—lost now and not to be regained. "Deep within the event signaled by Jerry Garcia's death and the end of the era his music signifies lies a singular irony: The world isn't beginning again. Beginnings now belong to a new century that is not ours, we rough contemporaries of Jerry Garcia. Beginnings belong to the new millennium." Mack Rosenthal, Bob's first real writing teacher, died abruptly after a surgery gone wrong. "Bob spoke quite emotionally at his memorial in New York," as Janice recalled.

Worst, on October 24, 1994, Deidre's husband, Luther Jones, died of premature heart failure at the age of forty-one. It was not wholly unexpected. "He had been sick for months, and Deidre was frantically researching heart transplants—who performed them, and at which hospitals. I think he was perhaps just too tired and ill. And I know he was skeptical of the medical system, as so many African Americans are." The loss was a catastrophe for the young family. Luther had no insurance. Deidre, with four children between the ages of four and ten, had no resources other than her parents. Even the house they rented, in Shutesbury, Massachusetts, was in jeopardy. The owner, who was going through a divorce, had been unable to keep up with the mortgage, and the house was slated for foreclosure.

The Stones had put the profit from the sale of their London apartment into the National Australia Bank. "That was to keep us from spending it, and interest rates in Australia were high." That nest egg had always been reserved for the purchase of a New York dwelling they hoped to make, first in partnership with the Gelbers and later on their own. As Bob grew disenchanted with his Johns Hopkins situation toward the end of 1993, they began looking at apartments on Manhattan's East Side. "They weren't as nice as our Baltimore apartment," Janice thought, but they brought the money back from Australia. With Deidre and her children on the verge of losing their home, "Bob and I realized that the best way to stabilize the situation was to buy the house. So instead of buying ourselves an apartment in NYC, we purchased the Shutesbury house at auction in the spring of 1995."

4

New Haven

In the fall of 1994 Bob began teaching as the Rosenkranz Writer-in-Residence at Yale. Despite the resounding title, the post did not have the same prestige as the position he'd given up at Johns Hopkins. Yale had no graduate creative writing program and its undergraduate offerings were somewhat unstructured. Moreover, Bob's position was not tenured and the five-year contract he had signed would see him only into his early sixties, a good few years short of retirement age. "The office he was assigned was small and dark," Janice recalls (though on the upside, it didn't have John Barth in it). "Bob seemed to be the low man on the totem pole."

"Basically I'm doing this because it would simplify our lives," Bob had told the *Baltimore Sun* on his way out of town. "My wife and I never really did move from Connecticut. It just makes things so much easier that I found it impossible to resist." Janice would surely have disputed the point about whether or not they had actually moved. But from Bob's point of view there was some truth to the simplification claim. Westport was less than an hour from Yale and it was possible to make the commute by train. The switch reduced the number of Stone residences from four to three if you didn't count the house in Shutesbury occupied by Deidre and her children.

The truth was that Bob, though he cared a great deal about the reception of his work, cared relatively little about academic prestige, and didn't particularly want to be permanently associated with a flagship program like the Iowa Writers' Workshop or the Johns Hopkins Writing Seminars. Yale's comparatively low investment in creative writing allowed him to be inconspicuous, although in the fall of 1995 he was assigned a better office in Calhoun College, "the opposite of the one he had the year before, spacious, beautifully furnished and carpeted, with many bookshelves. Finally there was a place to put all the books from the Baltimore apartment." Like many writers in the academy Bob was just as happy to teach talented undergraduates as compared to the more ambitious (and anxious) graduate students that a high-powered MFA program attracted. At Yale, "the students were excellent. On the whole he was pleased."

In January 1996, the Stones entertained Salman Rushdie, who was just beginning, very discreetly, to emerge from his years of immurement brought on by the fatwa, issued by Ayatollah Ruhollah Khomeini in 1989, exhorting faithful Muslims to slay Rushdie on sight. Janice: "Knopf was sending him cautiously on a book tour. Bob had a phone call from Sonny Mehta, saying that Rushdie would like to come to Key West and meet some writers. Could Bob help with this?" Security arrangements were not mentioned in this call, and the Stones decided to throw a large cocktail party at their condo, without revealing the nature of the occasion. Phyllis Rose and Laurent de Brunhoff (who continued to produce the famous Babar books in the style of his father) agreed to host a dinner in the waterfront house they were renting, without being told who the guest of honor would be. Laurent drew Babar place cards for the occasion.

"Bob found it hard to keep the secret. He was a storyteller, always wanting to entertain. I was a nervous wreck thinking he would let the word slip that famous/infamous Salman Rushdie was coming to Key West. If anyone learned of it, I was sure, everyone in Key West would soon know. Phyllis wrote later, in her book *The Year of Reading Proust*, that she thought Bob had lost his mind, he was acting so strangely." About forty people swarmed the Stones' small condo for the cocktail phase of the evening, and the dinner afterward was a success, although Phyllis was mildly, temporarily peeved at not being told ahead that she would be receiving Rushdie, which did after all entail some risk, despite the "security guys hanging from the trees outside." This episode may well have inspired a darkly comic incident near the end of *Damascus Gate*, when one of the principals creates a successful diversion by starting a rumor that Salman Rushdie is somewhere nearby, abroad on the dark streets of Jerusalem.

5
VIETNAM REVISITED

In January 1995, Bob signed up as a lecturer on a Yale-sponsored trip to Vietnam and Cambodia. It would be his first return to Vietnam since wartime 1971. Janice, who had never been there, went along—her expenses paid in her capacity as Bob's assistant. The group traveled on a cruise vessel, the *Bali Sea Dancer*, and obtained tourist visas without any of the difficulties that had scotched a PEN writers' expedition planned for 1991. The excursion had a carefully innocuous title: "Sacred Cities of Southeast Asia."

Bob and Janice flew to Bali and spent a couple of days touring that island before boarding their ship, which sailed along the north coast of Java, calling at Semarang, where the group visited the temples Prambanan and Borobudur. The ocean was rough from the day they left Bali, and continued to be as the ship steered toward the South China Sea. Bad weather put the voyage behind schedule and a couple of port calls were skipped, although some passengers, including the Stones, were able to spend a few hours ashore in Borneo. Bob, who had been initiated as a Trusty Shellback when the *Arneb* crossed the equator in 1956, was qualified to help administer the King Neptune Ceremonial Sacrifice when the *Bali Sea Dancer* rolled and pitched over the line, between Singapore and Kalamantan. Bob's navy experience stood him in good stead; he didn't get seasick, though he did become confused enough to sign someone else's cabin number to his bar checks, albeit in his name, so the problem was solved without malice.

On the approach to Ho Chi Minh City (formerly Saigon) Bob delivered two of the lectures that were paying his way, to whatever passengers felt well enough to emerge from their cabins: the first on the precolonial history of Vietnam and the second on various books about the country, with special attention to Graham Greene's *The Quiet American*, on which his opinions were strong. The *Bali Sea Dancer* docked in Ho Chi Minh City after dark. Debarking passengers were received by a crowd infested with pickpockets, to one of whom Janice lost her sunglasses before the Stones caught a pedicab for the Rex Hotel rooftop bar. "On the way, a motorbike shadowed us, and its driver made several attempts to steal my purse. The two of us were crammed together into a small seat, so Bob couldn't do much about it. I held tight to the flat and slippery bag, and the thief couldn't get a grip on it. The pedicab driver made no attempt to evade the man, and perhaps they had an arrangement."

Despite a certain prevalence of this sort of thing, "there was a sense of energy and optimism" in the air of Ho Chi Minh City. A growing economy was in evidence, propelled in part by a tourist trade that enthusiastically welcomed Americans for the most part, though the rap-prochement had its limits. When the Stones visited the Cu Chi tunnel site they were advised "to avoid the propaganda film there, as it was very anti-American."

Bob and Janice took a bus to Da Nang, checked into the Bach Dang Hotel, and made day trips along Route 1, "a road Bob remembered," visiting China Beach, the centuries-old seaport of Hoi An, and the old imperial city of Hue, also the site of some of the war's worst atrocities in 1968. Janice found it "serene and peaceful" in 1995; "we were grateful to have been able to travel overland by bus for a day or so, to see the countryside, with its dramatic mountains."

They rejoined the *Bali Sea Dancer* in Da Nang and sailed north to Haiphong, with the rough seas continuing. "The wind blew our lunch around as we tried to eat the buffet on deck." Some lecturers had to cancel because they were seasick; one, in the-show-must-go-on spirit, resorted to lying on the floor with his microphone. Bob managed to keep on his feet for his last performance, more controversial than the others because it addressed the war, American involvement, the peace process, and so on, about which he had very particular opinions. "This one got some push-back from a few passengers who had been in Vietnam before," some in wartime diplomatic service, but Bob was persuasive enough to sway most of them.

"When we arrived in Hanoi, Bob said it was like Saigon used to be. The streets were quieter. There were fewer vehicles, even fewer bicycles. There was a festive atmosphere, and people were carrying flowers for the Tet holiday. No one tried to rob us." Next stop Cambodia, where there was armed rebel activity against the government here and there; a tourist and guide had recently been killed in the vicinity of the ruins of Angkor Wat. Members of the Yale group had the option to skip this leg of the tour, but only one opted out. The rest caught the flight for Phnom Penh on schedule, despite Bob's being harassed for a bribe by an airport official.

Otherwise, the Stones' experience was calm enough, though "Cambodia had a very different atmosphere from Vietnam. The people appeared poor, stressed, and sad, as if they had not yet recovered from the war, or from the oppression." After a fairly standard tour of Phnom Penh and Angkor Wat, the Stones flew back to the States by way of Singapore.

6
LOVE, DOPE, AND OTHER DISTRACTIONS

Back home, Bob entered a phase of procrastination on the novel he was supposed to be writing, distracting himself with the opening of "a comic novel about a group of travelers on a cruise." He did complete a couple of chapters of this project, under the frivolous working title "Off to Zamboanga." This novel might have been, for better but probably for worse, Bob's rejoinder to Katherine Anne Porter's *Ship of Fools*. But he lost interest and the project petered out. Still, work on *Damascus Gate* did not move forward right away. Bob tinkered with the title—wanting for a time to call it *The Souls of Sparrows*.

The phrase was not without resonance, embracing the key biblical passage and also Bob's recurring interest in the bird and its call; he'd taken extra pains to work the song of the white-throated sparrow into the closing scene of *Outerbridge Reach*. Janice, however, was not buying it. As the muse, she wanted the artist who served her to produce great things. On the practical side, during the publication of Bob's last two novels she had essentially become his manager; she had a sense of what would sell and what would not, and a consciousness that Bob's publisher had placed a $600,000 bet on the table. *The Souls of Sparrows* was not a winner, in her view. "Like sparrows' souls, it was a small, modest title. I'd read what Bob had written so far and it was going to be a big book. *Damascus Gate* was a big title, a selling title."

Bob kept spending his energy on lesser things: a *New York Times* op-ed about Saigon and a long piece in *The New York Review of Books* about Wilfrid Sheed's memoir *In Love with Daylight*. The Stones had gotten to know and like Sheed in Key West; he also happened to be Eleanor Brooks's cousin. He had Catholicism in common with Bob (Sheed practiced, Bob did not) and alcoholism; *In Love with Daylight* is in part a story of recovery. The *Damascus Gate* project had immersed Bob in one of the most sustained and intense religious meditations of his life. His *New York Review of Books* piece found Sheed's Catholicism to be "lightly and gracefully worn, skeptical, anti-pietist, and nowhere offered as inspiration"—thus entirely approvable. On the subject of addiction, Bob allowed himself to generalize, beginning with the quip "As long as joy's hand is ever at his lips bidding adieu, people are going to want to get high," but then turning serious: "Addiction-depression is a hall of mirrors, an unfunhouse in the corridors of which the victim can lose hold of reality, a loss which is immediately and genuinely life-threatening. The emotions of childhood, the worst ones, emerge out of the past as torments unaccompanied by the optimism and resilience with which they were originally endured. The impulse is toward self-medication, which extends the arc of every mood swing. The subjective nature of feelings is difficult enough to grasp: What's the difference between a real and an artificial emotion? Is there one? May one speak in such terms? In the cycle of dope, perspective vanishes or appears in a Chirico landscape. Booze and drugs murder sleep just as Macbeth does."

A reader would have little doubt that Bob was describing his own experience here, and Janice didn't doubt it either. "I wished that Bob would take inspiration from Bill's book and give up drinking himself. And I wondered if he did, and started a sober life, if he would stay with me. It sometimes seemed to me that we had sailed through our entire married life on a wave of alcohol."

Something different happened instead. In 1996, Bob saw a psychiatrist a few times: Tina Strobos, who practiced in Larchmont, New York, not far from the Stones in Westport. Dr. Strobos was the mother of the writer Semon Strobos, an acquaintance of Bob's who had introduced them. She was an immigrant from the Netherlands, and in her childhood had helped her mother hide Jews from the Nazis in Amsterdam. She thought it possible that Bob might suffer from attention deficit disorder, a diagnosis coming into vogue for schoolchildren, though not so much for men in their middle fifties. Still, Bob's restlessness, volatility of mood, and sporadic difficulty concentrating could be added up to fit the syndrome.

Dr. Strobos prescribed Ritalin, a commercial name for methylphenidate, whose stimulating effects are somewhat similar to amphetamine, though its chemical mechanism is different. Ritalin had been used since the 1960s to treat children who were then called "hyperactive," which seemed paradoxical to some at the time, because the drug was casually understood to be an upper, thus apt to be considered a kind of speed. However, methylphenidate works as a dopamine reuptake inhibitor, and as such not only increases activity of the central nervous system but also can improve concentration and enhance performance (sometimes in combination with amphetamine, although this cocktail was not normally given to children).

Bob had used Ritalin recreationally in the 1960s, when he could get it via the Stones' friend Martus Granirer, whose mother was a doctor. Even Janice had tried it once; for her "it was certainly a great energizer." In the 1990s, Bob, in her opinion, "was mostly looking for a chemical lift in mood." His essay on Sheed's memoir, if nothing else, shows that he understood both the impulse to self-medicate and some of its risks. At the same time he was often in search of some panacea that would eliminate or reduce his need for alcohol. During the mid-1990s he was having frequent back pain on top of his episodes of sciatica and gout, and was beginning to connect with other doctors willing to furnish him a steady supply of prescription narcotics, which (at least sometimes) blunted his desire to drink. But he still used drink as a social lubricant, fueling his energy as a raconteur.

And also, sometimes, as a provocateur. Steve Goodwin remembers this not-atypical encounter in a DC bar: "The more he drank, the more eloquent he became. We must have gotten louder, too, or expressed unwelcome opinions, because the citizens at the next table began to mutter and then told us to pipe down.

" 'Kind sirs,' said Bob, a semi-Shakespearean voice coming to him in a twinkling, ' 'twas not our purpose to give offense but to entertain, and only ourselves; and if our mirth hath spilled over, why then, you are welcome to the overflow.'

"This further riled them.

" 'I am a peaceful man,' Bob said, 'but your words do buzz about me, and sting. Oh! Ow! I am pricked! I swoon! I stagger!'

"And so he did. I am guessing at the words, but not at the performance. Bob did stand and deliver, and he did stagger. He stayed in character, and the tension somehow went out of the confrontation, maybe because the other guys were simply dumbfounded."

Story was Bob's saving grace—the ones he wrote more than the ones he told, the latter being comparatively evanescent, the former durable, though he often wrote with difficulty, often with real pain. His writing life was "so lonely, so fraught, so demanding of energy and emotional investment that it hurts." In the summer of 1995 he signed up for a month at Yaddo—the same month that Janice brought the four grandchildren to Block Island. He wanted, urgently, to reconnect with the writing of *Damascus Gate*, but midway through his stay he wanted to bail out of the colony and return to his family. Janice thought it a bad idea. "I imagined him living in serene luxury, writing all the time, with good food and wine and conversation in the evenings. I envied him. Where I was, it was sandy and noisy, with the television set and the washing machine constantly running, the children squabbling. We were eating mostly macaroni and cheese. I suggested he stay where he was."

Later on it developed that Bob had managed to get himself entangled with two different women at once while at Yaddo. Such situations were not unheard-of or even unusual; the artists' colonies of the period were notorious for their *Love Boat* function, combining propinquity with isolation from ordinary life and obligation, and seasoning that with a dash of creative fervor. Bob's position was more awkward than normal, though, since (as he told Janice) one of the women disapproved of the other, "telling him that he should stay away from her, that she wasn't good for him."

Janice could appreciate the comedy here; this sort of *petite amourette* didn't threaten her, and in fact, Bob's friendship with the visual artist named Emily Cheng was platonic, though Janice would not necessarily have assumed that if Bob did not say so. Bob "may have had other thoughts," Cheng remembers, "but he found me easy to talk to, and enjoyed looking at my paintings. He said they gave him courage!" Their friendship would last a long time past those few weeks at Yaddo.

But something more serious came on the horizon when Bob returned to Yale in the fall. Bob told Janice "he'd been invited by the mother of one of his students to have a drink with her at a hotel bar in New York. I don't know if [a woman to be called in this text "Melisandra," not her real name] actually had a son in Bob's class, but she was the person who invited him. He described her as an attractive blond woman, maybe ten years younger than I was, whose story he had selected for some publication."

Melisandra was beginning to build a career as a fiction writer, with short stories appearing in the important annual anthologies. Toward the end of the 1990s, she would publish a bloody, romantic historical novel, a tour de force set in an obscure corner of the British colonial empire. If the fictional Gordon Walker could feel a sort of amused contempt for the novels of his occasional lover Bronwen, Bob Stone couldn't take that attitude toward this book; Melisandra's first novel (also as it happened her last) commanded his respect as a peer. Janice knew nothing of all that at the time—that is, while Bob did once in a while mention Melisandra as a younger writer he admired, he disguised his other encounters with her, although Janice eventually began to suspect that she might have been the other woman at Yaddo in 1995—the one his other woman friend in the colony thought "wasn't good for" Bob.

Emily saw Bob for the first time when he arrived late for a Yaddo reading, dropped into a chair, and promptly fell asleep. "I thought, Who is this arrogant man?" Later on, though, she was surprised to discover his sensitivity. A certain cliquishness expressed itself at Yaddo by who sat with whom at meals, as in a high-school cafeteria. Bob and Emily tended to end up together at a leftover table populated by those who had no investment in the cliques. They found they could talk freely about writing and art, more comfortably than if they had been measuring each other for status in the same discipline, as Emily felt some tended to do at Yaddo. Getting to know Bob, Emily found that he was "always watching and processing, but through a very normal face," a sort of poker face, inside of which was "a very attentive viewer."

Together they made a couple of excursions, visiting the Clark Art Institute in Williamstown, Massachusetts, to see a couple of Piero della Francesca paintings, and going out to dinner to celebrate Bob's birthday. Bob felt close enough to talk to Emily about his childhood, which he didn't do with many people, telling her about one of the episodes when he'd defended his home situation from Child Protective Services. Emily came away with a good sense of Gladys's volatile instability, and what that had meant to Bob as a boy, and even in later life.

Meanwhile Bob was also spending intimate time with Melisandra, whose electric personality made some residents think she was crazy. Maybe she was, at least sometimes, the same kind of crazy as Bob—though Emily thought it more likely that his long experience of his mother's mental illness had given him the habit and some skills in dealing with craziness.

Not long after that Yaddo residency, Bob told Janice "that it had been important to him to realize he was attractive to women. That surprised me, because he had seemed to get attention from women regularly over the years. I thought he was becoming more good-looking as he got older, with his beard turning a bit gray. He was distinguished. And he was such a great storyteller. He had a seriousness and honesty in his speech, but also a sense of humor, a sense of the absurd, and people were drawn to him. Certainly women found him attractive. He was, in 1995, fifty-eight years old." That age is not ancient, but neither does it represent the first spring of youth. Chris Lucas, Bob Stone's most obvious alter ego in *Damascus Gate*, is occasionally afflicted with impotence. It may be that Bob's amorous adventures in the late 1990s were no longer as successful as they had once been.

———•———

In the life of the mind he was as potent as ever; the problem was his energy kept scattering away from the completion of the novel he owed. In addition to "Off to Zamboanga" there was a more serious, though for the time being less coherent, project brewing in his brain. In the mid-1990s, Bob talked a good deal about Mary Rowlandson, the author of one of the first Indian captivity narratives in the mid-seventeenth century, and about American vitalism. He was contemplating a narrative of his own that would fuse these two themes, though how that would be accomplished was not yet very clear. Rowlandson's captivity was very much an ordeal, in which she saw the death of her six-year-old daughter along with the deaths of other friends and family members, sometimes by torture— yet the first phrase of her narrative's lengthy title is *The Sovereignty and Goodness of God.*

The philosophical idea of vitalism predates anything American by many centuries; it holds that living things, but especially human beings, are animated by a nonmaterial vital force that sets them apart from material things. Bob found such vitalism expressed in the works of the great authors of the American nineteenth century, Melville in particular, and connected to Mary Rowlandson's conviction that she had survived her captivity ordeal because she was, throughout, being held in the palm of a benign, omnipotent deity. The particularly American flavor of vitalism relates to the sense that (as Faulkner put it) we are destined not only to survive but to prevail, which in Robert Stone's construction includes an entitlement to life more abundant (though another phrase he used just as much is "nothing is free"). Bob had in mind a historical novel that would trace the braid of these ideas into the fiber of the American sensibility— the idea of being *chosen* also had application to the very different context of *Damascus Gate.*

Meanwhile there was that 1991 contract for a book of stories. Since his first beginnings as a serious writer, over the thirty years of his career so far, Bob had not written a great many of these. At heart he was not a miniaturist but an artist of grand scale. But there were better rewards for Stone short stories now—for example, "Helping" had made a splash when it appeared in *The New Yorker* in the 1980s. Nearly a decade later, his sluggish progress with the big novel was depressing him; he was also in frequent physical pain, mostly from his back but also from sciatica and gout; and he was depressing himself further with the prescription narcotics he took to relieve both kinds of suffering. Appraising this situation, Candida Donadio suggested that he write a few more stories to complete the contract and get a book out before the novel would be finished. Book publication tended to reassure Bob about his own vitality. He wrote a couple of very strong (and very different) pieces: "Miserere," a story of devout Catholics covertly gathering to give Christian burial to aborted fetuses, published in *The New Yorker*, and "Under the Pitons," a picaresque tale of drug-running in the Caribbean, selected for *Best American Short Stories* by Annie Proulx after it appeared in *Esquire*. Bob's volume began to take shape around a work of broader scope, a slightly longer story called "Bear and His Daughter."

During this period there was some confusion to be sorted out at Houghton Mifflin. On January 10, 1994, Houghton had shut down Ticknor and Fields as "redundant," firing John Herman among others. That event might have contributed to Bob's bad mood; to have a $600,000 contract orphaned in that way is not a happy event for any author. And the bad news was more widespread: New York publishing was going through a major late-twentieth-century contraction, and there were other massacres at other houses the same week.

Bob Stone was added to the caseload of Joseph Kanon, the executive vice president and director of Houghton's trade and reference division. When Kanon was ejected some eighteen months later, Bob was handed over to Kanon's successor, Wendy Strothman. His hands-on editor, though, would be Dawn Seferian, a younger woman who worshipped his work to the point of being slightly nervous about the assignment. Despite her mild jitters, Dawn was a capable and experienced editor and could offer Bob the credential that she'd published the paperback edition of *The Things They Carried*, the career-making Vietnam novel of Bob's good friend Tim O'Brien.

"I remember giving copies of *Outerbridge Reach* to friends with the promise it would change their lives. Well, it may not have changed theirs, but to no small degree, it altered the way I looked at certain things and thought about certain things and felt about certain things," Dawn wrote to Bob, early in their acquaintance in November 1995. "You know, sometimes I forget, when I get mired in paperwork and minutia and mountains of manuscripts the size of small boys, why it is that I got into this business. And then I'll read a paragraph, a page, a chapter of somebody like you, and I'll say to myself oh yes, I remember."

Compliments don't come closer to the heart than that. It was a good augury. Dawn Seferian would shepherd *Bear and His Daughter* into print, and a little later would take *Damascus Gate* almost all the way there.

7

BEAR AND HIS DAUGHTER

The composition of the stories in Stone's first collection spreads out over a couple of decades. The earliest is most likely "Porque No Tiene, Porque No Falta," the 1969 story set in something like the fugitive Kesey community in Mexico, its dialogue in flawlessly captured Prankster-speak and its story line braiding cannabis paranoia with the possibility of real conspiracies against the protagonist. ("Fletch," Janice has disclosed, "is a variation on the author at his most paranoid.") Some version of "Aquarius Obscured" probably existed earlier, since this story is either an outtake or an adaptation of a scene in *Dog Soldiers*. Stone stuck this pair of what might be called stoner stories in the middle of the volume, where they would be safe, and opened the collection with two stories saturated in different aspects of the Catholicism that had shaped parts of his own life.

All the incidents in "Absence of Mercy" are drawn directly from Stone's own experience, which would bring this story close to what Hannah Arendt called "an unbearable sequence of sheer happenings"—except for a clear conceptual intention. The story studies how helpless victims of violence become violent themselves in later years, and also the formation of what Stone sometimes called "the institutional man." Although Stone himself escaped into full personhood, his character ends the story by running wildly with no destination—having, like Stone, been battered into two different molds by the church and its orphanage first, and then the military. Stone's most thorough portrayal of an institutional man is Pablo Tabor in *A Flag for Sunrise*, but similar characteristics appear elsewhere; even in the bold and noble Owen Browne, who privately struggles with what is here called "a rat that lived near his heart," that is, a learned impulse to cowardice and cringing, instilled by brutalization in early childhood.

The dark energy of "Miserere" springs from a horrible episode the Stones heard about in Amherst; a friend of a friend lost her husband and child, who went through thin ice while skating and drowned or froze to death. In the fictional version they cling to the ice for hours, while their cries for help are taken for shouts of merriment by passersby who hear them in the distance. The total absence of mercy is again reflected. The widow Mary Urquhart, having lost "all her pretty ones," salves herself (none too successfully) by good works, including counseling pregnant girls against abortion and (illegally and quite dangerously) organizing proper Catholic blessing and burial for fetuses a cohort filches from abortion clinics in the area. This heartrending story presents a spectacle of extreme religious observance performed with little in the way of faith, and nothing at all of hope.

"Miserere" and "Helping" were fully realized, mature works; their publication in *The New Yorker* gave Stone some presence as a short-story writer. For "Under the Pitons," he acquired the key episode, which is structurally similar to the ice-skating catastrophe in "Miserere," from his *Outerbridge Reach* research: a true story of a group of feckless pleasure sailors who all went swimming at once, forgetting to lower a ladder or line. Unable to get back on board, all drowned. In the story, this fatal folly turns into a miniature image of a larger one—the sailors are running drugs around the Caribbean, in a scheme so half-baked it is bound to go wrong in some other way if not this one.

The collection's pièce de résistance is the title story, set in the wild Northwest to which Stone had been introduced by John Hildebrand, and starring the poet Smart, who's composed of some of the author's unrealized ambitions and some of his worst fears. "He was forever doing things wrong. Wronging students, brother poets, women. The world was rotten with anger." At the moment he's on a reading tour of colleges in "the mountain states," which stands to earn him $12,000 if he can get through it. But at the midpoint he slips into binge drinking, gets thrown out of a casino without knowing why, and decides to make a detour to visit his daughter, a ranger at a national park about five hundred miles away. Rowan Smart was not raised by her father. Perhaps Bob was thinking of Emily, his own daughter whom he rarely saw, when he wrote about Rowan, who in the story has her father's eyes, as did Emily.

During the long drive, Smart tries to revive in his mind a lost poem, about salmon returning up an Alaskan river to spawn, which he believes to have been his best. It was a long poem and the story is peppered with the fragments that Smart can remember.

> *What wisdom could be bound in a fish eye?*
> *It must be an illusion.*
> *For how could fish, these fish, under their long-lost ale-colored sky,*
> *In the strange light, coming home, coming back after all these*
>   *years,*
> *Have something in their cold old eyes I need*
> *Or think I need.*

Though he can remember many pieces, they won't assemble into a whole. "A man had to keep settling for less," he thinks bitterly. "You became a few scattered lines of your own poem." Yet this poem, itself describing quest, becomes one object of Smart's quest. The other is the image of his daughter.

Ranger Rowan is a hot mess herself. She begins to drink and take crystal meth at the same time that she is transferred from her usual post as a tour guide to law enforcement duty, for which she is issued a .357 caliber revolver. It happens to be her thirty-first birthday too. Rowan and Smart drink and snort some meth together, forgoing a planned meal. They discuss the lost poem, quoting more fragments. Her seductive behavior toward him is puzzling until it comes out in their conversation that sometime in the past he seduced or was seduced by her—or both; at any rate this father and daughter have been lovers, although in the present moment Smart seems to have actually forgotten it.

Rowan wants it to happen again. "Your poem," she tells him. "It's about me. It's about you coming back to me. Us both coming back where we belong. Which is together. Always. . . ." The crazed perversity of her intention repels Smart now, but then, what else has he come there for? He blames the impulse on the drink and drug, advising her, "I've got through many a night on many a drug." If they're sensible they can win through to morning. In the event, Rowan shoots Smart, fatally, after he has sunk into a drunken doze. At dawn she goes into the park and kills herself with the same pistol.

Rowan's boyfriend, a Wind River Shoshone named John Hears the Sun Come Up, is in charge of the denouement. His culture furnishes him a sort of fatalism that makes his reaction to the bloodbath measured and calm. "She loved him," John tells a park officer who's raging against Smart in the white man's way. And "he wasn't a bad guy," and "he wrote a poem about salmon I liked." Having John close the story seemed a curious choice to many readers (some critics angrily denounced Stone for it), but its effectiveness lies in the way his attitude places the whole question of whether any quality of art can vindicate such a wanton, recklessly destructive life.

"Bob himself had written a few poems," Janice recalls, "but lost most of them. . . . Bob was usually not entirely happy with his own poems and yet, like Smart, he mourned the lost ones. He always meant to rewrite them." The composition of Smart's lost poem was not a simple problem. "It had to be plausibly the work of a successful poet, but also obviously second-rate." A trick of the finished story is that no one can tell just how good or not that poem is because no reader of the story ever gets to see it whole.

Stone had talent as a poet, if incompletely realized. He admired the great poets of the past and the good ones of his own time, and a part of him wanted always to be more completely a poet than he was. A part of him also wanted to refrain from acting out his most destructive and self-destructive impulses. It was more important he succeed in that, and in that (sometimes with wrenching difficulty) he did succeed.

If *Bear and His Daughter* had been a first book, with no novels ahead of it, it would likely have been received as a debut as strong as that of Thom Jones, whose somewhat Stone-influenced collection *The Pugilist at Rest* was met with critical accolades in 1993. By contrast, readers of Stone's novels knew they could have *more*, and many of them wanted more.

———————

Bear and His Daughter appeared in the spring of 1997, to prominently placed but generally mixed reviews—typically written by admirers of Stone's novels who found in reading the short stories that they preferred him to work on a larger canvas. "Like the protagonist of his last novel,

Outerbridge Reach, the principal characters in Robert Stone's short-story collection are single-hand sailors on a course to disaster," wrote Richard Eder in the *Los Angeles Times*. After this robust start, the piece soon devolved into carping. "They are Hemingway heroes or heroines (the women in these stories are as macho as the men) on skid row. Their universal tragedy shrinks to the size of a half-pint bottle or a glassine envelope. They are Ancient Mariners, whose urgent tale is followed by a mumbled plea for a handout."

Stone's resemblance to Hemingway didn't go much deeper than the bushiness of his whitening beard, so this facile sort of comparison annoyed him, as did, still more so, the comparison to Graham Greene deployed by James Wood in *The New York Times*. Wood found that "these stories compact Mr. Stone's iron talents, and fracture them somewhat." Wood's review was sometimes perspicacious—he was one of few to note Stone's gift for milking the most from portrayals of male anger—but, on balance, persnickety to a weird extreme: "his taut, scrubbed work becomes oppressive, like a very clean person who also smells very clean." Say what? That sort of line made the review look something like a hatchet job, and Janice and Bob ventured to wonder whether Wood, of British origin, might be harboring old resentments from the *Outerbridge Reach* scandal in the U.K. Or maybe that was paranoid; in the same season Ken Kesey would tell a journalist that Bob saw "sinister forces behind every Oreo cookie."

Like many reviewers, Wood tacitly wished the stories to be novels (as several of them might have been), deciding that elements "that might waft free in a large novel" seemed "to have too controlling a stake in a narrower work." Vindication would come twenty years later from Atticus Lish, then an energetic newcomer to the literary scene, who chose *Bear and His Daughter* as "the book of a lifetime" for a 2016 piece in *The Independent*. In 1998, grudging reviews notwithstanding, *Bear and His Daughter* was a finalist for the Pulitzer Prize, in the end edged out by Philip Roth's *American Pastoral*.

Perhaps the best publicity the collection generated at the time of publication was a lengthy profile, "Romancing Robert Stone," in the March 1997 issue of *New York* magazine. The writer, Linda Hall, was a friend of the Stones' Westport friend Noel Parmentel, and the piece took a friendly approach, devoting some time, as its title suggested, to the symbiotic relationship Bob and Janice sustained, and reprising Michael Herr's compliment from the Bruce Weber interview, "Man, she's the patron saint of writers' wives." Bob, thirty-seven years into the marriage when Hall called on them in Key West, gave it a sober summary: "In a way we were both reluctant to make the commitment but once we did, it was plain we were in for the long haul."

Hall's hook for the piece was her idea of Bob's personal obscurity; "It has been Stone's peculiar fate to have great success without great recognition." She had the insight that Bob, unlike professional celebrities, had little interest in commodifying his personality. "The best of me goes into my books," he told her. "I'm not vain except in my work; there, I'm proud and touchy." Hall found the attitude admirable—"Although he has logged several book tours . . . Stone has never behaved as if life itself were one." At the same time she reported in detail on what Janice called "a hell of an interesting life," one in which, Bob told her, "I made it a point to be where things were happening."

Like many ambivalent reviewers, Hall was struck by the prevalence of alcohol and drug abuse in Stone's fiction. "Stone has unequivocally and repeatedly identified his subject as 'America and Americans.' In his fiction, though, he seems committed to depicting not so much all manner of Americans but all manner of American addicts." Still, the piece overall was revealing in a very positive way; not only did it boost *Bear and His Daughter*, it also set the stage for *Damascus Gate*.

The tour for *Bear and His Daughter* took Bob to Philadelphia, Boston, Austin, DC, New York, Los Angeles, San Francisco, and Miami. At a Coral Gables reading Kem Nunn and the director John McNaughton appeared with the news that Harvey Keitel was interested in starring in Kem's adaptation of *Children of Light*, but this project, like the movie options on *A Flag for Sunrise* and *Outerbridge Reach*, never made it to the first day of principal photography. Bob was pretty well out of the film business by the end of the 1990s.

Bloomsbury released *Bear and His Daughter* in Britain that spring, and Bob crossed the pond in May for a brief tour, with stops in London and a *New Yorker*–sponsored call at a literary festival at Hay-on-Wye in Wales. He returned to the States on June 4, and he and Janice moved into an apartment sublet from William Wright, a block from the 92nd Street Y, where Bob had become a frequent performer. There the two of them buckled down to the completion of *Damascus Gate*.

Janice's role in the procedure had become more systematic than previously. The file handle for the late draft chapters changed from "Holy" to "Jehu." Janice kept a printout of each chapter in a separate folder with a number—a tentative number since this novel involved more complicated crosscutting between different plotlines and groups of characters than Bob had ever attempted before. This system allowed her to present different arrangements for Bob to review, sometimes with notes on the order she herself thought preferable.

Alongside the work of copy editing and plot consultation, Janice was in charge of controlling the length of the whole—which at this late stage risked breaking a thousand pages, impractical and dangerously expensive to produce. Since each chapter was stored in a separate XyWrite file, this task required that she keep a parallel notebook from which a total page count could be calculated. The notebook could also be used to sketch chapter orders that could be taken in at a glance.

A heat wave blasted the East Coast that summer. The Stones, though they felt sorry for their tenants, were grateful to be away from Westport, where their house was not air-conditioned. Wright's apartment had a muscular cooling unit, so conditions were good for staying indoors, with noses to the grindstone. After five weeks or so Janice printed out copies of the finished manuscript and numbered all three of them by hand. The final draft, weighing in at 851 pages, was delivered to Dawn Seferian in mid-July. By the average standards of Bob's career, that hardly counted as late.

On August 19, Bob, still in considerable pain from an elbow he'd broken on a canoe trip earlier in the summer, rejoined Janice in Westport, where she had just returned from Block Island with a couple of grandchildren in tow. His Yale teaching schedule kept him closer to home in the fall, although he did manage to get out to the Harbourfront Festival in Toronto, and in December made a second, shorter run to Cuba.

The Cuban trip was sponsored by *The New Yorker*, by then in the charge of Tina Brown, late of *Vanity Fair*. Brown wanted Bob to get an interview with Fidel Castro—improbable, maybe, but he was willing to try. In a deftly respectful letter, forwarded to Cuba's president by Sandra Levinson, Bob explained that "my novels to date have reflected on the spiritual vacuum and lack of community in which the West finds itself. I have endeavored to explore these problems in prose fiction and speculate on their solution. I presume, with whatever relevance, to mention that like yourself, Mr. President, I was educated in part by the Marist brothers and the Jesuits. Although I no longer practice any organized religion, this may have some bearing on my concerns as a writer."

Bob spent five days at the Hotel Victoria in Havana, armed with a tape recorder and with Jim Maraniss standing by to translate, but despite the eloquence of his letter, Castro in the end did not receive him. Bob's first effort to write a piece on Castro without the interview didn't appeal to Tina Brown. *The New Yorker* eventually published Bob's piece "The High Cost of a Good Drink," a semi-satirical take on how the Helms-Burton Act of 1996 supported the Bacardi distillery's agenda to keep Cuban rum out of the United States.

———

The Grim Reaper's scythe passed near the Stones again in 1997. Candida Donadio's partner, Eric Ashworth, fell victim to the AIDS epidemic. He had joined the firm in 1980 and become a partner in 1989; during those years he'd worked closely with Bob. By 1997 better treatments were becoming available—for some it was possible to manage AIDS as a less than fatal disease—but for others it was already too late. The U.S. death toll hit 390,692 that year, with Ashworth contributing to that dire statistic. Too ill to keep working, he had retired from the agency some time before.

Janice's mother was old and frail by then, unable to withstand the summer heat wave. She died in June 1997. "Bob wasn't able to go to the funeral because of a previously scheduled reading at the Guild Hall of East Hampton. He particularly didn't want to disappoint one of the sponsors, Robert Rosenkranz, who funded his position at Yale. He was planning to apply for reappointment as the Rosenkranz Writer-in-Residence for another five years."

Bob, who turned sixty in 1997, was entering the fourth year of his Yale contract, and waking up to the fact that he no longer had the protection of tenure, which his position at Johns Hopkins had afforded. His career history showed that it would probably take him several years to deliver another novel after the immense effort of rolling *Damascus Gate* over the top of the hill. The enormous advance meant that the book would have to sell extraordinarily well to generate more income. The last dozen years had brought the Stones into an affluent situation, but Bob had known real poverty in childhood, and neither he nor Janice took their prosperity for granted.

At the same time Bob wanted, ever more urgently, to get a permanent foothold in New York City. This ambition was easier to project than to accomplish. Despite the huge income streams of the 1980s and '90s, maintaining four residences (with some debt on all of them) meant that the Stones' expenses were also toweringly high. The money from the sale of their London apartment had gone to the emergency purchase of Deidre's house in Shutesbury. Then again, if they were to make the New York City move, they didn't have forever to get it done. If one was no longer considered *old* at sixty, Bob's hard living and precarious health was a counterweight to that, and at the end of the 1990s the Stones were seeing family and friends expiring all around them.

Janice was very used to being Bob's quartermaster, accountant, and concierge. "Usually he would decide what he wanted and I was to figure out how to do it." They toyed with the idea of investing Bob's retirement account in New York real estate, but their accountant warned that the IRS was unlikely to smile on that plan. Deidre's home had to be sustained, while Ian and his wife and son were living in the Block Island house. The Key West condo was awkwardly small for year-round residence, never mind the crushing heat of the summer, and Bob needed the Westport house to perform his duties at Yale. This problem would not be easily solved.

———•———

Service requirements on a manuscript of more than eight hundred pages are apt to be somewhat laborious. Dawn Seferian returned a marked copy, with several pages of notes, in August. Bob moved quickly, for him; by September the book was in the hands of Larry Cooper. Dawn still wanted the book to move a little faster than it did. "My feeling is that we don't need everything explained—much can be gleaned from context and we don't want it to seem that you're offering the reader the benefit of your prodigious research for its own sake. A little murkiness is OK. You've never hewn to overstatement anyway."

Cooper, whose skills were reserved for Houghton's most important authors, weighed in with a vote of confidence. "Bravo!" he wrote in mid October, on his cover note to the copyedit. "*Damascus Gate* is remarkable. And what a ride. It's miraculous how you're able to pack religious fervor, great humor, love sacred and profane, mystical states and ideas, holy shrines, political shenanigans, communal violence, and more into an immensely readable story that kept drawing me in. This is a deeply thoughtful, hilarious, disturbing book." And in a clever allusion to Bob's story "Under the Pitons," Cooper finished, "You got the overstanding, mon."

There followed a dense three pages of an ace copy editor doing his job, in Cooper's words, "sniping and nagging and making mud pies of your prose." But the last paragraph returned to the sublime. Cooper either had a prior interest in the kabbalah or had been drawn into Bob's; and he had found his own little jewel "in one of Scholem's books. You might remember it:

" 'When I was studying with Rabbi Akiba, I used to put vitriol in the ink and he said nothing. But when I went to Rabbi Ishmael, he asked me: My son, what is your occupation? I answered: I am a scribe [of the Torah]. And he said to me: My son, be careful in your work, for it is the work of God; if you omit a single letter, or write a letter too many, you will destroy the whole world.'

"As if being a writer weren't hard enough!"

8
DAMASCUS GATE

Bob was still at work on the copyedited manuscript when he and Janice attended the National Book Awards on November 18, 1997. For once the dinner was a low-pressure event for the Stones; Bob was not a finalist, though Ward Just, another Houghton author, was for his novel *Echo House*. Charles Frazier's *Cold Mountain* took the prize that year. The Houghton table consoled itself with the prediction that Bob Stone would return in triumph the following year with the magisterial *Damascus Gate*.

Next day, the scythe that had been decimating publishing houses swung one more time. Dawn Seferian lost her job at Houghton.

Damascus Gate has a larger cast of important characters than any previous Stone novel, and therefore a more complicated convergence structure than the earlier works. In this case, though, the principals don't converge on one another across long distances, as in *A Flag for Sunrise*, but rather they circle about each other, making intermittent contact, as they wander the labyrinth of Jerusalem's Old City. Most of them are based in Jerusalem and its immediate orbit, though the action sometimes expands to Tel Aviv, the Gaza Strip, and other locations around Palestine. There is a certain unity of place.

The first pilot fish proposed to the reader is Chris Lucas, a middle-aged American journalist who's recently quit a major U.S. newspaper with the idea of writing . . . something different, he isn't yet sure what. In the beginning, his semi-aimless peregrinations around Jerusalem involve an undirected quest for a subject (as his author's first visits there must have done). He's magnetized by the several different kinds of religious energy suffusing the place. Lucas is a bit of a cynic but also a bit of a seeker, two more qualities he has in common with Robert Stone.

Happening haphazardly into a mosque, Lucas encounters what he takes to be "a young Arab woman"—actually Sonia Barnes, born in the Bronx of a mixed marriage, her father black, her mother Jewish, both Communists for a time, making Sonia a red-diaper baby. The Sonia of the present is something of a shapeshifter, with costumes that provide her "a cloak of invisibility" as she crosses boundaries between the Jewish, Christian, and Muslim quarters of the Old City. She also has a résumé as an international aid worker, having served in Africa and Cuba, and is now contemplating doing some similar work in the Gaza Strip.

The third chapter picks up a young clarinet player, also of American origin, Ralph Melker, Raziel in religious contexts, in the office of a psychiatrist, Pinchas Obermann. Raziel's an ex-addict, with chameleon qualities more aggressive than Sonia's, though he mocks Obermann: "You make me sound like a multiple personality." Their conversation reveals that Raziel is a friend of Sonia, that Obermann is trying to write a book about the various religious manias infesting the Holy City, and that Raziel has an acute interest in an older man waiting his turn to see Obermann— for whom he lies in wait outside.

The older man is Adam De Kuff, a bipolar wealthy descendant of a distinguished Jewish family and a religious seeker, something he has in common with his fresh young acquaintance. Both are tremendously erudite about almost every form of religion ever practiced, and both are pilgrims of a kind: Raziel was once a Jew for Jesus, while De Kuff, whose mother "is part Gentile," once made a conversion to Catholicism. The younger Raziel has a much quicker mind and a considerable bag of hustler's tricks (in the latter dimension he resembles a far more intelligent and less institutionally conditioned Pablo Tabor). In this long first encounter it's clear that on the one hand he is manipulating the older man, but on the other, there's something almost desperately sincere in his interest and attraction.

For his author's note to the Franklin Library first edition of the novel, instead of talking about thematic intention as he had done for the similar edition of *Outerbridge Reach*, Stone talked mostly about his sources, with one very specific remark on how he had applied them: "Readers familiar with the story of Sabbatai Sevi and his promoter and disciple, Nathan of Gaza, will see similarities between their story, as recounted by Gershom Scholem in *The Mystical Messiah*, and the characters Adam De Kuff and Ralph 'Raziel' Melker." Stone might have had his tongue in his cheek when suggesting that many of his readers would be "familiar" with Scholem's work, a difficult, arcane opus originally composed in Hebrew and in its English translation more than a thousand pages long.

The Sabbatean movement began in Smyrna in 1648, when Sabbatai Sevi proclaimed himself to be the messiah whose appearance had been predicted by the Zohar, the thirteenth-century foundational work of kabbalah. He began a migration around the Middle East, sometimes embraced by temporal rulers and sometimes proscribed by them. In Gaza he found a disciple, Nathan Benjamin Levi, who was eager to serve as his prophet. Nathan was a kabbalist and also a healer of sorts; a tradition has it that Sabbatai went to him first in the latter capacity, because (in Scholem's analysis) he was suffering from what would later be called manic-depressive psychosis, or bipolar syndrome.

Stone's characters, Raziel and De Kuff, begin to construct their own ecumenical cult on this model. If Lucas is the most obvious Bob Stone avatar in *Damascus Gate*, Adam De Kuff might also be a contender, sharing with his author an improperly managed mental illness (it's made very plain that De Kuff has stopped taking his prescribed bipolar meds a long while back); intermittent, inchoate, religious longings; a spellbinding, vatic power of speech when manic; and a great many very long, very dark nights of the soul. As Pablo did, though in a very different style, De Kuff could represent for Stone an alternative identity, a path not taken— mercifully: there but for the grace of something or other might have gone

I. With Raziel there is less authorial affinity (except, at moments, in the matter of his addiction); Janice thought this character to be partly based on Leslie Wolf, a hard-partying Amherst student who had been close to Bob in the 1970s. Wolf had crippled himself with a drug overdose in 1984 (and lived, with diminished capacity, until 2012); his circumstances may have contributed something to Raziel's tragic aura.

Raziel does manipulate De Kuff's illness to steer the older man onto a messianic path, as Nathan of Gaza is thought to have done with Sabbatai. Also like Nathan, Raziel becomes a true believer in the messiah he is helping to create, or at least deeply desires to be that. The impulse toward belief was shared by Robert Stone to some degree, particularly at this stage of his life. The kabbalah's elaborate technique for understanding the universe had a powerful appeal to the theologically inclined writer who would tell the interviewer Robert Birnbaum: "It is as though God has separated himself forever and would have to be put together by gathering up all these items of light, which is a virtually impossible task. That whatever that was, whether it was some kind of physical force, big burst, or blast we have seen the last of it, and yet it has conditioned the way we feel and what we want for all eternity."

Stone's peculiarly painful childhood had taught him plenty about exile—the fundamental condition of Sabbatai Sevi. The idea of some messiah opening a redemptive pathway of return had interested him for a long time too. "This was an old theme of his," says Janice, "of a charismatic leader like Dieter in *Dog Soldiers*—like Ken Kesey or Mel Lyman, or Jan of Leiden, whose story he had planned to use in the sixteenth-century novel he began but never finished."

Stone makes his characterization of Lucas a possible solution to the mystery of his own paternity. Gladys had once told him, in the last of her many inconsistent answers to the question, that his father had been "a Greek, a Jew, or a Lebanese." As Stone drenched himself in the kabbalah, the middle possibility began to attract him more and more. "If Bob's father had been Jewish, and his mother a Gentile, he would be like Lucas, half Jewish, but not a real Jew, since the religious identity is passed through the mother." Lucas is furnished with some other details of Stone's childhood: a father who's a rumor rather than a presence, periodic immurement in a school very like St. Ann's, punctuated by visits with his mother to the King Cole Bar of the St. Regis Hotel. This scattered background strands him without a tribe, a supporting culture, or an informing story—in Jerusalem at the end of the twentieth century, a city crawling with both religious and political fanatics, at a moment more fraught than ever with deluded millennial desires.

———

Lucas is located at the center of the web of the *Damascus Gate* narrative, able to see the many levels of doomed aspiration, both religious and worldly, but unable to commit, connect, or intervene. Or maybe Raziel and De Kuff and their messianic cult are at the center of the web, or maybe it's the set of conspirators planning to blow up the Dome of the Rock. Maybe the web has no center.

Lucas's journalistic interests open a couple of pathways into the labyrinth of the novel's plot. For one, there's an opportunity to collaborate on a book about the Jerusalem Syndrome with Raziel's psychiatrist, Pinchas Obermann. Obermann's example: "A young man of scant prospects receives a supernatural communication. He must go to Jerusalem at the Almighty's command. Once here, his mission is disclosed. Often, he is the second coming of Jesus Christ." In premillennial Jerusalem there is no shortage of subjects.

For another, Nuala (a former crush of Lucas's, an Irish international aid worker and hard-line communist) is urging Lucas to help her with an investigative report on Abu Baraka, the leader of a group that's regularly battering participants in the intifada in the Gaza Strip. Nuala is certain that the Arab name is a blind and that Abu Baraka is running an undercover enforcement squad for the Israelis.

Nuala's investigation has romantic appeal for Lucas, not only because he's attracted to her but because Sonia, his current crush, sometimes collaborates with her on missions of mercy in the Gaza Strip. Then again, Nuala is a magnet for the worst kind of trouble, and Obermann's project looks to be by far the safer of the two. Yet again, as Obermann warns Lucas, cults arising from Jerusalem Syndrome can have their own dangerous potency; some are "not merely a few lost souls but organized and powerful groups."

The story of religious mania and the story of political violence look very likely to converge on each other. Having consciously elected the first, Lucas keeps being drawn, sometimes unwillingly, sometimes unwittingly, toward the other. Both feature his new inamorata, Sonia Barnes, whose involvement in the Raziel–De Kuff cult relates to his Jerusalem Syndrome project.

De Kuff, his mania spiking and without any direct prompting from Raziel, begins to appear regularly beside the Bethesda Pool—one of Israel's most venerable holy places, where Serapis, "the great syncretic god of the East," had been worshipped during the late Hellenistic period. "Each year, it was believed, an angel descended to trouble the water with its wing. The water was good and healing. Beside it, Jesus cured a paralytic." De Kuff meditates there, recites from the Zohar, and preaches. His following is enlarged still more in religious rallies that he and Raziel present in the guise of concerts (both have professional musical experience, as does Sonia). On the Sabbatean model, De Kuff becomes known to his growing cluster of disciples as "the Rev" and is presented as the Messiah for Jews and Christians and also as the Mahdi for Muslims.

For a time, Sonia imbibes this Kool-Aid to the lees. Lucas is attracted to the cult not only because of his attraction to her but also from his own obscure religious longings and from recurrent weariness of his own "singularity." In conversation with a Catholic priest he discloses, "I was Catholic. I believed. I should understand faith but I can't remember it." Further, "Jewishness must mean something. It's always been the conduit between humanity and God." In the kabbalah he has come to find "the greatest interpretations of life and truth I've ever heard. And I find it brings me back to religious feelings I haven't had" since childhood.

These ideas and experiences Lucas most certainly shares with his author, but neither can ever quite discard his skepticism, though Lucas occasionally comes close: "Increasingly, the Kabbalist formulations delighted him, even as revised in the ravings of Raziel and De Kuff." But ultimately, as he has to tell Sonia, he sees De Kuff as "just a manic depressive. He's manipulated by Raziel." This difference interrupts the romance. Sonia, deep in an episode of magical thinking, interprets his impotence on their first attempt to make love as a sign from the universe that they must part.

Meanwhile there's a Christian component to the Jerusalem Syndrome story, which Lucas needs to explore. On that side of the tracks is a fundamentally fundamentalist organization called House of the Galilean, a group of "Christian Zionists," in Obermann's description. The place has been until recently run by two Americans, Reverend Ericksen and his wife, Linda, who have standard Stateside evangelical résumés. They are, more or less, the Christian counterparts to Nuala's group of secu-

lar NGO-niks, performing parallel good works—except that Linda has
recently left her husband and the House of the Galilean to pursue new
lovers and different interests.

Alongside his florid religious ravings, Ericksen feeds Lucas some
practical-seeming information. By him, the House of the Galilean mainly
exists to funnel U.S. donations toward a particular project: "They're trying to reconstruct Herod's temple. There's a Jewish effort and a Christian
one." Lucas is not inclined to take this stuff literally, and Ericksen is in his
own way cynical about the people remaining at the House of the Galilean,
calling them "just promoters," or less politely, con artists using the Second
Temple reconstruction chimera as bait. But Ericksen's sudden death from
a fall suggests that his fantasy of war in heaven may have a literal analogue.

Linda Ericksen has taken up with a Polish Jewish journalist named
Janusz Zimmer, a veteran of the world's worst situations—Vietnam, Africa,
Cuba—and a recovering Marxist-Leninist. He turns out to be manipulating a cabal that meets in the basement of the House of the Galilean—
including Linda, Raziel, and representatives of other lunatic-fringe sects,
including one group committed "to armed violence against the Palestin-
ians and, if need be, against the Israeli State." This sect is as inflamed with
apocalyptic millennialism as the others but more practically connected,
with "a few small but avid cells in the army and bureaucracy and especially among the pioneers in the harsher settlements of Gaza and the West
Bank, where the Arabs were many and the amenities few."

Zimmer knows that Nuala is smuggling explosives into the Gaza Strip
under the cover of her aid missions, an operation tacitly permitted by Sha-
bak as "their way of arming the one PLO faction they think they can control and that can keep order down there." (This subplot represents Stone's
take on the evolution of Hamas.) Through Raziel, Zimmer encourages
Sonia to accompany Nuala on these runs as often as possible, because Raziel has secretly agreed that his cult will falsely claim responsibility for the
eruption Zimmer's group is planning. The ultimate goal, as Zimmer puts
it, "is to destroy the enemy shrines on the Temple Mount. To wipe them
away and build the Temple of the Almighty."

Sonia has the influence to procure UN vans for Nuala's runs to Gaza;
when she discovers she's been played into the arms-smuggling scheme,
she's annoyed at first, but she and Nuala go too far back for a real rift to
develop over this deception. Sonia's fatalism in the situation is informed
by a Spanish proverb—"the slaves used to say it in Cuba," according to

her. "*Que tienen hacer, que hacer no morir.*" Bob Stone had learned it from Jim Maraniss, and it became one of his favorite expressions. He sometimes liked to render it in New York street talk: *What you gotta do—you gotta not die.*

Nuala, devout Marxist that she is, keeps pursuing her own agenda, which includes pursuit of the mysterious Abu Baraka, but neither she nor Sonia has any idea that they're being used by Zimmer's group. The runs in and out of Gaza continue. Lucas, who at this point would do anything to get next to Sonia, sometimes offers to drive. Eventually a group including these three plus Linda and another Zimmer confederate, a young American Jew with the cover name Lenny, get trapped in a riot in the Gaza Strip. Lenny, separated from the others, is made for a Jew and beaten to death by the mob.

Que tienen hacer, que hacer no morir. "It was the first time Lucas had ever seen the *shebab* rampant," he thinks, observing the kaffiyeh-masked youth swirling around the UN van. His erudition moves him to compare the present situation to the Zealots rising against Roman rule, inspired by the Lord of Hosts. "Mercy was his middle name—except on certain occasions, during special enthusiasms."

Nightfall overtakes them, still trapped in the Gaza Strip. Lucas, sufficiently Jewish in appearance to attract hostile attention, also gets separated from the others and is pursued by the mob on foot. Finally he manages to crawl out under barbed wire and into a settlement spinach field. Having survived a night of exotic misadventure, the next morning he's taken in (to custody as it turns out) by the settlers at Kfar Gottlieb. There's a dark comedy to the situation. Lucas hardly knows if he thinks of himself as a Jew or not. In the Gaza Strip the previous night, being a Jew would have been fatal. At Kfar Gottlieb, to be a Jew would be a far, far better thing than not. Lucas is soundly beaten there, and advised by his assailant, between blows, "You do not ever strike a Jew. For you to raise your fist, to attempt to injure a Jewish person, is to direct an injury against the Almighty Himself."

Eventually Lucas is confronted with Linda, also sheltering at the settlement, whose account of Lenny's death has been through enough distortion that Lucas is now being punished for it. But eventually the settlers stop beating him and start encouraging him to spin the story he's writing in their favor. "You were being programmed for a campaign of lies. Instead, you'll write the truth." Truth is relative; what the settlers want told is that the Raziel–De Kuff cult is conspiring to blow up the Dome of the Rock—the cover story devised by Zimmer's cohort.

In the aftermath of the riot, Nuala is abruptly expelled from Israel, then lured to Cyprus where, with her Palestinian lover Rashid, she is assassinated. Though Nuala's devotion is political and secular, this very powerful scene is reminiscent of Sister Justin's martyrdom in *A Flag for Sunrise.*

Apart from all these violent events, Raziel, De Kuff, and the other cult members have been living comfortably on De Kuff's inherited money, loafing and inviting their souls. With a little coaching from Raziel, De Kuff is, step by step, unfolding a series of universal mysteries: "Everything is Torah," "the time to come is at hand," "the Death of the Kiss," then, ecstatically at the close of a concert: "The mystery is one! You are of one faith! You are all believers in one heart! Not to believe together is to cease to be!" Raziel guides the group to a spot on the banks of the Jordan beneath Mount Hermon, where, with a little prompting, De Kuff proclaims, "He raised me up to be the Lamb of God returned, as it was foretold of Yeshu. And he has appointed me the Mahdi of the Merciful and Compassionate that the truth be made one! So as the Almighty is One, so also are the believers! The kings are resurrected! The vessels are repaired! The *tikkun* is restored!"

This oration refers to the kabbalist proposition of a primordial event when the vessels containing divine light shattered, the shards of them forming the basis for the material world and the light itself scattering. Regathering the light is one process of *tikkun*, and another is regathering the souls imprisoned in materiality by reason of that primordial catastrophe. Complete restoration of *tikkun* means entry to the messianic age and the return of the entire universe and its godhead to a state of spiritual perfection—the inspired De Kuff means to bring about no less than that.

A problem with this apotheosis is that Raziel has dosed his messiah, along with the rest of the group (including Lucas, who's along for the ride with Sonia), with Ecstasy to help make it happen . . . having lost confidence that the pure power of the contemplative soul will be sufficient. For the rationalist sensibility, which is Lucas's most of the time, miracles can't really happen; there is no "real" magic but magical thinking (certainly a property of both the kabbalah and the Gnostic beliefs also influencing the millennial cults) can always be enabled. To have an effect in the material world, magical thinking may sometimes require a boost from (say) heroin, or explosives.

Exhausted by the effort of actually believing in a messiah partly produced by his own charade, Raziel goes back to the needle. Fixing, "he felt a childlike rush of gratitude; creation in that instant became again a place of comfort, and he had found some quarter of a caring, providing world." Heroin also insulates him from the "violent aspect of the plan." At least metaphorically, there must be cataclysm in the reassembly of the vessels, as well as in their previous shattering, "an explosion that mirrored the accident at the beginning of time."

Back in Jerusalem, De Kuff is transported by his mania back to the Bethesda Pool (again): "I am the twelfth imam. I am the Bab al-Ulema. I am Jesus, Yeshu, Issa. I am the Mahdi. I am Moshiach. I have come to restore the world. I am all of you. I am no one." This time his audience is a rioting Palestinian mob, plus a force of Israeli soldiers trying to subdue the riot. De Kuff is pulled into the scrum and beaten or trampled to death, while Raziel, who has followed him, is clobbered into a coma.

Beneath this ground, meanwhile, the bomb plot is unfolding. Sonia, who has winkled some information out of Raziel, enters a maze of catacombs under the Temple Mount. Lucas converges on her there, as do a bomb squad they have alerted and the bombers themselves. The point of convergence is a fictitious underground shrine to Sabazios, a Phrygian deity who persisted through the ages in various syncretic avatars and who was—infrequently but significantly—called Sabaoth, the Hebrew Lord of Hosts. Stone therefore invented the shrine to represent the encysted origin of all the religions that De Kuff, Raziel, the Gnostics, the kabbalists, and all similar seekers and dreamers hope in vain to reunite.

The De Kuff cultists now and then refer to something called the "Uncreated Light," which is one of the objects of their quests. Some Christian theology identifies it with the nimbus surrounding the resurrected Christ on Mount Tabor, and also with the beam that struck down unbelieving Saul on the road to Damascus, transforming him into the Apostle Paul (who would be largely responsible for the development of Christianity as a mystery religion). The concept relates to "gathering up all these items of light," as Stone described it to Birnbaum, into the equivalent of critical mass.

But the bomb set in Sabazios's chamber turns out to be a fake, with just enough explosive to give Sonia some first-degree burns and produce a temporarily blinding flash, and the novel's plot devolves from this anticlimax into wholly material explanations. Janusz Zimmer turns out to have been playing an elaborate triple game, with the sole and successful purpose of returning one Israeli political faction to power at the expense of another.

In the aftermath, Sonia recovers from the mystical intoxication of the disbanded cult, but she will never join Lucas in his condition of unbelieving cynicism. She remains in Israel, while Lucas departs, returning to the secular world with a wistful kernel of earned wisdom: "a thing is never truly appreciated or defined except in longing. A land in exile, a God in his absconding, a love in its loss." If religion is the opium of the people, Lucas is headed for detox, leaving behind him "Jerusalem's Heaven . . . that rich, indifferent blue, the first and holiest of unresponding skies."

Damascus Gate is a work of art, and also a kind of thought experiment, perhaps; it was never intended as a prophesy, and it wouldn't have been very accurate if it had been. No explosion, sham or otherwise, occurred on the Temple Mount in the year 2000. But one year later there was a big one, in New York City, Stone's hometown.

PART SEVEN

———•———

BAY OF SOULS

1

SUCCUBI IN THE SHADOWS

On January 25, 1998, the Stones loaded their vehicle onto the Auto Train for the trip to Key West. Bob had spent much of the month struggling with *New Yorker* editors over transmogrification of the very short Cuba piece he'd filed in December and was ready for some R&R. However, he did make a couple of brief excursions, two to New York to consult with his publisher on the upcoming *Damascus Gate* tour in the spring, and another more arduous weeklong trip to Jerusalem, to brush up research for his *New York Times* piece, "Jerusalem Has No Past," which would appear in May. In between social engagements, Janice worked long-range with Houghton Mifflin's head publicist Lori Glazer to organize Bob's tour, while Bob did phone interviews with the *Los Angeles Times* and *The Boston Globe*. He was now a bestselling author on the eve of publishing a book about millennial chaos in an international political hotspot at the nexus of three of the world's great religions, and everything to do with that had become a very big deal.

Also on Janice's mind was the opening phase of a plan to get the Stones into a New York City apartment. The only solution she could devise was to sell their house in Westport. "That would get rid of one mortgage, and the place might sell for twice what we paid for it." To her surprise, Bob agreed to this idea, which Janice began to enact: If the house sold they would bank the profit, rent an apartment in New Haven for Bob's teaching semester at Yale, and look for a condo in Manhattan. They listed the Westport house before going down to the Keys for the winter of 1998, and in February an offer of $345,000 came in—comfortably more than twice what they'd paid for it: good news but also an injection of positive stress.

Janice worried about Bob's stress level that winter. The Key West retreat was meant to be a real vacation, but between a cascade of houseguests and his several side trips, it wasn't really turning out that way. The Stones' acceptance of the offer on their Westport house meant that they would be moving in the midst of Bob's tour, and pressure to promote the book was greater this time than ever before. As part of a general upping of the ante, he was asked and agreed to be coached for his appearances by the media trainer Bill Parkhurst. It all added up to the point that Bob certainly needed some way to calm down, but his inclination to soothe himself with prescription narcotics a Key West doctor gave him for back pain wasn't an ideal solution.

He may have been stressed for other reasons, which Janice couldn't yet discern. In the first week of April he made a preliminary tour stop in Boston, for an event revolving around the Literary Lights dinner at the Boston Public Library. "When he got back, he said to me, if anyone tells you I'm in love with a blond woman in Boston, it's not true. OK, I said. But—what?" This sort of preemptive disclaimer was totally unusual for Bob, whose occasional flings could be laughed off, shrugged off, or simply passed over in silence. "He explained that Phyllis Rose and Laurent de Brunhoff had also been in Boston, at the same event. He thought that they might say something to me about seeing him there with a woman. I knew that Bob was always pleased to be seen with attractive blondes. Over the years he had become friends with several—Annie Dillard, Jayne Anne Phillips, Jennifer Egan, Leslie Kopit—and was not in love with them either. I was prepared to trust him."

At the end of April, the Stones were put up in the grand and luxurious Biltmore Hotel in Coral Gables, for Bob's appearance at the local store Books & Books. Some woman had left a message for Bob to call her, and Janice was trusting enough that "it didn't occur to me to ask who she was." It was, after all, a period when dozens of publicists and reporters were calling for Bob. "I kept reminding him that he was supposed to make a phone call and he kept putting it off." It would be months before she attached any significance to this procrastination.

Viagra had recently come into vogue—delighting a good many middle-aged women a good deal less than their men. Janice, however, "felt quite the opposite. Bob's sex drive had been erratic for years, and that made us both unhappy. It's alcohol, I would tell him, and he would insist that it was nothing of the sort. Now we were back in business." Glad as she was to have their love life restored, Janice didn't consider that she might not be the only beneficiary. In any case, the Stones left the Biltmore for different destinations—Bob to begin a leg of his tour in Mississippi and Janice to catch the Auto Train back north. In the commotion of the coming months, one troubling phone call could easily be forgotten.

2

ON THE ROAD WITH DAMASCUS GATE

Damascus Gate appeared in April 1998 and, with all its publisher's energy behind it, was widely and generally well reviewed. Josh Getlin's review for the *Los Angeles Times* incorporated a snatch of interview conducted in Key West, including this observation: "Dressed in khaki shorts and a faded blue T-shirt, the bearded 60-year-old looks indistinguishable from the beach bums flooding into town on a sunny afternoon." (Not everyone would be pleased by that description but Bob probably was.) Bob was frank with the reporter about the difficulties of writing the novel: "Indeed, writing and researching the book caused Stone to reexamine his own beliefs—a blend of lapsed Catholicism and Jewish mysticism—and the experience was not pleasant. He had to confront adult demons, childhood conflicts and the stark consequences of his decision to live in a world without God."

It was somewhat surprising that he'd declare the extent of his commitment to the kabbalah, and also that he admitted to past "depression and heavy drinking" along with periods of "intense drug use." Identifying with his antihero Raziel, he mused, "There were times I thought: 'What have you done?' I was bringing out forces so deep within me, I was afraid of falling back into the old habits, of drinking too much. I feared I didn't have the strength, that I was losing it." That he had in fact fallen fairly deeply into those old habits didn't get a mention.

Michiko Kakutani turned in a largely descriptive review to *The New York Times*—fundamentally respectful, with a little carping about what she saw as the novel's slow, talky start. She connected Lucas accurately to previous Stone protagonists—"a detached outsider" like Frank Holliwell, "deep in the maw of a midlife crisis" like Owen Browne, and like John Converse "a burnt out case, determined to find an antidote to his ennui even as he's swept up in events he cannot control." Most perspicaciously, Kakutani found in Stone's Jerusalem an analog to the New Orleans portrayed in *A Hall of Mirrors*: "a city of secret labyrinths and mysterious subcultures, a place of extremes, where bizarre alliances are quickly formed and even more quickly dissolved, a realm where misinformation masquerades as fact and facts are passed off as truth."

The New York Times Book Review gave the novel to Jonathan Rosen, a younger novelist and journalist with an interest in and knowledge of the history of Jewish mysticism (and at the time the culture editor of the *Forward*). His piece was more energetic than Kakutani's, launching with this kind of verve: "Robert Stone doesn't need the approaching millennium to push him toward fantasies of Armageddon. Since starting out as a novelist in the 1960's he has been loaded for Leviathan, writing with Melvillean chutzpah, his harpoon aimed at the heart of apocalyptic America." Rosen deftly picked out the influence of religious impulses in Stone's previous work, leading to a fairly unusual comparison: "Stone has a lot in common with the great short-story writer Flannery O'Connor, whose violent, deeply Catholic, vaguely sadistic stories offer a kind of fatal salvation to many of her characters, for whom destruction comes as a perverse show of divine affection. If O'Connor had had a doubting, beatnik younger brother, he might have grown up to write like Stone, whose universe, however godless, possesses a murderous power."

The review asserted that "whatever his religious beliefs, Stone as a novelist writes with what can only be called conviction," while complaining that "there is a void behind the facade of authenticity in this novel that makes the setting a sort of false front. Stone seems to see religion mainly in terms of Manichaean collisions and ultimate questions, not in terms of daily accommodation. In this novel one is either a messianist or a nonbeliever." True enough regarding Stone's work, which itself was most likely true enough to the actual situation in Jerusalem two years shy of the millennium. Rosen had the background to understand how Raziel and De Kuff emerged from the figure of Sabbatai Sevi, who himself evolved out of the experience of Jewish exile, particularly from Spain. While recognizing the deep historical roots of the novel, he also called it "not merely ahistorical but in some sense antihistorical." Paradoxical maybe, but also in some sense astute, given that Bob's article, which ran in *The New York Times Magazine* a couple of weeks after Rosen's review, was entitled "Jerusalem Has No Past," and that Lucas has some similar reflections: "Other cities had antiquities, but the monuments of Jerusalem did not belong to the past. They were of the moment and even the future."

In somewhat dismissive conclusion, Rosen wrote *Damascus Gate* off as "an American religious fantasy." Both he and Kakutani paid attention to the novel's epigraph, from Herman Melville's epic poem *Clarel: A Poem and Pilgrimage in the Holy Land* (the longest poem in American literature, seldom read today).

> *Enigma and evasion grow;*
> *And shall we never find Thee out?*

Rosen argued that "it was easier for Melville, writing in the 19th century, to empty Palestine of its actual inhabitants and refill the landscape with American pilgrims enacting an American drama." Kakutani said, more simply and perhaps more accurately, that the novel "may have been inspired by that poem."

It was a good time to remember that all publicity is good so long as they spell your name right. Rosen's opinions, for example, mattered less than that the review was on the front page of *The New York Times Book Review*, with a dramatic, full-page illustration. Bob's essay for *The New York Times Magazine* was perfectly timed for the book's promotion, presenting him as an expert on fin de siècle Jerusalem, and possibly allowing some to read the novel as a political prediction or roman à clef. The *Times* magazine put a teaser for the essay on its cover: "Jerusalem's Past Is Irrelevant"—which annoyed Bob, as that was not at all what he (or Lucas) intended by the title phrase "Jerusalem Has No Past." But once again they spelled his name right and also the title of his novel.

Other coverage was similarly expansive and swelled as Bob went through tour stops in Jackson, Oxford, Memphis, Iowa City, Chicago, Ann Arbor, Minneapolis, St. Paul, Cincinnati, Washington, DC, Philadelphia, Boston, Los Angeles, San Francisco, and Seattle. The effort paid off—magnificently. *Damascus Gate* sold nearly 112,000 copies in hardcover, and paperback rights were sold at auction to Simon and Schuster for $357,500. As a cherry on this opulent cake: $100,000 for a Book-of-the-Month Club adoption.

3
Goodbye to Westport

On May 23, Bob limped back to Westport, where Janice was busy packing up the house, donating a thousand books to the Pequot Library, disposing of other domestic articles in the sort of yard sale where many of them had been acquired in the first place. Bob had his author's note to the Franklin Library edition to write and also several hundred sheets to sign for the same volume. His contribution to the moving operation was intermittent. Janice sent him out for more packing tape shortly before the movers were due to show up, but Bob didn't return for a long time.

"It was dark when he came back, hours later. The moving men had come and gone. He stood at the glass doors to the deck over the Mill Pond, and proceeded to put a curse on the house. As I watched in astonishment, he said something like 'If I can't have it. . . .' The rest of what he said was not audible. And I suddenly realized that he was regretting his decision—the sale, the move—that I must somehow have misread his wishes. Or that he himself had not known his own mind." Or, though Janice didn't say it, he simply wanted more than he could have (despite the great successes of that year) in a "life more abundant" sort of way. The curse was distressing to her, for both personal and practical reasons: Bob slipped easily from unhappiness to depression, which made it hard for him to work and might dial up his addictions. The moment was particularly dangerous because he didn't have sound footing in a new novel as yet.

In those years Janice would wryly describe herself as a "handmaid to genius"—the phrase was ironic on the surface but in fact she took this vocation with complete seriousness and had devoted most of her life to it. A sense of failure hurt. "I'd have been just as happy to stay in Westport. And now it was too late."

Or maybe it wasn't, because "Bob's curse seemed to have been effective" in that the house developed a leak soon after. At the closing "our buyer was unhappy. I told her I had had the problem fixed before and I was sure it could be fixed again. Or, if she wished, I could put the house back on the market. After a bit of negotiating, the sale went through." Bob, who had absented himself to San Francisco for some research purpose, probably never knew about the wobble.

The Stones had found lodging in New Haven's Taft Hotel, which opened in 1912, next to the Shubert Theater, and adjacent on the other side to the New Haven Green. After several decades of grandeur, the Taft had failed and stood empty for most of the 1970s, and was then renovated as an apartment building. It was a twenty-minute walk to Bob's office on the Yale campus and less than a mile to the train station. Janice set up the apartment while Bob was in California, perhaps in a slightly casual way— she'd let him know, after his chimerical decision to abandon Baltimore, that in the future she wouldn't be spending the same kind of homemaking effort she had applied to their apartment there, and with some exceptions she was true to her word. Still there was plenty to do to get settled in the Taft and only a couple of weeks of June in which to do it. In spite of all the yard sales and donations that Janice had recently organized, "I still had to rent a storage space in the basement of the Taft for the excess stuff we had accumulated in the Westport house over seventeen years."

By June 25 she was ready to make the annual migration to Block Island, where the grandchildren were as usual invited. Bob went too, though he "was able to escape the kiddie chaos when he wished by going down to the New Haven apartment." On January 25 they both went to the mainland, but with separate destinations. Bob was going to Manhattan, for a party at the United Nations honoring his German publisher, Michael Naumann. Janice, with her friend June Chapman, was going to yard sales in Connecticut, scouting for furnishings for the new apartment in the Taft. Bob "phoned me late that evening, after the party for Michael Naumann, to say he would be staying overnight at a hotel near the UN. There was something odd about his voice, and I suspected he wasn't alone." A couple of years later Janice read a similar scene in Bob's next novel, *Bay of Souls*, "where Michael Ahearn calls his wife, as his lover listens."

4

ARCTURUS, *UNFINISHED*

In the summer of 1998 the ultimate shape of *Bay of Souls* was still an idea in the mind of God. Bob was trying to work on a novel he'd been considering a few years before, set in 1930s Alaska for the most part, with the working title *Arcturus*. The story had the family of an Epis-

copal priest named Edward Dwight removing from a mission in China
to one in Alaska. The priest's personality bridged turn-of-the-century
American vitalism, with which Bob had long been fascinated, into the
worldwide rise of Fascism. According to Bob's notes, Dwight "sees, like
Henry Luce, the coming American century. Admires the Communists
in China and to some extent the Fascists. He's increasingly disenchanted
with Hitler. Believes in eugenics, social Darwinism tempered by compassion (somewhat condescending) toward the weak."

The wife is a daintier, more high-church sort of person. "In one aspect
a demure Yankee girl, in another a flamboyant creamy blonde who might
have been painted by Sargent." The idea was to see what happened when
such a couple was hurled from central China into the Alaskan wild. "The
settlement: mixed; a scattering of whites, several Métis families, (a Chinese trader?) Athabascan Indians.

"There is a deacon, an Indian Shaman. Reference is the Catholic Black
Elk. Believes that God speaks in whispers. The murmurs of the forest."

The priest, suffering a crisis of faith, consults his shamanistic deacon
and begins to learn strange and wonderful things, which Stone had discovered in his own exploration of Chukchi religion.

A potent cocktail was emerging from this mixture of ingredients. The
missionary impulse was to be thrust into the wilderness, there to encounter the earliest origins of religion in the form of ur-shamanism. The sort
of spiritual conflict that could develop from this cultural clash might have
been even more deeply seismic than what went on in *Damascus Gate*.

Stone created his missionary as the embodiment of a certain set of
American social ideals of the period, who, however, has seldom if ever
set foot in his homeland during the first thirty-five years of his life. In
faraway Golden, Alaska, he still stands to be buffeted by the sociopolitical turbulence swirling itself up into the storm of World War II. From a
long distance, the characters assembled in Golden can observe how the
fetishization of strength, which has a tendril of its roots in last-century
American vitalism, and an expression in the muscular Christianity apt to
be practiced by a missionary like Dwight, evolved into Fascism and all its
dire consequences.

There's a glimmer of how such conflation of religion with the accelerating violence of global politics could unhinge a man like Edward Dwight
and push him in the direction of shamanism. "Dawn Man. The Sun in
its divine aspect. Sea Festival. Represented on a skin. The Chukchi ele-

ment leads us back to the Bering Straits connection. Our answer may lead to the Caucasoid tribe, the Mandans, the fair and light-eyed. They are disappeared. Do they exist? Were they banished for cannibalism? Is cannibalism the knowledge of good and evil? Have they left to Athabascans a secret priesthood, of which Cuthbert [the deacon/shaman] is an adept?"

These were some mighty interesting questions, and Bob had been contemplating them since the early 1990s, before he got a running start on *Damascus Gate*. So many of his fascinations could converge in this project: American vitalism, the earliest origins of religion, the emergence of modern America from the cauldron of forces driving the twentieth-century world wars. The ideas feeding Mary Rowlandson's captivity narrative would work their way into this story. *Arcturus* would be a historical novel, but overlapping the period of Stone's childhood when he and the other unfortunates at St. Ann's had wanted to identify with the Nazis because they appeared to be strong.

So many promises were there in this beginning; moreover, as of August 1998, there was a contract with Houghton for a work described as "Untitled Alaska Novel." Candida Donadio's health was failing and Eric Ashworth had died the year before, so negotiations were handled by Neil Olson, a rising star at the agency. Neil tried for an even million for an advance but had to settle for $850,000—still not bad (and there were bonus clauses in case the novel should reach this or that place on bestseller lists when published). As usual for Stone's contracts the payout was stepped and included a salary-like component: thirty monthly payments of $6,667 each, beginning in January 1999. Stone received $250,000 on signing, and was to receive the same on delivery, then $100,000 on publication and $50,000 "upon the Author's completion of his tour to promote the work." No satisfactory-progress clause this time, just a delivery date of June 1, 2001 . . . when those thirty monthly payments would run out.

Here was the kind of guaranteed income that would reassure a New York City co-op board—and Bob still had his teaching salary from Yale to top it off. But the heft of the contract also brought pressure. In the past Bob had taken longer than thirty months from start to finish on a novel—sometimes a lot longer.

But first he took another trip to Montana, bringing Janice along this time. Janice was not immensely interested in rafting or camping, but they had civilized accommodations, first in Missoula and then Hanusa Cabin, on Nature Conservancy land west of Choteau. The "cabin" was commodious enough to hold Annie Dillard and Bob Richardson, Rust Hills and Joy Williams, Bill Barich, Kem Nunn and his daughter Jessica, along with the Stones, so this occasion was more of a house party than a camping trip, although Bob and Annie went out white-water tubing from Missoula, and some of the party saw a brown bear near Hanusa Cabin. There was a run to Glacier National Park, where there were warning signs about grizzlies, but no bears were seen. Annie painted watercolors and taught some tricks of that trade to Kem's daughter.

Bob had brought along a bound galley of Melisandra's novel. Janice read it while in Montana—not in order to furnish a reader's report to Bob as she often did but because Bob had read and admired it. She knew Melisandra was a passing acquaintance of Bob's, from Yaddo and had some glancing connection to Yale. She thought "it was excellent, a good read, a well-done historical novel. Bob complained that Melisandra didn't appear to take her writing seriously, and seemed so dismissive of her book that he began to feel disrespected himself. For Bob, nothing was more important than writing."

5
BENEATH THE WATERS

On August 15, the Stones returned east, making "the transition from the big world of Montana to the small world of New Haven." They settled into their Taft apartment and Bob, who turned sixty-one on August 21, fell into the routine of his Yale teaching as he tried to get a fresh grip on *Arcturus*.

But by mid-November he was in the Bahamas, making the deepest dive of his life, on assignment from *The New York Times*. It was arranged by the Stones' Key West friend Seward Johnson, who had a connection to the Harbor Branch Oceanographic Institute. The vessel was a Johnson Sea Link submersible, "a contraption suggesting the coupling of a jumbo prawn with a helicopter," in Bob's term. Scuba enthusiast that he was, Bob had thought a lot about the ultimate depths, in no way attainable with an aqualung. Yet "it's impossible to paddle around at the entryway to such a vast deep and not feel its dark invitation." Bob had a long-standing yen for "the place where the Creator appointed the seas their limit, the end, the bottom." The Sea Link wouldn't go that far, dropping a mere one thousand and forty-four feet to the bottom of a cliff in a trench evocatively known as the Tongue of the Ocean.

"For a while, the only light comes from the red instrument panels in the dive chamber, but then, through the port, we can see strange darts and twinklings in the pitch black. Little whirls go spinning, looking a bit like time-exposed photographs of traffic in impossibly distant cities. This darkness, whatever else it may be, is alive, and the light we're seeing is bioluminescence. The glow emanates from living creatures. Creatures we can soon see liberally populate what had looked like void." This imagery is reminiscent of the logos which, in Genesis, moves upon the waters to begin the process of Creation. "I have a vision of this dark stuff I'm in as the primordial soup, the solution from which life was formed, from which it is being formed now. Tomorrow, sitting in the dark in the sphere, which with its panoramic surface functions like a reverse fishbowl, I'll get a clearer look at these twinkling creatures and imagine myself transported back billions of years, into a warm Devonian sea at the dawn of creation."

As this language implies, the dive had a quasi-religious valence for Bob, and he also tended to talk about it in the manner of a near-death experience—as if he had entered the valley of the shadow, yet somehow been allowed to return. There was some real danger in the dive—in 1973, half of a four-man crew had perished from carbon dioxide poisoning in the first Sea Link submersible when it was trapped for twenty-four hours in the wreckage of a destroyer—but for Bob it had more to do with his sense of approaching the taproot of existence and getting a closer look at the unknowable than most mortals can commonly bear.

Damascus Gate was a finalist for the National Book Award that year. On November 18, New York publishing assembled in a ballroom of the Plaza Hotel for the banquet and awards ceremony. Finalists weren't informed of the outcome until the envelopes were opened after dinner (sometimes the outcome wasn't decided until close to the last minute) so it was a fairly stressful occasion for them and their families, editors, and publicists. More volatile non-winning finalists would sometimes bolt immediately after the announcement, but Bob and Janice stuck it out to the end, though *Damascus Gate* lost out to Alice McDermott's *Charming Billy*. Then they headed to Block Island to spend Thanksgiving with family, bringing along a laptop in hope that Bob might make some progress on *Arcturus.* He was stuck in the story and looking for alternative plotlines. Maybe the story would be set in Alaska, maybe somewhere else.

The Stones celebrated Christmas in the Taft apartment with Ian, his wife, Elizabeth, and their son, Cooper. On December 29, Janice and Bob drove Deidre's four children to New York. Janice wanted the children to see the Christmas tree at the Metropolitan Museum, and Bob had some other engagement. The plan was for Janice to bring the children back to New Haven by train (all four of them loved train travel) while Bob returned solo in the car. Instead he somehow flipped the vehicle on his way back up the West Side Highway. He was wearing his seat belt and the airbag deployed, so he wasn't seriously hurt, but he came to in a state of confusion, hanging upside down and looking at the dome light, which he thought was an ashtray on fire on the floor; he kept reaching to try to put it out.

Once he made his way out of the car, another driver stopped and let him use a cell phone to call home. The police were sympathetic when they came. Bob had wrecked in a spot where a chronic buildup of wet leaves on the pavement had caused other accidents in the past. He wasn't arrested or even ticketed—a lucky outcome, since although as he told me later "I was so sober everything had a black line around it," he was likely to have had prescription narcotics in his system. At that point he had doctors writing scrips for him almost everywhere he spent any time, so there were few interruptions of supply. The habit had become significant enough to worry Janice—enough to talk to Bob about it. "He had more of his share of pain during the 1990s, but his medicating himself was getting out of hand. He brushed off my concerns."

Bob got home late, bruised all over but without broken bones. To Janice he declared, "I was in perfect control of that car!," though circumstantial evidence cut into the credibility of that statement. Next day, while Janice drove the children back to Shutesbury in a rental car, Bob returned to New York to recover whatever he had left in the wrecked vehicle, catching a ride, as it happened, with Melisandra. "He hadn't mentioned that, but she called, trying to reach him. When Ian answered the phone, she thought it was Bob.

"Who was that? Ian asked. Well, what did she sound like? I asked. When I realized who it was, I was dismayed. There is this woman who is after your father, I found myself saying. Is she crazy? asked Ian. I was beginning to wonder about that, myself. I was finding her hard to ignore."

Janice was so busy in the next few days that she might have forgotten about it. The Stones had a January 4 reservation on the Auto Train—but now, no auto. Janice hastily purchased a 1996 Camry from a dealer in Shelton, Connecticut; "it turned out to be a good car." Once in Key West, Bob was fully occupied, with obligations to the Literary Seminars, an introduction to the paperback edition of *Damascus Gate*, and revisions to his *New York Times* piece on the deep dive in the Bahamas. Then Melisandra called again, this time from the Key West airport, with the idea of renting a place there for the winter. "No!" Janice told Bob, who was surprised himself, or professed to be. "Will you please tell her to go away? I asked. As far as I know, he discouraged her from spending time in Key West."

6
RENDEZVOUS IN HAITI

I was one of those readers who waited impatiently for Robert Stone novels to appear. I burned some midnight oil in Baltimore when *Damascus Gate* was published in 1998, devouring the novel. I hadn't seen Bob in the flesh for a couple of years by then, but when I finished my first read of the novel I had another, even stronger impulse to invite him on one of my trips to Haiti. I had been spending time there since 1995, in the service of a series of novels I was writing about the Haitian Revolution. Israel and Haiti don't seem very similar, but they do have in common a dangerously charged political situation unfolding in a religiously charged atmosphere—which seemed to be exactly what had attracted Bob to Jerusalem. I wrote to him along those lines, but I didn't really expect an answer, and I didn't get one.

But then Bob did call me, in January 1999, wanting to take me up on my invitation to Haiti. He had the particular idea of going to Jacmel for the Mardi Gras carnival, not much more than a month away. Short notice or not, I was thrilled; a trip anywhere with Robert Stone was not to be declined, and since most of my Haitian business was in the northern part of the country I had never been to Jacmel, a popular destination on the Caribbean coast, so it was a good excuse to go there.

Two days after the call I sent Bob an itinerary, maps, a chunk of my Haiti nonfiction writing that described the roads and the Haitian guide

I normally took with me, plus a color copy of one of the small Haitian paintings I was dealing at the time—an idyllic, Caribbean-paradise sort of scene. John Hildebrand prepared similar packages to entice Bob on hunting and camping trips . . . not that Bob needed much enticing. I was teaching in Baltimore one day a week so the maximum I could be gone was six days. That would allow us to go to Jacmel on an inland route by way of Forêt des Pins and Thiotte—the latter area, I'd been told by the Haitian scholar Michel-Rolph Trouillot, had escaped deforestation and was still very beautiful.

"The distances are negligible," I wrote Bob, "(all Haiti is about the size of Vermont). But the first leg, to Jacmel via Forêt des Pins will be very rough road and I'd guess it will take all day assuming nothing goes wrong. (Wrong would mean breakdown or truly impassable road which would require backtracking—I don't anticipate any political risk in this area.)" "Political risk" meant Haitian demonstrations, which could sometimes be extremely violent—for example, there was a $3,000 deductible on rental-car insurance in case of damage caused by *"mouvements de foule."* I had been caught in one of those situations a couple of years before and since then taken great care to avoid them. Bob had had a similar experience in Gaza (vividly reprised in *Damascus Gate*), and he didn't want to repeat his either. With that in mind I had recommended that we go the week before carnival, as carnival itself could be pretty volatile. Haiti was not especially dangerous in the winter of 1999 (election seasons were always the most turbulent times, and this wasn't one), but situations could change suddenly.

"The second leg, which is the more conventional way from Jacmel to Port-au-Prince, is more like a half day project if all goes well. However, there is some political risk on this route (very small and not to life or limb): if they happen to have a demonstration which blocks the road on the day we want to use it. I think that's unlikely—it's not hot right now, and those things almost never last more than a day, because after one day the demonstrators have to go looking for food again." Really my worst concern was being slowed down somewhere to the point of missing the return flight, meaning I would miss my weekly class, disappoint my students, displease my employer, etc. With that in mind I built a "safety day" into the itinerary. If nothing held us up on the circuit I'd planned we'd have "an extra day in Port-au-Prince on the way out, which is always valuable for avoiding the culture-shock bends, which can be fairly severe on return to the States."

Bob and I talked frequently over the next three weeks. He had a thing or two on his mind. First, he told me about his pain-pill habit, which till then was no more than a rumor to me. It unnerved me only slightly as these were prescription drugs. I told him, "so long as it's all in a pharmacy bottle with your name on it you should be all right, but be discreet. Drug jail in Haiti is not any fun and if you land there I won't be able to get you out." In Key West, Bob was busy getting the raft of vaccinations required for Haiti, and he also developed a worry that his occasional diverticulosis might act up during the trip. I told him I too was inclined to develop phantom symptoms on the eve of a Haiti trip; I figured they were psychosomatic, in my case and his. That seemed to settle him.

Next question: Bob inquired, very delicately, if he might bring a journalist friend along. She was an experienced third world traveler and would be no burden and maybe even helpful to have with us. In fact she was also a fiction writer, who'd just published an excellent historical novel . . . Sure, fine, I said, the more the merrier. I reserved an extra hotel room for her at the Oloffson and the Jacmelienne. I knew nothing of Bob's extramarital adventures then, and his presentation was so discreet I totally didn't get it.

I did order a copy of Melisandra's book, which I read with rapt admiration. The novel is based on the true story of a couple of English adventurers setting out to create their own kingdom in a farflung corner of Europe's colonial claims. It was full of romance and intrigue and violent action, had the gravitas of Conrad, and was very beautifully written. Hard to believe it was really a first novel. The author picture had a gravely urgent expression, with piercing, slightly strange light eyes. They looked like Lu Anne Bourgeois's "secret eyes," I told Bob teasingly, still clueless as to the real nature of this relationship. I thought Melisandra looked fascinating and dangerous in her author picture, doubtless because she wanted to look that way.

Then Bob called to let me know that Melisandra, feeling a bit uneasy about her security in a country that could sometimes be unsafe, had decided to take her own measures. She knew someone who knew someone in the Haitian National Police (HNP), and had, to use twenty-first-century parlance, "reached out." This news infuriated me because Bob knew, and she should have known, that I ran an exhaustive (indeed excessive) scru-

tiny of the security situation before every trip, using the "Corbett group,"
an e-mail list that included hundreds of Haitians and others who worked
in or for the country, and which reported daily in detail down to the
tremor of a butterfly's wing, not to mention the safety net I'd constructed
out of my own friends and colleagues down there. I had it covered, but my
reaction wasn't about injured pride. What Melisandra had done was a real
piece of foolishness, one that stood to be actually dangerous, because the
HNP of those days was a very mixed bag—a jumble of idealistic young
officers recently inducted and a very different class of people prone to
criminality and corruption. There was, for example, a great deal of police
cooperation with drug smugglers using Haiti as a transshipment depot.

Moreover, since the abolition of the Haitian Army by President Aristide in 1995, HNP was the only armed force standing, so every political
faction was scheming to get control of it. Not a good place to go for reassurance. What Melisandra had done, I explained to Bob, was the equivalent of announcing to God knows whom: I'm scared, here's where I'm
gonna be when, is it possible for anyone to hurt me? It was weird to be
shouting down the phone at the writer I admired most in the world but I
couldn't seem to help it. If the lady attracts sharks, I said, I'm pushing her
out of the boat.

Bob, apologetic on Melisandra's behalf, seemed to get it. I'd like to
think I apologized too. A few days later, and just a couple of days before
our flight out, he called again with some news report that had alarmed him
(or possibly given Melisandra the vapors). Whatever it was it didn't worry
me, but Bob was saying he thought we should "stand down." It took me
a minute to process the military-speak, and then I said I didn't agree, that
in fact as far as I was concerned we were already over the cliff . . . which
might not have been the most comforting image, come to think.

Bob and Melisandra met me on schedule at the Miami airport. Also
present was Herb Gold, a writer who'd been an amiable acquaintance of
Bob's for decades. Herb was ten years older and had published a couple
of dozen books, beginning in the 1950s. He'd spent time in Haiti since
the 1950s and had gotten a lot of attention for his 1991 book, *Haiti: Best
Nightmare on Earth*. Now he was making a sort of triumphal return, with
his son and a couple of other people, all clothed in those hundred-pocket
khaki vests that photographers on safari liked to wear.

Bob seemed a little uneasy about running into Gold (who was effu-
sively friendly), especially when it developed that his party would also be

staying at the Hotel Oloffson, but I still didn't get it. We boarded; Bob and Melisandra had seats together and I was in some other part of the plane. After takeoff I asked him to switch with me. I sat down with Melisandra, gave her a copy of my list of contacts in country (which included some people in both the Haitian government and the U.S. embassy, for reassurance's sake), explained who they were, and told her she needed to trust me and not fly around on her own. All that she seemed to understand and accept, calmly. I went back to my seat feeling better. The steely armature of her writing was to be found in her character as well.

Gesner Pierre, a guide attached to the Oloffson and at this point my old friend, met us at the Port-au-Prince airport. We climbed into a rented 4x4 Montero, me at the wheel, and headed across town to the hotel. The weather was pleasant and the windows were down. I was wearing a red bandanna tied over my head; the tight knot at the base of my skull seemed to help me concentrate in the always anarchic Haitian driving situation— also such a *mouchwa tet* would make bystanders think I might be a practitioner, which was in fact the case. I exchanged some elementary badinage in Kreyol with people who hailed me from the street. Bob later told me that when he saw me "doing the dozens" with these local boys, he was definitely convinced that I knew what I was doing and was not going to get us in trouble.

Then at the Oloffson, revelation. Bob wasn't planning to share a room with me as I had assumed, but with Melisandra. There was a moment of discomfiture, and nothing to do but swallow it. I was extremely unhappy to find I'd involved myself in betraying Janice, whom I liked and admired as much as I did Bob. But as I had said earlier, we were over the cliff. Also, since our conversation on the plane, I was beginning to think that Melisandra might really be the sound companion Bob had claimed, which turned out to be true.

Years after Bob's death, I turned up a page of *Arcturus* notes, which began with a statement of a Fisher King/Parsifal dynamic Bob had tentatively planned for two lovers in the novel, then slipped into a kind of prose euphoria: "Treasure waits outside. . . . Pole star man's place is over the divide where the waters run toward the arctic, across the lava beds, north. Other ocean.

"It's June in January because I'm in love, spring in my heart."

Impossible to know for sure but it does seem to me that Bob is talking about himself in that last sentence, which was probably written sometime shortly before we flew to Haiti, and that he may have seen Melisandra not only as a rejuvenating lover but also as a sort of panacea for his pain, on the model of the Fisher King/Parsifal relationship he was planning for the man and woman in his novel. Anyway, the next few days would prove that he was definitely hurting.

The Oloffson was a vast rambling gingerbread fantasy, built by one of Haiti's nineteenth-century presidents as a wedding present for his daughter, whose descendants still owned the place. It had served as a backdrop for Charles Addams's Gothic-flavored *New Yorker* cartoons. Aubelin Jolicoeur, a journalist and *debrouillard* close to the Duvalier regime (he was the model for Petit Pierre in Graham Greene's *The Comedians*, whose Hotel Trianon is also based on the Oloffson), still held nightly court in a central square of wicker furniture between the bar and the reception desk, twirling his gold-headed cane and receiving whoever would come to him (a dwindling number, since the Duvaliers' fall). He and Herb Gold, who was extremely well known at the hotel and occupied the best rooms in the place, were old friends and still cordial.

Our party dined on the wide gallery, overlooking the pool and a dense circular grove of tall palms, throbbing with verdant tropical energy. Afterward some people I knew turned up: Ephèle Milcé, the curator of the Saint-Martial library; Michelle Karshan, an American woman who was Aristide's secretary for foreign press; and the great Haitian novelist Lyonel Trouillot, who I thought would like to meet Robert Stone and who was hugely amused at my taking on the role of tourist guide to Haiti. Bob, who was consuming a good deal of the excellent local Barbancourt rum, became very ruddy by evening's end, which concerned me just a little. On average, I put away plenty of liquor myself but had learned to stick mostly to beer in the tropics. However, I had other things to worry about, and was beginning to see some advantage to Bob's bunking in with Melisandra.

Next morning we rose by starlight. The ways in and out of Haitian cities are the most dangerous, and I liked to have my wheels turning just a little before dawn, when most bad guys are still asleep and there's practically no traffic. Gesner showed up in a bit of a sweat, having heard that there was bandit activity on the inland road we were planning to take. We discussed workarounds but there were not good ones and we decided to take the main road to Jacmel instead, giving up Thiotte and the Forêt des Pins for now.

Our route out of town went through Carrefour and Martissant, where Gesner lived. We passed the crumbling upper wall of Habitation Leclerc, a vast luxury-hotel compound in the time of the Duvaliers, still containing some old-growth forest and now inhabited by squatters. There was a trench across the road so deep it took our truck down to the floorboards. That was a mere inconvenience by day but if you were to get stuck there at night, as Gesner and I explained to Bob and Melisandra, *zenglendo* would come out of the holes in the wall and kill you and take your shit.

We passed without incident in the rapidly brightening dawn. Our way led us near the *hounfor* where Gesner served the *loa*; we stopped there for an hour. The *houngan*, gravely courteous, let us look around the place. It was a classic lay: the large main room open space for drumming and dancing, and two closed chambers at the rear. On the right, the *Chamn Ginen*, for the service of the beneficent *loa*; this aspect of Vodou is compatible with charismatic Christianity, as indicated by the motto over the door: *Dieu qui donne et Dieu qui fait* (God who gives and God who makes). To be *Fran Ginen* is to have a clear spirit, and fortunate are those for whom this service is sufficient! But many *serviteurs* have occasion to go to the darker side, the *Chamn Bizango*, where you may appeal to the more malicious aspects of the twinned *loa*: to gain money, to gain power, to make people love you who don't. Over that door the motto read *Fok Nanpwen*, a Kreyol phrase meaning "There'd have to not be any for me to not get some."

It isn't a Manichean system, though; like their servants, the spirits incarnate both aspects from the time. In ceremonies on the open floor, one aspect or another may be summoned and celebrated; often enough they all flow together. Bob later sketched the floor plan of this *hounfor* from memory, and worked it into the climax of *Bay of Souls*.

Then we climbed back into the truck and crept through thickening traffic to the edge of the city and took the high road south past Léogâne. Route Nationale 4 had very recently been repaved, and was possibly the best-maintained road I'd ever driven in Haiti. But it was still arduous, as driving in Haiti usually is, since you share the roadway (more often than not with a sheer cliff ascending on one side and descending on the other) with goats and pigs and cattle and troops of uniformed schoolchildren spending half a day to reach a classroom and the other half to return; with files of women who danced and sang to amuse themselves, balancing great loads on their heads as they covered the miles to market; with ancient *madanm* riding sidesaddle on tiny donkeys they whipped up with crooked little sticks; with the Japanese mini-trucks from the 1980s, repurposed as tap-taps which might carry as many as forty passengers clinging to the superstructure butt-welded to the bed—these could appear very suddenly around the hairpins, with no warning but a fanfare of horn-blowing.

Over the years I had learned to negotiate this situation smoothly enough. Bob had gained confidence in my capability as a chauffeur/guide the previous day. He and Melisandra were calm in the back, soaking in the human torrent that flowed past us as we crossed the mountains. Gesner and I exchanged observations in either French or Kreyol; he gave me directions as needed. I stopped once to retrieve a crumpled straw hat from the roadbed (not sure why) and another time for gas; there was air in the tank that made it foamy, but the Montero seemed to be running just fine. We rolled into the Jacmelienne around midafternoon.

I checked into the room I was sharing with Gesner and fell into an oily black sleep. When I woke it was evening and I found Bob by the pool, which was level with the top of a twelve-foot stone wall that dropped to the beach. A little boy had scaled the wall like a gecko and clung there, lifting his head above the rim to tell Bob, with a cherubic smile, *"M'ap priye pou'w!"*

"What's he say?"

"He says he's gonna pray for you."

Bob, seeming very much pleased with this intention, gave the child one U.S. dollar, whereupon he vanished from our sight.

We dined on the veranda of the Jacmelienne, served by *femmes de couleur* wearing floor-length colonial-style gowns and the elaborate tall cloth headdresses from the same period—a hallmark of this particular hotel. The menu was the classic French-African fusion: *poisson gros sel, griot, cabrit en sauce, lambi* (the latter the only edible form of conch I have ever tasted, tender and delicious). There was a broad view of Jacmel Bay, with a derelict freighter heeled over in the shallows, slowly dissolving into rust.

After the meal we went for a walk on the beach (it's essential to exercise after eating in Haiti, I had learned at the cost of some suffering). There were few artificial lights along the shore and we could see the stars. We had circled around from the hotel's main entrance to reach the strand, but I knew there would be another, less obvious way to enter (there always was), and thought it would be instructional for us all to use it. Earlier I had seen a couple of hotel workers come over the pool wall in the same spot where that boy had stuck up his head. With a little exploration I was able to find the handhold and footholds that permitted the climb. Melisandra went up first, easily enough, and Bob after, with some lifting and pushing from Gesner and me. Bob was a little burlier than I'd realized, and huffing considerably by the time he reached the top. I began to feel downright grateful that Melisandra would be with him through the night.

Next day, another dawn departure. I wanted to try to reach Thiotte and the Forêt des Pins from the opposite direction. It seemed just feasible for a day trip . . . maybe. The rumored *zenglendo* activity was on the outskirts of the capital, as usual, so the excursion should be safe enough. The distance to Thiotte was just under seventy miles, though over roads of unknown qualities.

The eastbound road along the southern coast was under construction, meaning dirt surface, copious dust, a handful of men with picks and shovels, here and there broken-down hulks of heavy machinery, and less frequently one in operation. Not much traffic and it was flat, so we rolled along merrily enough. At Marigot we turned north and began to climb the mountain switchbacks. We were alone on this stretch of road and except for our diligent diesel engine it was eerily quiet. The forest was dense on the high side of the road, below the cliffs, the aqueous blue of the Caribbean fell farther and farther away, though still throwing up to us an occasional sparkle. It was calm in the car; I felt that the isolation and distance was making Melisandra a little uneasy, though she said nothing. Bob was still, in observation mode. When his attention was focused he didn't miss much.

The road through the mountains was unpaved, or so I thought, the surface covered with dirt and leaves, yet seemed surprisingly uniform and solid. Presently I began to pick a sort of checkerboard pattern under the debris—the outline of eighteenth-century *pavés*, the square stone blocks of which Royal, then Imperial, France was constructed. This road had been built to last, a good two centuries before, which seemed an encouraging sort of thing to point out to my passengers.

Eventually we emerged onto a plateau and after maybe another hour rolled into a village—Seguin, according to the inhabitants. We made our way to the market square and found beer. Oddly, one side of the market was raked with tall bleachers: the *Madanm Sara* had laid out their wares on the benches and everyone else picked their way up and down to make their purchases. Our little party sat near the top of the structure, drinking cold Prestige from napkin-wrapped brown bottles. From this height there was a long view and on the horizon a fringe of pines—undoubtedly the Forêt des Pins—but it was already midafternoon; it would take hours to return, and I had a strict rule to be off the road by dusk. If there was banditry, it would take place at points of entry to Jacmel during the first hours of darkness.

Melisandra relaxed perceptibly once we had passed Marigot again and were Jacmel-bound on the level coast road. An hour shy of sunset, golden light came slanting through our cab. Melisandra insisted Gesner try her sunglasses—big, bright yellow bubbly things. They made the world more beautiful, she assured him. When Gesner finally tried them, he chuckled with delight. Melisandra was a good sport when he assumed they were a gift and declined to give them back.

After dinner we checked out a nearby nightclub, where some *blan* (in Haitian parlance "foreign," though these were also white) NGO types were dancing among the Haitians in attendance. "My meat," as Bob told me he thought of such people—they'd served him as both guides and subjects in Israel, for example. But I was too tired to scrape acquaintance. Bob and Melisandra took a brief turn on the floor and then we all crashed early.

There was time to look around Jacmel the next morning. The town is on the small side, easy to navigate, and pretty, with many of the gingerbread houses of nineteenth-century Haitian architecture in unusually good condition. They were preparing for carnival in the central square, where Bob and I each bought gigantic papier-mâché masks—mine a classic lion's head I thought might please my eight-year-old daughter, and his a dangerously demented-looking bunny rabbit in lurid shades of pink and blue—this critter could have escaped from an acid flashback, which, come to think, might have been why Bob liked it.

In the afternoon we made a leisurely ride back to the capital, without incident except for a slowdown near Fondwa. Halted, we watched an ancient graybeard limping with his stick across the road, towing a long sack of the kind Haitians call *makout*. "That's Legba crossing our path," I told Bob, for the old gentleman was the spitting image of the description of Legba (the spirit of gates, crossroads, and passages, a rough equivalent of Hermes) found in Maya Deren's *Divine Horsemen*, which I had recommended Bob to read. "'Legba, limping along. It is a long time since we have seen you.' . . . They say he is an old peasant who has worked his fields hard all his life and is now at the end of his powers." My head was full of

Vodou lore and I had been dropping a lot of it on Bob, who used parts of it in *Bay of Souls* eventually. Legba's passage seemed a good omen. We were safe in the Oloffson enclosure by dusk.

Next day was the safety day I'd built into the schedule, lest we spend more nights than we planned on our loop to Jacmel. Bob and Melisandra found a ride to one of the beach resorts on the Côte des Arcadins, a few miles north of Port-au-Prince, maybe with some of Herb Gold's party, which was still in force at the Oloffson. I found I could spend a profitable day at the library at Saint-Martial. In the evening I rejoined Bob and Melisandra where they sat by the pool, drinking rum punches. Somewhere in the day's peregrinations he had picked up the rumor that Timothy Carney, then the U.S. ambassador, had when he first learned of this posting objected, "No way—Haitians are maggots."

Bob knew this morsel would get my goat, which it did. A possibility that we might go to some kind of embassy reception had been discussed. I snarled that I could easily buy an assault rifle on the street and bring it along if we decided to go (which was true; during that period destitute members of the disbanded Armed Forces of Haiti were selling their weapons for around $20 U.S.). Of course I didn't *really* intend to shoot up the American embassy, but Bob was devilishly pleased with the success of his sally; a touch of Gordon Walker had gotten behind his head. In the end we went no farther than the gallery, where we ordered another round of drinks.

Herb Gold dashed by, bright with enthusiastic energy. He loved Haiti and knew it well, and being there clearly gave him a lot of juice. Bob followed his passage with somber eyes. "What?" Melisandra asked him. *Sic transit gloriam*, said Bob, or words to that effect. "Herb used to be Mister *Playboy*," when Bob had first known him in the 1960s; everybody was talking about him and reading his work. Though the stream of his published books had barely slowed down, he hadn't been getting much attention for the past twenty years. His big Haiti book had brought him out of the shadows but briefly, and nearly ten years had passed since then. Melisandra, whose investment in literary reputation was lower than Bob's or even mine (peculiar, given her remarkable talent and achievement), still didn't follow.

"What are you talking about?" she asked, bridling a bit in her chair.

"You can outlive yourself." The line just sort of fell out of my mouth. Bob caught my eye with a look that said I'd nailed it. In that moment I knew that that was just the thing he was afraid of, and realized (for the first time) that I was afraid of it too.

On the other hand, Bob's chance of outliving himself didn't look so great that day; a bookie wouldn't have taken the bet. Earlier during our voyage Bob had explained to me his daily regimen: Ritalin in the morning for energy and concentration, pharmaceutical narcotics in the afternoon to bring him down from the Ritalin and blunt his appetite for alcohol. This system had worked as intended for several years, but he'd come to the point where, as the daily cocktail hour approached, "I ask myself, what else does life have in store?"

Life more abundant! In Haiti Bob had been drinking more and more heroically, on top of whatever his opiate dose might have been (the latter was consumed discreetly, per my suggestion prior to departure). At our last Oloffson supper together he pushed his food around the plate and tended to drop threads of conversation. Herb Gold appeared at our table and commenced an anecdote, but was barely through the expository phase when Bob's eyes rolled white and his bearded head crashed down to his sternum, as if some puppet master had loosed the supporting strings. Herb withdrew—disconcerted not by wounded vanity but by concern, I think; he was man of the world enough to guess the cause.

With Bob nodded out at the table, Melisandra and I walked down in the circular palm grove below the gallery—a liminal space, where leaves shivered in the breeze above and around us, sometimes whispering, sometimes clattering like swords. She looked at me intently, her extraordinary eyes full of love and fear. "I think he really might die this time," as if she'd read the sentence off my forehead. For a moment we were completely "in the same spirit," as Haitians often put it. I must have thanked her for the care she was taking of Bob—anyway I hope I did. She left me in the garden and took Bob away to bed.

In the morning everyone looked more or less all right. Still kicking and still breathing anyway. Word was that American Airlines had gone on strike so we headed to the airport early to see what could be done. It turned out that our flight to Miami was going on schedule; after that it was anybody's guess.

For *blan* like us, Haiti was either a nightmare from which to run away screaming or a very powerful bonding experience. This six-day run had cemented my friendship with Bob, and begun something of the sort with Melisandra, though the sequel to the latter was not obvious, given the loyalty to Janice I wanted to sustain as best I could. I shook hands with her as we boarded the plane in Port-au-Prince, and said with a smile (a sincere one, I swear!) that I looked forward to meeting her again someday.

What happens in Haiti stays in Haiti—that was my best idea. Melisandra didn't like that solution one bit, but there wasn't a lot she could do about it. In Haiti, Bob had found a moment to explain to me that the problem between him and her (and Janice and the rest of the world for that matter) was that Melisandra wanted status as his official mistress. She wanted to know and be recognized by his friends (most of them also Janice's friends) and to appear on his arm with her head held high—she had regal qualities enough to have carried off the pose on the arm of a French king. But this ambition was a bit much for Bob. Some of his previous affairs had lasted a while but were carried out with greater discretion, and none till this one had bid to change the dynamic of his and Janice's marriage. This very risky prospect both alarmed and excited him, I think, perhaps in equal measure. Also, if Melisandra wanted to get Bob's goat, she could and did threaten him with other lovers. A dedicated and adept equestrian, she played polo and could cause handsome young polo players to fawn on her at will. Although Bob was wise and lucid enough to see around the edges of such maneuvers, he was also sufficiently infatuated that they drove him mad with jealousy.

In Miami there was chaos; the strike had grounded most American Airlines domestic flights. Bob and Melisandra, taking different airlines to different destinations (Bob on a puddle-jumper to Key West), could make their flights if they ran for them. Bob was a few strides into his dash when he appeared to stop breathing. It was very likely his first real emphysema attack. I caught him up and gave him a blast from the albuterol inhaler I carried for asthma. The effect was magical—he hitched up his gear and ran on.

I had to run back to the American Airlines counter to see if there was any chance of my getting to Baltimore that night. There was not, but I got booked for the first morning flight and found a room at the airport hotel. A few more hours to decompress from this particular journey seemed like a boon. I would have time to get my first world personality on straight and still be able to teach my class, which met at night anyway.

The next day I learned that Bob had made a successful run for his plane and arrived safely back in Key West. A few days later I found out that he had been busted in the love affair—in flagrante—when Janice found

Melisandra's boarding pass stub with Bob's as she was going through his traveling clothes for the laundry.

7
BUSTED

Bob didn't have a journalistic assignment for the Haiti trip, but Janice thought he would likely pick one up. "He had had several phone calls before he went from a woman at *The New Yorker*, and I assumed he would do something for them." So Janice, in her managerial as well as her domestic role, was looking for his travel documents because they would probably be deductible tax receipts. Finding Melisandra's boarding pass with Bob's, she "confronted him with this, saying that he hadn't mentioned that she would be accompanying him and Madison to Haiti. He admitted that she had been traveling with them," but apparently no more.

"Later the same day the woman who said she was at *The New Yorker* phoned again. I told her that Bob was working and that I didn't want to disturb him. Maybe I could take a message. She said, Surely I can speak to him for a minute. In a very peremptory manner. No, you can't, I replied. I went downstairs and did interrupt Bob, to ask who on earth was this person at *The New Yorker*? It wasn't anyone from the magazine, Bob said. It was Melisandra."

Bad news. Bob's previous adventures had involved lies of omission, one might say, working in concert with Janice's general willingness to look the other way. This one looked like it had already spun out a quite elaborate web of deceit. "I had not expected that. Of all the nerve, calling our house and giving a phony name. I insisted Bob tell her that his wife had found out about them, and that their relationship had to end. Bob promised to do so. No argument. He seemed relieved to tell me about it. He knew this affair had gone too far.

"He soon phoned her, and reported her response. So your wife found out, she said. And she'll find out again. And she'll get used to it."

The good news was that Bob was telling Janice the truth again, as he had almost always done, and he doubtless felt better about that, as he resumed the "two against the world" defense posture. Not so good was the news that Melisandra was not planning to disappear gracefully. She was a very strong woman who did love Bob, and felt she had a right to.

Janice, meanwhile, had a quieter personality, but in no way a weaker one. She was angry. Bob, provocative to the bone, could and did make lots of people angry, especially when performing the Gordon Walker side of himself. Provocation was really part of his stock in trade, but Janice saw him in a different light and was seldom as angry with him as now. A wise forbearance was her usual stance. This time she felt aggrieved not only at Bob but also at a number of the Stones' good and old friends who had countenanced or enabled the affair with Melisandra—or so Bob reported to me. (Janice, long afterward, demurred on this point: "I don't remember cutting anyone off from my friendship. No one could have stopped Bob from doing what he wanted to do.") That development alarmed me, not for no reason, but Bob defended me by insisting that I hadn't known the score until it was well and away too late to do anything about it, which was true enough.

I was given to understand that Janice had no beef with me, to my immense relief, she being, independently of Bob, a friend I would not like to lose. A few months later she and I had a moment to talk privately; we were walking with a group somewhere in Manhattan, and the two of us fell behind the company. I think I began some sort of very elliptical apology, which Janice cut off, explaining that she and Bob had married very young indeed, at the beginning of a very turbulent time (indeed!); they had always given each other a good deal of leeway in romantic matters, so that both could stay in the marriage without either of them feeling a prisoner of it. "Our deal was always that he could do what he liked, and so could I. We did not own each other. We stayed together of our own free will, out of love for each other." That program might not have worked out for everybody (so-called open marriages often don't), but forty years on the Stones were still holding a steady course, even if Melisandra had rocked their boat a bit. Melisandra's determination to be a permanent and visible fixture in Bob's life was a step too far. Janice and Bob had agreed on that, and since Bob had been saying much the same thing in my other ear during this same period, it was easy enough to believe it.

Truth to tell, the conclusion hadn't come quite so tidily as that. In the weeks following Bob's return from Haiti, Janice (though there was not the slightest trace of it in her diaries) "was brooding as I waited for the problem to resolve itself. Usually these women moved on after a time. He said, I tell them I'm married. I tell them I'm *very* married." Melisandra, though, had not been much discouraged by this announcement so far.

Janice, with her preternatural ability to look coolly at her own risky passions, reflected that she had once been as powerfully attracted to someone else (that drummer in New York, during the Stones' London period). She could tolerate that it had happened to Bob—but not that it should keep on happening. In April she decided to accompany him to Boston for a conference on Ernest Hemingway's style, "thinking that perhaps he shouldn't go so many places on his own."

Bob didn't like other people comparing him to Hemingway but sometimes would covertly do it himself. "I think a lot about Hemingway," he wrote to the critic Sven Birkerts shortly before the event. "His work is the best argument I know for the principle that style represents moral perspective. That moral perspective may represent the writer's core beliefs, or it can be itself a fiction, part of the inventive process." Bob thought that "the influence of Gertrude Stein's mentoring "is hard to exaggerate but mainly undocumented. Hemingway, less original, more conventional and more professional, could make her linguistic eccentricities a commodity."

Beyond style, Bob was thinking particularly about Hemingway as a particular expression of the American vitalism that was also meant to be a force driving *Arcturus*, arguing that Hemingway had "become a modernist" in part "through being in Europe and paying attention to what was happening there on every level. . . . Being present when Europe's own anarchic vitalism (the *Rites of Spring* etc.) had undergone its own process of transformation in the First World War." Bob didn't want to sit in Papa's chair, but he was confronting many of the same issues, and these were not only aesthetic and philosophical.

A *Boston Globe* article covering the conference quoted an unused draft of Hemingway's 1954 Nobel Prize acceptance speech: "There is no more lonely man than the writer when he is writing except the suicide. Nor is there any happier, nor more exhausted man when he has written well." At that moment, Bob was not in a good place on this spectrum of possibility. The *Globe* began by announcing, "Countless writers have sought the mix of talent, war, wives, alcohol, Gertrude Stein, bullfighting and insight that was the elixir of Hemingway's work." Take away Stein and bullfighting, and Bob was imbibing a similar potion—and it was tending to turn toxic.

In respect to Hemingway's serial marriages, not to mention his suicide, Bob might well have been looking at Hemingway's personal life as an example to avoid.

Janice sat by him, as the event unfolded its array of speakers, "and, as I thought likely, Melisandra did turn up, but left immediately when she saw Bob had not come alone. I did not see her. I had no idea what she looked like. But this almost-encounter made Bob very nervous." Later in the month, the *Damascus Gate* paperback tour began. Janice could not go with him on all those many stops, and Melisandra would not necessarily require an invitation to turn up here or there.

During this time a friend asked Bob, "Why are you so unhappy? You have it all—a wife, a family, a beautiful mistress." But that wasn't the kind of *all* he wanted. Although Melisandra might tell him he could have it both ways, he really couldn't, as much because of his own temperament as what it was doing to Janice, who "was struck with jealousy, that unpleasant emotion I had mostly avoided." Melisandra had sent Bob a glossy of her author picture, and Janice, in her secretarial capacity, had inevitably discovered it. "Blond, sitting on the grass with her skirt spread about her, looking provocatively up at the camera. My possible replacement." Over four decades Janice had seen many marriages end that way. She was too practical to think that she and Bob would magically be immune. Jane Burton had once told her that "jealousy is a state very much like paranoia. I remembered that, as I was certainly feeling paranoid about this situation." She went to the hairdresser for her "first hair coloring ever. An unsettling experience. Fooling Mother Nature."

Eventually (and before that über-calm conversation I had with her on the New York pavement) there was another showdown. Janice told Bob to go if he must; if he wanted to, they could part ways, but it must be an absolute parting. Rather astonishingly, Bob asked if she would still be his secretary. Janice explained—logistically, keeping the emotional parts to herself—how that would be unfeasible.

Bob choked for a while. Maybe he was remembering the several characters he'd written for whom losing the Janice avatar meant death or the next thing to it. Then, finally, "he was clear. He did not want to end our marriage. He said, we are unbreakable."

In the same season Bob turned in a brief reflection on his writing for a Key West Literary Seminar brochure. "You can take the darkest impulses and turn them into art," he began. "I write a great deal about people's faith in one another. People coming through for people or not coming through for people. I write about the difficulty of behaving well. Let alone decently, let alone doing good. I write about people who are somewhat lost in terms of something they think they require. . . . They're looking for a kind of salvation."

Here was a pretty clear statement of issues plaguing Bob's life as much as his art. But clarity was hard for him to come by in those days. For one thing, he wasn't getting enough oxygen to his brain. His breathing problem was being treated as asthma, though he told me on the phone that he thought it might be early-onset emphysema—that huge old smoking habit coming back to bite him, though he'd given it up nearly twenty years before. His pill and alcohol habit was at its most dangerous peak ever. A whistle-stop book tour didn't help with that, nor did the stress of ending the affair with Melisandra. Then there was real pain to contend with: the recurring complex of lower back problems and sciatica. After an intoxicated evening (despite self-medication he was in such pain he could hardly stand to make conversation), he fell getting out of an elevator, taking a hard hit on one side. "The next day," Janice noticed, "he was, strangely, in much less pain. I conjectured that he might have hit himself solidly enough to knock the herniated disk away from the sciatic nerve. This improved the situation, for a while."

8

SKYDIVER DEVOURED BY STARVING BIRDS

Also on the upside, Bob was getting glimmers of what would eventually turn into a new novel. He'd returned from our February trip badly sunburned (despite the wide-brimmed straw hat I'd brought for him, which he wore with a Wild West rakishness that suited him very well) and with trouble in both legs from long hours sitting in the truck, but also "full of stories" he told Janice "about Haiti, a country that was really his sort of place, a place where Stone characters might spend time." In between bouts with *Arcturus*, he started a new story—one that had nothing to do with Haiti at all but was loosely based on the deer-hunting trip he and John Hildebrand had made in the Northwest a good many years before. By the end of March Janice was proofreading a first draft and (despite everything else on her mind at the time) recording it in her notes as "knock-out story." Published by *The New Yorker* as "Dominion," the story imported some elements from *Arcturus* into a modern setting and period: loss of faith and the principal couple's near loss of their only child, a boy in his early teens. Somehow or other, the Haiti material was going to find a way to converge with this story line.

In mid-March the Stones flew from Key West to New York, Bob to appear in *John Paul II: The Millennial Pope*, a documentary directed and produced by Helen Whitney; Janice to find a Manhattan apartment. Bob was impatient to make the move. Janice would have been happy "to shop around, look at everything available. June Chapman had looked at a hundred apartments, she told me, before she bought the one on East Sixty-Ninth Street that she sometimes loaned to us." They were looking in the Carnegie Hill area on the Upper East Side, more because of proximity to the 92nd Street Y and Bill Wright's apartment, where they often stayed, than that this area was in the boundaries of Bob's childhood neighborhood, with the site of St. Ann's twenty blocks down Lexington.

Janice was settling in for a long search when they were shown "a five-room co-op in a prewar building on Lexington Avenue and Ninety-Fourth Street that appealed to both of us. Bob was for buying it, immediately." Janice felt more hesitant. She had Carol Gelber look at the place; Carol thought it was fine. Janice looked for signs and portents, "some signal from the gods. I noticed that the vivid crimson paint on the walls of the entry and dining area was the same color as the dining-room walls of our former home in London, the flat on Redington Road. And, another coincidence, the amount of the monthly maintenance assessment on this apartment matched the number Bob and I regularly used as a PIN code, a number he had purposefully chosen years before." These auguries reassured her enough to enter a bid: $450,000, which in 1999 seemed expensive.

They left their money on the table and took the train to Washington, DC, for a party honoring Mary Lee Settle. On March 23 their offer was accepted, and they were both pleased at the prospect before them despite the heavy financial commitment. It wasn't the first time the Stones had thrown a hat over the wall, then pursued it into a happier situation.

Bob filed "Dominion" with his agents in the first week of April and then set off on the *Damascus Gate* paperback tour, which ran into May, enlivened in Miami by an encounter with "a man with connections to a group that hopes to blow up the Temple Mount in Jerusalem." The novel hit paperback bestseller lists in San Francisco and Los Angeles. Janice, extremely busy with details of the New York apartment purchase, couldn't go on most of the tour, but she did join him in Kentucky where they saw old friends Ed McClanahan, Gurney Norman, and Ed's ex-wife Kit Andrews.

Janice installed herself on Block Island at the end of June, preparing to receive the grandchildren. Bob was with her long enough for "a big discussion about how to maximize work time for the summer." The contractual deadline for Bob's next novel was still two years out, but progress on *Arcturus* had been slow, with Bob constantly traveling while trying to sweep his health problems under the rug; he had barely spent two weeks in the same place since the first of the year. Despite this concern, he was very soon on the move again, flying north to join John Hildebrand for a ten-day tour of British Columbia, driving the Cassiar Highway and floating the Stikine River.

Bob thought this region might suit as a setting for *Arcturus*, and John knew of two Indian tribes in the area that might serve as models for the lost tribe Bob was planning for the novel. They flew to Port Hardy, and there caught a ferry that conveyed them up the coast to Prince Rupert, where they rented a van, bought supplies, and drove the Cassiar Highway farther north, camping between stays at a couple of lodges. One of the lodge keepers showed Bob part of a manuscript by local memoirist Georgiana Ball, which when he wrote her after the trip Bob called a "fascinating history and remembrance"—a memoir of the very period in which *Arcturus* was set. He was hoping he might be able to see the complete work, to help him with what he described to her as "a novel set in the 1930s in a fictional British Columbia river town not unlike Telegraph."

After their river run, Bob and John removed to the Red Goat Lodge near Iskut, east of Mount Edziza Park and at the head of Eddontenajon Lake, where Hildebrand noticed that "only a few miles away, at Wolf Creek Retreat, an anthropologist and writer whose brochure informs us that he is 'often likened to a modern Indiana Jones' operates a lodge and cabins offering everything one might want to do in the wilderness from a base of authentically woodsy opulence. His wife and partner, adds the brochure, is a former Parisian fashion model . . . an anthropologist who studied Bedouin tribeswomen in the Saharan desert, and is 'active in dance and polarity massage.' "

It was none other than Wade Davis, a native of British Columbia and in truth and fact a very capable, sometimes brilliant anthropologist and ethnobotanist, who'd made his reputation with a 1985 book about Haitian Vodou, *The Serpent and the Rainbow*. I'd recommended it to Bob as one of the only two books in English (with Deren's *Divine Horsemen*) that really grasped the gestalt of the religion. There were caveats, though: To attract a popular audience, Davis had sensationalized his story a little here and there—not enough to damage its essential content but enough to annoy a good number of Haitians who had helped him. His enthusiastic involvement with an execrable horror movie by Wes Craven, very faintly based on his book but released under the same title, had cost him a lot of credibility among academics, Haitians, and anyone seriously interested in Haitian culture and religion.

Such a person might be an almost ready-made Robert Stone character. Bob and John went to Wolf Creek Lodge, "a lovely place on a mountain lake," as Hildebrand remembers, "and as we walked down to the beach, Davis paddled up in a canoe. The perfect entrance. He was ridiculously handsome—six-four at least, blond, square-jawed, an earnest squint to his blue eyes—so Bob started calling him Captain Canada. (Out of earshot, of course.) Davis was very friendly and even complimentary about a piece I'd done in *Harper's*."

Snickering in their sleeves, Bob and Hildebrand carried off a copy of the Wolf Creek Retreat brochure, so that Bob could spoof it in his article, "but when we left it in a café on the way back to Prince Rupert and had to retrace our path to retrieve it, we began to suspect Captain Canada had supernatural powers. This suspicion was further confirmed when a fox pelt Bob had bought in Telegraph Creek for Janice was somehow misplaced on the plane back to New York. The mysterious intervention, no doubt, of Captain Canada!" Against the odds, the fox pelt was recovered. "I have the remains of that fox still," says Janice. "I used it as a fur scarf, but my grandchildren treated the poor beast so roughly that its tail and feet fell off."

9

New York Is Now

Late summer took the Stones west, to the Squaw Valley conference and to Stanley, Idaho, among other places. Bob's difficulty breathing was becoming more obvious at the end of the summer of 1999, as Janice noticed when they hiked the hills around Lake Tahoe with Kem Nunn and other friends. "The altitude was high there, and he would get out of breath. Half as a joke, I would get behind him, put my hands on his back, and push him up the inclines." In Sun Valley, Bob's former student Stephen Byler took him fly-fishing. "Bob found the fishing strenuous. Again, he would get out of breath." For the time being, though, these symptoms were no more than mildly worrisome. "It seemed possible he might have asthma," nothing worse.

The Stones flew east at the end of August, and got a start on the furnishing of apartment 6F, 1435 Lexington Avenue. Their place was on the northeast corner of the building. On the wall outside the door hung a souvenir of Cairo: an ornamental banner rendering the Al-Fatihah in Arabic calligraphy—the verse that opens the Quran. Past the banner and through the door, a short foyer made a sharp turn to the right, leading to an open dining area on the right, galley kitchen and tiny guest room to the left. Thence, a straight shot to the master bedroom, which connected by way of a bath to the large room Bob used as his office.

It was a comfortable room—lined with bookcases of course, but also a large soft couch, conducive for recumbent reading or even a nap, a small stereo, and the Stones' vinyl collection. After Bob's death, Janice hung Eleanor Brooks's 1970s portrait of him in a central spot on the north wall of the office. Bearded and authoritative, Bob looks both ancient and ageless in it. At least one of the books he appeared to be expounding from was his own, but the aspect of the whole makes it seem like some sacred text, Bible, Torah, Quran, or kabbalah, and the plume of smoke from the cigarette in his hand might have risen from a burnt offering. Once, walking into the room as the sunset struck the surface of the painting, I thought I was seeing the very image of Adam De Kuff communing with the divine. The portrait was positioned and posed so that it would have appeared to look over the shoulder of flesh-and-blood Bob when he worked at his desk, for which reason he kept it wrapped and stowed behind the television during his lifetime.

———

In the fall of 1999, there was a windfall that came with a controversy: Dan Halpern of Ecco Press/HarperCollins approached Bob with the proposition that he write a memoir of the American 1960s, many of whose wildest gyrations he'd experienced directly or witnessed at close hand. Bob liked the idea—not least because of the $500,000 advance attached to it. Houghton Mifflin liked it not so much, for the excellent reason that the 1998 contract for the "Alaska novel" gave them an exclusive right of first refusal on Bob's "next full-length work, whether of nonfiction or fiction." As it happened, Houghton was not much interested in the memoir concept, nor did they have any notion of paying out another advance on the scale of what HarperCollins was offering (given that the $850,000 novel they'd contracted had yet to be delivered).

Houghton's first reaction was to stand on its contractual right, and Neil Olson needed all his diplomatic skill to cool things down to the point that the HarperCollins deal could go through. Olson negotiated that there would be no option clause in the HarperCollins contract for the memoir; instead the idea of a new multibook contract between Bob and Houghton could begin to be discussed (though certainly not consummated before that "Alaska novel" should be turned in). Bob promised in a general (and unenforceable) sort of way that he'd complete the novel for Houghton before beginning the memoir. The HarperCollins contract was not signed until March 2000, at which point Bob found himself in a brand-new positive-stress situation: owing two books, the one still in the beginning stages and the other entirely unwritten) to two different publishers, due one year apart—in 2001 and 2002, respectively, so neither date was comfortably far off.

Apart from that episode, the Stones spent the fall of 1999 fairly quietly—at least by their hyperactive standards. Janice served Christmas dinner in the just fully furnished New York place to Bob and her father and her niece Arwen Romes. The next day Bob went to the movies, ostensibly alone. Afterward Janice, who saved movie tickets to write off as research (Bob was a screenwriter, after all), found two stubs in his pocket. Green eyes illuminated, she confronted him with the idea he must have gone with Melisandra. Bob denied that, but had no other explanation for the extra stub. "It was farcical," Janice thought, for once almost bitterly. "It was beneath our dignity. I had to let it go."

The film, whoever had been to see it, was Neil Jordan's 1999 adaptation of Graham Greene's *The End of the Affair*. It might conceivably have been selected for a final parting. If Bob had anything more to do with Melisandra after that day, Janice never had to hear about it.

10
FIGHTING FOR LIFE

Bob sometimes felt a little surprised to find himself alive in the twenty-first century. His story about the deep-sea dive had appeared in *The New York Times* in 1999. Deeply impressed by this experience, Bob thought of it as a voyage to the roots of creation, perhaps with a capital C, and had discussed it in such terms during his talking-head appearance in Helen Whitney's documentary about Pope John Paul II. More privately he tended to frame it as a near-death experience, complete with resurrection. In the first weeks of the year 2000, he liked to quote Mickey Mantle: "If I knew I was going to live this long, I'd have taken better care of myself."

And, with Janice always willing to assist, he did begin making an effort: "When the weather was nice, we took long walks around the reservoir in Central Park. Bob bought a membership in the YMHA, two blocks from our building. He planned to swim regularly, but found the pool was often crowded and not the peaceful water exercise he wanted. He soon stopped going to the Y. In Key West he had the ocean at Zachary Taylor State Park within walking distance, or he could swim in friends' pools."

Breathing trouble, incipient emphysema or chronic obstructive pulmonary disease (COPD), was in the background of Bob's difficulty maintaining an exercise program. Meanwhile his drug and alcohol problems were still hovering at crisis level. In New York, he added a new doctor to his roster, a psychiatrist and "addiction specialist" who not only kept his painkiller and Ritalin supply refreshed but also wrote him prescriptions for antidepressants and Ambien. Bob had some history with sleeping pills of course—along with his quaalude habit he had sometimes taken benzodiazepine in the 1970s and '80s. During his recovery from colon surgery in 1990, he'd found Halcion effective for sleep. But after he'd recuperated, he found it hard to get that drug prescribed, as it was thought to interact poorly with alcohol, and "most of his doctors were aware that he was an alcoholic."

Bob's alcohol use was at least partly about combating the depressions to which he was prone, but he had tried specific antidepressants as well, sometimes "when he felt depressed enough to ask for a prescription." In the 1970s and '80s he also had taken amitriptyline, a tricyclic antidepressant. Now his new doctor could prescribe him the more effective SSRIs, first Paxil, "and when that did not mix well with alcohol, Zoloft."

Such drugs can take weeks to show the desired effect, even when not swirled into the complicated mix of other mind-altering substances that Bob was already consuming. In the winter and spring of 2000 his depression was severe enough to seriously interfere with his work. The breakup with Melisandra was likely to have been a factor. On the back of a manila folder he scrawled a notion for a new piece of fiction: "Guy writes a letter to his old sweetheart, saying goodbye, after he's committed a crime." The book he was supposed to be writing was not getting written. He didn't quite have the heart to follow up on *Arcturus*-related contacts he'd made on his recent trip to Alaska, nor to schedule the second visit he thought he wanted to make to the same region.

But he booked other travel like a man in flight from something: In March he ran up to New York from Key West for a few days, this jaunt including a reading at Wesleyan. In April another USIA-sponsored trip to Europe, this one to the Prague Writers' Festival in the second week of the month. Then a turnaround in New York for a couple of events at the 92nd Street Y, before flying to Frankfurt to tour for the German translation of *Damascus Gate*. In Germany he ran into Ward Just, who was spending a year on a Berlin Prize Fellowship and encouraged Bob to apply for one, "but Bob didn't follow through. Perhaps, as his secretary," Janice said, "I was foot-dragging on this. I had no desire to go to Berlin."

Early in May, Bob went to France for the French *Damascus Gate* publication, and then at the end of the month flew to Los Angeles for a reading at the Skirball Cultural Center "arranged by a booking agency called

Authors Unlimited. He had done a few readings for them, and they paid well. I remember cautioning him that he needed to moderate his pain pill/ sleeping pill intake on this trip to make a successful appearance. I don't recall what he said about the event when he returned, but I don't think Authors Unlimited contacted him again."

———•———

In the winter of 2000, Bob called Emily Cheng from Key West and told her that he had recently attempted suicide but was happy to have failed. The method he tried would most likely have been lethal overdose; the narcotics tolerance he'd developed over the last several years may well have saved his life. Afterward, "he was wandering around Key West in a sort of hallucination," says Cheng. "I also remember he was blissfully happy to have survived the attempt." Bob might also have confessed the episode to Annie Dillard, who wrote to him, "I pray for you every day with all my heart, and here's a report, however vatic:

"What has been lost to you will be replaced. Not restored, but re-placed, and at just that magnitude and at just that depth.

"That's the report. At the ordinary level, surely taking your own life at any speed is not only wrong but indecent.

"You can survive yourself, even this time in this pain, I think, and death is not only a waste of time but also would entail missing the joy, or whatever it is, supra, the promised reason to live."

If Bob said nothing about it to Janice, she'd have thought no more than Bob passed out and woke up again. For Bob, the delightful surprise of having his life back meant that he needed to change it.

He arranged to go to Serenity Knolls, a rehabilitation facility some twenty-five miles north of San Francisco, where Jerry Garcia, also a nar-cotics addict, had died a few years before. For Bob in his state of mind, the inauspiciousness of that example might almost have been a draw. In any case, the place came well recommended by Diana Barich, his old friend from the Perry Lane days. Diana lived near Serenity Knolls, and some of her friends were counselors there.

She picked Bob up at the San Francisco airport and drove him to Serenity Knolls. Before entering, he handed her his supply of pain pills, which Diana promptly destroyed. Within a week or so, though, Bob called her to come get him out. "He told me he had called Bill Barich," by then Diana's ex-husband, "but Bill wasn't comfortable 'rescuing' him. I agreed to it because I knew he could take a cab or otherwise get out if he wanted to." Bob was disappointed that he couldn't recover his pills from Diana, although with the many doctors he had writing for him, he'd be able to resupply soon enough. "I just wanted to give Janice a break," he told Diana, in explanation of his abrupt change of course. "He did seem very 'down,'" she thought, "discouraged more than depressed, but really under the cloud of a bad habit he couldn't break." Bob had stayed in rehab long enough to detox, but his use gradually crept back to previous levels.

11

Cap Haïtien

Given my 1999 experience, I was a little concerned about Bob's habits when we went to Haiti a second time in June 2000. But there were other things to think about; for this trip we had a stronger sense of purpose, though it wasn't the same purpose for both of us. Bob was by then trying to figure out how to incorporate some kind of Haitian world into the novel which . . . could not possibly be *Arcturus*.

Since he had started thinking about setting part of a novel in the Haitian world, Bob had also begun to worry that I might object—that I might think he was poaching, something like that. Considering that I myself was a *blan* foreigner in the midst of writing a version of Haiti's national epic, I didn't think it made any sense for me to object to anything Bob might do. What I did think is that if you do give any two writers the same piece of raw material they are not likely to do the same thing with it; moreover, I was submerged in the two-hundred-year-old Haitian Revolution, while Bob would be writing his own variation on Haiti today.

When he seemed to need better reassurance than that, I said, okay, to paraphrase Bob Dylan, *I'll let you be in my dream if I can be in yours*: Practically speaking, if you do write fiction about today's Haiti, make me a bit player in your story, and if I ever get around to doing that myself I'll do the same for you. Bob seemed to stop worrying about the trespass issue at that point, though I don't recall that he actually agreed to my proposition. Later on, I did keep my end of the bargain in a couple of short stories that revolve around a Stone-like character. And it added interest, reading

Bay of Souls, for me to keep an eye out for some avatar of myself in the narrative.

We were going to Cap Haïtien; in those days Lynx Air operated a nineteen-seat plane that flew out of Fort Lauderdale. Of necessity, Bob and I joined forces in a Fort Lauderdale flophouse the night before, as we were required to present ourselves at the airport at five a.m. The little plane's schedule was set by pilots peering at the horizon from the tarmac; it *might* take off at the crack of dawn, or also, possibly, several hours later than that. Once we checked bags we discovered that a bartender upstairs would allow us to carry go-cups of beer down to the curb at the lower level; an area served by tiny fleets like Lynx, it never had much traffic. We waited, comfortably enough, in this sort of no-zone familiar enough to both Bob and his characters, as in the close of *Damascus Gate*: "At Frankfurt airport, between planes, it was a different world."

From our previous trip Bob was familiar with the turbulent swirl of a Haitian arrival and trusted that once I had tightened my red cloth to the base of my skull I would be equal to deflecting unwanted offers and penetrating to what we did in fact want—to get into town and our hotel with a minimum of complication. Also we were met by a couple of my friends and retainers, which made the whole operation run more smoothly. And Cap Haïtien is in most ways smaller and simpler than Port-au-Prince, at the airport and its outskirts and in the town itself. Within an hour we had recaptured our luggage and were rattling toward town in our battered 4x4 Montero, having painstakingly inspected its essential components, all of which worked well enough except for the horn, which was too dust-clogged to manage more than a barely audible wheeze.

After some exploration of the town, I drove us to the Hotel Mont Joli, one of the couple of Cap Haïtien establishments that catered to foreigners and wealthier Haitians. After the evening meal both of us turned in early. Bob dithered a bit in the room, where I lay on my back, sinking toward sleep. He'd discovered a drawstring bag, which he thought Janice must have put in his kit, and he didn't quite know what to do with it. You should put your stuff in there, I said, you know: glasses, wallet, change purse, passport, knife and keys and all that kind of thing. Bob agreed that was a good idea and set about gathering his small essentials into the bag.

I felt cheered by this evidence of organization, as I had worried a bit over how well he would be able to take care of himself without Melisandra along. (In fact, as I understood better later on, it was typical for Bob to pull himself together whenever there was no woman around to look after him.) I had seen Bob's copy of the pink slip they give everybody at immigration floating around the room, and I meant to tell him to stick that in his passport for safekeeping, but somehow I passed out before I could manage to articulate this advice.

———

I took Bob to visit a small piece of property I owned, with a Haitian partner, a few miles out of town. The official site of Bwa Kayman, a vast Vodou ceremony that inflamed the revolution's first uprising, was a twenty-minute walk from the place. I had thought we might wander over—there was a giant sacred *mapou* tree marking the spot, a stone relief carved with an exhortation the revolutionary leader Boukman Dutty was supposed to have uttered, and some other items of interest—in fact it was a numinous place, in which Bob would have been interested. But Bob didn't appear to be up for the hike. Something seemed to have drained his energy. At the time I thought the narcotics might have turned him inward—he was dosing on pain pills during this trip, though not where I could see him do it, and drinking on top of the doses, though not in the same quantity as on our previous outing. In hindsight it also seems possible that the emphysema was sneaking up on him and making it hard for him to move around very much.

"*C'est son age*," my Haitian friend said: It's his age. We had drawn a little apart from where Bob sat nodding on a rock pile. I was slightly surprised at this conclusion, for although his beard and hair were white I did not think of Bob—then just entering his sixties—as old (besides which in Haiti a man might be gray-bearded and toothless at forty). To me he seemed in substantially better shape than during our last trip to Haiti (when, toward the end of it, Melisandra and I had both been genuinely frightened that he might die before our eyes). Today I had no reason to think that Bob might drop dead in the next few minutes; on the other hand, he was preoccupied with mortality, more so than usual. That deep descent in the submersible was still very much on his mind.

"You're so strong," Bob said to me, sometime during this excursion. I was flattered because it was an impression I sought to make on other people in general and of course there was no one I desired to impress more than Robert Stone. At the same time, I was distressed, because it was a false impression and when I saw it had succeeded with Bob I felt like I had lied to him somehow. Of course, he may have left unspoken *strong in your delusion*; he may also, as fiction writers are wont to do with their friends and acquaintances, have been trying the description just to see how it might suit me as a character. Then again, his reflections on strength planned for *Arcturus* were not altogether positive.

At the time the statement seemed to me to imply that Bob felt himself to be weak by comparison, which wasn't good because I would be leaving him on his own late at night. I couldn't take him into the ceremonies at Morne Calvaire, where I was fumbling my way through preliminary stages of Vodou initiation. In fact, that evening I was changing lodgings, to a hotel in the Carenage, less expensive than the Mont Joli and more convenient for slipping in and out in the small hours of the morning—so I reasoned. I thought Bob would be better off in the Mont Joli when I was elsewhere—he could observe rendezvous there and maybe sometimes join them.

Bob seemed slightly disconcerted by the news of this scheme. "I thought we were gonna hang out," he said. Indeed we were, I reassured him—I'd be on deck for drinks and dinner every evening; the ceremonies didn't get seriously underway until much later. If not good enough, it was the best I could do, although I did feel a little guilty about it, both at the time and again in reading *Bay of Souls*, where Michael Ahearn is temporarily stranded by Lara in a similar manner, on Bob's fictionalized island of Saint Trinity.

About halfway up the precipitous drive of the Mont Joli, a path cut horizontally across the slope toward a hilltop church, Saint Thérèse de la Croix, interrupted by a wall that enclosed a now abandoned house. From this wall, I demonstrated for Bob, he could look across into the *hounfor*, an oval arena with stadium seating, from a distance of thirty yards or so, and in the darkness he would not be seen himself. There were people stirring around over there already, though the drumming had not yet begun, and the Strawberry Moon, around which the ceremonies revolved, was rising toward the full.

Bob's ideas about religion had been hard for me to get a fix on. A Catholic childhood is apt to mark a person deeply; it can be a challenge, and sometimes a lifelong labor, to get out from under the guilt. If Bob didn't quite seem to be a case like that, he hadn't had a conventional Catholic childhood either. In conversation he was most likely to treat religious issues as philosophical questions, and in that fashion he thought about them very deeply. A person with no interest in religion doesn't write *Damascus Gate*, and sometimes a beautifully organic Christian symbol materializes, almost imperceptibly, in a novel, like the pelican flying across the sun at the close of *A Flag for Sunrise*. In Stone's work I often sensed a desire for faith that couldn't quite fulfill itself—inhibited by a skepticism acquired at the hands of hard experience. Frank Conroy, who knew Bob well, had once suggested something similar.

In any case I didn't think my project of total immersion in Haitian Vodou would have appealed to Bob for himself, though it was something he was interested to observe. We were crossing the Carenage Park in the dark (government electricity being out of service as was usual for that time), sidestepping puddles left from the evening rain, when Bob asked me if I was familiar with the concept of magical thinking. One might have called the question a sly one, but I'd seen Bob needle people before and I knew he wasn't needling me. I told him frankly enough that I did know what magical thinking was and that I also knew that at that moment I was in it a long way over my head. We laughed, I think. Years later, trying to answer a different question posed by someone else, I heard myself say that the reason I loved Haiti was that Haiti is a place where magical thinking actually works.

Bob's travel program for the summer of 2000 was as packed as it had been in the spring, so he could work in only four nights in Haiti. I was sticking around a bit longer. Getting Bob on the Lynx flight out of Cap Haïtien required the same hurry up and wait routine as in Fort Lauderdale. We rolled out of the Mont Joli at first light, with the idea of clearing the portal at La Fossette before the traffic really started. Dawn is a beautiful hour in Haiti: still cool, still breezy, the glorious light rising over the flowering trees and the pastel walls of the colonial houses. Some few people were stirring already, to get ahead of the heat, and we saw market women walking into town, with their fruit and vegetables and charcoal balanced in huge baskets or enamel pans on their heads. Some of them were driving tiny donkeys; most of them would have started their journey sometime in the middle of the night. Otherwise the streets of Cap Haïtien were almost empty, except for chickens or once in a while a pariah dog.

At that time the Cap Haïtien airport, situated on the plain about half-way between the two main roads leading out of town, was a cobble of tin-roofed, mostly open-air buildings. By the time we arrived the first swell of activity was beginning: porters, drivers, and market women all taking their posts. The day's heat was just starting to mount. In another hour every doorway of the place would be swarming with people who would spend all day there on the mere chance of some opportunity, so that getting in and out would become more challenging.

Lynx Air boasted a tin shed where passengers could wait. Bob and I were the first to arrive; we turned over his luggage, did the first phase of the paperwork, and settled down to wait. Looking to the right from the shed's doorway, one could see the small planes landing and departing, though so far none of them belonged to Lynx. To the left, just outside the leaky fence of the airport compound, was a hemispherical hillock about sixty feet high, with a few spindly acacias on which laundry was sometimes hung to dry in the dusty wind blowing over the flat, where a handful of people had gathered for no discernible purpose, unless to be spectators of the airport's activity.

Bob and I sat in companionable silence, both of us probably still half asleep. Bob was holding a white piece of paper on his knee—possibly a luggage check, or something to do with his ticket. It crossed my mind to ask him if he knew where that pink slip was—the one he'd been handed at immigration when we entered. The answer was no. Bob ran through his pockets, his carry-on bag, looked to see if he might have stuck it in his passport, where it was actually supposed to be. No such luck.

I wished I hadn't asked the question. By this time I had some experience of Bob's travel anxiety and I didn't want to set it off. I told him the form didn't matter much. In fact, on my first trip to Haiti I had lost my own pink slip and barely got a reprimand for the default. What I didn't say was that this episode had occurred in the Port-au-Prince airport . . . how the situation might play out here in the provinces I had no way of knowing.

Bob seemed calm enough, however. We sat quietly a little while longer. Then Bob, ruminatively, inquired if I had ever read Olivia Manning's *Balkan Trilogy*. I had not, although my parents had a copy in their house. Bob then gave me a dramatic paraphrase of the opening scene: A train, by night, rocketing across Eastern Europe; it is the eve of World War II. At a frontier crossing, soldiers move from car to car for a more or less routine document check. The aging, elegant gentleman in the compartment where the scene is set cannot seem to find his papers—though he is certain that he has them somewhere. Had them. He digs through multiple pockets of his jacket and trousers and of his sumptuous black overcoat, with no result. In the end (the end of this prologue, that is), the soldiers politely escort him off the train—never to be seen again. The rest of the novel, and the two that follow, concern themselves with the destinies of other characters.

I suggested to Bob that his was an insalubrious train of thought. We both managed a weak chuckle, I think. Then a slightly less comfortable silence resumed, during which I discovered that the ants that had infested the pouch of trail mix in my hand bag were the biting kind.

By the time the Lynx plane was ready to embark it had grown seriously hot under the tin. We wound through the spiralized space of the airport, accomplishing more procedures. The immigration checkpoint was in what must have started as a sort of dogtrot between two buildings, a small space now almost hermetically sealed and baking. The officer, a wraith in an immaculate military cap and uniform, accessorized with a pair of those aviator sunglasses the *macoutes* used to wear, waited in a plexiglass booth opaque with scratches and dried sweat. He was extremely tall and so perilously slender I assumed his honesty must be as perfect as his uniform.

On the way in Bob had reminisced about similar situations on other borders, where it sufficed to look up to heaven and ask wonderingly in Spanish, *Can nothing be done?* . . . meanwhile discreetly tucking an appropriate sum in U.S. dollars into the passport. I didn't think that was likely to work here. When the pink slip was requested I began to talk. Bob, who didn't understand the scramble of French and Kreyol in which the conversation took place, thought (ever after) that I was arguing his case with both fervor and eloquence, which was true up to a point. What he didn't know was that I kept changing my explanations as they were serially rejected by the officer: *He never received the pink slip in the first place. A maid in the hotel must have thrown it away. A crow flew in the window and carried the pink slip off to its nest.* Behind us the other passengers for the flight continued to wedge themselves into the small space—they were urgent to get through it because everyone knew that there was just a smidge of air-conditioning in the room beyond, the last pause before the plane. Soon we were getting glued together by funk and sweat like a mob of frat boys stuffing a phone booth, and the tin roof had hit a temperature to melt brass.

I shut up for a moment and took a mental step back (in the crush, it was no longer possible to move my physical person by even a centimeter), then declared: "*Bon. C'est un homme négligeant. Il l'a perdu.*" The only thing to be happy about was that Bob wouldn't understand what I had just said: *Okay. He is a negligent man. He lost it.*

The officer waited, eyes unreadable behind the teardrop lenses and the barely translucent plexiglass, then finally nodded, stamped the passport, and handed it back to Bob. "You may go," he said, and then, including both of us (somewhat unfairly) in the admonition, "But you must not tell lies."

Thanks to the delay the little plane was now boarding rapidly. Another officer took a cursory glance at Bob's passport, then he was through the door to the landing strip. I couldn't follow any farther, but Bob turned back. The brush with trouble had stimulated him, and of course he was giving me way too much credit for solving the pink-slip predicament. Across the doorway, we clasped hands. Bob had that fey light that sometimes came into his eyes, a manic shimmer of inspiration. All at once he seemed at the peak of his own powers. Then we had let each other go, and Bob slung up his shoulder bag and was walking through the blazing midday light across the tattered asphalt to the plane.

12

BUILDING ON "DOMINION"

Bob spent much of the rest of the summer apparently in flight from his desk, though he did stay on in New Haven, trying to work, for much of July while Janice was on Block Island with the grandchildren. There was another camping trip with John Hildebrand and a run to California with Janice for the annual Squaw Valley conference and visits to friends in San Francisco.

In the fall, a lighter travel schedule gave Bob time to write, but the *Arcturus* project was going nowhere. His most recent success with a piece of fiction was the story "Dominion," which had excited a good deal of interest and praise when it appeared in *The New Yorker* in December 2000. The story is in some sense a study of the shakiness of faith in twenty-first-century secular society. Kristin Ahearn and her son, Paul, are believers of a different stripe—Kristin a firm Lutheran, while Paul is in the midst of an early-adolescent infatuation with Catholicism, from which his father has fallen away. When Paul, following a reckless mission into a snowstorm, nearly dies of hypothermia, his father is plunged into the sort of crisis of faith that only a lapsed Catholic can have. Eventually he decides that what some project as Providence is really no more than random happenstance. That conclusion ties off the story firmly, without, however, exhausting its potential.

Janice and Bob "sometimes talked about how his stories had so much interesting material in them that some of them might well be expanded into novels. Regarding 'Dominion,' I asked him if he had considered what might happen next to the Midwestern couple who nearly lost their son. He was stalled on the novel he had been working on, and decided to consider that idea. He thought that Michael Ahearn, the main character, might go to a country like Haiti. He couldn't get Haiti out of his mind."

There were a few other things Bob couldn't get out of his mind, agglomerating close to critical mass to energize a swerve out of *Arcturus* into *Bay of Souls*. But when "Dominion" hit the stands, Bob was not in a position to work on this new idea. In December he had returned to Serenity Knolls, where everyone was expected "to work the program" full time—writing one's own work was not permitted (and perhaps considered a vicious habit).

He hadn't done the full hitch at Serenity Knolls the first time, and by now he'd backslid about to where he'd been before. There were signs of that when we were in Haiti, and I had run into him very discombobulated on the New Haven streets later in the summer. John Hildebrand had seen him collapse with what Bob thought (incorrectly) was a heart attack when they were fishing the Bois Brule River. Bob flew to San Francisco intending to reenter rehab but first spent a few nights in the Mandarin Oriental Hotel, where, Bill Barich remembers, he'd once stayed on a book tour and in his deluded condition thought they'd remember him.

Bob had called Bill from the Mandarin Oriental, "wanting to go out on the town for drinks, and I told him I couldn't do that, thought it would be wrong." Dinner with Kem Nunn and his daughter was a plan B. A day or so later, Kem picked up Bob from the hotel, then collected Bill from his home in San Anselmo. The three spent that night at Kem's in Tomales and the next morning set out for Serenity Knolls. In Barich's version, they "stopped in Point Reyes Station for breakfast, where Bob made a point of ordering a beer with his—like the condemned man's last meal. He bought a six-pack afterward and drank most of it on the way to rehab, so that our arrival was classic with Bob half drunk. When he opened the door of Kem's SUV, empty bottles cascaded onto the driveway with a great clatter, a scene I'm sure the folks at Serenity had witnessed many times before."

If it was an inauspicious beginning, Bob did stick it out for longer on this second visit. Kem thinks he picked Bob up at his request after only a couple of weeks; Janice remembers him staying for a month. She also remembers that the first thing Bob did when he joined her in their Key West condo in January was open a beer, an action she regarded with some cynicism. But in Bob's mind the main point of the rehab tour was to break his addiction to prescription narcotics, and that had at least been interrupted.

The turn of the year 2001 was colored with loss for the Stones. Longtime agent and close friend Candida Donadio was severely ill in December. On the eve of his trip to Serenity Knolls, Bob hadn't had time to go see her. Instead he called, "apologized for not visiting and explained that he was going to rehab. He promised to see her when he returned. He said, I haven't been the best steward of my talents, I'm afraid. He was at a low point, feeling like a failure."

Janice had stayed in New Haven for most of the time Bob was in California. They were giving up the New Haven apartment, and she had to move what was left of its contents into storage. "And I wrote to Candida, asking if we could visit in January. I promised her a new, sober Robert Stone. Her brother Louis wrote back to say that Candida was dying, no longer seeing anyone. Bob was still in California when the year 2001 began, and we were in Key West later that month, when Candida died." She had been more than a redoubtable ally—possibly Bob's biggest. When Janice told her that she always cried when she read Bob's novels, Candida said that she did the same.

After their return to New York that spring, the Stones attended a memorial service for Candida at the Church of All Souls on Lexington. Bob spoke about her on this occasion as did Michael Herr, Peter Matthiessen, Frank Conroy, and the celebrated editor Cork Smith. Bob's eulogy was brief and typed out in a sort of verse form, to lock in phrasing and probably also to accommodate shortness of breath. He praised

Her beautiful face, her eyes, like a reanimated Alexandrine
  portrait
Her lovely voice, her gestures—
She loved to say
To Trust is Good
Not to Trust is better—
Virtue diffident in the first line, a songbird on a limb
To Trust is good—
Then the turn, her jaw descending, the level gaze of the raptor,
  your fortune in the eyes of the sphinx
In the voice stern judgement
Like sung prophecy in half the parts of Don Carlo from the Grand
  Inquisitor to the Duchess of Eboli
Not that, I think she ever particularly believed that not to trust
  was better—
She just loved saying it.

And then Bob pulled up a set-piece:

Once, one-handed because she was talking to the man on the
telephone, she did a mimed impersonation, identifying him to an
onlooker.
   The man to whom she spoke being a man of great self-
importance, of a certain portliness, she made a curving single-
hand gesture to display—brought us together in a conspiracy
against this man's vast self-esteem, then blew it, dropped the
phone, spilled her coffee, danced, danced round —Oh Candida
   She had a show for us all—representing us all.

There were drinks beforehand with Herr and his family, but Bob was
in too much pain to go to dinner afterward. He was missing a good many
events for this reason, discouraged by pain.

———

   In the winter of 2001, Bob began to bear down on the writing of *Bay
of Souls*. On the desk of his Key West study, he set a page from a book
of poetry, a stanza of Tennyson's poem "Ulysses," including these lines.

Old age hath yet his honour and his toil;
Death closes all: but something ere the end,
Some work of noble note, may yet be done,
Not unbecoming men that strove with Gods.

The verse was suitable inspiration for an aging man who had seen his great powers atrophy, but was determined to recover as much of them as he could—a description that fit Bob Stone as well as his emerging protagonist, Michael Ahearn.

Arcturus was now definitively set aside. One reason was that Bob, on John Hildebrand's recommendation, had read Edward Hoagland's work on the region and admired it so much "that he didn't want to cover the same territory." But building a whole new novel on the foundation of "Dominion" did not go easily at first. Bob wrote fragments, which Janice organized on the computer, using the file name JACMEL. "Writing still seemed to be a struggle, and he was so depressed sometimes that I was afraid he would abandon this book also. I could never figure out if he became depressed because the writing wasn't going well, or if the writing wasn't going well because he was depressed."

On the pretext of proofreading, Janice got Bob's permission to print out the pieces and read through. She found the Midwestern sections to be solid, but "the sections he had done more recently about the island were less compelling. He was plainly losing track of his plot, perhaps losing interest." The island of "Saint Trinity" is a parallel-universe Caribbean place with a culture similar to Haiti's.

Janice "hoped that it would be a novel about a marriage." She was convinced by Ahearn's relationship with his wife (which derived from the preexisting short story). "When Michael slips into an affair, it's written as almost inevitable." Bob was hooked on a Haiti connection: "he still wanted to send Michael to the Island. He didn't call it Haiti. Why not? I asked him. Because Haiti is a real place, he explained. It has a real history. I can't just make things up about it." Although I didn't know of Janice's opinion then, I shared it, and was also trying to persuade Bob to use a real Haitian setting.

Janice, well used to supervising continuity in Bob's fiction, "put the best chapters in order. You have to read this, I told him. He didn't want to. I really had to push him. This is such a good start, I said. Finally he consented to read the somewhat shorter manuscript. I'd set aside probably almost half of what he had written. After reading what was left, he went back to work."

As always, there were distractions. Bob accepted an invitation from Dan Halpern to write an introduction to the Ecco Press edition of Paul Bowles's collected stories. Bob had mixed feelings about Bowles but "wanted to keep Dan happy. He still had a novel to finish for Houghton Mifflin. He had barely made a start on the memoir," although he had been mining the memories of Vic Lovell, Ken Kesey, and other friends from those days, while Janice unearthed memorabilia from the Stones' various residences and storage units. "The substantial advance from Ecco Press was supporting us as Bob wrote a different book." The monthly payments from the Houghton Mifflin contract would run out in June, and it would require a superhuman effort for Bob to meet the June 1 deadline for the novel that had morphed into *Bay of Souls.*

13
WORKING THROUGH PAIN

Bob's prescription narcotic habit had muted his pain for years, and with the pain pills temporarily out of the mix, "2001 may have been the all-time worst year for back pain, and that undermined his staying sober." Soon enough, though, the Key West doctor who was giving him steroid treatments also began prescribing pain medication, plus Ambien for sleep. Ambien, all by itself, can make some users behave like sleepwalkers in their waking lives. This symptom spiked at a panel Bob was on at the University of Miami. "It was as if quaaludes had returned," Janice thought. "I thought the Miami panel was a disaster, but Bob didn't seem to notice."

Bob's pain was real, sometimes real enough to become almost his only reality. "We were always having to leave parties and dinners early that winter, so that he could lie down. Convergences of different ailments could make matters much, much worse." On February 15: "Bob woke up with gout again this morning. Bad luck, on top of his back pain. The plagues of Job strike again."

Bob was fighting it, not only with drugs. He worked on the novel through the pain (indeed, much of the flavor of the finished work is filtered through pain's dark glass). In February, he started physical therapy with Bill Yankee, a personal trainer who served many of Key West's artistic and literary snowbirds. He sought advice from several fellow-suffering friends, including Philip Roth, who reported a reasonably happy result from a back surgery in New York. Bob considered surgery but never went through with it.

Janice, meanwhile, was having possibly the most hectic year of her life, not only because of Bob's woes and efforts to palliate them but also because of more extraordinary transformations in the Stones' living and real estate situation. Pain was certainly a factor in Bob's difficulty concentrating on his work in Key West—much as he struggled to surpass it. But he also needed a better workspace than their Truman Annex condo afforded.

Prices in Key West were soaring; in April the Stones accepted $340,000 for their condo, which Janice had had refurbished for the sale. On June 8 the Stones signed a contract to buy a house at 1523 Laird Street, in the Key West neighborhood of New Town. Almost immediately Janice rushed to New Haven, to orchestrate the move to an apartment they had found in Sheffield, Massachusetts—a pleasant rural location that would give Bob an easier commute on his teaching days at Yale. For Janice the two moves produced "endless work, putting books in storage space. . . . Bob spilled beer on his computer."

Bob continued as restless as ever, despite or because of drastically decreased mobility. His back pain was sometimes so severe that he had to spend the day in bed, and his breathing problems were becoming more difficult to ignore. Their building on Lexington Avenue was atop steep Carnegie Hill. When Beth and I called on the Stones in May, we went down the slope to a Third Avenue restaurant, after which Bob had real difficulty climbing back up, though he wanted to brush off assistance. He was grimly humorous about this problem, telling friends, "I'm finding lots of hills that didn't use to be there."

Bob still regretted losing the Westport house, somewhat unreasonably from Janice's point of view. "He complained so much I finally called him on it. I reminded him that we needed to sell the Westport house in order to buy the New York apartment, which was his idea." Janice was really not interested in one more move, in a year in which she was already managing two moves at once, but by way of a thought experiment she proposed that they could, in fact, sell one of their three properties (two very recently acquired) in order to return to Westport.

"I didn't think moving would really change anything. It would just put us in another location, but it would still be just ourselves again, the two of us—him with back pain, me tired and cranky. But if that was what he wanted, I would do it. As far as I was concerned, I said I didn't much care where we lived. Wherever *he* was, that was my home."

———

Bob was seeing so many doctors that spring, in both New York and New Haven, that the constant cycle of appointments was wearing him out. He tried "to get his thoughts together by taking a trip to Block Island with Ian. It didn't work out. He felt too bad to stay." In fact he had a big quarrel with Ian, from which both of them retreated, considerably rattled. Ian, whose marriage was breaking up at the time, wrote Bob a couple of letters afterward, whose insight and clarity of expression many professional writers might envy.

Epidural steroid injections helped the physical pain temporarily, enabling Bob to make the house-buying trip to Key West, and to fly to Las Vegas for an event staged by the Mandalay Bay Foundation, and to attend a concert by Terence Blanchard at the Village Vanguard, in the company of Tobias Wolff and his sons. Lucky patients may see their pain disappear permanently after a couple of these shots, but for many the good effects wear off in a few weeks, and Bob fell into the latter group. He was trying to maintain the physical therapy routine he'd begun in Key West, but this effort brought only limited relief.

Again, Bob was getting painkiller prescriptions from several different doctors and exceeding the recommended dosage (this opinion depended on which doctor was looking, and of course it was unlikely that any one doctor would know the whole story). When pain didn't interfere with his writing, his prescription cocktail, which also included antidepressants and Ambien, did. Bob was aware of this problem and worried about it, though he tried to keep the worry to himself. A doctor concerned about his pain-pill consumption referred him to an addiction specialist who "believed some people require opiates to live a normal life." In fact, in countries not prosecuting a war on drugs in the style of the United States, many addicts do live normal lives on a maintenance dose of narcotics. The specialist prescribed morphine sulfate, at a dosage Bob's other doctors thought excessively high. In the midst of this confusion, a friend of a Westport friend suggested a fentanyl patch, but Bob decided not to try it—perhaps for the best, as fentanyl soon emerged as a street drug more deadly than heroin.

14
9/11 AND AFTER

In the midst of this Job-like onslaught of suffering both mental and physical, Houghton's June 1 delivery deadline came and went, but Bob did manage to move the chains on his novel during this period. On September 8, he finished a first draft. By then the Stones had settled into a new term-time routine. On class days, if the ride to Sheffield seemed too long, they could spend a night or two in June Chapman's apartment in Stratford, if she was not there, or stay in a New Haven hotel. Then there were long weekends in the city. "But we were in the Sheffield apartment on September 11 as the World Trade Center fell. It was a teaching day for Bob, so we drove to New Haven. As I recall, his class did meet, while I went to the building designated for blood donations. There was no one there—everyone had left. There were so few survivors of the attack that they didn't need the blood. We stayed at the Omni that night, and then commuted from Sheffield to New Haven for two or three weeks, avoiding the police security checks at New York City's bridges."

The millennial explosion that *Damascus Gate* had predicted for Jerusalem had come a year late, to New York instead. It was a catastrophe still more immense than Bob, in the novel, had imagined, and it angered him for a long time afterward. "When I asked him some months after 9/11 whether we should go downtown to view the damage, the great hole in the ground, he became immediately angry. 'I'll go see it when it's in Mecca,' he snarled. We never did go see it."

His written response, a contribution to a *New York Times Magazine* special section, "The Way We Live Now: 9-23-01: Close Reading: Elements of Tragedy," was very much more measured. Bob elected not to treat the attackers as exemplars of pure villainy, which was a distinctly daring decision—less than two weeks after the event. "Though we are being judged," he wrote, "despite our grief and loss, we cannot really judge. We are steeped in relativism, as confined by our narrative as the murderers are confined by theirs. History is a story we have accepted; our lives are the stories we tell ourselves. . . ."

He gave a few examples of ways in which Judeo-Christian peoples have interpreted current events as fulfillment of prophecy. Then: "So in the Muslim world the sacred historical destiny of Islam is reasserted. The will of God is to be done on earth. One narrative continued in the Koran speaks of the people of Ad: 'Their sin is arrogance,' the book says. 'The people of Ad rely on their power and their material wealth to prevail in the world. They will be brought low.' " It would not have been difficult to apply this description to the United States, though Bob was cautious enough not to do so explicitly.

During the *Damascus Gate* period, Bob liked to talk about "the People of the Book," a term of Islamic origin that embraces Christians and Jews as well as Muslims. Times of such crisis as 9/11 tend to return people to their core beliefs; Bob's one unambiguous conviction was that human essence absolutely *is* the story we tell ourselves. "The internal narrative of our enemies, their absolute ruthless devotion to an invisible world, makes them strong. Our system too is a state of mind. We need to find in it the elements that will serve our actual survival."

———

Exhorted by President George W. Bush to return to shopping, the people of America soon did so. Deeply shocked as the nation had been, the national state of mind did not profoundly change. Life went on, as did less dramatic deaths. "In November we were on Block Island when Jane Burton phoned to tell us that Ken Kesey, who had cancer, had died not long after an operation to remove part of his liver. Bob wrote a letter to Faye, but he couldn't take time off from teaching to fly to Oregon for the funeral," and doubtless was in no condition to withstand a transcontinental flight. "It seemed to be the end of an era. We had known Ken since 1962."

At the moment of Kesey's death, Bob was reliving that era in memory, in service of the memoir he was soon to begin writing for Ecco Press. Ed McClanahan called later in November with a report on the funeral Bob had been unable to attend. In February 2002, Bob took part in a tribute to Kesey at the 92nd Street Y, alongside Ed McClanahan and Tom Wolfe.

Speaking off the cuff, at a moment when he was much concerned with having been a poor steward of his own talent, he offered explanations as to why Kesey had not written more significant fiction, after his spectacular first two novels.

Kesey "was not, I think, enough of an individualist by nature to want to be a novelist. I think he had preferred acting, in starting out, and I think he disliked the loneliness and the isolation of the writer's life. I think he was determined, somehow, to make it all happen faster, for everybody." Thus he had quite deliberately chosen a different path: "I think he tried somehow to short circuit the necessities of art. I think he believed that he could somehow invent a spiritual technology, an applied spiritual technology, somewhere between Silva mind control and the transistor, that would spare all the humiliating labor that went into the creating of art. I think he somehow thought that a lot of basic metaphysical mistakes had been made about the world, and that they could be righted."

Bob, by deep vocation, was a representational artist; Kesey, by contrast, wanted to make things happen directly in the world. His defining narrative, Bob proposed, "was both a Calvinist moral story and a science fiction story . . . those were elements that made up his life. But when you set forth with him, and when you went out with him—he always had this sense of doing something like *setting forth*, you didn't just go somewhere, you *set forth*. And it was as though we were out to resolve whatever had been overlooked between where we were and where we ought to be. I never knew anyone in my life, then or since, who was a dreamer on that scale, who really believed in possibility—the great American bugbear of possibility—to the degree that Kesey did." The evolving image of Kesey as "the prince of possibility" was feeding into Bob's portrait of him in *Prime Green*.

Janice's father had died on February 9. The Stones flew from Key West to New York for the funeral and for the Kesey tribute at the 92nd Street Y. Janice returned sooner, to receive a group of grandchildren in Key West, but Bob remained in the city to perform a couple of readings and to consult a lung specialist in the last days of his stay.

Laird Street was fully up and running by the time Bob returned to the Keys at the end of the month. The place had a generous open floor plan—dining room, kitchen, a pleasant living room overlooking the pool—plus three bedrooms and a workspace for Bob. It was an expansive change from the cramped quarters of the Truman Annex condo. And the pool was large enough for Bob to swim without feeling confined, whenever he didn't want to travel to the beaches.

The Stones stayed in Key West through the first week of June. Bob turned in his short story "Fun with Problems" to Bill Buford at *The New Yorker*, and dug into the overhaul of the novel. His back trouble had abated a good deal (regular swimming must have helped) but he had a couple of gout attacks, plus in April: "Bob has arthritis in his hands—it's getting hard for him to type. One problem after another. The plagues of Job."

In the first week of June, Bob was still adding new sections to the book, Janice printing and proofreading as he went along. The JACMEL file names had morphed to ESME—for "Esmerelda," a working title that evoked both the magical/mystical qualities of the female lead and, through slant rhyme, the emeralds that are part of the novel's thriller plotline. The Stones got back to New York on June 10, and Bob dove into work the next day. The book was just slightly more than one year late, which for Robert Stone was not an extravagant delay. As he and Janice put finishing touches on the manuscript, Bob thought of a new title, *Bay of Souls*, for the first time. The title embraced the broad harbor of Cap Haïtien, which Bob had been able to contemplate at leisure from the terraces of the Mont Joli, and the Vodou concept that the souls of the dead are gathered in Ginen anba Dlo—Africa Beneath the Waters.

On June 29, the Stones printed four copies, one for themselves, one for Neil Olson, one for the Houghton editor Janet Silver, and one for me. Always meticulous with verisimilitude, Bob used many experts for the various special subjects he portrayed. I had become his expert on Haiti, and Haitian religion in particular.

15
BAY OF SOULS

Bob and I had continued to discuss his hesitancy to invade (as he saw it) my Haitian territory. That compunction may have had something to do with his decision to create an entirely fictional Saint Trinity, though it's also true that a similar tactic had worked perfectly in *A Flag for Sunrise*. For further reassurance I had sent him a story of mine, "Top of the World," in which a Stone-like character is found in Haiti—pursuant to the *I'll let you be in my dream if I can be in yours* arrangement I had proposed. I didn't find myself in the *Bay of Souls* manuscript I received in the summer of 2002, which might simply have proved my contention that, more often than not, real people find themselves in fictional characters only when the writer intended no such thing.

"Jesus," Bob wrote in his cover note, "the end (but not really as you know) of three or four years of slavery to this thing." And a bit later, "I very much hope you will find this worthy. I've never sent a manuscript to another writer before, you're among the first to see it in the light of day."

To say I was bowled over by those last two sentences is a howling understatement. "Nobody imagines getting a letter like that from the living writer they most admire," I swiftly replied. At the time I had not much clue to the anxiety Bob was apt to feel about his finished work: It seemed unlikely for a writer who'd been turning in near-impeccable masterpieces for the past four decades. I did know that he had been generally depressed and anxious for the past several months, and sympathized in part because I'd been having similar problems during that time. The winter of 2002 had been exceptionally cold and dark for many in America, with the country still bleeding from its worst war wounds since Pearl Harbor, the anthrax poisonings, the shaky economy, the new terrors promised by the War on Terror in itself.

Then I sat down and read the novel, I think all in one burst. The night I finished it, I had, as I wrote to Bob, "one of those incredibly overpowering dreams of the kind that I usually only have when just back from Haiti. The key image was going down that column of light with the fish in it, when Michael is diving for the wrecked plane, and the soundtrack was 'Wete mò anba dlo'—just imagine that chanted with appropriate drumming." Bob had, I think without consciously knowing it, created in that dive scene a gorgeous image for the rite of bringing the dead back from beneath the waters—that is, from the undersea parallel universe which is the Vodou afterlife.

———

Neil Olson and Janet Silver, now Bob's editor at Houghton, had both come back with happy reactions to the novel, and not too onerous suggestions for a final revision. Even so, Bob kept worrying, more than usual, about the quality of the work. On the eve of publication, he reported a slight case of the vapors. "Well, I'm filled with fears of all sorts," he wrote to me, "trying to get my old confidence back, the old casual confidence of the hand, Yeats said. He put it better." I thought of the Psalm: "If I forget thee, O Jerusalem, let my right hand forget her cunning," and I'll bet Bob was thinking of that too. "You really do lose your nerve somewhat as you get older," he went on, "especially if you don't take care of yourself, keep in shape, etc. Take the word of an old scribbler."

Ghede is a Haitian spirit imported from Africa to represent both Eros and Thanatos; he has numerous personae, including Baron Samedi and Baron Cimitière, these two closely involved with graveyards and the rites of interment. To publicize *Bay of Souls*, Bob let *Entertainment Weekly* talk him into posing as Baron Samedi for a photo spread. It was probably not a good idea for an apprehensive unbeliever who'd recently had some very close brushes with death. The picture looked silly (as compared to the official jacket photo for the book, which was genuinely frightening), and (coupled with the headline "The Strange Voodoo of Robert Stone") was calculated to irritate people on the Haiti beat who might have been sympathetic to the novel, including Amy Wilentz (the author of *The Rainy Season*, a nonfiction work covering the background to Aristide's rise to notoriety and power at the end of the 1980s), who might have trashed it anyway, though previously her attitude toward Stone and his work had been worshipful.

Bay of Souls was Stone's first (and last) critical failure. The extraordinary achievements of his previous work might have raised expectations unreasonably high. The bad reviews had a tone of embittered disappointment, especially Wilentz's in the *Los Angeles Times*, which denounced the book as "a parody of a Robert Stone novel." Wilentz did take pains to acknowledge Stone's high ambition for the book, and the magnificence of his prior oeuvre. She singled out certain passages of *Bay of Souls* (all of them drawn from the non-Caribbean plotline) for sincere praise. But her conclusion was a complaint: "*Bay of Souls* addresses these eternal mysteries, but it doesn't push our understanding forward." Other pans, like Michiko Kakutani's in *The New York Times*, were unambivalently vicious: "embarrassing," she called the book, "a bad pastiche of Mr. Stone's own earlier fiction—a hodgepodge of characters, situations and themes cut and pasted together from his previous novels." Among major U.S. venues, only *The New York Times Book Review*, in the person of Norman Rush, approved of the book; Rush's essay focused on the novel's philosophical subtext rather than the plot, concluding that *Bay of Souls* moves a reader to look back on Stone's previous books "with a different sense of their burdens."

Hindsight suggests that Robert Stone's worst novel is still better than most of his contemporaries' best. *Bay of Souls* suffered especially from comparison to *A Flag for Sunrise*, his previous excursion into the Caribbean region, and an indubitable masterpiece. Certainly, *Bay of Souls* is less seamlessly finished than Stone's other novels. The circumstances of its composition were less than ideal; in the midst of the writing his health had hit its lowest point ever until his death a dozen years later, and also his marriage had come closer to fracturing than it ever had, or would.

Bay of Souls has its firmest footing in its Great Plains setting, "a little corner of nothing much," disparaged by protagonist Michael Ahearn as "Flyoverland." Like Holliwell in *A Flag for Sunrise*, Ahearn is one of Stone's slant self-portraits, a person of great intelligence and capacity whose inner life exceeds his outer one by a very wide margin. Ahearn is mildly disaffected from his job as a college professor of English and writing, but he's more or less happily married to Kristin, a native of the region descended from "prairie sodbusters," and a reasonably successful father to twelve-year-old Paul, their only child.

His employment at the college in their small town of Fort Salines has a time-serving quality that reflects, amusingly, Stone's own limited engagement with teaching. Ahearn can't always restrain himself from reacting to the mediocrity of student fiction and the self-congratulatory style of its discussion among the authors: "The personal needs and available life choices of these thin conceits were examined as though they were guests on the kind of television talk show whose participants murdered each other." After one of Ahearn's irritable outbursts, "The class sullenly dispersed ahead of schedule. He had failed to make himself clear. They had understood only that their youthful goodwill was being insulted. He had used abusive language. He had employed sarcasm. He had better watch it."

For a touch of spice, Ahearn has his beautiful student assistant Phyllis Strom, rumored to have once "posed for a *Playboy* spread, 'The Girls of the Big Ten.'" Despite Kristin's jealousy, Phyllis is now "a model of industry, modesty, sobriety and decorum"; moreover, "the new and rigidly enforced regulations required chastity in student-faculty collaborations," so Ahearn's attraction to Phyllis will never be consummated. He can honestly declare to Kristin that he would never "risk what we have for a little kid like Phyllis." Still, Ahearn is almost desperately "bored with pondering the etiology of his own hard-ons, his own insights, literary and otherwise. Bored with introspection." His whole situation cries out for some kind of radical disruption.

Approaching the downhill side of middle age, Ahearn is prey to episodes of existential dread, forever "trying to outrun the shadow inside him." Something lurks beneath the surface of his relatively tranquil life. "Perhaps the trouble was not pretty Phyllis but something else, something Kristin herself might not understand. The thought frightened him." His academic specialty is the strand of American vitalism to which *Bay of Souls* itself is assimilated in the Norman Rush review—Norris, Dreiser, Chopin, Cabell—but those well-worn books no longer vitalize him as they used to. Like Stone, Ahearn is a person with broad knowledge of religion but no faith. To him, Kristin's stern and wintry Lutheran background is a matter of anthropological interest. They send the adolescent Paul to a Catholic school, St. Emmerich's, "which meant laughing away the horror stories they liked to tell about their own religious education in the hope of winning a few apparent certainties for the next generation." Occasionally attending Mass, Ahearn suffers the internal writhings of an uncomfortably lapsed Catholic, "at the point of trembling, burning with shame and self-despising rage. The church that taught humiliation as a blessing was providing him all the humiliation he could bear."

Ahearn hunts deer, half-heartedly, going along to enjoy a walk in the woods and the company of men. He carries a loaded gun but seldom fires it. If an eligible deer appears he "would take his shot with the rest of them. He had never claimed one." This image of under-commitment is indelible and, at the end of the deer-hunting episode that opens the book, is soundly punished. During Ahearn's absence, Paul wanders out in the snow in search of a lost dog and ends up in the hospital near death from hypothermia. Doctors deem his chances poor, and Ahearn and Kristin spend hours of agony awaiting an outcome, wracked by terror and guilt over their possible, though ambiguous, negligence. Ahearn is particularly tormented by the idea that his own lukewarm attitude to everything might somehow have engendered the death of his son.

Paul's survival seems a miracle in the secular terms now normally used. For Ahearn, the resonance is more complicated: "Michael had been afraid, for a while, that there was something out there, at the beginning and end of consciousness. An alpha and omega to things. He had believed it for years on and off. And that night, he had felt certain, the fire would be visited on him. His boy would be taken away from him and he would know, know absolutely, the power of the most high . . . But now his son's life was saved. And the great thing had come of nothing, of absolutely nothing, out of a kaleidoscope, out of a Cracker Jack box. Every day its own flower, to every day its own stink and savor. Good old random singularity and you could exercise a proper revulsion for life's rank overabundance and everybody could have their rights and be happy."

Another writer could easily have milked a whole novel out of this amount of event and interpretation, concluding: "No one watched over us. Or rather we watched over each other. That was providence, what a relief." "Dominion," the short story, had ended on such a note. But in *Bay of Souls* this insight comes a scant thirty pages in. It constitutes the status quo ante, the baseline from which the rest of the narrative springs.

———

For Ahearn, Paul's brush with death only confirms the banality of his situation, where he "could be a serious person, a grown-up at last, and not worry about things that educated people had not troubled themselves with practically for centuries. Free at last and it didn't mean a thing and it would all be over, some things sooner rather than later." Radical disruption is brought to him by Lara Purcell, a character who shares with the real-life Melisandra a taste for fast horses and challenging men, a grand sense of entitlement expressed in a manner both charming and imperious, and large appetites with a strong determination to be satisfied. Lara is on the faculty of Ahearn's college; they first meet because "pretty Phyllis" wants Lara to serve on her thesis committee. The campus community is large enough for Ahearn and Lara not to have run into each other before but small enough for him to soon be advised, by his colleague and deer-hunting buddy Norman Cevic, of her local reputation as a femme fatale.

Composed in a period when Stone's health, both physical and emotional, had bottomed out, Lara's background is rather hastily executed. She hails from Saint Trinity, a dot of an imaginary Caribbean island with a baroque history no more incredible than some of the real ones. The fictional Saint Trinity received, in the late eighteenth century, an influx of French planters (with their slaves) fleeing the Haitian Revolution, an event that imparts a strong Haitian flavor to Saint Trinity's culture and religion.

Lara's family operates a hotel in a neighborhood resembling the Carenage of Cap Haïtien. The Purcells look European but have a drop of African blood from their Haitian ancestors; Lara and her brother practice the local variation of Vodou. Thanks to her American mother, Lara has dual citizenship, but she spent her childhood on the island, going to school in a Marist convent and later teaching there. She married a French Creole and went with him to Paris, where she studied at the Sorbonne. She and her husband then became small-time spooks run by Desmond Jenkins, "the wizard of influence agentry in the Third World and the United Nations" for "the socialist bloc." They pursued this career in Africa for a time. "Then she and her husband had changed sides and been bartered by the French services to the Triptelemos brigade"—Triptelemos being the nom de guerre of an originally Argentine thug with political/criminal interests all over the Caribbean, including Saint Trinity and the Purcells' hotel. Somewhere along the way the CIA has acquired a hold on Lara too, though to what purpose is never quite clear.

How does such a person end up teaching political science in an obscure university in "Flyoverland"? Well, as Norman Cevic and Ahearn explain to each other for the reader's convenience, the faculty once harbored a little nest of spy recruiters under the leadership of a legendary scholar/Cold Warrior called Nicholas Ridenhour. In latter days the university has become somewhere "you can place the casualties, the burnouts, the Men Who Know Too Much." Thus Lara, now divorced from her French husband and passing for a transnational academic courtesan in tiny Fort Salines.

Reviewers' accusations of self-parody found traction in this exposition. The international intrigues of *Damascus Gate* and *A Flag for Sunrise* might not be so much more substantial if it were possible to boil them down to bare facts, but in those cases Stone suggested them in a multilayered chiaroscuro so dense that a reader could not help but believe there must be fire underneath all the smoke. In *Bay of Souls*, a much shorter book, this material seems barely sketched in.

Stone captures the background detail of the Fort Salines region with a lot more conviction—if Michael Ahearn is a more convincing character than Lara, so too is his world more soundly constructed than hers. Stone's deep sense of American history serves him well in his rendition of the prairie at the turn of the twenty-first century, with its long descent of Germans and Slavs and Scots-Irish, the Lutheran sodbusters of Kristin's ancestry and a current population of Hmong refugees from the Vietnam War (recognizable to Ahearn and his fellow deer hunters by their habit of trailing their rifles by the barrel as they move through the woods), with its Catholic churches and various Protestant sects and cults that have struggled for a couple of centuries to beat back the dark. In this fertile milieu, Ahearn stands out as a character fully sculpted in the round, while Lara's characterization demands a more arduous suspension of disbelief.

Ahearn's love passages with Lara also proved easy to lampoon, although these scenes (bearing in mind that any erotic moment can be punctured by mockery) deserve to be read with an unjaundiced eye. The ignition of the spark between them, during apparently innocuous squash and racquetball games, is managed handily. After one such session, Ahearn, hanging Lara's fur in a sports bar, "could feel the warmth of her body against the coat's silk lining." Later, "the feel of her body took his strength away gram by gram." Stone's rendering of peripheral sensuous detail can also be quite powerful: "It was an odd little instrument, the strap. It had no buckle and apparently no holes to insert a metal tongue." Along with erotic strangulation, Lara likes to play in bed with a loaded gun. There's a little silliness in it all, but not too much, and Lara's cocktail of Eros and Thanatos stuns Ahearn like a cow in the slaughterhouse.

Like a good many men, artists or not, Stone liked to go out with ravishing women who were some kind of crazy, but preferred to go home to somebody sane. With the possible exception of Pablo Picasso, this pattern of behavior is not sustainable for anyone in the long term. Ahearn, who wouldn't dream of throwing his marriage away for Phyllis, knows full well how much he is risking for Lara. The element of self-destruction is part of the thanatoptic appeal. And Ahearn really does love Kristin (his one sex scene with her, though devoid of any special equipment or transgressive playacting, is the best in the book). He loves his son even more desperately. Even in the depths of his intoxication by Lara, the chain of that anchor pulls at him:

"In the darkness before his son's room he felt the vertigo of the shifting world. Stop, he thought. Go back. To the sweet order that had prevailed when life was innocent and carefree. Standing there, he could almost believe that things had been that way. Of course there was still time."

In his critique of "literary vitalism" (specifically contemplating Kate Chopin's *The Awakening*), Ahearn concludes that "solitary acts of personal liberation were what everyone must be spared or forbidden." His pursuit of Lara, however, is driven by a similar vitalist urge—and yet at the same time manages to be lukewarm and oddly fainthearted. He goes after Lara in the same style that he goes in the woods with a loaded gun he doesn't really intend to fire, passively setting himself up for a moment when consequences will become inevitable, overwhelming his lack of intention.

Stone's previous novels are structured on a convergence pattern, in which two or three clusters of characters begin the story with no knowledge of each other, and gradually accelerate their movement toward a climactic encounter. In *Bay of Souls*, Lara and Ahearn have to separate in order to reconverge, and here the structural machine doesn't quite run smoothly. The first shift into Lara's point of view, as she attends a faculty party reluctantly hosted by the Ahearns, feels like a bit of a lurch, though her appraisal of her rival Kristin ("a lofty, steel-eyed bitch") is tasty. In the Fort Salines faculty community, Lara operates with well-practiced Machiavellianism, fully in control of herself and taking a shrewd pleasure in manipulating others, but the closer she gets to the orbit of Saint Trinity, the more her consciousness begins to slip.

At Lara's suggestion, Ahearn has invented a dive trip as a pretext to rendezvous with Lara on her home island. They meet as planned in Puerto Rico, but flight cancelations out of San Juan force them to make the next leg of the journey separately. This device actually drains energy from the plot, since Ahearn, a stranger in a strange land once he reaches Saint Trinity, doesn't have much to do except hang around the hotel and wait for something to happen. (For these scenes, I fear, Bob drew on those evenings he finished alone at the Mont Joli while I was at the Morne Calvaire ceremonies.) Lara, meanwhile, has so many fish to fry that she might prefer to have a little time alone. Her brother John-Paul has died of AIDS the year before, and she's going to Saint Trinity to shut down the family hotel—which, however, is a linchpin in local politics, crime, and broader-based espionage. The Triptelemos brigade has an interest and expects to be paid off. The American intelligence agencies are interested too. On top of all that there's a touch of emerald smuggling and Saint Trinity is in the midst of a wee civil war, in which the American-backed Colonel Eustace Junot is challenging the junta currently in power.

But the spiritual side of the question matters more to Lara, as eventually it does to Ahearn too. She is planning to complete a Vodou ceremony for her brother, as she explains to Ahearn in San Juan: "the soul of people who died the year before are taken to a place under the sea called Guinée. After a year or so the souls are brought back from the sea. That's what our ceremony is for."

Marinette, who presides over Lara's family rite, is usually portrayed as an angry, vengeful spirit with skeletal twisted limbs, a member of the violent Petro pantheon, sometimes associated with the animal sacrifice at the 1791 ceremony where the Haitian Revolution was launched. The conceit of the novel is that Lara's brother, a person of "special powers" who "could do wicked things," gave her soul into the custody of Marinette. "I belong she," Lara tells Ahearn, slipping into Saint Trinity patois. "She began the killing. She drew the first French blood." Recovery of her soul is part of the mission. "I have to ask John-Paul to give it back when we take his *ti bon ange*, his soul, from Guinée."

From this point on, the part of the story taking place in ordinary space-time stops making very much sense at all. A plane carrying mysterious cargo from the Purcell hotel goes down just off the island, and Ahearn (rather improbably, as many reviewers complained) is drafted to make a night dive for the payload, under pressure from a posse of Colombian enforcers representing the Triptemelos brigade. In the background, Junot's military takeover plays out, with echoes of the Grenada invasion during the Reagan era—and an oddly prescient resonance with events that actually did happen in Haiti in 2004, a year after the book's publication. There's commentary furnished by Liz McKie, a venal American journalist; Stone normally excelled at this kind of characterization, here carried out somewhat perfunctorily. That Ahearn only recovers two out of three cases from the sunken plane causes a less than fatal "unpleasantness." At the long Vodou ceremony for her brother and herself, Lara, from Ahearn's point of view at least, appears to lose her mind.

Among Stone's retinue of luminous madwomen the closest to Lara is

Lee Verger/Lu Anne Bourgeois in *Children of Light*. Probably a schizo-phrenic, Lu Anne hears voices and sees apparitions from time to time. She is for the most part alone with this condition. Lara Purcell has a com-munity to receive her and a religious set and setting where her symptoms make sense—or maybe the religion has it right and Lara's paranormal experiences are the very truth. As Dostoyevsky would have done, Stone leaves this point for the reader to decide.

"Now that she had seen the temple at the lodge again, the *govi* jars in which the spirits were conveyed, she could not get the pictures out of her mind. She thought of her own soul, larvalike, breathing to the undersea rhythms. To meet one's soul again, what would that be like? She imagined it as a kind of judgment. I see myself in the mirror but my thoughts throw no reflection. My words cast no shadows, she thought. She imagined her present self as composed of two dimensions: an agent of influence, a pro-fessor of lies. Tomorrow she would be her former self, whoever that had been. Her eyes would change." Here is Stone's most successful imagining of how Vodouisant belief might organize the inner life.

Of Michael Ahearn, Lara thinks, "Because his situation was so like hers, the two of them together were no accident." This point may not be obvious until it is stated. But indeed, some sort of spiritual lack has punched a hole in the being of both characters. For Lara, religion offers a solution; she at least believes that she knows what to do. Ahearn, as usual, is clueless, if faithless wouldn't be a better word. His intellectual skepti-cism has drained all possible solutions of their potency.

———

On the material plane, the novel's denouement has Kristin find Lara's boarding pass along with Ahearn's, an event faithfully drawn from real life—except that Bob and Janice reconciled and stayed together, while Mi-chael and Kristin Ahearn don't. "Conniving son of a bitch," Kristin tells him. "You do not maintain a mistress on me, fella. Maybe your pals will think you're a sport. But I don't think you're a sport, I think you're weak."

Much earlier, Ahearn has rebuked Lara for mocking Kristin: "I don't like it when you demean people I love." By the same token, the wiser plan is not to portray people one loves in one's fiction. Janice-like figures in Stone's work are likely to remain offstage, or almost offstage, though they can still exert considerable influence from that position.

"He's ruled by a strong woman," Norman Cevic says to Lara, trying to explain Ahearn's situation. "She's good for him. He's a lucky man." Without Lara, whom Ahearn understands he has permanently lost by running away when the ceremony is disrupted by gunfire, "he would live a life suspended on the quivering air, the beat of loss, moment by moment." Without Kristin, he has to live without his good luck and without anything much left at all—Ahearn's arid, purgatorial situation at the end of this story is as good as anything Stone ever wrote.

Kristin drops on her soon-to-be ex this way: "Do you think I came to you with no dreams of my own? That all I wanted to do is plant roses? But finally I gave you everything. And everything involved you. Oh yes, I thought you were hot shit, fucker! I thought you were the beginning and the end and nobody really knew how great you were but me."

This dialogue has the ring of reality.

"I wanted more," Ahearn dares to tell her (life more abundant rearing its head once again). Previously, Stone has subtly laid in the evidence that Ahearn could have had all he wanted from Kristin, even on the spiritual side. The back-country Lutheranism of her raising has primal power enough to compete with the mysterious potential of Lara's island Vodou. Kristin is Ahearn's intellectual peer, whose "upscale Bible study group" reads Calvin alongside patristic literature in the original Greek. Better yet, she has faith enough to draw solace (or at least some sort of shimmering energy) from reading the Bible aloud when Paul is hospitalized with hypothermia. Even her beauty has a numinous quality: "like the Christus on a Viking crucifix." If he would accept it, Kristin could meet every last one of Ahearn's needs. The perversity of his refusal is the real subject of *Bay of Souls*.

———·———

For the faithless, resurrection is expressed in decaying flesh; there simply isn't another option. In Stone's world, this reality is not a recommendation for faith. As Bob told Robert Birnbaum (around the time *Bay of Souls* was published, in fact), "I think we go without it, we go with this longing and with this kind of half hallucination that we are seeing it out there. We want it to be there." Even though it's not.

In the opening sequence, as the deer hunters set out by canoe at dawn, Ahearn drops a flashlight in the stream, where it rests "on the bottom, seven, maybe eight feet below," too deep to be retrieved. The impression of this sunken light works into the crevices of Ahearn's brain. In his dive for the plane lost off Saint Trinity, the image is reprised: by the plane itself, whose instrument panel offers "a tiny red light" and "a faint green glow." Once underwater, "his light struck a rainbow. Following it with his beam, he saw that the rainbow was rising in a broad column toward the surface. For some reason, the prismatic column was crowded with fish. There were more than he had seen so far: parrotfish, wrasse, tangs and, in great number, angelfish. For some reason the fish were circling, remaining within the colored circumference." Shocked by the discovery that all this beauty is generated by fish feeding on the bloated corpse of the drowned pilot, Ahearn drops a second flashlight. "He had to hurry down after the tumbling illumination while its beam careened over the coral wall, lighting crevices where half-coiled morays darted, lighting pillars of sea snow, the tiny flakes ceaselessly falling."

In Saint Trinity's Vodou, as in its Haitian model, *wete mò nanba dlo* can be understood as a rescue of the soul from death. For Lara, this process seems to work the way it's supposed to. Ahearn gets a perverse inversion of it when the plane, and the corpse, are finally raised by higher authorities. "The surface did not at first hold it down. Whatever it was showed most of its length to the breathing world, then spun. . . . Then Michael realized that the rainbow jelly was oil slick, that the fish and other creatures were eating the creature. He caught a fraction of a second's whiff of foul breeze. It had a kind of face, Michael saw, a head and a body. Both were beyond imagining."

Unspoken, but driving all this imagistic machinery, is Stone's deep descent in the submersible, which for some inarticulate reason served him as a picture of mortality.

———

In *The New York Times Book Review*, Norman Rush defines Ahearn's trajectory as a "real-time vitalist adventure, undertaking a routine of death-teasing performances through which he hopes to win the love of a sexually perfect woman, an alpha female mysteriously but somehow authentically connected to a genuine metaphysical otherness reachable through the ecstatic practices found in voodoo trance ritual." Certainly Ahearn's desire for Lara has such an energy behind it: "In fact he wanted to share a taste of danger with her. To descend as far, to take as much of her as he could survive, and risk even more."

Rush argues that *Bay of Souls* amounts to "a symbolic validation of the vitalist project." Stone himself might not have agreed. "The literature of vitalism," he explains to Birnbaum, represents a process "in which one burns ordinary life for the life more abundant." He never says he thinks that's a good idea.

Élan vital is what carried the pioneers over the next hill; it also engenders chronic dissatisfaction. In a Robert Stone novel, the quest for life more abundant always turns out to be folly. In this way, American dream becomes nightmare.

———

The most successful engagement with Vodou in *Bay of Souls* is the portrayal of Baron Samedi in the climactic ceremony toward the end. When Ahearn hits the bottom of his dive into Eros and Thanatos, Baron, manipulating a wheelbarrow with the sacrificial goat, is there to receive him, perhaps permanently, into "the ranks of death." Ahearn runs from this encounter as fast as his legs will carry him, but he can't actually get away. The Ghede avatar goes with him, prodding constantly at his consciousness, in a sort of rape of the brain. The emigration official at the Saint Trinity airport assumes this guise.

"You got to have your pink form," Baron Samedi said. "Otherwise you can't fly."

Someone intervenes so that Michael can board the plane, but flying doesn't get him anywhere. Having burned his ordinary life, he has no way to reenter it. "You took me to hell," he tells Lara in the final scene, which by the novel's own standards of verisimilitude pretty well has to be a hallucination. "I'm still there."

Not for the first time, Stone had made of his main character an example to avoid.

In Jen Fong's jacket photo for the book, he looks exhausted, depleted, near the end of his rope. The otherworldly glitter of his eyes is still just barely perceptible but drastically weakened. It's the only widely circulated photo in which he looks vulnerable.

No wonder. Stone, like Ahearn, had been to hell. He had come to the edge of losing absolutely everything—not just Janice and his marriage but his very life and breath. Career death was also a possibility, if he had failed to complete the novel with a certain degree of success. *Bay of Souls* might not have been Stone's best work, but he felt, justly, that it was a sort of triumph to have pulled it together as well as he had. That accomplishment represented survival to him, and it also meant that he still had a future. He had hit the bottom of a very deep trench and was beginning the difficult process of resurfacing.

PART EIGHT

DEATH OF THE
BLACK-HAIRED GIRL

1
New Beginnings
and a Multibook Contract

Bob turned sixty-five on August 21, 2002. The Stones were in their New York apartment, "too busy to celebrate much—had filet mignon and mashed potatoes and spinach at home." They were consolidating the editorial revisions of *Bay of Souls* and there was plenty of other work to do—particularly that memoir, due to Ecco Press on December 1. Bob worked on it, but distracted himself with a new short story, plans for his next novel, and a project to produce "Helping" as a play, to be directed by Frank Corsaro if possible, and performed at the 92nd Street Y.

At the end of August, Janice "bought Bob a new briefcase for school so his students will stop looking scornfully at his ratty old (30 years?) one." At any rate, the old briefcase already had some wear on it when it appeared in that 1981 *People* magazine spread. Possibly more to the point, though, was that Bob, having beaten the odds and his own prediction to retirement age, could contemplate leaving teaching now, as Janice had been wanting him to do.

Nevertheless, the Stones fell into their term-time routine in September, rotating among New Haven, Sheffield, and New York. Bob was featured in *The New Yorker* Festival that fall; for the past couple of years he had been signing an annual "first reading agreement" with the magazine. "Fun with Problems" had appeared in the July issue, but Bob read from an earlier story, "Miserere," instead, performing on a double bill with Jhumpa Lahiri at the Bitter End. Beth and I were in the audience, and afterward went with the Stones to a party at Bill Buford's apartment.

Among the luminaries present was Aimee Mann, also participating in the festival. Her songs had an unusual literary bent, and she and I had exchanged a letter on that subject. After I went to speak to her briefly,

Bob inquired, semi–sotto voce, "Is that your connection?" For dope he meant—and the eagerness of the question meant he was looking for one for himself. I excused Aimee Mann from that role and pretended to be sorry I couldn't otherwise oblige. By and large, Bob seemed in pretty good shape that evening, though; he'd given a relaxed performance and was in condition to enjoy himself.

On the eve of *The New Yorker* festival, Bob and Janice dined with Janet Silver and Lori Glazer to talk over promotional plans for *Bay of Souls*, the cover art, jacket photo, and so forth. Bob described to them three new projects he had in mind: a book of stories, a childhood memoir, and a novel inspired by a sensational murder that had happened in New Haven in 1998. That latter part of the conversation wasn't casual. There were great expectations for *Bay of Souls* during this prepublication period, and Silver wanted Bob durably signed to Houghton for his next work or works. His agent, Neil Olson, was angling for a multibook contract.

In 1999, Silver had sent Olson a quite thorny letter, pointing not only to the breach of Houghton's option clause entailed by Bob's deal for a 1960s memoir then in process with Ecco Press but also "the moral obligation to honor a commitment that is as deep as ours in this author's career." Houghton's pockets had been deep in that commitment—$850,000 invested in the expected "Alaska novel." At the time, Silver's displeasure had been extremely understandable, and in settling the issue then, she had firmly underlined the point that the exception to Houghton's option clause granted in favor of the memoir left the clause in force with respect to any *other* future work by Stone.

Three years later, Houghton had its Stone novel in production, and the not yet written Ecco Press memoir threatened no competition with that. The atmosphere had become a lot friendlier. At that late-September dinner, Bob expatiated, with an eloquence few could match, on his plans for future work. By now he was well practiced at spinning yarns about the flamboyant 1998 Yale murder case that would be the core of his next novel. And the childhood memoir was an arresting idea. At that time very few people knew just how close to the edge (and sometimes over it) Bob's childhood had been.

For several decades he had been a distinguished and sometimes best-selling novelist, securely ensconced in academia like most of the breed. His intellect and erudition meant that if he didn't quite fit in among the profs, it was because his mind was quicker and bolder than most of theirs. Before the publication of *Prime Green*, only close friends knew he'd stopped short of halfway to an undergraduate degree. In terms of public information, the most radical thing about him was his association with Kesey and the Pranksters, and even in that case, because Tom Wolfe in *The Electric Kool-Aid Acid Test* had chosen to portray him more as observer than participant, there was a certain distance. Only alums of the Perry Lane scene knew just how complete and enthusiastic Bob's participation had been.

Writers and publishers alike get excited by the telling of secrets. Revelation has incontrovertible power, and the story of Bob's childhood was sure to be a good one. Bob spent October doing preliminary work on the novel and memoir and writing a proposal for the three books, delivering the latter to Neil Olson at the end of the month. To work on the new novel, he would slip out to the library of Bard College at Simon's Rock, not far from the Stones' apartment in Sheffield. In early November, he faxed what amounted to a chapter of the childhood memoir to Neil as well.

This latter piece, oddly enough, had been written on commission for *Architectural Digest* and published in 1996. The occasion was a reminiscent portrait of the Endicott Hotel, where Bob and his mother had spent his middle teens, but it appeared under the title "A New York Childhood," and Bob infused it with more than enough personal detail for it to serve as an excellent showpiece for the projected memoir—of which, unfortunately, he never wrote another word. The strange and marvelous Gladys Grant would be memorialized only in this one nonfiction piece and in her few cameo appearances in Stone novels.

The multibook contract, however, was going to be a go. At the end of November, Olson was calling Bob to consult on "probable delivery dates for the three books he is offering to write for Houghton Mifflin." There was a handshake agreement by the end of the year, and the contract—for a million dollars—was signed in February 2003, with the *Bay of Souls* publication and tour still a few weeks in the future.

In the fall of 2002, the Stones had begun to marshal their resources for retirement. Both of them put in for Social Security benefits. "Not that we were planning to retire"; that is, Bob had no notion of retiring from writing, nor Janice from her various support roles. The evolving plan for the future was more about adjustment of priorities. With *Bay of Souls* wrapped, Bob was generally in better shape, but Janice worried about him, for more than one good reason. "I was just happy that there *was* a book, finally. There had been times in the last few years when I doubted he was well enough, or thinking clearly enough, to finish another novel." In his rush of relief when *Bay of Souls* was accepted, Bob had told me much the same thing. It was scary to hear that from a master craftsman who normally had total control of every aspect of his text, down to the last punctuation mark.

———

Practically speaking, the Stones' most important income stream since *Outerbridge Reach* had come from Bob's book contracts, although his position at Yale was a well-paid gig. Both he and Janice knew, intimately, what it was to be stone-broke, even if they hadn't been in that situation for a long time. Bob continued to scout for ways to make extra money, usually involving travel which might also assuage his eternal restlessness. A reportorial trip to Indonesia interested him but he didn't quite commit. He was likewise tempted by a conference in Italy, but that trip was canceled in the wake of a December visit to the Yale New Haven Hospital emergency room.

A more severe than usual episode of shortness of breath on the Yale campus sent him there. The problem had been building for some time. Bob "had never considered Carnegie Hill to be a hill before this year, but walking in our neighborhood was becoming difficult. And commuting to New Haven twice a week was too much for him." For the latter reason Bob and Janice had been staying over at the New Haven Omni Hotel for Bob's teaching days. Yale New Haven Hospital released him without a conclusive diagnosis on December 5, but Bob was rattled enough to scratch the Italy trip and a few other upcoming commitments. In a follow-up visit to a pulmonologist, he was told he did have emphysema. That diagnosis isn't an absolute death sentence, and it was encouraging that Bob had not smoked cigarettes in several decades. Life expectancies vary, but a doctor is unlikely to tell an emphysema patient that he'll die of something else.

That news, plus writing obligations (including the unfinished memoir for Ecco as well as the three books in the planning stages for Houghton), helped Janice convince him to stop teaching at last. The big Houghton contract gave the Stones confidence for that step. In January, Bob let the Yale officials know that he would not be returning in the fall.

———

The Houghton contract called for UNTITLED NOVEL ("Book I"), UNTITLED MEMOIR ("Book II"), and UNTITLED STORIES ("Book III") to be completed and delivered in that order, though it was tacitly understood, at least by Neil Olson, "that Bob could be working on any number of books at once—as he did—and they would all be under contract!" Book I was due in January 2006, which would give Bob some breathing room, provided he managed to complete the Ecco Press book in reasonably short order. Books II and III were due in 2008 and 2009, respectively. As usual, a large portion of the large advance was structured in monthly payments (contingent on delivery after 2006 when the first book was due); Bob was one of the last few American authors to be, for all practical purposes, retained on salary by his publisher. The February signing date was "just in time," as Olson succinctly put it fifteen years later, "because *Bay of Souls* came out the same year and tanked."

Most of February Bob spent getting a start on the new novel. In March, with publication a month out, the mood was cautiously celebratory. Prepublication reviews had been favorable, and the positive review in *The New York Times Book Review* by Norman Rush came early; faxed to the Stones on March 28, it prompted a good number of congratulatory phone calls. Next day Bob and Janice threw a party, humongous even for them, receiving fifty-odd people from the Key West writer and artist community.

2
STONE ROLLS A LITTLE SLOWER

On the health front, Bob's luck continued, quietly, to wear thin. Although he was not yet using supplementary oxygen, during the April tour he'd had some difficulty finding enough wind to do the necessary speaking. Talk of a *Vanity Fair*–sponsored trip to Indonesia had revived in the summer of 2003. The plan appealed to Bob especially because he would be traveling with the photographer James Nachtwey, whose work he admired, and with whom he'd worked before. They had met for dinner in May to discuss the plan, and Bob was sorely tempted. On the downside, Nachtwey was going to cover a war and was not above getting shot at himself from time to time, while Bob was too short-winded for rapid, lifesaving maneuvers under fire, as he finally had to admit to himself, and to Nachtwey and the *Vanity Fair* editor, David Friend (who'd been Bob's student at Amherst decades earlier).

Instead, Bob and Janice went to Costa Rica in September, on a relatively mellow assignment from the *New York Times* Sophisticated Traveler. Risk was confined to zip-lining over the rain-forest canopy, and a volcano erupting near their hotel: "Rain clouds cleared enough for us to watch as lava flowed down the slope. Bob predicted that it was headed right for our room but I don't think he was actually worried." If Bob got winded climbing trails, Janice "went back to my old trick of getting behind him and pushing, as inconspicuously as I could."

Costa Rica was a good time, but a trip later in the fall proved more nerve-racking. Free of teaching in the fall of 2003, Bob bore down as much as possible on the overdue memoir and also worked on the beginnings of the new novel based on the Yale murder, but he was still eager to accept an invitation to lecture on a transatlantic cruise. Meant to be a profitable pleasure outing for both Stones, the trip's logistics seemed jinxed from the start. "Bob was not in good shape, and neither was I." The Stones flew to Lisbon by way of Paris, where one of their suitcases was lost; the rest of their luggage was left behind in Portugal when they embarked on the *Crystal Serenity*. The bags caught up with them in the Canary Islands, off the coast of Spain, but in the meantime "I had to buy Bob a Tommy Bahama shirt in the ship's store, and a long black skirt for myself, in order to look sufficiently posh."

Bob was addled on the crossing by his medication cocktail, including but perhaps not limited to a maintenance dose of morphine sulfate, Ambien, supplementary pain pills supplied by different doctors, and Seroquel, an antipsychotic that was new in the mix. His bewilderment was such that Janice thought it best for them to stay on board at the ship's intermediate ports of call, in the Canaries and then Nassau. "I don't know how the lectures went. I was too anxious and worried to attend. During one appearance, I sat outside the lecture room, praying. My prayer was that he not make a fool of himself. I thought he was in desperate shape, but he may have done OK. He was used to public appearances. And when he went to the ship's casino, two or three times, he played roulette and emerged each time with hundreds of dollars. Perhaps the Stone luck was going to carry him through."

The *Crystal Serenity* docked in Fort Lauderdale and the Stones headed south to Key West. Thanksgiving was celebrated chez Liz Lear, with Ian (who had recently turned forty) and several other snowbird literati. "I think it was that evening that Bob fell asleep at the table, to my embarrassment and Liz's annoyance. I convinced him to give up the Seroquel."

Nevertheless Bob soon fell asleep at the wheel of their new Honda and rear-ended the car ahead of him—a low-speed accident with not too much damage. The police bought his explanation of brake failure, and wrote him a ticket accordingly, though the shop found nothing wrong with the brakes. There were other mishaps in the winter and spring of 2004. Bob's sciatica came back, and he resumed sessions with trainer Bill Yankee. Despite the physical therapy he took a fall into the Laird Street pool, hurting his leg and breaking an oft-broken elbow one more time.

3

THE BAFFLED KING

On May 1, 2004, the Stones were with Judy Rascoe at their New York apartment when Bob had such a terrible breathing crisis that he was taken by ambulance to Lenox Hill Hospital. Doctors there diagnosed a blocked artery, then performed angioplasty and installed a stent. Before discharge he was warned about the increasing severity of his emphysema and given many new prescriptions, none of which, to his disappointment, proved to have any recreational value.

The stent helped; Bob was released May 5, feeling tired but okay. Incredibly he was determined to keep a West Coast engagement on May 8; he was scheduled to perform, with Calvin Trillin and Mary Karr, in a dramatic reading of Hemingway's correspondence with F. Scott and Zelda Fitzgerald. Janice doubted the wisdom of this trip but "somehow it didn't occur to me to try to talk him out of going. We were always inclined to believe that 'the show must go on.'"

His departure was delayed by multiple errors. Janice went to fetch the car to drive him to LaGuardia. Bob, blurry from a combination of Ambien and whatever new meds he'd brought home from Lenox Hill Hospital, came out to the curb without his plane ticket. The door locked behind him. The doorman was away from his post—a rare situation, so neither

Stone had a front-door key. That problem took time to solve, then Janice got stuck in the wrong lane on the FDR Drive, ended up crossing the wrong bridge, and had to stop, in unfamiliar territory, to ask directions.

They reached the airport twenty minutes before the flight's departure—not half enough time to get through post-9/11 security lines. Janice waited in the car for Bob to reappear, as surely he must, but he didn't, nor did he call her. His cell phone was off. Finally she concluded he must have somehow made the flight, but it didn't feel like much of a win. "I finally drove away, in tears. To distract myself, I turned on the radio, and heard for the first time a song by Leonard Cohen, 'Hallelujah'—but sung by another singer, Jeff Buckley. That song impressed itself on me. 'The baffled king composing Hallelujah'—that was Bob."

Calvin Trillin called the next day to ask what might be the cause of Bob's shaky state. Janice, as best she could from Trillin's description, guessed the problem was Ambien, rather than something potentially fatal gone wrong with Bob's heart or the stent inserted a scant week before. That was guesswork, but she also had to cover for Bob—a new, unpleasant necessity. She told Trillin "that Bob sometimes took more sleep medication than he ought to," describing the tip of a mighty big iceberg. Two performances were scheduled, in Portland, then Seattle. When Janice asked years later how Bob had come through, Trillin said only "He did what he had to do."

Although there had been a substantial history of social embarrassments, Janice had not had to worry until recently that Bob might fall apart in the middle of a professional engagement. For the most part, he could balance himself sufficiently to pull those off. He did drink less when he was taking prescription narcotics, but that trade no longer seemed like a good one. "Bob and I had been having a power struggle over pills and alcohol for years. I was losing." The positive effects of his two tries at rehab had by this time vanished in the air.

After reading a recent biography of Alexander Pushkin, Bob told Janice, "Writers always seem to die terrible deaths." Statistics may not support that contention, but it was a gloomy conclusion for Bob to have drawn. Pushkin had died young and by violence, in a duel over a woman. Such risks were receding from Bob's life, but if he didn't get control of his habits, he might well come to an ugly end from his blown-out body chemistry.

Death had already been much on Bob's mind when in the year 2000 he'd given a reading of an episode from Proust: the death of the novelist Bergotte, who rises from his sickbed to attend an exhibition of Vermeer: "His dizziness increased; he fixed his gaze, like a child upon a yellow butterfly that it wants to catch, on the precious patch of wall. 'That's how I ought to have written,' he said. 'My last books are too dry, I ought to have gone over them with a few layers of colour, made my language precious in itself, like this little patch of yellow wall.' Meanwhile he was not unconscious of the gravity of his condition. In a celestial pair of scales there appeared to him, weighing down one of the pans, his own life, while the other contained the little patch of wall so beautifully painted in yellow. He felt that he had rashly sacrificed the former for the latter."

Bob, underconfident in his own recent work and always suspicious that he'd squandered his talent, would have connected particularly to the last sentiment above, and more generally to the whole passage's calm mood of infinite resignation. A few more lines into Proust's text, Bergotte, quietly enough, expires.

4

GIFTS OF THE GODS

Houghton's publicist Lori Glazer also passed through Key West that season, relaying optimistic predictions that the paperback would outperform the hardcover when released a few months later. Bob, meanwhile, was working on a couple of small assignments. If long-term deadlines for book-length projects could sometimes paralyze him for a while, short-term deadlines often helped him focus.

In Key West he had two of those, an introduction for a new Penguin Classics edition of *The Quiet American*, and the completion of the Kesey section of his memoir, eventually to be published in *The New Yorker* as "The Prince of Possibility." The preface was peculiarly demanding because of Bob's complicated attitude to Graham Greene; it took longer than an occasional piece should have done but also turned into one of the finest pieces of criticism he ever wrote. Here he took a more judicious view of Greene than in his early savaging of *The Human Factor*. The nature of this assignment would not have permitted a wholesale trashing, besides, Bob had some respect for *The Quiet American*, and his late-stage view of Greene was tempered with a kind of sympathy. The finished introduction amounted to a capsule critical biography, full of sharp insights like this one:

"At Berkhamsted School, where his father was headmaster, young Graham Greene was tortured almost to suicide by a classmate whose name he remembered all his life. Another boy, one whom he had deeply trusted, laughingly betrayed him. His rendering of all the American characters as pathetic straight men, helpless before irony, blinking in the pure light of the British characters' ordinary, instinctive decency and wholesome common sense has a darkly familiar tone. It suggests the delight of the long ago, storybook public school bully at recognizing an elaborately vulnerable mark. Greene knew that satisfaction from the victim's point of view, not as a literary conceit but from life. He understood the reverse angle as well. His awareness and fascination with the tormentor was something close to admiration, he tells us in one autobiographical work, *A Sort of Life*. This admiration, detected by the sadistic classmate, would have made Greene an attractive object."

Writing about the early days with Kesey and company allowed Bob imaginative reentry into his youth—as writing *A Moveable Feast* had done for Hemingway, late in life, when he was tiring and, apart from this one exceptional reminiscence, writing very poorly, his meticulous craft smudged by decades of successive head injuries and an alcohol habit so heroic it dwarfed even Bob's. Late Stone was in fact a lot better off than late Hemingway—in much better command of his writing craft, no matter what he applied it to. But the writing of the memoir turned out to be well timed.

"The Prince of Possibility" might have had an elegiac feel, given Kesey's recent demise, but instead its effect is to bring Kesey boldly back to life. Bob hit the high spots of his friend's career with affection, admiration, and the perspicacious insight of one who had been there for much of it. His reservations, sometimes considerable, were muted in this remembrance: "He felt his own power and he knew that others did too. Certainly his work cast its spell. But, beyond the world of words, he possessed the thing itself, in its ancient mysterious sense. . . . Kesey's extraordinary energy did not exist in isolation—it acted on and changed those who experienced it. His ability to offer other people a variety of satisfactions ranging from fun to transcendence was not especially verbal, which is why it remained independent of Kesey's fiction, and it was ineffable, impossible to describe exactly or to encapsulate in a quotation. I imagine that Fitzgerald endowed Jay Gatsby with a similar charisma—enigmatic and elusive, exciting the dreams, envy, and frustration of those who were drawn to him. Charisma is a gift of the gods, the Greeks believed, but, like all divine gifts, it has its cost."

5
CIRCLING THE NEW NOVEL

The Stones spent much of May on a book tour in France, with a sidebar excursion to see paintings in Bruges, and were back in New York on June 5, a couple of days before *The New Yorker* with Bob's Kesey piece hit the stands. The publication drew a lot of praise from companions of those days, which renewed Bob's enthusiasm to return to the memoir.

The Yale murder novel was hanging him up considerably at this point. The story idea had its origin in a case that had by then grown cold. On December 4, 1998, Yale senior Suzanne Jovin had been found murdered on the corner of Edgehill Road in New Haven, with seventeen stab wounds and a slit throat. The frenzied assault suggested a crime of passion, but it was not easy to fix on a suspect (the case remains unsolved to this day).

Earlier on the day she was killed, Jovin had submitted a thesis about the terrorist leader Osama bin Laden, but though that factor was intriguing, investigators could not translate it into a motive for her murder. Bin Laden was not yet a household name in the United States. It was interesting, though, that Jovin's thesis adviser, James Van de Velde, was a career intelligence officer who had assigned her class to "think like a terrorist group" and plan an attack. They had the idea of using crop dusters to spray poison on some large outdoor gathering. Years later this option turned out to be one the bin Laden group had considered, but coincidentally: Jovin never had any connection to the group. Van de Velde pointed out that if she had conducted any interviews for her thesis she would have announced and footnoted them; she had not. The thesis had no dangerous disclosures to make; that bin Laden had called for the killing of Americans anywhere and everywhere was already public knowledge.

In absence of another candidate, investigators developed a notion that Van de Velde and Jovin had been having an affair that went wrong in a way that inspired him to butcher her. Jovin had a boyfriend, and neither he nor anyone who knew her believed this theory, nor was there any other evidence for it. Nevertheless Van de Velde became a center of such scandal that the university dismissed him. Never charged, but presumed guilty by the public, Van de Velde left academia and eventually went to work for the State Department, then for a private consulting firm, always in the counterterrorism field. In 2013 his suit against Yale and the City of New Haven was settled for a large though undisclosed sum, effectively clearing his name.

For months, Yale and New Haven had talked of nothing else, and Bob was as fascinated as anyone, though for slightly different reasons. A case unsolved in fact could always be solved in fiction, and a professor/spy might make an excellent Robert Stone protagonist. There was surely a novel in this material, a novel described in Bob's Houghton Mifflin contract, indeed. But by this time, as he admitted to Janice, "the plot was giving him trouble. He talked about various possibilities, motives that might explain why someone would kill the girl. He was less interested in the plot than in the predicament of a man accused of murder who is most likely not guilty." That meant that his story line was running fairly close to the real-life predicament of James Van de Velde. For the moment the memoir seemed a path of lesser resistance.

In the fall, Bob's sciatica and back pain returned with a vengeance, so severe that he was unable to attend a September performance of *The Tempest* in Greenfield, in which Ian and his son Cooper both had parts. The pain also caused short-notice cancellations of a good number of social engagements that season and was generally bad enough for Bob to consider surgery, but his doctors thought the anesthesia too risky for someone in his stage of emphysema. For a couple of months he was truly impaired.

I'd arranged a reading for Bob at Goucher College in early October, tapping a donor fund for a healthy honorarium. Assisted by Janice, Bob limped into our house with his sciatica-plagued leg as rigid as a peg. He touched Beth for a couple of Percocet left over from some dental adventure. For years I'd heard of him making this play from other writers out on the circuit, but it was a little disheartening to see it in action now (Janice was also visibly and vocally displeased). And yet he was clearly in terrible pain. He had to deliver his reading from an armchair—from pain, not pills, as I can confirm from my own bout with sciatica a decade later. His performer's chops kicked in and, as Calvin Trillin had remarked, he did what he had to do. Or maybe he did better than that, because fifteen years later a young Baltimore writer buttonholed me to say that Stone's reading back then was the very best that he and his friends had ever attended.

In November a couple of cortisone shots brought Bob some relief, and on December 9 he got to play the role of Lord Justice Johan Steyn in *Guantanamo: 'Honor Bound to Defend Justice,'* which was running off-Broadway at the Bleecker Street Theatre. The play, by Victoria Brittain and Gillian Slovo, was an assemblage of actual testimony from Guantánamo detainees, which had come to New York from the Tricycle Theatre in London. The Steyn role was brief but critical: three fiery paragraphs introducing the play.

Steyn was an Afrikaner who'd grown up under apartheid in South Africa. In 2003 he had denounced the Guantánamo prison in a lecture to fellow jurists—a more or less private event that, however, soon became international news. Steyn called Guantánamo "a monstrous failure of justice, which is a hellhole of utter lawlessness," and defined the American military tribunal there as "a kangaroo court which makes a mockery of justice." There was more—fourteen page's worth—and the opening speech of the play was taken verbatim from the document.

A conceit of the New York producers was to have the Steyn opening monologue performed by a different player every night. Bob, cold sober for the occasion, carried it off with panache, although he narrowly missed a fall in leaving the darkened stage. Despite his myriad health problems, no one would have called Bob frail; in his worst incapacity he still had the furious energy of Lear on the heath, but Janice "had become anxious about his tendency to fall."

6

THERE ARE NO METAPHORS

The Stones took the train to Key West on December 18, a bit earlier than usual. Bob dug into winter work on his memoir, and stayed on the rock for the next few months, as he was not in good shape to travel. *Bay of Souls* had been voted best American novel of 2004 by the Chinese Publishing Association and the People's University Publishing Company. Bob was sorely tempted to attend the January 12 ceremony in China, but had to recognize that his back wouldn't respond well to forty-odd hours in an airplane seat. In April he did make a trip to Austria for the Vienna Writers' Festival, and toward the end of May went to the Amherst College commencement to receive an honorary degree, instigated for him by William Pritchard and Jim Maraniss.

The night before the ceremony he gave a lecture; the title announced ahead of time was "Unteachable Unknowable Echoes of Beckett," but the speech as delivered mentioned Samuel Beckett not at all, although Bob did discuss the structure of jokes as a radical, accessible form of narrative. The audience got good value anyway, as Bob managed to compress his most heartfelt beliefs about artistic practice into the talk, often connecting them gracefully to Amherst College: "If I was apprenticed here as a teacher, I was a journeyman of a writer, learning my trade as I hope I am still." Although: "You can't teach writing, as some athlete of perception brightly discovers every second week and is moved to remind us. In advanced composition classes, writing workshops or whatever such assemblies can be called, there is very little technology to impart. . . . In fact we have no matter beyond what we all already know. If we have somehow managed not to know it, or not to know we know, there's nowhere to proceed."

And for the first time in public he revealed the origin of a scary sentence he'd presented as a graffito on the wall of a tunnel in *Dog Soldiers*: THERE ARE NO METAPHORS. Turns out he had first seen it "inscribed on one of Johnson Chapel's interior walls. . . . I had to wonder—I still have to wonder—what kind of fiendish youthful mentality had evoked this horror. Carried to its ultimate reduction that assertion means that no word or act can represent anything more than itself." There was more, a good deal more, though Bob never quite got to Beckett. He closed with a passage from Conrad he often used for such occasions. Bob was on his game that day and knocked a few balls out of the park. The occasion mattered to him, more than most. Janice: "It was the only college degree that he ever received, and he was really very pleased about it."

———

Bob had accepted a six-week residency at Beloit College in Wisconsin for the fall of 2005. He didn't really need the paycheck, although his chronic anxiety about running out of money was always a factor. In October, they moved into a small guest apartment on campus. The residency's obligations weren't too heavy, so he had time to write, without much distraction, as they had no close friends in the area. Near the end of their stay Bob did finish the memoir, and Janice filed copies with Neil Olson and Ecco Press.

There was no particular celebration of finishing the book this time. In some respects their weeks in Beloit were difficult. There were no doctors there to refill Bob's pain-pill prescriptions, and despite Janice's careful husbanding, he ran out. "Fortunately his back pain had lessened." Ambien was also in short supply, since the local pharmacist "insisted that the 'senior dose' was half a pill," while Bob was accustomed to . . . more than that. Janice, meanwhile, was stressed out of her mind by a bad situation in Key West. While driving cross-country to Wisconsin, they'd been notified by cell phone that the Laird Street house had finally been tagged by a hurricane, Wilma this time, which had put eighteen inches of water inside. Janice's first impulse was to rush to the scene, but Bob needed her assistance in Beloit, so for several weeks she left the problem in the hands of her niece Arwen Romes and Arwen's husband, Mike Hebden, who had been staying on Laird Street during the Stones' absence.

When Beloit classes ended in December, Bob and Janice headed east, skating over icy roads as they tried to outdistance a snowstorm. On January 1 they caught the Auto Train to Key West, where they would live as Gypsies for the winter and spring. The water in the Laird Street house had receded, but a foot and a half of drenched wallboard made the place uninhabitable, and there was more damage yet to be discovered.

The Key West Literary Seminars put them up for the first couple of weeks, as Bob was performing for them in January, and then they began zigzagging between friends' temporarily vacant guesthouses and short-term condo rentals.

Fond as he might be of constant motion, this series of local dislocations made it hard for Bob to settle into work. There were glitches in his retouching of the memoir: Responding to a call from Dan Halpern, Bob forgot to push the Save button and lost a whole day of work. "Damn technology," quoth Janice, who was mightily distracted by the struggle to rehabilitate the Laird Street house. To her mind "this year was already shaping up to be one of our worst."

7

REHAB REDUX

Bob was having a different editorial experience than usual with Halpern, who'd returned the memoir manuscript annotated with requests for changes. "Editing by his editor," Janice, startled, noted in her diary. "This is new—more like journalism than fiction." Apparently Bob's novels had gotten no such penciling from acquiring editors, or had not for a long time (though anyone publishing in *The New Yorker* ought to have been inured to that sort of thing—not to mention the meticulous notes of Larry Cooper). Irritated, Bob called Neil Olson to complain, but then settled down to work on the edit, if grumpily. Janice came to think Dan's suggestions "were usually sensible," and Bob turned the job around by the end of January.

In the first week of February, Bob flew solo to California for a reading and award ceremony at Cal Poly in San Luis Obispo. The day of the event Bob called Janice from his hotel, deeply discombobulated by pain pills and Ambien. "I tried to make him understand that he needed to stop taking any more pills—immediately—if he was going to speak at the school." In the end the event had to be canceled and Cal Poly made the award to Stone in absentia.

Kem Nunn got a call from one of the organizers. The situation: "Bob was on one of his benders and the guy didn't feel that he could put Bob in front of a group without humiliating him and, being a great admirer, he didn't want to do that but wasn't sure what to do." Bob had a flight out of Los Angeles the next day and Kem agreed to come up and fetch him. At the time, Kem was working on projects with David Milch, a producer of *Deadwood* among many other series, who already had a glimmer of interest in getting Bob to write for that show. Kem needed to ask Milch for a day off to run his mission of mercy up the coast. "David had been a huge fan of *Hall of Mirrors* and he and Bob had met one time on the East Coast somewhere and slammed some dope together. So David said, why don't you go get him and I'll put him up at the Casa Del Sol which is this very high end hotel on the sand in Santa Monica. We'll all have breakfast together the following morning and maybe we can talk about getting Bob into rehab, which I will pay for if Bob can't swing it financially."

Milch shared many of Bob's enthusiasms: substances, gambling, music, fine art, literature, and film. He had studied with literary critic R. W. B. Lewis at Yale. His profligacy was often on a very grand scale, but what Kem thought more important was "his incredible generosity. He may have blown a lot but he also put people through rehab, paid medical bills, bought people cars and houses and gave them jobs." Thus encouraged, Kem went with a friend named Amy to collect Bob and bring him to Santa Monica. "We got him into a room and it was quickly becoming one of the half-tragic, half-comic scenes that Bob so often seemed to engender. He wanted to get a drink. I kept telling him we were going to have breakfast with David in the morning and that he should really try to get some sleep. I had to use the bathroom and remember giving Amy strict orders to keep Bob out of the mini bar. You can imagine what happened next. I was gone for about five minutes and came back to find the mini bar open, Amy with a helpless expression on her face, and Bob standing there with a small whiskey bottle in one hand and a small bottle of wine in the other—the image has remained etched in my mind."

The breakfast meeting happened anyway. If Bob was still in rocky shape, Milch, who had gone a few rounds with his own addictions, remained sympathetic; "he extended the offer to put Bob through rehab. Bob declined but was very impressed with David who was still, at that point in his life, a very impressive guy." Kem got Bob on his flight to Miami, and Milch even paid for a driver to bring him all the way to Big Coppitt Key, where Bob and Janice were staying. Bob arrived in disarray, missing his watch, two pairs of glasses, at least one bottle of prescription meds, and the medal from the Cal Poly award.

In the wake of this fiasco he was depressed, for cause and also probably clinically. His pills had run out, and Janice tried treating his depression with Saint-John's-wort. He no longer had the memoir to sustain him through workdays, though he did make a start on a short story. There was an argument with Ecco Press over the memoir's title; Bob wanted to resurrect *Skydiver Devoured by Starving Birds*, but Halpern and others were not enthused. On February 16, driving from Big Coppitt to the Key West Library, he had an accident, rear-ending a truck. Janice called Arwen, "who met him at the nearby gas station and apparently charmed the policeman who came to the scene. Bob didn't receive a citation." He was sober at the moment with regard to all substances, so the accident, which took place in broad daylight, was mysterious; maybe the truck had pulled in front of him as abruptly as he claimed.

The new deluxe Honda turned out to be totaled from the insurance company's point of view. (Janice eventually sprang for a brand-new Camry sedan, as used cars in the Keys at the time were all suspected of saltwater damage.) Bob got off with bruises and a somewhat worse injury to his knee, which became infected and required some doctor's visits later in the month. In March, settled at Hidden Beach, he worked on his short story and a review of John Updike's *Terrorist*, then, returning from a swim in Cecelia and Seward Johnson's pool, tripped on some hard-to-see twine demarcating a section of pavement under repair, fell, and broke his elbow for the fourth time. As with the car wreck, sobriety or the lack thereof did not appear to be a factor in this accident, although Bob did get a fresh supply of pills for the pain, there being no other treatment for the break besides the sling. It seemed that 2006 was indeed shaping up to be one of the Stones' worst years.

In April the Stones flew north. Bob was to consult with Halpern and the Ecco team about publication of the memoir; the title *Prime Green* had by now been agreed on. Janice scoured their storage for memorabilia, coming up with Bob's merchant marine card and a few old photos for possible use in the book. Ron Bevirt, aka Hassler in the Prankster days, produced a few more photos from that period. Bob's Vietnam press card had been stolen years before, unfortunately, along with a small stash of cocaine that had happened to be in the same drawer.

With *Prime Green* wrapped, Bob found himself in an awkward place where he'd been before, unsure what novel he really wanted to write. He hadn't made any kind of start on that childhood memoir built into the three-book contract. The first book on that contract, due in January 2006, was already a few months late: another familiarly discomforting situation.

His determination to regain and conserve his health, specifically for the purpose of writing those books, had succeeded up to a point. His back pain and sciatica had abated, though not altogether disappeared. His emphysema was still manageable without supplementary oxygen. His heart health was improved, which allowed him to stop some medication, but his addictions were always standing by to fill any time not occupied by a full-bore writing project.

In the second week of May the Stones went to Sheffield, hoping for cool weather and that Bob could hole up and work, but they left their computer keyboard behind in New York, and Bob was "in a slump anyway, and not getting much done." He tinkered with possible reviews and with a very short *Prime Green* excerpt (about the penguin sighting from the *Arneb*) to appear as a side-bar in a special *New Yorker* travel issue. By the end of the month he was on the phone with Kem Nunn, discussing "a possible therapeutic trip to L.A." In Kem's recollection, Bob "felt that he'd hit some new kind of bottom and asked if I thought David's offer was still good. It was and Bob flew back out to go to rehab.

"David provided me with a car and driver and we got Bob into Las Encinas later that night where he remained for the next few weeks. From what I saw, and I visited him a number of times there, the Las Encinas stay went pretty much according to plan. There was a moment, after the first ten days of detox and before the commencement of the twenty-eight days . . . I got a call from Bob saying that he thought it might be a good idea to take a little break, go visit some friends in the Bay Area. . . . He was thankfully dissuaded from this plan and remained at Las Encinas." That program allowed him time to write, which for Bob was a good incentive to stay with it.

A while later, Kem went to visit him "at a point when he was able to go off campus for lunch. He'd been reading a book on the various religious movements involved in the American Revolution, various pastors and churches and such. At any rate, there he was, and he was clearly not feeling all that well, but he was rattling off from memory a litany of names and dates, and talking about why this interested him and it was just one of those moments when you could step back and admire the man's mind, the depth and breadth of who he was."

8

SUFFERING TOGETHER

On June 7, the day Bob flew west to start rehab, Janice stopped drinking herself in New York, "partly in solidarity, partly as magical thinking, as if somehow my not drinking would help him stay sober. I very much wanted the treatment to succeed this time." She had no other recreational drug habits to give up by then. She did have a worrisome medical appointment to look into a breast lump, and, not long after Bob's departure, was diagnosed with cancer.

Bob and Janice had met Leonard Cohen at a dinner hosted by Ecco Press in May, and Cohen had signed his book to the Stones: "Suffering together." If this phrase now seemed prophetic, Janice didn't obviously take it that way. Though Bob was periodically in touch by phone from Las Encinas, she didn't tell him anything about her illness. After all, she didn't feel sick, and "he had more than enough to deal with in rehab, where he told me he had been warned that if he didn't quit now, future detox treatment at his age could kill him." She didn't take any of the emergency measures most other people would have either, but instead flew to the West Coast to join Bob on July 26.

By then Bob had been released from Las Encinas, had spent a week or so in a sober-living house, and on July 14 moved into a house David Milch rented in Santa Monica to put up occasional guests. During this period he and Milch had been discussing various screenwriting projects, including work for *Deadwood* and a notion to adapt the Faulkner novel *Light in August*. The day before Janice's arrival, Milch put him on the payroll of his production company, Redboard. He also loaned Bob one of his spare cars, "an old Jaguar" Bob drove to the office and to meet Janice's flight. She immediately took the wheel, however. "I didn't think he should be behind the wheel of a car yet." Bob was sober and drug-free except for a vastly reduced dose of Ambien for sleep, which the Las Encinas doctors thought would do no harm. On July 27 he clocked into his first day of work at Redboard. "I'm not sure what he worked on there," says Kem Nunn, but that sort of arrangement "was just one of the ways in which David would support writers that he liked." Nunn himself was deep in writing the script for the soon to be released HBO series *John from Cincinnati*, along with Milch and several other writers.

———

Janice and Bob settled into the Santa Monica place, with Bob, who was in pretty good shape these days, commuting most days to the Redboard offices to work. Although no fruit of this labor ever came to light, he was scoring a weekly paycheck of $2,500, with Janice cheerfully noting the receipt of each in her diary. Kem Nunn remembers these few weeks as "a good time. Bob was clean and sober and going to AA meetings." He had lunch every day with a group of writers on *John from Cincinnati*. "Everyone liked him and liked having him around. We had a great party one night at the little house in Santa Monica. One of our writers, Regina, prided herself on her Italian cooking. We had a great meal and good talk afterward with David and Bob kind of taking center stage. Bob told me later that it was a kind of revelation for him to see how much fun he could have while remaining sober."

Bob might have dug into Hollywood for a years-long stint—as literary novelists from William Faulkner to Richard Price had done before him. There were many tantalizing projects beyond *Deadwood* and the *Light in August* adaptation. Bob and Kem were discussing a surfer series (surfer culture being a specialty of Kem Nunn novels) and Kem had found a couple of other possibilities for getting his *Children of Light* script produced.

There was no doubt that Bob could have kept busy and productive with this steady employment in L.A. The routine of a regular office schedule helped him stay clean. But it wasn't going to get the three books in the new Houghton contract written. On August 21, Bob celebrated his sixty-ninth birthday by going to work at Redboard. A couple of days later the first copies of *Prime Green* arrived and on August 26, Bob and Janice were headed back to the East Coast.

Bob went with Janice to the Yale New Haven Hospital for the lumpectomy she had deferred to go west. Though she was still anxious about his driving, he did drive her home from the procedure, and she found "his driving was okay. He made only one wrong turn. We had a bit of a tour through the city of Waterbury until he found his way back to Route 8."

Chemotherapy was prescribed for Janice's condition. "Sitting there in the idiotic pink bathrobe provided to all breast cancer patients, I was pissed off, and reverted to my usual anti-medical-establishment position. I figured my immune system could handle this. The disease had probably been set off by my taking hormone replacement therapy, recently found to be implicated in breast cancer. So I had reluctantly quit the estrogen and progesterone, after fourteen years of artificially extended middle age. And I had another thought—Bob had emphysema, which we knew would eventually be fatal. Breast cancer in older women, I had read somewhere, tended to develop slowly. With a bit of luck, maybe we could die at the same time. I don't think I shared that notion with Bob," although it would have been a complement to his suggestion, many years before, that they plan deliberately so as to leave the living world together. For Bob's part, "if he expected the worst (as he did about so many things) he did not even hint at that to me. We got through it together, as we did every other setback.

"In any case, I didn't want to be sick with chemo side effects when Bob had a new book coming out. I had radiation treatments in New York, at Sloan-Kettering. I walked down to the hospital and back five days a week in November and December, saving taxi fare and getting plenty of exercise. Then I took an estrogen blocker for five years."

The Stones spent the fall of 2006 shuttling between New York and Sheffield. Their social life was a bit quieter than some years, maybe because Bob wasn't drinking at all. He was working, mostly on short stories that autumn. When in Sheffield he and Janice went to the movies a good deal, usually in nearby Great Barrington. Ecco Press was not planning a whistle-stop tour for *Prime Green*—a relief to Janice, who worried he might have trouble staying sober on the road.

But Bob held steady in that department. "No one was prescribing for him now," and when in New York he attended AA meetings with some regularity. He'd broken off with the doctor who'd tried to keep him on a maintenance dose of morphine sulfate. That sort of controlled drug dependence had never really had much appeal for him. Janice by now understood "that moderation was not Bob's style. He didn't want regular doses of opiates that his body would adjust to, or to live his life in a more orderly fashion. He wanted to shake things up, to get high." But for the most part, he wasn't getting high, apart from one episode: When Janice "was prescribed a few opiate pills after my surgery, I found Bob helping himself one day. Aren't you ashamed of yourself? I said, with an attempt at righteous indignation—your wife has cancer, and you're filching her pills. But I wasn't really angry with him. I no longer had pain, maybe no longer had cancer. And he had been watching me. He knew I'd stopped taking the medication. I was just annoyed that I hadn't been quick enough to do what I usually did when I had any pills—squirrel them away for emergencies."

Bob stayed sober through a fairly heavy travel schedule that fall. At the end of October he bought a bottle of single malt scotch to entertain Mark Levene, who was visiting in New York, but did not partake himself—which Janice noted as something of a milestone. "He was six months sober on December 7, 2006. It was the longest I had known him to go without drinking. He had promised to quit alcohol and pills for a year but wouldn't commit to anything longer." The Stones got through the holiday season without drinking, and went to the Carlyle Hotel to ring in the New Year with Seward and Cecelia Johnson—"without champagne."

9
GREEN FOLIAGE OF YOUTH

Prime Green appeared in January 2007. The book made a brief appearance on the *New York Times* bestseller list, leaving Bob and Neil Olson a little frustrated because they thought that if more copies had been printed in the first run the book might have listed for longer. The book got cheeringly better press than *Bay of Souls*. Michiko Kakutani's coverage for *The New York Times* was a little grudging in some particulars but finally admitted "What Mr. Stone excels at is conjuring the mood of specific times and places, capturing the attitude he and his friends shared as well as the larger zeitgeist." Walter Kirn, a more wholehearted Stone admirer whose own career as a literary wild child had launched in the 1990s, wrote a piece for *The New York Times Book Review* which was both more complimentary and more astute, picking out "this memoir's peculiar power, its singular mood of soulful sarcasm. Erudite but blunt, both tender and hard-boiled, the part-time tabloid hack turned novelist knows how to stick a sentence. He knows how to fly down the high road of ideas, then suddenly crank the steering wheel of style and take us for a tough ride along the ditches. He's great on people—on joining their abstract insides to their outsides—and he's even better on places, both when they're populated, like New Orleans, and when they're almost deserted, like stretches of the Pacific coast of Mexico."

The last setting was the inspiration of the title, as Kirn underlined: "named for the light at early dawn as glimpsed above the ocean from Kesey's lair." Bob's own take in the book was considerably more lavish: "In the moments after dawn, before the sun had reached the peaks of the sierra, the slopes and valleys of the rain forest would explode in green light, erupting inside a silence that seemed barely to contain it. When the sun's rays spilled over the ridge, they discovered dozens of silvery waterspouts and dissolved them into smoky rainbows. . . .

"All of us, stoned or otherwise, caught in the vortex of dawn, would freeze in our tracks and stand to, squinting in the pain of the light, sweating, grinning.

"We called that light Prime Green; it was primal, primary, primo."

Prime Green is subtitled *Remembering the Sixties*, a semi-in-joke based on the line "if you can remember it, you weren't really there." This opening riff set the tone for the book, which runs from darkly humorous to acerbic—a relatively narrow range for Stone prose, though achieved with impeccable craft. Stone covers his life and times from his late-1950s navy hitch through his return from Vietnam in 1971, delivering a generous baker's dozen of years for the decade promised in the title. There are chapters on the *Daily News*, the New Orleans year, the San Francisco Perry Lane scene, Kesey of course, the Stones' expatriate period in London, a hilarious episode about *The National Mirror*, and Bob's formative tour of Saigon during the war.

Prime Green presents a remarkably vivid and comprehensive account of cultural change in the United States (mostly) from the late 1950s to the early 1970s; its author appears as an actor on those scenes in a very limited way. Bob may have understood that to be the assignment. In any case he drew a picture of a period, more than of himself. The reader gets a panoramic view of how the American dream turned Technicolor in the early and mid-1960s, then darkened again, as if bloodstained, at the time of the Manson murders, under the looming shadow of the Vietnam War.

Stone does pass an occasional judgment. Of the civil rights struggle in the South, succinctly: "I was there and did nothing to help," though he does claim *A Hall of Mirrors* as "a modest shot from the right side." Of 1960s aspirations to reconceive the world for the better, intensely concentrated by Kesey and his entourage: "We had gone to a party in La Honda in 1963 that followed us out the door and into the street and filled the world with funny colors. But the prank was on us." The liberating drugs of those halcyon early days "were forged into a weapon for use of the darkest forces in American society, the witch-hunting, punitive-minded hypocrites who promptly gave us the war on drugs as they had given us Prohibition." It wasn't all bad: "My generation left the country better in some ways, not least in destroying the letter of the laws of racism and sexual discrimination," despite or maybe because of a risky tendency "to exalt freedom over order, to demand more of the world than it may reasonably provide. We saw—may we not be the last to see—the country as blessed in its most generous hopes."

From reading *Prime Green*, one might infer that Robert Stone was hatched in the womb of the navy, which to some extent he did feel and believe. His childhood appears in a couple of over-the-shoulder glances (of course the decade packaging of the project precluded much expansion on this theme). There are a few pages on Gladys Grant, and we learn that Bob, while living in the St. George Hotel, took the trouble to look up his birth certificate, unenlightening as it proved. Conclusion: "Not knowing your father's real name was common enough where I came from." On the other hand, "not knowing your mother's real name surely indicates a degree of social pathology."

Clipped references to his early hardships, in SRO hotels, on the street, in the hands of the Marists at St. Ann's, are delivered with a wit whose bitter edge is almost undetectable. There is none of the pathos of his story "Absence of Mercy." Elsewhere, Stone presents himself consistently and almost exclusively as the protagonist of ironic anecdotes. One would learn more about his inner life by reading almost any of his novels. He was not about to make himself a tragic hero—not in a work of nonfiction.

———

Bob's memoir was, among other things, fueling a revival of interest in Ken Kesey, and about a year after *Prime Green* was published, the filmmaker Alex Gibney came to New York to interview Bob extensively for *Magic Trip*, a documentary that finally succeeded at incorporating the film footage and audiotape from the 1964 bus odyssey into some kind of coherent narrative, which others, including Ken Babbs and Kesey himself, had failed over decades to do. Later on he did a phone interview with Lawrence Downes, who'd gone to the scene of Kesey's Mexican exile to soak up color for a piece in *The New York Times* Travel section. "Although he listened kindly when I called," Downes wrote of Stone, "he could not answer all my questions about addresses and landmarks. He confessed that it had been 40 years ago, and he too had been stoned a lot of the time. The buildings were already ruins in '66, he said. 'We weren't much into infrastructure.'"

10
BLACK ICE

The Stones were able to move back into the Laird Street house in January 2007, and Bob was well enough to resume a near-frantic travel schedule for the next few months: Washington, DC, Corfu, London, Wales, Dublin. . . . Most of his intermittent writing time was going into short stories during this period; the collection owed to Houghton was beginning to take on a shape. A good thing, because Bob needed to begin formulating some sort of progress report for his new book editor, Rebecca Saletan, who'd replaced Janet Silver when Houghton merged with Harcourt Brace. Alice Turner had left *Playboy*, and Bob began revising his story "Charm City" to suggestions of the new fiction editor, Amy Loyd. Between stories, he dabbled in a novel set in a rehab facility featuring a poet or painter (the vocation changed among versions) who'd crashed and burned at a public event and so found himself undergoing rehabilitation in a situation not dissimilar to Las Encinas; the plot trigger seemed based on Bob's misadventure in San Luis Obispo a year or so back.

In May, Bob read from one of his new stories at an event sponsored by the magazine *Open City*, the brainchild of fiction writer Tom Beller, at an opulent Greenwich Village town house where I lurked at the rear of the audience. Bob was in good form, his voice strong and compelling. His text was a portion of "High Wire," whose heroine Lucy is based on Lucy Saroyan—I am reasonably certain that she was the woman Bob had told me about years before, who regularly invited him to "chase the dragon," an expression for smoking heroin off tin foil. The line in the story "She was my heroine" would cease to be fiction if you dropped the *e*. Bob had sustained an intense though intermittent friendship with Lucy Saroyan since they'd first got to know each other during production of *Who'll Stop the Rain* in the 1970s, and "High Wire" is in some sense an elegy for her.

Lucy had died in 2003, not directly from an OD but from a couple of user's maladies: cirrhosis and hepatitis C. "Chasing the dragon" gets its evocative name from the conceit that the heroin vapor rising from the heated foil takes on the form of the dragon, which the user then pursues with a straw. In the course of 2008, Bob would inhale the vapors of more ghosts than one.

In February, Paul Newman left an ominous phone message for the Stones in Key West. "Black ice," he said. When Bob was finally able to reach him he learned that Paul had been hospitalized with a heart problem. "He didn't see Paul often now, since we had moved from Westport, but his old friend had shared some rueful thoughts about aging—'You keep settling for less,' he said." Returning to New York that summer from Block Island, Bob put himself in a bad mood by losing several hundred dollars at the Foxwood Casino and decided to skip a planned call on the Newmans in Westport. Paul died in September, and Bob never saw him again.

Staying in Bill Wright's Pennsylvania home that summer, Bob wrote a couple of occasional pieces, both war-related—an introduction to a new edition of Michael Herr's *Dispatches* (Bob had long been a big fan of both the book and the author) and a review of *The Forever War*, an account of the conflicts in Iraq and Afghanistan by the journalist Dexter Filkins. He met a couple of times with Becky Saletan to discuss, perhaps somewhat delicately, publication prospects for the three books owed to Houghton Mifflin Harcourt (as his publisher was now called). The novel due in 2006 was a long way from completion; in fact Bob was still oscillating between a couple of other novels he might write instead of the Yale murder story described in the contract. The UNTITLED MEMOIR was also now due, but Bob had not written a line of that, other than the 1996 *Architectural Digest* piece, used to give the flavor of what that book might be. Short stories he'd been finishing and publishing (two in *Playboy* and one in *The New Yorker*). A couple more were well underway: "The Wine-Dark Sea" (very loosely based on a 1972 episode when some outraged citizen had tried to hurl Secretary Robert McNamara into the drink) and a clip of some of Bob's rehab fiction material into a story called "The Archer." It looked likely that the short-story collection, scheduled as the third book in the contract, would be finished and published first. As it happened, Saletan left HMH at the end of 2008, and for a while after that Bob didn't have an editor to pressure him.

Though the Stones had been a little disappointed in the promotion of *Prime Green*, the book did win a prize: the Ambassador Book Award, given by the English-Speaking Union of the United States for works "that have made exceptional contributions to the interpretation of life and culture in the United States." The organization bought and distributed copies to libraries in thirty cities around the world—a rather nice boost for *Prime*

Green in itself. Bob was genuinely pleased. At a ceremony in New York on September 28, he read the book's closing passage: "We learned what we had to, and we did what we could. In some ways the world profited and will continue to profit by what we succeeded in doing. We were the chief victims of our own mistakes. Measuring ourselves against the masters of the present, we regret nothing except our failure to prevail."

Spoken toward the end of the reign of George Bush the Second, that last line had both bitterness and bite. There was some muttered carping that selections for the Ambassador Book Award were tilting too far to the left. But a bigger change was in the pipeline than anyone expected. In November "we watched the presidential election returns on television. Bob was pessimistic about Barack Obama's chances. At 11 p.m. I suggested we might open a bottle of champagne. Bob's response was, Maybe we should wait another half hour. But it was soon evident that Obama had done it."

Later that month, Janice had a hip replacement. She was skeptical about the operation and had tried to treat her symptoms with herbs, vitamins, and supplements, passing on the pain pills furnished by one of the Key West doctors writing prescriptions for Bob, who "was using both alcohol and pain pills again, but he drank less alcohol if pain pills were available." For that and other reasons some friends suggested that the Stones should hire a nurse for Janice's recuperation. "Bob smilingly insisted that he would be the one to take care of me. And so he did." He ran errands and did laundry and organized takeout food. Janice could walk, with some difficulty, once she'd returned from the hospital, but she had trouble getting into bed for several weeks. "So now if I got up at night I had to wake him. I hated to do it because he was such an insomniac. Getting enough sleep was always a problem for him. But he would cheerfully awaken and get me back in the bed."

11

THERE STANDS THE GLASS

Bob stepped off the wagon to toast the advent of 2009. The Stones found the Key West artist and writer community euphoric over Obama's election, and, another positive development, Bob's story collection, now titled *Fun with Problems*, was in preproduction, supervised by

Tom Bouman, Bob's new editor at HMH. Bouman sent down first-pass cover art: "a disembodied hand with a few bandaged fingers. Ouch! Bob didn't approve this one." A new design, featuring a dartboard, pleased both Stones better. There was movie interest too.

Bob had an idea for a different novel, working title "Havistock," set in London during the same period the Stones had lived there, nearly forty years earlier. The story began with an arresting description of a man found crucified on Hampstead Heath; materials involved a staple gun and a surprisingly well-made mahogany cross. A longer scene described Antoni, "an American who, in literal but misleading fact had once been connected to military intelligence," watching an anti–Vietnam War demonstration take shape through the windows of a Hampstead pub. This panoramic view of the social elements—bourgeois college kids, "the Moms and Dads of northwest London," expat Americans, working-class Londoners, soccer thugs, skinheads, a sprinkling of Middle-European types, and so on—promised a story as complex as *Damascus Gate*.

Bob worked on the project during a spring 2009 residency at the Civitella Ranieri Center in Umbria, but didn't get very much of it done. He was out of touch with Janice during his stay. She'd bought him a Blackberry but he couldn't figure out how to operate it. Another resident showed him how to Skype, but Janice had trouble catching on to that. He spent most of his time working on an introduction for a new edition of his old teacher Wallace Stegner's first novel, *The Big Rock Candy Mountain*, and an essay for *The New York Times* about Malcolm Lowry's *Under the Volcano* (in honor of the hundredth anniversary of Lowry's birth), and falling down stone staircases in the medieval castle in which the center was housed. He "was black and blue when he got home to Key West," but for once had no bones broken, and he'd enjoyed the outing.

In the summer of 2009, he went camping with John Hildebrand around Lake Superior. "This was the last of our trips," says Hildebrand. "I picked Bob up at the airport in Minneapolis and we drove north with my son in a van that I'd outfitted so Bob wouldn't have to sleep in a tent. The weather was terrible at the start of the trip—rain and wind—and we'd had the bad luck to travel on a Canadian holiday so campgrounds were full despite the stormy weather. Bob's emphysema had gotten worse and he couldn't walk very far, especially if there was any slope. There were pictographs on a cliff on the eastern side of the big lake that he would have liked to see but didn't trust his footing so he stayed in the van. Driving back across the Upper Peninsula, we stopped in the little town of Seney, the starting point for Hemingway's best story 'Big Two-Hearted River.' The river that runs through Seney, however, is the Fox and it's not proportioned anything like the fictional stream. Nevertheless we stopped beside the river and had my son Jack read a passage from the story. Jack had just finished a year at a college he didn't like and I remember how solicitous Bob was of an eighteen-year-old, asking questions and listening patiently to the answers."

Bob and Janice spent most of the fall of 2009 in the city. *Fun with Problems* was just about wrapped up, and Bob, abandoning his "Havistock" project, went back to work on some version of his Yale novel. The Stones' fiftieth anniversary rolled around in December 2009. Busy as they were, they had planned no festivity, but their recently deceased friend Michael Buller's widow turned out to be trying to sell a special bottle of champagne online. "I consulted Bob, and he agreed this might be a way to do Jennifer a small favor, and also to celebrate our anniversary. On December 11 we drank 1996 Roederer Cristal at our apartment with Cecelia and Seward Johnson."

The Stones had planned to head for Key West a few weeks earlier than usual but were delayed when Bob fell ill. This time the problem was relatively easy to address, and after having his gallbladder removed in an outpatient procedure at the Yale New Haven Hospital, he felt well enough to pick a favorite hot and sour soup from a restaurant near the Taft on their way back to New York. He and Janice made it to Key West by December 25, only a week later than planned.

Bob remained slightly under the weather for the first few weeks in Florida, recuperating from the gallbladder surgery. *Fun with Problems* appeared in January, and Bob observed the publication mostly from a distance. HMH had only scheduled a couple of February events on the West Coast, and although Bob suggested adding a few cities, he wasn't really in shape to take on more travel.

Reviews landed from New York: on January 25, a pan in *The New York Times* daily. Michiko Kakutani, who had frowned in Stone's direction before, decided to eviscerate this volume and did so somewhat cleverly, making invidious comparisons of the stories to the handful of his novels she continued to admire (treating "High Wire" as a weak reprise of *Children of Light*, for example). Under the headline "When Impulse Control Goes Awry," Kakutani announced: "Unfortunately for the reader, *Fun with Problems* is a grab-bag collection that's full of Mr. Stone's liabilities as a writer, with only a glimpse here and there of his strengths." Individual stories were dismissed as "ridiculous," "preposterous," "wobbly," etc. "We are not given the full arc of his people's lives," she complained; "we get only snapshots of their drunken nihilism and puerile self-pity. It's certainly not enough to make us care, not even enough to engage our voyeuristic curiosity; it's simply dismal and depressing."

Such a review might drive a man who wasn't already there to drink, but the Stones could take heart from Antonya Nelson's review that appeared in the Sunday *Times* a few days later. Nelson, whose own fiction might have owed something to a close reading of Stone, had an unerring apprehension for the best qualities of Bob's work: "A Robert Stone character is often in a position to do harm or good, and his inclination is often to choose harm. This harm is as frequently to the protagonist himself as it is to others—the characters in Stone's new collection, *Fun with Problems*, are, like many in contemporary fiction, dangerous mostly to themselves. But what distinguishes Stone's men and women is that they realize it. They are conscious of their bad decisions, which prevents them from resembling that more ordinary fictional bungler, the still-waters-run-deep guy hatched by Hemingway and subsequently adopted by an unending stream of male American story writers."

The most potent expression of the Hemingway lineage in 2010 was the opus of Raymond Carver; Nelson was astute in contrasting Stone's work to his. "If you thought that Raymond Carver's men would be happier if only they had a little help—if they'd been educated, cultured, programmed, employed in white-collar rather than blue-collar jobs, sent to talk therapy and prescribed antidepressants—well, Robert Stone is here to tell you that none of that guarantees anything.

"Which feels awfully true. Readers don't exactly want to know this, but once they do, they can never not know it. Reading a Robert Stone story might ruin you for the likes of Raymond Carver. Stone's heroes are disallowed any form of sentimentality or nostalgia, especially those encouraged by omission or ellipses."

Curiously, although it's unlikely that either writer knew enough of Bob's personal history to do so with full intention, both reviews tended to assimilate the work to the author's own life, not entirely a fallacious thing to do in this case. By 2010 Bob had been sowing the wind with doubtful "impulse control" for a very long time, and was reaping some harsh consequences, particularly with regard to his health. Nelson, unlike Kakutani, could read the moral courage that accompanied all that, story by story: "*Fun with Problems* is a book for grown-ups, for people prepared to absorb the news of the world that it announces, for people both grateful and a little uneasy in finding a writer brave enough to be the bearer."

In exactly opposite ways, both reviewers were expressing what Tatjana Soli (a novelist who'd worked with Bob at KWLS some years before) had called the "dream of all fans, the conflation of the author with his creation, which we secretly believed to be the same thing all along." Bob's late short stories were in some ways a little sketchy; as a generally favorable *Los Angeles Times* review put it, "Stone is no miniaturist, after all." But the heart of the best of them had to do with his measuring himself against the world, and doing so, as Nelson perceived, unflinchingly and without compromise. That winter Bob read the title story, which revolves around a relapsed alcoholic luring an unfortunate woman he happens to pick up back to the bottle, at a fund-raiser for the Key West library. Janice "was struck again by how bleak it is, how sad the ending, how despairing and cynical the main character." Certainly the story expressed that bitter inclination to do harm.

Bob put time and energy into recovering his health that spring, swimming regularly and working out at Bill Yankee's gym. "Bill Yankee's father had emphysema, so he was knowledgeable about the challenges of that condition. And Bob liked talking to Bill. Going to the gym was not a chore." But in April he was set back by a bad fall, though at first it seemed relatively minor. "We were going to dinner with Bill Wright, and as Bob entered the bar he tripped over the step, which was not awfully well marked. The waitress hovered throughout the meal, assessing Bob's injuries, which he played down, and getting him to sign a statement. Proof against a lawsuit, I suppose. Bob joked that he might fall when walking out of a bar, but usually not when walking in." Next day the joke wore thin when Bob, convinced by Janice to visit a doctor, learned that he had broken three bones in his hand. "More pain pills were forthcoming. Now it was difficult for him to type, which further slowed down his progress on the novel."

Surgery was contemplated but not undertaken, and the hand seemed to be healing by the time the Stones went north in June. Bob was advised by his New York pulmonologist that his emphysema, if no better, was at least no worse. But his health continued to be shaky that summer.

12
A SOJOURN IN TEXAS

In August they loaded the car for another long cross-country drive—this time to San Marcos, Texas, where Bob had signed on to teach at Texas State University. The distance was 1,700 miles, Janice the sole chauffeur. The Stones spent their first night on the road in Lexington, Virginia, and the second in Nashville, where they tried to get into the Bluebird, a legendary music venue that Bob had visited with Ed McClanahan some years before. Long lines outside the tiny place discouraged them. Despite the early night in Nashville, Bob had another fall the next day, disembarking from the car at a Best Western in Hope, Arkansas. "He wasn't hurt, but he'd also fallen out of bed the morning we left New York, which had never happened before. Bob was intrepid about his falls, but they distressed me. There seemed to be nothing I could do about them."

Bob's contract with Texas State University was somewhat unusually detailed, stipulating for example that "All works written in part or completed during Mr. Stone's tenure at Texas State will include an acknowledgement of the university's support, such as 'Thanks to the English Department at Texas State University–San Marcos for its generous support during the writing of this book.' " Bob was required to be "in residence at Texas State during the fall and spring semesters"—apparently Austin, where they found lodgings, was close enough—and details of his obligations (workshops, class visits, readings, interviews, and the like) were punctiliously and exhaustively spelled out. It was as if Texas State wanted to be certain it could contain, if not constrain, the notorious rolling Stone it had hired, or maybe it was Bob who wanted a definition of the limits of his duties, or maybe there was concern on both sides. There had been some negotiation, which raised his salary (health insurance included) from $120,000 to $125,000, and reduced the number of his spring workshops from four to two.

In the fall, Bob taught the weekly graduate fiction workshop in the

MFA program. Teaching plus "the change of scene seemed to have got Bob writing again." Janice had seen little of the novel but he told her it was going well, "albeit slowly." On the side he continued working on the rehab material. A portion of that had been used for a short story, "The Archer," which was included in *Fun with Problems*, but Bob had a much longer narrative in progress, with the thought that Kem Nunn might adapt the story for television.

It was hot in September, the mercury hitting 105, and Bob turned out to have an allergy to the leaves that fell into the pool at the Austin house. By the time the trees were bare, it was too cold to swim. The Stones might reasonably have hoped that the dry climate would improve Bob's emphysema, but that idea was trumped by Texas State's steep slopes. "Bob wasn't able to negotiate the campus very well. He complained that whenever he tried to walk from one building to another, it was uphill and he ran out of breath." Twice weekly Janice drove him to the door of the English Department building, where there was an elevator. Bob was still doing without supplementary oxygen. Texas State's insurance plan bought him a large amount of dental work: a new bridge, an extraction, and a fresh source of pain pills.

But in Key West that winter, Bob drifted into the doldrums; he was depressed and had lost momentum on his writing projects. His efforts to brighten his mood with substances were not succeeding very well, and he wasn't getting much work done either. In March, Janice "printed out what Bob had written of his novel, and put the chapters in order. It was nowhere near finished." It was also now quite drastically overdue to HMH, a situation that didn't do much to cheer Bob up either.

Tim Tankosic visited Key West in April, and arranged for Bob to try another hitch in rehab, this time at Spirit Lodge, in Spicewood, Texas. Tankosic was an alcohol counselor who had worked with Bob as he emerged from his most recent West Coast rehab, and had become a trusted friend. Bob "phoned Tom Bouman to say he would be further delayed in turning in the novel. I don't know if he told the editor the reason." As luck would have it, the Spirit Lodge "rules allowed him to write when not attending meetings," so he was able to move the book a little way forward. In Key West, Janice "did some copy editing on the chapters he had written. It seemed to me that he was possibly halfway through a very interesting novel."

Bob could swim at Spirit Lodge, emphysema notwithstanding, and he got on well with the doctors, staff, and other residents. Janice felt somewhat alarmed when she took stock of the number of drugs he was on, even in rehab: "Hydroxine, Phenobarbital, Sober-Ease, Ativan, Lamictal, Neurontin, Doxepin, Advair, Combivent, Lisinopril, Atenolol, aspirin, Sertraline, Spiriva, Medrol, Indocin, Androgel, Remeron, Cipro, Lotrimin cream, and Difulcan. Some of these were to treat his emphysema, or gout, or an infection. But holy cow! A drug cocktail. The list didn't include those he'd given up during treatment: hydrocodone, methphenidate, and Ambien." He wasn't drinking either, of course. He stayed at Spirit Lodge from May 4 to June 14, and was happier and healthier once he got out, though when he reached New York that summer his pulmonologist prescribed oxygen for the first time because his blood oxygen levels had begun to drop dangerously after exercise. "Bob didn't use oxygen frequently at this point, but he needed to have it available."

The Stones left Key West separately in the summer of 2011. Bob flew to Rhode Island for the Ocean State Summer Writing Conference hosted by the University of Rhode Island at Kingston. His old friend Bob Leuci (late of the NYPD and the subject of *Prince of the City*) was also attending, and his introduction of Bob to the audience featured a description of the martyrdom of Sister Justin at the end of *A Flag for Sunrise*, "in much more gruesome detail and at greater length than he had actually written." Nonetheless, Bob enjoyed spending time with Leuci. They could commiserate about the chronic obstructive pulmonary disease they shared, "and Leuci gave him some Adderall, an energizing drug he used to deal with the condition. Bob found it helpful too, but wasn't able to get Dr. McDowell to prescribe it."

Adderall might have taken the place that Ritalin had occupied in Bob's turn-of-the-century daily drug schedule, but he had not been taking Ritalin for some time, and Janice hoped to phase out a few others on that scary long list of prescriptions, simply because "the interactions between them were unknown, and it was known that senior citizens couldn't metabolize drugs as well as younger people." Bob never had Kesey's enthusiasm for injectable drugs—he didn't like needles—but "he seemed willing to swallow anything he was prescribed," though he also "considered himself moderate in his use compared to some of the people he'd met in rehab." But with Janice's encouragement he weaned himself off the antidepressant Zoloft, which he had been taking for ten years without being certain it was helping him much.

Janice, who had read up on such things, tried to substitute "nutritional supplements that I hoped could replace the prescription drugs, that might work more gently, with fewer side effects—SAMe for depression, ginseng or guarana for energy, etc." She hadn't given up alcohol herself when Bob went to Spirit Lodge in 2011, because "I had become pessimistic about his quitting for the long term." Unencumbered with any sort of addictive personality, Janice had no more than a couple of glasses of wine in the evening anyway. "But I did not drink in front of him, because I hoped for the best. I don't recall how long he stayed sober. Dr. McDowell prescribed Antabuse, but he didn't take it for long. He did attend some AA meetings."

Janice returned north with the Stones' vehicle on the Auto Train, having stayed a little longer in Key West to set up a rental of the Laird Street house for the few months of their absence—"to augment our finances." The fat HMH contract signed in 2003 made it seem that the Stones had left their lean years behind them for good, but Bob was so drastically behind on his delivery dates that it now looked like skinnier times might return. The monthly payments on Book I, the novel, had finished in March 2006, with said novel nowhere in sight. Delivery of *Fun with Problems* had started another sequence of monthly payments, and the publication and tour released a couple of healthy lump sums, but the monthly payments had run out again in 2009. Bob wanted to buy another residence (in November they closed on a house in Chesterfield, Massachusetts, having sold their Block Island house at a profit during the previous year), and the Stones were still subsidizing their children and grandchildren to some extent. This situation had been a motive for Bob to take the teaching residency in San Marcos, and it now moved him to take all the paying work he could get.

Although Bob wasn't yet dependent on supplementary oxygen, he couldn't stray too far from the relevant machinery, a factor that cramped his style a little in the summer of 2011. The Stones shuttled between Sheffield and New York, where they were out and about fairly often.

Friends from the old days were busy dying: "Carol Southern died in New York, and then Fran Landesman in London. When Eleanor Brooks phoned, she said Fran had seemed a bit lost without Jay, who had died in February, and was probably ready to go. Fran was quoted in her *New York Times* obituary saying, "It was a good life, but it wasn't commercial.""

13
NAUTICAL DIVERSION

In September, Bob had remained in New York while Janice and Deidre cleared out the Block Island house in preparation for the closing. There were thirty years of lares and penates to be shifted or disposed of. Alone in the apartment, Bob had a flash of inspiration and began work on a new novel, working title "Wreck," inspired by a news story he'd read sometime before. Although the novel he was supposed to be writing was now five years overdue, he was still captivated by the new project in Key West that winter.

The manuscript had a catchy start, narrated by twelve-year-old Janey, who delivered snappy, cynical takes on her hapless father, depressed mother, and little brother, drawn as something of an idiot savant. This group embarks on the *Trade Winds*, a small craft whose captain is already indulging heavily in rum and cocaine on their first day out from Sheffield Harbor, a fictional location somewhere in the Caribbean. This tiny ship of fools is undoubtedly headed for the wreck projected by the working title. This story was an interesting departure for Bob, who had very seldom written in first person, and certainly never from the point of view of an adolescent girl. There was an opportunity to explore nuclear family dynamics in a way he had not done before either, and perhaps to return to aspects of a father-daughter relationship he'd dealt with so explosively in *Bear and His Daughter*.

But eventually he put "Wreck" aside in favor of the Yale novel, which was probably the more practical choice, striking into what was becoming *Death of the Black-Haired Girl* with fresh commitment. "He wanted to publish a book soon, for his own satisfaction, and so his readers wouldn't forget him, something he often worried about. In February he sent 118 pages of the novel to Neil Olson."

Outings in Key West were now accompanied by a portable oxygen concentrator that Bob could carry on a shoulder strap. There was a larger one too, which needed a car to move it. Despite the encumbrance, the Stones saw many old and new friends, and had houseguests, notably Jim Maraniss, who always cheered Bob up. But when Jim departed, Bob dropped into a depression. Health problems dragged at him. The COPD was bad enough, but on top of that his vision problems had not been solved by a recent cataract operation, and the Texas dental work was acting up. He tried acupuncture and did his best to keep working out with Bill Yankee. The prednisone he sometimes took to relieve the COPD also had an erratic effect on his mood.

In spite of these difficulties, Bob finished a first draft of the novel by the beginning of May; after years of false starts the writing had gone rather quickly. Some uncertainty about their plans had caused the Stones to miss reserving their usual bedroom on the northbound Auto Train. They, or at least Janice, would have to travel sitting up in coach—a hardship for Bob with his back and breathing trouble. Although his traveling alone was now a dubious proposition, they decided he would fly to Washington for the May 4 PEN/Faulkner Award ceremony, then take the train to New York, while Janice finished copy editing the manuscript and packed up to leave Key West.

Bob lost his wind making his way out of Penn Station and uptown by taxi. He called Janice from the New York apartment, sounding "distressed and confused. I told him he'd better call 911. He agreed that was a good idea, adding—I can't just go around falling down." An ambulance took him to Lenox Hill Hospital, where he stayed a week, being given intravenous steroids. By the time Janice got back to the city, he was eager to get out, and came home perked up by a big dose of steroids.

They had closed on the Chesterfield house in January, and on May 14 went to look it over, staying with Jim Maraniss and Gigi Kaeser, as the Stones' new place was unfurnished. Bob enjoyed the memory foam mattress their hosts put him on, but his shoulder was hurting him, increasingly. He didn't remember exactly what had happened before his ambulance ride a couple of weeks prior, but a neighbor down the hall had found blood on the floor when she came into the Stones' apartment to pick up some things to take to Bob at Lenox Hill. So he must have had a fall, a fairly bad one. The Stones cut their Chesterfield visit short and went to an orthopedist in New York, who found a hairline fracture in Bob's shoulder.

Bob refreshed his stock of pain pills from two different doctors and went back to work on his book. "Without opiates it was hard for him to type, or concentrate on his work." With opiates, "he continued to work on the novel, doing several variations on an ending for the book. He finally decided to send his philandering hero, Brookman, to Siberia." Janice had her doubts about that outcome, although in fact it comes off with a certain panache in the finished volume. By the second week of June she had printed a clean copy for Neil Olson to pick up, accompanied by a diskette and a key to the separate chapters stored therein. Against probability, the Stones were still finding ways to use their antiquated word-processing program XyWrite, which, a dozen years into the twenty-first century, would pose some interesting problems for the HMH production team.

14

HAMM AND CLOV

With the book delivered, Bob and Janice returned to Chesterfield, where Janice set about furnishing a new abode—for the umpteenth time certainly, but experience can lead to expertise. She got Bob the memory foam mattress he wanted for the king-size bed. "Bob hung out with Jim Maraniss, who read *Death of the Black-Haired Girl* aloud to him." Bob was waiting, in some trepidation as in the case of *Bay of Souls*, for word on the book from HMH. Tom Bouman had left the company and Bob had been assigned a new editor.

In July, Bob had his first meeting with Lauren Wein, a captivating young woman with a tough mind and great editorial skill behind her very compelling charm. They hit it off, and Bob took her list of suggestions for the novel with good grace. Wein entered the lists with a certain caution: "I don't know how your editorial relationships have worked in the past, but basically I'm not about to tell Robert Stone how to write a novel." That sentence opened a seven-page letter in which Wein (albeit tactfully) pinpointed every weakness in the manuscript and relayed her ideas for bracing its strengths. The work occupied Bob for the rest of the summer. Janice saw that "he needed more backup from his editor on this book than he usually required. I had done what I could to point out what I thought needed fixing, but I didn't want to overwhelm him with every little detail. I could make some cuts, but I would never add a single word—Bob's writing was sacrosanct to me." In fact, though, Janice had been in charge of assembly and continuity in Bob's more recent novels, and she could accomplish a good deal by cutting.

She "had agonized over a long chapter about Steve Brookman's wife,

Ellie. It was too long. It was exotic, almost as if he were writing about a character from *Arcturus*, the novel he began writing years before about the northwest in the 1920s. Ellie, as Bob had written her for this section, seemed possessed by supernatural forces." This problem could not be solved with scissors alone. Janice persuaded Bob to pay attention to it. "He saw the problem immediately once he read it again, and rewrote it in a few hours." These successes reassured him that he still had command of his craft, what his semi-alter-ego Strickland had called "the casual confidence of the hand."

Acceptance of the manuscript turned the HMH money tap back on. Bob got a check for $87,500 right away, with $67,500 to come on publication and another $20,000 on completing the publicity tour. "Bob didn't care much about money, in the day-to-day income and spending sense. He rarely bought anything or wrote a check himself. But he seemed to have an existential fear of running out of it."

Janice had long since become the family accountant (as well as quartermaster, travel agent, secretary, and copy editor). She managed them through the lean years: "we did come very close to running out a few times." Occasionally impatient with the situation, and concerned how Bob might manage if he ever had to do it without her, "I began to say to him, what if I get hit by a bus? You wouldn't have a clue! Finally he said, OK—where's the money. I brought out the bank statements, and he had a quick look. Then he said, If we have all this money, why don't we go somewhere? He was always planning his next trip."

———

A couple of trips stalled out in the planning stages, as Bob was not well enough to follow through on them. The Stones spent most of the summer and fall of 2012 between New York and their new house in Chesterfield, with Bob doing his best to address the complex of health problems that was holding him back. At the end of July, he had some sort of seizure, never explained, in the Chesterfield kitchen; he was sitting down when it happened so there was no fall. "He was inclined to brush it off." But on the drive back to New York he had a real breathing crisis; his inhaler didn't help; the portable oxygen machine wasn't working . . . and they pulled into Norwalk Hospital, where Janice recharged the oxygen concentrator and Bob recovered enough for them to get back on their way.

This incident unnerved Bob more than others. He got opinions from two new lung specialists; one recommended a course of pulmonary rehabilitation exercises at NYU Langone Orthopedic Center. Bob bought in for three sessions a week, beginning in August; the Stones could still spend the weekends in Chesterfield. The shoulder he'd hurt when he fell in May was still bothering him and he undertook an additional physical therapy routine for that. Then, "in mid-September, I was walking behind Bob on East Seventy-Third Street, where a section of the sidewalk was narrowed by scaffolding. A woman with a baby carriage impatiently attempted to squeeze past us, and Bob was caught by surprise. In trying to avoid falling onto the baby, he lost his balance and fell forward, away from me, into the street. I was speechless with surprise as I registered that the occupant of the carriage was not a baby but a small dog."

This time Bob got off relatively lightly, with a fresh shock to his shoulder and a scraped elbow. The dog-loving woman, who was near her own building, brought a wet cloth to clean the wound, which got infected anyway and required a course of antibiotics. Other vicissitudes included bouts of dizziness, probably caused by the ear Bob had blown up in a dive several decades earlier. Another doctor suspected nerve damage in the troublesome shoulder and thought that physical therapy for that was doing more harm than good.

One of the new pulmonologists had finally answered Bob's question about how long he might have to live: two to five years. "No other doctor had been willing to venture a guess," and of course a guess was just what it was. The dark prediction motivated Bob to stick with the pulmonary physical therapy, which did seem to be helping. "We would go by taxi to the hospital, but Bob sometimes felt well enough after the exercise to take the bus back uptown." In August, they celebrated Bob's seventy-fifth birthday by dining at Sfoglia with their new neighbor Ruth Pratt. It was another milestone Bob had hardly expected to reach, having spent most of his life on a "die young, stay pretty" program. His spirit of adventure was as vigorous as ever, though locked into a body that no longer much wanted to play.

Hurricane Sandy's strike on Manhattan didn't affect the Stones directly—during floods there's an advantage to living on top of Carnegie Hill. But NYU Langone was closed by flooding, which put an end to Bob's pulmonary rehab sessions. The Stones headed for Key West earlier than usual, on November 17. Bob resumed his workouts with Bill Yankee and was cheered by the upcoming publication of his next novel; the New Year season found him relatively optimistic about the future. He was still enthused about the "Wreck" project, and worked on it when he was able, and also on an article about New York in the 1960s, commissioned by David Friend for *Vanity Fair*. Addressing the theme of "disruption" in both the destructive and creative senses, the piece emerged as one of Bob's most succinct and pointed observations of this troubled, fertile period.

Illness hindered his work a good deal during the winter of 2013. Despite the mild climate of the Keys, Bob's weak lungs made him susceptible to colds and these could turn into respiratory infections that might lay him up for days at a stretch. They added a day to their return north, stopping overnight in Fort Lauderdale before driving the next two hundred plus miles to catch the Auto Train. "Bob was no longer willing to get up at five in the morning and leave before six for the drive to Sanford." Likely he was no longer able, either. Janice "began to see that if we were to take a trip, it would have to be a cruise whether I liked it or not, because any other travel would be so difficult for him."

There were meetings with publishers in New York, which both of them attended: "By now Bob and I were going everywhere together, so that I could carry the portable oxygen concentrator. He thought that carrying the machine on his own expended as much of his energy as the oxygen provided," although to healthier Janice the weight was negligible, "hardly more than my handbag." Bob wanted to tour *Death of the Black-Haired Girl*, to support the book and because he had always enjoyed that kind of direct connection with his audience.

To prepare, he resumed the pulmonary physical therapy routine, this time at Cooley Dickinson Hospital in Northampton, Massachusetts, which was in easy range of the Chesterfield house, where the Stones spent much of the summer of 2013. It was a five-acre property, much of it wooded. "When we sat on the screened porch, Bob would say he felt like the Lord of the Manor." He used the pool regularly, but walking remained a problem. "The clean air of the country somehow did not improve his breathing." Country air in New England can be quite thick with allergens, which might have been a factor. When Jim and Barbara Wolpman came to visit in July, the foursome attended concerts over three days at Tanglewood. "I bought Bob a walker to help him get around the concert grounds, but he found it aggravated his shoulder pain. He managed with the assistance of Jim and Barbara, who would stay with him while I parked the car. He really couldn't walk very far. I thought it did not bode well for the upcoming book tour."

Bob liked to recall having been told by one of his doctors "that the liver is a very forgiving organ." In the summer of 2013 he was warned by another that his liver might be reaching the end of its long tolerance. He stopped drinking for a couple of days—long enough for his test results to improve. By that time he was drinking mostly beer when he did drink, but his pain-pill consumption had climbed again since the Spirit Lodge stay.

"I sometimes said to Bob that we were in our Hamm and Clov period—referring to *Endgame*, my favorite of Samuel Beckett's plays. If Clov had been a woman, of course. Hamm constantly asks for his painkiller, and Clov refuses him. Finally, *Clov*: There's no more painkiller. *Hamm*: But the little round box. It was full! *Clov*: Yes. But now it's empty."

Mimi and Rodolfo; Stanley and Stella; now Hamm and Clov. If the romance was fading, the literary values remained high. Bob was a keen (and acutely insightful) admirer of Beckett, though he may not have entirely enjoyed this particular allusion. "Bob would hold a new prescription bottle of pills for a week or so, and then, seeing the supply rapidly decreasing, would give them to me. And I would dole them out, trying to make them last. I wanted to give him enough to make him relatively pain-free but not so much that he would have another fall." The inconvenient truth was that Bob now required narcotics both to concentrate enough to compose and to blunt his physical pain enough that he could type.

Again, he was undecided about what to write. The HMH contract stipulated the childhood memoir (supposed to have been the second book and now to be the third) but Neil Olson, after tactful inquiry, let Bob know that a novel would also be acceptable to the publisher. "Wreck," in Bob's conception of that work, was more likely to come out at novella length, although he might always fill out a book around it with short stories.

The article on which the memoir had been sold was written back in the 1990s and had cooled off considerably since then. Furthermore, Bob was hampered by the fact that his only ready source for this project was his own memory. That had also been the case with *Prime Green*, only not entirely because Bob could refer to letters, documents, memorabilia, books and films by others, and the memories of many companions of those days. For his childhood, there was next to nothing of that sort. The Ann Greif manuscript, in which much of the story was told in Bob's own words, had temporarily dropped out of sight.

Bob "thought that he might try to obtain his mother's records from the Board of Education in New York to see if they revealed anything about her career as a teacher. Perhaps he could find out whether she had been hospitalized, and where, and why she lost her job. He'd had his DNA tested by 23andMe to see if the results provided any insight into his mysterious father's origin. To his surprise, the report said he had some Basque heritage. He was also surprised to learn that he had no trace of Jewish ancestry." With that, Lucas's strange status as a sort of hidden Jew in *Damascus Gate* went up in smoke, or rather became a work of pure fiction. The same was true of Holliwell's encounter with his might-be Jewish father in the first movement of *A Flag for Sunrise*. Bob's deep connection with the metaphors of the kabbalah no longer could be explained by bloodline, though that was authentic enough in itself not to require such explanation.

Neither the memoir nor the novella made any real headway in the summer of 2013. It was normal (though none too pleasant) for Bob to write in fits and starts, sometimes for years, before he could identify his next big book and dig himself entirely into it. That situation was okay so long as he had plenty of time, but now he knew he didn't. Now even the exercises he was trying to keep up for pulmonary fitness would sometimes provoke a breathing crisis.

For some reason his breathing was a little better in New York in the fall, and the imminent publication of *Death of the Black-Haired Girl* provided a happy distraction. The book was touted by the publisher as a comeback: Bob's first novel in ten years. There was a gratifying stir of interest, and Bob did a good few interviews for print (*Publishers Weekly*, *The Observer*, *Tablet*, *Tin House*, *Interview*, and *The Times-Picayune* in New Orleans), plus a couple for public radio and *The Bob Edwards Show* on Sirius.

In October, Bob and Janice went to Bryn Mawr College for a reading arranged by Karl Kirchwey. Publication of the novel was still a month off, but this appearance served as a dry run for the limited tour HMH had scheduled. "The reading did not go as well as we'd hoped. Bob's voice was weaker than usual." His backlist books were on sale and it worried Janice that not many people were buying them. *You can outlive yourself*, Bob might have been reminded.

15
DEATH OF THE BLACK-HAIRED GIRL

As he had done several times before, in *Death of the Black-Haired Girl* Stone split aspects of his own personality between the two male principals: Steve Brookman and Ed Stack. Brookman is a travel and adventure writer, somewhat oddly placed in a tenured position at a college much resembling Yale, in Amesbury, a town much resembling New Haven. Stably and more or less happily married with a ten-year-old daughter, Brookman is also having an affair with one of his students, his first ever in a long teaching career. He's a practicing, high-functioning alcoholic, a point that doesn't make enormous difference to his story line. Stack is a widower, with a daughter, Maud (the black-haired girl of the title and also Brookman's illicit student lover); he's also a retired NYPD veteran and recovering alcoholic, with terminal COPD he picked up as a responder at the World Trade Center on September 11.

The next most important character, other than Maud, is Jo Carr, a person very like what Sister Justin of *A Flag for Sunrise* might have become if she had lived. Jo has spent several years of her youth as a teaching nun (in Justin's fictional order, the Devotionists) in remote villages of the Andes. There she had some relatively slight involvement with a religiously flavored but murderously violent guerrilla movement with attitudes and tactics reminiscent of Shining Path, and a very special feeling that its destiny was written in the stars. Back in the States she put off her habit and acquired some social-work qualifications. The present finds her a counselor of long standing at Amesbury's college. "Now and then she had the feeling that some people at the college regarded her with caution. It was no secret she had been a nun. She was resolutely secular in the counseling she dispensed."

With respect to faith she feels an ambivalence short of agnosticism. The off-and-on skirling of Andean flutes played by South American Indian minstrels around the town takes her back to a time when "Spying out the heart of evil in the sacred lines of heaven made her suspect that perhaps the religious life was not for her. On the other hand, she thought, maybe it was."

As usual in a Stone novel, the principals are on a convergence course, though not across long physical distances, as in *A Flag for Sunrise*. They are all living in the same region when the story begins, though with limited awareness of one another at first. The wandering of Maud Stack, a black Irish beauty of tremendous intelligence, talent, verve, and recklessness, is the thread that stitches the others together.

Maud leaves her dorm room on a wintry morning shortly before Christmas break and passes by Brookman's office, lingering for a brief dalliance, a little romantic postcoital talk, and a taste of a lovers' quarrel to come. Not a habitual philanderer, Brookman has "been crazy about Maud for a year, not only because she was beautiful and sexually inspired but because of her youth, her moments of sheer brilliance, the unquiet being behind her eyes." Now, however, he needs to break off the affair, because his wife is unexpectedly (but happily) pregnant. Since he is Maud's thesis adviser among other things, that operation won't be easy. Maud for her part is "seriously, determinedly in love with him. Too young to know better." Advised that Brookman's wife is returning from a trip to see her parents in Saskatchewan, Maud insists rather childishly, "But I want to see you."

There will be trouble, and more than one kind. Leaving Brookman, Maud repairs to the offices of the college newspaper to finish an article attacking the sort of right-to-lifers who like to brandish "cute-kid pictures of fetuses" in their demonstrations. She is a gifted if immature writer, with a flair for satire, writing "No offense intended to . . . the denizens of megachurches nor of the Holy Roman Megachurch itself." (Maud is a fallen-away Catholic . . . very far away.) She inserts a few choice images of her own—infants whose crippling or fatal birth defects have taken them well beyond the grotesque, and in her peroration alludes to "Christ Torturer the Lord of Unending Piss-Off. This personage is watching your every move for an excuse to fry your ass, not just for an hour, not just for a year, but always." And to conclude: "So, folks, see how the great Imaginary Paperweight in the Vast Eternal Blue has all his little ones covered, so let's make sure they join us. There's life after birth! That's what jails and lethal injections are for!"

She delivers the piece for Brookman's reaction, but Brookman, preoccupied with his wife's condition, is inclined to avoid Maud now and doesn't open the envelope. The piece runs in the paper without any commentary from him. Advised by her roommate that some mayhem might be provoked, Maud calls on Brookman again, to be told by him, "I want to be your teacher. I want us to be something in each other's lives. We cannot be lovers now."

The line reminds Maud of another philandering milksop, Abelard. "I'll become a nun like Jo Carr used to be and I'll get my father to cut your prick off and we'll live in France and write cool letters to inspire future generations of assholes. Like you and me, Prof." That said, she leaves Amesbury to call on her father, still inhabiting her childhood home in Queens. Like some recovering alkies do, Ed Stack keeps a sealed bottle of Jameson as a test of his willpower. Maud vacuums that up overnight and on the morrow quarrels with her father over her article, which has reached him with the morning mail, bolts to spend a few days in Manhattan, and then returns to Amesbury.

Death threats have been coming in on their dorm-room phone, she learns from her roomie, and Jo Carr, who counseled Maud briefly a year or so back, wants to see her. Maud, highly agitated and still soaked in booze, is persuaded to respond to Jo's call. After remonstrating with her about the article ("you don't have to be quite so mean"), Jo takes her to the hospital to be checked out for alcohol poisoning. But Maud slips away from both the doctors and Jo and heads for Brookman's house, determined to make a scene.

Blissful scenes chez Brookman have already been slightly disrupted by Elsa, Brookman's wife, reading Maud's article. Elsa Bezeidenhout was raised in and is still a member of a fairly far-out-there Canadian Mennonite sect. There's a very slight tension between faithful Elsa and unbelieving Brookman, similar to that between Kristin and Michael Ahearn in *Bay of Souls*. But both feel blessed by Elsa's pregnancy, if not in exactly the same way. "I too still believe that God wills what I must do," Elsa tells him. Her deep and rather simple conviction is offered to Brookman as a sort of moral compass, though it's not easy for him to avail himself of that.

Elsa knows that Maud is Brookman's advisee and wonders if he ought not to have advised her against the article (at a moment when Brookman is certainly feeling remiss for not having read it ahead of publication). She doesn't yet know about the affair, but just as her suspicion begins to awaken, Maud shows up outside, part of a flow of pedestrians departing from a hockey game, and begins shouting taunts at the house. Brookman reluctantly goes out to try to calm her and keep her away from his hearth, home, and family. Maud throws him a couple of punches; Brookman tries to control her physically; Maud breaks away and recoils into the street (supposed to have been temporarily closed to vehicles for the duration of the game and its exodus) where she is struck and killed by a hit-and-run driver.

Foul play or simple accident? In the real Yale murder story there was no such doubt, the victim having been multiply stabbed with a Swiss Army knife. At a glance it appears that almost nothing is left of the story Stone had first meant to fictionalize. For one thing, Maud's death can't be legally constructed as a murder, though there are some inconclusive efforts to do that, on the part of police and others, and though Brookman comes away from the catastrophe with a sizable dose of guilt. What remains of the Yale story is what was most important to the author: the ambiguity of the event itself, the impossibility of assigning it a single cause, and the complete disruption of the life of a suspect who (in the fictional version, not the real one) though innocent in the legal sense is morally culpable in ways that he himself finds difficult to define.

The hockey crowd produces plenty of eyewitnesses, a couple of whom claim Brookman pushed Maud into the path of the speeding car. The investigation, conducted by Ed Stack's former partner, Lou Salmone, now an Amesbury police officer, exonerates him of that much. Other suspects: a politico-religious fanatic, known as "the Mourner," from Jo Carr's South American period; someone much resembling him calls on Jo shortly before the accident, uttering obscure menaces inspired by Maud's article. Jo reports the visit to Salmone but by then the man has disappeared and it turns out that the real Mourner has a sound alibi hundreds of miles away. Still, it's a possibility that some other outraged right-to-lifer might have been at the wheel of the car. There were those death threats after all. Maud's roommate's deranged ex-husband (himself a member of another obscure Christian cult) calls in a confession, but he also was too far away at the time of the accident to be a contender.

The agony of Eddie Stack is something to behold—when notified, "although he knew perfectly well what he had been told in the captain's soft professional tone, he kept thinking that the thing that had been announced had been his own death." It's something Stone took personally. His own children were alive and well, but Stone was long familiar with rage against unrightable wrongs. He invested Stack with his own lung disorder, which makes his rage an almost helpless one.

Bereft of his only daughter, Stack has no family left and practically no one close to him, and he has his own special fund of guilt and suspicion.

If he had not quarreled with Maud over the article she would probably have stayed in Queens over Christmas and avoided her rendezvous with death. Also, Stack has for some years been accepting money (applied to the gap between Maud's financial aid and her total expenses) from a cabal of crooked cops, whom Stack—himself an honest cop—knows to have looted corpses during 9/11. Improbable as it may be, the notion that corrupt police may have had some hand in Maud's death plagues him.

What really eats Stack's liver, though, is Brookman—whose affair with Maud has generally leaked. Having talked the evidence through with Salmone, he understands that Brookman can't be found guilty of Maud's death under the law. Just as certainly the accident could never have happened without Brookman's involvement. "What if he walks away from this, Sal?" Stack rails to his ex-partner. "He's laughing. He's . . . laughing." Armed with his police-issued Glock, he limps and wheezes his way to Amesbury, where with the help of Jo Carr he finds his way to Brookman's house and waits outside for the professor's return. Warned by Jo, Salmone rolls up on him in an unmarked car, disarms him, and drives him to catch a train back to Queens.

Stack, however, "was not going to miss his appointment with Brookman, even if it was just an announcement of things future." He calls Brookman from the station and arranges to meet him at the professor's college office. Brookman, well stocked with firearms from his sporting life and sensing Stack's possibly lethal intention, brings a pistol to the encounter. Stack, who has thought of doing Brookman some damage with his cane, isn't up to it. A man of action no more, he's thwarted by a crisis of his emphysema, and departs after making a few obscure and empty threats to have Brookman punished by others—leaving Brookman cringing with shame at having brought a weapon to meet this lack of threat . . . plus everything else he has to be ashamed of.

Nothing is left for Stack to do but settle Maud's ashes beside her mother's, but making that happen in a Catholic Church turns out to be more than a notion, given the notoriety of Maud's violently blasphemous article—the last words she ever wrote. Mary Pick, the Amesbury dean's wife and a practicing Catholic, joins forces with Jo Carr to intervene, and finally Maud's ashes reach their consecrated destination in a suburban cathedral. The brief and modest service on that occasion is somewhat paradoxically reminiscent of the covert funerals held for aborted fetuses in the earlier story "Miserere."

As for the hit-and-run driver, he turns out to be a young combat veteran, self-medicating his PTSD with pills and alcohol at the time of the accident. There's no conspiracy, no intentional murder; Maud's death is thus rendered completely meaningless, unless one believes (with Elsa Bezeidenhout Brookman) that everything that happens is an expression of God's will.

Brookman, after all, doesn't walk away unscathed. Times are changing in academia and even a nonlethal fling with a student has become grounds for dismissal. Shorn of tenure, he returns to adventure reporting. Elsa stays with him and a second daughter is born, "whom she and Steve named Rosalind after the witty heroine of _As You Like It_." Brookman begins reporting from Kamchatka. "Over time he grew steadily more obsessed with tigers and planned more Siberian adventures, sometimes taking Ellie and the children along." The choice of Siberia was something of a joke, based on the colloquial use of "Siberia" as a marker for exile. Stone wanted to show he was still enough of a magician to make an audience believe in Brookman's presence there, and he did so.

———

Though not as long or as fulfilling as the novels of Stone's peak, _Death of the Black-Haired Girl_ does collect and address a good number of his late-career concerns. The first sentence—Maud's roommate telling blanket-clad Maud "You look like a white captive"—would be his last gesture in the direction of the Mary Rowlandson narrative. A good deal of _Arcturus_ material was worked in too, though much of it was removed from the published version. The opening features a rich rendition of New England social texture, which had been a feature of the unfinished novel-length extension of "Helping" and of a couple of later stories. Stone is deft and efficient in creating the sense that his Amesbury is relatively recently ripped from a wilderness where the apostles of European civilization still had to contend with aboriginal resistance to their aims. That atmosphere gave the novel something in common with the great narratives of nineteenth-century New England, and inspired reviewers to think of it as a modern morality play.

Such was indeed the case. Brookman, called "a weak man" by Jim Maraniss when he was reading the manuscript back to Bob, isn't a completely worthless person. His moral cowardice vis-à-vis Maud and his own family has a high cost to himself and others, but his survival, and the salvage of his marriage, really does amount to a kind of redemption. With that, Stone probably intended to forgive certain aspects of himself. Meanwhile there's a drop of Stone in Maud, to whom he assigns a particular blasphemy he himself had uttered in real life—and has her fatally punished for it. For Eddie Stack, who shared Stone's grim resignation in the face of terminal lung disease, the denouement is brief and noncommittal: "Stack died three months after his daughter. His ashes were placed with those of his wife and daughter in the crypt at Holy Redeemer."

The book was dedicated, very simply, "For Ian."

16
FAREWELL TOUR

Press for *Death of the Black-Haired Girl* was generally good. Michiko Kakutani, writing for *The New York Times* daily, had not quite let go of her old grievances, but was willing to see merit in this book and even to rank it with Stone's most celebrated work: "This novel is not a big, ambitious excavation of the American soul, like *A Hall of Mirrors*, *Dog Soldiers* or *A Flag for Sunrise*, and it takes as its presiding muse not Conrad or Graham Greene, but Nathaniel Hawthorne.

"What *Black-Haired Girl* does have in common with the rest of Mr. Stone's work is a fascination with the existential and religious yearnings of the human heart, and with what Melville called Hawthorne's fascination with the 'great power of blackness' rooted in man's capacity for sin.

"After a melodramatic and embarrassingly overwritten novel, *Bay of Souls* (2003), and a wobbly collection of stories, *Fun with Problems* (2010), *Black-Haired Girl* also marks Mr. Stone's rediscovery of his voice—or, rather, a retooling of his voice for the purposes of creating a taut novel of psychological suspense."

Claire Messud, in *The New York Times Book Review*, was more muted in her approval, finding several key characters inscrutable in their rendering, while picking out some strong values through a close reading of the story. To her the stories of the two male protagonists, father and lover of the lost girl, are "residually Christian narratives, but they're ultimately examples of our human need to find meaning in what threaten to be incomprehensible events, to frame the world's brutality in some ennobling fashion." Kakutani went further with this sort of interpretation, asserting that the book "explicates its characters' hope that life is not completely random—'people always want their suffering to mean something,' as one character puts it—and their contradictory awareness of the dangers of religious certainty; their understanding that choices have moral consequences and that innocents frequently are tangled and hurt in the crossfire. The result is at once a Hawthorne-like allegory and a sure-footed psychological thriller."

Mark Saunders, in *The Washington Post*, found the moral/historical seriousness lurking in Stone's thriller plot: "Over Stone's novel hangs the dust of Sept. 11, 2001, the ultimate blowback. In his self-lacerating estimation, Maud's father, the acutely sympathetic Eddie Stack, may have given in to the forces of corruption on that terrible day and brought on his daughter's death. No matter who drove the car that killed Maud, there is plenty of guilt to go around, but which solution are we to believe? A standard-issue interpretation of the wages of empire? Payback for ripping our land from its native inhabitants? Judeo-Christian moral retribution in a fallen world? What is America's secret culture as revealed by Robert Stone? After reading this harrowing novel, one is tempted to say: all of the above." Priscilla Gilman, in *The Boston Globe*: "At once unsparing and generous in its vision of humanity, by turns propulsive and poetic, *Death of the Black-Haired Girl* is wise, brave, and beautifully just."

———•———

Critical consensus had it that Robert Stone the writer was back, in full force or something very close to that. Bob Stone the physical man was still in serious difficulty. A breathing crisis sent him to the hospital in New York on November 15, three days after the official publication date. He was determined to make his first scheduled tour stop four days later, but medical advice was against his flying, so HMH hired a driver to convey the Stones in a car loaded with oxygen equipment to the Philadelphia Public Library, where Bob read briefly and was interviewed onstage by a rising young novelist, Andrew Ervin. It seemed to come off well enough, and Bob sold and signed a good number of books. One of the officials involved in Bob's twentieth-century USIA excursions turned up and, so long after the fact, "was able to confirm Bob's suspicion that the trip to Albania years before had had another, secret agenda." The filmmaker Merrill Greene, Bob's former student, also appeared, glad to see him but sorry that he was too exhausted to go for a nightcap afterward.

Running bookstore appearances in a quasi-talk-show format was then becoming a fad, and for Bob it was helpful, since he didn't have to read for very long and could take time to catch his breath while his interlocutor was speaking. Christopher Lydon played the part at the Harvard Book Store in Boston, and rising star Rachel Kushner at the Strand in New York, and in Washington, DC, it was me.

I had dinner with Bob and Janice beforehand at the George Hotel near Union Station. It was the first time I'd seen Bob since he went on oxygen, and his aspect was somewhat alarming. In the course of the meal I understood that the real brilliant Bob was still in there somewhere, but having serious trouble getting out. Janice was worried too, most immediately for the performance's sake. At a Barnes and Noble in New York, Bob had gone "into a long riff about his character Brookman, about redemption. Redemption—he kept repeating the word. I couldn't figure out the problem, and only later realized that it wasn't alcohol or pill interfering with his thinking, but rather lack of oxygen."

Bob huffed as much oxygen as possible in a back room of Politics and Prose; he didn't want to take the concentrator onstage with him. The reading and talk came off well enough. Bob was rather more willing to be led in the talk than he would have been if he'd had all his faculties. Janice had counseled me to keep him off the topic of redemption at all costs, but finally I couldn't stop him. At the end of the conversation, he raised his face toward the ceiling and assumed a faintly beatific expression, as if some invisible light shone on his countenance, and wondered very tentatively if it might not all be about . . . some sort of . . . redemption. He pronounced (and indeed repeated) the word with the air of someone reciting a novena. Afterward I wondered, improbable as it might seem, if I had not witnessed an act of piety.

Later I asked myself why that line annoyed Janice so much, since she generally tended to embrace her own religious sensibility, while Bob spent so much energy fighting off his. Late in life, though, he seemed to have evolved away from the muscular atheism that got him expelled from St. Ann's in his teens, and even from the more guarded skepticism of his adult life. Maybe all his works had been meant to please the Creator, whom he regretted, in a late nonfiction fragment, having referred to as a flying Babylonian paperweight.

As bad a shape as Bob was in that night, it somehow didn't occur to me that I might not see him again on this earth.

—•—

The Strand appearance wrapped the East Coast leg of the limited tour. On November 28 the Stones caught the Auto Train for Key West. There were a couple more appearances for the book, the first in New Orleans, revolving around a reading at Tulane, where Tom Beller, writer, *Open City* editor, and Stone aficionado, was their host. The event turned out *Hall of Mirrors* fans who asked interesting questions. Bob went to the French Quarter, where the Stones had lived long ago, for a radio interview. All in all, it was a pleasant visit, and Bob and Janice thought well of the restaurant at the Windsor Court Hotel where they were staying. "But when we tried to take a walk in the city, Bob couldn't do more than six blocks."

The tour wrapped on December 17 with an appearance at Mitch Kaplan's Books & Books in Miami, which was simulcast on the Internet, so that Bob could sign books for listeners in remote locations, as well as those physically present. This event was a success, too, but the Stones went into the Christmas season utterly drained by all the exertion. Janice had begun to wonder if they were entering old age—they were both, after all, in their seventies. "On New Year's Eve we went down the street to Bill Wright's house, and we both drank too much. Bob had been upset when his book was not listed as a notable book, or an editor's favorite, at the end of the year. He had angrily poured himself a whiskey, in spite of my protests. Hard liquor affected him badly now, and he soon went back to beer."

17

FALLING

Soon after New Year's Bob got out of bed sometime after midnight, went into the kitchen, and fell, knocking himself out. When Janice roused him, he told her he couldn't feel his right arm, except for a burning sensation in the hand. At the hospital, where he spent three days, it was discovered he had dislocated his right shoulder and broken his humerus. He had no sensation in his right arm when he was released— gone, that casual confidence of the hand, most literally. This episode was a rather eerie episode of life imitating art, for Bob had earlier written a similarly incapacitating fall for Steve Brookman in the Siberian wilderness.

As Brookman lies helpless on the frozen ground, "The dark surrounding forest served to illuminate his shame.

"Shame that he would never again elude. After that day's fall the thought of what had happened would be a scourge to him as it had not been before, and every step he took thereafter would be edged with shadow. He had discovered the place to which his own capacity for excusing himself, his self-indulgence, could not penetrate.

"He did not die there in the pain and the cold as he expected but found his way to the cabin and to Ellie. Sleep failed him. His arm for weeks remained useless to him. He was, in a way, never the same again, though only he and Ellie would understand that."

———

Not long after, in real life, Bob suffered "a seizure-like event, like the one he'd had in Chesterfield during the summer." The paramedics, despite Janice's warnings, managed to dislocate his shoulder again as they struggled him into the ambulance. In the intensive care unit (for ten days this time) Bob had a breathing tube and a heart catheterization, which found nothing wrong. Bob's heart was strong, never mind for a man of his years. Still, Janice quietly canceled an Istanbul–to-Venice cruise they had booked for May, while Bob was an inpatient. "I didn't mention it to Bob—he was bummed-out enough already." Refusing to be transferred to Miami for more tests, Bob, who'd had enough of hospitals, came home and a few days later fell again, but this time got off with a mere broken rib. "Dr. Shapiro jokingly suggested that Bob and I belt our ankles together when we went to bed, so Bob couldn't get up without my being alerted."

Bob was told that it might take a year or two for him to regain the use of his right arm, which still had no feeling. Darlene, a new physical therapist, advised a wheelchair. By now Bob had fallen so many times he was no longer dismissing the incidents and had lost confidence in his own mobility, to some degree. Janice fought off the wheelchair. "He had always had strong legs and surely he could walk."

The Stones had no pulmonologist in Florida; "the Key West doctors were a mixed bag to say the least." Janice wheedled a prednisone prescription out of a doctor in New York. Physical therapy was going poorly until Darlene suggested aquatic exercise. Bob "was happy to be back in the water, his familiar element. Darlene gamely turned up in her swimsuit twice a week. But with only one functioning arm, when he tried to swim he went round in circles. But he could exercise in the pool, and regained some strength."

Bob's handicaps curtailed the Stones' social life in the winter of 2014. They begged off the regular big parties, often at the last minute when Bob felt too poorly to attend. He was a bit weary of those anyway, if Janice was not. "We watched a lot of TV that spring. CNN, MSNBC. There was the disappearance of flight 370. The invasion of Crimea. The war in Ukraine." For someone like Bob, watching the news was not a passive activity.

Though Bob was relatively housebound, they still saw plenty of their friends. Jane Burton came from the West Coast to stay a few days. Deidre came. Two couples, Ann Beattie and Lincoln Perry, and Edward Hower and Alison Lurie, were especially attentive. "Ann has a good reading voice and would read to him. He requested that she read him a story by Henry James, 'The Jolly Corner.' Edward set him up with various amusements— audiobooks, etc.—though Bob was finally disinclined to use them. He read on his Kindle, which he could do one-handed, and he continued to try to write. Using his left hand, it was a slow process."

Most writers need to become unconscious of their physical materials, be it stylus or keyboard. The synapse between the imagination and the text in progress needs to disappear. Understandably, Bob was having trouble getting into that state. His fragments from that winter go on sensibly enough for a page or so, then collapse into disjointed phrases embedded in cat-typing. Looking at those pages now it's easy to see him slipping in and out of consciousness at his desk.

He wrote part of a piece, working title "Coda," which began with a reflection on his youthful reading of Thomas Wolfe and continued into a kind of philosophizing:

"They say among the suffering ill, Jews on the one hand complain incessantly. The Irish on the other deny feeling any pain at all.

"This has nothing, understand, to do with 'who's tougher.' Because

Christ I think we all know by now how tough we all are, which is plenty and not enough. The reason for the difference they say is this: the Jews believe they can make things better, with effort, reason, argument, change the world. Even a little pointless agitation can't hurt. The Irish think they know that nothing under the rain will change, from this time until the last. So they deny their pain lest it be increased on them by perverse strangers. When at last, trained to be each his own and her own stranger, they act on pain scalded in silence, they can do heartless spiteful things."

Certainly, at this point Bob knew plenty about pain as well as its limited, dangerous panaceas. And he was still grappling with the perverse choice to inflict pain on others. But in this late essay, he constituted his relationship with readers as a loving one.

"I presume to say these things, having acquired a variety of genetic material out of the dark past. So I appropriate to myself a variety of inappropriate opinions. As a reasonably obscure writer with a small loyal band of readers on whose love I have lived, as I see it, I wish I had done more. I live in hope, as may surprise some. It isn't despair so much that interests me. I know the line about Thomashevsky's deathbed: dying is easy, comedy is hard. Let me say that I interpret the actor's joke as artistic metaphor. Before death I have nothing to offer but dread reverence. But the practice of hope, of life against death, of edges and surviving, were what I wanted to write about.

"Except that we are all against our will adventurers, it was not so much the adventurer's edge—though who coming after Hemingway could resist trying themselves against that? But I've spent considerably more time trying to stay awake in quiet rooms than spying on birds, let alone lions. When you have read this through you will have a sense of how drug ridden, boozy and wasted a lot of this life has been. When I thought of beginning this coda about Wolfe's reference to suffering it was of drugs and alcohol I was thinking.

"The edges I pursued were of the mind and heart because I believed they were where insight resided. Insight was my God when I felt deserted. I fell in love with the word in William James or somewhere, with the thing itself in Joyce or somewhere. It was survival, I thought."

In this sense, then, Bob saw himself as what he'd dubbed a couple of his protagonists, an athlete of perception, but without the sting of irony this time. He was writing in acute consciousness of death, *sub specie aeternitatis*, a term that Bob would likely have encountered at St. Ann's.

One feels the near approach of death in the body, and through the corporeal element, in the whole being. Bob wasn't giving up: "Neither do I end this coda as a farewell. It may be that. It's not meant to be."

————•————

Janice, seeing the terrible frustration Bob felt at the physical barrier that had come between him and the act of composition, "would try to persuade him that he didn't need to try to write anything more. He had written so many excellent books already. He didn't agree. He thought he hadn't written enough. He had so many ideas, and was intensely frustrated that he couldn't put them into writing. I don't think he knew what to do with his brain, without a writing project. He'd always had a story going, in his imagination."

In 2014, aside from his disabled right arm and hand, he was vacillating between projects: "Wreck," the contracted childhood memoir, or maybe he'd return to the adaptation of "Helping" as a play, or to the historical novel *Arcturus*. The "Coda" manuscript suggests a run at a very different kind of autobiography than what Houghton was expecting.

By March, Bob was feeling distinctly better. The Stones began dining out with friends again. They could go to see HD Metropolitan Opera at the Regal. Bob began to talk about going on a cruise (he seemed to have forgotten the one Janice had canceled in January) or taking another trip to Costa Rica.

But early in May another breathing crisis landed him in the hospital . . . where, however, he refused a breathing tube—his past experience of that had apparently been worse than the chance of death. Janice: "They tried to get me to okay it. He might die, the EMT told me. I said I was not going to overrule Bob." With better luck they'd have been en route to Istanbul for the cruise that had been canceled. Instead she sat at Bob's bedside, overhearing nurses muttering about end-stage COPD. "This illness seemed to be something we were not going to outrun."

The better part of valor might have been to stay through the summer and fall in Key West, "but Bob wanted to go north. He got bored staying in one place, especially when most of our friends left for the summer." Travel was in fact dangerous, particularly the long legs by car, when Bob would not be in close range of a hospital if he happened to need one at short notice. On top of which he caught a cold on the eve of the departure, increasing the risk.

In the end he survived the trip without incident. The Stones stopped in Pipersville, Pennsylvania, to deliver a walker Bill Wright had left in Key West, and then went on to Chesterfield, where they spent most of the summer, with occasional trips down to the city. They spent a great deal of time with the Maranisses—one plan that had worked as intended. The great frustration was that Bob could not use the Chesterfield pool. His right arm was still dead and the pool ladder had no handrail. The one time he went in turned scary—Janice had to use all her strength and ingenuity to get him back out.

Death of the Black-Haired Girl had won the Paterson Prize for Fiction (awarded by the Poetry Center of Paterson, New Jersey) over the winter, and was now to be published in the U.K. Of course there was no question of going over this time, but Bob did some interviews by phone. He was still trying to get back into a good writing groove. Janice bought an iPad, in hopes that Bob could use the Notes dictation app. "Bob couldn't adjust to it. Every time he paused to compose a thought, Notes would assume he was finished dictating and end. He found the iPad useless."

In the fall the Stones heard of a COPD treatment that involved putting a stent in the lung. They explored that possibility for Bob, but it looked uncertain. Generally speaking, Bob was not a good candidate for any sort of surgery—a reason that nothing of the sort had been attempted for his shoulder and paralyzed arm. He might not be accepted into a lung stent program and to attempt it would mean deferring departure for Key West. Doctors recommended against that, and Janice "was anxious to get out of New York before cold weather could set off a breathing crisis."

They caught the Auto Train on November 16, after some complications to do with replacing a key piece of Bob's oxygen equipment. Back in Key West, they put some time into getting the new iPad to cooperate with the rest of their computer setup. They had Elena Castedo and Denny Ellerman in for Thanksgiving, and Judy Blume and George Cooper for their December 11 anniversary—their fifty-fifth. "George gave Bob a book on drawing with the left hand."

His right hand was still useless, but he wanted to work. Among other prospects, he now thought of returning to the Dr. Tom Dooley story. But he was not in shape to make a real start on anything. Janice was perennially tired—life had been harder for her once Bob went on oxygen—but she believed what Tim Tankosic had recently told her that the longer she worked the longer she'd live. Bob "once proposed that he have a second wife. As he described her, she would be younger, hardworking, and very respectful of the elder wife—me, that is. Oh, and Chinese. . . . Another amusement of his was to ask me about all the lovers I had ever had. I think there's one you didn't tell me about, he would say. He was so persuasive, he even had me wondering if I'd forgotten somebody. But I think he was just fishing. I wish now I'd made more of an effort. Invented someone for his entertainment."

Invited to Liz Lear's for Christmas, Bob in the end was not up to the outing. "We spent the day lying in bed, holding hands, listening to music channels, or watching whatever was on the news. I thought if he died on Christmas, it would somehow be appropriate. I don't know why I thought that."

Instead, Bob rallied. Jim and Barbara Wolpman came for a week's visit on December 26, and Bob was able to get out and about with them—to dinner at a Geiger Key restaurant and a New Year's Eve party chez Bill Wright and in the company of Phyllis Rose and Laurent de Brunhof. Janice had been treating Bob's crippled arm with Saint-John's-wort oil, which she massaged into the muscle at bedtime. "One night I asked him if he could feel his fingers, and he thought perhaps he could. Squeeze my hand, I said. And he did. A small squeeze, very weak, but I could feel it."

David Wolkowsky's annual rooftop blow-out was held on January 9, 2015. Wolkowsky was a collector, connoisseur and bon vivant, whose forebears had been Key West merchants, and who, beginning in the 1960s, had done much to rehabilitate his ancestral village. He had become a good friend of the Stones in Key West, and he loved to throw elaborate parties for the local writers and artists. This year, Bob didn't feel well enough to attend, despite some urging. In fact, he didn't feel well enough to get out of bed. The rally he'd produced for the Wolpmans' visit had faded soon after they left. The news of the day was the terrorist assault on the offices of *Charlie Hebdo* in Paris, in which most of the satirical magazine's staff had been slain. Janice: "I should have got a clue that Bob's condition was getting worse when he was uninterested in following this horrifying story on TV from his bed."

Edward Hower came over to keep Bob company while Janice ran a few quick errands with Alison Lurie. That much accomplished, she was preparing for an early bedtime with Bob, when she found him "standing in the bathroom with a strange expression on his face. Something had happened. He said nothing, but sat down, and then tried unsuccessfully to stand. His legs seemed to have lost their strength, and I tried to help him up. He slid gently down to the floor, and lay down quite gracefully and closed his eyes."

Janice called Edward, who with Alison left the Wolkowsky party and came to assist, but their best efforts couldn't get Bob off the floor, not even when more reinforcements were called. "Bob tried to cooperate with us, but he was dead weight. He lay down again, peacefully. I didn't want to call 911, as he had explicitly told me not to several times that week." That would have been his informal version of a Do Not Resuscitate order. The friends helped Janice tuck pillows around him and then went home. Janice connected him to his oxygen supply, then "turned off the lights, lay down on the floor next to him. And I fell asleep too. Waking up several times during the night, I heard his difficult breathing. I thought, he'll wake up. We'll deal with this in the morning. Bob Stone always wakes up."

But this time, he didn't. One imagines that his pain stopped then, along with his labored breath.

On January 10, after Bob's body was removed from the Laird Street house, Bill Wright asked Janice if she'd like to stay at his place, rather than be bereaved and alone at home. "I most definitely wanted to stay where I was, in the room where Bob had last been. I wanted to be alone with him. He was gone, and yet I felt as though he were still here.

"That night I had the oddest sense that I could feel the earth turning under me, that it was taking me away, and leaving Bob behind. I was supposed to be with him, I was sure. I wanted the earth to stop turning. Stop, I said. But it carried us away from each other."

Bob's body was cremated, and there was a small memorial at the West Martello on Higgs Beach, not far from the Laird Street house. Several of the Stones' writer friends spoke, including Annie Dillard, Hal Crowther, and Bill Wright. The Stones' daughter, Deidre, closed the program and there were drinks afterward at the Johnsons'. Janice returned north in

May, according to old custom. She had come to prefer Key West among all their residences, but the summer months there were really too hot, and of course there was always work to be done in the other places.

Excellent archivist as she unsurprisingly turned out to be, Janice had organized Bob's papers in the New York apartment for the use of an eventual biographer. I began to spend a good deal of time at 1435 Lexington Avenue, apartment 6F. When Janice was in Chesterfield or Key West, Beth and I could stay there and often did. If a set of rooms can express a state of being numb with grief, the Stone apartment did so during the first year following Bob's death. After that time had elapsed, Janice made a quite ferocious order-and-organization effort before heading for Florida. Among other things, she cleared off all the cards and photos from the refrigerator door and left only a short poem by Kay Ryan, "Tree Heart/True Heart," which had recently appeared in *The New Yorker* and which concluded:

> *A*
> *real heart does not*
> *give way to spring.*
> *A heart is true.*
> *I say no more springs*
> *without you.*

This sentiment alarmed me some, when I discovered it on the fridge—Janice herself having made her departure for the Keys. She had spoken to me a time or two about her deep desire not to survive Bob, or not by long. But she'd also talked about how the biography project, plus another project to collect his occasional nonfiction pieces into a final volume, was keeping her going. It wasn't just something to do; Janice was still working for Bob, and so still feeling his presence. She was rereading all his work, and writing her own very eloquent memoir of fifty-five years of symbiosis—for better, for worse, for richer, for poorer, in sickness and in health, and the whole nine yards of traditional marriage vows, with one of the world's most brilliant, difficult, extraordinary men.

CODA

Nothing is free.

Those three words had been a Bob Stone mantra for a very long time. Their application is extremely broad. The pleasure of intoxicating substances, for example, isn't free. Eventually a bill comes due and must be paid. The magical bar that Malcolm Lowry imagined for a poem, "where one can drink forever without owing/with the door open and the wind blowing," does not exist in reality.

"You spend a lot of time getting into intense emotional states by yourself," Bob once told an interviewer, "and I think that's why many writers tend to substance-abuse. They tend to drink; they tend to get stoned. It's a way of ending the day." It's ironic that the addiction that finally killed him was the one he had successfully broken, and that many decades before. No doubt he didn't miss that joke. As a man he appreciated irony, and as a writer he traded in it.

Moral cowardice and intellectual dishonesty aren't free either. That conviction might have originated in the Catholicism of Stone's childhood, although it evolved a good deal in the kind of personal existentialism he devised for living his life. In such a system, courage both moral and physical is something to aspire to—difficult to achieve and even harder to sustain. The truly brave are those who master fear, not the ones who never feel it. Nervous traveler that he was, Stone logged time in some of the world's more terrifying places. Loath to lie to himself ever (except in the standard, banal ways all addicts do), he spent much time in the scarier places of his own mind. "Insight was my God when I felt deserted," as he wrote late in life. His inspiration came from that practice, which was, undoubtedly, often painful; he needed painkillers for that too.

Malcolm Lowry's bad habits killed him a lot faster than Stone's did him, and in writing about Lowry and *Under the Volcano* in 2009, Stone took the matter under consideration. "We can speculate that in a not uncommon irony it was his hunger for experience, for life more abundant, that drove him to addiction. It's no surprise that experience failed him. Let's say his own experience did not speak well for the writing life. It taught him about suffering."

And a masterpiece novel came out of it all. There, Stone's admiration is unstinting. "Writers with problems like Lowry's sometimes produce work that is narcissistic and entirely self-referential. In *Under the Volcano*, Lowry used the grim experiences he had gone through to express his love for the world. He applied his considerable learning and generosity of spirit to a hundred things beyond his own despair, even if the experience of despair informs it."

As Stone saw it, Lowry "was destined to endure the humiliations of the addict." To be charitable about Lowry's weakness was to take a similar attitude toward his own. "As Auden wrote, 'time loves language.' It forgives much in exchange, he says. So we pardon Lowry his unhappy life. The alcohol was bad luck. He believed that the experience of life was a labyrinth at the heart of which identity dwelled, and he lost himself in his own darkness."

High aspiration and the impulse to self-destruction have their equally potent seductions. Many lives oscillate between those two poles, but for most, the amplitude is pitifully small. Whatever Bob did, he did on a grand, a Lear-like scale. No wonder he loved that play so much.

———

With a relatively small body of work, Michael Carlson wrote in an obituary for *The Guardian*, Robert Stone "established himself as one of the most important novelists to emerge from the chaotic changes of 1960s America. His work combined a unique journalistic eye for places of conflict where the country's power was turned into vulnerability, and a writing style combining expansive realism with narrative experiment. As he put it: 'That is my subject. America and Americans.'

"He understood that subject to its core. His books were populated by its disillusioned, idealistic, cynical, stoned and wasted products, people chasing an American dream and inevitably doomed to failure."

"Writing is how I justify my existence," Hillel Italie quoted Stone in a *Los Angeles Times* obituary. "This is a basic hunger for most people; they want their suffering to mean something. You go through all these things and the idea it's utterly of no consequence is very difficult to work with."

It's reasonable to locate Stone's aggregated opus on a spectrum between these two statements. The tattered veil of the American dream engaged him in practically everything he ever wrote. In his engagement with suffering, very possibly a deeper concern, is an echo of his lapsed Catholicism.

The editor and critic Gerald Howard thinks of Thomas Pynchon and Don DeLillo as Stone's "true peers"—which may seem a little odd, given that Pynchon and DeLillo are formal innovators, while Stone is not. But all three emerge from the "silent generation"—coming of age in the 1950s, having lived through World War II but as children, too young to fight or be killed in it. These three novelists share, in Howard's view, the perception that "being a postwar American is a complicated and crazy-making and morally dubious condition." That moral dubiousness was a subject inexhaustibly attractive to Stone.

The psychedelic revolution and the Vietnam War were pole stars of Stone's maturation as a man and an artist. Unlike some of his contemporaries who went through the same psychedelic looking glass, the writer Stone emerged intact as a conventional representational realist (as did his close friend the writer Ken Kesey, though Kesey would abandon the literary muse in his attempt to manipulate the world itself as artistic material). If a hallucination happens in a Stone novel, it's not going to engulf the whole text but (as Howard puts it) be safely contained inside someone's head. At the same time, Stone is easily distinguished from important contemporary realists like Raymond Carver or Richard Ford.

Since his 1986 novel *The Sportswriter* set the template, Ford's characters are apt to spend tremendous energy pondering moral choices without ever doing much of anything about them. In marked contrast, Stone's characters spend tremendous energy not only cogitating about moral choices but also trying to translate them into some kind of action in the world. Carver was wont to write down to his characters in a way Stone does not. In a Carver work, Stone's Pablo Tabor would appear as the equivalent of a marble rolling through a maze, with no awareness of the surrounding and controlling structure. Stone for his part puts the reader entirely inside Pablo's very complex subjective experience—yes, he is a pawn in somebody else's game, but his struggle for agency is what makes him fascinating.

In Stone's long view of the world he lived in, American conscience reshapes itself around the problem of Vietnam—or more precisely, around an inability to process the moral problem that our conduct of the war presented. Among Vietnam writers Stone is probably closest to his two friends, the war reporter Michael Herr and the novelist Tim O'Brien, although even there the differences may be greater than the similarities. Vietnam is everywhere and nowhere across the body of Stone's work—a sort of perpetual haunting.

Stone shares an interest in measuring America against its near neighbors with the Joan Didion of *Salvador* and *A Book of Common Prayer*, and the Peter Matthiessen of *At Play in the Fields of the Lord*. But he was never inclined to push form as far as Matthiessen does in *Far Tortuga*, nor political engagement as far as Matthiessen does with *In the Spirit of Crazy Horse*. Like Tom McGuane, Stone adopts a politically aloof stance in his fiction (perhaps not so much in other writing), though McGuane's *92 in the Shade* can be seen as a companion piece to *Dog Soldiers* in its accounting of the unacknowledged but high and bitter cost of America's euphoria during the 1960s.

The artist's mantle as public intellectual was already threadbare when handed down to Stone's generation by Norman Mailer and Gore Vidal. Stone's most obvious peers in this arena are Joan Didion and Susan Sontag. He rose to certain public occasions (9/11 for example) eloquently, but these were occasional sallies; he was always first and last an artist.

Stone's claim to be a theological novelist is far from frivolous. Yet he cannot very well be grouped with convinced Catholics like Mary Gordon, Wilfred Sheed, or Flannery O'Connor. His position of semidetached inquiry may be closest to Marilynne Robinson's. Any apparent descendance from Graham Greene is (like any apparent descendance from Ernest Hemingway) superficial. Yes, both Greene and Stone set politically edged stories in exotic locations, and both have a Catholic background, but the fact that Stone is a lapsed Catholic while Greene is a convert means that both their approaches and their conclusions are almost always opposite.

It may be that Stone's most typical American quality is being a complete maverick. The unique circumstances of his childhood helped make him so. Comparisons finally serve best to set him apart. At the end of the day, Robert Stone was his own man, and his own writer. As for the work, there is nothing else quite like it in the entire American canon.

———

Accepting his honorary degree from Amherst in 2005, Bob had talked very frankly about what mattered to him in the métier he had chosen. "Literature exists. We are able to entertain narratives about other people's lives, even imaginary people's lives, and recognize elements familiar to us from our own hopes, fears and dreams. Past lives, imaginary lives are seen to contain messages for us, metaphorically speaking. Our understanding may draw upon them. This is the importance of fiction, that it offers meaning." And further: "This process of recognizing ourselves in stories about other people is the beginning of all wisdom. As soon as we understand that we may draw meaning from other lives, we begin to wonder if life itself may not have an underlying meaning. It's a congenial notion. Most people suffer and would very much like it if their suffering meant something."

Stone would of course continue to earn his right to that last statement over the ten years to come. During that time his study of the process of human being kept pulling him back in the direction of Scripture. "Adam is supposed to have named all the creatures of the garden in order to assert his dominion over them. Language is a way of rationalizing life, subjecting the chaos around us to the control of grammar and reason. Fiction carries this process one step further by suggesting a moral relationship between people and things. Those who assert that good fiction can work its way free of moral valences are mistaken. From the most simplistic narrative with its good guys and bad guys to the most decadent and arcane poetry, wherever fiction exists, judgment is in progress. It's inescapable, built into the language, into the grammar."

The value of storytelling is particularly built into the foundational texts of the Judeo-Christian tradition. "The western Bible assumes that human action matters, matters even on a cosmic scale. In its view of the universe, life is not an illusion nor does the universe consist of endless cycles eternally replaying dreams. Its God, unlike many, is directly concerned with humanity. So our ancestors examined the strange stories in the Bible for their meaning, their message. They felt certain that every story was intended as a lesson and guide."

Of course the most durable stories of Scripture aren't openly or obviously didactic, any more than Robert Stone novels are. If not wholly inscrutable they are resistant to certain or exhaustive interpretation. Holding a mirror to the world and the people in it, they reflect the mystery there contained. In his *New York Times* obituary, Bruce Weber quoted Bob expanding on this theme: " 'I see this enormous empty space from which God has absented himself,' Mr. Stone said in a *New York Times Magazine* interview in 1992. 'I see this enormous mystery that I can't penetrate, a mystery before which I'm silent and uncomprehending. This, in any case, is where I find myself in my sixth decade.' "

"The sensation of being seduced by a fiction is very satisfying and can be surprisingly intense," Stone told his Amherst audience. "Most literate people can remember being possessed by a novel." At a turning point in his own life, Mark Powell (a novelist who'd been a student of Stone's at the Key West Literary Seminar) was thus possessed by the novels of Robert Stone. "It's a bit dramatic to say I felt lost in a vast wood, but it's not exactly untrue either. I had discarded the evangelical Christianity of my boyhood with such a thoroughness I had begun to feel the rough grain of my decision. It was difficult for me to believe, and yet it was impossible not to. I felt the necessity of choosing something—anything—on my skin like a rash. What I discovered in Stone was that I didn't have to. It was perfectly acceptable to live in the tension of unknowing, doubt scaled against faith, neither attempting to resolve the other. Belief in God, Karl Rahner wrote, is orientation toward mystery. If there is any central line present throughout all the work of Robert Stone it is, I believe, an orientation to mystery."

An athlete of perception in a very Stone-like way, Powell puts his finger on the "tension of unknowing" that his writer/hero inhabited. In his interview for the PBS program *John Paul II: The Millennial Pope*, Stone said, "When I was about fifteen or sixteen, for the usual rationalist reasons, I stopped believing—at that time under the impression that belief and faith were the same thing. I since understand that they are not the same thing. But I thought they were. And I stopped believing in all this stuff. And I felt tremendously liberated. And only somewhat later, only years later, did it come to me that half of my head was missing, that I had just cut myself off, from a tremendously important part of myself that was no longer available."

He had begun to recover the missing piece during his deep dive in the Johnson Sea Link submersible: "capable of going to enormous depths. And it's totally dark, except for the bio-phosphorescent creatures that live there, tritons and cedapods and creatures like this. You feel like you're in the ocean at the dawn of creation. What it made me think of is when God confronts Job. God asks him [and at this point Stone's voice becomes deep and incantatory], Can you draw Leviathan with a hook? Who made Behemoth? Have you seen the springs of the ocean? And I thought, well, huh, I'm seeing the springs of the ocean. And I thought that this creature has as much life, is as perfectly formed, as complete in its destiny, in its place in things, as I am. And it made me think, surely there is a Providence underlying all these wonders. And that tempted me to faith."

Being tempted to faith is not the same thing as embracing it, no more than faith and belief are the same thing. Stone had told a *Paris Review* interviewer years before that "it's almost as hard to stop being a Catholic as it is to stop being a black." But the point of the deep-dive experience was not a reversion to the Catholicism of his childhood. Late in life, Stone was working his way toward a relationship to faith that would not require returning to belief in the corpus of mythology that is its usual medium. In the draft of his "Coda" (which did after all turn out to be a farewell), he wrote: "Perhaps it was rash of me to describe the fisher of Leviathan as a GIANT INVISIBLE BABYLONIAN PAPERWEIGHT. I propose to go on serving, to serve better. God must in appallingly stranger mercy understand that he is the one joke by which we live and that he, agent or principal, is at the center of it."

In 2008, Mark Powell, then a stranger to Stone, wrote him a letter about how Bob's work had helped him resolve his own religious crisis. He expected no answer and was surprised to receive one, in which Stone "thanked me for my letter and spoke of his need to be of service. That his writing might be something other than an indulgence—that was his hope. To the extent that he could pray—that was his prayer. I thank you from the bottom of my heart—so closed the letter—and may God, wherever He has gone, bless you."

———

Absconded God, of course, can't be expected to furnish magical solutions to anything. There is not much indication that Robert Stone expected anything of that kind, even at the end of his life when he had begun
sometimes to mutter about the possibility of redemption. His life and his
work take place in the real human world, where magical thinking is dangerous folly, where we have no one to turn to but each other, where "the
thing that you have to do is not die."

When Bob first ran that line by me, I asked him to say it in Spanish,
and was surprised when he couldn't pull it out. Jim Maraniss, who was in
the vicinity, did it off the cuff: *El importante es no morirse.* This sentence
raised my meager stock of Spanish to about twenty words, so I had no
right to be suspicious of it, but it felt to me like a retranslation, somehow.
Years later I asked Jim again and he replied: *"Lo que hay que hacer es no
morirse.* I learned this from Antonio Benítez-Rojo, who knew Cuban folk
sayings, of course." Bob had used this version in his article "Havana Then
and Now," with the gloss that it was something Cuban slaves used to say
to themselves and each other, which makes compellingly good sense.

Then, some while after Bob had died, I stumbled on it somewhere
else, maybe as a scrap of dialogue in some semi-bilingual story: *El merito
es estar vivo.* This has to be it, I said to myself, the very thing I didn't quite
know I was looking for—the same idea but expressed in positive terms.

The virtue is to be alive.

This version, old friend, I will bring you in the next life, if there is one.

ACKNOWLEDGMENTS

Janice Stone, who served Bob as muse, secretary, personal assistant, travel agent, copy editor, proofreader, archivist, and organizer until his death in 2015, began undertaking most of those roles for this project later the same year. Without her work, it is safe to say, this biography would not exist (and probably much of Bob's work wouldn't either). She had her archive of Stone drafts, correspondence, travel records, contracts, and everything else organized to a degree that only a biographer in possession of a magic lamp would have the nerve to wish for.

Janice is herself a writer to reckon with, with a style completely unlike Bob's—her remarkable memoir of her life with him, which she began in 2015, became the first armature for this volume. Her companionship during the years of my work was as much a joy as her support was essential. When (while I was burrowing my way through one more file of correspondence) a liverwurst sandwich mysteriously appeared at my elbow, I had an inkling of how completely Bob must have depended on her in small things, as well as great. Thanks to her generosity I was able to spend many months going over the archives in the Stones' New York City apartment, and I also got to write the last line of this biography sitting at Bob's desk and sharing his view of the distant Triborough Bridge.

Ian Stone is first on the list of a great many people who took the time to talk to me extensively about their relationships with Bob Stone, mostly but not exclusively via written correspondence (a tremendous convenience for me). Ian is also a redoubtable writer, whose style does have something in common with Bob's, as do the strength of his convictions and his fluency of expression. Also the host of Bob's friends of youth and later years (Bob had a great gift for friendship): Robert A. Bell, Grace Schulman, Michael

Horowitz, Merrill Gerber, Chloe Scott, Diana Barich (née Shugart), Dirk van Nouhuys, Ed McClanahan, Jane Burton, Bill Barich, James Wolpman, Gurney Norman, Joan Michelson, Eleanor Brooks, Jim Maraniss, Ruth Pratt, Andrew Ervin, Annie Dillard, Arlo Haskell, Chris Offutt, David Blistein, David Wolkowsky, Elena Castedo, Lauren Wein, Bob Gottleib, John Martini, Kem Nunn, Emily Cheng, Mark Powell, Neil Olson, Mark Levene, Paul Sweeney, Philip Tsiaris, John Monroe, Sandra Djikstra, Tatjana Soli, Tim Tankosic, Tom Alderson, Tom Jenks, Bob Richardson, Edward Hower, and whomever I forgot (and I'm sure there are a few).

William Heath was kind enough to let me have early drafts of his definitive collection of Stone interviews, *Conversations with Robert Stone*, and also the final page proofs of that work—and a very great kindness it has turned out to be. These materials have been invaluable to me in many ways, not least in assembling the endnotes to this volume.

My thanks also to Tal Nadan and the rest of the staff of the Brooke Russell Astor Reading Room at the New York Public Library for their skillful and discreet support of my work with NYPL's extensive Robert Stone collection.

Thanks to the Leon Levy Center for Biography, for the generous grant given me in 2011–2012 to support my writing of a biography . . . not this one, as it turns out, but here's this one for what it is worth—something to show for the Levy Center's investment in me as a biographer.

I'm indebted to Philip Gaskill for some critical logistical support in time of urgent need, to Alexandra Truitt for expert research on the photos included in this volume, and to Anna Young for sleuthing out old bits of press I'd half forgotten and could not find.

Copy editing a book like this one is no joke, and Karla Eoff has done a thorough and excellent job of it, with the thorough and excellent collaboration of Bette Alexander.

Thanks to my agent, Deborah Schneider, especially for finding the ideal editor for this book in Gerald Howard. Gerry and I have been friends for decades, but here is the first book we have done together. He took his dismay at receiving a nearly thousand-page manuscript more or less in stride. When I proposed, *You cut; I'll suture*, he was willing to take that approach—where most editors nowadays would have just said, *Call me when you've got it down to half the length*. A good editor doing his job will piss a writer off once in a while, but Gerry very seldom stung me for no reason. This book is much the better for his meticulously attentive reading and astute judgment—in three passes that add up to one of the best editorial experiences of my career.

NOTES

Five general categories of source are frequently quoted in this biography.

1. A thus far unpublished memoir by Janice Stone (see below).
2. The collection of Stone papers that Janice Stone had organized and which she allowed me to use for many months before it was put on its pathway to join the Robert Stone archive already at the New York Public Library (see below).
3. William Heath's early and final iterations of an essential volume of interviews ultimately published as *Conversations with Robert Stone*.
4. "Unpublished interviews" conducted with Stone's friends and family members (named in the preceding acknowledgments) from 2015 to 2019; these exist only as digital files in my personal system.
5. Robert Stone papers, 1950–2012, held by the New York Public Library's Manuscripts and Archives Division (nypl.org).

The following abbreviations appear in these notes:

BaHD	Robert Stone, *Bear and His Daughter* (New York: Houghton Mifflin, 1997)
BoS	Robert Stone, *Bay of Souls* (New York: Houghton Mifflin Harcourt, 2003)
CoL	Robert Stone, *Children of Light* (New York: Alfred A. Knopf, 1986)
CwRS	*Conversations with Robert Stone*, ed. William Heath (Jackson, MS: University of Mississippi Press, 2017)
DG	Robert Stone, *Damascus Gate* (New York: Houghton Mifflin, 1997)
DotBHG	Robert Stone, *Death of the Black-Haired Girl* (New York: Houghton Mifflin Harcourt, 2013)

DS	Robert Stone, *Dog Soldiers* (Boston: Houghton Mifflin, 1973)
EYE	*The Eye You See With: Selected Nonfiction of Robert Stone*, ed. Madison Smartt Bell (New York: Houghton Mifflin Harcourt, 2020)
FFS	Robert Stone, *A Flag for Sunrise* (New York: Knopf, 1981)
Greif	"Thomas—Case #6," Ann Greif (unpublished thesis, circa 1978), NYPL/Lopez
HoM	Robert Stone, *A Hall of Mirrors* (Boston: Houghton Mifflin, 1964)
NYC	Robert Stone, "A New York Childhood" (*Architectural Digest*, October 1996)
NYPL	Robert Stone Archive, New York Public Library
NYPL/Lopez	Robert Stone archive being prepared, at the time of this writing, by bibliographer Ken Lopez for offer to the New York Public Library
OR	Robert Stone, *Outerbridge Reach* (New York: Ticknor & Fields, 1992)
PG	Robert Stone, *Prime Green: Remembering the Sixties* (New York: HarperCollins, 2007)
WWI	Robert Stone, "The Way the World Is," *Once a Catholic*, ed. Peter Occhiogrosso (New York: Houghton Mifflin, 1987)
Weber	Bruce Weber, "An Eye for Danger," *The New York Times Magazine* (January 19, 1992): pp. 19–24
Woods	William Crawford Woods, "Robert Stone, The Art of Fiction, No. 90," *The Paris Review* 27 (Winter 1985)

Quotations without citations in the notes below are from Janice Stone's unpublished memoir of her life with Robert Stone.

EPIGRAPHS

ix   "its story about itself": Robert Stone, "1984," in EYE, 129.

ix   "in order not to fall": Robert Stone, "The Reason for Stories: Toward a Moral Fiction," *Harper's Magazine* (June 1998).

PREFACE

xiv   "slothful perfectionist": Robert Stone, conversation with Madison Smartt Bell.

xv   "burning the unburied grain": Robert Lowell, "Children of Light," *Lord Weary's Castle* (Boston: Houghton Mifflin, 1946).

PART ONE: A HALL OF MIRRORS

3   "then I was out again": WWI, 43.

4   "looking out for me": Greif, 19.

4   "difficult to be very clear": Ibid., 10.

4   "Sy had been his mother's lover": FFS, 28.

4   "affirming two different names": PG, 27.

5   "age of forty or what not": Greif, 14.

6   "something she had grown up with": Ibid., 13. NB: And all preceding quotations in this paragraph.

7   "useful to me outside that world": Ibid., 16.

7   "serious fashion which was engaging": Ibid., 13.

7   "I didn't not like her": Ibid., 16.

7   "a center I could not contact": Ibid., 18.

7   "She was a great actress": Ibid., 19.

8   "basis of their relationship": Ibid., 50.

8   "no contact with her family": Ibid., 10.

8   "various hearings": Ibid., 23.

8   "for the size I was": Ibid., 18.

8   "punch him around": Ibid., 32.

9   "that was the scene": Ibid., 23.

9   "hit them on the hands": WWI, 44.

9   "bloody never learned it": Greif, 39.

10   "beyond your age capacity": Ibid., 31.

10   "extremely chauvinistic": Ibid., 35.

10   "kind of lost paradise": Robert Solotaroff, "An Interview with Robert Stone," in CwRS, 123.

10   "for my mother's benefit": Greif, 22.

10   "TURGENEV": "Coda," in EYE.

10   "I could never get it through": Greif, 30.

11   "bigger than I was": Ibid., 31.

11   "thing going with that bear": Ibid., 32.

11   "I wasn't taken out": Ibid.

11   "orphans about to be beaten": BaHD, 30–31.

11   "suffering more than I": Robert Stone, letter to Brother Vincent Jerome, July 5, 1998, NYPL/Lopez.

12   "prefects and procurators": Greif, 45.

12   "one ongoing story going": Ibid., 31.

12   "I just kept it up": Ibid., 37.

12   "going to school to": Ibid., 45.

12   "running story games to play out": Ibid., 44. NB: Pseudonyms are used for all players in the Greif manuscript, including for Stone.

13   "which seems kind of unfair": WWI, 43.

13   "about Renaissance painters": Greif, 36.

13   "slapped you around in the classroom": Solotaroff, in CwRS, 121.

13   "in its way good": Maureen Karagueuzian, "Interview with Robert Stone," *TriQuarterly* 53 (Winter 1982).

13   "I realize it now": Weber, 19–24.

13   "kick the son of a bitch": Woods, 28.

14   "what you have to do": WWI, 44–46. NB: For all quotations in this paragraph.

14   "no need for this": Greif, 25.

15   "I didn't want it": Ibid.

15   "that is what I did": Ibid.

15   "made them hit you": Ibid., 26.

15   "all the more troublesome": Solotaroff, in CwRS, 124.

16   "when there weren't any systems": Ibid.

16   "emotionally crippled individual in American life": Charles Ruas, "A Talk with Robert Stone," *The New York Times Book Review*, October 18, 1981, nytimes.com, accessed May 21, 2019.

16   "that I recognized in others": Greif, 27.

16   "being the deserving poor": OR, 35.

17   "tradition of conning": Greif, 27.

17   "but quite eventful": George Rhoades horoscope, NYPL, box 22, folder 2.

17   "lonely, solitary people": Greif, 28.

18   "not getting married": NYC, 50–56. NB: And all other quotations in this paragraph.

18   "as it were, afar": Ibid., 54. NB: And all other quotations in this paragraph.

18   "Museum of Natural History": Ibid.

19   "stress and confusion to me": Robert Stone, untitled essay fragment, NYPL/Lopez.

19   "in an unpleasant way": Greif, 49.

19   "fondness for Catholicism": Ibid., 41.

20   "their own personal idiosyncrasies": Ibid., 38.

20   "poetry in Latin": Steve Chapple, "Robert Stone Faces the Devil," *Mother Jones* 9 (May 1984), 35.

20   "true literary experience": Robert Stone, letter to Brother Vincent Jerome, July 5, 1998, NYPL/Lopez.

20   "provocative, and strange": Ruas, in CwRS, 52.

20   "weirdo": Greif, 37.

21   "everything they stood for": Ibid., 42.

21   "hitting me all the time": Ibid., 37.

21   "off her black suit": Stone juvenilia, "The Vulture," NYPL, box 44, folder 12 (folder mislabeled "box 41").

21   "mercy for them at all": Greif, 38.

21   "winning any arguments": John Gavin, letter to Robert Stone, October 22, 1998, NYPL/Lopez.

22   "clients infuriated us": NYC, 55. NB: And all other quotations in this and the previous paragraph.

22   "girl's good looks": Ibid., 55–56.

22   "any crazy shit": Solotaroff, in CwRS, 123.

22   "war counselor": Greif, 47.

22   "safe by today's standards": NYC, 56.

23   "occasion of sin": Greif, 49.

23   "an idealized version": Solotaroff, in CwRS, 128.

24   "try things together": Robert Stone, "The Two Smartest Kids on the Block,"

unpublished short story, NYPL, box 44, folder 3 (folder mislabeled box 41). NB: And all quotations in the preceding four paragraphs.

25   "than anything else": Chapple, "Robert Stone Faces the Devil," 40.

25   "for Calvary Cemetery": WWI, 54.

25   "grand inquisition": Greif, 41–42.

25   "I was a superhero": Ibid., 42.

25   "thrown out of school": Ibid.

26   "more solid way": Solotaroff, in CwRS, 125.

26   "bad, it was": Greif, 51.

26   "than I am now": Ibid., 53.

26   "somewhere in my head": Ibid., 43.

26   "mannered and artificial": Ibid., 19.

27   "next morning feeling older": Robert Stone, "The City Is of Night," *Good Themes* (New York: New York University, 1954), 20–25.

27   "intensely Salingeresque": Solotaroff, in CwRS, 125.

28   "do with his time": Stone, "The City Is of Night," 20–25. NB: And all quotations in preceding five paragraphs.

28   "really set me up": Solotaroff, in CwRS, 128.

28   "acceptable and secure": Ibid., 125.

28   "kiddie cruise": Greif, 58.

28   "Corny old Navy stuff": Christopher Bollen, "The Total Anti-Totalist," in CwRS, 199.

29   "I really needed them": Robert Stone, untitled essay fragment, NYPL/Lopez.

29   "over again": Solotaroff, in CwRS, 157.

29   "an instinctive cringe": Ibid., 121.

29   "really shocked them": Ibid.

29   "stacked up on the hull": Ibid., 126.

29   "as plain as dumpsters": Robert Stone, "Uncle Sam Doesn't Want You," *The New York Review of Books*, September 23, 1993.

30   "de facto leadership": Ibid.

30   "angry about that": Greif, 56.

30   "very bad indeed": Ibid.

30   "nobody much cared": Stone, "Uncle Sam Doesn't Want You."

30   "like a cooze": Ibid. NB: And all other quotations in this paragraph.

32   "and you make it art": Robert Stone, "Me and the Universe," *The Writer in Our World*, ed. Reginald Gibbons (New York: Atlantic Monthly Press, 1986), 215–17. NB: And all quotations in the preceding six paragraphs.

32   but not the one at Port Said: In a different account, Stone says that the events he saw happened in Ismailia; however, the *Chilton* did not call at either port during the Suez Crisis. Since the *Chilton* was present for an action at Alexandria during the same period, it is most likely that what he describes happened there.

32   "Greece, for example": Solotaroff, in CwRS, 128.

32   "not political": James Maraniss, unpublished interview.

33   "everyone was nice": Robert Stone, "Havana Then and Now," *Harper's Magazine*, March 1992.

33   "into imaginary ones": Ibid.

34   "the lovely, deadly night": Robert Stone, "The Good Neighbor," unpublished short story, NYPL, box 44, folder 7. NB: And all quotations in the preceding two paragraphs.

34   "or whatever": Woods.

34   "prophecy at its core": Robert Stone, untitled essay fragment, NYPL/Lopez.

34   "I understood it!": Ibid.

35   "people to hang with": Bollen, in CwRS, 199.

35   "in the navy": Ruas, in CwRS, 39.

35   "what it was": Solotaroff, in CwRS, 127.

36   "the poles of my desire": PG, 21.

36   "in New Zealand and Australia": Robert Kinsloe Bell, unpublished interview.

36   "took them to a movie": Robert Kinsloe Bell, *Ask and Accept* (Orlando, FL: Bells, 2003), 86.

36   "man just disappeared": Ibid., 93.

36   "by his mother": Woods.

37   "no limit to the supply": Claude Bristol, *The Magic of Believing* (Princeton, NJ: Princeton Cambridge Publishing Group, 2010), 48.

37   "winter day in New York": Solotaroff, in CwRS, 127.

37   "outskirts of Cheyenne": Robert Stone, untitled essay fragment, NYPL/Lopez.

37   "look at the penguins": Solotaroff, in CwRS, 127.

38   "lonely place to die": Robert Stone, "The Trojan Letter," unpublished short story, NYPL, box 44, folder 5.

38   "beautiful, terrible sight": Robert Stone, untitled essay fragment, NYPL/Lopez.

39   "great Melbourne tennis player": Bell, *Ask and Accept*, 111.

39   "the dingy gym": PG, 3.

39   "Not like most blokes": Ibid., 6.

40   "The horror": Ibid., 16–18.

40   "no way to have breakfast": Solotaroff, in CwRS, 129.

40   "I walked away": Robert Stone, untitled essay fragment, NYPL/Lopez.

40   "no beef with the French": PG, 20.

41   "put together an education": Robert Stone, untitled essay fragment, NYPL/Lopez.

41   "had a bad time": Bollen, in CwRS, 199.

41   "tremendously helpful": Solotaroff, in CwRS, 129.

41   "when I came out": Greif, 59.

41   "out in me": Solotaroff, in CwRS, 128.

41   "no hassle": Greif, 61.

42   "free again": Robert Stone, untitled essay fragment, NYPL/Lopez.

42   "years to come": PG, 29.

43   "the morgue for instance": Solotaroff, in CwRS, 130.

43   "come out for death": Ibid.

43   "child like me": PG, 32.

44   *Star Trek* uniform": Ibid., 41.

46   "rhythm of a treadmill": Ibid., 29.

46   "rest of my life": Grace Schulman, tribute to Mack Rosenthal in a pamphlet privately printed for a memorial service.

46   "teacher for me": Robert Stone, tribute to Mack Rosenthal in a pamphlet privately printed for a memorial service.

46   "beaten up be": Mack Rosenthal handwritten notes on Robert Stone, "A Walk in the Street," unpublished short story, NYPL, box 44, folder 6.

47   "poetic passages": Ibid.

47   "pretty standard": Ibid.

47   "response to the death": Mack Rosenthal handwritten notes on Robert Stone, "The Trojan Letter," unpublished short story, NYPL, box 44, folder 5.

47   "write the letter": Ibid.

47   "Oscar Wilde-ism": Ibid.

47   "frozen in silence": Ibid.

47   "wordy": Ibid.

48   "loves the bastards": Robert Stone, "The Dark Winter of Corporal Rafferty," unpublished short story, NYPL, box 44, folder 4.

48   "Read your book": Ibid.

48   "ain't part of": Ibid.

48   "too horrible": Ibid.

48   "I'm an intelligent guy": Ibid.

49   "subsequently married": Stone, tribute to Rosenthal.

50   "18-year-old undergraduate": Wallace Stegner, quoted in "History of the Stanford Writing Program," creativewriting.stanford.edu, accessed May 2, 2019.

55   "good feelings for each other": Greif, 66.

56   "changed my life": Ruas, in CwRS, 43.

57   "conversation with him": Greif, 70.

59   " 'cause he was so": Ibid., 66.

60   "the next day": Ibid., 67.

60   "romantic newlyweds": PG, 43.

61   "really dirty": Greif, 74–75.

61   "more than anything": PG, 56.

61   "sangfroid to try": Greif, 56.

62   "whites and blacks": Ibid., 47.

62   "word to anybody": Ibid., 48.

62   "system was about": Solotaroff, in CwRS, 130.

62   "some population": Ibid., 40.

63   "mourn and pray": PG, 61.

64   "either, luckily": Janice Stone, letter to the Burrs, April 27, 1960, private collection.

64   "the poor went there": PG, 58.

65   "isn't everyone else's": Janice Stone, letter to the Burrs, April 27, 1960, private collection.

66   "since Reconstruction": PG, 52.

66   "to spring us": Ibid.

67   "the bar pillars": Ibid., 59.

67   "slamming shut forever": Ibid., 62.

68   "see her again": Ibid.

68   "as he chooses": Greif, 73–74.

68   "going down in New Orleans": Ibid., 75.

68   "burned the poetry": Ibid.

68   "begin a novel": Kay Bonetti, "An Interview with Robert Stone," in CwRS, 77.

69   "me to go there": Maureen Karagueuzian, "Interview with Robert Stone," TriQuarterly 53 (Winter 1982).

69   "my own scam": PG, 69.

69   "wouldn't have to work": Janice Stone letter to her aunt Helen, June 8, 1961, private collection.

70   "chicken-wired hotels": PG, 67.

70   "than most whites": Ibid., 68.

70   "anything I ever saw": Ibid.

70   "your good stuff goes": Ibid., 69.

71   "write a novel": Woods, 27.

72   "many in California": Alec Hanley Bemis, "What It Was Like to Study Under Robert Stone," The New Republic, February 9, 2015.

74   "that'll be it": HoM, 14.

75   "off the Stanford Campus": Ed McClanahan, "The Day the Lampshades Breathed," in I Just Hitchhiked In from the Coast: The Ed McClanahan Reader (Berkeley, CA: Counterpoint, 2011), 40.

75   "weird time-future": Robert Stone, foreword to My Vita, If You Will: The Uncollected Ed McClanahan by Ed McClanahan (Berkeley: Counterpoint, 1998).

75   "You had to be there": Robert Stone, introduction of Ken Kesey reading at the 92nd Street Y, 1992, unpublished manuscript, NYPL/Lopez.

76   "understand all the words": Vic Lovell, "The Perry Lane Papers (II): Wayward Girls," One Lord, One Faith, One Cornbread, eds. Fred Nelson and Ed McClanahan (Garden City, NY: Anchor Press, 1973), 120.

76   "Sin Hollow": Rick Dodgson, "Ken Kesey and the Sexual Mores of Perry Lane," Utne Reader (October 2013).

76   "writing papers": Lovell, "The Perry Lane Papers," 120.

76   "sleeping with everybody": Dodgson, "Ken Kesey and the Sexual Mores of Perry Lane."

77   "group love affair": Ibid.

77   "it usually did": McClanahan, 44.

77   "to their lairs": Ken Kesey, One Flew Over the Cuckoo's Nest (New York: Viking Press, 1962), frontmatter.

77	"It was grand": Jane Burton, unpublished interview.
77	"against your cheek": McClanahan, 41.
78	"didn't mind": Burton, unpublished interview.
78	"rictus of terror": PG, 75.
78	"soprano sax riffs": Ibid.
79	"every novel I've written": Ruas, in CwRS, 44.
81	"offer his advice": Merrill Joan Gerber, *Gut Feelings* (Madison, WI: University of Wisconsin Press, 2003).
81	"the class was transfixed": Merrill Joan Gerber, unpublished interview.
82	"three of the Viking editors": Malcolm Cowley to Robert Stone, March 22, 1963, NYPL/Lopez.
82	"on a literary fellowship": Paul Brooks to Robert Stone, April 9, 1963, NYPL/Lopez.
82	"completed manuscript": Ibid.
83	"playing my flute": Diana Shugart Barich, unpublished interview.
83	"chased *them*": PG, 78.
83	"raise their hands": McClanahan, 46.
83	"in jubilation": Gerber.
84	"I was the only one": Diana Shugart Barich, unpublished interview.
85	"charm for women": Jane Burton, unpublished interview.
85	"had an infant": Diana Shugart Barich, unpublished interview.
85	"over the years": Jane Burton, unpublished interview.
85	"along with Jane Burton": Gurney Norman, unpublished interview.
85	"scores a knockout": Gordon Lish to Robert Stone, November 18, 1963, NYPL/Lopez.
86	"so it seemed to me": Jane Burton, unpublished interview.
87	"any of the other people": Dirk van Nouhuys, unpublished interview.
88	"A cure": PG, 104.
88	"transcendent friendship": Jane Burton, unpublished interview.
89	"up at Kesey's": Robert Stone to Janice Stone, 1964, NYPL/Lopez.
89	"not a bad way to look at it": Ibid.
90	"with that action": Ibid.
90	"to get done": Ibid.
90	"pad in the Mexican mountains": Ibid.
90	"same old shit": Ibid.
91	"haunt your dreams": PG, 105.
91	"a major dereliction": Ibid.
91	"in the way of the life force": Jane Burton, unpublished interview.
91	"changing that": Ibid.
92	"home on wheels to me": PG, 107.
92	"ongoing first novel": Ibid., 111.
92	"great work in progress": Ibid., 117–18.
93	"unspoiled New York City": McClanahan, 101.
95	"miss the kids": Robert Stone to Janice Stone, 1964, NYPL/Lopez.
95	"Papal splendor": Ibid.

96   "liberator for the generation": *Magic Trip*, directors Alex Gibney and Alison Ellwood (Magnolia Pictures, 2011).

96   "thing of the past": Ibid.

98   "Beside Hell's fireside": Randall Jarrell, "Cinderella," *The Complete Poems* (New York: Farrar, Straus and Giroux, 1969), 217.

98   "guest writer in residence": Joan Michelson, unpublished interview.

100   "fit like a nail": PG, 134.

100   "he had invented it": Dirk van Nouhuys, unpublished interview.

101   "to the intellect": PG, 133.

102   "intellectual Zorro": Robert Stone, unpublished draft of "The Man Who Turned on the Here," NYPL/Lopez, 27.

102   "You've turned on the Here": Ibid., 9.

103   "laudanum heads": Ibid.

103   "Everything": Ibid., 4.

103   "it will hear": Ibid., 13.

103   "in absolute control": Ibid., 5.

103   "world of the future": Ibid., 9.

104   "the name of the future": Ibid.

105   "good old Boise": Robert Stone, "The Man Who Turned on the Here," *One Lord, One Faith, One Cornbread*, eds. Fred Nelson and Ed McClanahan (Garden City, NY: Anchor Press, 1973), 55.

105   "any tempo I choose": Marshall McLuhan, *Understanding Media: The Extensions of Man* (Boston: MIT Press, 1964), 15.

105   "Tell it to a neutral reader": Harold Hayes to Robert Stone, 1966, NYPL, box 22, folder 2.

106   "quaintly menacing": PG, 165.

107   "sends her love": Robert Stone to Jim Wolpman, 1966, NYPL/Lopez.

108   "went into it": Robert Stone, "The Reason for Stories: Toward a Moral Fiction," *Harper's Magazine*, June 1998.

110   "turned her face away": HoM, 10.

110   "dropped dead": Ibid., 181.

111   "how beautiful I am": Ibid., 47.

111   "I'll be goddamned": Ibid., 102.

111   "eagles and lightning": Ibid., 109.

112   "ground their teeth at him": Ibid., 141.

112   "We do that": Ibid., 143.

112   "field service overseas": Ibid.

112   "to you, Mr. Rainey": Ibid.

113   "absolutely impervious": Ibid., 149.

113   "Lester Clotho, colored": Ibid., 157.

113   "reform-minded attitude": Ibid., 163.

113   "bringing her along": Ibid., 179.

114   "question marks and things": Ibid., 23.

114   "from the blade": Ibid., 41.

114   "don't believe in it": Ibid., 172.

114   "presence of virtue": Ibid., 174.

114   "when I find out": Ibid., 175.

115   "damn thing started": Ibid., 245.

115   "strike this down": Ibid.

115   "from passing cars": Ibid., 267.

116   "nigger neighborhood": Ibid., 299.

116   "bolt for the exits": Ibid., 298.

116   "extremist niggers": Ibid., 299.

117   "and falls dead": Ibid., 367.

117   "never so pretty as in May": Ibid., 368.

118   "feel anything there": Ibid.

118   "primary process": FFS, 228.

118   "survival and so forth": HoM, 377.

118   "Individual initiative": Ibid., 377.

118   "make you feel sad": Ibid., 394.

118   "What, dead?": Ibid., 395.

119   "would have said Gogol": Ruas, in CwRS, 44.

119   "author's vision of America": Christopher Lehmann-Haupt, *The New York Times*, September 12, 1967.

120   "to the body politic": Howard Junker, *Newsweek*, October 9, 1967.

120   "an historical moment ago": Ivan Gold, *The New York Times Book Review*, September 24, 1967.

PART TWO: DOG SOLDIERS

125   "it was entirely different": Alec Haley Bemis, *L.A. Weekly*, January 17, 2007.

127   "In sorrow and woe": Ronald Vickery, "All Things Are Quite Silent," in *Notes from the Isle of Laev, Part I: Lammas* (Lulu.com, 2017), 185.

128   "they could do that": Robert Stone, unpublished manuscript, NYPL/Lopez. NB: All quotations from the Dunaway profile.

129   "disheartening to most Americans": Robert Stone, "We Couldn't Swing with It: 'The Intrepid Four,'" *The Atlantic* 221, No. 6 (June 1968). NB: And all quotes from this article.

130   "a frustrated one-novel novelist": Sybil Steinberg, "An Interview with Robert Stone," *Publishers Weekly*, March 21, 1986, 72–73.

134   "to save her life": Janice Stone, letter to the Burr family, November 1968, private collection.

137   "I did not see them": Ian Stone, unpublished interview.

138   "it totally knocked me out": Ibid.

140   "not very with-it graduate student": PG, 181.

141   "squid in threatening situations": Ibid., 183.

141   "mocked by Nathanael West": Ibid.

142   "somehow connected": Ibid., 184.

142   "point was their ambiguity": Ibid., 185.

142   "stories we wanted to tell": Ibid., 183.

142   "peculiar frisson": Ibid., 184.

143   "just like real rain": Janice Stone, letter to Deidre and Ian Stone, May 1969, private collection.

143   "without you here": Eleanor Brooks to Robert and Janice Stone, July 1969, private collection.

143   "it was worth it": Janice Stone, letter to the Burr family, June 1969, private collection.

143   "sleek-looking sedan": Ian Stone, unpublished interview.

143   "without air-conditioning": Janice Stone, letter to the Burr family, June 1969, private collection.

143   "it was all over": Solotaroff, in CwRS, 144.

144   "nearest equivalent cliché": Jim Schumock, "A Conversation with Robert Stone," *Story Story Story: Conversations with American Authors* (Seattle, WA: Black Heron Press, 1999), 72–81.

144   "of poison oak": Janice Stone, letter to the Burr family, July 8, 1969, private collection.

144   "about to witness": PG, 188.

145   "psychodrama marathons": midpeninsulafreeu.com, accessed May 6, 2019.

145   "John the Baptist to Werner Erhard": Dirk van Nouhuys, unpublished interview.

145   "joy, love and peace": Peter Smart, "Chung: Psychodrama Letter #1," *The Free You* 3, No. 6 (May 1969): 4–5.

145   "psychodrama in disarray": Jim Wolpman, unpublished interview.

146   "ensconced in moguldom": PG, 197.

146   "in a handful of dust": PG, 198.

146   "indifferent episode of *Matlock*": PG, 197.

146   "fall short of *The Manchurian Candidate*": Roger Greenspun, *The New York Times*, November 2, 1970.

146   "and the best": John Walker, ed., *Halliwell's Film Guide* (New York: Harper Perennial, 1977), 1276.

147   "god-awful movie": William Heath and Michael Berryhill, "An Interview with Robert Stone," in CwRS, 12.

147   "twice in the ad": Alfred Butler Burr, letter to the Stone family, October 25, 1970.

149   "communist-inspired": Ibid.

149   "more than a place": Eric Schroeder, "Keep the Levels of Consciousness Sharp," in CwRS, 44.

149   "changed my life": Chappell, 39.

150   "poorly laid-out": Janice Stone, unpublished London journal, private collection.

151   "Robert has departed": Ibid.

151   "on board": PG, 208.

151   "paid their dues": Robert Stone, "There It Is," *The Guardian*, July 17, 1971, 9.

152   "insane exhilaration": Ibid.

152   "head shorthand": Ibid.

152   "do justice to": Heath and Berryhill, in CwRS, 21.

153 "discount any of them": Weber, 22.

153 "extremely dislocating": Stone, "There It Is."

153 "outraged humanism": Ibid.

154 "washed-over bloodstain": Ibid.

154 "didn't have to be": Robert Stone, "No Such Thing as Peace," *Esquire*, March 1, 1983.

154 "did in Saigon": Sybil Steinberg, "An Interview with Robert Stone," *Publishers Weekly*, March 21, 1986, 72–73.

154 "it seemed betrayal": PG, 206.

155 "spirit of the war": Ibid., 221.

155 "on the hotel wall": Stone, "There It Is."

155 "got the inside dope": Janice Stone, unpublished London journal, private collection.

156 "my name on it": PG, 207.

157 "a different country": Ruas, in CwRS, 48.

159 "didn't have time for her": "Coda," in EYE, 539.

159 "financially uneventful year": Janice Stone, letter to Irving Zand, February 6, 1972, NYPL/Lopez.

159 "things were actually about": Heath and Berryhill, in CwRS, 4.

161 "of me, at least": James Maraniss, unpublished interview.

163 "loyalty toward each other": HMCo Advance Report from the Editors, March 29, 1974.

164 "best novelists under forty": Richard Locke, "Dog Soldiers," *The New York Times Book Review*, November 3, 1974. NB: All quotes from Locke's review.

164 "Flowers of Evil": Paul Gray, "Flowers of Evil: Dog Soldiers by Robert Stone," *Time*, November 11, 1974, 111.

164 "capture in *Dog Soldiers*": Rust Hills, "Writing," *Esquire*, December 1974, 9.

165 "novel of the year": William McPherson, "Dog Soldiers," *The Washington Post Book World*, December 22, 1974.

166 "if they get the chance": DS, 39.

166 "gets by me": Ibid., 172.

166 "existentialist caves": Stone, "There It Is," 9.

166 "Skydiver Devoured by Starving Birds": DS, 128.

166 "all there had ever been": Ibid., 186.

166 "instrument of agonizing death": Ibid., 185.

166 "I'm so glad that I'm here": Robert Stone, "Me and the Universe," in *The Writer in Our World*, ed. Reginald Gibbons (New York: Atlantic Monthly Press, 1986), 215–17.

166 "dead lions": DS, 186.

166 "therefore I am": Ibid., 42.

167 "want to get high": Ibid.

167 "death's head harlequin": Ibid., 96.

167 "psychopath": Ibid., 172.

168 "it's gone funny": Ibid., 57.

168 "no sense of irony": Ibid.

168   "huge erect phallus": Ibid., 116.

168   "Our land is your land": Ibid., 161.

169   "the next bag of bones is you": Ibid., 110.

169   "obsessiveness, a thinker": Ibid., 114.

169   "the heroin scene": Ibid., 190.

169   "old roshi": Ibid., 230.

170   "shattered cerebration, entombed": Ibid., 293.

170   "mortars, rockets, tank guns": Ibid., 299.

170   "Not Different From Form": Ibid., 318.

170   "*Chieu hoi*": Ibid., 301.

171   "Like everything else": Ibid., 315.

171   "he concentrated his pain": Ibid., 308.

171   "the hardest thing to get by": Ibid., 324.

171   "lies about themselves": Ibid.

171   "see you do it": Ibid., 325.

171   "hold its shape": Ibid., 327.

171   "if you only knew it": Ibid., 329.

172   "help their friends": Ibid., 306.

172   "we fought the war": Ibid., 307.

172   "like all men": Ibid., 15.

172   "I wanted to please her": Ibid., 133.

172   "dope for Charmian": Ibid., 185.

173   "The thing itself": Ibid., 96.

173   "a merely superstitious—esteem": Ibid., 261.

173   "thought and action for him": Ibid., 271.

173   "to embody absolutely": Ibid.

173   "get straight": Ibid.

174   "passed the 19,000 mark": Austin Olney to Robert Stone, January 22, 1975, NYPL, box 22, folder 3.

174   "Vietnam and drugs": Austin Olney to Candida Donadio, ibid.

174   "complain about that": Ibid.

176   "infinitely painful stumbling toward it": Robert Stone, National Book Award acceptance speech, 1975, NYPL/Lopez.

176   "only each other": FFS, 431.

177   "reaction to the period": Robert Stone, "The Reason for Stories: Toward a Moral Fiction," *Harper's Magazine*, June 1998.

177   "guys like that": Bettina Drew, letter to Robert Stone, March 23, 1999, NYPL/Lopez.

PART THREE: A FLAG FOR SUNRISE

181   "but trying to cooperate": Janice Stone, letter to Burr Family, March 23, 1974, private collection.

182   "suitable progress": Alfred A. Knopf contract with Robert Stone for untitled novel, January 8, 1976, NYPL/Lopez.

182   "Candida's ultra-tricky ways": Robert Gottlieb, e-mail to Gerald Howard, December 10, 2018.

182   "as good a place as any I guess": Robert Gottlieb, letter to Robert Stone, October 3, 1975, NYPL/Lopez.

183   "probably at poolside": Candida Donadio, letter to Robert Stone, July 31, 1974, ibid.

186   "sarcasm and loathing": Robert Stone, introduction, Graham Greene, *The Quiet American* (New York: Penguin Books, 2004), xv.

187   "replete with expletives": Philip Tsiaris, unpublished interview.

189   "walking across campus": David Blistein, unpublished interview.

192   "from the nearest habitation": Robert Stone, "Keeping the Future at Bay: Of Republicans and their America," *Harper's Magazine*, October 1988.

193   "border of a great mystery": Robert Stone, "Under the Tongue of the Ocean," *The New York Times Magazine*, June 6, 1999.

197   "In fact I'm thrilled": Robert Gottlieb to Robert Stone, March 15, 1977, NYPL/Lopez.

197   "quickens the blood": Robert Stone, "Far Tortuga," *The New York Times Book Review*, May 25, 1975.

200   "and on weekends only": Carl F. Brandfass Jr., MD, report to the Minnesota Mutual Life Insurance Company, July 19, 1977.

200   "a slothful perfectionist": Madison Smartt Bell, "A Memory of Robert Stone," *The New Yorker*, January 14, 2015.

200   "perks up when he's on": Frances Chastain, "'The Homecoming' Full of Funny Shocks," *The Amherst Record*, May 3, 1978.

201   "embattled crustacean": Stephanie Kraft, "The Homecoming," *The Valley Record*, May 3, 1978.

201   "a woman responds to them": Ibid.

201   "the eloquence of the unspoken": John Lahr, "Demolition Man," *The New Yorker*, December 24, 2007.

203   "will clear your head": Charles Ruas, *Conversations with American Writers* (New York: Alfred A. Knopf, 1985), 265–94.

204   "Vietnam screwed them up": Roger Ebert, "Who'll Stop the Rain," rogerebert.com, August 2, 1978.

206   "aren't speaking to her": Robert Stone, letter to Janice Stone, undated (1979), NYPL/Lopez.

206   "day in Paradise": Ibid.

207   "and ate them": Ruth Pratt, unpublished interview.

209   "was wearing it": Ibid.

209   "palm of God's hand": Ibid.

209   "and things like that": WWI, 49.

211   "best I'm capable of": BaHD, 100.

211   "through the darkest night": Ibid., 103.

212   "promiscuity of his thoughts": Ibid., 90.

212   "little justice and no mercy": Ibid., 114.

214   "with your snores, Bob": Tom Riley, letter to Robert Stone, undated (1981), NYPL/Lopez.
214   "They come to you": FFS, 166.
214   "pardon the expression—intelligence": Ibid., 156.
215   "before the war": Ruas, CwRS, 49.
215   "both sides of the Pacific": FFS, 28.
216   "involved here for so long": Robert Stone, "The Reason for Stories: Toward a Moral Fiction," *Harper's Magazine*, June 1998.
216   "it is the world": Ruas, CwRS, 55.
216   "the price for it": Ibid., 58.
216   "a common cause": FFS, 168.
217   "institutional personality": Ruas, CwRS, 53.
217   "affectless sociopath": Woods, 46.
217   "sweet with love": Robert Stone, typescript of unfinished play, NYPL/Lopez.
217   "keep in line": FFS, 98.
218   "good intentions seriously": Ibid., 40.
219   "Fear. Prey.": Ibid., 227.
219   "turning me around": Ibid., 64.
220   "under the reef": Ibid., 256.
220   "favored by God": Ibid.
220   "without mortality": Ibid., 316.
221   "as though she deserved it": Ibid., 342.
221   "always going for": WWI, 48.
221   "yes I am": FFS, 264.
222   "dangerous for him": Ibid., 340.
222   "I'm waiting": Ibid., 402.
223   "the way things are": Ibid., 372.
223   "Me. I am": Ibid.
223   "the handmaid of the Lord": Ibid., 416.
224   "special, young Justin": Ibid., 434.
224   "you don't exist": Ibid., 435.
224   "its own reward": Ibid., 437.
224   "educated people": WWI, 53.
225   "deal with them": Ibid., 51.
225   "world is this way": Ibid., 50.
226   "terrible bad news": Ibid., 52.
226   "how it was meant": FFS, 428.
226   "The thing itself": Ibid.
227   "only each other": Ibid., 431.
227   "the other shark said": Ibid., 432.
227   "Ape stuff": Ibid., 425.
227   "the greatest horror": Ibid., 437.
227   "eye in the sun": Ibid., 438.
228   "I require rescue here": Ibid., 439.

228 "much of the dialogue": "Robert Stone: *A Flag for Sunrise*," *Kirkus Reviews*, undated (1981), kirkusreviews.com, accessed May 22, 2019.

229 "any other kind of imperialism": Richard Poirier, "Intruders," *The New York Review of Books*, December 3, 1981, nybooks.com, accessed May 22, 2019. NB: And all quotes from this review.

230 "escaped from Omsk": John Leonard, "Books of the Times," *The New York Times*, October 18, 1981, nytimes.com, accessed May 22, 2019.

230 "even un-American": Jonathan Yardley, "Gun-Running and Jungle Fighting," *The Washington Post*, November 1, 1981, google.com, accessed May 22, 2019.

231 "I wish *I'd* written it": Tim O'Brien, letter to Robert Stone, December 3, 1981, NYPL/Lopez.

PART FOUR: CHILDREN OF LIGHT

235 "one think one is": FFS, 245.

235 "ruddy complexion of the country": Charles Ruas, "A Talk with Robert Stone," *The New York Times Book Review*, October 18, 1981, nytimes.com, accessed May 21, 2019.

236 "hassle me": Jim Calio, "Robert Stone Lives in Peaceful Seclusion, but His Novels Inhabit a Shadowy and Violent World," *People*, February 22, 1982. NB: And all other quotes from this article.

236 "on my face, too": Nan Emanuel, letter to Robert Stone, undated, NYPL, box 22, folder 4.

237 "coming out again": Daphne Ehrlich, letter to Robert Stone, June 3, 1975, NYPL, box 22, folder 5.

238 "very angry": Curt Suplee, "Voices of the Dark and Light," *The Washington Post*, November 15, 1981, G5.

240 "so much international attention": Tracy Ullveit-Moe, letter to David Rosenthal, March 18, 1982, NYPL, box 13, folder 1.

240 "get on your wavelength": Robert Stone, "What Fiction Is For," *Bohemian Club Library Notes* No. 78 (Winter 1994).

240 "a far-flung place": Robert Stone, letter to Dr. Mary Ann Ignatius, May 20, 1981.

240 "drugs, gays, etc.": Andre Brezianu, letter to Robert Stone, April 14, 1981.

240 "most ghastly places on earth": Robert Stone, unpublished essay, NYPL/Lopez, 8.

241 "a potential foreign friend": Ibid., 7.

241 "memory of that meeting": Ibid.

241 "turn in the keys to the police": Ibid., 8.

241 "like evil itself": Ibid., 7.

242 "an émigré typesetter": Ibid., 8.

242 "helping out in the first place": Ibid., 9.

242 "at Lang Vei in 1971": Ibid.

242 "We insist on it": Ibid., 11.

243   "satisfactory progress": Alfred A. Knopf contract with Robert Stone for un-
       titled novel, December 7, 1981, NYPL/Lopez.
243   "from blindness to sight": Tom Jenks, "Remembering Robert Stone," *Literary
       Hub*, July 24, 2015, lithub.com, accessed May 10, 2019.
244   "no list of rules to follow": Ibid.
244   "public premeditated act": Robert Stone, manuscript in spiral notebook num-
       bered 79, NYPL, box 21, folder 2.
244   "And he raised it to art": Jenks, "Remembering Robert Stone."
246   "when he got there": Kem Nunn, unpublished interview.
246   "and thought he'd have a look": Ibid.
246   "see what happened": Steve Goodwin, "Remembering Robert Stone," *The
       American Scholar*, January 14, 2015.
246   "anything I'd imagined": Kem Nunn, unpublished interview.
247   "and a sense of humor": John Hildebrand, unpublished interview.
248   "the celebrated novelist Robert Stone": Sylvie Drake, *Los Angeles Times*, July
       28, 1982.
252   "the reasons for their reaction": USICA American Participant Report, a
       guidelines document in use in 1982, NYPL/Lopez.
253   "particularly viable these days": Robert Stone, undated report to USICA,
       1982. NB: And all quotes from this report.
253   "imaginary Latin American revolution": Inge Eriksen, letter to Robert Stone,
       "mid-November 1982," NYPL/Lopez.
253   "*The Whore from Gomorrah*": Inge Eriksen, letter to Robert Stone, June 28,
       1983, NYPL/Lopez.
253   "a real human being": Inge Eriksen, letter to Robert Stone, "mid-December
       1983," NYPL/Lopez.
253   "unfold in the next": Ibid.
253   "you've seen them all": Robert Stone, letter to Inge Eriksen, undated (1984),
       NYPL/Lopez.
256   "albeit a funny one": John Gregory Dunne, *Quintana and Friends* (New
       York: Dutton, 1978).
260   "Plan Charlie": NYPL, box 13, folder 3.
261   "he might die quite soon": CoL, 5.
261   "alcohol and cocaine": Ibid., 8.
262   "Walker had seen the bodies": NYPL, box 1, folder 6.
262   "paralyzed with the fear of death": Bill Barich, unpublished interview.
262   "and, well, there you go": Arlo Haskell, unpublished interview.
262   "the people who loved you": CoL, 9.
262   "they were life": Ibid., 8.
262   "mind drugs and transfigurations": Ibid., 11.
262   "I need downers": Ibid., 71.
262   "a medical hit man": Ibid., 101.
263   "what he had come to see": Ibid., 129.
263   "something almost as good": Ibid., 130.

263   "Your movies": Ibid.

263   "the Long Friends": Ibid., 122.

264   "perish in its tumult": Kate Chopin, *The Awakening* (New York and Chicago: Herbert S. Stone, 1899), 33–34.

264   "soft, close embrace": Ibid., 301.

265   "not Rosalind": CoL, 81.

265   "Edna Pontellier before her": Ibid., 95.

265   "she would sometimes forget them": Chopin, *The Awakening*, 47–48.

265   "chickenshit and crazy": CoL, 98.

265   "Walker's notes said": Ibid., 121.

265   "concealed beneath black cloth": Ibid., 113.

265   "the sight of the stuff": Ibid.

266   *"a kind of exaltation"*: Ibid., 120.

266   "To go for it was dying": Ibid., 121.

266   "her moves, her aura": Ibid., 147.

266   "his dark angel": Ibid., 12.

266   "strength of character": Ibid., 154.

267   "daylight hour or so": Ibid., 178.

267   "through a drinking straw": Ibid., 182.

268   "gas and imagination": Ibid., 215.

268   "for some time thereafter": Ibid., 228.

268   "Sacred to me": Ibid., 233.

268   "This is where the flow goes": Ibid., 245.

269   "I lost her": Ibid., 254.

269   "shiny and hung up there": Ibid., 236.

269   "secret eyes": Ibid., 235.

270   "the place of excrement": William Butler Yeats, "Crazy Jane Talks with the Bishop," in *The Collected Poems of W. B. Yeats* (New York: MacMillan, 1933).

270   "vulgarize pure light": CoL, 213.

271   "a voyage on the Nile, and so on": Tom Jenks, unpublished interview.

273   "crush of heretics": Robert Stone, unpublished manuscript submitted to *Esquire*, 1983, NYPL/Lopez.

PART FIVE: OUTERBRIDGE REACH

278   "I anticipate using not at all": Barth Healey, "Smiling Through the Apocalypse," *The New York Times Book Review*, March 16, 1986.

278   "the apostle of strung out": Jean Strouse, "Heebiejeebieville Express," *The New York Times Book Review*, March 16, 1986.

279   "taken for psychiatric testing": "Missing 'Superman' Actress Found Frightened in Bushes," *The Independent*, April 25, 1996, independent.co.uk, accessed May 15, 2019.

279   "mislead readers": Janice Stone, unpublished memoir, private collection.

280   "self-indulgent": Al Alvarez, "Among the Freaks," *The New York Review of Books*, April 10, 1986.

280 "hopeless bitterness": *People*, "Picks and Pans Review: *Children of Light*," April 14, 1986.

281 "a middle-aged man": Weidenfeld and Nicolson contract with Robert Stone for untitled novel, August 8, 1986, NYPL/Lopez.

282 "doing so through complacency": Robert Stone, handwritten draft of untitled lecture, transcribed by hand by Janice Stone, delivered at the "Letteratura, Tradizione, Valori" conference in Palermo and Acireale, Sicily, May 20–23, 1986.

284 "up and coming American writers": Raymond M. Lane, "Tough Talk from the Literati," *The Boston Globe*, April 28, 1987, 25–26.

284 "whoredom of the lecture circuit": Ibid.

285 "our golden age": Ibid.

285 "sometimes a bloody one, in Russia": Ibid.

285 "you become the porter": John Hildebrand, letter to Robert Stone, March 30, 1987, NYPL/Lopez.

286 "if for nobody other than ourselves": John Hildebrand, unpublished interview.

286 "informing story": Robert Stone, *Outerbridge Reach* typescript, variant of page 472, NYPL, box 17, folder 5.

286 "attempt to rationalize it": John Hildebrand, unpublished interview.

287 "Help is my middle name": Robert Stone, "Opus 5," aka "Charlie Manson's Gold," unpublished fragment of typescript, NYPL, box 45, folder 9.

287 "Fascism and astrology": Ibid.

287 "only the shadow of both": Ibid.

288 "that one was always alone finally": Ibid.

288 "helping professions": Ibid.

288 "You've come to the right man": Ibid.

288 "but it was so paltry": Ibid.

288 "would die with it": Ibid.

289 "inspiration had better strike me soon": Robert Stone, letter to Ed Bacon, undated (1987), NYPL/Lopez.

290 "reflected in their work": Robert Stone, "Changing Tides," *The New York Times Magazine*, April 24, 1988.

290 "whose prosperity raised them": Ibid.

293 "bumps into the Mississippi": John Hildebrand, unpublished interview.

293 "Midwestern Gothic anyway": Ibid.

293 "makes a terrible roar": Ibid.

293 "we were gutting the doe": Ibid.

294 "we mistake it for our own": Robert Stone, "Keeping the Future at Bay: Of Republicans and Their America," *Harper's Magazine*, November 1988.

295 "deserves no less": Robert Stone, letter to John Banville, March 9, 1988, NYPL/Lopez.

296 "admire and love the writing": Sam Halpert, interview with Robert Stone, in... *When We Talk about Raymond Carver* (Layton, UT: Gibbs Smith, 1991), 38.

296 "to the other side": Robert Stone, unpublished typescript tribute to Raymond Carver, undated (circa 1988), NYPL, box 45, folder 10.

296 "alarmed and shocked": Halpert, . . . *When We Talk about Raymond Carver*, 38.

296 "success in the bookstores": Adam Begley, "Ann Getty: Publish and Perish," *The New York Times Magazine*, October 22, 1989, nytimes.com, accessed May 16, 2019.

297 "against my will": Robert Stone, letter to Robert Massie, December 1, 1990, NYPL/Lopez.

300 "I found that this was so": Robert Stone, "Enter the Muse: Janice Stone," *Esquire*, June 1990, 146.

300 "has nowhere to turn": Robert Stone, "Fighting the Wrong War: How the President's War on Drugs Repeats the Mistakes of Vietnam," *Playboy*, July 7, 1990.

303 "Your ear is perfect": Larry Cooper, letter to Robert Stone, July 30, 1991, NYPL, box 19, folder 1.

303 "Quod petis hic est": Larry Cooper, letter to Robert Stone, September 17, 1991, NYPL, box 17, folder 7.

304 "Bob and Janice went for a walk": Janice Stone, tax diary, 1991, NYPL/Lopez.

304 "sensibility in our time is Robert Stone": Mona Simpson, "God and Man in Provincetown," *The New York Times Book Review*, February 4, 1991, nytimes.com, accessed May 16, 2019.

304 "very dark, very dark": Weber. NB: And all quotes in this and the next two paragraphs.

306 "losers, losers, losers": OR, 130.

306 "it makes her seem crass": Ibid., 131.

306 "losing is a nobler condition": Ibid.

306 "not to let on": Ibid., 132.

306 "Did you win that one": Ibid.

307 "on the edge of a slum": Ibid., 12.

308 "and the Navy at war": Ibid., 6.

308 "honor, duty and risk": Ibid., 101.

308 "cleaning spittle off their dress blues": Ibid., 11.

308 "America fail to win the war there": Ibid.

308 "since the last century": Ibid., 73.

309 "failed him in that regard": Ibid., 44.

309 "He wanted more": Ibid., 45.

309 "the way to recoup": Ibid., 100.

309 "he would never live to see": Ibid., 45.

309 "the intersection of his desires": Robert Stone, *Outerbridge Reach* (New York: The Franklin Library, 1992).

309 "But it's unforgiving": Weber, 23.

309 "a penitent Jansenist princess": Robert Stone, *Outerbridge Reach* manuscript, NYPL, box 16, folder 4.

310 "it would be her fault": OR, 190.

310   "children and fuckups": Robert Stone, *Outerbridge Reach* manuscript, NYPL, box 15, folder 3.

310   "their own misery and mediocrity": OR, 208.

310   "She required victory": Ibid.

311   "you really open them up": Ibid., 29.

311   "make them dance": Ibid., 83.

311   "he could never rest": Ibid.

311   "it never lied": Ibid., 79.

311   "As a man": Ibid., 140.

311   "upright, *uptight*, got it": Ibid.

311   "How we gonna fuck 'em": Ibid., 134.

311   "locatable in the novel": Weber, 24.

311   "the sound of Browne": Ibid.

311   "patronized him as a half-wit": OR, 83.

312   "news they didn't want to hear": Ibid., 326.

312   "the proper measure of respect": Ibid., 171.

312   "and remotely dangerous": Ibid., 172.

313   "and called her a bitch": Ibid., 278.

313   "absconded presence obsessed her": Ibid., 279.

313   "had been to bed with him": Ibid., 76.

314   "what she wanted": Ibid., 298.

314   "dangerous quality that pleased him": Ibid., 271.

314   "bloated and shrill": Ibid., 343.

314   "afraid of losing her": Ibid., 330.

314   "and he was afraid": Ibid., 167.

315   "who you think you are": Ibid., 168.

315   "to spend the rest of his life with it": Ibid.

315   "looked good after the fact": OR, 167.

315   "from becoming a prison": Ibid., 309.

315   "there was the radio": Ibid., 283.

315   "coursed down his cheeks": Ibid., 285.

316   "his teeth set in rage": Ibid., 286.

316   "and even outside ordinary reality": Ibid., 287.

316   "a liar burning in hell": Ibid., 300.

316   "his own first, best customer": Ibid.

317   "laughed away our holy things": Ibid., 301.

317   "the one he actually was": Ibid., 333.

317   "That was survival": Ibid., 334.

317   "DREAMS OF YOUR YOUTH": Ibid., 349.

318   "connected certainly with any other": Ibid., 371.

318   "even outside ordinary reality": Ibid., 297.

318   "I'll make myself an honest man": Ibid., 384.

318   "Nothing did": Ibid., 385.

318   "I'm silent and uncomprehending": Weber, 25.

319   "lost regard": OR, 388.

319 "it was survivable": Ibid.

319 "port known to Whitman and Melville": Stone, "Changing Tides."

320 "informing story": OR, 344.

320 "for a meaning to our suffering": Stone, note to Franklin edition.

321 "stretched to the end of darkness": OR, 74.

321 "but could not call to mind": Ibid.

321 "urge toward excellence and transcendence": Stone, note to Franklin edition.

321 "piece of literary art": William H. Pritchard, "Sailing over the Edge," *The New York Times Book Review*, February 23, 1992, nytimes.com, accessed May 16, 2019.

322 "the public domain": John Sutherland, "In Dangerous Waters," *The Times Literary Supplement*, May 1992.

323 "avoid copyright infringement": Robert Stone, letter to Deborah Rogers, June 3, 1992, NYPL/Lopez.

323 "that clumsy replication of 'real life'": Robert Stone, "The Genesis of *Outerbridge Reach*," *The Times Literary Supplement*, June 7, 1992.

PART SIX: DAMASCUS GATE

327 "both in the Kesey crowd": James Maraniss, unpublished interview.

328 "referred to ungenerously as *come mierdas*": Robert Stone, "Havana Then and Now," *Harper's Magazine*, March 1992.

328 "on visits to Eastern Europe": Ibid.

329 "the boy replies: 'A foreigner'": Ibid.

329 *"Lo que hay que hacer es no morirse"*: James Marannis, unpublished interview.

330 *"Ustedes quieren tomar algo?"*: Ibid.

330 "serve no purpose, have no place": Stone, "Havana Then and Now."

330 "I'd like to get going more or less at once": Robert Stone, letter to John Herman, June 7, 1992.

330 "known as 'Luce'—as in 'loose'": Ibid.

331 "They called her 'Firefly'": Ibid.

331 "true erudition and genuine insight": Ibid.

332 "It's not a silly question for me": WWI, 53–54.

333 "Stone's law": Robert Stone, letter to Kate Lehrer, May 10, 1992.

333 "melancholy chords": "The Best American Short Stories 1992," *Publishers Weekly*, October 5, 1992.

333 "a treatise on extinction": Janet Silver, letter to Robert Stone, October 21, 1992.

333 "the literary life": Robert Stone, *Best American Short Stories 1992* (New York: Houghton Mifflin Harcourt, 1992), xvi.

335 "the notion of human responsibility": Robert Stone, "Jerusalem Has No Past," *The New York Times Magazine*, May 3, 1998, 55.

335 "Whose Jerusalem?": Ibid.

336 "Professor in the Writing Seminars": William C. Richardson, letter to Robert Stone, March 26, 1992.

339 "Esprit and morale are high": John Barth, letter to Robert Stone, November 10, 1992.

340 "from behind dark sunglasses": Hampton Sides, "Dog Scholars," *Baltimore Magazine*, December 1993, 41.

340 "from Tweedledee to Tweedledum": Ibid., 48.

340 "brutal": Ibid., 43.

340 "weren't a writer in the first place": Ibid., 49.

341 "presumably ad inf.": John Barth, letter to Robert Stone, November 10, 1992.

343 "them being pissy and me being": Conversation with Madison Smartt Bell.

343 "So there is a God": Ibid.

343 "Geraldine hangs herself with": Ibid.

343 "you can be free": Ibid.

345 "the new millennium": Robert Stone, "The End of the Beginning," *Rolling Stone*, September 21, 1995.

346 "I found it impossible to resist": Tim Warren, "Novelist Robert Stone Leaving Job at Hopkins for Writing Post at Yale," *The Baltimore Sun*, March 17, 1994, baltimoresun.com, accessed May 17, 2019.

351 "just as Macbeth does": Robert Stone, "Looking the Worst in the Eye," *The New York Review of Books*, April 6, 1995, nybooks.com, accessed May 27, 2019.

352 "were simply dumbfounded": Steve Goodwin, "Remembering Robert Stone," *The American Scholar*, January 14, 2015, theamericanscholar.org, accessed May 17, 2019.

352 "that it hurts": Stone, letter to Lehrer, May 10, 1992.

353 "they gave him courage": Emily Cheng, unpublished interview.

354 "Who is this arrogant man": Ibid.

354 "a very attentive viewer": Ibid.

357 "oh yes, I remember": Dawn Seferian, letter to Robert Stone, November 10, 1995, NYPL/Lopez.

357 "sequence of sheer happenings": Hannah Arendt, "Isak Dinesen: 1885–1963," *Men in Dark Times* (New York: Penguin Books, 2001), 106.

357 "the institutional man": Woods, 35.

358 "a rat that lived near his heart": BaHD, 36.

358 "all her pretty ones": Ibid., 19.

358 "rotten with anger": Ibid., 180.

359 "of your own poem": Ibid., 176.

359 "Always": Ibid., 216.

359 "on many a drug": Ibid.

360 "wrote a poem about salmon I liked": Ibid., 220.

361 "a mumbled plea for a handout": Richard Eder, "Bear and His Daughter," *Los Angeles Times*, April 6, 1997, latimes.com, accessed May 17, 2019.

361 "who also smells very clean": James Wood, "A Rage to Live," *The New York Times Book Review*, April 20, 1997, nytimes.com, accessed May 17, 2019.

361 "sinister forces behind every Oreo cookie": Linda Hall, "Romancing Robert Stone," *New York*, March 31, 1997, 54.

361 "in a narrower work": Wood, "A Rage to Live."

361 "the book of a lifetime": Atticus Lish, *"Bear and His Daughter* by Robert Stone, the Book of a Lifetime," *The Independent*, February 11, 2016, independent.co.uk, accessed May 17, 2019.

362 "patron saint of writers' wives": Hall, "Romancing Robert Stone."

362 "in for the long haul": Ibid., 55.

362 "to be where things were happening": Ibid.

362 "but all manner of American addicts": Ibid.

364 "my concerns as a writer": Robert Stone, letter to His Excellency Dr. Fidel Castro, December 9, 1997, NYPL/Lopez.

365 "hewn to overstatement anyway": Larry Cooper, letter to Robert Stone, October 15, 1997, NYPL/Lopez.

366 "the overstanding, mon": Ibid.

366 "making mud pies of your prose": Ibid.

366 "weren't hard enough": Ibid.

367 "a young Arab woman": DG, 18.

367 "a cloak of invisibility": Ibid., 21.

367 "a multiple personality": Ibid., 27.

368 "is part Gentile": Ibid., 33.

368 "Ralph 'Raziel' Melker": Robert Stone, author's note, *Damascus Gate* (New York: The Franklin Library, 1997).

369 "what we want for all eternity": Robert Birnbaum, "Robert Stone on *Damascus Gate* 1998/2009," identitytheory.com, accessed May 17, 2019.

370 "the second coming of Jesus Christ": DG, 45.

370 "but organized and powerful groups": Ibid., 49.

371 "Jesus cured a paralytic": Ibid., 148.

371 "but I can't remember it": Ibid., 261.

371 "religious feelings I haven't had": Ibid., 262.

371 "in the ravings of Raziel and De Kuff": Ibid., 179.

371 "He's manipulated by Raziel": Ibid., 248.

371 "Christian Zionists": Ibid., 48.

372 "a Jewish effort and a Christian one": Ibid., 153.

372 "just promoters": Ibid., 154.

372 "against the Israeli State": Ibid., 228.

372 "the Arabs were many and the amenities few": Ibid., 229.

372 "build the Temple of the Almighty": Ibid., 204.

373 *"que hacer no morir"*: Ibid., 241.

373 "Lucas had ever seen the *shebab* rampant": Ibid., 313.

373 "during special enthusiasms": Ibid., 314.

373 "against the Almighty Himself": Ibid., 340.

373 "you'll write the truth": Ibid., 345.

374 "the Death of the Kiss": Ibid., 267.

374 "is to cease to be!": Ibid., 271.

374 "The *tikkun* is restored": Ibid., 401.

375 "violent aspect of the plan": Ibid., 373.

375   "at the beginning of time": Ibid., 431.

375   "I am no one": Ibid., 474.

375   "Uncreated Light": Ibid., 62.

376   "a love in its loss": Ibid., 500.

376   "holiest of unresponding skies": Ibid., 373.

PART SEVEN: BAY OF SOULS

381   "live in a world without God": Josh Getlin, "The Conflict Within," *Los Angeles Times*, April 30, 1998, latimes.com, accessed May 17, 2019.

381   "that I was losing it": Ibid.

382   "facts are passed off as truth": Michiko Kakutani, "*Damascus Gate*: Believers and Cynics on the Road to Rebirth," *The New York Times*, April 14, 1998, nytimes.com, accessed May 17, 2019.

382   "possesses a murderous power": Jonathan Rosen, "Jerusalem Syndrome," *The New York Times Book Review*, April 26, 1998, nytimes.com, accessed May 17, 2019.

382   "but in some sense antihistorical": Ibid.

382   "of the moment and even the future": DG, 55.

383   "an American religious fantasy": Rosen, "Jerusalem Syndrome."

383   "enacting an American drama": Ibid.

383   "inspired by that poem": Kakutani, "*Damascus Gate.*"

386   "toward the weak": Robert Stone, typescript notes for unfinished novel with working title *Arcturus*, NYPL/Lopez.

386   "painted by Sargent": Ibid.

386   "The murmurs of the forest": Ibid.

387   "is an adept": Ibid.

387   "to promote the work": Houghton Mifflin contract with Robert Stone for "Untitled Alaska Novel," August 11, 1998, NYPL/Lopez.

389   "the end, the bottom": Robert Stone, "Under the Tongue of the Ocean," *The New York Times Magazine*, June 6, 1999, nytimes.com, accessed May 17, 2019.

389   "at the dawn of creation": Ibid.

390   "everything had a black line around it": Conversation with Madison Smartt Bell.

392   "any political risk in this area": Madison Smartt Bell, letter to Robert Stone, January 7, 1999, NYPL/Lopez.

393   "on return to the States": Ibid.

395   "spring in my heart": Robert Stone, handwritten notes for unfinished novel with working title *Arcturus*, NYPL/Lopez.

398   "he's gonna pray for you": Conversation with Madison Smartt Bell.

400   "at the end of his powers": Maya Deren, *Divine Horsemen* (New York: Chelsea House, 1970), 99.

401   "Haitians are maggots": Bob Shacochis, *The Immaculate Invasion* (New York: Grove Press, 2010).

406   "her linguistic eccentricities a commodity": Robert Stone, letter to Sven Birkerts, April 2, 1999, NYPL/Lopez.

406   "transformation in the First World War": Ibid.

406   "the elixir of Hemingway's work": "Hemingway in our Time," *The Boston Globe*, April 10, 1999.

408   "a kind of salvation": Key West Literary Seminar brochure, 1999, 26.

410   "the Temple Mount in Jerusalem": Janice Stone, tax diary, May 17, 1999, NYPL/Lopez.

410   "work time for the summer": Janice Stone, tax diary, July 3, 1999, NYPL/Lopez.

410   "not unlike Telegraph": Robert Stone, letter to Georgiana Ball, undated (1999), NYPL/Lopez.

411   "active in dance and polarity massage": John Hildebrand, unpublished interview.

411   "a piece I'd done in *Harper's*": Ibid.

411   "no doubt, of Captain Canada": Ibid.

413   "whether of nonfiction or fiction": Houghton Mifflin contract with Robert Stone for "Untitled Alaska Novel," August 11, 1998, NYPL/Lopez.

415   "after he's committed a crime": Robert Stone, handwritten note, NYPL/Lopez.

416   "to have survived the attempt": Emily Cheng, unpublished interview.

416   "the promised reason to live": Annie Dillard, letter to Robert Stone, April 8, 2001, NYPL/Lopez.

417   "a bad habit he couldn't break": Diana Barich, unpublished interview.

418   "it was a different world": DG, 500.

426   "had witnessed many times before": Bill Barich, unpublished interview.

433   "the stories we tell ourselves": Robert Stone, "The Way We Live Now: 9-23-01: Close Reading: Elements of Tragedy; The Villains," *The New York Times*, September 23, 2001.

433   "They will be brought low": Ibid.

433   "serve our actual survival": Ibid.

434   "and that they could be righted": "The Boys Octet," in EYE, 168.

434   "to the degree that Kesey did": Ibid.

434   "the prince of possibility": Robert Stone, "The Prince of Possibility," *The New Yorker*, June 14, 2004.

436   "in the light of day": Robert Stone, letter to Madison Smartt Bell, undated (2002), NYPL/Lopez.

436   "living writer they most admire": Madison Smartt Bell, e-mail to Robert Stone, undated (2002), NYPL/Lopez.

436   "chanted with appropriate drumming": Madison Smartt Bell, letter to Robert Stone, July 24, 2002, NYPL/Lopez.

437   "He put it better": Robert Stone, e-mail to Madison Smartt Bell, January 28, 2003, NYPL/Lopez.

437   "Take the word of an old scribbler": Ibid.

437   "push our understanding forward": Amy Wilentz, "Voodoo But No Real Magic," *Los Angeles Times*, April 20, 2003.

437   "pasted together from his previous novels": Michiko Kakutani, "Farewell,

Midwest. Hello, Isle of Voodoo and Intrigue," *The New York Times*, April 1, 2003.

438 "a different sense of their burdens": Norman Rush, "Possession," *The New York Times Book Review*, April 6, 2003.

438 "Flyoverland": BoS, 77.

438 "prairie sodbusters": Ibid., 8.

438 "He had better watch it": Ibid., 47.

439 "sobriety and decorum": Ibid., 35.

439 "student-faculty collaborations": Ibid., 8.

439 "little kid like Phyllis": Ibid., 45.

439 "Bored with introspection": Ibid., 42.

439 "outrun the shadow inside him": Ibid., 47.

439 "The thought frightened him": Ibid., 45.

439 "for the next generation": Ibid., 2.

439 "all the humiliation he could bear": Ibid., 114.

439 "He had never claimed one": Ibid., 5.

440 "have their rights and be happy": Ibid., 31.

440 "what a relief": Ibid.

440 "some things sooner rather than later": Ibid.

440 "pretty Phyllis": Ibid., 45.

441 "the Triptelemos brigade": Ibid., 129.

441 "the Men Who Know Too Much": Ibid., 66.

442 "against the coat's silk lining": Ibid., 52.

442 "took his strength away gram by gram": Ibid., 56.

442 "apparently no holes to insert a metal tongue": Ibid., 58.

443 "Of course there was still time": Ibid., 97.

443 "literary vitalism": Ibid., 58.

443 "must be spared or forbidden": Ibid., 50.

443 "steel-eyed bitch": Ibid., 73.

444 "That's what our ceremony is for": Ibid., 120.

444 "could do wicked things": Ibid.

444 "his soul, from Guinée": Ibid., 121.

444 "unpleasantness": Ibid., 190.

445 "Her eyes would change": Ibid., 151.

445 "were no accident": Ibid.

445 "I think you're weak": Ibid., 234.

445 "when you demean people I love": Ibid., 57.

446 "He's a lucky man": Ibid., 71.

446 "moment by moment": Ibid., 232.

446 "how great you were but me": Ibid., 234.

446 "I wanted more": Ibid.

446 "upscale Bible study group": Ibid., 90.

446 "Christus on a Viking crucifix": Ibid., 30.

446 "We want it to be there": Robert Birnbaum, "Robert Stone on *Damascus Gate* 1998/2009," identitytheory.com, accessed May 17, 2019.

447 "maybe eight feet below": Ibid., 15.

447 "a faint green glow": Ibid., 181.

447 "within the colored circumference": Ibid.

447 "the tiny flakes ceaselessly falling": Ibid., BoS, 185.

447 "Both were beyond imagining": Ibid., 206.

447 "practices found in voodoo trance ritual": Rush, "Possession."

448 "and risk even more": BoS, 118.

448 "of the vitalist project": Rush, "Possession."

448 "for the life more abundant": Birnbaum, "Robert Stone on *Damascus Gate* 1998/2009."

448 "the ranks of death": BoS, 173.

448 "Otherwise you can't fly": Ibid., 229.

448 "I'm still there": Ibid., 248.

PART EIGHT: DEATH OF THE BLACK-HAIRED GIRL

453 "and spinach at home": Janice Stone, tax diary, August 21, 2002, NYPL/Lopez.

454 "in this author's career": Janet Silver, letter to Neil Olson, September 30, 1999, NYPL/Lopez.

455 "to write for Houghton Mifflin": Janice Stone, tax diary, November 21, 2002, NYPL/Lopez.

457 "they would all be under contract": Neil Olson, unpublished interview.

457 "came out the same year and tanked": Ibid.

461 "sacrificed the former for the latter": Marcel Proust, *In Search of Lost Time*, Volume 5: *The Captive, The Fugitive* (New York: Modern Library Classics, 1999), 245.

462 "made Greene an attractive object": Robert Stone, introduction to Graham Greene, *The Quiet American* (New York: Penguin Classics, 2004), xiv.

463 "like all divine gifts, it has its cost": Robert Stone, "The Prince of Possibility," *The New Yorker*, June 14, 2004, 70.

463 "think like a terrorist group": Paul Bass, "The Bin Laden Connection: Bin Laden, Crop Dusters—and the Last Work of Suzanne Jovin," *Silicon Investor*, September 27, 2001, siliconinvestor.com, accessed May 20, 2019.

465 "makes a mockery of justice": Martin Childs, "Lord Steyn: Judge Who Opposed Tony Blair and George Bush over Iraq War and Guantanamo," *The Independent*, December 3, 2017, independent.co.uk, accessed May 20, 2019.

466 "there's nowhere to proceed": Robert Stone, typescript of 2005 lecture at Amherst College, NYPL/Lopez.

466 "anything more than itself": Ibid.

468 "if Bob can't swing it financially": Kem Nunn, unpublished interview.

469 "the image has remained etched in my mind": Ibid.

469 "a very impressive guy": Ibid.

471 "a possible therapeutic trip to L.A.": Janice Stone, tax diary, May 29, 2006, NYPL/Lopez.

471 "and remained at Las Encinas": Kem Nunn, unpublished interview.

471   "breadth of who he was": Ibid.

472   "support writers that he liked": Ibid.

473   "while remaining sober": Ibid.

475   "as well as the larger zeitgeist": Michiko Kakutani, "The Haze and Tumult, Revisited," *The New York Times*, January 2, 2007, nytimes.com, accessed May 20, 2019.

475   "the Pacific coast of Mexico": Walter Kirn, "Stone's Diaries," *The New York Times Book Review*, January 7, 2007, nytimes.com, accessed May 20, 2019.

475   "from Kesey's lair": Ibid.

476   "primal, primary, primo": PG, 167.

476   "modest shot from the right side": Ibid., 49.

476   "But the prank was on us": Ibid., 161.

477   "in its most generous hopes": Ibid., 228.

477   "a degree of social pathology": Ibid., 27.

477   "We weren't much into infrastructure": Lawrence Downes, "In Mexico, on the Lam with Ken Kesey," *The New York Times*, March 23, 2008, nytimes .com, accessed May 20, 2019.

478   "She was my heroine": Robert Stone, "High Wire," in *Fun with Problems* (New York: Houghton Mifflin Harcourt, 2010), 169.

479   "life and culture in the United States": Susan Leckey, ed., *The Europa Directory of Literary Awards and Prizes* (New York: Routledge, 2015), 10.

480   "except our failure to prevail": PG, 229.

481   "Moms and Dads of northwest London": Robert Stone, unfinished novel typescript, working title "Havistock," NYPL/Lopez.

482   "listening patiently to the answers": John Hildebrand, unpublished interview.

483   "dismal and depressing": Michiko Kakutani, "When Impulse Control Goes Awry," *The New York Times*, January 25, 2010, nytimes.com, accessed May 20, 2019.

483   "male American story writers": Antonya Nelson, "Bad Choices," *The New York Times Book Review*, January 29, 2010, nytimes.com, accessed May 20, 2019.

483   "encouraged by omission or ellipses": Ibid.

484   "brave enough to be the bearer": Ibid.

484   "Stone is no miniaturist, after all": David L. Ulin, "Fun with Problems," *Los Angeles Times*, January 10, 2010, latimes.com, accessed May 20, 2019.

485   "during the fall and spring semesters": Memorandum of Agreement between Robert Stone and Texas State University at San Marcos, February 6, 2009, NYPL/Lopez.

488   "but it wasn't commercial": Douglas Martin, "Fran Landesman, Lyricist with a Bittersweet Edge, Dies at 83," *The New York Times*, August 1, 2011, nytimes.com, accessed May 20, 2019.

491   "how to write a novel": Lauren Wein, letter to Robert Stone, August 7, 2012.

497   "secular in the counseling she dispensed": DotBHG, 39.

497   "she thought, maybe it was": Ibid., 52.

498   "Too young to know better": Ibid., 15.

498   "I want to see you": Ibid., 21.

498   "the Holy Roman Megachurch itself": Ibid., 37.

498   "what jails and lethal injections are for": Ibid., 38.

499   "Like you and me, Prof": Ibid., 79.

499   "you don't have to be quite so mean": Ibid., 118.

499   "God wills what I must do": Ibid., 95.

500   "had been his own death": Ibid., 133.

501   "He's . . . laughing": Ibid., 190.

501   "an announcement of things future": Ibid., 245.

502   "heroine of *As You Like It*": Ibid., 275.

502   "Ellie and the children along": Ibid., 276.

502   "You look like a white captive": Ibid., 1.

502   "a weak man": James Maraniss, unpublished interview.

503   "in the crypt at Holy Redeemer": DotBHG, 281.

503   "a taut novel of psychological suspense": Michiko Kakutani, "For a Professor, a Messy Affair," *The New York Times*, November 25, 2013, nytimes.com, accessed May 20, 2019.

504   "in some ennobling fashion": Claire Messud, "Blood Debt," *The New York Times Book Review*, November 15, 2013, nytimes.com, accessed May 20, 2019.

504   "a sure-footed psychological thriller": Kakutani, "For a Professor, a Messy Affair."

504   "all of the above": Mark Saunders, "*Death of the Black-Haired Girl* by Robert Stone," *The Washington Post*, November 13, 2013, google.com, accessed May 20, 2019.

504   "and beautifully just": Priscilla Gilman, "*Death of the Black-Haired Girl* by Robert Stone," *The Boston Globe*, November 9, 2013, bostonglobe.com, accessed May 20, 2019.

507   "would understand that": DotBHG, 277.

509   "they can do heartless spiteful things": "Coda," in EYE, 360.

509   "It was survival, I thought": Ibid.

510   "It's not meant to be": Ibid.

CODA

515   "with the door open and the wind blowing": Malcolm Lowry, *Under the Volcano* (New York: HarperCollins, 2007), 304.

515   "It's a way of ending the day": Alec Hanley Bemis, "Stone, Warm, Sober, 2007," *L.A. Weekly*, January 17, 2007.

516   "It taught him about suffering": Robert Stone, unpublished typescript on Malcolm Lowry, 2009, NYPL/Lopez.

516   "the experience of despair informs it": Ibid.

516   "lost himself in his own darkness": Ibid.

517   "inevitably doomed to failure": Michael Carlson, "Robert Stone Obituary," *The Guardian*, January 14, 2015, theguardian.com, accessed May 20, 2019.

517 "very difficult to work with": Hillel Italie, "Robert Stone Dies at 77," *Los Angeles Times*, January 11, 2015, latimes.com, accessed May 20, 2019.

517 "morally dubious condition": Gerald Howard, unpublished interview.

519 "their suffering meant something": Robert Stone, typescript of 2005 lecture at Amherst College, NYPL/Lopez.

519 "into the grammar": Ibid.

519 "as a lesson and guide": Ibid.

520 "in my sixth decade": Bruce Weber, "Robert Stone, Novelist of the Vietnam Era and Beyond, Dies at 77," *The New York Times*, January 10, 2015, nytimes .com, accessed May 20, 2019.

520 "being possessed by a novel": Stone, typescript of 2005 lecture at Amherst College.

520 "an orientation to mystery": Mark Powell, unpublished interview.

521 "that was no longer available": Robert Stone, in *John Paul II: The Millennial Pope* (PBS Home Video, 2003).

521 "And that tempted me to faith": Ibid.

521 "stop being a black": Woods, 49.

521 "is at the center of it": "Coda," in EYE, 362.

521 "wherever He has gone, bless you": Robert Stone, letter to Mark Powell, undated 2008, NYPL/Lopez.

522 "Cuban folk sayings, of course": James Maraniss, unpublished interview.

INDEX

RS indicates Robert Stone.

ABOUT THE AUTHOR

Madison Smartt Bell is the author of numerous novels,
including *All Souls Rising* (1995), nominated for a National
Book Award and the PEN/Faulkner Award, and *Freedom's
Gate* (2007), a biography of the Haitian revolutionary Toussaint
L'Ouverture. He teaches writing at Goucher College in
Towson, Maryland, and is married to the poet Elizabeth Spires.